The Aleutian Warriors

A History of the 11th Air Force & Fleet Air Wing 4

Part I

To
William Weedon Cloe
Let us now praise famous men,
and our fathers in their generation.

(Ecclesiaticus 44.1)

To General Brown,
With Best Wishes and
thank you for your continued
support

15 June 1994

The Aleutian Warriors

A History of the 11th Air Force & Fleet Air Wing 4

by John Haile Cloe

Part I

LIBRARY OF CONGRESS CATALOG
CARD NUMBER 90-60028

ISBN 0-929521-35-8

First Printing: June 1991
Second Printing: October 1991
Third Printing: June 1993

All royalties from the sale of this book support the
Anchorage Chapter's annual scholarships given to the
youth of the Anchorage area in honor and memory of:

Major Michael F. Monaghan
Robert C. Reeve

*The art work on the front and back covers was done by Ogden
Pleissner, an Army Air Forces artist, who spent three months
in the Aleutians during the late Spring and Summer of 1943.
During this period, he completed hundreds of sketches from
which he developed more than forty paintings, many of which
later appeared in* Life Magazine.

*The cover painting, "Sweating in the Mission," shows the
landing of B-25s at Adak. Paintings shown on the back cover
are: "War Hawks at Amchitka," upper right; "Muddy Roads of
Amchitka," center right; and "Clearing Weather at Adak,"
bottom. All the paintings are from the U.S. Army Art
Collection.*

Published jointly by:
ANCHORAGE CHAPTER—AIR FORCE ASSOCIATION
and
PICTORIAL HISTORIES PUBLISHING COMPANY, INC.
713 South Third Street West, Missoula, Montana 59801

FOREWORD

His devotion to accuracy in fact and detail, the clarity and easy style of his writing, his understanding of the events of World War II, his personal knowledge of the Aleutian Islands gained from visits to all the World War II bases including Kiska, his military background and education as an infantry officer, and his experience as a military historian for the U.S. Air Force make John Haile Cloe eminently qualified to write the history recorded in this book.

It was my good fortune to serve with him on the advisory board to the production of the motion picture film *Alaska At War*, a 58 minute documentary of World War II fighting in Alaska. I introduced John to a number of my former Japanese enemies, now my good friends, such as Masatake Okumiya, air officer on the staff of Admiral Kakuta who commanded the two carrier task group which raided Dutch Harbor on the 3rd and 4th of June, 1942, and Hiroichi Samejima who led the "Kates" and Zenji Abe who led the "Vals" in those attacks.

John Cloe's thoroughness and devotion to accuracy saved us from making embarrassing errors on more occasions than one during the review of the script to *Alaska at War*. When studying the electrifying effect of the Doolittle raid of 18 April 1942, on the home islands of Japan, it was easy to assume that it caused the Japanese to undertake the Midway-Aleutian operation. The Midway-Aleutian operation of the Japanese began with a diversionary strike against Dutch Harbor on 3 June, 1942, and the main attack, that on Midway, on 4 June 1942.

One could assume that the Doolittle raid caused the Japanese to undertake the Midway-Aleutian operation. Not so, said John Cloe, and produced the date of the decision by the Imperial Headquarters to undertake the Midway-Aleutian operation. It preceeded the date of the Doolittle raid.

In the early days of World War II the Japanese Zero fighter demonstrated superior performance to our U.S. fighters. One success we had, and there were few, in the Aleutians, was the recovery of a flyable Zero fighter against which our pilots could fly and devise tactics to defeat it.

Flight Petty Officer Tadayoshi Koga, IJN, flying a Zero and returning with his flight to his carrier, the *Ryujo*, from the attack on Dutch Harbor, found that his fighter was damaged so badly that he would not be able to make the flight back to his ship. The Japanese had an emergency plan for the occasion. He was to land on Akutan, the next large island east of Dutch Harbor, destroy his airplane, walk to the shoreline and be picked up by a Japanese submarine. Koga picked a sizable meadow and prepared to land. What the nineteen year old naval aviator did not know was that most flat land on the Aleutian Islands is a bog with heavy grass growing out of water and mud. He made the mistake of lowering his wheels. these sank into the bog on contact, flipped the fighter on its back, and Koga was killed. Thirty days later a passing Catalina from VP-41 Squadron, piloted by Lieutenant Bill Thies, USN, spotted the downed Zero on its back. The third try at salvage was successful. The navy fighter was taken by ship to the Naval Air Station, San Diego, and became the first Zero to be flown in the U.S. — in late September.

For some time after Koga's Zero was found, and I believe developed from superficial evidence established by the earliest visitors to the crash site, gossip prevailed that a .50 caliber bullet had severed the lightweight small diameter tube to the oil pressure gauge on the instrument panel of the aircraft. Thus Koga could have made it back to his ship even though his oil pressure read zero.

This myth was dispelled by the report of a meticulously conducted examination of the recovered Zero by a group of intelligence experts. All damage was from .50 caliber bullets which entered the fighter from above as well as from below. Mortal damage was done by a round which ruptured the oil return line from the oil cooler to the engine.

Who exploded this myth? John Cloe, who found the report of the experts, and generously reproduced a copy for me and others.

So it is that John Cloe has, in the pages which follow, a very readable book, with every attention given to ensure the correctness of the accounts given. I have enjoyed reading it and I am sure that you will.

Admiral James Sargent Russell, USN Ret
Tacoma, Washington

The biography of Admiral Russell is one of remarkable achievements that span the development of Naval Aviation. Born the year the Wright Brothers first flew at Kittyhawk, Russell graduated from Annapolis in 1926, earned his wings in 1928 and then became the first Naval aviator to land aboard all six pre-war carriers. He assisted in the design of the *Essex* class carrier, served as a patrol squadron commander in the Aleutians; and then after a tour in Washington, returned to the war, serving aboard carriers. He commanded the escort carrier *Bairoko* and then the fleet carrier *Coral Sea*. He authored the North Pacific portion of the U.S. Strategic Bombing Survey (Pacific). In 1957, as Chief of the Bureau of Aeronautics, he shared in the award of the Collier Aviation Trophy, for the development of the first supersonic carrier fighter, the F8U "Crusader." In 1958, Admiral Russell became Vice Chief of Naval Operations. He retired in 1965, but remained active in Naval affairs. He was inducted into the Naval Aviation Hall of Fame in 1990.

INTRODUCTION

· · · · · · · · · · · ·

Not much is known about the Aleutian Campaign or about the men who fought along the chain of islands that stretch over a thousand miles from mainland Alaska towards Asia.

The Aleutian Campaign occurred during the early years of the war. What was accomplished there has been obscured by time and overshadowed by the more dramatic events of other war theaters. It was the only campaign fought on North American soil during the war. It was primarily an air war where young men battled not only each other, but also the terrible, unforgiving elements of the storm-lashed, primeval place.

The war in the Aleutians has been referred to as the forgotten war, and the terror of the air battles that were fought in the lonely skies unfortunately have not summoned up the power and the glory of other theaters of conflict as was so recently expressed in the movie *Memphis Belle*. However, those who fought there remember. One veteran, Jack Roberts, in a letter to the editor of the *Anchorage Daily News*, expressing appreciation for a memorable article by Al Haley on the reunion of Eleventh Air Force veterans in Anchorage, perhaps best summed up their feelings.

> Most young people do not know of the Japanese bombing of Dutch Harbor, the invasion of Kiska and Attu and the battles for the Aleutian Islands. As a nation we were not isolated then and have not been isolated since.

A handful of popular books were written about the campaign during World War II. A very few have been written since the war. Notable among these is *The Thousand Mile War* by Brian Garfield. While it provides a dramatic and well written account of war in the Aleutians, the book also suffers from factual errors and misconceptions. It, nevertheless, remains the only book to cover the Aleutian Campaign in its entirety. Another book, *The Forgotten War*, a pictorial history of the war years in Alaska and northwest Canada, by Stan Cohen, includes the Aleutian Campaign. It has enjoyed considerable success and has gone through fourteen printings. A sequel, *The Forgotten War, Part II*, is in its second printing.

Three other books that address Aleutian Campaign topics have recently been published. Jim Rearden's *Cracking The Zero Mystery* documents the recovery of an intact Zero on Akutan Island and its exploitation for intelligence purposes. His other book, *Castner's Cutthroats*, is a fictional account of the Alaska Scouts in the Aleutians. The third book, *Home from Siberia*, by Otis Hays, tells for the first time the saga of American aircrews interned in Russia, most of whom flew from Aleutian bases against Japanese bases in the northern Kurile islands and were forced to divert to Petropavlovsk when they ran into difficulties.

Despite these efforts, no published book to date has focused on the air war fought over the weather-tortured Aleutian Islands. This book is a history of the Eleventh Air Force and Fleet Air Wing Four and the men who braved the hostile skies only to be ignored and forgotten by history. It is also a history of the Canadian airmen who honored their commitment to a common cause, and of those Japanese flyers who fought with great valor in a strange and terrifying place.

Most of the research for this book was completed during the late 1970s and early 1980s, and then set aside for other projects and the demands of employment. It was not until the fall of 1988 that I began writing on what was intended to cover the history of the Eleventh Air Force and Fleet Air Wing Four during their involvement not only in the Aleutian Campaign but also the later air offensive against the Kurile Islands. Unfortunately, time and space did not permit both accounts to be included in one book. As a result, the Kurile operations will be published as Part II to the *Aleutian Warriors*.

Until recently, Alaska's historical community has ignored the impact of World War II on Alaska, and the history of the military in general and its contributions to the development of the state. Alaska's rich aviation history has suffered a similar fate despite a popular interest in the subject and the missionary zeal of a few enthusiasts, notably Ted Spencer, Director of the Alaska Aviation Heritage Museum in Anchorage. He has also championed the cause of the Aleutians Warriors and the contributions made by military aviators. The Interior Alaskan and Arctic Aeronautical Foundation of Fairbanks has also made significant contributions to the understanding of Alaska's aviation past in promoting the remembrance of the Lend Lease transfer of aircraft to Soviet aviators at Ladd Field during World War II.

Fortunately, there has been an awakening of interest in Alaska's military heritage and the impact that World War II had on the sparsely populated territory. The Alaska Region, National Park Service, has devoted a considerable amount of its resources to the documentation and preservation of cultural resources associated with the military's activities in Alaska during the war. There is talk of establishing a World War II interpretation center at Dutch Harbor. The Secretary of Interior has designated several of the Aleutian military sites as National Historic Landmarks. Likewise, the State Office of History and Archeology has made efforts to preserve war-related sites and create public awareness of the military's role in the development of Alaska. Also, the Alaska State Legislature, at the urging of Brigadier General Benjamin B. Talley, whose contributions are covered in this book, appropriated funding for the production the film on the impact of World War II on Alaska. The Alaska Historical Commission, with state funding and monies raised from private sources, oversaw the production of *Alaska at War*.

Books are generally joint ventures, and this one is certainly a case of team effort. Stan Cohen, who has the theory that "if it is Alaskan, military and aviation, it will sell," willingly agreed to publish the book even before the work of writing it began. Stan's Pictorial Histories Publishing Company is essentially a two person operation that has produced over 120 titles, 16 of which are Alaskan. Many have been authored by Stan. Virtually all have been successes.

This book represented a challenge for Stan in that it contained a considerable amount of text, endnotes, an index and the other historiographical adornments not normally found in a pictorial history. Stan despite comments to the effect, "it's getting to be too long," never faltered in seeing the project through to completion. He was responsible for overseeing typesetting, doing the layout, and arranging for printing and distribution.

Bill Brooks, who promised his wife, Lorraine, their marriage would never be boring, and who arrived with her in Alaska in 1970 with modest means to make their fortune, provided not only financial support for the publication of this book, but also moral encouragement. A World War II pilot who races sports cars for a hobby, and who at the age of 72 established the world speed record for the Corvette at 244.198mph and now plans to run the first water powered car (an experimental innovation) on the Bonneville Salt Flats, Bill owns and flies his DeHavilland Beaver to remote locations in Alaska on a routine basis. He was quick to recognize the importance of Alaska's rich aviation history and the military's contributions to it. Bill has generously given of resources and time not only for this project but for the others that support Alaska's aviation heritage.

His full support of a previous book sponsored by the Anchorage Chapter, Air Force Association, *Top Cover for America*, resulted in the means for the chapter to award annual scholarships in memory of Bob Reeve and Maj. Mike Monaghan to deserving youth of Anchorage.

Colonel Ed Monaghan, USAF Ret, a National Director, Air Force Association, fighter pilot and veteran of the air war over Korea, and a sustaining force behind the association's Anchorage chapter, provided invaluable editorial and technical support. He and his wife, Mary, also contributed financially to the book's publication as did Enid and Vic Davis. Mary, as treasurer, also kept track of the bills.

Admiral James S. Russell, who is the ranking veteran of the Aleutian Campaign, in addition to being one of the few experts on the subject, read every word of the manuscript. He offered not only personal encouragement but constructive criticism on the book's coverage of Naval aviation. Herman Thompson, a wise and dedicated retired Air Force Chief Master Sergeant with 31 years of service to his nation, prepared the index. Captain Monica Aloisio, Deputy Public Affairs Officer, Eleventh Air Force, was responsible for the Air Force policy review and also volunteered much appreciated editorial comment in her usual cheerful and professional manner. Carl Bradford, Jr., a strong supporter of the military in Alaska, proofed the final book galleys. Finally, I owe a great deal to my wife, Cay, who sacrificed time and her dining room table for the cause. The book was written during the early morning hours before work and during the evenings and weekends.

Much of the material used in the book is from the memories and personal papers of those who served in the Aleutians during the war. Many furnished photographs that are used in this book. They are noted in the credits. Other photograph credits include AAF for Army Air Forces, AC for Army Air Corps and AAHS for Alaska Aviation Heritage Museum.

Information for the book was also gleaned from the unit histories that were produced during the war, and in one case long after the war, by the men of the 406th Bombardment Squadron when their commander, Doug Courtney, discovered his unit history had been lost. Also used were the correspondence files of the commanders and their organizations and the mission and intelligence reports.

It has been a privilege over the years to meet, talk and correspond with many of those who served in the Aleutians. They are of a remarkable and passing generation who came of age during the Great Depression, went off to fight in the greatest war ever inflicted on mankind, and then came home to make America the strongest nation in the world.

JHC, Eagle River, Alaska

TABLE OF CONTENTS

· · · · · · · · · · ·

1

OLD ALASKA NEW ALASKA

· · · · · · · · · · · ·

The Landing

It was very unusual for Robert Atwood not to be there. The young enterprising owner and publisher of the small town newspaper, *The Anchorage Daily Times*, had featured a series of front page articles, covering the construction of a nearby air base and the arrival of military units. Somehow he missed the landing of the old bomber and its three-man crew that August morning at Merrill Field. It had been an eventful Spring and Summer for Anchorage and for Alaska. Like the rest of the nation, the town and the territory had been caught up in worldwide events that meant the ending of one era and the beginning of another.

America, after twenty years of self-imposed isolation, had begun a massive rearming program that Summer in response to far away events in Europe and Asia. The nation had become disillusioned after its participation in World War I; a war that had devastated Europe, ripping apart the world's fabric and sowing the seeds of despair. America now faced the sad prospect of being drawn into another war.

Germans, humiliated in defeat and borne down by economic depression, had turned to Adolf Hitler, who restored their pride and created a nightmare. His armored columns had smashed through the blue and white painted border gates of Poland on September 1, 1939. Within twenty-four days, that hapless nation ceased to exist. World War II erupted; and Europe, almost over night, lost the leadership of mankind.

On the other side of the world, Japan had become a warrior nation as a solution to its economic problems. Supremely confident in their small, austere islands that they were the superior race, the Japanese righteously looked upon their militarily weaker but resource rich neighbors as the source of manpower and raw materials for building their national might. They quickly occupied Manchuria in 1931, and embarked on an inconclusive war

with China in 1937.

For Anchorage and for Alaska, the gathering storms of war would forever change the town and the remote territory. The year in which Major Everett S. Davis and his two companions landed at Merrill Field marked a turning point in the remote territory's history; one that separated old Alaska from new Alaska. Nineteen hundred and forty was the beginning of an era that the Alaskan economist and historian George Rogers termed the "Military Alaska." It would last well into the Cold War years of the 1950s and end with the achievement of statehood.[1]

Major Davis, his flight engineer Staff Sergeant Joseph A. Grady and radio operator, Corporal Edward D. Smith, landed at Merrill Field in their obsolete B-10 bomber at 10:55 AM August 12, 1940. The event went unrecorded in *The Anchorage Daily Times*. Davis and his men were the advance party for the 28th Composite Group and the start of what would later become the Eleventh Air Force. They had flown down from Ladd Field near Fairbanks, where Major Davis was to have assumed command from Major Dale Gaffney. General Henry "Hap" Arnold, the Army Air Corps' new Chief of Staff, in one of his typical last minute decisions, decided that Major Gaffney should remain at Ladd, then in the process of being constructed as a cold weather test facility.

Arnold instead picked Davis, who had entered the Army in 1918 as an enlisted man, gained a commission and had gone on to flight school and assignments with various aviation units during the austere inter-war years. The major, who had just graduated from the prestigious Army Command and General Staff School, was the ideal man for the difficult job ahead.[2] He was in the words of Brigadier General Benjamin B. Talley, who served with him during the early days in Alaska, a "muy hombre . . . a great man . . . a very forceful leader," whose role in Alaska's history has never been properly recognized.[3]

General Arnold was already familiar with Alaska and

Colonel Everett S. Davis help found what would later become the Eleventh Air Force. In 1976, as part of the Bicentennial Year celebration, the headquarters building for the Alaskan Air Command was named the "Davis Building" in his honor. Somehow, the new name never caught on and the building is still referred to by its numerical designation, "Building 5-800." Other than a bronze plaque on the building, the memory of Everett S. Davis and what he accomplished during the early years of the Air Force in Alaska is generally unknown.
AAF photo

Lieutenant Colonel Henry "Hap" Arnold, led a flight of ten YB-10s on a 7,360-mile round trip flight from Bolling Field, Washington DC to Fairbanks, Alaska during the Summer of 1934. One of the purposes of the flight was to look for possible military field sites in the territory. Arnold, in the cockpit of his YB-10, became the Chief of Staff, Army Air Forces and a five star general. AC photo

its strategic importance as the "air crossroads of the world." He had led ten B-10 bombers on an epic round-trip flight from Bolling Field, Washington DC to Fairbanks during the summer of 1934. Among the recommendations he made upon his return was the construction of air bases in Alaska. At the time, Alaska's sole defenses consisted of two infantry companies at Fort Seward near Haines. Although they had included Alaska in their defense plans, the military had done little during the Depression years other than develop staff studies, conduct survey flights, and testify before Congress along with Alaska's voteless delegate, Anthony Dimond, and the visionary Brigadier General Billy Mitchell.[4]

Major Davis' Martin B-10B, which he landed at Merrill Field on August 12, 1940. The photograph was taken in May 1942, after a minor accident. The wing tips and tail of the aluminum-finished bomber had been painted orange for better visibility. The obsolete aircraft was used for survey flights, served as a transport, employed on search and rescue missions, and on occasions used as a "control tower." The bomber was "written off" in late 1942, after being damaged in a wind storm. AAF photo

It was not until the spring of 1939 that Congress appropriated four million dollars to build a cold weather test facility near Fairbanks, thus fulfilling a long-standing need that went back to 1929, when the military had to admit, much to its embarrassment, that it did not have the cold weather flying expertise needed in the search for the pioneer bush pilot, Carl Ben Eielson and his mechanic, Earl Borland. The two had disappeared off the northern coast of the Chukchi Peninsula while attempting to recover a cargo of firs from the stranded schooner, *Nanuk*.[5]

Preliminary construction and land clearing was begun for Ladd Field during the summer of 1939. The field had been named for Major Arthur K. Ladd, who had been killed when his pursuit aircraft crashed near Dale, South Carolina in 1935. Major Gaffney arrived in April 1940 to assume command, and construction began in earnest. By August the runway had been paved, and Ladd was declared operational on September 4. Major Gaffney made the first landing in an O-38 observation aircraft.[6]

Fort William H. Seward near Haines in southeastern Alaska was the last "Gold Rush" military post to be built and the last one to be closed. It provided a military "presence" in the Territory of Alaska during the prewar years. In 1922, it was renamed Chilkoot Barracks. During the war, it was a National Guard facility. It was sold after the war to a group of investors. Those who served in the two infantry companies stationed there generally found life pleasant in the leisurely routine of the prewar Army. Elinor Dusenbury, the wife of one of the commanders, wrote the music for "Alaska's Flag," which later became the state song. The photograph was taken on June 22, 1929 during a Navy survey flight. USN photo

The Navy began routinely deploying flying boats to Sitka on training missions in the mid-1930s. A small naval air station was built on Japonski Island in 1937, and was later expanded in compliance with a recommendation of the Hepburn Board. It was the first military air facility to be built and operated in Alaska. Normally, the Navy deployed half a squadron, around six flying boats, at a time to Sitka from its Northwest bases. One of the earlier float planes was the Consolidated P2Y-3 Ranger, shown here at Sitka in 1937. The Ranger was replaced on Alaskan duty by the Consolidated PBY-5 Catalina float plane in the late 1930s. Jim Magee collection via AAHM

While Ladd Field fulfilled the cold weather testing requirement, there was still a need for an operational air base in Alaska. Presidential Executive Order 8102, dated April 22, 1939, withdrew 43,495 acres of land adjacent to Anchorage, which the military, after several fact finding visits, had deemed suitable for the construction of a permanent air base.

By early 1940, the American public and their leaders had become concerned about the war in Europe and the growing Japanese militarism. The military, which had spent about $225 million on defense facilities on the Hawaiian Islands, had invested only $1.5 million in Alaska, most of which was civilian related. The Army planners had found "it hard to shake their long held conviction that Alaska was not a critical area."[7] The Navy had shown a little more interest. They had conducted a number of surveys of the Aleutian Islands, and their 1935 Fleet Problem XVI had been held in Aleutian waters. The Hepburn Board, headed by Admiral Arthur J. Hepburn, formed to study Naval aviation and readiness, had included in its

Ladd Field as it looked during the Summer of 1941. The field was the first permanent modern military facility to be built in Alaska and was intended as a place for cold weather testing of Army aircraft and equipment. It was also used during the war as an Air Transport Command base and as the transfer point of Lend Lease aircraft destined for the Soviet Union. According to figures kept a Ladd, 7,926 aircraft were signed over to the Russians there. Ladd Field was transferred to the Army in 1960 and renamed Fort Wainwright. AC photos

1938 recommendations that the small seaplane base, which the Navy had established at Sitka the previous year, be expanded and other bases be built on Kodiak Island and at Dutch Harbor in the eastern Aleutian Islands to protect America's northern flank in the Pacific.[8]

The Army was also concerned, because of the rapid advances being made in aviation technology, that Alaska was becoming vulnerable to air attacks; and that either Japan or Russia might establish advance bases there which would threaten the rest of Alaska and the population centers of the west coast of the U.S. and Canada.[9]

In late February, General George C. Marshall, who had assumed his duties as Chief of Staff of the Army September 1, 1939, the day Germany invaded Poland, testified before Congress on the Army's need for additional funding. He was asking for slightly more than nine hundred million dollars for fiscal year 1941, which was scheduled to begin in July 1940, and run through the following June. One of the line items in the budget was $12,738,000 for an air base near Anchorage. General Marshall spoke of the need for the base and the Army's plans to build other air fields throughout the territory. The committee members of the House Appropriations Committee questioned him at length on why the money should be spent on the Anchorage base when the Navy was already building one at Kodiak. They also believed that Ladd Field was sufficient for the Air Corps' needs. As a result, the funding for the Anchorage base was deleted from the Army's budget.[10]

Robert Atwood, in his paper, greeted the decision with dismay. For years he and other Anchorage boosters had been championing the idea of a military base near the small town of approximately 4000 persons. Atwood believed that Anchorage would grow and prosper like so many other frontier communities that had sprung up around Army posts.[11] His paper carried a series of front page articles in which Representative Dimond and the Territorial Governor, Ernest Gruening, expressed their dismay at the budget cut. In one article, Gruening noted: "The government spent $400,000,000 fortifying Hawaii while Alaska on the shortest route to the Orient is practically undefended."[12]

Others before him had also recognized Alaska's strategic location. In 1867, Secretary of State William Seward, in his efforts to persuade Congress to purchase Alaska from Russia, pointed out that in order to defend the United States, Alaska was needed "to dominate the North Pacific." In 1909, Homer Lea in his book, *The Ignorance of Valor*, predicted the Japanese would one day invade the United States by way of the Aleutian Islands and Alaska.[13] Brigadier General William Mitchell, who had served in Alaska at the turn of the century and termed the remote territory "the most strategic place in the world," also cautioned that the Japanese could easily use the islands as an invasion route to Alaska and the rest of North America. He believed that air power provided the only means for stopping such an invasion.[14]

Ladd Field was named in honor of Maj Arthur K. Ladd, killed when the pursuit aircraft he was piloting crashed near Dale, South Carolina, December 13, 1935. He was a promising young officer, with a bright future. He was married and the couple had one child. "Jimmy" Doolittle, who knew the Ladds, referred to them as "Maw and Paw Ladd." Somehow, during the transfer from Air Force to Army control in 1960, the field did not keep the designation Ladd Army Air Field as has been the custom at other Army posts with military fields. Colonel Victor E. Micol Jr, the Senior Army Advisor, Alaska Army National Guard and an Army aviator, corrected the oversight in 1989. AC photo

Brigadier General William "Billy" Mitchell in his element. As a young U.S. Army Signal Corps lieutenant he helped build the Washington-Alaska Military Cable and Telegraph System. He gained an appreciation for Alaska, believed in its strategic importance and prophesied that the Japanese would use the Aleutian Islands as an invasion route. AC photo

Later, the Japanese occupation of the western Aleutian Islands and the publication of such books as *Alaska, Back Door to Japan, Bridge to Victory* and *Short Cut To Tokyo* would lend credibility to Mitchell's predictions. Dimond and others had noted that when one looked at the world globe, it quickly became evident that the shortest route to the Orient was through Alaska. The distance from San Francisco to Tokyo by way of Alaska was 1,400 miles shorter than the traditional air route across the Pacific. The Arctic explorer, Vilhajalmur Stefansson, prophesied that with the development of aviation, the Arctic Ocean would one day become another Mediterranean because the shortest distances between Europe, North America and the Orient lay across the polar regions.[15]

Many of Alaska's leaders believed Alaska was America's "Achilles Heel." Dimond, in stressing the need to fortify the territory, pointed out that: "By bombing plane, one corner of this great territory is less than fifteen minutes from the Soviet mainland, another corner is about three hours from a Japanese naval station, and a third corner is about three hours from Seattle."[16]

However, during the spring of 1940, Congress and the military were more interested in the events unfolding in Europe than they were about the Japanese threat to Alaska, or the alleged Soviet military buildup in Siberia that some Alaskan supporters were trying to use as a pretext for garrisoning the territory.

On April 9, German troops invaded Norway and Denmark, ending the phony war that had existed in Europe since the conquest of Poland the previous September. One month later, Hitler sent his divisions slashing into Holland and Belgium; and on May 13, other divisions tore into France, driving all before them to a humiliating defeat. By June 17, it was all over. Germany dominated the continent. England, weakened and alone, began preparing for an invasion. Germany, in little over three months, had achieved what it had been unable to do in four grinding, bloody years of trench warfare during World War I. Most of the rest of the world, in shocked disbelief, began preparing for war.

Americans, who had based their hopes on a broad ocean, a relatively powerful navy and the military forces of England and France to protect them from becoming involved in another European war, suddenly became concerned for their own safety. Although still reluctant to go to war on behalf of a beleaguered England, they were much more ready to prepare for war and to become, in the words of President Roosevelt, "the arsenal for democracy."

Congress, who in March had been unwilling to approve a two billion dollar budget for the Army and Navy, quickly voted an appropriation for ten and a half billion dollars. The President, who had declared a state of limited emergency when the Germans invaded Poland, now proclaimed an unlimited national emergency. Industry geared up to produce 50,000 aircraft a year; shipyards began laying the keels of the Essex class carriers, the Iowa class battleships and other warships needed for a two-ocean Navy; the National Guard was federalized; the Reserves called up; and the first peacetime draft in history approved, thus beginning a buildup that would totally mobilize the nation for war and put nine million men and women in uniform.

The Senate approved the budget on May 21. It contained the funding for the Anchorage base and the construction of Navy facilities at Kodiak and Dutch Harbor. Shortly afterwards, the House of Representatives voted their approval.[17] A new era had begun that would transform Alaska from an often ignored and exploited territory into its rightful place as the 49th state.

One contemporary author, noting the change, would comment that while "the Gold Rush gave Alaska its mystique, the military put it on the map."[18] In the war years ahead, the military would spend over a billion and a quarter dollars to develop a permanent modern defense network that would also provide an infrastructure of roads, airfields, harbors, and communications systems.

Anchorage benefited the most. The initial appropriations for the Anchorage air base would swell to forty-five million dollars, or ten million more than had been spent on the construction of the Alaska Railroad. Anchorage would become the fastest growing community in Alaska and the dominant economic power, a condition that would not have been possible without the presence of the military.[19]

Fourth Avenue, Anchorage, as it looked in 1942. The Signal Corps photograph was taken in front of the City Hall. Jack Boyd collection

As a result of the military build up, Anchorage enjoyed one of its several "boom" economies. Bars and other establishments of lesser repute flourished on the paychecks of military personnel and construction workers who flocked north. Joe E. Brown, on his first visit to Alaska, was reputed to have said, "My, what a large bar."

Jack Boyd collection

Alaska, 1940

Alaska in 1940 was a remote, sparsely populated place whose economy was dominated by "outside" interests. About 70,000 people lived in the territory that year, many of whom were seasonal employees of the fishing and mining industries, Alaska's two major economic mainstays. The majority were controlled by outside interests. Most were located in Seattle, Washington. "Cap" Lathrop, Alaska's first millionaire, viewed the migratory workers and absentee owners as people who regarded Alaska as "a treasure box," from which they could take what they wanted before winter set in and they had to go home. Ernest Gruening compared them to 17th Century Spaniards who exploited the territory and left nothing in return.[20]

The Federal government played a dominant role in the affairs of Alaska. Over 50 agencies operated in the territory with an annual budget of twelve to fifteen million dollars. The Alaskans often resented the decisions made in Washington to which they had little input. Much of it was focused against Secretary of Interior Harold Ickes, who was responsible for supervising the affairs of the territory.

Their sentiments were echoed by the Nome newspaper, *The Nome Nugget*, which paraphrased the Aleut saying of the Russian American days: "God is high and the Czar far away," with "God is afar and it's a long way to Washington."[21]

There were only four sizable communities in Alaska: Anchorage, Fairbanks, Ketchikan and the territorial capital of Juneau. The latter, with a population of 6,000, was also the largest town in the territory. The next largest was Ketchikan with 5,000. The other, much smaller, communities were scattered throughout the 586,400 square miles of remote and often inhospitable territory. Southeastern Alaska, because of its relatively large population and closeness to Seattle, was the dominant economic and political force in the territory.

There were very few roads. The only major one was the Richardson Highway; an unpaved, two-lane road between Valdez on Prince William Sound and Fairbanks in the interior. Altogether, including the Richardson Highway, there were 10,171 miles of roads and trails in Alaska, of which only 2,212 miles were suitable for vehicular traffic. There was no road connecting Anchorage and Fairbanks. The two towns, however, were joined by the Federally owned Alaska Railroad, which had been built in the early 1920s to open interior Alaska to further economic development. Seward served as the ocean terminus for the 470-mile long, single-track railroad. The inland waterways provided the major means of travel during the ice-free summer months.

The Alaska Steamship Company furnished the principal link between Seattle and Alaska. The Northland Steamship Line and the Northland Transportation Company, to a lesser extent, also provided passenger and freight service between the two locations. They were seasonal, however, with only a limited number of ships in operation during the winter months. Pan American Airways Clipper Service furnished the only air link with the outside. The service was limited to the larger communities in southeastern Alaska.[22]

For much of Alaska, the airplane supplied the only

General Mitchell, reaching out to grasp Captain Streett's hand, was among the notables who greeted the Black Wolf Squadron members on their return from their 9,000-mile round trip flight from Mitchell Field, New York, to Nome. From left to right are: Lieut. Ross C. Kirkpatrick, Sgt. Edmund Henriques, 2nd Lieut. Erik A. Nelson, Captain Streett, Sgt. Joseph E. English, 1st Lieut. Clifford C. Nutt and 2nd Lieut. Clarence E. Crumrine. Sgt. James D. Long is hidden behind Lieutenant Nutt. SC photo

Carl Ben Eielson learned to fly in the Army Air Service. After mustering out, he moved to Fairbanks, where with the help of local businessmen, he started an air service with a surplus Curtis JN-D "Jenny." On February 24, 1924, he made the first mail flight in Alaska. In April 1924, Eielson achieved international acclaim as the pilot for Sir Hubert Wilkins on the first flight across the high arctic from Point Barrow, Alaska to the Spitsbergen archipelago northeast of Norway. He was killed in an aircraft crash on the coast of Siberia on December 9, 1929. Griffin's Photo Shop, Fairbanks

reliable year-round means of transportation. The arrival of a flight of four DeHavilland DH-4s in the territory during the summer of 1920 had firmly established aviation as a way of life in Alaska. Brigadier General William Mitchell, the Assistant Chief, U.S. Army Air Service, had conceived the idea of a New York to Nome flight as part of an effort to draw public attention and support to his service which was suffering from severe budget reductions. General Mitchell, because of his belief in the strategic importance of Alaska, wanted to prove that the then remote territory could be linked with the rest of the United States by the airplane.

The highly successful 9,000-mile round-trip flight of the Black Wolf Squadron proved his point. It also firmly introduced the airplane as a revolutionary new means of transportation in the territory and marked the beginning of its emergence as the dominant military force in Alaska.[23] Other flights of significant importance, military and civilian, would be made in the next two decades that would vindicate General Mitchell's contention that Alaska was "the most central place in the world for aircraft."[24]

Two years after the Black Wolf flight, a former Navy aviator, Roy Jones, arrived in Ketchikan with a surplus Navy Curtiss MF flying boat to form Alaska's first commercial aviation venture, Northbird Aviation Company. While Jones was pioneering commercial aviation in southeastern Alaska, Carl Ben Eielson, for whom Eielson Air Force Base would later be named, arrived to teach high school in Fairbanks. Shortly afterwards, with the help of several local businessmen, the ex-Army pilot purchased a surplus Curtiss Jenny and began flying for hire.[25]

They were the forerunners of a breed of pioneers who would revolutionize travel in Alaska. The late 1920s and the 1930s were the golden years of the Alaskan Bush Pilot. Men such as Jim Dodson, Bob Ellis, Harold Gilliam, Alex Holden, Jack Jefford, Russ Merrill, Al Monson, Ray Petersen, Frank Pollack, Bob Reeve, Art Woodley, and Noel Wien provided the foundation upon which Alaska's military aviation was built.[26]

By the late 1930s the dog team, the road houses, and the river boats were rapidly fading into history. The airplane was firmly entrenched in Alaska. The Civil Aviation Administration, which had begun regulating commercial aviation in Alaska in the early 1930s, sent Marshall Hoppin to Alaska in 1938 as the head of their first office in Anchorage. That same year, the agency began an ambitious five-year program to develop an infrastructure of airfields and navigational facilities throughout the territory. At the time, there were only four airfields that could be considered adequate. They were located at Anchorage, Fairbanks, Juneau and Nome. The other approximately 100 fields in the territory were often little more than clearings in the wilderness that had been built by miners and fishermen for their own use.

By 1940, the number of airfields with runways of 2,500 feet or more had grown to ten. However, there was much work left to be done before Alaska would have an adequate aviation infrastructure. The arrival of the military in 1940, and realization that the airplane was the key to military operations in the vast territory, greatly accelerated the development of commercial aviation in Alaska.[27]

Alaska Under Arms

The men of the 28th Composite Group at March Field, California wondered about what they would encounter when they arrived in Anchorage. The group had been activated February 1, 1940. Shortly afterwards, the men were notified that they were being sent to an air base that was to be built near Anchorage. They, like most military personnel who are about to leave for a new duty assignment, were concerned about housing and what their new surroundings would be like. They began writing letters to Bob Atwood and the President of the Anchorage Chamber of Commerce, seeking information. However, it would not be until the following year that the group would actually leave California. There were other more pressing matters that had to be attended to, the major of which was the construction of an air base to accommodate the group and its aircraft.[28]

Although nothing had been done to properly garrison the territory until 1940, the military planners had already decided how Alaska would be defended. Military plans are normally based on a threat assessment. The two nations that posed a threat to Alaska at the time were Japan and the Soviet Union. However, Alaska's vast expanse and rugged terrain discouraged any large scale invasion. Additionally, both countries would have found it extremely difficult to logistically mount and sustain such an operation, a lesson that Japan would later learn in the Aleutian Islands. America's military planners figured that the most likely attack would come in the form of air strikes or small-scale ground actions against remote, hard to defend locations, and they would come only if the Navy lost control of the North Pacific.

To meet such a threat, the planners were faced with two choices: station a strong, highly mobile force near Anchorage or build a series of military installations throughout the territory. The chose the latter. They planned that the Anchorage air base would serve as the major operational and support base for the other military installations in Alaska.

By early 1940, Army planners had developed a defense concept for Alaska which recognized Alaska's strategic location, took into consideration the great potential of military air power, and emphasized that forward basing and air power were the key to Alaska's defenses and the defense of the North Pacific area. The Army's long range planning objectives for Alaska became the establishment of a major air base near Anchorage to support operations throughout Alaska, the development of a network of air fields at forward locations from which aircraft could operate, and the stationing of garrisons to protect these fields and the Navy's bases at Sitka, Kodiak and Dutch Harbor.[29]

Work on the first major operational air base in Alaska began June 8, 1940, when 25 local men were hired to begin off-loading equipment and supplies from four Alaska Railroad cars at the Whitney Station House. Major Edward M. George had arrived the previous day from Ladd Field to supervise the construction effort. He established an office in Anchorage and set about hiring additional men to clear the land and begin work on the building of facilities and the laying of runways of what would become the largest military base in Alaska.[30] By June 10, forty to fifty men were at work. By the end of August, their number had swelled to 3,415. Virtually all construction was done under contract with the firm of Bechtel-McCone-Parson.

The men rushed against time to complete the projects before the onset of winter halted their efforts. The paving of the east-west runway was begun on September 20. The first snow fell on October 10. Work continued. Jackhammers and steam jets were used to break and thaw the frozen ground. Construction of the first set of barracks was completed in early November. By then it had become too cold to continue. Major construction work was halted until the following spring as was the Alaskan custom in those days.[31]

The first troops to man the new base had arrived at the

Alaska Railroad depot at 7:00 AM June 27 from the 3rd Infantry Division, Fort Lewis, Washington. The 4th Infantry Regiment, commanded by Lieutenant Colonel Earl Landreth, disembarked from the U.S. Army troop transport Saint Mihiel at the Port of Seward on June 26. The troops and their equipment were immediately loaded aboard an Alaska Railroad train for the trip north through the twilight of an Alaska summer night.

Many Anchorage citizens, including Bob Atwood, were on hand to greet the soldiers as they alighted from the train. They were the beginning of a flood of military personnel who would swell the population of Anchorage in the years ahead.[32]

The troops pitched their tents in a hay field that had once been part of the Arthur Marsh homestead. Their headquarters was established in the nearby farm house. The adjacent barn was turned into an ordnance warehouse. Colonel Landreth and his men quickly settled into a routine while they awaited the arrival of the man who would oversee the dramatic buildup of the Army in Alaska.[33]

The U.S. Army transport Saint Mihiel, *off-loading troops and supplies at Seward. The transport was a familiar sight in Alaskan waters. It had brought the Matanuska Valley colonist to Alaska in May 1935. Five years later the Saint Mihiel landed the first troops at Seward for the build up of the military forces in Alaska. During the war the passenger and cargo transport continued to ply between the West Coast ports and Alaska.* USA photo

Arrival of troops at the Alaska Railroad Depot, June 27, 1940. Russ Dow photos

The first encampment in what would later become Fort Richardson and Elmendorf Field was established in a hayfield just off the Loop Road adjacent to Anchorage. Note the farm house to the extreme right. It served as the first headquarters. Russ Dow photo

Tents provided shelter until the civilian construction workers could build wooden barracks. Russ Dow photos

Elmendorf Field as it looked July 8, 1940. AC photo

Nearby Ship Creek provided a ready source of salmon which was put to good use supplementing the soldiers' diet.
Russ Dow photo

Field kitchens were set up to feed the troops. Russ Dow photos

The Silver Stallion

By temperament and background, the strapping, ruddy-complexioned, white haired Colonel Simon Bolivar Buckner Jr. was well suited for his first major command after thirty-three years of military service. The fifty-four year old Kentuckian was an avid outdoorsman with an extensive academic background as a student and instructor in the Army's school system.

His father had achieved dubious fame by accepting unconditional terms from his West Point class mate, General Ulysses S. Grant, for the surrender of Fort Donalson. Buckner and Grant were forever linked with the term "unconditional surrender." The Confederate general, who had once loaned a destitute Grant money, bitterly commented after the surrender, that if it had not been for his men, he would not have accepted such "ungracious and unchivalrous terms."[34]

Following the war, Buckner senior entered politics, became the adjutant general of Illinois and later governor of Kentucky; and as a sixty-two year old widower, married a twenty-eight year old woman and fathered his namesake. The junior Buckner, an only child adored by his aging father and mother, grew up in the rugged outdoors of the rolling, wooded hills of Kentucky where he developed a lifelong passion for the outdoors. Glib of tongue and quick of mind, he did well in the rural schools. After almost two years at the Virginia Military Institute, Buckner received an appointment to West Point where he graduated in 1909, ranking 57th in his class of 107.

Commissioned in the infantry, Buckner served in a succession of infantry assignments where he developed a reputation as a strict but fair taskmaster. He spent World War I in the States with the fledgling Army Air Service trying to instill a sense of discipline in would be aviators. During this time he learned to fly, but when the war was over, he reverted back to his beloved infantry. The brief experience, however, left him with an appreciation for the potential of military aviation.

During the next twenty years, Buckner served two tours at West Point as an instructor and Commandant of Cadets, attended the Army Command and General Staff School for two years, stayed on for another three years as an instructor, and graduated from the Army War College where he remained for three years as the executive officer after graduating with honors. The experience earned him the

The Marsh homestead barn was used as a temporary ordnance store house. AC photo

The soldiers participated in their first Fourth of July parade in Anchorage within a week of arrival. The building to the left of the towed 105mm howitzer is the city hall. Russ Dow photos

reputation as one of the Army's leading schoolmasters and provided him a thorough theoretical knowledge of operations and tactics.

Because of this background and his rich vocabulary, Buckner's brother officers, who served in a profession not known to be very articulate, were inclined to accuse him of possessing too much surface brilliance.[35] Buckner also suffered from a lack of tact, which did not help him in his dealings with others; and reflecting his cultural background, a racial bias towards minorities. Protesting DeWitt's plans to send a Black artillery unit to Alaska, Buckner feared their presence would "result in a serious and lasting race problem, since they will interbreed with the Indians and many of them will probably settle here."[36] His attitude towards Alaska's Natives was not much better, much to the disgust of Governor Gruening.[37]

Buckner's shortcomings, however, were far exceeded by his drive and dedication to building Alaska's defenses. Enjoying his newly acquired title, "The Silver Stallion of Alaska," Buckner was constantly on the move. He advocated the defense of Alaska to a fault, to the exclusion of a broader strategic view which had relegated the territory to a lower priority.

He was also an apostle of the vigorous life. While Commandant of Cadets at West Point, Buckner was horrified to discover that some of the cadets were using cold cream and after shave lotion. He immediately banned them, claiming that, "Cadets should work and smell like men."[38] Buckner was also hard on himself and hard on others. He handed out demerits so unmercifully at West Point that one cadet's parents complained, "Buckner forgets that cadets are born and not quarried."[39]

Soldiers fish in Ship Creek near Anchorage. AC photo

General DeWitt, left and General Buckner, right, review troops at Fort Richardson May 23, 1941. General DeWitt was one of three general officers who were veterans of the Spanish-American War to remain on active duty during World War II. General Buckner was killed in action on Okinawa, one of two three star Army generals to die in battle during World War II.

Jack Boyd collection

At the time of his selection to command Army forces in Alaska, Colonel Buckner was serving as the Chief of Staff, 6th Infantry Division at Fort Lewis, Washington. Lieutenant General John L. DeWitt, Commander, IX Corps, had decided that the aggressive, outdoor inclined Buckner was the ideal man for Alaska. The general, from his headquarters at the Presidio, California, was responsible for the defense of the western United States and the territory of Alaska. It was from his command that the forces would be drawn to garrison and defend the territory, and the general would insist on retaining operational control of the northern area long after military wisdom dictated that Alaska be made a separate theater of operations.[40]

As Colonel Buckner was preparing to come north, General Arnold and a party of four staff officers arrived at Ladd Field on an inspection trip to observe construction and discuss the Army Air Corps' future role in Alaska. After spending four days at Ladd, they flew down to Anchorage on July 15 in their C-47. They spent the next day inspecting Elmendorf Field. That night, the Anchorage Chamber of Commerce hosted them at a dinner and dance at the Idle Hour Club. General Arnold departed the following morning for Fairbanks with Colonel Otto Ohlson, manager of the Alaska Rail Road. They drove north in Ohlson's DeSoto automobile, which been converted to run on the railroad tracks.[41]

General Arnold and his party, using Fairbanks as their base, visited Circle, McGrath, Talkeetna, Tanana, Seward, Iliamna, Cordova, Yakutat, Juneau and Sitka to look at potential air field sites. Arnold, who later wrote an account of his trip in the October 1940 edition of *National Geographic*, never returned to Alaska during the

Major General Buckner in the observation blister of a PBY somewhere over the Aleutian Islands in 1942. By the time he left Alaska in 1944, he had earned his third star as the builder of the military in Alaska. USA photo

war.[42] There were too many other pressing duties. As Chief of Staff of the Army Air Forces, his responsibilities would ultimately embrace more than 2,300,000 men and 72,000 airplanes; the mightiest air force ever assembled to wage a global war.

General Arnold, however, never lost his appreciation for the strategic importance of Alaska or the importance of air power to its defense. In a speech to the Fairbanks Chamber of Commerce during his July visit he noted that:

> In Alaska must be situated the great flying fields and air terminals which shall eventually bind and serve vast airways connecting industrial centers. Here too must be situated the great air bases equipped to defend these same air frontiers from sky invasion by any possible enemy of the U.S.[43]

Colonel Buckner arrived on July 22, 1940 to assume command of the newly created Alaska Defense Force. Shortly afterwards, he announced to the Anchorage Chamber of Commerce his plans for building Alaska defenses, and noted that of all the assignments, this was the one he would have chosen. Buckner went on to say . . . "we are starting from scratch and it will be a most interesting job."[44] After turning down an offer of a house in Anchorage, the colonel moved into a tent on Elmendorf Field to be nearer his men. On August 31 he pinned on the stars of a brigadier general and celebrated the occasion by going duck hunting.[45]

The gregarious Buckner quickly made friends with Anchorage's leading citizens. After his men had moved into their barracks, he left his tent for more suitable quarters in a rented house in Anchorage, and sent for his wife, Adele, and their 16-year-old daughter. And with bourbon in hand, began actively entertaining his newly acquired friends and a succession of visitors who came north to see first hand what was going on.[46]

The Alaska Defense Force was redesignated the Alaska Defense Command in February 1941. It would remain a subordinate command under DeWitt's IX Corps, later changed to Western Defense Command, until November 1943. The Alaska Defense Command was responsible for defending United States military and naval installations in Alaska.[47]

When Major Davis and his two enlisted assistants arrived at Merrill Field on August 12, 1940, they found that very little if anything had been done to accommodate them. The field at Elmendorf was still under construction and there was no office or housing available. They obtained the use of a portable one room building on Merrill Field which served as their headquarters, storage area and sleeping quarters.[48]

Major Davis immediately dispatched a message to General Arnold to let him know that he had arrived, and to inform him that until facilities were available on Elmendorf, he would operate out of Merrill Field. Davis also asked Arnold when the first units would arrive, and requested another officer along with enlisted clerical and supply personnel to help him prepare for their arrival.[49] In a note to a friend on General Arnold's staff, Davis commented that he was . . . "just finding out how damned little one man could do without a clerk and other trained help."[50] However, it was not until November that help finally began arriving. In the interim, the major did his best with what little he had. He spent most of his time making survey flights in his B-10, looking at potential air field sites.

It was a difficult period. Besides the lack of help, Major Davis' duties were never clearly defined. He had to depend on General Buckner, who he served as the senior Air Corps representative in Alaska, for his authority. This hampered his dealings with General Arnold's staff. Major Davis, commenting to one of his friends on the staff, remarked that:

> If you can find out for me exactly what I'm here for and what reports are expected of me, let me know. At present I'm occupied in learning the territory and trying to see it all from the air and also as air officer, Alaska Defense Force, making plans to receive and train the squadrons when they arrive. My position as a member of the Alaska Defense Force headquarters does not permit me to make direct reports nor to transmit anything direct except requisitions for Air Corps property. Officially everything is very pleasant as is and I have no intention of chancing a trip to the doghouse by going over anyone's head without specific authority. To do so would reduce my usefulness to zero.[51]

Davis, Grady and Smith moved their portable building to Elmendorf Field. Additional help arrived in early November in the form of Lieutenant John Bowen and nine enlisted men. Later that month the 4th Infantry Regiment detailed additional men to help them unpack and sort out the equipment and supplies that had been accumulating. By the end of the month Major Davis' "command" was composed of one officer, nine sergeants, a corporal and sixteen privates. The two officers lived in the infantry bachelor officer quarters, the men in the infantry and artillery enlisted barracks. A flight line garage was set aside for their use. Davis and his men began preparing for the arrival of the first Air Corps units.[52]

General Buckner, on December 1, designated Davis as the Commanding Officer, Elmendorf Field. He now had the authority to begin implementing the Army Air Corps' plans for Alaska.[53] By then the War Department had taken steps to officially name the field, which initially had been referred as the Anchorage Air Base and later informally as Elmendorf Field. The Adjutant General's office announced November 9 that the Army installation near An-

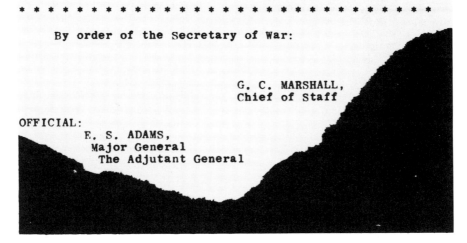

```
                                                           (G.O. 9)

GENERAL ORDERS )                              WAR DEPARTMENT
     NO. 9     )                  WASHINGTON, December 12, 1940

                                                      Section
Designation of military reservation as Fort Richardson-- I
Designation of flying fields ------------------------------II
* * * * * * * * * * * * * * * * * * * * * * * * * * * * *

    I.--Designation of military reservation as Fort Richardson.
The military reservation located at Anchorage, Alaska, is
announced as a permanent military post under the provisions
of paragraph 2c, AR 210-10, and is designated Fort Richardso
in honor of Brigadier General WILDS P. RICHARDSON, United
States Army.  Post Office address:  Anchorage, Alaska.

    II.--1. * * * * * * * * * * * * * * * * * * * * * * * *

         2. The flying field at Fort Richardson, Alaska, is
designated "Elmendorf Field" in honor of Captain HUGH M.
ELMENDORF, A.C.  Captain Elmendorf was killed in an airplane
accident at Wright Field, Ohio, on January 13, 1933.


    * * * * * * * * * * * * * * * * * * * * * * * * * * * *


    By order of the Secretary of War:



                                      G. C. MARSHALL,
                                      Chief of Staff

OFFICIAL:
     E. S. ADAMS,
        Major General
        The Adjutant General
```

Photostatic copy of the original order designating Fort Richardson and Elmendorf Field as military installations. The original was almost destroyed in a fire.

chorage would be named Fort Richardson in honor of Brigadier General Wilds P. Richardson, former head of the Alaska Road Commission. The airfield and facilities were named after Captain Hugh M. Elmendorf, a promising Air Corps officer who had been killed January 13, 1933, while testing an experimental pursuit aircraft near Wright Field, Ohio. War Department General Orders 9 dated December 12, 1940 made it official.[54] No one, according to the *Anchorage Daily Times*, knew why the field had been named after a man who had never lived in Alaska or contributed to its development.[55]

General Buckner spent most of his first months traveling throughout Alaska to become familiar with the territory. He joined Major Davis in making survey flights, one of which involved a flight over the Bering Sea islands of Little Diomede and the Russian owned Big Diomede three miles to the west across the International Date Line. The *Nome Nugget* had reported from "reliable sources"

that the Russians were constructing an air base and radio station on Big Diomede.[56] The report proved false.

In September, Buckner accepted an invitation from his Navy counterpart, Captain Ralph C. Parker, to accompany him on a visit to Dutch Harbor where the Navy was building a base on Unalaska Island in the eastern Aleutians to support its operations in the North Pacific. The trip was made aboard one of Parker's old World War I destroyers. The seas were rough, the Navy officers aboard the destroyer did not have suitable charts, and there was a scarcity of navigational markers and radio beacons. As a result, they exercised caution as they steamed through the unfamiliar waters along the Alaska Peninsula and around the eastern Aleutian Islands. Buckner, who was probably the first Army officer to visit the Aleutians and who managed not to become seasick, informed General DeWitt, after his arrival back at Elmendorf on October 3, that:

Captain High M. "Elmie" Elmendorf was among the group of bright young Army Air Corps officer who contributed to the development of air power during the inter war years when the military was starved for funding and a neglected segment of American society. He was noted for his achievement in aerial gunnery and the establishment of a new high altitude record. He was killed while flight testing the experimental YP-25 twin-seat pursuit aircraft near Wright Field, Ohio on January 13, 1933. photo courtesy of Hugh M. Whittingham

The Navy officer had an instinctive dread of Aleutian waters, feeling that they were a jumping off place between Scylla and Charybdis and inhabited by a ferocious monster that was forever breathing fog and coughing up williwaws that would blow the unfortunate mariner onto uncharted rocks and forever destroy his chances of becoming an admiral.[57]

His comments about the Navy were symptomatic of a deeper national problem of a rivalry that existed between the two services, made even more acute by the competition for limited funds during the inter-war years. Traditionally, the Army had contended that the Navy existed to support its effort to seize and hold territory. The Navy looked upon itself as the first line of defense and the major means for projecting power. Each service jealously guarded its prerogatives and their rivalries often received more attention than the nation's defense. A Joint Army-Navy Board had been established in the late 1930s to resolve difficulties and coordinate joint operations. Later, during the war, it would evolve into the Joint Chiefs of Staff, modeled after a similar British staff system. The rivalries would remain, however, and would be particularly noticeable in Alaska where personal egos often got

in the way of military necessity.

Like Buckner, Captain Parker was new to his job, having assumed command of the newly created Alaska Sector, 13th Naval District, in September 1940. Parker's headquarters were located aboard the *Charleston*, and he reported to the district headquarters in Seattle, Washington. The captain had a small fleet of ships built around the *Charleston*; and as with Buckner, he was responsible for overseeing the expansion of the Navy in Alaska. Both commanders were given a considerable amount of local autonomy; and to a certain extent, their joint plans and operations depended on mutual cooperation. Despite their friendship, they were hampered by the flaws in the system that stemmed from service differences and methods of operations.

By 24 October, Buckner had learned enough to submit a list of recommended airfield locations to General DeWitt. They included Nome, Bethel, Kodiak and Unalaska as the first priority. The second established McGrath as an intermediate field between Elmendorf and Nome, and Ruby between Ladd and the Bering Sea coast field. The third priority proposed airfields for Big Delta and Northway to serve the interior route and Cordova to link with the airfields under construction at Yakutat and Annette Island along the coastal route.

General Buckner had coordinated the list with Marshall Hoppin. The Civil Aviation Administration was engaged in an $18 million civil airfield construction program. Virtually all the sites had been surveyed during 1930s. They fit into the general scheme of building civilian and military fields which could be used to the advantage of both for the common good of Alaska. They complied with the War Department's concept of relying on forward bases and air power to provide the main defense of Alaska. Finally, they met the need to provide air defense for the Navy bases.

For the most part, the sites selected posed no particular engineering problems. However, the Navy base at Dutch Harbor was a major concern. Amaknak Island on which the base was located was too small. Unalaska Island was too mountainous. The only alternative left was to shave off the lower slope of Mount Ballyhoo on Amaknak Island to make room for a short tactical field; a project the engineers were not yet ready to tackle. General Buckner and his engineers had to look elsewhere for a place to build the airfield needed for the protection of Dutch Harbor.

By early September, the general had formulated his concept of defense of Alaska. It was similar to that developed by the War Department. He believed that Alaska's vast distances, forbidding terrain and harsh climate precluded any major land invasion, and that Alaska could only be attacked if the Navy lost control of the North Pacific. However, his concept differed from the War Department in two points. He believed the principle threat would be an air or parachute attack, or the combination of the two, launched without warning to seize a forward base. Secondly, he felt that an enemy would use the base for attacking targets along the west coast of Canada and the United States.[58]

The infantry general considered Alaska, because of its terrain and strategic location, to be a theater of air operations. This was the driving force behind his plans to defend the territory. He would later comment to General Marshall that he would rather have a heavy bombardment squadron than an Army division. He believed in striking first, and in a letter to General DeWitt he emphasized his point, stating:

> About twenty years ago, I could have easily knocked out Joe Lewis when he was young and weak. Since he has grown up, I would hesitate to meet him in the ring. The same principle applies to hostile expeditions against Alaska. If we hit them while they are at sea and weak, we can destroy them, but if we wait until they are on shore and strong, our chances for a heavy-weight championship are not particularly good.[59]

The gun boat Charleston *not only served as Captain Parker's flagship but also his headquarters as well from August 1, 1940, when the Alaska Sector was established, until December 1941, when Parker moved ashore at Kodiak following the Japanese attack on Dutch Harbor. The* Charleston *(PG 51) was commissioned July 8, 1938. It was three hundred and twenty-eight feet, six inches long and had a displacement of two thousand tons. The gunboat was equipped with four 6-inch guns, sonar and depth charges. She also carried a Curtiss SOC-1 Seagull amidships but no catapult. The* Charleston *was first based at Seattle upon assignment to the Alaska Sector. At the outbreak of war, she was operated out of Kodiak and Dutch Harbor for the duration of World War II. Her 236 man crew complement contained a detachment of Marines.*

USN photo via Leon Davis, USMC Ret

The Douglas OA-5 amphibian (#33-17) arrived in early November 1940. It was the only one of its kind, having been developed as a prototype of the OA-4. General Buckner and Major Davis intended to use the amphibian in their survey work and for transporting personnel and cargo. General Buckner disliked the Pelican and referred to it as a "tropical bird." The OA-5 was difficult to maintain and did not operate well in cold weather. Nevertheless, Davis and others used the amphibian to land on bodies of water near places than did not have an air strip. It was this aircraft that Davis and Buckner's engineer, Talley, used the following year to examine Otter Point on Umnak Island as a possible landing field site. They landed on a small lake there. Note the insignia of the 1st Air Base Group, Langley Field, Virginia, on the aft section of the fuselage.

Keith T. Petrich photo taken at Juneau via James Ruotsala

The Air Force Arrives

On 8 November *The Daily Times* reported that a Douglas OA-5 Pelican had made the first landing at Elmendorf Field that day.[60] The twin engine amphibian had been sent north for use by General Buckner and Major Davis in making survey flights. It did not operate well in cold weather, and Buckner referred to it as a "no good tropical bird." He elected to use other means of transportation to include a converted yacht named the *James Clark*, which DeWitt sent him during the late summer of 1941.[61] *The Anchorage Daily Times* recorded the landing of one of the two Boeing B-17Bs at Ladd Field on November 26. The big four-engine bombers were undergoing cold weather testing at Ladd.[62] The landing and the rapid progress that had been made in construction meant that the air base could accommodate tactical units. Major Davis had already established a temporary headquarters in one of the flight line garages while waiting for the headquarters building to be completed. His handful of men spent their time inventorying the equipment and supplies that were arriving for the 28th Composite Group and maintaining Davis' B-10, the OA-5 and the O-38 on loan from Ladd Field.

The Douglas O-38F (#33-324) was the first aircraft to be assigned to Alaska. It was shipped to the territory in April 1940 for use by the Cold Weather Test Detachment at Ladd Field. Later in the year, the observation aircraft was loaned to Major Davis. On June 16, 1941, Lieut Milton Askin and his mechanic Sgt Raymond A. Roberts were flying seventy miles southeast of Fairbanks when the O-38 experienced mechanical difficulties. They managed to make a crash landing and walked out safely. Twenty-seven years later a recovery team from the Air Force Museum retrieved the aircraft. It was taken to Wright-Patterson AFB, Ohio where it was restored and placed on display at the museum. AC photo

The latter duties became an increasing hardship with the approach of winter. The temporary hangar had not been completed and construction had just begun on the three permanent hangars, forcing the men to work outside on the aircraft. Additionally, they were responsible for maintaining the runway; and in the absence of markers, they had lined up cut spruce trees along its edges.

They spend much of their time knocking snow off the trees, and realigning them every time the prop wash from one of the Ladd Field B-17s blew them down.[63]

Bob Atwood and his paper reported almost on a daily basis the progress of construction and the arrival and planned arrival of more units. On September 23 he announced that the 73rd Bombardment Squadron (Medium) at McChord Field, Washington had been alerted for deployment to Alaska.[64] On October 4, Atwood informed his readers that the 23rd Air Base Group at Moffett Field, California had been selected for Alaska duty.[65] The next day's paper carried an announcement that the 36th Bombardment Squadron (Heavy) from Lowery Field, Colorado, was coming to Alaska.[66] Finally, on 29 October, Atwood notified his readers that the 18th Pursuit Squadron was scheduled to depart Hamilton Field, California in early 1941 for Elmendorf Field.[67]

Lieutenants Frank L. O'Brien (copilot) and Joe G. Schneider (pilot) were the first to arrive. They landed at Elmendorf Field on February 19, 1941, in one of the 73rd Bombardment Squadron's B-18A Bolos to make the advance arrangements for the rest of the squadron. The two pilots and their crew had departed McChord Field two days earlier. Since there was no control tower, MSgt Delmar E. Wolders, one of Davis' men, used the B-10's radio to issue landing instructions. Davis took O'Brien and Schneider to the 4th Infantry Regiment Officer's Club, which was located in one of the temporary barracks. O'Brien later remembered that everyone seemed "real happy," to see them. Davis was finally getting an air force.[68]

Two days later, the first unit, the 18th Pursuit Squadron, arrived. The squadron had been activated at Moffett Field February 1940, as part of the rapid buildup of the Army Air Corps. At the time it was commanded by Captain Norman D. Sillin and assigned along with the 20th and 21st Pursuit Squadrons to the 35th Pursuit Group. During September, the group and its squadrons moved to Hamilton Field. Shortly afterwards, Captain Sillin received orders to deploy his squadron to Alaska. The other two squadrons were sent to the Philippines in October, where in less than a year they would fall prey to the Japanese invasion and cease to exist. Sillin, who retired as a major general, later recalled that he could have easily ended his career as a prisoner of war if it had not been for the quirk of fate that sent his squadron to Alaska.[69]

Captain Sillin and his men departed San Francisco aboard the U.S. Army transport *Chirikof* on February 8. Their twenty P-36 Hawks were stored in the hold of the transport, an ex-fish hauler converted for Army use. The *Chirikof* arrived in Seward on February 20 after stopping at Seattle and Yakutat. The men, the crated P-36s and the squadron's equipment were loaded aboard an Alaska Railroad train. They reached Elmendorf Field the follow-

The first bomber crew deployed to Alaska arrived at Elmendorf Field, February 19, 1941. Lieuts Frank L. O'Brien is third from right and Joe G. Schneider, fourth from right. Other members were Sgts L. Little and L. W. Williams, engineers; and Pvt Johnson, radio operator. Joe Schneider collection

The Douglas B-18A in which the first bomber crew arrived. AC photo

Sergeant Howard D. Nelson with a P-40E from the 11th Fighter Squadron. Howard Nelson moved with the 18th Fighter Squadron, sometimes ahead of it, from Elmendorf Field to Kodiak and then on to Cold Bay, Umnak, Adak and finally Amchitka. He and the other mechanics assigned to the Eleventh Air Force and Patrol Wing Four suffered many privations at the advance bases, but they always kept their aircraft in the air. Howard Nelson collection

ing day, earning for themselves the distinction of being the first Air Corps unit to be assigned to Alaska. Sillin's men immediately began reassembling the P-36s.[70]

Howard D. Nelson, who had joined the squadron on its activation, remembered the experience. The men of the 18th were greeted on arrival at Elmendorf Field by bleak rows of barracks. The only hangar was unheated and its floor was frozen mud. There were no widow panes on the windows. It was under these conditions that Nelson and the other crew chiefs set to work reassembling the P-36s.

The Hawks had been flown to the Sacramento Air Depot, California prior to their shipment to Alaska. There they were dismantled, covered with protective grease and crated. Nelson and the other mechanics hand washed the

Pilots of 18th Pursuit Squadron aboard the Chirikof, en route to Alaska. Captain Sillin is third from left, front row. Howard Nelson collection

P-36A Hawks, 18th Pursuit Squadron, at Elmendorf Field in crates beside what is today Hangar Four. The emblem of the 55th Pursuit Squadron, Hamilton Field, can be seen under the aft section of the canopy of the Hawk in the foreground. The two bands indicate that it was assigned to a squadron commander. The 55th Pursuit Squadron converted to P-40s in 1940 and the 18th Pursuit Squadron inherited the older aircraft. Howard Nelson photo taken late February 1941

The Hawks at Elmendorf Field, shortly after being reassembled. Howard Nelson photo taken March 1941

The 18th Pursuit Squadron P-36A Hawks lined-up at Elmendorf Field, Summer of 1941. The aircraft in the foreground belonged to the squadron commander, Maj Norman Sillin. AC photo

In Resurrection Bay, entering the Port of Seward. Howard Nelson collection

Captain Sillin's P-36A. Howard Nelson photo

grease off with kerosene. They then rigged a chain hoist and with brute force began connecting the wings, engines and all the other pieces of the aircraft. Everything was cold: the hangar, the barracks and the flight line. Fingers, ears and faces froze and life was generally miserable.[71]

The 28th Composite Group arrived two days after the 18th, ending its long wait since activation at March Field the previous February. Because of the expansion of the Air Corps, the group had lost two of its original squadrons, the 34th Pursuit and the 37th Bombardment Squadron (Medium) to other groups, leaving it with the 36th Bombardment Squadron. The 18th Pursuit Squadron and 73rd Bombardment Squadron were reassigned to the group.

The 28th Composite Group, commanded by Major Donald W. Titus, had boarded the *Saint Mihiel* the morn-

P-36As at Juneau, Summer 1941.
Keith T. Petrich photo via James Roustsala

Members of the 36th Bombardment Squadron at McChord Field, Washington, en route to Alaska. From left to right: Sgt Davis, MSgt Halliwell, MSgt Henry Johnson, TSgt Fretwell, Cpl Randall, Sgt Gus Hewen, Maj Benneth, MSgt Leland B. Culp, Capt William M. Price, MSgt Norman Thruwitt, Lieut Frederick Andrews, Sgt Richard F. Davis, Maj William O. Eareckson, MSgt Clehon, Lieut Frederick R. Ramputi, TSgt Keith Pickett, Lieut Russell A. Cone, Capt Clark, Lieut Frank L. Luechen, unidentified, Capt Giffen, Lieut Nickseson, unidentified, Capt Madison, unidentified, MSgt R. W. Muiller.
AC photo via Richard F. Davis

ing of February 12; and, with an Army band playing at dockside, had sailed for Seward. The trip north was pleasant. The *Saint Mihiel*, after dropping off a group of civilian workers at Ketchikan, arrived at Seward February 22. The next day the 28th Composite Group, which consisted at the time of a headquarters squadron, along with the 23rd Air Base Group and the advance party of the 36th Bombardment Squadron, arrived at Elmendorf Field. Major Davis and his men had done their work well; everything was prepared for the new arrivals, and the men were able to move immediately into their quarters and work places.[72]

Major Davis was particularly glad to see the 23rd Air Base Group and its commander, Major John L. Davidson. The group and its assigned and attached service and service support units meant that Elmendorf Field could now function as a proper air base. The group also provided Davis with a better means for handling the rapid buildup of Air Corps units in Alaska. By the end of February there were 1,301 personnel assigned to his command and more were on the way.[73]

After Lieutenants O'Brien and Schnieder had made their arrangements, the ground echelon of the 73rd Bombardment Squadron arrived March 14. Captain Jack Donohew, the squadron commander, landed at Elmendorf Field on March 30 with eight B-18s after an uneventful three day flight from McChord Field. Again Major Davis' B-10 was parked along the side of the runway and its radios used to provide landing instructions.[74]

The ancient bomber continued to serve on. Davis and others flew it on missions ranging from hauling cargo to searching for downed aircrews. It was painted in Arctic markings, its wing tips and tail day glow orange and the rest silver. Parts were hard if not impossible to find. One of the fuel pumps for the two engines gave out, and the remaining pump had to do double duty. Finally, a wind

Douglas B-18As of the 36th Bombardment Squadron head for Alaska. The 28MB on the vertical stabilizer of the lead bomber denote that it was assigned to the 28th Composite Group, the parent unit of the 36th. Richard F. Davis photo

The 36th Bombardment Squadron arrives over Elmendorf Field. Richard F. Davis photo

storm blew it into the side of a hangar in late 1943; and the relic from the formative days of the modern bomber was salvaged for its few remaining usable parts.[75]

The ground echelon of the second bomber squadron allocated to Alaska, the 36th Bombardment Squadron, arrived March 17 aboard the *Chirikof*. On May 26, Major William O. Eareckson led his squadron's six B-18As to a landing at Elmendorf Field. One of Eareckson's pilots, Lieutenant Fred Ramputi, who later retired from the Air Force as a colonel, remembered the trip north as a pleasant experience with several stops along the way to enjoy the scenery.

Ramputi, as a young bachelor just out of flight school, recalled being "volunteered" for Alaska. He,, along with the other squadron pilots and their crews, had picked up their winterized B-18s at the Sacramento Air Depot. From there, they departed on May 22 for Alaska, stopping

briefly at McChord Field where they had their picture taken. From McChord the squadron flew to Prince George, British Columbia where the town constable took them fishing. Whitehorse was remembered for its moose steak for breakfast, dinner and supper. The next stop was Ladd Field, were Lieutenant Ramputi remembered being taken out on the town by a free spending major. At the time he thought it was part of the welcome. He later learned that the major had been apprehended for check forgery.[76]

The 36th Bombardment Squadron was the last flying unit deployed to Alaska in 1941. Also, no other aircraft were sent to Elmendorf Field that year. General Buckner and his air officer, Major Davis, would have to make do with the small number of obsolescent bombers and pursuits on hand until after the Japanese attack on Pearl Harbor. Alaska was the last overseas theater to receive aircraft and it was also at the bottom of General Arnold's priorities. The Army Air Corps chief of staff was coping with the problems of managing a rapidly expanding air force while at the same time contending with the fact the many of the new aircraft coming out of the factories were being sent to England to assist that embattled nation in her lonely struggle against Germany.

The general kept the bulk of his forces in the states with the idea that they could be rapidly deployed to any trouble spot should the need arise. The Philippines, the Panama Canal and the Hawaiian Islands had priority on anything that went overseas. General DeWitt tried to convince Arnold that Alaska needed more flying units and modern aircraft. The Air Corps chief of staff finally agreed in September that he would send another bomber and pursuit squadron, but it was not until early 1942 that the units arrived.[77]

Jack N. Donohew, shown as a major just after receiving the Distinguished Flying Cross, was one of the few Army Air Force officers who served in the Aleutians to achieve general officer rank. He graduated from the University of Missouri in 1933, then went to West Point where he graduated in 1938. He earned his pilot wings in 1938, later served as the Commander, 28th Composite Group. He left Alaska in May 1943. He attained the rank of major general and served as the Commandant of the Air War College

Frank O'Brien collection

-23-

The Viking Warrior

Except for Colonel William Olmstead Eareckson, the campaigns of the North Pacific produced few heroes. In addition to earning the Distinguished Service Cross, the Navy Cross, the Silver Star and the Distinguished Flying Cross, he also won the love and admiration of those who served under him if not the gratitude of his superiors.

The soldierly looking major, who had the build of a 175-pound halfback, celebrated his fortieth birthday four days after his arrival in Alaska. In the next two years he would leave his unforgettable mark in Alaska. Of Viking decent, he was born in Baltimore, Maryland, and grew up on lands that had belonged to his family since 1690. His ancestors had first migrated from Sweden to England and then had accompanied Lord Baltimore in the founding of the Catholic colony in Maryland during the 17th Century. During 1914-1917, he attended St. Johns College, a preparatory school in Annapolis, Maryland, with the idea of going to West Point. However, he quit in February 1917 to join the Army. In April, the United States declared war on Germany.

The seventeen-year-old Eareckson was sent to France. However, except for a brief period when he went absent without leave to the front, the frustrated young private had to sit out the war in the rear area. Mustered out shortly after the Armistice in 1918, he reenlisted with the idea of gaining an appointment to West Point. In 1920, Eareckson finally realized his dream when he entered the Military Academy on a Presidential appointment. His cadet years were not distinguished by academic brilliance; he ranked 284 out of the 407 members of his class who graduated in 1924. He played intramural football and was on the boxing team but did not qualify for the Academy monogram. He sang in the glee club for four years and served as his class historian. When asked later on a biographical questionnaire if he had achieved any honors at West Point, Eareckson, scrawled, "Graduated!!" However, he looked back at the experience as "the most formative years of my life."[78]

Shortly after graduation, he entered flight school at Kelly Field, Texas, where he was "washed-out" in 1925 for "inherent lack of ability to become a military aviator." Typically undaunted, Eareckson, who had listed the three choices of assignment upon graduation from West Point as "Air Corps," "Air Corps" and "Air Corps," applied and was accepted for balloon school, from which he graduated as an observer and pilot. He spent the next five years at Scott Field, Illinois, the Army Air Corps center for lighter than air operations and training. In 1928, Eareckson and Captain William E. Kepner represented the United States in the Gordon Bennett International Balloon Race. The two came in first, earning them The King Albert of Belgium Trophy and letters of commendation from the Chief of the Army Air Corps.

Eareckson, who had never given up hope of becoming an airplane pilot, was finally accepted for the second time for flight training in 1930. He was twenty-nine years old, well above the normal age for those undergoing the rigorous training. This time, however, he easily won his wings, explaining that the instructors had by then been taught to teach. He spent the next nine years as a bomber and pursuit pilot and was serving as a bomber instructor at Lowery Field when he was selected to command the 36th Bombardment Squadron.[79]

Colonel Eareckson, bare headed, briefs members of his bomber crews on their next mission over Kiska. His leadership style did not impress his superiors and he never made general officer.
AAF photo

He was a man of action who preferred the cockpit of an airplane over a desk, and an officer who strongly believed that the best way to lead was to set the example by going in "harms way." In his letters to Major General William Butler, later to assume command of the Eleventh Air Force, Eareckson vented his frustrations over what he perceived to be too much red tape and unnecessary discussions.[80]

While his men, who called him Colonel "E," revered him and his friends addressed him as Erick, his superiors referred to the impetuous Eareckson as "Wild Bill"; resenting his brash, no-nonsense manner, and sometimes criticized him for spending too much time in an airplane when he should have been on the ground tending to the tedious but necessary administrative and operational details that often spelled the difference between success and failure of a mission.

Apparently reckless and independent in a profession that demanded conformity and team work, Eareckson was innovative in his tactics and a dedicated professional when it came to getting the job done. Ramputi thought him a dynamic leader, and credited him with introducing precision low-level skip bombing and forward air control procedures in the Aleutians before they became common practices in the other war theaters. Whatever his genius or faults were, Eareckson was the right person for a difficult job in a very lonely theater of operations.[81]

Immediately upon his arrival, Eareckson took command of the 28th Composite Group, replacing Major Titus who became Major Davis' deputy. Davis' two-man command from the previous August had grown to 2,087 men by June 1. Earlier, on March 3, shortly after the redesignation of the Alaska Defense Force as the Alaska Defense Command, Buckner appointed Davis as the command's Chief of Aviation. The general also recommended him for promotion to lieutenant colonel.[82]

Quick-Drying Cement

While Major Davis was building his air force, other units were continuing to arrive as fast as transportation could be found. Construction on Elmendorf continued, weather permitting. General Marshall, in early January, was quoted by *The Anchorage Times* as saying that Alaska's defense buildup was a year ahead of schedule with 3,000 assigned military and that:

> This force represents a development more important than the numbers would indicate. With funds made available in the latter part of June, we have succeeded in delivering material and labor to that isolated northern region in time to construct shelter and develop airfields before winter closed in last November.[83]

A considerable amount of progress had in fact been made on the building of Elmendorf Field. Most of the temporary buildings were up and the foundations had been laid for several of the permanent structures. The east west runway had been graded and a 60 by 4,980 foot section paved.[84] However, despite the efforts that had been made and General Marshall's optimistic words in The Anchorage Times, there was a great deal more that had to be done, and the man who was to accomplish it arrived on January 7.

Captain Benjamin B. Talley was the right man for the difficult job of building Alaska's Army defenses. The thirty-eight year old captain had been commissioned in the regular Army in 1926, through competitive examination shortly after graduating from the Georgia School of Technology as an electrical engineer. He was assigned to the U.S. Army of Corps of Engineers, in which he would serve faithfully for thirty years.

During the next fourteen years he served in various engineering assignments that included surveying an alternate route for the Panama Canal through Nicaragua, becoming an authority on the use of aerial photographs in map making and lecturing at Harvard. In September 1939, he became the executive officer at the Seattle District, U.S. Army Corps of Engineers, whose chief, Colonel John Lee along with others had just conducted a survey of Alaska to select air base sites.

The following October, Colonel Lee sent his hard driving captain to supervise the construction of the coastal route air field at Yakutat. Talley and Company B, 28th Engineer Regiment arrived on October 23 and began carving an air field out of the coastal wilderness.[85] Before taking on the Yakutat project, the engineer captain had visited Elmendorf Field that summer. He found conditions far from ideal. The cold drizzling summer rains, typical of the Anchorage area during late summer and early fall, had made life miserable. Mud was everywhere, and Talley later remembered that it was "the most uninviting military camp that I had ever seen until I saw the U.S. Marine Corps camp in Vietnam during the monsoon of 1965."[86]

Talley got his opportunity to do something about the conditions he had found at Elmendorf Field when the War Department decided to transfer the supervision of construction of Army facilities from the Quartermaster Corps to the Engineer Corps. Until that point, the latter had primarily been involved in large scale civil and military construction projects. The change placed Talley in charge of all Army constructions in Alaska. The captain assumed his duties as Resident Engineer in Alaska for the Seattle District on January 15. The following day, he was quoted in *The Anchorage Daily Times*, as being "very gratified with work at the Anchorage base and I am taking over a well organized and smooth running organization."[87]

The engineer captain, however, was faced with a con-

Captain Benjamin B. Talley, center, probably engaged in one of his numerous survey flights. He was one of the few "ground" officers assigned to the Alaska Defense Command who was placed on flight status. He is an honorary member of the Eleventh Air Force. Benjamin Talley collection

Civilian construction workers toiled into the winter months of 1940, laying out runways, erecting barracks and building other facilities. When Captain Talley arrived in January 1941, Major George had already laid the foundation of what would be the largest permanent military installation in Alaska. Talley completed the project. Russ Dow photo

A temporary hangar was built. It was here that Sgt Howard Nelson and the other mechanics reassembled the P-36. The hangar is still in use today. AC photo

Work resumed on the pouring of concrete for the runways at Elmendorf Field during the Spring of 1941. AC photo

A steam system was used during the Fall of 1940 to thaw the ground so than work could continue. AC photo

One of the three permanent arch hangars that were built. The photograph was taken July 10, 1941. George Sullivan, later mayor of Anchorage during the 1980s, was a construction worker on one of the hangars. Note the P-36s parked on ramp. AC photo

View of barracks construction May 5, 1941. AC photo

The heating and power plant and the post laundry as they looked in June 1941. The power plan was torn down in 1986. The former base laundry now houses the base reproduction and publications facilities. AC photo

A view of what the accommodations were like in an Elmendorf Field barracks during 1941. AC photo

Elmendorf Field was built as a permanent air base. The headquarters building above now houses the headquarters of the 21st Tactical Fighter Wing. When the photograph was taken June 13, 1944, the building had been painted in camouflage colors. AAF photo

The two aerial photographs, one taken on May 27, 1941 and the other a month later show the progress in construction of *Elmendorf Field that had been accomplished in less than a year, first under the direction of Major George and later Captain Talley. In the photograph above, Ship Creek and Anchorage can be seen in the upper center and Merrill Field in the upper left. The photographs were taken by the 1st Photographic Squadron.* Frank O'Brien collection

siderable number of problems that ranged from labor unrest to an unresponsive bureaucracy. One of the biggest problems was the emergency nature of the construction projects. As with most such efforts in Alaska, there was a considerable lag between planning and execution.

Then there were the traditional problems of transportation and weather. Alaska was undeveloped, and almost all the construction material, as well as the workers, had to be brought from the "outside." The difficulties did not end once the men and materials reached Seward. They then had to move over Colonel Ohlson's railroad into the interior. The continual shifting of transportation modes and the distances involved, invariably led to delays.

The major problem, however, was not the amount of supplies being delivered but in the manner in which they were delivered. In the absence of enough local longshoremen, Buckner had to press his infantry troops, to the detriment of their training, into unloading the equipment and materials that were arriving at a rate of a thousand tons a day at Anchorage and then transporting them to Fort Richardson where the storage sheds stretched for a half mile. Unfortunately, the shipments were not delivered in an orderly manner, and vitally needed components were often sent in different ships or were missing altogether. Also, unlike the states, where missing items could readily be replaced in days, it sometimes took months to obtain them in Alaska. This often delayed, or worse, stopped construction work.

Many projects had to be halted during the sub Arctic winter months, usually signaled by snow on the mountain tops which was aptly referred to as "termination dust." This resulted in a frenzy of activity during the summer months as workers worked around the clock in shifts to complete their projects.

General Buckner, an impatient man who took pride in his newly acquired nickname "The Silver Stallion of Alaska," was not pleased with the delays and the red tape he was encountering in his efforts to fortify Alaska. To his dismay, he found that his engineers lacked the authority to make changes on designs, and that procurement decisions were being made by the U.S. Army Corps of Engineers office in Seattle and at General DeWitt's headquarters at the Presidio.[88] He wanted the authority and the construction projects under his control. The general decided to go directly to General Marshall. In a November 24 letter to the Army chief of staff he quoted Talley, stating, "that quick-drying cement did him very little good in speeding up construction unless some quick-drying ink was used on the approval of his plans."[89]

General Marshall, after consulting with his staff and General DeWitt, decided in late December to transfer the Western Defense Command's construction responsibility to Alaska. Buckner's control was further strengthened

when he succeeded in May 1942, in having Talley's engineer office transferred from the Seattle District to his direct control. The ambitious and highly energetic Talley, who was advancing rapidly towards his colonelcy, now had complete charge of all Army construction in Alaska. With typical bulldog determination, he was to oversee a remarkable $300 million building program, which would provide much of the modern military infrastructure in Alaska.[90]

Another of Buckner's problems was solved when he gained control of the Civil Aviation Administration's $18 million construction program in mid-1942. The agency was engaged in building a series of badly needed civilian air fields. Although the 3,000-foot strips were suitable for commercial aviation, they could not accommodate the heavier military aircraft. Buckner wanted 6,000-foot strips and he wanted them paved.

While the relationship between Buckner and Hoppin was cordial, those at the national level were not. The administration rightly considered the needs of commercial aviation first and were unwilling to accommodate the military. Additionally, they were not building air fields fast enough or in the right places to suit the aggressive general. With a war on and Alaska threatened, Buckner finally proved his point. The agency agreed to relinquish its authority for local construction to Hoppin. This allowed the general and his civilian counterpart to work out their differences without outside interference and to coordinate their efforts more effectively.[91]

As the construction proceeded at a rapid pace, General Buckner continued his campaign to obtain more and better aircraft for Alaska. Here he was less successful in his efforts. Despite General Arnold's words of support the previous year, Alaska remained at the bottom of the priority list. General Arnold was contending with an expansion program that would ultimately take the clubby, bomber-oriented prewar organization of less than 20,000 officers and men to a force of 2,372.292, the mightiest of its kind ever sent into battle.

Arnold's plans to husband his resources in the states, and only send them to overseas locations when needed did not sit well with Buckner. To him, Arnold and his staff were "obsessed with an unfortunate degree of optimism," and had dismissed Alaska with the idea "that if anything happens we will rush a lot of planes up there to take care of the situation." Buckner felt aircraft could not "be rushed . . . and if anything happened it would be too late to do much about it."[92]

Of the original twenty P-36s and fifteen B-18s allocated to Alaska, fifteen of the pursuits and ten of the bombers were serviceable by July. Although considered one of the best fighters in the world when it was first delivered to the Army Air Corps in May 1938, the radial engine P-36 was being phased out of the inventory in 1941, in favor of its derivative, the P-40 Warhawk. With two cowl-mounted 30 caliber machine guns, the P-36 was grossly under-armed in comparison to fighters of other nations. The B-18 was a derivative of the Douglas DC-3, which Congress had foisted on the Air Corps as an economy measure in lieu of the more expensive four-engine B-17. With a 4,400-pound bomb load and a 600-mile radius, the slow and vulnerable twin engine bomber was unsuitable for combat operations in 1941.

The best that Davis could do was use his small fleet of obsolescent warplanes to train his pilots to fly under Alaskan conditions. Taking advantage of the long summer daylight hours, Davis divided the training into two shifts so as to maximize the use of his limited number of aircraft. The first shift rose early and flew until 11:00 AM, when the second shift, who had slept late, took over and flew until late in the evening. The pilots quickly gained operational experience that they would later pass on to the newer pilots.[93] Buckner, pleased with their progress and acknowledging a debt to the Alaskan Bush pilots, commented to DeWitt in July, ". . . the splendid performance of our own pilots, and as they gain in experience, we are less and less dependent upon local flyers."[94]

Despite the progress in training, Buckner and Davis had serious doubts about the ability of the small number of obsolescent aircraft to meet a determined attack. Writing to General Marshall in late July, Buckner pointed out that his, ". . . immediate concern [was] to build up an Air Force sufficiently strong to make any hostile expedition against Alaska shores too hazardous a venture as to remove it from the realm of probability."[95]

He was arguing a lost cause in 1941. General Marshall was sympathetic. "The War Department is appreciative of the importance of your problem . . . is doing everything . . . your command has been given a high priority [but] . . . deliveries to Alaska have been delayed because of more pressing demands in the Philippines."[96]

The Douglas B-18A Bolo was obsolete when it was sent to Alaska in 1941. Fortunately it was replaced with more modern bombers before the Eleventh Air Force entered combat with the Japanese. It continued to serve on as a squadron transport and perform other utilitarian duties. Charles Pinney provided an account of flying one in this role in his article "A Military Bush Pilot on the Forgotten Front," in the Spring 1975 edition of the Aerospace Historian. AC photograph

A display of emergency equipment carried in a B-18 in Alaska. The 36th and 73rd Bombardment Squadrons personnel flew wide-ranging missions throughout Alaska after their arrival supporting air field surveys, transporting personnel and familiarizing themselves with Alaska's rugged and unforgiving terrain. They and the men of the 11th and 18th Fighter Squadrons provided a trained cadre for the personnel of the units who arrived later to fight the war in the Aleutians. AC photo

One of the missions assigned to the B-18 crews was to fly support for the 1st Photographic Squadron. The squadron had been deployed from Grey Field on Fort Lewis, Washington, during the Summer of 1941 to take aerial photographs of Alaska air field sites and the proposed Alaska Highway route. Frank O'Brien recalled that one of the missions involved returning some of the squadron's support personnel and equipment back to Grey Field during the Fall of 1941. O'Brien, two other pilots, Lieuts Edward P. Clark and Gene Yarborough, the mission commander, took off from Elmendorf Field and stopped in Juneau. The next day, a few miles from Prince Rupert, one of Clark's B-18 engines quit and the heavily loaded bomber began losing altitude. Fortunately, he managed to land it on a sandbar during low tide. The passengers and cargo were safely removed before the tide came in. Clark and his crew succeeded in making the bomber waterproof. The Royal Canadian Air Force from Prince Rupert provided a barge, which was sunk under the floating bomber. When the tide went out, the barge with the B-18 on it was left high and dry. The barge was then drained and on the next high tide it was towed to Seattle where the bomber was repaired at the nearby Boeing plant. Frank O'Brien collection via AAHM

This photograph shows a B-18 in olive drab at the far left somewhere in the Aleutians. In the foreground is a B-26 being used as a temporary control tower. In the distance is a C-47 and a PBY. AAF photo

The Last Summer of Peace

General Marshall had reason for concern. The Japanese were becoming increasingly aggressive. The small island nation within the past one hundred years had emerged from feudal isolation to become the leading industrial nation in Asia with a powerful army and the world's third largest navy. Racked by the world-wide depression of the late 1920s, Japan's democratic ideals had given way to military solutions. By the early 1930s, the military, primarily the Army, capitalizing on the economic depression and social unrest, had gained the upper hand through political intrigue and assassination. Its leaders controlled national affairs and dictated international relations. Imbued with a warrior spirit and an arrogant outlook toward its Asian neighbors, Japan embarked on a plan to seize, by force, the resources its barren lands could not provide and to establish itself as the dominant power in Asia.

The Army moved into Manchuria in 1931, on the pretext that the Chinese had tried to sabotage the Japanese owned railroad there. When the League of Nations protested, Japan withdrew in 1934 from the unpopular 1922 Washington Arms Limitation Treaty and embarked on a massive navy expansion program. This expansion coupled with the possession of the former German owned Caroline, Marianas and Marshall Islands in the Central Pacific, ceded to her for token participation in World War I, gave Japan a dominant position in the western Pacific. It effectively isolated the American forces in the Philippine Islands.

After the occupation of Manchuria, Japan began placing increasing demands on China; and having failed to gain her ends by diplomatic means, used another fabricated military pretext to invade the hapless nation in 1937. With an industrial base geared for a minor war, Japan's otherwise well trained and modernized military force soon became bogged down in a protracted war against the weak but resilient China.

The United States, while suffering though its own depression, watched the events in the Far East with a growing concern. Because of its long association with China, founded on economic interest and the activities of her missionaries, the nation sympathized with that country's plight. The relationship between the U.S. and Japan became increasingly strained over the latter's atrocities against the Chinese and its mistreatment of American citizens living in China. The distrust was further fueled by racial misunderstandings and a refusal to comprehend each other's capabilities and intentions.

In 1939, the United States, exasperated over Japan's aggressions in China, declared its intention to abrogate its 1911 Trade Treaty; and the following year, imposed a limited embargo on goods shipped to Japan. Hitler's lightning conquest of continental Europe during the Spring of 1940 completely upset the balance of power in the Far East. With France and Holland defeated and England preoccupied, Japan took advantage of the situation to coerce the weak French Vichy government into allowing her to occupy northern Indo-China. This gave her bases from which her bombers could interdict the Burma Road, over which American supplies were moved into China. At the same time, Japan sought unsuccessfully to have the entire oil output of the Dutch East Indies diverted to her use. The United States blocked the attempt.

Japan further consolidated her position on September 27, by signing the Tripartite Pact with Germany and Italy, which she unrealistically believed would deter the United States from interfering with her plans to extend her influence in the Far East.[97] The United States, having embarked on a massive build-up of its military forces, was not impressed. President Roosevelt in early 1940, in response to the growing Japanese menace, had quietly shifted the U.S. Fleet from its West Coast ports to Pearl Harbor. On February 1, 1941, the U.S. Fleet was redesignated the U.S. Pacific Fleet. Efforts were also begun in earnest to reinforce the isolated and vulnerable Philippine Islands.[98] The Japanese in turn began planning for war with the United States, which she considered morally weak and more interested in her material needs than her commitments to others.

To secure her northern flank, Japan entered into a nonaggression pact with the Soviet Union in April 1941. The treaty ended years of tensions which had been brought to a head by the Khalkhin-gal incident in the summer of 1939, when a series of border incidents along the ill-defined Manchurian-Outer Mongolian border erupted into a short but violent war between Japan and Russia. A Soviet army led by General Georgi Zhukov utterly defeated the Japanese.

Smarting from the drubbing at the hands of the Red Army, Japan turned her attention to the more vulnerable western colonial possessions in Southeast Asia and the Pacific and entered into negotiations with the Russians. The resulting nonaggression treaty allowed her to transfer a million men elsewhere. The Russians in turn scrupulously observed its terms, much to the displeasure of her allies, until the very last days of the war against Japan, when like a vulture, she took advantage of the impending victory to attack that desperate nation and acquire her share of the spoils of war.

In July, following the German invasion of Russia, Japan occupied the rest of Indo-China. This gave her access to bases from which her air forces could dominate the South China Sea and the surrounding resource-rich countries she coveted. President Roosevelt reacted on July 25 to this blatant act of aggression by placing a complete embargo

Captain Parker acquired additional Grumman J2F-6 Ducks. This one is shown at Juneau later in the war. USN photo via AAHM

on goods being shipped to Japan and freezing her assets in the United States. There would be no more trade and no more oil from America's refineries. The British imposed their embargo the next day and the Dutch government in exile followed suit the day after.

It was the last summer of peace. With an awful certainty, the United States and Japan moved toward war, each misjudging the others' intentions. A philosophy of war permeated Japan, and the oil embargo had pushed its people to the brink of despair. Even the most antiwar Japanese generals and admirals were convinced that war was inevitable. The proud, industrious and highly disciplined Japanese faced the sad prospect of giving up all they had gained in Manchuria and China, and perhaps becoming a third-rate power in exchange for the lifting of the embargo. Instead, the small island nation decided to take on a sleeping giant, who although initially confused, would strike back with terrible, uncompromising vengeance.[99]

During the last week of August, Colonel Hedeo Iwakuro, an influential colonel in the War Ministry, who had already made dozens of speeches before top-level military, political and industrial groups urging that Japan continue its negotiations with the United States, attended a conference where he contrasted the vast differences between the two nations. In steel, the U.S. out performed the Japanese 20 to 1; in coal, 10 to 1; aircraft production, 5 to 1; shipping 2 to 1; labor, 5 to 1; and oil production, 100 to 1.[100]

The Japanese through sheer force of will could make up most of their deficiencies. However, they could do little without oil. They were importing at the time 80 percent of their oil from the United States. Much of the rest came from the Dutch East Indies and British oil fields in the Mid East[101]. Japan's oil production in 1941, which included Formosa, was a paltry 5,455 barrels a day compared to the United State's 3,842,000.[102] Yet, she was consuming

over 75,000 barrels a day. At the time of the embargo, Japan had built up a reserve of 50,000,000 barrels, which by careful rationing she could make last for at least two years.[103]

However, the Imperial Japanese Navy was a prodigious user of oil, accounting for over half of the nation's consumption. The Navy's statisticians calculated that at its current consumption rate the Navy would run out of oil in six months.[104] To conserve its allocation of oil, the Navy restricted its training activities to the waters near the home islands.[105]

The tensions between the United States and Japan continued to build as summer turned into fall. Alaska, far to the north, remained low on everyone's priority list. Reinforcements, particularly airplanes were being rushed to more endangered places in the western Pacific. The Alaska Defense Command began its second winter with only a handful of antiquated warplanes despite promises from Arnold, Marshall and others that Alaska been not been forgotten. Arnold in a November 15, 1941, letter to Buckner summed up the dilemma he was facing.

His rapidly growing force had finally achieved an equal footing with the ground forces when the Army Air Corps was redesignated the Army Air Forces on July 20, as part of an overall reorganization of the Army in preparation for the coming conflict. However, the demands of the Lend-Lease program and the need to equip and man the new units left little for Alaska. Nevertheless, he did promise to send another fighter and a bomber squadron to Alaska and to replace the B-18s and P-36s with modern aircraft in the near future.[106]

Captain Ralph Parker had even less success obtaining aircraft for the Navy. In addition to a Curtiss SOC-1 Seagull scout plane aboard the USS *Charleston*, he had a Vought OS2U-3 Kingfisher at Sitka and a Grumman J2F-6 Duck at Kodiak. The two were only suitable for utility duties and limited off-shore patrolling. His appeals for more aircraft met a negative response from his superiors. The Navy, which was also undergoing its own expansion program, did continue to deploy Catalina PBY patrol planes to Sitka and Kodiak on training missions from Sand Point Naval Air Station, Washington.[107]

If General Buckner and Captain Parker were disappointed with the air support they were receiving, they could be proud of the rapid expansion of their forces. By the end of September, there were 21,565 men assigned to the Alaska Defense Command and 13,260 to the Alaska Sector. More were on their way.[108]

By then proposals had been put forth to make Alaska a separate theater of operations. In April, War Department planners suggested the idea for the first time. Shortly afterwards Brigadier General Carl Spaatz, then Chief of the Air Staff, recommended an Alaska Department be created under an Army Air Force general. He reasoned that Alaska, because of its vast size, was more suited for air than ground operations. General Buckner in his letters to General DeWitt also suggested a separate theater. DeWitt, not wishing to see his responsibilities diminished, countered that since he was furnishing the forces and Alaska was vital to the defense of the western United States, he should retain overall control. In mid-August, the War Department relented, and DeWitt, for better or worse, was to retain control of Buckner and the Alaska Defense Command for the next two years.[109]

The uncertainties of the command relations were particularly difficult for Major Davis. As Chief of Aviation, Alaska Defense Command, he had little command authority over the air units. With the rapid buildup of forces during the first half of 1941, the need for a command headquarters became apparent. As a result, the Air Field Forces, Alaska Defense Command was established May 29. It was responsible for the training, maintenance, plan-

The P-36s continued to serve after the arrival of the more modern P-38s and P-40s. They were painted olive drab and used to build flying time. The P-39 pilots who arrived on temporary duty with the 54th Fighter Group after the Japanese attack on Dutch Harbor flew the fighters in order to familiarize themselves with its conventional landing gear. The P-39 was equipped with tricycle landing gear. Gradually, over a period of time, most of the original complement of twenty Hawks were damaged beyond economic repair. Those that survived were eventually transferred elsewhere. AAF photos

ning and the executing of air defense plans. However, the 23rd Air Base Group and other air support units remained under the control of the Fort Richardson commander. Consequently, Major Davis had no direct control over the ground units that supported his air operations.[110]

The problems came to a head when two of General Arnold's staff, Colonel Frank M. Kennedy and Lieutenant Colonel Harold L. Clark, arrived in August on an inspection trip. Both were familiar with Alaska, and Colonel Clark had accompanied General Arnold on his trip to the territory the previous year. The two found the conditions under which Major Davis operated "deplorable." Tactical operations were being neglected because of administrative requirements, such as the survey flights that Buckner had ordered. In addition to not having direct control over the ground support units, Davis had not been given an adequate staff to assist him in his duties.

In their report to General Arnold, the two colonels recommended that the Alaska Defense Command be made a separate theater of operations under an Air Force general. They also recommended that Davis be given more command authority over the Army Air Forces units in Alaska.[111]

While General Arnold did not act on the first he did take action on the second recommendation. The ground units were placed under Davis's control, more staff personnel were provided and the name of the headquarters was changed to the Air Force, Alaska Defense Command on October 17. Shortly afterward, Davis received his much-deserved promotion to lieutenant colonel. He now had the rank, the authority and an organization to carry out his duties as commander of a force that had grown to 2,278 officers and men.

In the wake of the change, Major Eareckson assumed command to the 23rd Air Base Group, replacing Major Davison who became Davis' assistant. Major Sillin replaced Eareckson as Commander, 28th Composite Group on November 7. Major Titus became the Chief of Aviation, Alaska Defense Command.[112]

Even though many of his problems had been solved, Colonel Davis was still faced with a shortage of aircraft and air crews. In a letter to an old friend on Arnold's staff, Davis noted in November that only six of his original fifteen B-18s were flyable. Five had been damaged in accidents and the others were grounded for various reasons, leading Davis to comment, "Don't figure on getting any serviceable B-18s back from us. We have been hard on them."[113]

The 18th Pursuit Squadron had experienced similar problems with their P-36s. Many were grounded due to the lack of spare parts and several had been involved in accidents. The squadron's first fatality occurred in late November when Lieutenant William A. Anderson spun out of control over Chatham Bay, south of the Kenai Peninsula, after encountering severe turbulence during a training mission. His squadron mates observed his aircraft falling into the waters in three pieces. Davis ordered an immediate inspection of the other P-36s. The mechanics found eight with popped rivets. One had a buckled wing. Davis, commenting on the accident, voiced the general concern about the Hawk's suitability for Alaskan operations. "The boys have lost their faith in the ruggedness of the P-36s."[114]

The Alert

While Davis trained his pilots and Buckner continued his relentless program to build Alaska's defenses, Hitler launched operation Barbarossa in the early dawn hours of June 22. In the biggest campaign of mankind's biggest war, Hitler committed 121 divisions and 3,000 aircraft in an invasion of Russia across a 2,000-mile front that stretched from the White Sea in the north to the Black Sea in the south. For a moment it appeared that Hitler's prediction that "if you kick in the door, the rest of the rotten edifice will fall," might come true.

Rolling forward as much as forty miles a day, the Germans easily overwhelmed their confused foe. However, by the end of the summer, Russian resistance began to stiffen, and as fall changed into bitter winter it solidified. With German patrols probing the outskirts of Moscow, the Russians launched a massive counterattack in December that stopped the onslaught. The Germans, ill-equipped for the minus forty degree temperatures and worn out by over six months of unrelenting combat, settled into defensive positions. The horror, however, would continue; and before it was over, it would consume the lives of twenty million Russians, lay waste to their most productive lands, further justify their paranoia of being surrounded by potential enemies, and help plant the seeds of the Cold War.

General Marshall and his staff were alarmed at the rapidity of the German advance into Russia during the opening days of the war. They feared that Japan might, under the guise of the Tripartite Pact, take advantage of Russia's plight to seize her bases in the Pacific. On July 3, he ordered an alert. DeWitt immediately notified Buckner to inform all his garrisons of the "increasing danger of total Russian collapse and subsequent possibility of Axis operations in direction of Alaska."[115]

While Hawaii and Panama were quick to respond to General Marshall's alert order, the Alaska Defense Command took four days to notify its forces of the impending danger. The Alaska Communication System, geared for peacetime operations, had failed its first military test.[116]

U.S. Army Signal Corps telegraph delivery men stand ready in front of the Signal Corps Office in the Federal Building, downtown Anchorage. From 1900 to 1970, when the Alaska Communication System was sold to a private firm, the military provided all long-line communication services in Alaska. USA photo

ACS telegraph office & qtrs at Flat, Alaska
Oct 1943

A typical Alaska Communication System office and quarters. This one was located at Flat in interior Alaska. At the outbreak of the war, the Army had two Signal Corps companies in the territory. Its personnel were located in the widely scattered and remote communities throughout Alaska. USA photo

Since the days when General Mitchell helped build it, the Army Signal Corps had maintained and operated Alaska's long distance communications system. Initially known as the Washington Alaska Military Cable and Telegraph System, or WAMCATS, the name had been changed to the Alaska Communication System in 1936. The system consisted of remote radio stations located throughout Alaska manned by approximately 200 Signal Corps personnel. Although originally intended to provide communications for the Army garrisons that were built during the Gold Rush, the system actually supported the civil sector. It provided the only means by which Alaska's far-flung and isolated communities could communicate with each other and the rest of the world. It was also slow and expensive to operate, so much so that Bob Atwood, who received most of his national and international news over the Anchorage to Seattle radio link, had devised a code to reduce the number of words in order to save money.

Although the system was adequate for peacetime use, it could not meet the requirement of war. There was no backup system and the radios used could easily be monitored by an enemy. Land-line communications had been abandoned in 1923, because of maintenance difficulties in favor of the cheaper radio system, which some jokingly referred to as DBR, or damned big rush, since it was installed in a hurry without proper testing. With the military buildup, the Alaska Communication System was taxed to the limit. Traffic increased by 200 percent between 1939 and 1940.

To meet the greatly increased needs, additional funds were allocated and the Alaska Communication System staff was increased to 599 by January 1941. It would continue to grow in the years ahead. A tactical communications network that linked the military bases was established; and the underseas cable between Anchorage and

Seattle, which had been deactivated in favor of a cheaper radio link, was reactivated to provide the military with a secure means of communications. In addition to the Signal Corps efforts, the first men of the Army Airways Communication System began arriving in mid-1941 to provide air traffic control and weather reporting services.[117]

However, the Army's communications still could not keep up with the demand placed on it by the growing number of bases. The problem became more acute in the Aleutian Islands. The Signal Corps did rig a system between Dutch Harbor and the base Talley's engineers were building at Otter Point on Umnak Island, but it was destined to fail at a critical moment when the Japanese attacked Dutch Harbor.

The Navy was better prepared since their ships' radios were more efficient and it had developed a considerable amount of experience with its radio station at Dutch Harbor. Later, the Army was able to establish a tactical and administrative network that linked its posts throughout Alaska. However, lack of supplies and equipment and the vast distances that had to be covered in Alaska would hamper both services in the years ahead.[118]

The alert had also exposed the weaknesses of the air defense system. Aside from the handful of P-36s, there was no early warning radar system in Alaska to provide warning of an air attack. The Signal Corps, however, had begun work on establishing one in 1940. The vast distances and sparse population in Alaska made it difficult to establish a ground observation corps as had been the practice elsewhere in the United States. By August 1940, the Corps had developed its initial plans for providing a series of radar sites near the bases that were being built in Alaska. They called for the construction of eight radar sites, later increased to twelve in January 1941. Generals DeWitt and Buckner had wanted twenty. The number was finally scaled back to ten after the start of the Aleutian Campaign.[119]

In December 1940, site construction was authorized for Aircraft Warning Service fixed SCR-271 long-range aircraft warning radars at Cape Chiniak on the northeast coast of Kodiak Island, Mount Harbor at Sitka and Cape Winslow north of Dutch Harbor. Site construction was also authorized for a mobile SCR-270 long-range aircraft warning radar on Pedro Dome near Fairbanks and a radar filter center on Elmendorf Field where the information could be collected and the necessary orders issued. In March 1941, construction of additional sites were authorized for Cape Hinchinbrook at the entrance of Prince William Sound, Yakutat and Forrester Island in south eastern Alaska, Lazy Bay on the south coast of Kodiak Island and Nushagak on the lower end of Bristol Bay. These sites were intended to provide minimum warning of the approach of enemy aircraft to Elmendorf and

Ladd Fields and the Navy bases at Dutch Harbor, Kodiak and Sitka.

Other sites were planned for the west coast of Alaska. However, after the Japanese attacked Dutch Harbor and occupied Attu and Kiska, the priorities were changed. Emphasis was shifted to locating the sites on the Alaska Peninsula and the Aleutian Islands.[120]

The 691st Aircraft Warning and Reporting Company arrived in March 1941. The first site, a mobile SCR-270 long-range aircraft warning radar, was installed on Fort Richardson in November 1941. A fixed SCR-271 long-range aircraft warning radar was installed on Cape Chiniak, Kodiak in February 1942. They were the only operational sites by the time of the Dutch Harbor attack. Most of the sites that were built in Alaska during the war were located in remote locations, which in some cases were accessible only by boats. As a result, the mobile radar sets intended for temporary locations wound up becoming a permanent fixture for the duration of the war. In practice the early warning radar system proved to be inadequate because of the vast area it had to cover, the atmospheric conditions and the limitations of equipment at that time.[121] In any case, even after the start of the war, visual observations continued to be the most reliable, if not the best means of detecting an air attack.[122]

General Mitchell as a Signal Corps lieutenant in Alaska. The photograph entitled "ready to mush" was taken near Fort Egbert, Alaska in the winter of 1903. It was found by Lyman Woodman, an Army historian living in Anchorage, in the Mitchell family album.

Photograph, probably taken in March or April 1942, shows, from left to right, Capt Leslie E. Gehres, Commander, Patrol Air Wing Four; Lieut Charles E. Perkins, Executive Officer, VP-42; Lieut Comdr James S. Russell, Commander, VP-42 and Capt Russell Cone, Commander, 36th Bombardment Squadron.

James S. Russell photo

The Gentle Warrior

Finally, the alert exposed the problem over who had the authority to order off-shore air patrols in Alaska. In the absence of suitable Navy aircraft, Buckner ordered his B-18s into the air. Elements of the 36th and 73rd Bombardment Squadrons were sent to Nome to conduct patrols over the Bering Sea. After accumulating approximately 5,000 hours over the frigid waters, the B-18s were withdrawn from their duties in September. Although accomplishing little operationally, the patrols did provide valuable training in over water flights, something which would later prove useful in the Aleutians.

While Captain Parker had readily agreed to General Buckner using Army aircraft for patrolling the Bering Sea, his superiors all the way up to Admiral King thought otherwise. They quickly pointed out that it was their mission to fly over water and the Army's mission was to restrict itself to operations over land. General DeWitt intervened, Buckner continued to send his B-18s out on missions over the waters off Alaska, and the Navy began deploying patrol aircraft to Alaska in earnest.[123]

Beginning in July 1941, Consolidated PBY-5 seaplanes from the Sand Point Naval Air Station, Washington based VP-41 and VP-42 patrol squadrons began routine operational deployments to Alaska. Operating from Sitka, Kodiak and Dutch Harbor, the Catalinas were flown on missions over the Gulf of Alaska and along the Aleutian Islands as far west as Attu.[124] One of the men who came north with VP-42 was Lieutenant Commander James Russell, who would later become one of the key players in the Aleutian Campaign, and as a full admiral following the war, its ranking veteran.

Born the year the Wright Brothers made the first powered flight, James Russell grew up in Tacoma, Washington. After graduating from high school, he served as a merchant seaman during World War I. In 1922, he entered the U.S. Naval Academy from which he graduated 15 out of a class of 450 in 1926. Three years later he became a Naval Aviator. A summary of the quiet, gentle man's career reads like a list of "firsts" in Naval Aviation, starting with being among the first Academy graduates to receive flight training and the first aviator to land on all six of the Navy's prewar carriers.

Following flight school, Russell served in various observation squadrons with the fleet before the Navy, taking advantage of his brilliant mind, sent him to graduate school where he earned a masters degree in aeronautical engineering. He would later put it to good use in assisting in the design of the Essex class carrier; and after the war, the F8U Crusader, the first supersonic carrier-based fighter for which he shared the Collier Trophy in 1956.

After earning his graduate degree in 1935, the Navy sent Russell back to sea as a member of a fighter-bomber squadron aboard the carriers *Ranger* and *Lexington*. He was then assigned to the Bureau of Aeronautics where he worked on the development of the Essex class carriers which were to play a pivotal role in the Pacific during the coming war. In early 1941, as his tour at the bureau was coming to an end, Russell learned that there was an opening for him at the Sand Point Naval Air Station.[125] On asking for the assignment, the personnel officer informed him: "Want to go to that rainy country? Why not!" Remembering later, Russell felt he, "did not want to burden him with the information that I was a native of Tacoma and my family home was there."[126]

About mid-way through his leave in Tacoma, Lieutenant Russell decided to visit his new unit, VP-42. After driving to Seattle, he reported to its commander, Lieutenant Commander Alan R. Nash, who informed him that the squadron was preparing to deploy to Alaska. Instead of the pleasant assignment near his home town, Russell, like so many of his generation, found his life suddenly changed by the winds of war. Cutting short his leave, he left for Alaska with the rest of his squadron in mid-July on a four month deployment, one of the many the Seattle based naval aviation units would make in the years ahead.

After spending the night at Sitka, the flight of five Catalinas flew on to Kodiak. The squadron got its first taste of Alaskan weather on its trip across the Gulf of Alaska, when a lowering ceiling forced the crews to fly just above the waves. As the squadron navigator, Russell was responsible for guiding the others in for a safe landing in Womens Bay at Kodiak. The only navigational aid available was an uncalibrated radio range station on Woody Island offshore of Kodiak Harbor. Using this Russell was able to lead the flight to within sight of the coastline. Soon rocks and stunted spruce trees appeared out of the fog on the left and then the same scene came into view on the right side. "The squadron fell out of the air like a flock of wounded ducks," Russell later remembered.

The pilots of three PBYs landed straight ahead. One reversed course to come down into the wind. The squadron commander in the fifth patrol plane continued on up the bay in search of an opening in the fog. Finding none, he returned and landed where the others were waiting on the water. Shortly afterwards, a Mr Nelson rowed up in a dory to Russell's PBY. After consulting with him and looking at the charts, the newly initiated navigator to Alaskan flying learned that they had landed in the channel between Afognak and Kodiak Islands.

The two squadrons had been preceded to Kodiak by two seaplane tenders, the USS *Gillis* and USS *Williamson*. Both were World War I destroyers from which the two forward boilers had been removed to make room for aviation gasoline tankage. In addition to carrying gas for the PBYs, they also provided other stores to keep their charges in operation while away from their normal support bases. It was the *Gillis* which came to the rescue of the stranded VP-42. However, as the crew of the seaplane tender began dropping the anchor, the fog lifted, and the pilots started their engines and made their own way into Womens Bay. The squadron remained there until October when it was relieved by VP-41.[127]

The alert was called off in early July when it became apparent that the Japanese were not going to side with the Germans in their war against Russia. However, nothing was the same again. With Russia removed as a threat to Alaska, plans to build a military base at Point Barrow were cancelled and the construction of bases at McGrath and Nome received less attention. The military turned its attention to Japan as the primary threat in the Pacific, and General Buckner and his staff began seriously considering the Aleutians as their first line of defense against the Japanese invasion they expected would come from that direction. Thinking ahead, Buckner also began considering the islands as a potential invasion route against Japan.[128]

The seaplane tender USS Gillis *(AVD-12).* USN photo

The seaplane tender USS Williamson *(AVD-2). Both tenders were converted in 1940 from World War I destroyers and displaced 1,190 tons, hence the similarity in appearance. They were assigned to Patrol Wing Four and one tender was normally allocated to a patrol squadron. They allowed the PBY crews to operate away from land bases.* USN photo

Lieutenant Commander James S. Russell's Consolidated PBY-5 Catalina flying boat over a glacier near Prince William Sound. The number 42 near the nose designates its assignment to VP-42. The 3 is its number within the squadron. Russell kept six at Kodiak, two at Sitka to cover southeastern Alaska and four at Dutch Harbor to patrol the Aleutian Island during his second deployment to Alaska in February 1942 as Commander, VP-42. His squadron covered 2,000 miles of coastline. USN photo

The harbor to the Kodiak Naval Station in Womens Bay. The photograph was taken later in the war. USN photo

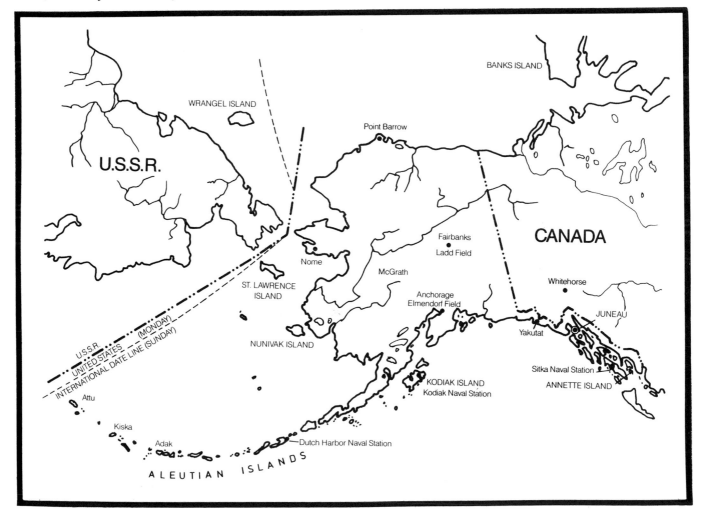

A PRIMEVAL BATTLEGROUND

· · · · · · · · · · · ·

The Lonely Islands

On the map they look deceptively simple, a string of islands bridging the gap between North America and Asia, a potential invasion route to both continents. The Aleutian Islands stretch 1,100 miles from the Alaska Peninsula almost to the Kamchatka Peninsula. There are 279 islands ranging in size from the largest, the 1,474 square mile Unimak Island, to unnamed rocks. Included in this grouping are the Komandorskies, a logical extension of the world's longest archipelago, which are generally omitted because they are across the International Date Line in Russian territory.

On the United States side of the date line, the Aleutians are divided into five major and eight lesser island groups. The major groups, named by the Russians who explored and exploited the islands for their fur seals during the Eighteenth Century, are from west to east the Near Islands, Rat Islands, Andreanof Islands, Islands of the Four Mountains and Fox Islands.

The Near Islands, so named because of their closeness to Russia, consist of the large mountainous islands of Attu and Agattu and the small, flat Semichi islands of Alaid, Nizki and Shemya. The next grouping, except for Buldir, a lonely speck of an island, are separated by a wide expanse of ocean. The Rat Islands, principal of which are Kiska and Amchitka, were named for the large number of rodents the Russians found there. The next group, which includes the lesser Dearof Islands, are the Andreanof Islands, named after the Russian merchant Andreian Tolstyk who explored them in 1716. The major islands in this 310-mile, multi-island chain are Adak and Atka. The Islands of the Four Mountains are the most spectacular island group in the Aleutians. The four major and three lesser islands, located in close proximity to each other, are almost perfectly formed volcanic cones that rise straight out of the ocean. The last major group, named for

the large number of foxes found there, are the Fox Islands. This group contains the largest islands of the Aleutians, the major of which are Umnak, Unalaska and Unimak. The latter is separated from the Alaskan Peninsula by the narrow, unnavigable False Pass.[1]

The Aleutians were first inhabited by the Aleuts, a fierce and proud warrior race, whose ancestors had migrated from coastal Asia to the islands sometime between 8000 and 6000 BC. Adapted to their environment, the Aleuts were expert seafarers who traveled the sea in search of food and raided each other's villages for slaves. They were equally adept at using the resources provided by the land to sustain themselves and their rich culture despite the harsh environment. By 1700 there were between 6,000 and 12,000 Aleuts living on virtually every major island with a source of fresh water. By then their culture had evolved into two separate languages. Those on the central and western islands spoke Atkan and those living on the eastern islands spoke Unalaskan.[2]

Like so many others, the Aleuts way of life was interrupted and changed for the worse with the coming of the white man. Beginning in 1728, the Russians began to probe eastward into the North Pacific. The returning explorers brought news of the many fur-bearing animals they had found in their travels. The first hunting expedition reached Bering Island in the Komandorskies in 1743. By 1745 they were on Agattu and Attu Islands, and were pushing further eastward in search of sea otters.

The Aleuts fiercely resisted the Russian incursions. The first blood is believed to have been spilled on Agattu in 1745. Massacre Bay on Attu was later named to commemorate the destruction of an Aleut village there. By 1763, the Russians had penetrated to the eastern Aleutians. When the Aleuts destroyed four of their ships, the Russians retaliated by ravaging the villages on Unalaska and Umnak. The Aleuts scattered throughout the Aleutians and lacking modern weapons were not able to contend

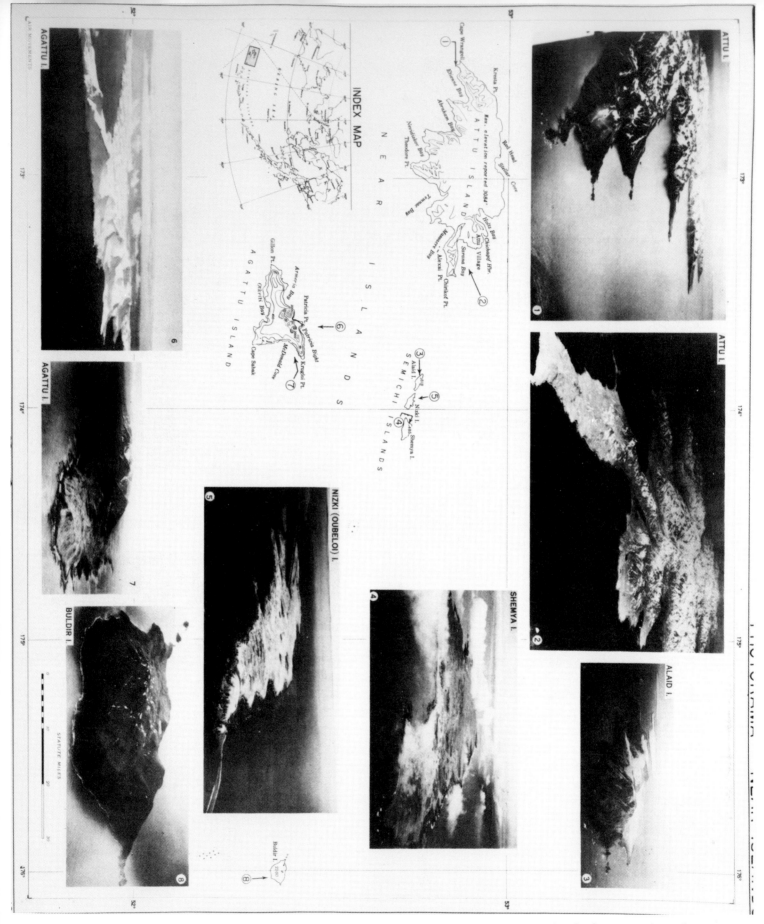

The principal islands of the Near Islands, named by the Russians because of their closeness to their land mass, are Attu and Agattu. Tiny Shemya is one of the few flat islands in the Aleutian Chain. A major air base was built on the island during World War II. It is still in use today as Shemya Air Force Base. photo from air pilot manual, April 43

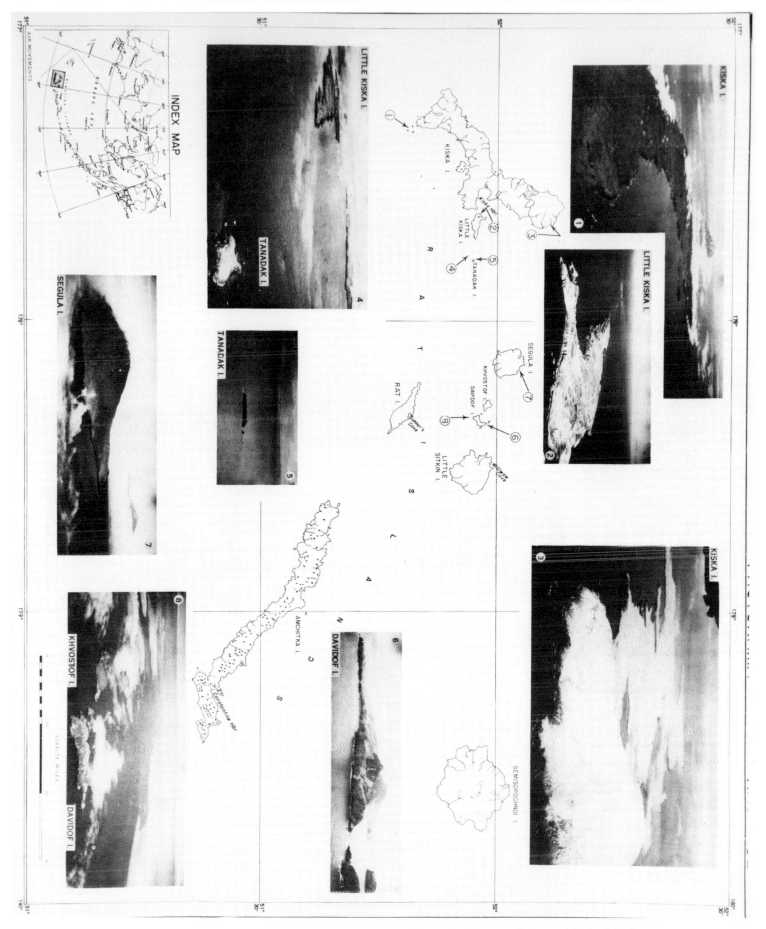

The Rat Islands group contains Kiska where the Japanese built a major base in the Aleutians. It is one of the few islands which has a natural harbor. photo from air pilot manual, April 43

The Andreanof Islands were named after a Russian merchant who explored them in 1716. They are among the most rugged groups of islands in the Aleutians, and best illustrate the difficulty of conducting large scale military operations.

photo from air pilot manual, April 43

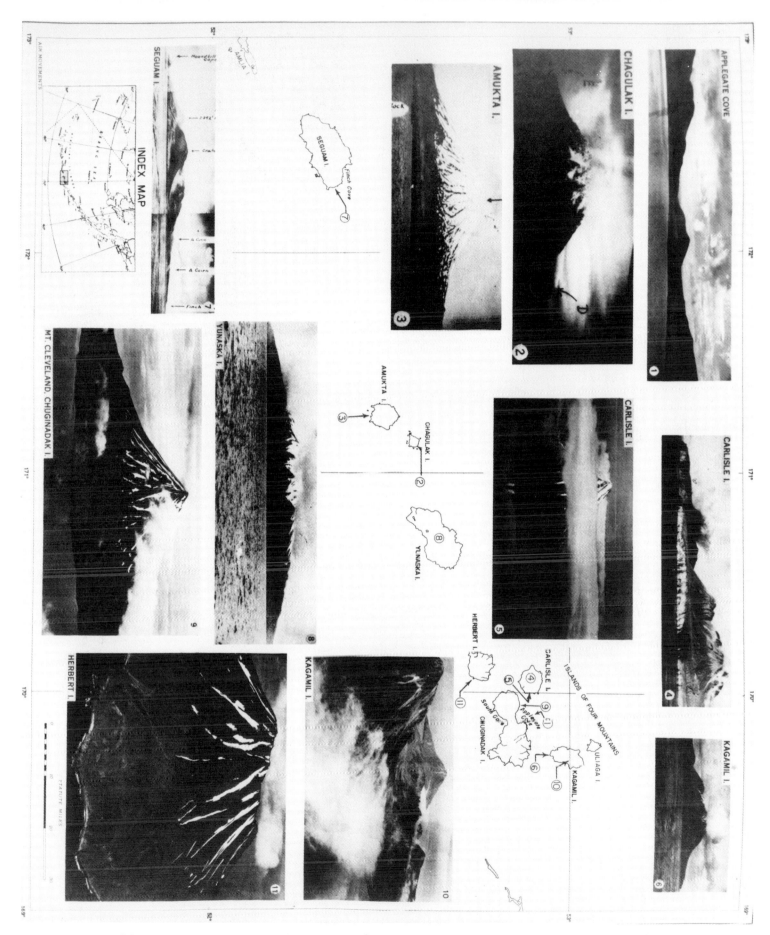

The Islands of the Four Mountains are the most spectacular of the Aleutian Island groupings. They contain no natural harbors or places where air fields can be built. photo from air pilot manual, April 43

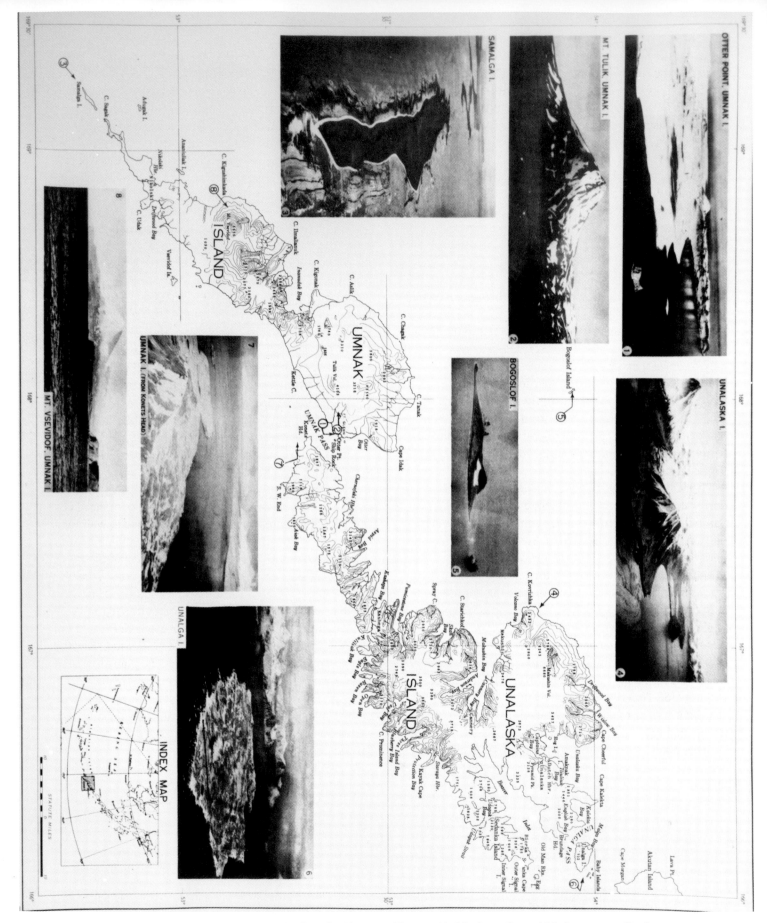

The Fox Islands contain the largest islands in the Aleutians. They provided the bases from which the counter offensive against the Japanese was launched. Dutch Harbor on Amaknak Island in Unalaska Bay on the northern side of Unalaska Island was established as a major naval base. photo from air pilot manual, April 43

with the onslaught of the greedy and often brutal fur traders, who subjected them to virtual slavery and in the process greatly weakened their culture and their pride.

In 1867, the Russians tired of an unprofitable fur business, discouraged by other failed economic ventures and under pressure from others interested in Alaska, sold their remote territory to the Americans. By then, the Aleut population had declined to about 2,000; victims of Russian abuse, introduced diseases and general despair. The only sustaining force was the Russian Orthodox Church whose priests were able to mitigate the depredations of their fellow countrymen. The Americans treated the Aleuts with paternal benevolence but did little to help them regain their cultural identity[3].

The military's attitude was one of ambivalence. While it was concerned for the Aleuts' safety and well being, it also considered them inferior as reflected in an Army report issued in 1942, which described them as a "mentally undeveloped people."[4]

The Aleuts were to suffer further indignities in the coming years, including being forcibly removed from their lands. However, the war years, for the Aleuts, as with so many other racially repressed minorities, would mark the beginning of a long and difficult journey back to their former glories.

The military's general attitude to the Aleutians Islands during the prewar years can be reflected in Naval historian Samuel Eliot Morison's postwar comment that the Aleutians should have been left to the Aleuts. The U.S. Army, until the Navy announced that they were building a base at Dutch Harbor and needed their protection, had never seriously considered the Aleutians as a theater of operations despite General Mitchell's warning that the Japanese might one day use it as an invasion route. The Navy took a more active interest in the islands because of their strategic location in the North Pacific. Beginning in 1853, while Alaska was still a possession of Russia, the Navy sent the USS *Fennimore Cooper* into the western Aleutians on a series of surveys to determine if bases could be established there to facilitate trade in the western Pacific.

Other Navy ships visited the Aleutians during the last half of the Nineteenth Century for a variety of reasons that ranged from searching for lost Arctic explorers to establishing a communications link with Siberia. It was not until the beginning of the Twentieth Century that the Navy began seriously considering the military possibilities of the Aleutians.[5] They selected Kiska Harbor for a coaling station, and the USS *Petrel* and a collier were sent there in 1904 to start the construction. However, the project was dropped in 1907 because of a lack of funds. The Navy, however, did support the establishment of a wildlife refuge, provided that its interest in the islands were protected. They also constructed a radio station at Dutch Harbor.[6]

On March 3, 1913, President Taft signed an executive order which set aside the Aleutian Islands ". . . as a preserve and breeding ground for native birds, for the propagation of reindeer and fur bearing animals and for the encouragement and development of fisheries." The order ended, stating: "The establishment of this reservation shall not interfere with the use of the islands for lighthouse, military, or naval purposes . . ."[7]

Very little else was done during the next twenty years. Although the Navy acknowledged their strategic importance, the Aleutians' harsh environment posed too many problems. The United States easily wrote them off during the 1921-22 Washington Naval Armament Limitation Treaty negotiations by accepting Japan's proposal to limit the fortifications of the islands the United States possessed in the eastern Pacific, including the Aleutians. The Hawaiian Islands were exempted. The Japanese, in turn agreed not to fortify the Caroline, Marshall and Marianas Islands. The major term of the treaty that was intended to make it impossible for the participants' navies to fight an offensive war, however, was the establishment of a 5:5:3 ratio for naval ships between the U.S., Britain and Japan. The latter's democratic government agreed to the terms, although it meant scrapping a large number of war vessels, including their monster battle ship, *Mutsu*, already launched and over ninety percent complete. The military bitterly resented the terms, but had to wait for a more opportune time to assert itself.[8]

By the early 1930s, the U.S. Navy, responding to a growing militarism in Japan, began to seriously consider the Aleutians as the northern anchor of a defensive line in the Pacific. Plan Orange had been published in 1928. Although its main purpose called for the U.S. Fleet to sail west to engage the Imperial Japanese Navy in battle and secure the defense of the Philippines, the plan also made provisions for the establishment of a defensive line bounded by the Panama Canal in the south, the Hawaiian Islands in the center, and Alaska in the north. Only the northern end of the triangle was undefended and would remain so for the next twelve years.[9]

Between 1931 and 1936, the Navy sent four expeditions into the Aleutians. They were focussed primarily on flying conditions, since the Navy had come to realize that:

> . . . in the event of war between this country and an Asiatic nation, aviation operations in the area might well be of great importance. In such an event, it would be of vital interest to the Navy to have a definite knowledge of sites suitable for the establishment of landplane and seaplane bases, whether it is decided to occupy these sites ourselves or to deny them to the enemy.[10]

Three of the seaplanes from the 1934 U.S. Navy expedition on the beach at Kiska Harbor. Note the fox trapper cabins. The last trapper, a man and his daughter, left Kiska Island in April 1942. A Navy Seabee unit built two ranch-style houses and a generator shed 300-yards from the shore line in 1941. It housed a Navy weather detachment. The Japanese established the seaplane ramp on this beach and built their main camp behind it. USN photo

The first expedition in 1931 was a modest effort consisting of the minesweeper USS *Gannett* and two seaplanes. The next one in 1933 was larger with four ships. In 1934, the Navy dispatched a fleet of seven ships and six seaplanes under the command of a rear admiral to the Aleutians where it operated from early May until the end of September. While Hap Arnold and his flight of ten B-10s were photographing mainland Alaska and looking for potential air field sites, the Navy flyers were exploring the Aleutians in detail from Unalaska to Attu. A large number of aerial photographs were taken and a considerable amount of information on flying conditions collected. The next year the Navy selected the North Pacific as the location for their annual fleet exercise. The exercise, Problem XVI, was designed to show how they would defend the area against a Japanese attack.

Although the Navy was able to compile accurate charts, their expeditions and the exercise convinced them the Aleutians, because of their notorious weather and forbidding terrain, were not suited for Naval operations in general and air operations in particular.[11]

Unfortunately, in less than six years the lonely, storm-whipped islands would be turned into a primeval battleground where the antagonists were more at war with the elements than themselves. To an arm chair strategist in the safe confines of warm surroundings, the howling winds and raging seas seemed insignificant; but to those actually engaged it was another matter, especially to those airmen, Allied and Japanese, who were called upon to commit their lives to that terrifying and strange place.

Asked by a ground crew how he felt about flying combat in the Aleutians, Flying Officer Arthur C. Fanning, a Royal Canadian Air Force P-40 pilot, perhaps summing it up for the rest, responded that he was "scared every time I get over Kiska because I don't know whether I'm going to find a place to land when I get back."[12] Many did not

and one unit, the 54th Fighter Squadron, would suffer grievously. Of the thirty pilots who came north with the first P-38 squadron to see action in World War II, almost half would be dead a year later.

Combat and accidents took their toll, but it was the weather which claimed most of the young lives. The section on the war in the North Pacific in the U.S. Strategic Bombing Survey for the Pacific, authored by Navy Captain James S. Russell, who served there, summed it up:

Early experience in the Aleutians campaign also developed clearly the disadvantages of the northern short route to Japan. The prevalence of fog in the summer and great storms in the winter was known, but the effect on air operations was not fully appreciated. Significant was the ratio of total theater loss to combat loss in aircraft of the Eleventh Air Force. The ratio was 6.5 to 1, as against 3 to 1 for an average of all Pacific theaters. Reflected in it were unusual hazards due to weather, visibility at base, icing, storm damage, poor maintenance, conditions of the runway, and the hazards of operating from a sparse number of airfields strung along a single line of islands which paralleled the direction of the target. Significant also was the number of days upon which successful bombing missions could be flown: for a period of 19 days, 11-30 June 1942, during the early attempt to bomb the Japanese out of Kiska, only six successful heavy bombing missions were completed. Likewise in the critical period of the Attu occupation, weather permitted air bombardment and support on only 11 out of 19 days.[13]

Of all the places that the military could have picked to fight a war, the Aleutian Islands was one of the worst in the world. The terrible weather and the forbidding terrain were not at all conducive to large scale military operations.[14]

Cold Siberian winds blowing down over the frigid Bering Sea from the north clash with the warm air and waters

This section of steel matting, weighing approximately eight tons and covering three thousand five hundred square feet, was ripped up and rolled back by the force of the Aleutian wind. AAF photo

This Consolidated PBY-5 seaplane was picked up from its mooring and flung onto the beach by the force of the wind. There were jokes about using 500-pound bombs as wind socks in the Aleutians. USN photo

of the Japanese Current flowing eastward across the North Pacific. The unholy interaction results in high winds, dense fog, mist, rain and snow that can torment those not prepared or able to cope with its ferocity. "Never speak of the wind. If you do, there probably will be a storm," was an expression used by the Aleuts to describe the weather.

Clouds cover the Aleutians twenty to ninety percent of each year with cold, drizzling, persistent rains occurring during the summer months. That, with the sleet and snow that sweep the islands from November to April, accounts for the average of forty to fifty inches of precipitation that falls around two hundred days each year. Fog is a common feature. July and August are the worst periods. Temperatures average fifty degrees Fahrenheit during the summer and thirty-three degrees during the winter months. It seldom dips below zero.

It is the incessant wind, however, that is the most noticeable scourge to human sanity. Coming down from the north with an average speed of twelve knots, they frequently blow at twenty-four knots for twenty-four hours

and more. The Aleutian Islands are the only place where high winds and fog occur at the same time. Another phenomenon is the williwaw, a local name given to the fierce winds that originate in the mountains and gust up to a hundred and forty knots. There are two general types, cold and warm, with the cold being the most dangerous of the two since its circulation is spiral and its direction unpredictable regardless of the gradient wind direction.

If the weather does not discourage military operations, the very features of the Aleutians surely will. Formed in Quaternary and Post-Tertiary times as a result of volcanic activity, the Aleutians are part of the seismic "Ring of Fire" surrounding the Pacific. Frequent earthquakes, the occasional eruption of some the fifty-seven volcanoes and the action of remnant glaciers continually change the landscape. With few exceptions, the islands, reflecting their origin, are mountainous with irregular shorelines and rocky cliffs that extend straight out of the heaving seas. Streams flow down to the sea in deeply incised valleys between mountains whose summits average two to three

Scenes from a calm day. The Aleutian Islands are of volcanic origin and still contain active volcanos. Paul L. Earle collection

Shemya Island, as it looked in 1942, is one of the few flat islands in the Aleutians.
AAF photo

Kiska as seen in an a aerial photograph taken July 25, 1943. The island has one of the few natural harbors in the Aleutian Islands. The air field that the Japanese tried to build on North Head can be seen on the far right side of the photograph as a small white rectangle. Little Kiska is in the foreground. AAF photo

thousand feet.

There are few beaches over which amphibious operations can be conducted and fewer even which can sustain such operations for prolonged periods of time. For the most part the larger islands do provide some form of sheltered anchorage, but they are generally narrow, and the approaches are filled with jagged pinnacle rocks that can easily rip the bottom out of any vessel unfortunate enough to be caught on one. Strong and dangerous undertows add to the problem. The only suitable natural harbors are located at Akutan Harbor on Akutan, Dutch Harbor on Unalaska, Nazan Bay on Atka, Kuluk Bay on Adak, Constantine Harbor on Amchitka, Kiska Harbor on Kiska and Massacre Bay on Attu.

Inland the problem becomes worse. There are few places where men and vehicles can easily move on the mountainous islands. The low areas generally consist of muskeg under which are layers of waterlogged slimy volcanic ash, mud, sand and finally, volcanic rock. In many instances stream beds, alluvial fans, beaches, spits and other such areas provide the only relatively flat and firm foundations for movement and the construction of facilities. There are very few islands flat or large enough which lend themselves to the construction of airfields. Amchitka and Shemya are the exceptions. Elsewhere, it requires a considerable engineering effort to build them.[15]

The Aleutians can also be a hauntingly beautiful place, beyond belief. On a cold, bleak day they seem like one of Paul Gustave Dore's romantic and macabre etchings of some faraway, seldom visited fantasy land. From the air they appear one after another on the horizon, out of the mist, some with smoke trailing from volcano tops; and from the sea they can be seen at a distance as a long string of lonely, cloud covered mountains. Yet it is when the rains stop and the sun comes out, that the islands take on their greatest, almost breathtaking beauty, one of deep green grass, and blowing white clouds against the cobalt blue of the sea and sky, of rainbows rising from seldom visited mountains and valleys; a place described by the Alaskan author and publisher Robert Henning as:

. . . sometimes unbelievably blue skies and fluffy clouds and a stillness broken only by the sounds of the seabirds, the gentle wash of surf on black sand beaches—a faraway place suspended between the worlds of the East and West, visited rarely, even largely unknown by the people of Alaska . . .[16]

Make Mine Moet

The Aleutian tranquility would be disturbed in the coming years, for the Navy, despite their initial reservations, had decided that a base, after all, was needed to secure their flank in the North Pacific. They needed a place from which their patrol aircraft and submarines could operate in northern waters. Dutch Harbor, protected from the worst of the Aleutian storms and near Unimak Pass, the entry way into the Bering Sea, suited their needs.

The natural harbor, located on Amaknak Island, had been used since the Gold Rush days as a stop-over point for ships bound to and from communities along Alaska's western and northern coast. The North American Commercial Company established the original settlement there to support its sealing operations in the Bering Sea. Jack London is said to have given the small island's most prominent feature, Mount Ballyhoo, its name during the filming of the "Sea Wolf." The Navy built a radio station there

in 1911, part of a network of three in Alaska to furnish navigation support in the North Pacific and Bering Sea areas. Large radio towers were erected and a handsome brick building that contained six family quarters was constructed. The brick building, the only one in the Aleutians, still stands.

The Navy established a weather station there in July 1939. The next year the Navy purchased the North America Commercial Company's lands on the island for $78,973.00 and assumed ownership of the rest of the public domain lands. Siems Drake-Puget Sound workers arrived in August 1940, to begin base construction. A Marine detachment arrived October 12, 1940. Naval and Army personnel began arriving shortly afterwards, and on August 21, 1941, Commander William N. Updergraff assumed command of the Naval base.

When the construction of the forty-four million dollar project began in September 1940, there were around twenty-five to thirty people, mostly Navy, assigned to the communications and weather stations, living on the island. A larger, predominantly native community was situated immediately across a narrow channel that separated Amaknak from the main island of Unalaska

The aerial photograph of Amaknak Island and the village of Unalaska was taken by the U.S. Navy in 1934. The Church of the Holy Ascension can be seen just to the left of the plane's wing tip. Amaknak Island is located just across the narrows from the village dock. The Navy radio station was located on the lower right hand side of the island near the small lagoon and pier. Farther up the island was Dutch Harbor and the North America Commercial Company settlement. Note the ships in the harbor and the spit. Beyond is Mount Ballyhoo. It should be compared with the photograph in Chapter IV.
USN photo

Dutch Harbor as shown on a 1940 post card purchased by Paul L. Earle in the Unalaska Curio Shop shortly after his arrival with the 250th Coastal Artillery Regiment, California National Guard in May 1941. Earle remained at Dutch Harbor until 1943, as the engineer in charge of harbor defense. Paul L. Earle collection

Another view of Dutch Harbor and the North America Commercial Company complex from the dock. It was here that the Navy built their base. The house on the far left was left standing. The ship Northwestern *was later moored in front of where the store is located.* Paul L. Earle collection

The Navy radio station at Dutch Harbor as it looked in 1929. It was the only military installation on Amaknak Island that the Japanese had any real knowledge of before their attack. USN photo

The village of Unalaska and the Russian Orthodox Church of the Holy Ascension. Unalaska was, and still is, the largest settlement in the Aleutians. Paul L. Earle collection

along a narrow crescent of sea frontage. The village, by the same name, was then and still is the largest community in the Aleutians. At the time it had a year round population of approximately 200 which swelled during the summer months with the increase of fishing, shipping and governmental activities. Known as the "Metropolis of the Aleutians," Unalaska had existed since the time of the Russians as the religious, commercial and governmental center for the Aleutians.[17]

While the Navy could deal with the surface threat, they had only a limited capability to defend their bases against an air attack. That responsibility belonged to the Army, more specifically the Alaska Defense Command, part of whose mission was the protection of Naval bases in Alaska. General Buckner, from his previous visit in September 1940, had already determined that there was no suitable place to build an airfield near Dutch Harbor short of razing the village of Unalaska, which even in

those days of a more liberal eminent domain policy was not a suitable option.

A potential airfield site existed at Chernofski Bay on the west end of the island. The Navy ruled it out as too expensive and too exposed to raids from the sea. There was also the possibility of carving out a runway on the lower slope of Mount Ballyhoo near the Navy base. The Army contended it would not be long enough to support its planes and there was not enough room to park and maintain the aircraft. In the interim, the Navy began installing a catapult and arresting system near the seaplane ramp from which its carrier based fighters could be operated. It was not completed by the time the Japanese bombed Dutch Harbor. General Buckner and Colonel Talley decided to look elsewhere.[18]

With winter over, Buckner volunteered Lieutenant Frank O'Brien, now an old Alaskan hand, to go aboard the USS *Charleston* on a survey of potential airfield sites

Lieutenant Frank O'Brien shortly after being decorated with the Distinguished Flying Cross for his part along with Lieut Gene Yarborough in recovering Lieut Elmer Booth from an ice flow in Turnagain Arm near Anchorage. The P-36 pilot had bailed out of his airplane. O'Brien, among the first Army Air Corps pilots to arrive, married a former Miss Alaska, and spent most of World War II in the territory. O'Brien Collection

as the Air Force "expert." The USS *Charleston* sailed in early May, making its way westward down the Aleutians. O'Brien was checked out in the gunboat's aerial spotter aircraft, a Curtiss SOC-1 Seagull. Along with the two Naval aviators aboard the Charleston, Lieutenant Commander William Miller and Lieutenant Kenneth Musick, O'Brien made an aerial survey in mid-May 1941, of each potential site as the gunboat proceeded down the Chain. The three examined potential sites on Unalaska, Umnak, Adak, Tanaga, Amchitka and Kiska.

On his return to Elmendorf Field, O'Brien submitted a report on May 19 in which he recommended Otter Point on the eastern end of Umnak Island as the most suitable location for an air base. It was the logical choice despite the fact that it was also exposed to raids from the sea and there was no suitable harbor nearby on the island. The closest place that provided any shelter from the sea was Chernofski Bay across the strait from Umnak. Otter Point did, however, have a large, flat and relatively stable expanse of land, a rare commodity in the Aleutians, on which a large air base could be built. It was also 70 miles as the crow flies from Dutch Harbor.[19]

While O'Brien was still in the Aleutians, General DeWitt arrived to see first-hand the progress that General Buckner had been making and to discuss plans and future requirements. Shortly after his return to Elmendorf Field, O'Brien was awakened at 4:00 AM and told that the two generals wanted to be briefed an hour later on what he had found out during his trip to the Aleutians. Miller was also asked to be present. The young lieutenant arrived at the headquarters building to find the entire Alaska Defense Command staff assembled and the two generals waiting. After O'Brien had completed his presentation, DeWitt looked at Miller and asked: "Is the kid right?" The Navy lieutenant commander said "Yes," and the plans were set in motion to build an air base at Otter Point.[20]

Shortly afterward, Buckner submitted his plans to DeWitt to build a forward base at Otter Point and to use Cold Bay, where the Civil Aviation Administration was planning to construct a field, as a staging base. Buckner also asked that another staging base be built at Port Heiden, further down the Alaska Peninsula. DeWitt, replying on July 18, noted that he . . . "looked upon this piece of paper as the most important paper I now have to act upon in connection with the defense of Alaska."[21]

The Charleston's *SOC-1 Seagull in the Aleutians during the survey.* O'Brien collection

Both Buckner and DeWitt agreed with the Navy that it was the Navy's responsibility to defend the Aleutians and other off-shore islands. The Army would take care of the rest of Alaska. They also agreed with their Navy counterparts that the defense of the mainland was dependent on securing the eastern Aleutians, for the loss of Dutch Harbor would isolate western and northern Alaska.[22]

However, they were in disagreement with the Navy over the construction of an airbase in the Aleutians. The Navy opposed an airbase at Otter Point. They were concerned about the lack of harbor facilities, feared that the base would place an undue strain on their supply system and were anxious about the lack of naval forces to protect the sea approaches to the base. The War Department also opposed the idea. Buckner and DeWitt continued to insist that not only would an air base on Umnak provide a good air defense of Dutch Harbor, it would also prevent the Japanese from establishing one there; and, if necessary, it could be used as an offensive base should the need arise.

General DeWitt bombarded General Marshall with a series of personal letters and memorandums, seeking approval and funding to proceed with the construction of the Otter Point base and the others at Cold Bay and Port Heiden. On July 24, DeWitt, angered over the lack of support for the bases, noted to General Marshall: "If the attitude still persists in the War Department contrary to my judgement in the matter, a survey should me made at once by air or boat by those opposed, because the question does not permit prolonged discussion—the times are too critical and there is no time to waste."[23]

While General DeWitt argued his case, General Buckner dispatched Talley, now a major, on ground survey of Otter Point. Colonel Davis made his OA-5 available and the two departed Elmendorf on September 11 with stopovers at Kodiak, Bethel in southwestern Alaska and Sand Point in the Shumagin Islands. They arrived at Otter Point on the 17th. After Talley examined the place in detail, they departed the 21st for Elmendorf Field.

They stopped at Sand Point for the night. When the two returned from the village the next morning, they found that waves had bashed the amphibian against a rock, knocking a hole in the hull. After pumping out the water from the half-filled hull, the two enterprising men patched the hole with a piece of tin roofing and stove bolts and caulked it with oil soaked rags, all of which they had obtained from the local store. They then flew straight back to Elmendorf Field. The trip convinced the engineer

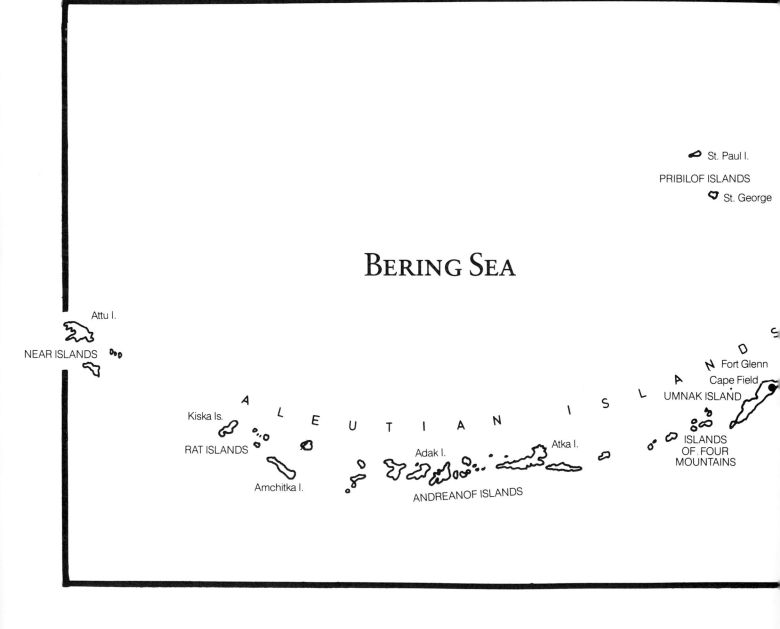

St. Paul I.

PRIBILOF ISLANDS

St. George

BERING SEA

Attu I.

NEAR ISLANDS

N Fort Glenn

Cape Field

UMNAK ISLAND

Kiska Is.

RAT ISLANDS

A L E U T I A N   I S L A N D S

Adak I.

Atka I.

ISLANDS OF FOUR MOUNTAINS

Amchitka I.

ANDREANOF ISLANDS

Talley that an airbase could be built at Otter Point. Shortly afterwards, he dispatched a survey party to begin laying out the runway and other facilities.[24]

General Buckner, with General DeWitt's concurrence, decided to send Major Talley to Washington to present the case for Umnak directly to General Marshall and his staff. General Buckner also instructed Talley to ask for a garrison for Nome to protect the airbase that was being built there and for a squadron of badly needed air transports. At the time, the B-18s and even Davis' tired old B-10 were being used to move cargo and personnel. Buckner had learned that the Army had somehow obtained a number of German Ju-52s from South America, and he felt they would be ideal for the rugged conditions of Alaska.

Major Talley departed in mid-November. After stopping briefly at The Presidio, during which General DeWitt placed a phone call to General Marshall confirming General Buckner's requests, Talley went on to Washington. Tensions with Japan were increasing when Talley arrived. He had to wait a few days until General Marshall was available. It was not until the day before Thanksgiving that he was summoned into the Army Chief of Staff's spartan office in the old Munitions Building. General Marshall, after apologizing about the delay and noting that he had been conferring with the president over the Japanese, asked Talley what Generals Buckner and DeWitt wanted. Talley explained his mission; the Chief of Staff asked one or two questions and then called DeWitt. On hanging up, he set up a conference for Talley to see his operations officer, Major General Leonard T. Gerow and the Chief of the Army Air Forces, General Arnold.

General Gerow agreed that the airbase at Otter Point was necessary, and asked Major Talley where he was go-

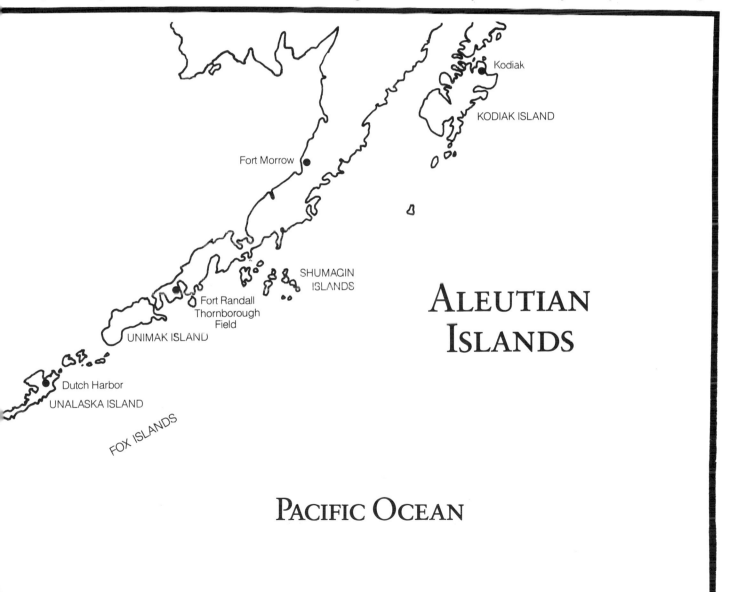

ing to get the troops to construct it. Talley replied that they would come from Yakutat as soon as that base was completed. Gerow also agreed to the garrison at Nome as soon as troops could be provided. General Arnold, who asked one of his bright, young staff officers, Colonel Lawrence Kuter, to be present, was less cooperative. When Talley asked for the transports, Arnold replied, "what would you do with them if I gave them to you?" Talley then reminded General Arnold that Elmendorf and Ladd Fields could accommodate them and they were needed to support the forward bases. The Army Air Forces' chief, perhaps having been the recipient of many other similar requests, shot back, "now look, don't tell me what's up there. Remember, I've been up there too."[25]

The meeting lasted about thirty minutes. Talley then met briefly with General Marshall, after which he left to spend Thanksgiving Day with his family and to meet with General DeWitt. He arrived back in Alaska on the 28th.[26]

On November 26, while Talley was en route back to Alaska, the Joint Army-Navy Board approved the construction of the Otter Point airbase, ending almost a year of debate and opening the way for the Alaska Defense Command to move into the Aleutians. General Buckner, however, would have to wait until the next year for his Nome garrison and transports.[27]

At the time only Elmendorf and Ladd Fields could support combat operations. Annette Island and Yakutat in southeast Alaska lacked support facilities. The fields that the Civil Aviation Administration were building at Bethel and Naknek in southwestern Alaska were little more than cleared strips as were those at Gulkana and McGrath in interior Alaska and Cordova in the southeast. The Agency had halted work at Nome for the winter due to the extreme cold. The field that the Navy contractors were building at Kodiak was not yet ready. In addition to Fort Richardson, Army garrisons had been also established at Dutch Harbor, Kodiak, Nome, Seward and Sitka.

The Canadians had built fields at Grand Prairie, Fort St. John, Fort Nelson, Watson Lake and Whitehorse, and had refurbished the civilian field at Edmonton to support the Northwest Staging Route to Alaska. The five fields were in a primitive stage of development, and they were not connected by a road.

Originally, the joint civil-military priority list for completing fields in Alaska that supported military operations had listed the fields in the following order: Yakutat, Nome, Kodiak, Annette Island, Cordova, Naknek, Bethel, Cold Bay and Otter Point. Other intermediate fields were planned at Galena and McGrath. However, with the shift of emphasis to the defense of the Aleutians, Cold Bay and Otter Point were moved to the head of the list.[28]

Morrison-Knudson construction workers arrived in

NORTHWEST STAGING ROUTE

The photograph of Cold Bay, taken February 4, 1947, graphically demonstrates its bleak and wind swept environment. Even then the conditions were primitive. AAC photo

September to begin work on carving out an airfield at Cold Bay, aptly named for its location on a cold, bleak, wind swept patch of land at the tip of the Alaskan Peninsula, 200 miles northeast of Dutch Harbor. Their noisy bulldozers and earth-moving equipment soon drove away the only human inhabitant of the area, a navy pensioner who had sought solitude there.

Although at the time it was of little use for civil purposes, Cold Bay's strategic location between Kodiak and Dutch Harbor made it an idea site for a military field from which aircraft could cover the seaward approaches to both bases. Also, it, along with smaller fields later constructed at Port Heiden and Port Moller farther up the Alaskan Peninsula, provided an intermediate field between Elmendorf and Otter Point. Later, Cold Bay would support the other bases that were built in the Aleutians and serve as one of the transfer points for Lend Lease ships destined for Russia.

With the increasing emphasis on Cold Bay, Major Talley's engineers assumed responsibility from the Civil Aviation Administration for completing the field. The 151st Engineer Combat Regiment arrived in early February 1942, to take over from Morrison-Knudson, as part of an overall effort to transfer the construction effort from civilians to the military following the outbreak of war. By then, the workers of Morrison-Knudson had made remarkable progress, despite the considerable hardships of weather, the remote location and loss of equipment and materials to the storms that raged across the bay.

Their military replacements labored around the clock.

By early March, they had completed work on a 3,200 foot strip of runway. Colonel Davis was given the privilege of making the first landing. By April the runway had been extended 5,000 feet and another 5,000 foot runway that crossed it had been completed. The workers began pouring asphalt.[29]

The asphalt had originally been intended for McGrath. However, with the Russian threat eliminated, the need for airfields in western and northern Alaska had assumed a lesser importance. Plans for an airfield at Point Barrow were dropped and other projects were scaled back. Buckner and Talley decided that McGrath could do without a hard surface. The money could be put to better use paving the runways, taxiways and hardstands at Cold Bay. They were needed to support the bombers and fighters that Buckner was planning to send there, as soon as General Arnold could provide them.[30]

Because of the need to obtain the Navy's concurrence, the construction of the airfield at Otter Point, 70 miles southwest of Dutch Harbor, had gotten off to a slower start. Major Talley, as soon as he returned from Washington, began plans to move the 807th Engineer Aviation Company from the Yakutat project to Otter Point. The War Department gave its official go-ahead December 9, and the company began its movement in late December. On January 18, the first contingent, 64 officers and men, arrived at Otter Point to begin carving an airfield out of a bleak, treeless, wind swept wilderness. The conditions

East Base, Great Falls, Montana. AAC photo

Grand Prairie, Alberta, Air Field. AAC photo

Fort St. John, 50 miles north of Dawson Creek. USA photo

*Fort Nelson, British Columia,
halfway between Fort St. John
and Watson Lake.* USA photo

*Watson Lake, 300 miles
southeast of Whitehorse.*
USA photo

*Northway on the Alaska side
of the Alaska-Canada border.*
USA photo

The infantry usually inherited the job of laying Marston mats. Lieutenant Colonel Otis Boise, U.S. Army Retired, and an infantry veteran of the Aleutians, remembered that it provided a diversion to the dreary routine of Aleutian duty. It became a competition to see how much could be put down in a day's time. USA photo

A cargo ship off the coast of Umnak Island near Otter Point. Unalaska Island can be seen across the body of water that separated the two islands at their narrowest point. There was a fear at the time, unfounded, that the Japanese would try to occupy Umnak Island and build an air field there. It provided an incentive for General Buckner to rush construction of the field. USA photo

The air strip, upper right corner, that was built at Otter Point was primitive and the accommodations austere, but the project was completed in time for the Japanese attack on Dutch Harbor. The structures shown near the tents are Yakutat huts. The sixteen by sixteen foot buildings could be quickly assembled from prefabricated wooden panels.
USA photo

The "secret air strip," Otter Point.
USA photo

under which they had to work were heartbreaking, for it was neither the best place or the best time of the year.

Since there was no natural harbor at Otter Point, the Army engineers had to unload their equipment at Chernofski Bay, reload it onto barges for the trip across the eleven miles of rough water that separated Unalaska Island from Umnak Island, then off-load everything in the pounding surf and move it overland across the frozen tundra to the construction site. The men worked in three shifts, around the clock, seven days a week, often in driving snow storms and howling winds. Bulldozer operators, working to scrape the top layer of tundra off and form a firm foundation for the runway, sometimes became lost for hours in the blinding snow that whipped across the land.

A transport arrived at Chernofski Bay in early March. In its cargo hold was eighty thousand sections of Marston mats.[31] The matting was one of those pedestrian but revolutionary World War II innovations that contributed greatly to the winning of the war. Neither the Germans or the Japanese had anything like it. The U.S. Army had first tested the matting near the small North Carolina town of Marston during the Carolina Maneuvers in November 1941. It fulfilled the Army's need for a hard runway surface that could be laid down in a hurry on a prepared surface by inexperienced personnel. Each mat weighed 66.2 pounds, was ten feet long and fifteen inches wide and covered a 12.5 square foot surface that resembled Swiss cheese stamped out of steel. The slots on one side and the bent hooks on the other side allowed the matting to be connected with relative ease. All that was needed was a prepared surface, sledge hammers, pry bars and a lot of hard labor. A 5,000 by 150 foot runway could be laid down in a few days with 60,000 sections of the mats. The Marston mats literally provided the foundation on which America projected it air power to the far corners of the world during the war.[32]

Although the Army had used Marston mats to a limited extent on the Atlantic coast, it was employed operationally for the first time in the Aleutians. Major Talley had originally intended to surface the Cold Bay runway with the matting. However, when General Buckner decided not to pave the runway at McGrath and sent the materials to Cold Bay instead, the Marston mats were diverted to the Umnak project.

By mid-March, the entire 807th, now upgraded to a battalion, had arrived. They, along with men from an infantry and an artillery unit that had arrived to protect Otter Point, were put to work unloading the matting from the heaving barges that plied between Chernofski and the beaches at Otter Point. From there the matting was dragged by crawler tractor to the runway site. The men began laying the matting on March 23. By the end of the month they had completed covering a 100 by 5,000 foot runway.[33]

The next day, clear and bright for a change, a C-53 piloted by Lieutenant Joe Schneider bumped to a landing. Out of it stepped General Buckner and Talley, now a colonel. Talley had bet a Navy friend a case of champagne that the field would be operational by April 1. Shortly afterwards, he sent a radio message to Kodiak, stating, "make mine Moet."[34]

Talley had sent the message in the clear. If he had provided any further details, he would surely have been chastised by his superiors for committing a breach of security, since the activities at Cold Bay and Otter Point had been hidden from the public view as much as they could, even though they were large construction projects involving many personnel, military and civilian. Until the summer of 1941, military activities in the Territory had been a rich source of information for the news media. However, because of the growing tensions with Japan, Buckner, DeWitt and other responsible military authorities decided the time had come to begin hiding their activities behind a wall of secrecy and censorship.

The Japanese had used their fishing activities to explore the Aleutian Islands during the prewar years and there was a general fear that their agents in the United States were seeking to gain more information. General Buckner's intelligence officer, Colonel Lawrence V. Castner, suggested the shipment of equipment and materials destined for Cold Bay and Umnak be disguised as a commercial operation to mislead any Japanese agent trying to ferret out information at the West Coast ports. As a result, fake fishing canneries were created. The shipments destined for Cold Bay bore the name of Saxton and Company while those sent to Otter Point had Blair Packing Company stamped on the manifests and crates. Headquarters, Alaska Defense Command was given the fictitious name Consolidated Packing Company. The ploy worked, and Buckner provided an account in the April 1943 edition of *Scholastic* on how it had fooled the Japanese, who were unaware of the airfields when they struck Dutch Harbor.[35]

Talley's engineers continued to work on improving air base facility at Otter Point, later named Cape Field. Additional runways were built and the original field became an auxiliary strip. The photo shows a P-40E from the 18th Fighter Squadron landing at Otter Point. USA photo

There Is Nothing We Can Do Now

The oil embargo had pushed Japan to the limits. When Admiral Isoroku Yamamoto learned of it, he commented: "There is nothing we can do now."[36] The fifty-seven-year-old Commander of the Combined Fleet was probably in the best position to judge Japan's capabilities to wage war against the United States. Yamamoto had spent nearly a quarter of his thirty-seven years of service abroad, much of it in the United States. He had participated in the 1921-1922 Washington Naval Armament Limitations Treaty negotiations, and the 1930 London Naval Conference, where the five great naval powers agreed to extend the terms of the earlier treaty. The admiral had traveled extensively in the United States, observed its production capabilities and spent a semester at Harvard studying the English language. He had opposed Japan's military extremists, contending that they were leading the nation to its doom. They responded with veiled threats of assassination, and at one point the admiral had been sent to sea for his safety. With the sad possibility of war becoming a reality, the Admiral Yamamoto continued trying to convince his military colleagues of the folly of taking on the United States. Speaking to his Nagaoka schoolmates on September 18, 1941, the admiral warned:

> It is a mistake to regard Americans as luxury loving and weak. I can tell you that they are full of spirit, adventure, fight and justice. Their thinking is scientific and well advanced. Lindbergh's solo flight across the Atlantic was an act characteristic of Americans, adventuresome but scientifically based. Remember that American industry is much more developed than ours, and unlike us, they have all the oil they want. Japan cannot vanquish the United States. Therefore we should not fight the U.S.[37]

However, the military, particularly the Army, was determined to go to war. The Army's officer corps was drawn mostly from the lower and middle classes of Japan's stratified society. They had come up the hard way, and generally showed little interest in anything outside their profession other than the acquisition of power and the furtherance of nationalism. Many, as they rose through the ranks, had seen their parents borne down by the economic depression that swept the nation during the late 1920s and 1930s. They wanted a stronger Japan, one that had ready access to natural resources, and one that dominated the other Asian nations. Above all, they regarded themselves and Japan as superior, particularly when it came to the West, including the United States, which they regarded decadent, weak and morally bankrupt. In reality, they knew little of their potential enemy nor did they care about its industrial capacity. Substituting blind faith for reason, courage for common sense, they firmly believed that their martial spirit would prevail.[38]

On September 12, Admiral Yamamoto met with Prime Minister Fumimaro Konoye in Tokyo. Konoye, who was as concerned as Yamamoto about the prospects of war, asked the Commander of the Combined Fleet what chances Japan had for winning the war. The admiral responded: "If you insist on my going ahead, I can promise to give them hell for a year or a year and a half, but can guarantee nothing as to what will happen after that."[39]

Konoye, the moderate, also did not want to go to war with the Americans. However, there was little he could do to prevent that "gang of idiots," a label bestowed by Admiral Yamamoto on the Army, from taking control of the government. Since the 1937 invasion of China, Japan had been in a state of war. This had given the military extraordinary powers over the nation. The military, abetted by an avaricious industrial complex, dominated the Japanese Cabinet, the ruling body of Japan. Its prime ministers were drawn from the active ranks of either the Army or Navy, and the cabinets fell at the whim of the military since the resignation of a prime minister meant that a new one had to be formed.

Admiral Isoroku Yamamoto, the Commander of the Combined Fleet was the ablest of Japan's war leaders. Short of stature (five foot three inches), highly intelligent, mischievous, blunt of speech, sentimental, earthy and a professional, he led the Imperial Japanese Navy in a war he did not approve of. NA

The prime minister clashed with General Hideki Tojo, his war minister in the cabinet. The dogmatic, unimaginative Army general was bent on war as a means of resolving Japan's difficulties. On October 12, Konoye in an effort to stop the drift towards war, tried to persuade Tojo that the best way still lay through negotiations. The next day the cabinet met. Tojo remained firm and Konoye resigned. A new cabinet had to be formed, and the advisors to the Emperor made the fatal decision to recommend that Tojo be made prime minister in the belief that he could control the Army. Emperor Hirohito gave his consent; there was little else the forty-year-old monarch was able to do under the circumstances.[40]

Although he was revered as a god and regarded as the supreme head and embodiment of the state, Hirohito's actual powers were obscured and he had no active voice in the conduct of public affairs. Tradition and ceremony shielded him and he found it difficult to obtain accurate information. His own personality made it hard for him to assert the power of the throne that had been steadily eroding since his grandfather, the Emperor Meiji, had pulled Japan from feudalism into the modern mainstream. Although he usually presided over meetings where important national decisions were made, Hirohito limited his actions to providing advice and comment. Yet all actions were taken in his name and his position was used to inspire the inordinate sacrifices his countrymen were called upon to make during the war years.[41]

The ascension of General Tojo to power set Japan firmly on the course to war with the United States. Admiral Yamamoto's staff set about the task of putting the finishing touches to their plans to destroy the United States Pacific Fleet, some 10,000 miles away at Pearl Harbor.

Japan had already begun planning for war in the Pacific. By the fall of 1941 her military planners had developed the major objectives. They included the seizure of the Southern Resource Area that encompassed the oil rich Dutch East Indies, Indochina, Malaya, Thailand and Burma; the destruction of the United States Pacific Fleet; the isolation and the occupation of the Philippines; and the establishment of a defensive perimeter that would extend from the Kurile Islands through the Marshall, Gilbert and Solomon Islands, New Guinea, the Dutch East Indies and the Malayan Peninsula to Burma.

Once this was accomplished, Japan could then consolidate her perimeter, isolate China and complete the conquest of that nation while the United States and Britain battered themselves against the outer defenses and the powerful Imperial Navy. Japan anticipated that the Americans would soon tire and negotiate a peace.

Japan might have to give up some of their gains on the periphery, but the core of their empire, the Greater East Asia Co-Prosperity Sphere would remain firmly established. The plan appeared unbeatable on paper. The major unknowns were the perseverance of the United States and the endurance of Japan.[42]

The Imperial Japanese Army and Navy were placed in a state of readiness to strike early in December. Those in Washington DC, who were privy to the deciphers of the Japanese diplomatic code, knew of Japan's intentions, but not where or when the attack would come.[43]

Alaska At War

The United States called a Pacific-wide alert on November 26 in response to the growing tensions with Japan. General Buckner put his command in a state of increased readiness. By then the Alaska Defense Command boasted a force of 20,000. Most of the major construction had been completed at Fort Richardson and Elmendorf Field. Ladd Field was ready and the fields in southeastern Alaska were operational. However, there were still serious weaknesses, particularly with Colonel Davis's small force of approximately 2,300 officers and men. Other than the one fighter and two bomber squadrons he had only one other flying unit, the 15th Tow Target Squadron, which had arrived at Elmendorf Field November 1 without any aircraft.[44]

On December 6, Colonel Davis put down his thoughts in a hand written memo, stating:

> The air force is so small, consists of such old equipment, and is in such poor conditions as to constitute a cadre sent to the territory in advance of the main body for the purpose of gaining information of the geography, developing a technique of cold-weather operation, and principally to develop a plan and facilities for the operation of the main force on its arrival. By no stretch of the imagination can it be accepted as a force able to defend the territory against any attack in force.[45]

The next day the Japanese bombed Pearl Harbor. Conceived in January 1941 by Admiral Yamamoto, the attack had not been incorporated into the overall plan until October. In the interim, Yamamoto had carefully selected the men and trained them well for their mission of neutralizing the Pacific Fleet. Vice Admiral Chuichi Nagumo's carrier task force, built around six large carriers, was alerted in mid November. On November 27, as Japanese diplomats carried out last minute negotiations, the task force departed its assembly area at Tanakan Bay on Hitokappu Island, in the bleak cold southern Kuriles. Following the 40th parallel, well out of normal shipping lanes, it turned southeast shortly after crossing the International Date Line.

By 6:00 AM on December 7, the carriers had reached their launch points 200 miles north of Oahu Island. The first of the 360 aircraft began flying off. The first wave roared in over their objectives at 7:40 AM, followed by the second wave at 8:50. The attacks were well planned and executed. In exchange for a loss of six submarines (five of them midget types) and twenty-nine aircraft, the Japanese had achieved a stunning if not complete victory. When the last of their aircraft departed at 9:45 AM, eighteen ships had been sunk or seriously damaged, one hundred and eighty-eight aircraft lay in ruins and 3,581 men had become the first American casualties of a war that would unite the nation as never before or after.

Yet the Japanese had failed to sink the three American carriers which were elsewhere in the Pacific at the time. Neither did they destroy the large fuel storage tanks and the extensive repair facilities at Pearl Harbor. All would be crucial during the next six months. Of the seven battleships sunk or damaged, all but two would be placed back in commission. However, the mighty vessels of war, the pride of the fleet, were already obsolete by the time Yamamoto's young Naval aviators had savaged them. It was the majestic aircraft carrier that would rule supreme in the war in the Pacific. The Japanese had been the first to demonstrate its effectiveness. The Americans would use it with a vengeance.[46]

For the Americans, the attack on Pearl Harbor came as a thunderclap. Never since the War of 1812 had United States territory been so violated. For a moment, Americans were frightened and confused. A thirteen year old boy raced through the streets of Florence, Alabama shouting that the Japanese were heading up Four Mile Creek towards the town. In Georgia, a citizen's army known as the State Guard began preparing defenses along the Atlantic coast in preparation of an expected German invasion. A high ranking American Legion official in Wisconsin appealed for the creation of a guerrilla force composed of the state's 25,000 licensed deer hunters. In San Francisco, an over-zealous sentry shot a woman who was too slow at stopping at a check point, and in Los Angeles, an anti-aircraft battery blasted away at an imaginary target.[47]

In Alaska, news of the Japanese attack came not from the military but from an enterprising twenty-four-year-old radio engineer, August "Augie" Hiebert. Austin E. "Cap" Lathrop, Alaska's first millionaire, had opened Fairbank's radio station KFRAR on October 1, 1939. The station, under the slogan "From the Top of the World to You," was located several miles outside of Fairbanks. Hiebert came in early that morning. Since the station was not scheduled to go on the air until 2:00 PM, he began turning the dial of the short-wave receiver. At about 9:27 AM, one hour earlier than Hawaiian time, a drama program he was listening to was suddenly interrupted by an announcement that the Japanese were attacking Pearl Har-

bor. Hiebert called the duty officer at Ladd Field, and Alaska went to war.[48]

General Buckner immediately went into action. Orders were issued to recall all the troops that were away from the bases. Fighting positions were manned and aircraft launched. That night a blackout was ordered, and the citizens of Alaska, like their fellow Americans elsewhere, worried and wondered what the future would hold for them. It was a period of uncertainty. *The Anchorage Daily Times* reported two days later that the Japanese were near the Aleutian Islands. An invasion was expected any day.

The skies over Anchorage "bristled with warplanes out for business."[49] The communities' civil defense organization swung into full action. Some three hundred men reported to the city hall armed with a variety of weapons. The American Legion called a special meeting to determine what they could do for the war effort.[50] The communities' first casualty occurred when fifty-eight-year-old John D. DeHay dropped dead on the street from a heart attack during an air raid alert December 10.[51]

Strange aircraft were sighted; reports circulated that the Japanese had attempted to launch a carrier attack but bad weather had prevented the planes from taking off; and news was received from "outside" that Alaskan cities had been bombed. Representative Dimond told Congress, "My people feel they occupy a battle field."[52]

In a sense he was right. In one of his first acts, General Buckner ordered the evacuation of all dependents of military and construction workers from Alaska. The only exceptions were those who could claim the territory as their home of record or who were otherwise engaged in a line of work that was critical to the war effort; otherwise everyone else went south, including the general's wife and two sons. With the exodus of the wives and children, the husbands could devote more of their time to their military duties. "In a raid," according to Buckner, "I want the men to think of their posts, not their families."[53]

General Buckner next ordered another far less merciful evacuation. The West Coast had been thrown into a state of hysteria following Pearl Harbor. The public turned its suspicions on the Japanese and their descendants who had settled in the coastal states. There was suspicion among some in positions of power that there were those among the Japanese-Americans who would conduct sabotage and espionage operations. Latent and overt popular prejudice fueled the problem. The end result was their forced movement to internment camps . It was a sorry episode in American history in which Alaska shared.[54]

Since the territory was part of DeWitt's command, General Buckner was required to order all Japanese-Americans removed from Alaska. The warnings of the pending troubles came in early January when military and civilian authorities began confiscating guns, ammunition, cameras and radios. The blow fell on April 7 when the Alaska Defense Command issued a public proclamation notifying the 263 Japanese-Americans who called Alaska their home that they had less than twenty days to settle their affairs. The first groups began leaving in late April, and by July all had been relocated, the majority going to the Minidoka Internment Camp in Idaho.[55]

Few, if any of Alaska's Japanese-Americans could be considered disloyal. Most were hard working, and many were highly respected members of a society that prided itself on its frontier spirit. They and the Aleuts who would be removed from their homes in the Aleutians were victims of the harsh, often mindless realities of a war that reached deeply into the lives of all Americans. Personal freedoms, normally taken for granted in peace, were subordinated to the national effort of defeating enemies whose totalitarian governments threatened the very foundations of democracy. The alternative in the words of Winston Churchill, was the sinking of civilization "into the abyss of a new Dark Age made more sinister, and more protracted by the lights of perverted science."[56]

The war years also imposed other hardships, of which censorship was the most irksome. A normal wartime practice, it was carried to extremes in the remote territory. As early as August 1941, General DeWitt had informed Governor Gruening:

> That until further notice, there is to be no publicity with reference to Army stations in Alaska; and no newspaper or magazine correspondent, radio commentator, or other publicity agent is to be given any special access to Alaska stations or to be authorized to publish or broadcast any information concerning the defense establishment there.[57]

Until then the news media had covered the buildup of military forces and the construction of facilities in considerable detail. Following Pearl Harbor, there was a virtual blackout of information. It was the beginning of what one author, Otis Hays Jr, called "the silent years in Alaska." Even tighter restrictions were imposed in June 1942, after the Japanese attack on Dutch Harbor and the seizure of Attu and Kiska, when General Buckner issued a proclamation designating Alaska a military area. Travel was tightly controlled, letters were opened and read, film confiscated and the news tightly censored.[58]

The censors went to the point of cutting out articles on Alaska that appeared in popular magazines before they were sent to the territory. Governor Gruening, much to his annoyance, found his copies of *Time* and *Newsweek* full of holes. Even Buckner was not immune to the zealous personnel who worked in the Office of Censorship in Seattle, Washington. He became enraged when he found that they had clipped a section from a roll of film he sent to be developed. The section, showing a dog team, had been removed on the grounds that the Japanese might find

out that dog teams were still being used as a means of transportation in Alaska. The height of absurdity was reached when copies of *The Seattle Post Intelligencer* containing an account of the Dutch Harbor attack were sent to the base with all the pictures of the attack clipped out.[59]

Gruening complained frequently and bitterly, stating on one occasion, "censorship in Alaska has been and is, in my judgement, unusually repressive, wasteful—since many are employed in carrying out its provision—and wholly unnecessary."[60] Finally, in late 1943, he turned to his Congressional friends to apply pressure on those in authority. He did gain some concessions, but at the expense of his relationship with President Roosevelt, who backed the head of the Office of Censorship, Byron Price.[61]

The reporters and authors who had to contend with the censors, particularly after Dutch Harbor, found the experience even more frustrating. Joseph Driscoll, in his book, *War Discovers Alaska*, wrote that while the news media in other theaters of war had ready access to information, the censorship in Alaska was so strict that it "gave rise to all sorts of rumors."[62]

Following the Pearl Harbor attack, the jitters soon turned to determination. The Matanuska dairy farmers announced plans to increase milk production so shipping could be freed to move more ammunition to Alaska. Alaskans began buying bonds to purchase a B-17 to be named the "Spirit of Alaska," and a group of Eskimo women showed up at the recruiting office in Nome to volunteer for the Army.[63]

Governor Gruening began recruiting a Territorial Guard to replace the Alaska National Guard which had been inducted into federal service in September 1941, barely two years after its formation. At the time the Guard consisted of the 1st Battalion, 297th Infantry and a territorial headquarters. Plans had been made to form an observation squadron, the 129th, and funds had been appropriated in April 1941, to recruit and equip a flight of observation aircraft at Elmendorf Field and another at Ladd Field. However, Generals DeWitt and Buckner objected. They felt the National Guard squadron would draw too many scarce resources away from the active forces. The plan was dropped.[64]

After the shock of Pearl Harbor wore off, Alaska, like the rest of the nation, settled in for the duration of the war. Isolation, remoteness, censorship, population displacements and the Japanese occupation of the western Aleutian Islands posed their hardships; however, the territory enjoyed one privilege that was denied the 48 states. There was no rationing. The officials reasoned that it would be too hard to control. Many Alaskans bought their staples in bulk to last for a year. Although there were shortages from time to time caused by shipping delays, there were no restrictions placed on the quantity of such items as gasoline, cigarettes and meats, that could be bought. Alaskans enjoyed a booming economy. There was no shortage of jobs, and people flocked to the territory.[65]

We Have Had Very Poor Luck

General Buckner, writing to General Arnold the day after Pearl Harbor, vented his frustrations over his air units and their obsolete aircraft: "At dawn this morning I watched our entire Alaskan Air Force take to the air so as not to be caught on the field—six medium bombers and twelve pursuit planes."[66] Buckner believed at the time the Japanese force that had attacked Pearl Harbor was going to turn north and strike Alaska. The small and dwindling number of old aircraft could not have fought off an attack. Sticking to his premise that air power was the key to Alaska's defenses, Buckner ended his letter to the Army Air Forces chief of staff by stating:

> I would rather be reinforced by one heavy bombardment squadron than a division of ground troops since the only striking force that we can use is bombardment aviation and the enemy is always at a disadvantage when he is in the water and we are on land.[67]

Captain Parker's Alaska Sector forces were even less prepared to counter the Japanese threat. From his headquarters aboard the *Charleston* at Kodiak, he commanded a small surface force of old destroyers and the gun boat, his flagship. His staff was making plans to confiscate fishing boats, arm them with light weapons, paint them grey and turn them into patrol boats. He had also under his control the six PBYs of VP-41 commanded by Lieutenant Commander Paul Foley Jr., whose turn it was to conduct patrols over the Gulf of Alaska and the North Pacific from Kodiak.

The seaplane tender *Gillis* was also at Kodiak. Lieutenant Commander Russell had taken his squadron, VP-42, back to its home base at Sand Point, Washington. Both squadrons, plus VP-43 and VP-44 at San Diego, California, were assigned to Patrol Wing Four at Sand Point. Captain Leslie E. Gehres had assumed command of the wing on November 9, 1941.[68]

Colonel Davis continued to make do with his small force until the bomber and fighter squadrons and the more modern aircraft that General Arnold had promised Buckner could arrive. After the initial excitement of Pearl Harbor, operations settled down to a routine. The handful of B-18s were loaded with 300-pound bombs and sent out to join the PBYs in patrolling the Gulf of Alaska. Others were committed to patrolling the Bering Sea from Nome. The P-36s were placed on a twenty-four hour ground alert at Elmendorf Field. It soon became apparent, however, that the Japanese were not interested in Alaska, but were more intent on carrying out their Far East operations.[69]

The fear, however, remained that the Japanese, as soon as they finished their conquests, would turn their attention to Alaska. On January 21, 1942, General Marshall informed President Roosevelt that the Army was "anticipating at any moment a destructive raid . . . especially at Dutch Harbor where our state of preparedness is far from complete."[70]

The Japanese, likewise, feared the Americans would use the Aleutian Islands as a route for attacking them. On March 1, 1942, Rear Admiral Tanetsuga Sosa, in an interview with the *Japan Times* warned that the Americans were preparing bases in Alaska and the Aleutians for such an effort. He felt, however, the attack could easily be smashed since Japan's navy was far superior.[71] In its May 6, 1942, edition, *The Anchorage Daily Times* carried a reprint of an article by a Japanese military correspondent, Schichiji Ito, noting the possibility that Japan could be invaded from Alaska. Like Admiral Sosa, he believed that it would be too difficult because of the distances involved and the poor transportation facilities. Rather, he felt it would be the Japanese who would invade Alaska by way of the Aleutians.[72]

Generals Buckner and DeWitt noted all of this, and continued to use it in their justification for reinforcing Alaska's defenses. General DeWitt's IX Corps had been upgraded to the Western Defense Command four days after Pearl Harbor in recognition of the important role it would play in the defense of the West Coast and Alaska. At the time, there was a fear that the western United States was opened to a Japanese attack. DeWitt's command, in addition to Alaska, included nine western states and three air forces: the Second Air Force, the Fourth Air Force and the Alaskan Air Force.[73]

Buckner, who had been promoted to major general in August, proposed shortly after Pearl Harbor that he be given overall responsibility for all military forces in Alaska. At the same time, General Arnold's staff recommended that Buckner be replaced by an Army Air Forces general who was more attuned to air operations. Their proposal, like the previous ones for creating a separate unified command in Alaska, fell on deaf ears. DeWitt, not wanting to see his authority diminished replied on January 3 that "instead of unity of command, it is essential that the closest and most cordial cooperation be maintained. Therefore, it is desired that no further action be taken on this subject."[74] General Marshall, his long time colleague, supported him; and Buckner, not wanting to offend his boss further, did not press the issue. The lack of an unified command would remain one of the major stumbling blocks in the coming Aleutian Campaign, primarily due to the egos of the principal commanders and their inability to get along with each other.[75]

Colonel Davis also saw his small force grow in stature following Pearl Harbor. The first improvement came when General Buckner issued a directive, freeing his men of many administrative duties, which included providing their own base defense. The duties were assigned to the Army's ground forces. Davis scribbled a short note to his adjutant on the margin of the directive, "Jack, this is sort of a Bible, file carefully."[76] The real breakthrough came on December 28 when the Alaskan Air Force was formed at the direction of the War Department. It replaced the Air Force, Alaska Defense Command which had been created locally two months earlier to provide Davis with a headquarters and an organization to manage his forces. The War Department order provided a formal organization and more authority to its commander, Colonel Davis. He reported administratively to General DeWitt and answered operationally to General Buckner.[77]

General Arnold also came through on the promised additional squadrons and more modern aircraft. DeWitt informed Buckner that the squadrons were on the way accompanied by five badly needed Douglas C-53 twin engine transports. In addition to the B-26s and P-40s that were coming north with the squadrons, others were being winterized for Alaskan duty. DeWitt also told Buckner that until the situation could be stabilized in the Pacific, Alaska would play a passive defense role.[78]

It was a beginning. At long last Buckner was getting the air units he needed. In late December the 11th Fighter Squadron and 77th Bombardment Squadron began deploying to Alaska. The 18th Fighter Squadron was scheduled to received Curtiss P-40Es in replacement for its tired old P-36s, the 36th Bombardment Squadron would replace its few remaining B-18s with the four engine B-17Es and the 73rd would receive B-26s.[79]

Following the hectic days after Pearl Harbor, the two new squadrons were ordered to deploy to Alaska on short notice despite one of the coldest winters on record, a lack of en route air facilities and the inexperience of the young air crews who were required to make their way over the frozen, sparsely settled and unfamiliar lands of the Canadian Yukon and Northwest Territories. Their experience more than proved General Buckner's warning to Arnold and others that air units could not be rushed to Alaska.

Typical was the deployment of the 11th Fighter Squadron from Key Field, Mississippi. The squadron had been activated January 15, 1940, at Selfridge Field, Michigan. It moved to Key Field, Mississippi in early October 1941, only to be informed December 18 that it was being reassigned to Elmendorf Field. Lieutenant Edgar A. Romberg and the ground personnel departed Key Field on December 19 by rail. Reaching Seattle four days later, they boarded the *Saint Mihiel* on Christmas Eve after being allowed to see the sights of Seattle. For most, according to the squadron historian, it was their "first time away from home and certainly the first Christmas." Most were new to the Army, and although they accepted the simple sacrifice, any one of the young men would "have given a year's pay to be somewhere in the states." Buckner sent them a message: "I know that you and your garrison have the guts to take it, the punch to hand it out and the stuff to carry the war into the enemy's country before 1942 is over." The historian noted: "One wonders what meaning this had to the men of the 11th Pursuit Squadron, once of Selfridge Field, Michigan, formerly of Key Field, Mississippi, and now of Elmendorf Field, Alaska."[80]

The *Saint Mihiel* pulled into the dock at Seward on December 29, and the men finished their long journey to war aboard the Alaska Railroad. The little band of men, 227 strong, arrived at Elmendorf Field at 10:30 PM. that evening and began preparing for the arrival of the pilots

As he was about to board the ship for Alaska, John Melter's sister handed him a small black dog. Bomber became Melter's companion as the 11th Fighter Squadron mechanic moved from base to base. He slept under Melter's cot at night and roamed the squadron area during the day. Dogs of every description and breed were a common sight in the Aleutians. They provided companionship and a source of love for the young men who suddenly found their lives changed by the harsh realities of war. Bomber was struck and killed by a truck on Adak in late 1943. John Melter never forgot him. John R. Melter collection

The 11th Pursuit Squadron's area at Key Field, Mississippi. It was quite a contrast to the place the men of the "Aleutian Tigers," would soon find themselves. John R. Melter collection

Bomber and a kindred soul. One of the 18th Fighter Squadron's P-40s in the background. John R. Melter collection

Colonel Eareckson also had a dog named Scootch, which he sometimes carried with him on his missions over Kiska. Scootch is shown in a photograph of unknown origin making his mark on the only tree on Umnak Island.

who would man the squadron's aircraft.[81]

The task of supervising the ferrying of the squadron's twenty-five Curtiss P-40 Warhawks to Alaska went to Lieutenant John S. Chennault, the son of Major General Claire L. Chennault. He was one of the few experienced pilots in the squadron, having entered flight school at Randolph Field, Texas as a cadet in March 1934, at the age of 20. Following graduation from flight school in 1935, Chennault was assigned to Selfridge Field where he remained until he was ordered to lead his group of inexperienced flyers on their long and difficult journey to Alaska. Those who knew him at the time described him as a "big framed man . . . healthy and powerful . . . a man's man," who "loved to fly and spent every possible minute in the air," and although not talkative, still took in everything that was happening, was always friendly and always took the time to listen to others. The squadron historian, remembering him, noted: "John Chennault was a good soldier and a true leader of men. His eight months as squadron commander was something of a golden era."[82]

Six days after Pearl Harbor, Chennault learned that he was to lead his men north. While his close friend, Edgar Romberg, was preparing to depart Key Field with the bulk of the squadron, Chennault set about the task of collecting the pilots and picking up the P-40s that were being winterized at the Sacramento Air Depot.

> I was very puzzled about the future when I left Selfridge on 13 December 1941. My orders were to pick up my 24 pilots, plus myself, get them to Sacramento, equip them with 25 P-40s supposedly chaffing at their bits, and set out for Alaska. Upon arrival at Sacramento, I was stared at somewhat coldly, not many people knowing my mission. The P-40s were scattered around the field, pickled, and a long way from being ready as they weren't even modified for winter operations. We had to get them modified and that took up to the beginning of 1942. The whole deal was screwed up considerably.[83]

Most of Chennault's pilots had just graduated from flight school. Only three had about eight months of experience in the P-40. Eighteen averaged less than eight hours in the fighter and three had less than three hours apiece when they departed for Alaska. Their route north took them over some of the most rugged terrain in north-

Now a major, John S. Chennault went on to become the first commander of the 343rd Fighter Group. Here he stands in front of one of the 11th Fighter Squadron's P-40s. The squadron earned the nickname, the "Aleutian Tigers," for their service in the Aleutians. Their emblem, a tiger's head, was designed by Edward Lange and Gerlad Webber. It was painted on the nose of the Warhawks. AAF photo

west Canada in the dead of winter. Airfields were few and far between, often little more than clearings in the wilderness. Navigation aids, when there were any, were primitive and the charts inaccurate. The en route facilities were not much better. Remembering the experience, Chennault later commented: "We fueled our planes from drums, slept in rude huts and bedding rolls and froze all the time."[84]

Albert Aiken, then a young second lieutenant, was one of the few pilots who was experienced in the P-40. He had been flying it since graduating from flight school earlier in 1941. He was transferred into the squadron on December 13. Aiken recalled that the P-40s were divided into three flights for the trip north. Each was accompanied by a C-53, which carried the mechanics and baggage. Aiken's flight consisted of six P-40s when they left Sacramento on New Years Day. When they reached their first destination, Medford, Oregon, it was dark. Two of the inexperienced pilots promptly ground-looped their fighters on landing. Fortunately, the damages were minor.

The flight waited at Medford for two P-40s they had left behind at Sacramento to join them. The two novice pilots, however, lost their way and, low on gas, landed in a corn field near Mount Shasta in northern California. Aiken and another experienced pilot borrowed a truck, filled it with 55 gallon drums of fuel, and went to look for the two stranded pilots who had somehow managed to bring their planes down between stacks of corn stalks. After refuelling the P-40s and clearing a strip through the corn field, Aiken and his companion took off in the P-40s, leaving the two lost flyers to drive the truck back to Medford. One of them was John Cape, who would lose his life in the opening days of the Aleutian Campaign.

The next leg took them to Spokane. By then, three of the original twenty-five P-40s had been so damaged that they were unable to continue. Chennault decided to have Aiken serve as the "the clean up man to pick up any stragglers along the way." Aiken and two other P-40 pilots accompanied by a C-53 took off after the others had departed. They made it to Calgary and Edmonton, Alberta and on to Fort St. John in British Columbia without any further incidents.

They were promptly weathered in by a heavy snow storm at Fort St. John. After almost a week of enforced idleness in the small, isolated community, they managed to take off for their next destination, Fort Nelson, where one of the P-40s plowed into a snow bank, damaging the engine and prop. The pilot finished the journey in the C-53. Aiken and his remaining companion continued on to Whitehorse and finally arrived at Elmendorf Field without any further incidents.[85]

By February 4, only thirteen of the original twenty-five P-40s had reached Alaska. Seven had crashed en route,

Albert Aiken represented the finest of a generation that grew up during the Great Depression and then was called on to fight in the greatest war ever inflicted on mankind. Like the great majority of the others who were caught up in the war's triumphs and tragedies, Albert Aiken performed his duties with dedication and honor. He remembered his men and they remembered him. Garvis H. Aman took Aiken's wife, Patricia, aside at a reunion of the 18th Fighter Squadron forty-five years later, and told her that her husband had been a "very brave young man." The photograph of Captain Aiken was taken during a May 1943, ceremony in which he and Lieut Glenn M. Rynerson were presented the Distinguished Flying Cross by General Buckner. Rynerson, except for his boots, is hidden by Buckner. photo courtesy Patricia L. Aiken

three of which were a total loss. Five were still somewhere in Canada.[86]

The 77th Bombardment Squadron experienced even more problems. Activated January 15, 1941, at Fort Douglas, Utah, it was one of the first medium bomber squadrons to be equipped with the Martin B-26 Marauder. The 77th moved to Gowen Field, Idaho in June. In October, Lieutenant Elbert Owen Meals, the acting commander and two other lieutenants went to the Glenn L. Martin plant near Baltimore, Maryland to be checked out in the B-26 and begin ferrying the squadron's complement of the new medium bomber back to Gowen Field. At the time the 77th was equipped with B-18s.[87]

Compared to the other medium bombers of the day, the twin engine B-26 was a revolutionary new design. Hardly out of the prototype state when Meals and the others began flying it, the B-26 was a "hot" aircraft to handle, a "widow maker," referred to by many as the "Baltimore Whore" since it had "no visible means of support." The version assigned to the 77th Bombardment Squadron was a particularly difficult aircraft to handle, especially in the primitive conditions of Alaska. Its sixty-five foot wing had to support, when the bomber was fully loaded, a weight

of 27,200 pounds. This resulted in an unusually high wing loading of fifty pounds per square foot that raised its landing and stall speeds considerably. The problem was never really corrected in later models, despite the fact that the wing span was increased to seventy-one feet, the engine output raised from 1850 to 1920 horsepower and slotted flaps added. The advantages were cancelled by the additional weight of more armament and other improvements.[88]

The assignment of the B-26 to the Alaskan theater was a mistake, as events would later prove. With its high landing speed and tricycle landing gear it was a difficult aircraft to operate from the landing fields at the forward locations. The propellers, whose tips cleared the ground by only nine inches, threw loose gravel against the fuselage with great force, endangering the crew. The medium bomber also lacked the range needed in the Aleutians to effectively carry out a mission. One pilot, Richard D. Salter, found the bomber to be "a good airplane in the wrong theater."[89]

After receiving their B-26s, the men of the 77th Bombardment Squadron spent the rest of 1941 flying training missions. Despite this, most of the pilots who had come straight out of flight school still had not completely mastered all the skills required to operate the tricky and at the time unproven medium bomber.

The ground crews consisting of 194 officers and men under the command of Captain Ray S. Bartholomew departed Gowen Field on December 15 by train, and arrived in Seattle in time to join the men of the 11th Fighter Squadron for the trip north aboard the *Saint Mihiel*. The air crews, thirty-nine officers and sixty-five enlisted men led by the squadron commander, Major Robert O. Cork, left for Sacramento on December 20 to pick up fourteen winterized B-26s. Along with the 11th Fighter Squadron pilots they departed for the 2,300 mile trip to Alaska on

The Marauders deployed to Alaska in early 1942 were from the first 201 (40-1361/1561) off the Martin production line. They bore no model number. Three (40-1453, 40-1459 and 40-1464) were crash landed in "Million Dollar Valley" near Watson Lake, British Columbia. They were recovered in 1972 through the efforts of David Tallichet of Chino, California. The one flown by Lieutenants William J. Danner and Howard F. Smiley (40-1464), above being run-up, was restored to flying condition. Tallichet flew it for the first time April 28, 1992. Not much is known of the pioneering efforts of the crews who flew the first production B-26s in Alaska and the Aleutian Theater.

Photo via Maj Gen John O. Moennch, USAF Ret.

January 1. The planned route included stops at Spokane, Edmonton and Whitehorse. The problems began immediately. Four of the bombers experienced engine problems even before they reached Spokane. After spending the night there, Major Cork departed with ten B-26s for Edmonton. The temperatures at Edmonton hovered at thirty degrees below zero; ahead lay more intense cold and the frozen wilderness of northwestern Canada.

Major Cork decided to wait for the other four bombers and for the temperature to rise. The four B-26s made it in from Spokane on the fourth. Finally, on January 12, all fourteen bombers took off on the next leg of their journey, the thousand-mile flight to Whitehorse in the Yukon Territory. In the absence of aeronautical charts, the crews had to use crude maps drawn by Canadian bush pilots familiar with the route. They got as far as Ft. St. John, midway to Whitehorse, where they were grounded for another two days by the extreme cold. Only eleven made it into Watson Lake, another small landing strip on the way to Whitehorse. The crews of three of the bombers became hopelessly lost in a snow storm. With fuel and daylight running out, they decided to make a wheels up landing in a shallow valley. Appropriately enough, the place, 90 miles south-east of Watson Lake, was later named "Million Dollar Valley."

Two of the bombers landed safely; the third nosed over, injuring the pilot and copilot. The crews fashioned shelters out of the wing covers and settled down with their emergency rations to wait to be rescued. Chennault, in a flight that was following the bombers ordered his pilots to fan out in a search pattern. A flight of four fighter pilots spotted the three downed bombers. A Canadian bush pilot, Russ Baker, and another pilot landed near the bombers in a ski equipped single engine Focker. The two injured pilots were evacuated to Watson Lake. A C-47 on skis landed on a nearby lake and picked up the rest of the men.[90] Later, a salvage team from Elmendorf Field was sent out to recover what they could before abandoning the B-26s to the wilderness. The B-26 crews had spent two days in the wilderness. While waiting to be rescued, they amused themselves by shooting at the wrecked bombers with 50 calibre machine guns to see if the armored plating worked.[91]

A fourth bomber was damaged while landing at Watson Lake and the fifth suffered the same fate at Whitehorse. The remaining nine finally made it to Alaska January 29th.[92] However, by February 4, when Buckner wrote to DeWitt, expressing what was probably an understatement: "We have had very poor luck with our reinforcement airplanes,"[93] only five had made it to Elmendorf Field. The others were at Ladd Field. All were grounded for faulty gas line installations, and could not be flown until the parts could be sent to Alaska. Buckner figured that because of the inexperienced pilots and the condition of the aircraft, it would take two months to make the squadrons operational.

In the interim, the numbers of the tired old P-36s and B-18s continued to dwindle. In the week before Buckner's letter to DeWitt, one of the Hawks had crashed in flames; its pilot escaping by parachute. Several days later the engine on a B-18 quit on takeoff. The bomber was wrecked and one man killed. Buckner decided to send some of the old aircraft to Kodiak and use the newer aircraft for training. At the same time, the two fighter squadrons exchanged pilots so that the 11th would have one Alaskan-experienced pilot per flight to pass on his knowledge to the new arrivals.[94] Albert Aiken was among those who were transferred to the 18th Fighter Squadron. For him and the others, the transitioning into the P-36s did not pose any particular problems and the exchange went smoothly.[95]

Nevertheless, for Aiken and the new arrivals and those who followed them, Alaskan flying would prove to be a difficult and dangerous occupation, one that had to be mastered in order to survive. Joe Schneider, who along with Davis and a few others had been one of the earlier arrivals, remembering forty years later the death of a comrade, noted:

I don't remember his name. But, of those of us who were here early enough to become acquainted to Alaska's flying conditions, most survived. The boys who came directly from sunny California, and the other states where the weather wasn't so bad sometimes didn't even get a chance to learn how to cope with the situation.[96]

In the postmortem that followed the deployment debacle, everyone agreed that it had been poorly planned and the problems compounded by inexperienced air crews, inadequate facilities and the extreme cold weather.[97] General Arnold was furious. His concept for rapidly sending air reinforcements to Alaska had failed; it was not at all like the well planned and supported flight of B-10s he had led to Alaska in the summer of 1934. If any more aircraft were to be sent to the territory, he wanted to make certain they all arrived safely and on time.

On February 10, Colonel William O. Butler, Chief of Staff, Fourth Air Force was summoned into Arnold's office and directed to solve the problem. Butler and his staff quickly drafted a plan that worked. Fourth Air Force pilots flew the winterized planes to Spokane. There they were met by experienced Alaskan pilots and mechanics. After the mechanics were satisfied that the planes had been properly winterized and were in top mechanical condition, they were turned over to the pilots. The planes were then flown north over the inland route in groups of six and accompanied by a transport plane carrying the mechanics and spare parts.[98]

Albert Aiken was among those dispatched to ferry the new aircraft to Alaska. He left Elmendorf Field in early March aboard a C-53. The weather deteriorated and the Goony Bird pilot, Lieutenant Bud Giffen, decided to land at Burwash Landing in the Yukon Territory. They came down on a small landing strip covered with snow. One of the local natives met them with a dog team and informed them that they had landed at the wrong place.

The right place was on a strip marked out on the nearby frozen lake. He offered to show the pilot the right place if he would allow him and his wife to fly with them. Giffin agreed and Aiken and a pilot from the 11th Fighter Squadron volunteered to drive the dog team back into town. Neither had handled a dog team before, and before they could stop the dogs they had gone almost completely through the town.

After spending a brief time at Burwash Landing where Aiken and the others dined on the toughest meat he had ever eaten before or since, they went on to Whitehorse, Edmonton and Spokane where they thoroughly enjoyed a week's layover. After picking up the P-40s they flew as a group back to Alaska without any serious incidents.[99]

By the end of April the two fighter squadrons had received a full complement of P-40Es, and the 73rd Bombardment Squadron was equipped with B-26As. The 36th Bombardment Squadron had to make do with the B-18s until the four engine Boeing B-17Es that it had been promised arrived.[100] In January, General Arnold's staff, as an interim solution, diverted three LB-30s to Alaska from a shipment of 139 Lend Lease versions of the Consolidated B-24 Liberator that had been intended for England. They also found a spare prototype B-17E for Alaska, and the Cold Weather Test Detachment at Ladd Field agreed to transfer its remaining B-17B, "Old Seventy," to the 36th Bombardment Squadron. It was one of the thirty-nine early model Flying Fortresses manufactured by Boeing during the late 1930s. Two were sent to Ladd Field for cold weather testing, one of which was lost in an accident.[101]

The B-17E arrived from Wright Field, Ohio in early March. It had been undergoing testing there. The three LB-30s and "Old Seventy" arrived in May. They were equipped with the British designed SCR-521 air-to-surface vessel, or ASV radar; a recent innovation designed to extend the search range of the bombers and provide a better margin of safety in the event the weather turned bad. Airborne radar was still in the initial stages of development and was difficult to use and not very reliable. It still provided a much needed feature that would prove useful in the foul weather of the Aleutians. Cameras were also installed and "Old Seventy" was used. She became an RB-17B — a reconnaissance aircraft. The 36th Bombardment Squadron, which had moved to Kodiak in early February, now had a mixed bag of old B-18s and the recent arrivals to carry out its mission of patrolling the Gulf of Alaska and the North Pacific.[102]

The arrival of the two squadrons and newer aircraft and the promise of B-17Es gave Buckner the forces he needed to defend Alaska. The lack of an air transport squadron was solved with the C-53s that had deployed with the 11th Fighter Squadron and the activation of the 42nd Troop Carrier Squadron at Elmendorf Field on May 2 under the command of Captain Philip T. Durfee. It was the first flying squadron to be activated in Alaska.[103] The squadron was immediately pressed into service transporting passengers and cargo to the bases under construction in the Aleutians. It was a pioneering effort since many of the fields in Alaska were little more than cleared strips of land. In the months ahead, the 42nd would be committed to long hours in the air. One C-53 would log 187 hours in 17 days.[104]

Another transportation problem was solved when President Roosevelt gave the go-ahead to build the Alaska Highway. The idea for a highway that would connect Alaska with the states had originated during the 1930s, when the United States and Canadian governments established commissions to investigate its feasibility. However, it took Pearl Harbor to make it a reality. On

Two of the thirty-nine B-17Bs that Boeing built were assigned to the 36th Bombardment Squadron while the squadron was still at Lowry Field. They, along with their crews, were sent on detached duty to Ladd Field for cold weather testing during the Winter of 1940-41. The purpose of testing was to determine how well a squadron of the big bombers would operate under Arctic and sub-Arctic conditions. This one (#38-216) known as "Old Seventy" and still in its Cold Weather Detachment markings, later served in the Aleutians. It was the only "B" model to see combat. It crashed on July 18, 1942 as it was returning from a mission over Kiska. The other (#38-217) was destroyed in a crash near Lovelock, Nevada February 6, 1941. Captain Richard S. Freeman and his seven man crew were en route to Wright Field when the accident occurred. All perished. AC photo

LB-30, foreground, and B-17E, 36th Bombardment Squadron at Otter Point, early June 1942. The LB-30 was one of three originally intended for England, but diverted and sent to Alaska instead. AAF photo

The crews of the C-47s and C-53s of the 42nd Troop Carrier Squadron and later the 54th Troop Carrier Squadron flew long hours under very hazardous conditions in the Aleutians. Their contributions have never been fully recognized.
AAF photos

of engineering skill and determination. It also was a demonstration of the close cooperation that had developed between the United States and its Canadian ally.[106]

The 1st Photographic Squadron was deployed from Grey Field, Fort Lewis, Washington in May 1941 to fly photo reconnaissance missions over Alaska and chart a route for the Alaska Highway. The squadron remained in Alaska on temporary duty until December 1941. It employed the Beachcraft F-2 photo-reconnaissance aircraft, two of which are shown over the Kenai Peninsula June 5, 1941. AC photo

Allies In A Common Cause

The cooperation had proceeded the outbreak of hostilities when Canadian Prime Minister MacKenzie King and President Roosevelt created the Permanent Joint Board of Defense in August 1940, following the collapse of France, to provide a forum for discussing mutual defense needs. Pearl Harbor had also shocked the Canadians, who until then were more concerned with the war in Europe and her commitment as a former colony and as a dominion of the embattled British. Canada had declared war on Germany September 10, 1939, one week after Great Britain.

January 16, 1942, President Roosevelt asked his Secretaries of War, Navy and Interior to study the need for the highway. They quickly determined that because of the vulnerability of the sea lanes to Alaska to Japanese submarine attack and the need to support the staging airfields in the Canadian Northwest and Yukon Territories the highway was a vital necessity. The disastrous attempt to rapidly deploy the 11th Fighter and 77th Bombardment Squadrons to Alaska in the dead of winter provided a clinching argument. At the time there was a critical shortage of supplies and equipment at the partially completed fields at Ft. St. John, Fort Nelson, Watson Lake and Whitehorse. The highway provided the only practical way in which they could be resupplied and sustained on a regular basis.[105]

An advance party arrived at Dawson Creek at the southern terminus of the planned highway on March 9. Shortly afterwards, U.S. Army engineers began pushing north from Dawson Creek and south from Whitehorse. On September 24, "amid the roar and thunder of the big cats and the swishing crash of the giant trees," they met at Contact Creek, 50 miles east of Watson Lake. Several days later, a truck which had left Dawson Creek, crossed the stream and continued on to Whitehorse. It took seventy hours to make the thousand miles over the primitive road. On November 25, the engineers met at Beaver Creek just across the Canadian side of the border, completing the final link between Whitehorse and Big Delta in Alaska. It had taken the engineers, working in the sub-zero temperatures of winter and the mosquito infested summer, eight months to carve a road through the wilderness. Even for a wartime project, it was a considerable achievement

Following Pearl Harbor, Canada began reinforcing the Western Air Command. The command had been formed in early 1938, and was responsible for the air defense of western Canada. By 1942, its commander, Air Commodore L. F. Stevenson had five regular and three auxiliary (reserve) squadrons to defend a thousand miles of coast line. In early January 1942, a joint plan was drawn up for the defense of the western United States, Canada and Alaska. It furnished the basis for the future commitment of Royal Canadian Air Force units to the defense of the territory.

Hardly had the plan been agreed to than it was implemented. With the Port of Seattle strained to the limits, the United States turned to Canada for use of Prince Rupert. The British Columbia coastal city and its port was

2,000 miles from the Anchorage area, and it provided an alternate to Seattle, a thousand miles to the south. It was officially opened on April 5. Air Commodore Stevenson, who was concerned about the air defense of the area, proposed to General DeWitt that the RCAF be allowed to base a fighter squadron at the Annette Island airfield as an interim measure until the Americans could provide one. At the time, the Canadians did not have an airfield near Prince Rupert that could accommodate military aircraft. DeWitt and Buckner, faced with a shortage of aircraft in Alaska, readily agreed to the Canadian use of the one on Annette Island, which was located at the southern end of southeastern Alaska and some 60 miles northeast of Prince Rupert.

Stevenson selected Number 115 Fighter Squadron, commanded by Squadron Leader E.M. Reyno, for deployment from Rockcliffe, Ontario to Annette Island. The squadron, which had been reformed in August 1, 1941, was equipped with fourteen twin-engine Bristol Bolingbroke Mark IVs, a long range fighter version of the British manufactured Blenheim bomber. The obsolescent medium bomber had been modified for its fighter role with a belly-pack of forward firing machine guns. The air commodore and his staff realized that the unwieldy Bolingbrokes had limited value as a fighter, but they felt it

would do until a more modern fighter could be obtained for the squadron. Squadron Leader Reyno and his men began moving into Annette Island in April. By May 5, they were operational and flying anti-submarine patrols over the Gulf of Alaska.[107]

The first deployment of a Canadian flying unit to American soil had not been without its humorous side. An officious American customs agent, overly concerned with the letter of the law and present when the squadron began arriving, insisted the Canadians pay duty on their equipment. The matter was referred up through State Department channels until it finally landed on Secretary of State Cordell Hull's desk, who settled it by declaring the Canadians "distinguished visitors"; but not before a wag in his department suggested "the agent be sent to the Philippines after the war to confront any new invader with a copy of the tariff act."[108]

Number 115 Squadron remained under the operational control of the Prince Rupert Defenses, and Annette Island, in essence, became an RCAF base during the war. For General Buckner, the squadron's deployment was another step in the strengthening of Alaska's defenses. For both nations, it was the beginning of close cooperation for the common air defense of North America.

The Alaska Highway under construction. Someone with a sense of humor placed the sign along the Glenn Highway. The highway was built to connect Anchorage with the Alaska Highway. USA photo

Bristol Bolingbroke Mark IV, No 115 Fighter Squadron, RCAF, being de-iced prior to patrol from Annette Island, Winter, 1942-43. H. P. Clark collection vie Canadian Directorate of History

Annette Island, October 10, 1943. The air field became an RCAF base during the war. AAF photo

3

THE SIDE SHOW

· · · · · · · · · · · ·

The Smallest Air Force

Colonel Davis' forces were growing. In addition to the establishment of the Alaskan Air Force, a provisional fighter interceptor command had been activated on December 31, 1941. Besides being responsible for air defense, it controlled blackouts and imposed radio silence. More importantly, it reflected the growing importance of air power in Alaska. Colonel Davis' command, compared to the ground forces, had assumed a responsibility far out of proportion to its limited size.[1]

The time had come for the creation of a major headquarters. On February 5, 1942, the short lived Alaskan Air Force, formed on December 28 the previous year and activated January 15, was redesignated the 11th Air Force. In one more change, the 11th was again redesignated the Eleventh Air Force on September 18, 1942. The Eleventh, one of the oldest, certainly the smallest, was destined to become the least known of the World War II Army Air Forces' numbered air forces.[2]

Eleventh Air Force headquarters was authorized seventeen officers and one hundred and fifty enlisted men, which was considerably more than what was actually assigned. Shortly afterwards, the War Department sent General Buckner a manning list of what they felt was a proper headquarters. It contained spaces for eighty officers and six hundred enlisted men. After looking at it, Buckner snorted: "When we get enough planes for such a headquarters, we then can request it."[3]

The Eleventh Air Force at the time of its creation consisted of a headquarters squadron; a provisional interceptor command, commanded by Lieutenant Colonel Norman D. Sillin, which included the 11th and 18th Fighter Squadrons; the 28th Composite Group, commanded by Lieutenant Colonel William O. Eareckson, composed of the 36th, 73rd and 77th Bombardment Squadrons; and the 23rd Air Base Group. The Alaskan Air Depot provided administrative and maintenance support. Altogether,

there were 3,067 persons assigned to the Eleventh by the end of February.[4]

The headquarters list that the War Department sent to Buckner contained a general officer position. No one in Alaska was qualified to fill it. Davis, Eareckson and Sillin, old hands now but still junior lieutenant colonels, were not qualified even in those days of fast promotions to wear the stars of a general officer. Despite the fact that he had spent almost two years creating the Eleventh Air Force, Davis had to step aside after two days as its commander when he was replaced by a more senior recent arrival, Colonel Lionel H. Dunlap.[5]

Even Dunlap's tenure was short lived, for on March 8, Colonel Butler, the former Chief of Staff, Fourth Air Force arrived from San Francisco to assume command of the fledgling air force. Dunlap was reassigned as Commander of the Alaskan Air Depot and Davis, promoted to colonel, and became Butler's chief of staff. Six days later General Buckner pinned the stars of a brigadier general on his air new commander.[6]

Slow and methodical, the large-framed forty-six-year-old Virginian and 1917 West Point graduate exercised leadership a different way from the free wheeling style of Davis and Eareckson. Talley described Butler as a "commander type," one who gets the job done but does not excite the imagination or provide inspiration.[7]

Butler did not impress the younger pilots who had preceded him. Shortly after he arrived, Colonel Davis asked Frank O'Brien to fly Butler around Alaska on an orientation trip. The next morning the newly promoted Butler showed up at O'Brien's aircraft, an ex-American Airlines DC-3 which the military had taken over. After sliding into the copilot seat, he ordered O'Brien to take off. Other than to fool with the engine instruments he left the flying to O'Brien, who kept calling him colonel much to the new general's irritation. O'Brien, his hands full with flying the airplane and concerned about what Butler would do with the engine instruments, had not noticed that

A formal photograph of General Butler. AAF photo

his copilot had been promoted.

From Elmendorf Field they flew to Big Delta where a field was being constructed. Just before they arrived, Butler spotted an emergency strip and ordered O'Brien to land. Much against his best judgment, O'Brien managed to get the plane down and back into the air again. Colonel Talley, who had been riding in the back, as soon as Butler was out of sight, commented: "Nice going O.B., I always wanted to know how short you could make it into one of these."

After spending the night at Ladd Field, where Butler could not produce his "short snorter," a dollar bill that was passed around for signatures, and had to buy the Officers Club bar a round of drinks, they went on to Nome where the temperature was forty-five degrees below zero. After finally getting the engines started the next morning, O'Brien got into an argument with the general over the oil pressure warning lights. O'Brien, who understood the aircraft, insisted on taking off with the indicator lights on. The lights finally went off just before they reached McGrath.

Butler, now in a better frame of mind, spotted a road house near the runway and ordered O'Brien to land for lunch, which he offered to buy for everyone on the aircraft. Unfortunately, he did not realize in that remote location lunch averaged around $2.50 instead of sixty to seventy

General Butler and his subordinate Colonel Eareckson were of different temperaments. Butler was thoughtful and slow moving; Eareckson was fiery, a poet, impetuous and a leader by example. AAF photo

cents elsewhere. There were twenty-one people on the plane.

On arrival over Elmendorf Field, Butler and O'Brien got into another argument about which direction they were suppose to circle to land. O'Brien as the pilot and the more experienced with Alaskan flying conditions insisted he was right. Butler reluctantly agreed. Later, O'Brien commented: "He never really liked me after that flight." He also noted that Butler was a "good man."[8]

Butler brought with him an impressive list of accomplishments. After graduating from West Point in 1917; he had seen combat as an artillery officer during World War I; had rapidly risen to the rank of captain; and had commanded a balloon company before returning to the states in July 1918. Butler transferred to the Army Air Service in 1920, and was sent to the Airship School at Langley Field, Virginia. After graduating in 1921, he remained there as an instructor and in July 1922, he assumed command of an airship company.

More progressively responsible command and staff assignments followed. He attended the primary and advanced flight schools; graduated from the Air Corps Tactical School in 1932; attended the first year of the Command and General Staff School at Fort Leavenworth, Kansas and was among the few selected to remain for another year of instruction. Acceptance to Leavenworth, then as now, was highly competitive. It was a great separator of officers' careers. Those who graduated, for the most part, were assured of future advancements. The rest, other than exceptional cases, were destined to plod through mediocre careers.

After graduating, Butler went on to command a bombardment group in the Panama Canal Zone and to serve as the executive officer of the 1st Bombardment Wing at March Field, California and as the Chief of Staff, Fourth Air Force before his assignment to Alaska.[9]

General Buckner welcomed his new commander and shortly afterwards commented to General DeWitt that he was "very much pleased with General Butler" and thought that he was "a good practical soldier and will do a good job."[10] The general faced a number of problems, the most immediate of which was a shortage of pilots, planes and bases.

Forty-three pilots were assigned to the two fighter squadrons, each of which was authorized twenty-five aircraft. The three bombardment squadrons were better off. They had sixty-five pilots and more were en route to man each squadron's allocation of fifteen bombers. However, there was a shortage of crew members. The aircraft, those that were still flyable, were kept in the air as much as twelve to fourteen hours a day on training and operation missions. As Buckner had done before him, Butler asked for more pilots and planes.[11]

He got essentially the same answer. General Arnold and his staff felt that Alaska had enough squadrons. In April, the Army Air Forces, with a global war raging, could only field seven bombardment groups and seven and a half fighter groups. Alaska had one bombardment group and half of a fighter group, and that was enough. President Roosevelt and Prime Minister Churchill and their senior military advisors, meeting in Washington during the dismal Christmas after Pearl Harbor, had already decided Alaska's fate. In the military priority of things, Europe came first, then the Pacific and Alaska was at the bottom of the list in the Pacific. The decision had been made despite an initial but unfounded concern that the Japanese would attack Alaska. Everyone, including Buckner, had come to the conclusion that the Japanese would not be that stupid to commit forces to a war in a place that was far from their nearest support bases in the Kurile Islands. It would be a difficult, hazardous and useless undertaking, doomed to failure. General Marshall and his war plans staff looked at the Alaskan situation and decided to withdraw forces for use in more active theaters.[12]

Buckner, ever the parochial champion, countered with a proposal that Alaska be used as a staging base for an invasion of Japan. In a statement reminiscent of Billy Mitchell, the Alaska Defense Command commander pointed out that: ". . . to look on Alaska merely as a territory to be defended . . . ignores the strategic position of this territory as a potential base for offensive missions."[13]

The water tower above Fort Greely on Kodiak Island. Commander Paul Foster noted in his report that the tower could easily be seen and used as an aiming point by the Japanese. The tower was later taken down. AAF photo

Captain Parker agreed, and together they submitted their plan to General DeWitt who passed it on to General Marshall. In summary, it called for negotiating airbase rights in the Soviet Far East with the Russians, completing the Alaskan bases as soon as possible, and reinforcing Alaska so that offensive operations could be launched against Japan by way of the Aleutian Islands.

General Marshall sent a copy of the plan to his Navy counterpart, Admiral Ernest King, Commander-in-Chief, U.S. Fleet, for comment, and gave another to his Chief of War Plans, Brigadier General Dwight D. Eisenhower. Admiral King noted that the Russians were unlikely to jeopardize their nonaggression pact with Japan by allowing the Americans to use her Far East bases. General Eisenhower, in view of the other higher priorities and the limited forces then available, recommended the idea be dropped. General Marshall agreed. The issue was set aside, but not for long.[14]

Butler made do with his limited forces, a difficult if not impossible job of trying to cover all the contingencies. The fighters, a mixed bag of P-36s and P-40s, pulled alert at Elmendorf and Kodiak. Half of the B-26s were held in readiness at Elmendorf. The others were used for training new aircrews. The 36th Bombardment Squadron, commanded by Captain Russell Cone, was sent to Kodiak in early February 1942, to join VP-42 in patrolling the Gulf of Alaska. Cone's squadron flew an inner search pattern with their B-18s, while Russell's squadron flew the outer pie shaped pattern with their new, radar equipped PBY-5A amphibians. Later, after the two B-17s and the three LB-30s had arrived, the 36th Bombardment Squadron extended its patrol range.[15]

Captain Cone and his men, after the austere conditions on Elmendorf, found the living "easy." The Navy paid more attention to creature comforts than the Army. The squadron diarist and historian, Lieutenant Billy Wheeler, commented that the men "lived high on the hog" at the Navy base, but not for long. More Navy units came in, and the squadron was moved to less desirable quarters. Even at Kodiak, the "weather never seemed to improve," according to Billy Wheeler."[16]

Generals Buckner and Butler continued their efforts to obtain more pilots and units for Alaska and met with some success. General Arnold's staff agreed to send the pilots. They arrived shortly after the Japanese bombed Dutch Harbor. In late March 1942, Butler's staff developed a plan for deploying units from the Fourth Air Force to Alaska in the event of an emergency. It was submitted to DeWitt who met with Major General George C. Kenney, the Commander of the Fourth Air Force. General Kenney selected two Washington based groups: the 42nd Bombardment Group at McChord Field and the 55th Fighter Group at Paine Field. The 42nd Bombardment Group had already provided the 77th Bombardment Squadron from its ranks and would provide the 406th Bombardment Squadron before it was in turn sent to the South Pacific in early 1943. Only one of the 55th Fighter Group's squadrons, the 54th Fighter Squadron, would be sent to Alaska. It and the 406th arrived too late to be of any real assistance during the Dutch Harbor attack.[17]

Kodiak Naval Air Station. Barometer Mountain is located at the end of the runway. Old Womens Mountain is to the left foreground. USN photo

Running Wild

Yamamoto's September 12, 1941, predictions to Konoye that Japan would give its enemies in the Pacific "hell" for the first year and a half seemed to becoming true. Starting with surprising the Americans at Pearl Harbor, the small island nation literally ran wild in the Pacific for the next six months. One day after Pearl Harbor, Japanese fighters and bombers from Formosa savaged the Far East Air Force in the Philippines, knocking it out of the war as an effective fighting force. Four days later, Japanese troops began landing at Lingayen Gulf north of Manila, and on December 26, General Douglas MacArthur declared the Philippine capital an open city and withdrew his forces into the Bataan Peninsula for a protracted, heartbreaking defense whose only outcome promised death or captivity.

Elsewhere, the Japanese landed on Guam, a lonely American enclave surrounded by the other Japanese held islands in the Marianas. Only 365 Marines opposed the 5,000 Japanese who came ashore on December 10. Their heaviest weapons were 30 calibre machine guns. After suffering 17 casualties, they surrendered. The garrison on Wake Island farther to the east held out longer. When the Japanese attempted to land on the 10th, Marine artillery and a handful of Grumman Wildcat fighters promptly sank two Japanese destroyers. The Japanese, expecting an easy victory, pulled back and regrouped. A rescue force was dispatched from Pearl Harbor, but its commander, Rear Admiral Frank Jack Fletcher paused to refuel as he approached the island. The next day, December 22, the Japanese landed in the early morning hours and quickly overwhelmed the American garrison.

Striking simultaneously on all fronts, Japanese landed on Hong Kong Island on December 18. The garrison commander surrendered the crown colony on Christmas Day. Elsewhere in the British Far East empire, the Japanese went ashore on northern beaches of the Malayan Peninsula on December 8, turned south and rapidly moved through the jungles towards Singapore. The British had spent two hundred million dollars fortifying the place and as a last minute effort had dispatched he battleship *Prince of Wales* and the battle cruiser *Repulse* to shore up its defenses. The Japanese promptly sank both. The elaborate defenses did the British little good since they were facing the sea. The Japanese came in from the jungles behind. By February 15, 1942, Lieutenant General Arthur E. Percival called a halt and his 80,000 men laid down their arms. The British had lost an empire which they would never regain.

The Japanese moved into Thailand without opposition, and used that country to launch an invasion of Burma during January 1942. The British, reinforced by two Chinese armies under the command of Major General Joseph Stilwell, fought back; but by May they were forced to retire into India. The Japanese cut the Burma Road, isolating China from the rest of the world. The only way in was by air.

In occupying Burma, the Japanese gained control not only over Asia's largest rice exporter, but more importantly, its oil fields. They rapidly completed their conquest of the rest of the resource rich southern areas. The vast expanse of the Dutch East Indies, rich in oil, rubber and other strategic materials drew the Japanese like a magnet. In December 1941, they established forward bases on the northern shores of Borneo. The allies responded by forming the American-British-Dutch-Australian Command (ABDACOM).

The improvised joint command was short lived. Moving rapidly southward, the Japanese captured Dutch airfields which they used to support their naval operations and to wipe out the feeble allied air opposition. Airborne forces were used to seize critical facilities.

The navy moved relentlessly through the Makassar Strait and Java Sea in support of a converging operations to capture the Dutch East Indies islands to the south. The allies managed to surprise and sink five transports. However, Japanese air and naval units in a series of attacks sent thirty allied ships to the bottom. Among the number was the United States' first aircraft carrier, the *Langley,* which had been converted to a seaplane tender and was being used to ferry aircraft to the allies.

The end came on February 27, 1942, when Dutch Rear Admiral K. W. F. M. Doorman took his worn down fleet out to meet the Japanese onslaught. He was overwhelmed in the Battle of Java Sea. The Japanese swarmed ashore on Java, and the Dutch surrendered on March 9. The Japanese gained the resources they needed and drove a wedge between the British in the Indian Ocean and the Americans in the Pacific.

While Japanese forces crushed the hopelessly gallant allied efforts in the Pacific, others drove southward beyond the East Indies to capture bases in the Solomon Islands and on the island of New Guinea. On January 23, 1942, the Japanese seized Rabaul on New Britain Island in the northern Solomons. This gave the Japanese one of the finest natural harbors in the western Pacific which they quickly turned into a major bastion from which they would conduct operations in the years ahead. On March 8, Japanese forces landed at Lae on the northern coast of New Guinea and began developing an airfield to support further operations aimed at capturing Port Moresby on the southern coast. The Japanese in their southward movement intended to isolate Australia.[18]

On March 26, 1942, after supporting operations in the East Indies, Admiral Nagumo turned his carrier force west and headed into the Indian Ocean on a large scale raid that was intended to destroy the British Eastern Fleet. Nagumo concentrated his five fleet carriers against the British naval bases at Colombo and Trincomalee on Ceylon Island and sent the small carrier *Ryujo* with a force of cruisers on a commerce raid into the Bay of Bengal. After attacking the two bases and sinking two cruisers and the old aircraft carrier, *Hermes*, Nagumo headed back towards the Pacific in mid April for the next phase of Japan's grandiose plans of conquest. The foray into the Indian Ocean demonstrated that British carriers with their outmoded aircraft were hopelessly outclassed by the Japanese. The United States Navy and its major instrument of war, the aircraft carrier, would carry the war across the vast reaches of the Pacific in the years ahead.[19]

However, the United States had precious few carriers in the Pacific during 1942. The Navy began the year with three. The Japanese torpedoed the *Saratoga* in early January, and she had to be returned to the states for repair. Fortunately, the *Yorktown* arrived from the Atlantic to join the *Enterprise* and *Lexington*. Until more carriers arrived, Admiral Chester Nimitz, who had assumed command of the Pacific Command in the wake of Pearl Harbor, used the three he had to carry out a series of raids. The first was on February 1 against Japanese installations and shipping in the Marshall and Gilbert Islands. The inexperienced Navy aviators overestimated the damage inflicted on the Japanese and the press inflated the score. It, however, boosted the morale of a nation that was witnessing one defeat after another. More raids were conducted against Japanese positions on Wake and Marcus Islands and on New Guinea. On April 18, a carrier task force under the command of Rear Admiral William Halsey launched a raid that helped to change the course of the war in the Pacific.

No one realized the effect that the war was having on American morale more than President Roosevelt. Shortly after Pearl Harbor he asked the military to strike back at the Japanese homeland. The Navy, reeling from Pearl Harbor, did not want to risk sending their carriers deep into Japanese waters past the picket boats that patrolled the perimeter 700 miles off the Japanese coast. Their aircraft did not have the range for the type of operations that were being contemplated. At best, it would have been a suicide mission.

Captain Francis Low, one of Admiral King's staff officers, suggested that Army bombers could be used. At first the idea of launching a bomber at gross weight off a heaving 809-foot carrier deck seemed crazy. However, General Arnold greeted the idea with enthusiasm. The Army had three medium bomber types at the time, of which the B-25B Mitchell was the best suited. It required

less take off distance and it had the range to reach the intended targets, provided there was a place for it to land.

General's Arnold and Admiral King's staff, working together, determined that if Navy carriers could get them close enough to Japan, the B-25 crews could take off from a carrier deck, fly to and bomb their targets, and then continue on across the East China Sea to airfields in the unoccupied parts of coastal China. Lieutenant Colonel Jimmy Doolittle, who had given up his executive position with the Shell Oil Company to return to active duty, volunteered to lead the mission. He had ten weeks to work out all the details. The feisty forty-five-year-old reserve officer selected B-25 crews from the 17th Bombardment Group and 89th Reconnaissance Squadron to man the sixteen medium bombers. They were put through an intensive training program at a remote strip on Eglin Field, Florida during March, concentrating on the techniques of using the least amount of take off distance.

On April 1, the B-25s were loaded aboard the deck of the Navy's newest carrier, the *Hornet*, at Alameda, California. The *Hornet*, which had been commissioned just prior to Pearl Harbor, sailed west under the Golden Gate Bridge the next day to join a carrier task force built around the *Enterprise*. Halsey and his group departed Pearl Harbor on April 8. The rendezvous was made on the 13th. The Japanese by then, through radio intercepts, were aware that a carrier task force of two to three carriers was approaching their shores along a route that was the reverse of the one they had used to strike Pearl Harbor. They could do very little about it since Nagumo's carriers had not arrived back from the Indian Ocean. During the early morning of the 18th (Japan time), the crew of the picket boat *Nitto Maru* spotted Halsey's force while 650 miles off the shores of Honshu. They managed to get off a message before their vessel was sunk by one of the cruisers escorting the carriers.

Rather than risk his force to a land based attack, Halsey, with Doolittle's concurrence, decided to order the B-25s to take off in a forty knot gale before they reached the planned 400-mile launch point. The original plan had been to launch the bombers at dusk on the 19th. The bomber crews would strike their targets independently at night and continue on to their recovery airfields. The early launch meant that in all probability that the bombers could reach their targets but would have to ditch in the waters off the China coast without any hope of rescue.

At 7:25 AM, Doolittle took off in the first bomber. By then the Halsey's force had approached to within 623 miles of the Japanese coast and were 688 miles from the heart of Tokyo. Although the Japanese had been forewarned, they expected that the Americans would not launch their attack until they were within carrier aircraft range of the home island. When Doolittle's bombers roared over Tokyo, Kobe, Nagoya, Yokohama and Yokosuka, their air defense forces were not ready. After dropping their general purpose and incendiary bombs, the Doolittle raiders continued on safely across Japan and the East China Sea where a tail wind helped extend their range. However, as Doolittle's raiders approach the coast they ran into deteriorating weather and darkness. The crew of one B-25 with fuel problems diverted north to Vladivostok where it was interned by the Russians. The crews of the other bombers, unable to find the intended landing fields, either bailed out or made force landings in the coastal provinces of Chekiang and Kiangsi. The Japanese captured two crews. The others, aided by the Chinese, made it to safety.[20]

The Doolittle raid, despite the loss of all the aircraft and the minimum amount of damage it inflicted, boosted the morale of America when it was needed the most. Alaskans were particularly proud since Jimmy Doolittle had spent his boyhood in Nome. They were quick to point out that ". . . the two qualities, fighting and flying, which have distinguished his every act since childhood, were acquired in that hell-roaring mining camp of Nome."[21]

The Japanese were shocked and angered. Their country had never been violated by a foreign power. Their reaction was swift and terrible. The eight crew members who had fallen into her hands were tried as war criminals. Three were executed and the rest sentenced to life imprisonment. An offensive was launched against the costal provinces to capture the airfields and punish those who had aided the Americans. The Japanese knew where the attacks had come from and they wanted to make certain that they did not occur again. Nearly a quarter of a million Chinese civilian and military persons died as the direct result of the raid. Generalissimo Chiang Kai-shek, who had opposed the Americans using Chinese fields for the recovery of Doolittle's men, informed the United States government that the Japanese troops had "slaughtered every man, woman and child in those areas."[22]

Victory Disease

President Roosevelt, when pressed to explain where Doolittle's raid had originated from, humorously announced that they had flown from "Shangri-La." Some then and since may have thought the president's reference to the mythical Tibetan city in James Hilton's novel "Lost Horizon" meant the Aleutian Islands. They were mistaken, for the Japanese through their radio intercepts and the warning from the *Nitto Maru* knew exactly where the raid had come from. Neither did the Japanese launch their Aleutian-Midway operation in direct response to the Doolittle raid as has been recounted in some scholarly sources;

although it did provide a final convincing argument.

With the exception of the stubborn but hopeless American resistance on Bataan and Corregidor, the Japanese had it all their way in the Pacific. Their well-trained Army, supported by the Navy, had been victorious on all fronts. Originally trained to fight a continental war in the isolated and cold wind swept expanses of Manchuria and Siberia against the Chinese and Russians, the Army had quickly adapted itself to the use of small unit tactics in the steaming jungles of South East Asia where they had excelled against their surprised and confused foes. The Army was a blend of the Prussian system after which it had been modeled and the Samurai spirit and tradition which sustained it.

The Japanese tactics stressed the primacy of the infantry, and the soldiers who fought during World War II, often against hopeless odds, were warriors in the truest sense. Primarily from peasant stock, they willingly endured hardships and harsh discipline from a military society that demanded self-discipline, unshakable loyalty and great valor.

However, flesh and blood and ardent spirit were no match against the hot steel of superior firepower and manpower that was brought to bear against them in an increasing ascending levels of violence during the course of the war. Light, mobile but lacking the ability to sustain itself, and led by well trained but dogmatic officers imbued in the Samurai spirit and influenced by the Bushido code, the Imperial Japanese Army fought either with great brilliance or blind fury throughout the war.[23]

The Japanese had a magnificent Navy which they had built in less than a hundred years, using the British as a model, to be the third largest in the world. Their warships were faster, more heavily armored and better armed than their American and British counterparts. They had the best torpedoes and their optical devices were superb. Their submarines outclassed those of the Americans. The large I boat class could cross the Pacific with ease, something that the Americans were not able to achieve until the last years of the war. Their carrier force was probably the finest naval weapon of the war at that time. The Zero fighter far surpassed anything the allies had and their carrier based torpedo and dive bombers were deadly. In comparison to the Americans, the pilots were better trained and many had experienced combat in China.

Yet there were problems. The Navy clung more closely to the mystique of the battleship than their American opposites. The Americans, having lost most of their battleships at Pearl Harbor and under the pressure to conduct warfare over the vast expanses of the Pacific Ocean, quickly relegated their battleships to a supporting role, and built their offensive capability around the faster and more flexible carriers. The Japanese, while experts at

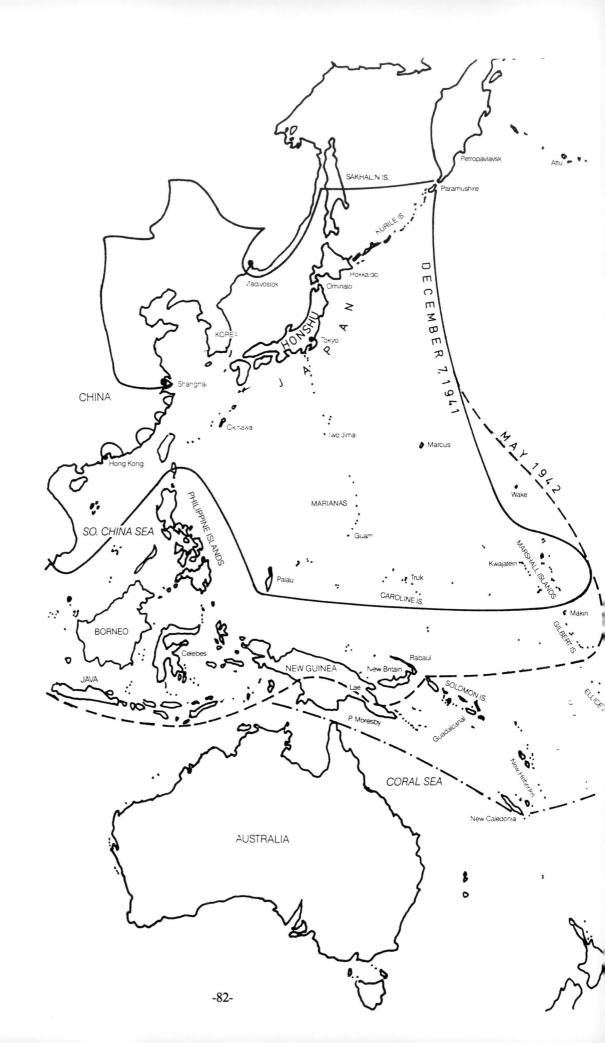

SAKHALIN IS.

Petropavlavsk

Attu

Paramushire

KURILE IS.

Vladivostok

Hokkaido

Ominato

DECEMBER 7, 1941

KOREA

HONSHU

Tokyo

J A P A N

MAY 1942

Shanghai

CHINA

Okinawa

Iwo Jima

Marcus

Hong Kong

Wake

PHILIPPINE ISLANDS

MARIANAS

SO. CHINA SEA

Guam

MARSHALL ISLANDS

Kwajalein

Palau

Truk

Makin

CAROLINE IS.

BORNEO

GILBERT IS.

Celebes

Rabaul

ELLICE

NEW GUINEA

New Britain

JAVA

Lae

SOLOMON IS.

P. Moresby

Guadalcanal

New Hebrides

CORAL SEA

New Caledonia

AUSTRALIA

JAPANESE EXPANSION PLANS

NO. PACIFIC OCEAN

Seattle

San Francisco

Los Angeles
San Diego

Kodiak

Unalaska
Umnak

Adak

Amchitka

Attu

Midway

HAWAIIAN ISLANDS

Hawaii

PLANNED EXPANSION

PHOENIX IS.

Samoa Is.

FIJI IS.

Vice Admiral Chuichi Nagumo, direct, gregarious, sentimental and uncomplicated was the instrument of Japan's bid to obtain dominance in the Pacific. Between December 7, 1941, until the Battle of Midway, his Carrier Strike Force operated across 120 degrees of longitude from the Hawaiian Islands to Ceylon in the Indian Ocean. It conducted strikes against ships and shore installations at Pearl Harbor, Rabaul, Ambon, Darwin, Tjilatjap, Colombo and Trincomalee and emerged victorious from every naval engagement. Allied losses included five battleships, two carriers, one cruiser, one aircraft tender and eight destroyers sunk or very heavily damaged; three battleships, one carrier, three cruisers and one destroyer damaged; and thousands of tons of auxiliaries and merchant ships sunk. Additionally, the allies lost hundreds of aircraft and suffered the damage and loss of docks, hangars and base facilities. Until the Battle of the Coral Sea, not one of Admiral Nagumo's ships was sunk or damaged. It was a remarkable display of naval power, unequalled in modern warfare; made even more so by the fact that Admiral Nagumo was not fitted by background, training and experience for waging carrier warfare. He had been brought up in the traditions of the battleship and the one decisive naval surface battle to which the aircraft was only an auxiliary. When confronted for the first time with the management of a major carrier battle against a foe on equal terms, Admiral Nagumo failed to grasp the complexities of naval warfare. After Midway, he lost favor. He committed suicide July 6, 1944, while commanding the ground defenses on Saipan. He was one of Japan's most formidable and courageous leaders.

night fighting, lacked proper radar equipment. The Americans were quick to recognize the importance of radar and overcame the advantages the Japanese enjoyed in night operations. The Japanese never learned to use their submarines effectively. The Americans, after some initial problems with their torpedoes, used their fleet submarines with a vengeance to interdict and destroy the Japanese supply lines. The Japanese lacked a training system to replace their pilot losses. The Americans quickly adopted one that proved far more effective in turning out well-trained and aggressive aviators. The Japanese aircraft proved fragile. The Americans produced better and more robust planes.[24]

But, perhaps fatally, the Japanese suffered from a bad case of overconfidence. The victories had been too easy, and they had fostered what the Japanese later referred to as "victory disease." The Japanese, using interior lines of communication and the element of surprise, had been able to commit superior forces against every objective. The allies, on the other hand, had been forced to withdraw from one base after another, then reorganize and reestablish their communications. The Japanese in the first six months of the war skillfully employed their naval, ground and air forces in combined operations against objectives over widely separated areas; and in doing so, demonstrated to the world that the allies faced a progressive and aggressive foe who had set the standards for the war in the Pacific.

By April 1942, the Japanese had achieved all her objectives with only a minimum loss to herself. Never before in military history had so much been gained in exchange for so little. Japan's military forces were intact and on the offensive and the nation's morale was sky high. Impressed by what they had achieved and their own invincibility against the perceived weakness of America and her allies, the Japanese began making plans to further expand their empire.[25]

The Supreme War Council met in early March 1942, to assess what had been accomplished and decide Japan's next course of action. The council was composed of high ranking military leaders from both services whose responsibility it was to formulate military policy. It operated by mutual consent. If one of the services objected, nothing could be accomplished. The Army wanted to stick to the original plan of consolidating the gains, preparing defenses and starting negotiations with the United States and Great Britain to end the war on favorable terms. Admiral Yamamoto and most of the Navy wanted to expand the original perimeter line and complete the job of destroying the United States Pacific Fleet.[26]

The Japanese had a fixation with the latter and Admiral Yamamoto was its chief proponent. The Commander of the Combined Fleet was an ardent gambler, a master at bridge and poker, who at the same time was a fatalist who believed Japan's only chance at winning the war was a decisive and quick victory over the United States. The son of a schoolmaster, the admiral had graduated from the Japanese Naval Academy in 1904, just in time to participate in the Russo-Japanese War. He was wounded at the climactic naval battle of Tsushima Straits. The Russian Baltic Fleet had sailed half way around the world in a vain effort to relieve the Japanese naval blockade of Port Arthur on the Liaotung Peninsula. The Japanese fleet, commanded by Admiral Heihachiro Togo, intercepted the Russians in the straits between Japan and Korea, and in one mighty engagement, defeated it. The Russians sued for peace, and Japan emerged as a power in the Pacific.[27]

Tsushima had been a remarkable victory, considering the fact that the Japanese had only begun to build a navy thirty years prior. By 1904, the Imperial Navy had become a well-equipped, well-trained and well-led, highly disciplined fighting force. The only thing that it lacked was a tradition. Tsushima gave it one; it provided a Nelson and a Trafalgar for future generations to aspire to.[28]

Tsushima firmly established the Japanese Imperial Navy as a premier fighting force and one of the most formidable in the world. It also fostered in Japan a belief that wars could be won by decisive naval engagements. This belief would haunt the Japanese during World War II. Initially, the concept of the big naval battle paid off during the first six months of the war; but as America regained the initiative in the Pacific the Japanese went from one defeat to another.

Shortly after the meeting of the Supreme War Council, Admiral Yamamoto directed his senior operations officer, Captain Kameto Kuroshima to develop a plan for expanding the defensive perimeter and luring the Pacific Fleet into a battle of annihilation. Captain Kuroshima completed the plan in early April. Yamamoto presented the navy plan to the Imperial Headquarters on April 13. The headquarters was the apex of the Japanese military system. Composed of the Emperor and the Chiefs of Staff of the Army and Navy, it was responsible for the direction of joint operations. The Emperor served as the titular head, but his authority was so defused and ambiguous that he had little real power. The real power belonged to the military members. However, like their junior members on the Supreme War Council, their decisions were reached only by mutual consent and force of personalities. The Japanese, more so than the Americans who also suffered from their own unity of command problems, lacked a viable unified command system for the planning and conduct of joint operations despite their earlier successes.

The Imperial Headquarters, on April 16, issued the Midway-Aleutian directive. The Army had reluctantly agreed to Yamamoto's plan. If they and the minority in the

Navy had any further doubts, they quickly vanished in the aftermath of the Doolittle Raid two days later. The raid and the others before it reinforced the need for a new defensive line. The April 16 directive had called for a defensive line that would run from the western Aleutians through Midway south to the Samoan and Fiji Islands, and then double back westward by way of New Caledonia to Port Moresby on the south coast of New Guinea. The plan for implementing the directive was complex and demanding.

It required the operations to be conducted in three phases. The first dictated that Port Moresby be taken by mid-May in order to complete the conquest of New Guinea and the Bismarck archipelago. The next involved the capture of the tiny Midway atoll, the destruction of the Pacific Fleet and the seizure of the western Aleutian Islands. The Japanese hoped to complete this phase by early June. It would give them control of the central and northern Pacific. The final phase involved the capture of the Samoan, Fiji and New Caladonia Islands by late July. This would completely isolate Australia from its allies. The successful conclusion of these operations would place Japan in an ideal position to bargain for peace terms that were favorable to her interests.[29]

The Japanese began experiencing problems from the start. Admiral Nagumo arrived back from the Indian Ocean on April 18, but many of his carriers needed overhaul after almost six months of constant operations across 120 degrees of longitude from Hawaii to Ceylon. Only two large and one small carrier could be spared for the Port Moresby operations. The Americans, who had broken the Japanese Naval code, figured out what was being planned. Admiral Nimitz dispatched Admiral Fletcher with a force built around the *Lexington* and *Yorktown* to intercept the Japanese invasion force.

The Japanese initiated the Battle of the Coral Sea by sinking a destroyer and an oiler on May 7. Fletcher's pilots found and sank the 13,950 ton light carrier *Shoho* which was escorting the landing force. The next day pilots from the opposing sides carried out a series of attacks against each others carriers. The Americans badly damaged the *Shokaku*, and the *Zuikaku* lost most of its complement of pilots. The Japanese in turn sank the 33,000-ton *Lexington* and damaged the *Yorktown*. Although the Japanese had won the tactical victory, the loss of their newest carrier, the damage to the *Shokaku* and the heavy losses in pilots and aircraft were too heavy to bear. They postponed the Port Moresby invasion. With the turning back of the invasion force, the Japanese had suffered their first major strategic setback of the war. To compound the problem, the two large carriers would not be available for Midway.[30]

Despite this, the Japanese occupied the tiny island of Tulagi in the southern Solomon Islands. Shortly afterward they started building airfields there and on nearby Guadalcanal, threatening to cut the supply line between Australia and the United States. The Japanese Army began making plans to take Port Moresby by crossing the forbidding Owen Stanley Mountains from their strongholds on the north coast of New Guinea. And the Japanese decided to proceed with the second phase of their operation against Midway and the Aleutians.

Admiral Yamamoto had argued against postponing the operation. He feared another Doolittle raid. The authors of the United States Strategic Bombing Survey in the Pacific would later write:

> The reserve strength which should have been used in consolidating the positions seized in the initial phase was dissipated in the unsuccessful attempts at further expansion. In view of the limitations of Japanese military strength, shipping and national economy, this attempt to expand an already too big strategic sphere brought about unsolvable problems. At the time when the defense of those areas, which had to be held at any cost, were left wanting, operations for the capture of Port Moresby, Midway and the Aleutians were undertaken, thereby further dissipating the nation's strength. Thus, it was conceded that the expansion program, which was intended to strengthen the Japanese defense positions, actually weakened it.[31]

A State of Fleet Opposed Invasion

Admiral Yamamoto began assembling his force during early May. It included virtually every ship in the Japanese Imperial Navy. The two hundred ships were manned by 100,000 officers and men, many by now seasoned veterans of the battles of the Pacific and Indian Oceans. Some seven hundred aircraft were embarked on the five heavy and three light carriers. It was the largest armada ever of its kind to be committed to battle, and it would use more precious oil in the coming operation than had been consumed annually during peacetime operations.

Admiral Yamamoto's staff had developed one of their typical complex plans, which spread his Combined Fleet all over the Pacific Ocean in five different groups. None of the groups were within easy supporting or reinforcing distance of each other. The Main Force consisted of the bulk of the eleven battleships that had been committed to the operation. Its mission was to finish the job of destroying the Pacific Fleet. It had a secondary mission of intercepting any forces sent to the aid of the Americans in the Aleutians. The Carrier Striking Force with the four heavy carriers *Akagi, Kaga, Hiryu* and *Soryu*, under the command of Admiral Nagumo was responsible for blasting the defenses on Midway into oblivion and paving the way for the landing of the occupation troops by the

Midway Invasion Force. The Advance Submarine Force was responsible for scouting ahead, sending back intelligence and sinking any ships that came their way. Finally, the Northern Force was committed to the Aleutians.[32]

Vice Admiral Moshiro Hosogaya had his work cut out for him. Until then his small Fifth Fleet had bided its time keeping an eye on the Russians while the rest of the Japanese Imperial Navy had rampaged across the Pacific. Finally, the Fifth Fleet was being given its opportunity for glory. On May 5, the Imperial Headquarters issued the Navy Directive Number 94 for the Aleutian operations. The Japanese, fearing that the Americans would use the islands as an invasion route — Attu lay 675 miles by sea from their base at Paramushiro in the northern Kuriles — intended to "capture and demolish any points of strategic value on the western Aleutian Islands in order to check the enemy's air and ship maneuvers in this area."[33]

The Aleutian operation, as the Japanese had originally planned it, was to be a reconnaissance in force with the objectives of destroying a suspected American garrison on Adak, launching an diversionary raid against Dutch Harbor and seizing the islands of Attu and Kiska. Although they had gained a considerable amount of in-

formation on the waters around the Aleutian Islands from their pre-war fishing activities, the Japanese knew little about the islands and what was on them. They had sent the seaplane tender *Kimikawa Maru* into Aleutian waters in early May on a reconnaissance mission. A float plane was launched on May 10, and aerial photographs were taken of Adak. However, a similar mission planned for Kiska was cancelled due to weather. They knew little of what was going on at Dutch Harbor other than the Americans were building a base there and bringing in troops. From their limited intelligence, the Japanese were convinced that Dutch Harbor was garrisoned by an Army division with smaller garrisons defending Adak, Attu and Kiska. They also believed there were two small carriers in the North Pacific area. However, the Japanese were completely unaware that Talley's engineer troops had built an airbase on Umnak.

The Japanese intentions in seizing Attu and Kiska were to secure their northern flank and protect their forces on Midway. They planned to bring in long-range flying boats and use them to conduct patrols between Kiska and Midway 1,400 miles to the south. However, initially, the Japanese had intended to withdraw their forces from Attu and Kiska before winter set in. They overrated the

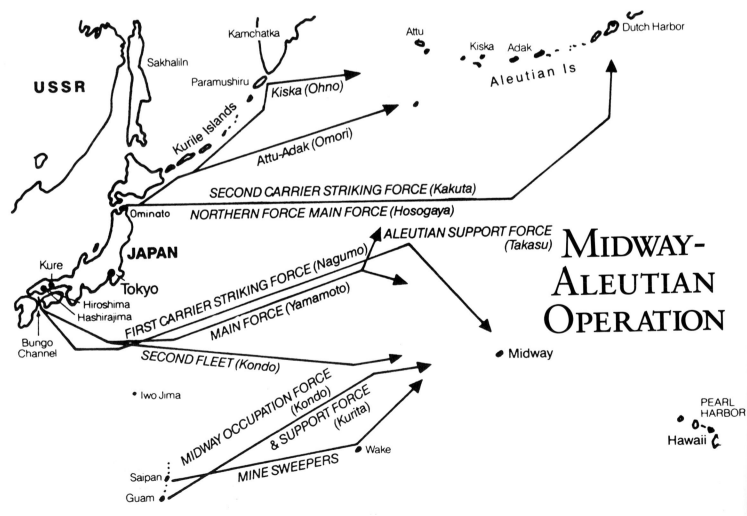

severity of the weather in the Aleutians. They made the mistake of comparing the Aleutians to their own Kurile Islands which were closer to the mainland, and therefore experienced colder and more severe winter weather. Some believed that Kiska Harbor would freeze over in the winter. All agreed that there were no icebergs in the region. They also believed that the Aleutians were an unsuitable place for military operations. Their lack of knowledge of the Aleutians hampered their planning.

By attacking Dutch Harbor one day ahead of their Midway operation, the Japanese expected to divert the Americans away from the main Midway battle area, planned for the following day. Additionally, they hoped to destroy any American forces there that might interfere with their operations in the North Pacific. Finally, the Aleutian operations provided a side benefit of isolating the Americans from their Russian allies in the Pacific.[34]

By May 20, Admiral Hosogaya's staff had completed its work, and the orders were issued for the Aleutian operations. It was to be conducted in three phases. The first called for the occupation of the western Aleutians and the bombing of Dutch Harbor; the second, the consolidation of the defenses; and the third, the establishment of bases from which the Japanese could control the North Pacific

and the approaches to their home islands. For the first phase, Admiral Hosogaya had organized his forces into four groups.

The main group under his control, consisting of the cruiser *Nachi* and two destroyers, was to proceed to a point halfway between Midway and the Aleutians, so it would be in a position to intercept any American forces coming from either direction. The 2nd Carrier Division, commanded by Rear Admiral Kakuji Kakuta, consisted of the heavy carrier *Junyo* and the light carrier *Ryujo*. They were supported by two heavy cruisers, three destroyers and an oiler. Its mission was to conduct the air strike against Dutch Harbor. The landings on Adak and Attu were entrusted to the Adak-Attu Invasion Force. Commanded by Rear Admiral Sentaro Omori, it was composed of a light cruiser, four destroyers, three transports and a seaplane tender. It was responsible for landing 1,200 Army troops on Adak, and once the suspected American garrison there was destroyed, transporting them to Attu. Captain Takeji Ohno commanded the Kiska Invasion Force, which consisted of two light cruisers, two converted cruisers, four destroyers and three converted gunboats. Captain Ohno was responsible for putting the Navy's five hundred man Third Special

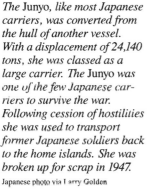

The Junyo, *like most Japanese carriers, was converted from the hull of another vessel. With a displacement of 24,140 tons, she was classed as a large carrier. The* Junyo *was one of the few Japanese carriers to survive the war. Following cession of hostilities she was used to transport former Japanese soldiers back to the home islands. She was broken up for scrap in 1947.*

Japanese photo via Larry Golden

The Ryujo *was the first aircraft carrier that the Japanese built from the keel up. She was a light carrier with a displacement of 11,700 tons. She was sunk August 24, 1942 during the Battle of the Eastern Solomons.*

Japanese photo via Masatake Okumiya

Landing Force along with seven hundred construction personnel ashore on Kiska.

Admiral Hosogaya was also allocated additional forces to support his operations. Six large I class submarines were detailed to scout ahead as far as the Seattle area. The seaplane tender *Kimikawa Maru* with eight seaplanes aboard was assigned the general mission of supporting the landings, and a detachment of six four-engine Kawanishi H6K4 Mavis seaplanes from the Toko Seaplane Squadron were given the responsibility of locating and attacking any American shipping in the area.[35]

Admiral Yamamoto began assembling his giant armada in early May. Sixty-eight ships sailed into their anchorage in Hashirajima Bay, near the city of Kure on the Inland Sea. Among them were the *Junyo* and *Ryujo*.

The *Junyo* (Free-flying Falcon) was brand new. She had been converted from the hull of one of Japan's largest passenger ships, the *Kaskiwara Maru* at the Mitsubishi Nagasaki shipyard. The use of hulls from other types of vessels was a common practice that both the United States and Japan used during the war to expedite aircraft carrier production. Although the *Junyo* had a displacement of 24,140 tons and was 885-feet long, which classified her as a large carrier, she could only accommodate fifty-three aircraft. Construction work was finished on May 5, and the *Junyo* was rushed to Hashirajima before her crew could complete all the requirements needed to certify her as operationally ready.

While the *Junyo* was new, the *Ryujo* (Prancing Dragon) was an old veteran. The 600-foot long light carrier with a displacement of 11,700 tons had been commissioned in 1933 at the Yokohama Dockyard as Japan's fourth and the first aircraft carrier to be built from the keel up. She could accommodate forty-eight aircraft. The little carrier had seen action from the western Pacific, where she had launched the first carrier based attack against American installations in the Philippines on December 8, to the Indian Ocean, where she was used to raid commerce in the Bay of Bengal.

The two carriers, after taking on stores and provisions, which included heavy winter clothing, departed Hashirajima for Ominato on the north coast of Honshu Island where Admiral Hosogaya was assembling his Northern Force. The *Junyo* carried a compliment of twenty-one Aichi D3A1 Val dive bombers, commanded by Lieutenant Zenji Abe, and twenty-four Mitsubishi A6M2 Zero fighters under the command of Lieutenant Yoshio Shiga who also commanded the air group aboard the carrier. Loaded aboard the *Ryujo* were twenty-one Nakajima B5N2 Kate torpedo bombers and sixteen Zeros. The Kates, which could also be used as horizontal bombers, were commanded by Lieutenant Masayuki Yamagami. Lieutenant Minoru Kobayashi commanded the Zeros and

the air group aboard the *Ryujo*. The carrier also served as Admiral Kakuta's flagship.

Admiral Hosogaya had assembled every ship he could beg or borrow from Admiral Yamamoto, who was concentrating on the Midway operations. He had originally been promised another carrier division, but with four heavy and two light carriers committed to Midway and the remaining two heavy carriers out of commission, there were none to spare.

After putting his amphibious forces through a series of practice landings, Admiral Hosogaya began dispatching his forces. Admiral Kakuta's carrier force, with the longest distance to travel, was the first to leave on May 24. (Please note that all departure dates are those west of the International Date Line, one day behind those at east of the line.) Captain Ohno's Kiska invasion force departed two days later, swinging north to refuel at Paramushiro before proceeding to Kiska. The next day, Admirals Hosogaya and Omori headed out into the stormy North Pacific with their forces.

Admiral Yamamoto's forces to the south had gotten underway on May 25 when Admiral Nagumo's carrier force departed the Inland Sea. The elements of the Midway occupation force departed from bases on Guam and Saipan in the Marianas. On May 26, Admiral Yamamoto celebrated Navy Day, the anniversary of Admiral Togo's victory at Tsushima, by drinking a toast with his senior officers from cups that the Emperor had presented to him. The next day he led his force out into the central Pacific on a course that followed Admiral Nagumo.[36]

At Pearl Harbor, Admiral Nimitz and his staff waited and watched the events as they unfolded. Although heavily outnumbered, the admiral had one big advantage. He knew the outline of Admiral Yamamoto's plan. Commander Joseph J. Rochefort's Combat Intelligence Unit, code named "Hypo," had been working around the clock since Pearl Harbor to break the Japanese Navy JN 25 code and cipher which the Japanese had changed shortly after the Pearl Harbor attack. By April 1942, the cryptography unit in the basement of the admiral's headquarters building were able to decipher about thirty percent of the Imperial Japanese Navy radio transmissions. By analyzing the bits and pieces of coded communications intercepts, they had pieced together the Japanese plans for the Port Moresby operations.

Initially, the Midway-Aleutian operations eluded them. However, the Japanese contributed to their own undoing. During May, Admiral Yamamoto's staff, pressed for time, sent an inordinate number of radio messages directing the deployment of forces. In normal circumstances, they would have used couriers to carry their highly sensitive operations plans. From these intercepts, Rochefort's staff were able to piece together an amazing picture of what the

Japanese were intending to do.

For a time, they were stymied by the code letters AF, AL, AO and AOB; and at one point figured the Japanese were planning to attack Alaska. By May 12, they were able to identify the letters AF as Midway by having the radio operator at Midway send a message in the clear, stating the seawater distillation plant there had broken down. One of the Japanese radio listening posts intercepted the message, coded it, and retransmitted it. The Americans, in turn, intercepted the coded message, and Rochefort's staff learned what AF stood for. The other letter combinations were determined to be locations in the Aleutians.

Admiral Nimitz and his staff knew by the end of May the names of the four carriers committed against Midway, the main target. They were aware that the *Ryujo* and an unknown carrier would be used to launch a diversionary attack against Dutch Harbor. They also knew that the Japanese were planning to occupy the western Aleutians. Finally, they figured the attacks would come in early June.

On paper, the odds appeared hopeless. The Japanese had eight carriers to three and eleven battleships to none. The Americans were equally outnumbered in cruisers and destroyers. However, by spreading his forces all over the Pacific, Admiral Yamamoto had reduced the odds. Admiral Nimitz decided to position his carriers, *Enterprise, Hornet* and the hastily repaired *Yorktown* northwest of Midway where they could intercept Admiral Nagumo's four carriers and destroy them before Admiral Yamamoto, sailing two days behind, could bring his force of battleships to bear. In addition to the two hundred and fifteen aircraft aboard the carriers, Admiral Nimitz could count on the strike capabilities of seventeen Army B-17s, four B-26s and twenty-seven Marine dive bombers and six Navy torpedo bombers based on Midway. Finally, the thirty PBYs on Midway gave the Americans an edge in locating the Japanese.

He designated Admiral Fletcher as the overall commander and placed the *Yorktown* and its escorts under his direct command. Rear Admiral Raymond A. Spruance, an experienced cruiser admiral with no experience in carriers, was given the command of the *Enterprise* and *Hornet* and their escorts, the first of a succession of important commands he would have in the coming years.[37]

Admiral Ernest King, Commander-in-Chief, U.S. Fleet, set the tenor for the command relationship problems that were to exist throughout the Aleutian Campaign, when, on May 21, he issued a directive to Admiral Nimitz which informed him that a "state of fleet opposed invasion existed." It required Admiral Nimitz to form a task force commanded by a Navy admiral to counter the Hosogaya's thrust into the North Pacific; and it effectively shunted General Buckner aside, placing him in a supportive role to the Navy. He would have no direct control over the

combat operations which he spent most of his life preparing for, nor would he have any real control over his forces committed against the Japanese in the Aleutian Islands. The directive, which bore the concurrence of General Marshall and the approval of his plans officer, General Eisenhower, placed the Eleventh Air Force and the other Army forces in the Aleutians under the operational control of the Navy. General Buckner's role in the forthcoming Aleutian Campaign and North Pacific operations was that of providing and supplying the Army forces the Navy needed for their operations.

General Buckner could only console himself with the fact that Admiral King's directive had specified he would be in charge of operations in the highly unlikely event the Japanese decided to invade the mainland; otherwise the remote string of islands in the North Pacific was a Navy show. Finally, Admiral King admonished all concerned that the "command relationship between the remainder of the Army Forces in Alaska and the North Pacific Forces is to be by mutual cooperation . . .[38] It might have worked except for the tender egos of those involved.

North to Alaska

Admirals King and Nimitz realized the Japanese intentions in the North Pacific were a "side show" to their main operations in the Central Pacific. However, they could not ignore the fact that it was aimed at North American soil, even if in the final analysis the thrust was strategically unimportant and could be easily contained. If they had ignored it, the political price they would have had to pay might have been too much.

Admiral Nimitz elected to spare a token force of cruisers and destroyers and dispatch them north to Alaska, where along with the Eleventh Air Force and Captain Parker's meager forces, they could be formed into a task force to counter the Japanese. He selected Vice Admiral Robert A. Theobald, Commander Destroyers, Pacific and ordered him to form Task Force Eight and proceed at once to Kodiak where he was to establish his shore headquarters.[39]

Known to have one of the best minds and worst dispositions in the Navy, the crusty, fifty-four-year-old Theobald, a native of San Francisco, was one of the Admiral Nimitz's most able and energetic flag officers. The highly intelligent admiral had graduated ninth in a class of eighty-six from the U.S. Naval Academy in 1907. Following graduation, he had gone to sea for five years and then returned to Annapolis where he served until 1915, when he was given his first command, the destroyer *Walke*. During World War I he served as gunnery officer aboard the battleship *New York*, flagship of Battle Ship Division Nine, United States Atlantic Fleet. He was present when the

Admiral Theobald was a man with a promising future when he arrived in Alaska. Less than seven months later, his career side tracked, he was banished into obscurity. The Aleutians were a destroyer of careers. Theobald's inability to get along with Buckner was part of his downfall. The lack of a unified military command in Alaska contributed to his problems. The formal photograph was taken in the admiral's office December 20, 1942. The relief map of Kiska in the background was made from aerial photographs. USN photo

Germans surrendered their fleet to the British at Scapa Flow in November 1918.

By now Theobald had been promoted to lieutenant commander with a bright and promising future ahead of him. He spent the next two years at Annapolis as the executive officer of the Naval Postgraduate School, and then went back to sea again for a two year tour in Asian waters as a destroyer commander. Despite his nickname, "fuzzy," Theobald was brilliant, a fact that the Navy was quick to recognize. Promotions came quick and prestigious assignments followed in rapid succession. By 1921, he was a commander, and by 1924 he was the head of the Naval Postgraduate School. He left in 1927 to serve two years as the executive officer aboard the battleship *West Virginia*. He then attended the prestigious Naval War College; and after graduation, reported to the Navy Department in Washington DC in 1930, where he served a two-year tour in the war plans division. He was promoted to captain in 1932, and spent the next two years at sea before returning to the Naval War College for another year of study.

Following graduation from the Navy War College's senior course, Captain Theobald stayed on for two years as head of the Naval Strategy Department. In 1937, he achieved one of the most prestigious jobs in the Navy, the command of a battleship, the *Nevada*. He was a marked man, destined for elevation to the rarified levels of flag rank. By December 1941, he was a rear admiral commanding the destroyers in the Pacific.[40]

For Theobald, the Aleutians proved to be a very difficult theater of operations; a destroyer of careers. In addition to having to make do with very slim resources and contend with a convoluted command arrangement, the admiral had to deal with an aggressive General Buckner. Nimitz, according to Admiral Russell:

Commander Paul L. Foster, far right, was sent to Alaska to assess the situation. He was one of several who arrived there during 1942 to look into the problems that were reaching political and military leaders in Washington. He visited most of the major bases, including Yakutat, where this photograph was taken. The aircraft are RCAF Bolingbrooks. USN photo

. . . had at Pearl Harbor a number of admirals sitting on the bench, and as various operations came up, he'd assign them. If the fellow who had been warming the bench turned out to be a good commander, he would go on to bigger and better things. Admiral Theobald was one of those on the bench and he was sent up. We felt rather badly because he adopted the attitude that General Buckner knew nothing about fighting Naval battles. General Buckner was so aggressive, something we appreciated very much. And Theobald was quite the other way.[41]

Task Force Eight was formed on May 21, and shortly afterwards, Admiral Theobald departed Pearl Harbor aboard the light cruiser *Nashville* for Kodiak. Admiral Nimitz promised him two heavy and three light cruisers, fourteen destroyers and submarines. However, they had to be assembled from various parts of the Pacific, and several did not reach their destination until early June. In Alaska, General Buckner and Captain Parker, who had been alerted two weeks prior, had done everything possible to prepare their forces for the coming conflict.[42]

General Buckner was also playing host to a visiting dignitary, who, although low ranking, was on an important mission and deserving of the general's attention. President Roosevelt had dispatched one of his aides, Naval Reservist Commander Paul L. Foster, to Alaska to assess the military situation and determine if the Aleutians, as Buckner claimed, could be used as an invasion route to Japan. Commander Russell met him at Sitka with one of his squadron's PBYs and took him on to Yakutat where Foster visited with the Canadian squadrons. From Yakutat, they went on to Elmendorf Field, and then to Kodiak where General Buckner met them. Foster wanted to visit the Aleutian Islands as far as Attu. The Commander, Alaska Defense Command, saw the opportunity to see the islands first hand and invited himself along. Russell, who was responsible for transporting the commander aboard one of his PBYs, was reluctant to take the general along. He feared for Buckner's life because of the pending Japanese thrust into the Aleutians.

General Buckner, typically, would hear of nothing else. He arrived at Russell's amphibian in high spirits and equipped for the field with a hunting rifle and a down sleeping bag, looking forward to his first visit down the entire length of the Aleutian Islands. Lieutenant Commander Russell had picked one of his top pilots, Lieutenant Samuel E. Coleman, to accompany the party in another PBY in case of maintenance problems or an emergency. He also brought along VP-42's best navigator, Lieutenant Clark "Joe" Hood. They set off for their trip on May 18. After stopping at Dutch Harbor, they took off for lonely Attu Island at the end of the Aleutian Chain. They had just passed Kiska, when

Mike Hodikoff, left confers with officers in the pilot house on the bridge aboard the Casco. *At Hodikoff's right are Ensign Mullaero, logistics officer, Comdr Theda Combs, and Comdr Charles E. "Squeaky" Anderson who was along for the ride. Mike Hodikoff was fated to die in Japan.* James Russell collection

deteriorating weather forced them back into the safety of Kiska Harbor where the crew of the *Williamson* was off-loading supplies for the weather detachment at Kiska. General Buckner, accompanied by Russell, Foster and Coleman went ashore to visit with Aerographers's Mate William House and his nine man weather detachment.[43]

In addition to Kiska, Captain Parker had established a weather detachment on Kanaga, which he intended to move to Adak. He had also planned to establish others on Attu, Amchitka and Umnak to track and report on the predominantly eastward-moving weather. Captain Parker kept the number of men and the facilities at each location to the minimum on the theory that in the event of an enemy attack or raid it would be better to "have only four buildings burned and ten throats cut, than ten buildings and one hundred throats."[44] His theory was soon to be put to the test.

The weather continued to deteriorate at Kiska. Commander Russell became increasingly concerned for the safety of his high ranking charges. After consulting with Commander K. N. Kivette, the Commander of the *Williamson*, he convinced the reluctant general to return aboard the seaplane tender to Kodiak. Commander Foster elected to go along. They departed the afternoon of May 19 as a storm from the west slashed into Kiska Harbor. Russell and Coleman remained at Kiska for another four days as the storm raged. The *Casco* came rolling and pitching into Kiska Harbor on the way back from Attu. The *Casco's* commander, Commander Theda Combs and his crew had taken an Army survey party there. Their work done, Commander Combs reembarked the survey party. He offered to take aboard the forty-two Aleuts and their white school teacher, Etta and her husband, Charles Foster Jones. However, the village chief, Mike Hodikoff, declined the offer.

Vice Admiral Charles S. Freeman, right and RAdml Robert Theobald, left, meet at Kodiak August 19, 1942. USN photo

Ensign William C. Jones, a radio technician aboard the *Casco*, went ashore to help House and his men set up new radio equipment. On an earlier trip, he had presented the men with a dog named "Explosion." After stopping to pose with House and his men for a picture, Jones went aboard the *Casco*. Shortly, afterwards, Combs ordered the seaplane tender to pull up anchor and head for Dutch Harbor. Russell and Coleman had already departed on the 23rd. For House and his men and the villagers on Attu, the men of the *Casco* would be their last contact with free Americans until after the war.[45]

By mid-May, what had been perceived as a nebulous threat to Alaska had hardened into reality. General Buckner's intelligence officer, Colonel Lawrence V. Castner figured that the Japanese would certainly strike Dutch Harbor, possibly occupy the base, and might even venture as far east as Kodiak. Everyone agreed that the Aleutians were in jeopardy and the attacks would come in early June.[46] General Butler began moving his forces to Cold Bay and to Otter Point. Captains Russell Cone and Donald Dunlap from the 36th Bombardment Squadron had already conducted several B-18 flights to Cold Bay and Otter Point to determine if the fields could accommodate heavy aircraft. On May 15, Captain Jack Marks flew the squadron's B-17E to Otter Point. It was the first time that a heavy four engine aircraft had been landed there. The Marston matting buckled and heaved but held.[47] General DeWitt, according to the established plans, ordered the 54th Fighter Squadron and 406th Bombardment Squadron to Alaska. At the same time he began searching his command and seeking assistance from the Canadians for other air units that could be sent north to help repel the Japanese invaders.

Vice Admiral Charles S. Freeman, Commandant, Northern Naval Coastal Frontier and 13th Naval District, also moved to reinforce Captain Parker's forces in Alaska. Captain Leslie E. Gehres, Commander, Patrol Wing Four left Tongue Point near the mouth of the Columbia River on May 25 with three members of his staff and four PBYs from VP 41 for Alaska. Captain Gehres arrived at Kodiak two days later and established his headquarters. The remaining Catalinas from Lieutenant Commander Paul Foley's squadron flew in shortly afterwards. They brought the total Catalinas in Alaska to twenty. Up until that point, Patrol Wing Four had been engaged in flying anti-submarine patrols off the Northwest Coast. It now had a far more demanding mission in a very difficult theater of operations. The wing would remain in Alaska for the duration of the war.[48]

Commander Russell, who had relieved Commander Foley in early February, was busily engaged with his squadron in patrolling the icy reaches of the North Pacific. The number of Catalinas assigned to VP-42 had been increased to twelve of the newer PBY5A amphibians. A similar number were assigned to VP-41. All were equipped with the British designed SCR-521 ASV radar.

After the PBY-5, Russell remembered the amphibian as "a joy to be able to fly from airfields ashore with greatly simplified maintenance, yet we retained the ability to operate from the sea and our seaplane tenders."[49] Commander Russell and his men found flying conditions over the North Pacific brutal and dangerous. For the most part they operated out of Dutch Harbor or from one of the seaplane tenders. The *Casco* arrived in April to join the *Gillis* and *Williamson*. The patrols were long and uncomfortable due to the cold. Despite the fact that everyone was

The Casco *(AVP-12) was commissioned in 1941 as a seaplane tender that could accommodate a twelve-plane squadron. A small tender of the* Barnegat *class, she displaced 2,800 tons. The* Casco's *crane could lift a PBY out of the water for repairs.*
USN photo

A PBY-5A amphibian from Patrol Wing Four over the snow covered mountains of the Aleutian Islands. The antennas for the SCR-521 air-to-surface radar can be seen under the wings. USN photo

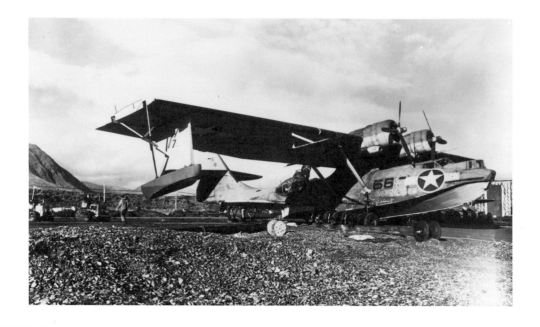

Another view of a Catalina seaplane in the Aleutians and its beaching gear.
USN photo via AAHM

Pilots of the 54th Pursuit Squadron stand beside one of their P-43s at Hamilton Field, California. Captain Thomas Jackson is the pilot third from the right. The pilot second from the left is Lieut Francis Poe who led the first flight of P-38s to Alaska.
Photo via Maj James Hazen, 54TFS

The officers of VP-42 at Kodiak June 1941. Front row, from left to right: Lieut (JG) Michael Vicent, Lieut Norman F. Garton, Lieut Comdr James S. Russell, Lieut Alan R. Nash (squadron commander at the time), Ensign Francis Grisko and Ensign Marshall Freerks. Back row, left to right: Ensign Edwin R. Winter, Ensign Wiljo Lindgren, Ensign David A Brough, Lieut (JG) Samuel E. Coleman, Ensign Royal A. Letti (jg) and Ensign Frederick A. Smith. Winter, Brough and Smith were to die in the Aleutian Islands. Coleman was killed in the South Pacific.
James Russell collection

Thomas W. Jackson as a major. He commanded the 54th Fighter Squadron from May 1, 1941 to September 14, 1942.
Lyle A. Bean collection

Two fighter pilots. Note the 54th Fighter Squadron emblem on their P-38. It was changed with the reactivation of the squadron in 1987 as a tactical fighter squadron equipped with the F-15 Eagle. AAF photo

A closer view of the deadly end of the P-38. The tapes over the gun mussels protected them from the elements. AAF photo

Lieutenant Herbert Hasenfus, 54th Fighter Squadron, in his P-38 Lightning. The four 50 caliber machine guns and the one 20 millimeter cannon in the nose packed a tremendous wallop with their concentrated fire. AAF photo

bundled up in heavy, fleece lined leather flight jackets, pants, gloves and boots, everyone returned half frozen. A typical patrol, according to Paul Carrigan.

> . . . droned for six hours just above the vicious, storm-tossed, cold grey waves on the outward leg, made a ninety degree turn at the end, flew another hour of so on the short cross leg, then made another ninety degree turn to start the long homeward leg.[50]

The patrols lasted thirteen hours or more and were made by dead-reckoning navigation, often in the snow, sleet, fog and the savage winds that plagued flying operations. They were made with only rudimentary navigation aids, very few check points over the featureless expanse of the cold, heaving North Pacific waters. Instead, the navigators depended on course flown, time, distance, air speed and estimated wind drift to find their way out and back over the ocean. Paul Carrigan "always hated the implications of the term 'dead reckoning navigation,' especially after he overheard one of the navigators remark, 'Oh, you know, I reckon I'll get us back or I reckon we'll be dead.'"[51]

On May 10, Ensign Edwin Ray Winters and his co-pilot, Ensign Edwin C. Sindel and a crew of six took off from Dutch Harbor on a routine patrol and disappeared, never to be heard from again. The tragedy came hard on the heels of another loss. Captain Gehres arrived at Dutch

Harbor April 22 on a visit to VP-42. Commander Russell suggested he go along on one of the patrols as a means of boosting morale. To be more democratic, he asked the captain to randomly pick a sector and crew to fly with. A storm blew in that night and covered everything with ice.

Commander Russell woke the next morning to find the wind blowing and a heavy front moving in. He cancelled all flying for the day. Several of the PBYs had already been warmed up on the ramp, included one piloted by Ensign Frederick A. Smith. The young, impetuous Smith was disappointed. He figured he would be the one to take Captain Gehres on the patrol. After talking the duty officer into allowing him to make a quick, local patrol, Smith opened up the throttles of the two the Pratt-Whitney Twin-Wasps to full power. In his haste, Ensign Smith and his crew had not cleaned of the ice off the amphibian. They never made it off the water. Smith stubbornly kept trying to lift the heavily laden Catalina until it finally crashed into a sand spit that ran out into the harbor. The PBY caught fire. Commander Russell, who had taxied one of the other PBYs to the scene of the crash, found Smith and the others in the front of the Catalina burned beyond recognition. Those in back had managed to scramble to safety. Almost fifty years later, the Admiral would remember the names of the men of his squadron and the details of their deaths in the Aleutian Islands.[52]

Of the Army units that deployed to Alaska that late Spring of anxiety, the "fighting 54th" was the first to leave. The fighter squadron had been activated January 15, 1941 on a foggy, cold and damp day at Hamilton Field, California. Lieutenant Thomas W. Jackson assumed command the following month. The squadron moved to Portland, Oregon in May and then to Paine Field, Washington in January 1942. The 54th was one of the first units to be equipped with the revolutionary new Lockheed P-38E Lightning. Up until then, Lieutenant Jackson and his men had been flying a collection of P-36s, P-40s and P-43s that were cast-offs from other squadrons. The squadron historian noted that:

> February 13, 1942 didn't seem like much of a day and probably no one even remembers it except the 54th. On that memorable day, rumors died, fingers could be uncrossed and chests could really swell; we had our first P-38. Others of course were quick to arrive and soon we had our share, but this first beauty was our darling. We crawled up her bowels, out her exhaust, in one boom and out the other. All this may have been a little hard on her but we just had to know all the secrets of this then reportedly fickle devil. There were a few bugs, of course, but we were soon confident that the P-38 would soon prove itself the most honest plane ever built.[53]

Initially, some of the pilots had reservations about the twin engine fighter. Their confidence was further shaken by several fatal crashes that occurred shortly after the P-38s arrived. Colonel Ben Kelsey, who had been assigned to the Lockheed development team, visited the squadron and demonstrated the true potential of the fighter and proved that, if handled right, it was a safe aircraft to fly.

On April 9, Captain Jackson and three others left for Elmendorf Field on a "secret mission." They returned on the 22nd. Shortly afterwards, Jackson prepared a report on the conditions that the squadron could expect if it was suddenly deployed to Alaska. By now, word had leaked out that the squadron might at some future time be called to move north. The rumors hardened into reality by mid-May. The squadron historian noted:

> Our assignment was to be somewhere in the Alaska Frontier, many of the line personnel had misgivings concerning the climate, the hardships and isolation confronting them but this was very effectively counteracted by the promise of combat duty at long last; the chance to test and prove our months of intensive training against a foe who as yet hadn't accomplished more than threatening the far reaches of our Aleutian Island Chain. Little did we realize then that our far reaching crescent of islands would mean more than the fur adornment for our mercenary fairer sex.[54]

The 54th was brought up to full strength with the issuing of the deployment orders. A complement of twenty-five P-38Es was assigned to the 54th Fighter Squadron. The pilots flew them to the Lockheed factory at Burbank, California where long range tanks were installed and the fighters winterized. The squadron began its deployment to Alaska on May 23 when the pilots took off from Paine Field, stopping at Edmonton and Watson Lake. The maintenance personnel accompanied them in transports.

The remaining ground crew assembled in front of their barracks in the drizzling rain on the 25th after having been fed breakfast at 5:00 AM. They climbed aboard Army trucks for the first leg of their long journey to the Aleutians. On reaching the Port of Seattle, they boarded the S.S. *Columbia*. The Alaskan Line ship stopped at Kodiak, its destination, on the 29th. The men then boarded the S.S. *Coldbrook*, a rusty relic of forty Alaskan summers. By the early afternoon of the 31st, they were peering over the rails at Anchorage. They could see in the distance airplanes taking off and landing at Elmendorf Field. By the 3rd of June, the squadron was temporarily settled at Elmendorf Field preparing to move to Cold Bay and Otter Point. The pilots flew their first operational mission that day, when in response to the Japanese attack on Dutch Harbor, they took off on a two hour patrol over the Cook Inlet area.[55]

While Captain Jackson and his men had been notified days in advance that they were being deployed to Alaska, Major Doug Courtney had no warning at all. Colonel John V. Hart, Commander, 42nd Bombardment Group called the Commander, 406th Bombardment Squadron at 11:00 AM June 2, and ordered him and his squadron to depart at once for thirty days of temporary duty in Alaska. At first, Major Courtney thought his commander was joking since there were only a few flyable aircraft at Paine Field. The squadron had been released on May 4 from anti-submarine patrol duty so that it could begin transitioning from A-29s to B-25s. The squadron at the time had six A-29s and two B-18s. Two B-25s were on loan for transition training. Colonel Hart advised the young major that ten additional A-29s and two more B-18s were en route to Paine Field. When Courtney realized the orders were serious, he immediately went into action.

By 3:00 PM, Major Courtney had dispatched Captain Harry Mitchell with a flight of four B-18As north and began selecting and preparing the A-29s that were in the best mechanical condition and had all their equipment for deployment to Alaska.

When Major Courtney assumed command of the squadron on May 17, 1942, it had been in existence since its activation January 15, 1941, at Fort Douglas, Utah as the 16th Reconnaissance Squadron. From there the squadron moved to Gowen Field, Idaho in early June 1941. The squadron started out with B-18s, and for a brief time in late 1941 and early 1942, was equipped with B-26s. A few of the B-18s were retained. The Marauders were assigned to other units after the squadron moved to Paine Field in late January 1942. It was reequipped with Lockheed A-29s, modified as Hudson IIIs, which had originally been intended for Lend Lease shipment as the Hudson II to England. The 16th was assigned an anti-submarine patrol mission; and on April 22, 1942, it was redesignated the 406th Bombardment Squadron.[56]

Ward T. (Tommy) Olsson had joined the squadron on May 7. Just out of flight school, he and the other new pilots had looked forward to belonging to "a tactical unit." They were disappointed to learn that the 406th was equipped with "some old Douglas B-18s," and Lockheed A-29s. Despite his disappointment with the aircraft, Tommy Olsson found duty with the squadron pleasant after the hectic pace of flight school. Olsson and the other young lieutenants enjoyed the prestige and life style of their newly acquired rank. The Northwest was a pleasant place to be in the spring, and Seattle, twenty miles to the south, offered a nice weekend diversion to the routines of Paine Field.

As Olsson recalled, "Our routine was dramatically changed on June 2nd," and "A hectic scene unfolded at Paine while the members of the squadron frantically packed their belongings and checked out for an extended

Lockheed A-29 Hudson, 406th Bombardment Squadron at Kodiak during a survey trip prior to the squadron's deployment to Alaska. The light bomber-maritime reconnaissance aircraft could carry a 1,200-pound bomb load. It had a crew of four. Other than off-shore patrolling it was not suited for Aleutian operations. The 406th Bombardment Squadron had to wait until February 1943 when it converted to B-25s to be committed to the war in the Aleutians. In the interim, its crews flew combat missions with the other squadrons. Douglas Courtney

TDY assignment."[57] Olsson was among the air crews of the eight A-29s that roared down the Paine Field runway at 9:00 AM on June 3. Major Courtney led his squadron north over the now familiar Northwest Staging Route.

Their route took to them to Great Falls, Montana and then across the border to Calgary, Edmonton, Fort Nelson, Whitehorse and back across the border to Ladd Field and south to Elmendorf Field. The flight was made without any incidents despite the fact that all the ground navigation aids had been turned off. Major Courtney arrived at Ladd Field June 5 with four A-29s. The other four A-29s arrived shortly afterwards. The remaining A-29s at Paine Field departed on June 6 for Alaska with additional equipment and support personnel.

Immediately upon arrival at Ladd Field, Major Courtney received an urgent message from General Butler directing him to "proceed immediately to Elmendorf and report as soon as possible." Captain Schneider met Major Courtney and informed him General Butler wanted to see him at Kodiak. Schneider flew Courtney to Kodiak in the general's personal plane. The Commander, Eleventh Air Force was happy to receive another squadron, but was also surprised that it was not equipped with B-25s as he had been led to believe. At first some of his staff members were reluctant to keep the squadron because of the limited capabilities of its aircraft in Alaska. However, General Butler decided to assign the squadron to flying anti-submarine patrols over the Gulf of Alaska and the Bering Sea until it could be reequipped with B-25s. Detachments were dispatched to Yakutat, Naknek and Nome. The thirty days of temporary duty stretched into seventeen months. The squadron's ground personnel, who had been left behind at Paine Field, arrived in early November.[58]

The Canadians also rushed forces to Alaska. President Roosevelt, at a meeting of the Pacific Council in Washington on April 1, 1942, mildly suggested the Canadians take a more active role in the Pacific defense, especially Alaska and the Aleutian Islands. The Permanent Joint Defense Board discussed the topic during their meetings on April 7 and 27. The military representatives from both nations, after some discussion, agreed that Canada would come to the aid of Alaska in an emergency. Air Commodore Stevenson was reluctant about releasing squadrons from the Western Air Command. His forces were already stretched to the limit trying to guard the Canadian west coast from a possible Japanese attack. He and his superiors felt that Canada's contributions should extend no further north than southeastern Alaska. Nevertheless, he notified Number 8 Bomber Reconnaissance Squadron, Number 14 Fighter Squadron and Number 111 Fighter Squadron that they might be committed to Alaska's defense. Representatives from the Western Air Command and the squadrons visited Elmendorf Field to discuss their plans with Generals Buckner's and Butler's staff.

The Americans, after some initial hesitation, decided to inform the Canadians of Japanese plans in the Pacific. Air Commodore Stevenson was alerted on May 21 of the Japanese Midway-Aleutian operations. The Canadians were concerned about the vulnerability of the Prince Rupert area. An eight day debate ensued. DeWitt and Buckner wanted the Canadians to send two squadrons to Yakutat, midway between Annette Island and Anchorage. Air Commodore Stevenson and his superiors wanted them no farther north than Annette Island where they would be in a better position to protect Prince Rupert to the south. They decided to move Number 8 and Number 111 Squadrons north from their bases at Sea Island and Patricia Bay, British Columbia. Number 118 Fighter Squadron was ordered west from its base at Dartmouth, Nova Scotia to Sea Island, and Number 132 Fighter at Rockcliff, Ontario received orders to replace Number 111 Fighter Squadron.

Generals DeWitt and Buckner continued to persist in their arguments that the Canadians send their two squadrons to Yakutat. Buckner especially wanted the

Number 118 Fighter Squadron P-40 Kittyhawk at Annette Island during Winter of 1942-43.

M.W. Thompson collection, Directorate of History, National Defense HQ

Curtiss P-40 Kittyhawks of No 111 Squadron, RCAF over Alaska 1942. Note the one below the other top two.

Canadian Forces photo

Bristol Bolingbroke IV of No. 8 Bomber Reconnaissance Squadron shortly after arrival at Elmendorf Field June 7, 1942. Canadian Forces photo

The air field at Yakutat was constructed under the supervision of Captain Talley. In addition to being a staging field on the southeast Alaskan air route, it was used by the Eleventh Air Force and RCAF as a base for conducting anti-submarine patrols over the Gulf of Alaska. FAA collection, Anchorage Museum of History and Art

Visit of Canadian officials to Elmendorf Field July 4, 1942. From left to right the Honorable C.G. Powers, Minister of Defense, General Buckner, Air Marshall Breadner. USA photo

authority to send them to Elmendorf Field, Kodiak, Cordova and Cold Bay in the event their services were required at those locations. He and General Butler were stripping Elmendorf Field of its fighter and bomber forces and sending them to Cold Bay and Otter Point. On June 1, General DeWitt telephoned the War Department and asked for its assistance in getting the Canadians to comply with the Permanent Joint Defense Board decision. He promised that the Canadian squadrons would not have to remain at Yakutat past June 8, by which time the 54th Fighter Squadron and the 406th Bombardment Squadron would have arrived. Other American squadrons had also been alerted and once they arrived, the Canadians would no longer be needed. This was the first mention of a limited commitment.

The Canadians agreed. Squadron Leader deM Molson and Number 118 Fighter Squadron had already departed Dartmouth in their P-40s for the 4,000-mile trip across Canada to Sea Island. They were diverted to An-

nette Island and Number 8 Bomber Reconnaissance Squadron was ordered north to Yakutat. The squadron departed on June 2 with ten Bolingbrooks. They were followed by two transports carrying support personnel and equipment. Squadron Leader Charles Willis and his squadron flew north from the RCAF base at Sea Island, stopping at Annette Island and Juneau. The squadron arrived on June 3, the same day the Japanese launched their first attack against Dutch Harbor. The American commander asked Squadron Leader Willis to fly a local patrol. The Canadians committed one of their bombers to the mission, the first to be flown in support of the Eleventh Air Force. The next day, June 4, Wing Commander G. R. McGregor, holder of the British Distinguished Flying Cross and a veteran of the Battle of Britain, arrived at Yakutat to assume command of the two Canadian squadrons that were being committed to the defense of Alaska.

Number 8 Bomber Reconnaissance Squadron had hardly settled at Yakutat when General Buckner ordered it and Number 111 Fighter Squadron to Elmendorf Field. Wing Commander McGregor immediately asked the Western Air Command for permission. Elmendorf Field had become the staging base for units deploying to the Aleutians, and if the Canadians were to get in on the action, they would have to move there. His request was approved. Number 8 Bomber Reconnaissance Squadron arrived at Elmendorf Field on June 7. The American units had either departed or were about to depart for the Aleutians, and the squadron began flying anti-submarine patrols over the Gulf of Alaska from Elmendorf and Kodiak. The action was elsewhere in the Aleutians. The

Bolingbroke and B-26s, 73rd Bombardment Squadron at Elmendorf Field Summer 1942. Raiford Perry collection via AAHM

squadron diary entry for June 7 noted: "possibilities of unit seeing combat whilst based here seems extremely remote."

Squadron Leader A. D. Nesbitt, another Battle of Britain veteran, led the P-40s of Number 111 Fighter Squadron into Elmendorf Field on June 8. Nesbitt and his men had departed Patricia Bay five days earlier with only one suitable map between them. They proceeded without incident through Prince George, Watson Lake to Whitehorse where Wing Commander McGregor met and provided them with maps for the rest of the trip. The deployments "brought home to the Canadians the greatest hazards of Alaskan operations: long distances between bases and generally poor weather conditions, compounded by inadequate meteorological information, especially en route forecasts."

Wing Commander McGregor established Wing X as a provisional wing at Elmendorf Field to serve as an intermediate headquarters between the Eleventh Air Force and the squadrons. General Butler promptly ordered the red centers on the top wing roundels of all the RCAF painted over. He was concerned that they might be mistaken for Japanese markings. The Americans had already discarded the old Army Air Corps red center in the star for the same reason.

The short stay in Alaska was proving to be much longer than anticipated, Wing Commander McGregor began having reservations about the role that Buckner and Butler intended for his command. From all appearances, they expected the Canadians to remain in the rear areas so that the American squadron could be sent to the forward areas.[59]

Admiral Theobald arrived at Kodiak on May 27. He was met by Generals Buckner and Butler and Captain Parker. The new commander tried to be diplomatic. Buckner resented his presence. For two years he had been building Alaska's defenses only to see them slip from his grasp and into the hands of another who was his opposite in temperament and personality. The rambunctious "Silver Stallion of Alaska," could not get over the fact that he had been reduced to playing a supporting role to the cautious and cerebral Theobald. Buckner, ever the aggressive infantryman, wanted action. Theobald proved to be more slow moving. Later, in frustration born of not being in charge, Buckner would turn and criticize his Navy opposite for his lack of aggressiveness. Theobald, in defense would reply: "Man and boy I've been to sea for forty years," to which Buckner would retort: "That's right, you've been to sea for forty years."[60]

General Talley remembering years later the difference between the two, attributed it not only to a difference in personalities but also difference in philosophy between the Army and the Navy. The Army could afford to withdraw from a battle that was not going well while the Navy could not, least they run the risk of complete defeat.

Admiral Nimitz in his orders to Admiral Theobald cautioned him not to risk his fleet unless there was a certainty of victory.[61]

Admiral Theobald held a conference at his shore base headquarters at Kodiak the day after he arrived to plan a counter to the expected Japanese thrust into the North Pacific. Buckner, Butler and Parker and the newly arrived Gehres along with their key staff members were in attendance. The conference lasted four days.[62]

The intelligence estimate was briefed. The analysts, basing their estimates on the information they received from Admiral Nimitz's staff, stated that the Japanese were expected to bomb Dutch Harbor and occupy the western Aleutians. Theobald was incredulous. He wondered why anyone would want to capture the desolate islands. He believed it was a ruse to draw his forces westward so that the Japanese could land their forces at Dutch Harbor, Kodiak or even the Alaskan mainland. The Japanese intentions, the admiral felt, were to seize one of the bases by amphibious assault, then bring in land-based aircraft for further strikes against mainland Alaska and even the west coast of Canada and the United States.[63]

Admiral Nimitz's intelligence chief, Commander Edwin T. Layton, was equally perplexed that Theobald would ignore the estimate that his staff had developed based on the decoding of the Japanese radio intercepts and follow his own hunch. "Theobald," Layton recalled over forty years later, "had been briefed that our reliable sources indicated the enemy intended to capture Kiska and Attu and raid Dutch Harbor. But without telling us, he decided to ignore our intelligence estimate." It was the new commander's first blunder.[64]

The plan, *Task Force Operations Plan 1-42*, which Admiral Theobald's staff developed was designed to counter a Japanese thrust in the eastern Aleutians and the Alaska Peninsula area. It ignored the possibility of the Japanese landing troops in the western Aleutians. Completed by June 1, the plan was almost as complex as the one the Japanese had developed for the Midway-Aleutian operations. It called for the deployment of six separate groups. Admiral Theobald assumed command of the Main Body (Task Group 8.6) which consisted of the two heavy and three light cruisers and four destroyers. He decided to position this force 400 miles south of Kodiak Island, where it would be in a position to "exploit opportunities." General Buckner objected. He thought the force should be southwest of Dutch Harbor. Admiral Theobald believed otherwise. He figured that the Japanese would try to draw the American forces westward so that they could get behind them, land troops somewhere between Umnak and Cold Bay and attack and occupy Dutch Harbor. He wanted to be in a position to intercept the Japanese.[65]

Admiral Theobald also faced a very difficult situation

because of Admiral Nimitz warning not to engage in battle unless he was certain of victory. The Commander of Task Force 8 felt he could not commit his small force of cruisers and destroyers against Admiral Kakuta's carrier task force. The odds favored the Japanese. General Butler did not have the capability of providing a combat air patrol over Theobald's force to ward off attacks from Kakuta's carrier planes. The Army fighters were too few, did not posses the range, and the pilots were not trained for naval aviation operations. Theobald ruled out another possibility: engaging Kakuta's force in a night operation. There were not enough hours of darkness in the northern latitudes. It all came down to placing the initial reliance on Gehres' PBYs to locate and track the enemy ships and Butler's bombers to hit them. After that, Theobald might find an opportunity to use his guns.[66]

Admiral Theobald formed two search groups whose mission it was to locate the Japanese force and direct General Butler's bombers against it. Captain Gehres commanded the Air Search Group (Task Force 8.1) consisting of his twenty Catalinas and the 36th Bombardment Squadron's two LB-30s and one B-17E at Kodiak. The B-17B, "Old Seventy," was dispatched to Otter Point to fly patrols down the Aleutian Chain. Four Catalinas operated from the *Casco* at Cold Bay, four from the *Williamson* at Sand Point in the Shumagin Islands and twelve from the *Gillis* at Dutch Harbor. Admiral Theobald tried, without success, to have the other two squadrons of Patrol Wing Four sent to Alaska in time to counter the Japanese.

On May 28, Gehres increased the patrol flights to cover the hours of darkness, which in the northern latitudes at the time, depending on the cloud cover, lasted from 10:30 PM to 2:30 AM. The crews of the slow, lumbering, lightly armed amphibians took off from Cold Bay, Dutch Harbor and Otter Point at dusk, droned out at low level for 400 miles through the twilight darkness, and turned on a short base leg, before heading back. The day patrols took off in the early morning as the night patrols were returning. They arrived back in the late evening. The handful of PBY crews at Kodiak were committed to patrols out to 400 miles over the Gulf of Alaska. The 36th Bombardment Squadron four engine bomber crews flew patrols out to seven hundred miles.[67]

The Surface Search Group (Task Force 8.2) was composed of Captain Parker's "Alaskan Navy," and consisted of the *Charleston,* his flagship, five Coast Guard cutters, an oiler and a motley collection of fifteen Navy YP patrol and requisitioned fishing boats. Their mission was to establish a picket line 150 miles south of Dutch Harbor and north into the Bering Sea. Captain Parker, up until then, had kept his small fleet busy escorting the freighters and transports that carried equipment and personnel to Alaska. The *Charleston* was the only vessel equipped with sonar and with guns larger than three inches. None had radar. The YP, or Yippy boats, were commanded by Commander Carl "Squeaky" Anderson, a colorful naval reservist of "infinite resource, energy and cunning," who, before his recall to active duty, had been a salesman in Los Angeles, California. General Buckner objected. He felt the picket line would be useless, given the weather conditions and the lack of radar.[68]

Admiral Theobald urged General Butler to commit the entire Eleventh Air Force, which made up the Air Striking Group (Task Group 8.3), to the defense of the Aleutians. The Eleventh, particularly the bomber force, composed his only real offensive force. Butler was uncertain. He had already dispatched part of the 11th Fighter

In addition to dispatching them to various locations in the Aleutians and on the Alaska Peninsula, Captain Gehres also ordered his PBYs to disperse to nearby bays to reduce their chances of being discovered and destroyed by the Japanese. Note the Kingfishers in the background. USN photo via AAHM

The Marston mat runway at Otter Point as seen from the nose of a B-24. AAF photo

A P-40E from the 18th Fighter Squadron takes off from Cold Bay. AAF photo

Umnak on a rare clear day. Mount Tulik is in the background. Larry Reineke Collection

The conditions at Otter Point were primitive. Men lived in tents which did not stand up well to the high winds in the Aleutians. Later, conditions were improved. USA photo

Squadron's ground complement to Cold Bay and Otter Point. By May 25, one hundred and seventeen of the squadron's personnel arrived at Cold Bay and the following day there were thirty-one at Otter Point. Major Chennault flew in with the P-40s shortly afterwards. By the end of the month the squadron's twenty-four P-40s were evenly divided between the two fields.[69]

John R. Melter, an 11th Fighter Squadron mechanic, remembered leaving Elmendorf Field with ... "a group of about five men for Cold Bay on a B-18 the latter part of May. We were made self sufficient by being supplied with two bags of soft coal, a Sibley stove and a case or two of rations." Melter and his comrades remained at Cold Bay until after the first Japanese attack on Dutch Harbor, following which they were loaded into a C-47 and flown to Umnak.[70]

The conditions at both fields, particular at Otter Point, were primitive. Talley's engineers had managed to build revetments for the aircraft; and there was sufficient gasoline, ammunition and bombs, but little of anything else, especially radio sets. The communications personnel had rigged an underpowered, "field expedient" set at Otter Point to communicate with Dutch Harbor until a planned undersea cable could be laid. The radio receiver was especially weak.[71]

General Butler, who had just completed an inspection trip to the two fields, was convinced they were not ready to receive the large numbers of aircraft Theobald wanted. The engineers had not completed paving the runway at Cold Bay and the Marston mats that had been laid over the hastily prepared surface at Otter Point did not provide a stable runway. The pilots who landed there had to fight for control as their aircraft bounced wildly in the air. It was like landing on a trampoline. Take-offs proved equally challenging, since the matting had a tendency to ripple up in front of the wheels. Space was even more of a problem. According to Butler, the pilots who landed at Otter Point "were forced to land one after another like carrier planes, as on a deck of a carrier, and then taxi back, so that their wheels were just on the edge of the runway to make way for other ships." The aircraft were packed so close that Butler feared one good dive bombing attack would destroy the lot.[72]

If there was one thing General Buckner and the admiral did agree on, it was the need to deploy the bombers and fighters as far forward as possible so they could strike the Japanese ships and protect the bases in the Aleutians. There was no way that Butler's forces at Elmendorf Field and Kodiak could have reached their intended targets in time to influence the outcome of the battle. The Eleventh Air Force commander relented and agreed to send part of his small force to the two fields.[73]

Butler moved an advance headquarters of the Eleventh Air Force to Kodiak, placed Colonel Davis in charge of it, and ordered Colonel Eareckson to move forces of his 28th Composite Group westward. Eareckson dispatched a flight of P-40Es from the 18th Fighter Squadron at Kodiak to join the twelve P-40Es from the 11th Fighter Squadron at Cold Bay. The fighter squadrons had been placed under his control for the coming operation. Seven B-26s from the 73rd Bombardment Squadron arrived at Cold Bay on May 28, and the following day, Captain Owen "Jack" Meals, Commander, 77th Bombardment Squadron passed through from Elmendorf Field with six B-26s en route to Otter Point. By the early hours of June 3, as Admiral Kakuta prepared to launch his aircraft, there were twelve P-40s, six B-26s and a B-17B at Otter Point. Captain Cone, who had brought the big bomber in on May 27, began flying daily reconnaissance patrols down the Aleutian Chain.

Colonel Eareckson set up a small advance tactical headquarters of the 28th Composite Group at Cold Bay. He and Commander Russell decided to establish a joint communications center and moved into it with their bedding so that they could better control and coordinate air operations. There were twenty-one P-40s and twelve B-26s at Cold Bay. Butler kept the remainder of his P-40s at Kodiak to augment a squadron of twelve F4F Wildcats which the Navy had brought in to provide air defense of their base on June 1st. The 54th Fighter Squadron and the remaining B-26s of the two medium bombardment squadrons were left to guard Elmendorf Field. The 36th Bombardment Squadron also remained at Kodiak. On June 3, the six new, long awaited B-17Es arrived and were sent on to Kodiak. The bombers were equipped with SCR-521 radars. They were immediately put to work flying combat patrols.[74]

The atmosphere at Kodiak, Billy Wheeler recorded in his diary, was "tense, expectant and hurried in preparation for immediate offensive action." The bombers were placed in camouflage revetments, bomb bay tanks taken out and five hundred pound bombs hung in their place. Old, experienced crews were assigned to them.[75]

While General Butler was deploying his aircraft, Commander Wyatt Craig led his fleet of nine destroyers into Makushin Bay, Unalaska Island and ordered his commanders to drop anchor and wait. His command, the Destroyer Striking Group (Task Group 8.4), had been assigned the task of breaking up any Japanese attempts to land troops at the western bases.

Commander Burton G. Lakes' Submarine Group (Task Group 8.5) consisting of six vintage S class submarines of little endurance and suitability slid out of Dutch Harbor into the cold waste of the North Pacific. They joined Captain Parker's force in forming a line that stretched south and north of Dutch Harbor. In addition to keeping a lookout for the Japanese, Commander Lakes and his submariners had another mission of sinking any hostile ships that came their way.[76]

Admiral Theobald boarded his flagship, *Nashville*, and steamed out into the Gulf of Alaska on June 1 to join the rest of his fleet, which was still in the process of assembling. The admiral, adhering to Navy doctrine, imposed a strict radio silence to prevent Admiral Hosogaya from knowing his plans. Unfortunately, the silence, to be broken only when action against the Japanese was initiated, put him out of touch with his other forces during the initial stages of the coming battle. By then, it was so far removed from the main scene of action, that it "proved about as useful as if it had been in the South Atlantic."[77]

Jack Chennault's and Owen Meal's men waited. The living conditions at the forward bases were primitive, especially at Otter Point. The men of the 11th Fighter Squadron set up their tents on the bleak windswept muskeg and settled into a routine of flying daily fighter patrols out over the North Pacific and Bering Sea.

While stationed at Elmendorf Field, the men had lived in barracks and enjoyed the amenities of the "Kashim" service club and the company of local young women who were outnumbered by the men ten to one. Compared to Elmendorf, "Umnak was nothing like that." Lieutenant William S. Johnson, the squadron historian, later recalled the experiences of the men at Otter Point during the first several weeks:

> The men and officers lived in tents which were always blowing down and there were no floors in them because there was no wood to be found on the island. The tents were as close as possible to the planes and the pilot and his crew chief slept in one tent right by their airplane. If and when they were called during the night, they could get up and move out together. They slept in sleeping bags which had four thicknesses and four set of zippers. Some of these had a colorful, extravagant lining of blue silk which conclusively proves that someone in the Army supply system had a sense of humor. These were placed directly in the damp, spongy tundra, although some of the men tried to add a layer of dried grass or paper.[78]

"The kitchen was housed in a wall tent which had the annoying habit of blowing over at mealtime, so that the men occasionally had to go over and eat with the engineer company." The four mess personnel finally obtained wood to build a floor for the tent. It helped. Two wooden tables were installed, but the men ate out of their mess kits for the duration of their stay at Umnak. The food in the early days consisted mostly of "chile or corn beef or powdered eggs."

The squadron's only means of transportation was a Jeep which "had been illegally acquired." The mess personnel, among others, used it to haul sandwiches and coffee out to the flight line. "The usual way of going places was by foot." Recreational facilities "were entirely absent." The first mail did not arrive until three months after the squadron reached Otter Point. A small post exchange was set up, but it "seemed to deal mostly in shoe strings and none of the things which the men wanted, such as cigarettes, candy, razor blades or soap."[79] Owen Meals remembered:

> We had one runway which ran north to south. It was a steel landing mat 4,500 feet long and possibly sixty feet wide. It was later abandoned except for emergency use when regular runways were constructed. There were no base operations. We were not set up to function at all. There was no traffic control or runway lights. Our only lights were the candles in our tents and Quonset huts. The weather was typical-almost continuous rains squalls. We ate—when we ate—in the engineers' mess located about two and a half miles from our Quonset hut. During that critical week of the Dutch Harbor attacks we practically lived on bread and peanut butter. Ground crews worked under extreme difficulties. They labored on our planes right out there in the rain. Facilities such as hangars, repair shops and maintenance supplies were totally lacking.[80]

The conditions were not much better at Cold Bay. According to Lieutenant Johnson, for the men of the 11th Fighter Squadron, their stay at the windswept base at the tip of the Alaskan Peninsula:

> . . . was a stark, bleak period, and the men who were stationed there for three months felt that it had been a lifetime. It was crude and rough, and the weather was the worst-constant fog, mist and rain. No one remembers having seen the sun at Cold Bay. Personal bathing was performed in buckets of water because there was no shower house. The men never had cigarettes or candy, for a familiar reason, that the small PX was stocked only with soap and shoes strings. In the evening there was no entertainment except bull sessions in a wet tent with a candle for light. When it came time to leave Cold Bay in August, no one regretted it."[81]

Compared to Cold Bay and Otter Point, Dutch Harbor was a paradise. The Navy contractors, Siems Drake Puget Sound, had been hard at work since July 1940, constructing a variety of wooden buildings and the other facilities needed to house the Navy garrison and a small contingent of Marines. The first Army troops arrived in May 1941 to man the coastal and anti-aircraft defenses. It was a place of flush toilets, relatively comfortable accommodations, nightly movies and the limited diversion offered by the nearby village of Unalaska.

Among the attractions of the village of fifty whites and one hundred and fifty Aleuts were Blackies Bar and the Cameo Theater. There was usually a long line outside of

Blackies, as each man waited to get his drink before moving on or rejoining the line. The Cameo contained two hundred plush seats, but was plagued with intermittent power which interrupted the showing of movies. An enterprising madam had set up a what was probably the only bawdy house in the Aleutian. To reach it, those in need paid fifty cents to be rowed across the narrows that separated Dutch Harbor from Expedition Island where the house of ill repute was located. The return trip cost two dollars. The Japanese spoiled everyone's fun. Shortly after the attack on Dutch Harbor, the military evacuated all nonessential civilians, including the madam and her five girls.[82]

Commander William N. Updegraft, the Naval base commander had given his deputy, Lieutenant Commander Thomas Carson Thomas the job of preparing the base for the anticipated Japanese attack. Thomas had arrived at Dutch Harbor on March 24, and had immediately set about improving the base defenses and security. His "dynamic and frequently vitriolic personality grated on the personnel who had become accustomed to an easy way of letting things slide." A rigorous training program was implemented, trenches were dug, concrete pill boxes erected, observation posts established on high points around the base and a daily 6:OO AM full alert for all base personnel implemented. The Naval personnel were moved out of the barracks and dispersed to quarters elsewhere. Thomas' work was credited with saving lives and limiting damages when the attacks were launched.[83]

Despite the precautions, Dutch Harbor was far from ready to meet a determined attack. Commander Foster in his report noted that the base was "still in its infancy and was far from being an air station or a submarine base." The outstanding deficiency Foster noted was the lack of an air defense system. He felt the Otter Point air field had been a mistake. Even at 70 miles distance, it was too far removed from the base it was intended to protect. Too much time would be wasted in transit, and the 140-mile round trip limited the time the fighters could spend defending Dutch Harbor. He recommended a runway be build at Dutch Harbor. The second major deficiency was the lack of anti-aircraft artillery practice due to a lack of tow target aircraft and a shortage of ammunition.

An early warning system was practically non-existent. The SCR-271, scheduled for installation near Dutch Harbor, was still in its packing crate. The three short ranged SCR-268 anti-aircraft searchlight radars that provided the only ground based coverage were masked by nearby mountains. Although observation posts had been established, there was no command and control system to process and disseminate the information. Communications were entirely inadequate, particularly between Dutch Harbor and Otter Point. In short, according to

Foster: "Control of aircraft operations and communications between Army planes and the Navy Air Station, between Army and Navy planes seemed to be only in the kindergarten stage of development."[84]

Ready or not, Alaska braced for war. By June 1st, all military installations in the territory were on full twenty-four hour alert.[85] All up and down the west coast of Canada and the United States, there was a fear that the Japanese were planning an invasion. Military leaves were cancelled, radio stations silenced least their signals guide the Japanese to their targets, yachts were requisitioned and sent to sea as picket boats, and the Western Defense Command urged the public to report any unusual activities.[86]

By late May Rear Admiral Shigeaki Yamasaki's six I boats had reached their patrol points which stretched from the Pacific Northwest coast to the western Aleutians. Admiral Yamasaki proceeded up the Aleutian Chain in the I-9, his flagship, stopping to launch air reconnaissances of Attu, Kiska and Adak with the I-9's Yokosuka E14Y1 Glen scout float plane.

The small, two place monoplane, its wings folded back, was carried in a water proof hangar on the deck of the submarine. When ready to launch, the plane was pulled out, its wings unfolded, and then it was catapulted off the deck. On completion of their mission, the crew landed the Glen on the water and taxied over to the submarine to be hoisted aboard by a small crane.

The crew of the I-9 had completed their scouting missions of the three islands by the 25th. The Glen had been flown over each island without observing any military installations or activities.[87] House and his men on Kiska had seen the Glen circling overhead on 25th and reported it to Dutch Harbor. The radio operator at the Navy base asked for confirmation, which House then gave. The navy command post at the base then wanted to know what type of plane had overflown Kiska to include particulars on its speed, course and altitude. House stated that he believed it was a Glen. All this took a considerable amount of time since radio transmissions had to be coded and decoded, a tedious and time consuming process. Finally, the radio operator at Dutch Harbor tapped out: "Did you really see a plane?" House signed off without replying and turned the radio off.[88]

The I-9 then took up its patrol position south of Kiska where Admiral Yamasiki could direct the operations of the other submarines. The I-15 prowled around Adak while the I-17 patrolled the waters off Attu. Commander Seigo Narahara headed his submarine, the I-19, for the waters off Unalaska. His mission was to intercept and destroy any American ships sent north in response to the planned Dutch Harbor attack.

Elsewhere, the captain of the I-25 launched a Glen on a reconnaissance mission over the naval facilities at

Kodiak on the 26th. The float planes crew reported seeing a heavy cruiser and a destroyer entering the harbor and another destroyer and three patrol boats in Womens Bay. Two other patrol boats were noted. No PBYs were sighted and no hangars or airfield facilities noted. The I-25 then continued on to Seattle where it took up station to observe any warships heading north. According to Japanese sources, its Glen also conducted an overflight of Seattle Harbor. The I-26 also headed for the Seattle area. While en route, the captain, Comdr Meiji Togami, reporting seeing two heavy cruisers seven hundred miles northwest of Seattle heading towards Alaska.

On the 2th, Commander Narahara maneuvered I-19 into the waters off Dutch Harbor and raised the periscope. What he saw was considerably less than the division the Japanese thought was there. He relayed the information and the fact the weather at Dutch Harbor was favorable to Admiral Kakuta whose carrier task force was moving into position to launch their aircraft.[89]

Early the next day, Captain Cone and the crew of "Old Seventy," lifted off from the rain soaked runway at Otter Point in the early morning hours and headed down the Aleutian Chain on their daily reconnaissance flight. The weather had turned bad. Another cold front was moving in from the west. The ceilings ranged from five hundred feet to zero. Visibility was down to five miles. Captain Cone and his crew flew on. House and his men, from their lonely post on Kiska, heard the bomber pass overhead. Cone and his men could see the American flag waving below through the swirling mist. To the east, Admiral Kakuta's carrier pilots were attacking Dutch Harbor.[90]

A PBY-5 Catalina flying boat from VP-42 on an early deployment to Dutch Harbor. The PBY flying boat was slightly faster than the amphibian version and could carry more weight. However, beaching and sea handling were difficult on the frigid waters of the north. The amphibians could be operated from land, a method of choice in the Aleutian Islands. USN photo via AAHM

EXTRA Anchorage Daily Times **EXTRA**

"READ BY ALASKANS EVERYWHERE"

TWENTY-SIXTH YEAR — ANCHORAGE, ALASKA, WEDNESDAY, JUNE 3, 1942 — PRICE TEN CENTS

RAID DUTCH HARBOR!

WASHINGTON, D.C., June 3. (AP)---The navy announced today that four Japanese bombers and about 15 fighters attacked Dutch Harbor at approximately 6 o'clock this morning.

The attack lasted 15 minutes, the communique said. No other details were available at this time.

The Navy announced that the Dutch Harbor attack caused no serious damage. There were only a few casualties.

The second communique based on reports received to 6 p. m., eastern time, said "further reports on the Japanese air attack at Dutch Harbor state there were but few casualties. A few warehouses were set afire but no serious damage was suffered. There is nothing to report from other areas."

BLACKOUT TONIGHT

400 Planes Hit Essen In New Raid

Promise Nazis 30,000 Planes Every Month

"Weeping Women of Kerch" Bemoan Dead

Ask 8 Billion For 500 More

Call For War Against Three More Nations

WASHINGTON, D. C., June 3 (AP)—The House of Representatives today voted without oppo... to add Bulga...

City Must Be Dark As Pitch, CD Orders Say

Raid Wardens Get Patrol Instructions, Close Loop Road

...ers for a total blackout in

Weather

Continued rather warm today.

Highest, 82; Lowest, 70

The State

'For Columbia and South Carolina'

18,662—FOUNDED FEBRUARY 18, 1891 — COLUMBIA, S. C., THURSDAY, JUNE 4, 1942 — DAILY, 5c; SUNDAY, 10c

Japanese Bomb Alaska Twice

Libyan Battle Now Struggle For Position

Score Still Stand-Off Between Tanks

Court Denies Rehearing In Santee Cooper Case

All Out of Sheep

By Thomas

America Declares War on Axis Satellites

Bulgaria, Rumania and Hungary Added to List of United States Foes

Second Raid Made 6 Hours After First

Few Casualties, Little Damage Inflicted at Dutch Harbor by Four Bombers and 15 Fighters

4

MANY FOOLISH THINGS

· · · · · · · · · · · · ·

We Can Launch Now

Another series of cold fronts swept across the North Pacific during late May. The 2nd Carrier Division, since leaving Ominato on May 25, had been steaming at a steady ten to eleven knots towards Dutch Harbor. Admiral Kakuta had taken his carrier strike force into the leading edge of the front. There, hidden by heavy clouds, fog, rain and sleet, his force had easily slipped undetected through Theobald's picket line of ships and submarines. Without radar, the Americans bobbing on the heaving, grey, cold ocean in their small vessels were blind to anything that was not in their immediate area.

Captain Gehres' PBY crews also suffered from the effects of the cold front. Kakuta's men had heard one of the amphibians pass overhead on June 2 as his ships were being refueled at sea in preparation for the attack on Dutch Harbor the next day. Two Zeros had been launched, but the pilots were also stymied by the thick fog that hid friend and foe alike. Somehow, the radar operator aboard the PBY failed to detect the ships below. That night, Lieutenant Jack Bingham of VP-41 and Ensign Marshall C. Freerks from VP-42 had managed to get airborne despite the poor weather. Neither PBY crew spotted Kakuta's carriers as they were maneuvered into position 180 miles south of Dutch Harbor to launch their attacks.

Lieutenant Commander Masatake Okumiya was worried as he examined the forbidding, fog filled, sub Arctic sky from the bridge of the *Ryujo*. As the admiral's aviation officer, it was his responsibility to recommend whether or not the mission should proceed as scheduled. The timing had to be just right if the pilots were to have enough visibility to locate Dutch Harbor, bomb it, and then find their way back to the carriers. Admiral Kakuta had earlier ordered the speed increased to twenty-two knots to get ahead of the front and into clear weather. The sunrise was to occur at 2:58 AM. Takeoff had been scheduled for 2:33 AM. On the flight decks of the two car-

riers, the mechanics were preparing the aircraft for the attack. The pilots, bundled up against the morning cold, were waiting to go.

Admiral Kakuta anxiously tapped Okumiya on the shoulder amid the roar of engines being warmed up, and asked, "Can the attack get off in time?" Okumiya looked at his watch. It was 2:28 AM. Sunrise was thirty minutes away. The normal twilight skies for that time of the year at that latitude were still dark due to the heavy fog. Both were concerned. The sooner the aircraft were launched, the better chance their pilots would have surprising the defenders at Dutch Harbor. They had enough troubles as it was without the delay.

The weather at Dutch Harbor was an unknown factor. The pilots had never operated in that high latitude before. Their maps of Unalaska Island showed only a coast line, often broken with dots that the cartographers had placed on the map as an educated guess. The map of Dutch Harbor was based on a chart that was made around 1920. They also had a photograph that a crew member of one of their merchant ships had taken about the same time. The report they received from the submarine reconnaissance the day prior helped, but not much. They still did not know the exact layout of the base. They would have to find this out when they got there. At best, the attack was a calculated risk; which, if all went according to plan, would draw Admiral Nimitz's forces north, away from Midway and gain a strategic victory for Kakuta and his men. It might even inflict enough damage at Dutch Harbor to make the whole investment in men and equipment worthwhile from a tactical point of view.

Admiral Kakuta, a Naval officer of the old school, was impatient. Brought up in the tradition of Admiral Nelson, he believed that whatever strength he had under his command should be used decisively. His fleet had come a long way since leaving Ominato ten days prior. The stern, thick set admiral did not intend to waste the effort, even if it meant the sacrifice of his aircrews to the uncertainties of

Rear Admiral Kakuji Kakuta, Commander, 2nd Fleet. Japanese photo via Larry Golden

the Aleutian weather. Too much depended on attacking Dutch Harbor.

Finally, Okumiya turned to Kakuta, and said, "Sir, we can launch now." By then the task force had moved out of the outlying fog of the cold front.[1] The outline of the *Ryujo* was visible a thousand feet away in the early morning light. The still morning air became alive with roaring engines and planes began thundering down the decks of the two carriers. Lieutenant Yoshio Shiga cleared the flight deck of the *Junyo* at 3:25 AM in his Zero, climbed, circled and waited for the other twelve fighters and Lieutenant Zenji Abe's thirteen Val dive bombers to join up in loose formations. The first of Abe's bombers lifted off the deck of the *Junyo* at 3:45. Each carried a single 550-pound bomb.

Lieutenant Hiroichi Samejima on the *Ryujo*, waited for the Okumiya's signal to go. The 1938 Japanese Naval Academy graduate had been aboard the carrier since January and was a seasoned veteran of the Dutch East Indies and Indian Ocean operations. Unlike most of his contemporaries, he would survive the war, and rise to the top of the post-war Japanese Self Defense Force as a full admiral. Finally the signal came, and at 3:40 AM, Samejima opened the throttle of his Kate. The torpedo bomber, which had been configured for level bombing, rumbled down the carrier deck with its load of one 550 and four 150-pound bombs. The other six Kates followed in rapid secession. One lost engine power immediately on takeoff and went into the ocean. A nearby destroyer was rushed to the scene in time to save the three man crew. Samejima gathered his remaining torpedo bombers and headed

north, flying three hundred feet above the surface of the ocean. At 4:10 AM, shortly after the last Kate had cleared the deck, the first of the six *Ryujo's* Zeros led by Lieutenant Minoru Kobayashi began rolling down the flight deck. At 4:30 AM, Lieutenant Masatake Yamagami, led the second wave of seven Kates off the carrier deck.[2]

The two carrier groups flew in a loose formation into deteriorating weather. Finally, Lieutenant Zenje Abe ordered his pilots to return to the *Junyo*. Although the submarine report from the previous day had reported good weather conditions at Dutch Harbor, the experienced veteran of the Pearl Harbor attack and carrier operations in South Pacific saw no reason for continuing on. His dive bomber pilots needed at least a six thousand foot ceiling to start their diving attack. Abe doubted that they would find that at Dutch Harbor.[3] Eleven of the *Junyo's* Zero pilots also turned back. Two others continued on.

The weather began to clear as Samejima's group of pilots approached the southern shoreline of Unalaska Island. Admiral Kakuta had instructed them to go after the airfield and airplanes the Japanese thought were at Dutch Harbor. Samejima's secondary target was the radio station. The *Ryujo's* first wave of attackers began climbing to six thousand feet to clear the mountains. The plan called for Samejima's and Yamagami's bomber pilots to make high level bombing attacks from different directions while the Zero pilots were to streak in at low level, strafing everything in sight. The force flew north east along the east coast of the island, then turned northwest over Udagak Strait and headed up the strait across Beaver Inlet and the low mountains behind Dutch Harbor.[4]

Lieutenant Otis Boise had arrived the evening before with the 3rd Battalion, 37th Infantry Regiment aboard the transport *President Fillmore*. The battalion, which had departed Seattle five days prior, had not been told where

Marines and sailors wait and eat breakfast in the early morning hours of June 3, 1942. USN photo

Elsewhere, an Army 37mm anti-aircraft gun crew searches the sky, waiting. USN photo

A Navy crew mans their fifty caliber water cooled machine gun at the foot of Mount Ballyhoo in anticipation of the impending attack. It was a round from a gun like this that severed the oil return line in Tadayoshi Koga's Zero. USN photo

When Lieutenant Samejima and the other pilots arrived over Dutch Harbor, they saw a scene very similar to this one. The photograph was taken before the attack. Fort Mears and Margaret Bay are in the foreground. Above them is the Dutch Harbor Naval Operating Base. The long building is the reinforced concrete power plant. It currently (1990) houses the Unalaska Power facility. The Northwestern is moored along the shore near the power plant. Another ship is moored to the dock. The old Navy communications station and its antennas can be seen to the right of the base. The location of the Oil Dock Tank Farm and dock area where the fuel tanks were destroyed by Zenji Abe's dive bombers during the second day attack can be seen further to the left of the small lagoon at the tip of the island. The seaplane ramp is located to the left of the Naval Base at the narrow point in the island. Construction had not begun on the hangar when the photograph was taken. Although Dutch Harbor had a fine, deep harbor, it was not suited for air operations. The sandspit and the swells on the bay outside made seaplane takeoffs and landings difficult. The mountainous, uneven land inhibited runway construction. Navy Seabees later constructed a runway that ran from the harbor shore line across the neck of the island and along a carved out strip on the lower slope of Mount Ballyhoo. USN photo

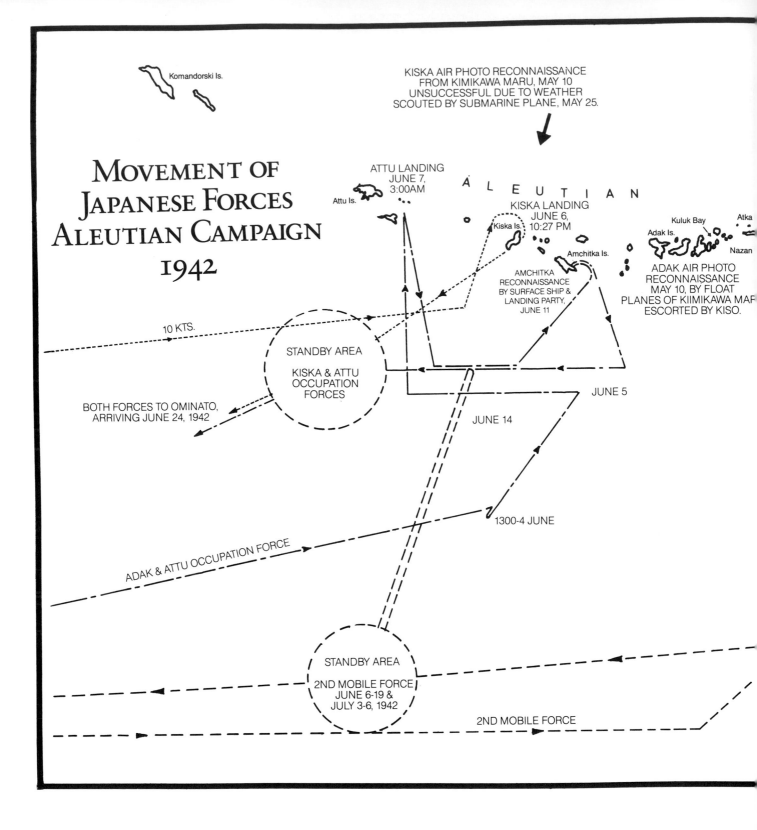

Movement of Japanese Forces Aleutian Campaign 1942

Komandorski Is.

KISKA AIR PHOTO RECONNAISSANCE
FROM KIMIKAWA MARU, MAY 10
UNSUCCESSFUL DUE TO WEATHER
SCOUTED BY SUBMARINE PLANE, MAY 25.

ATTU LANDING
JUNE 7,
3:00AM

A L E U T I A N

Attu Is.

KISKA LANDING
JUNE 6,
10:27 PM

Kiska Is.

Amchitka Is.

Kuluk Bay

Atka

Adak Is.

Nazan

AMCHITKA
RECONNAISSANCE
BY SURFACE SHIP &
LANDING PARTY,
JUNE 11

ADAK AIR PHOTO
RECONNAISSANCE
MAY 10, BY FLOAT
PLANES OF KIIMIKAWA MARU
ESCORTED BY KISO.

10 KTS.

STANDBY AREA

KISKA & ATTU
OCCUPATION
FORCES

JUNE 5

JUNE 14

BOTH FORCES TO OMINATO,
ARRIVING JUNE 24, 1942

1300-4 JUNE

ADAK & ATTU OCCUPATION FORCE

STANDBY AREA

2ND MOBILE FORCE
JUNE 6-19 &
JULY 3-6, 1942

2ND MOBILE FORCE

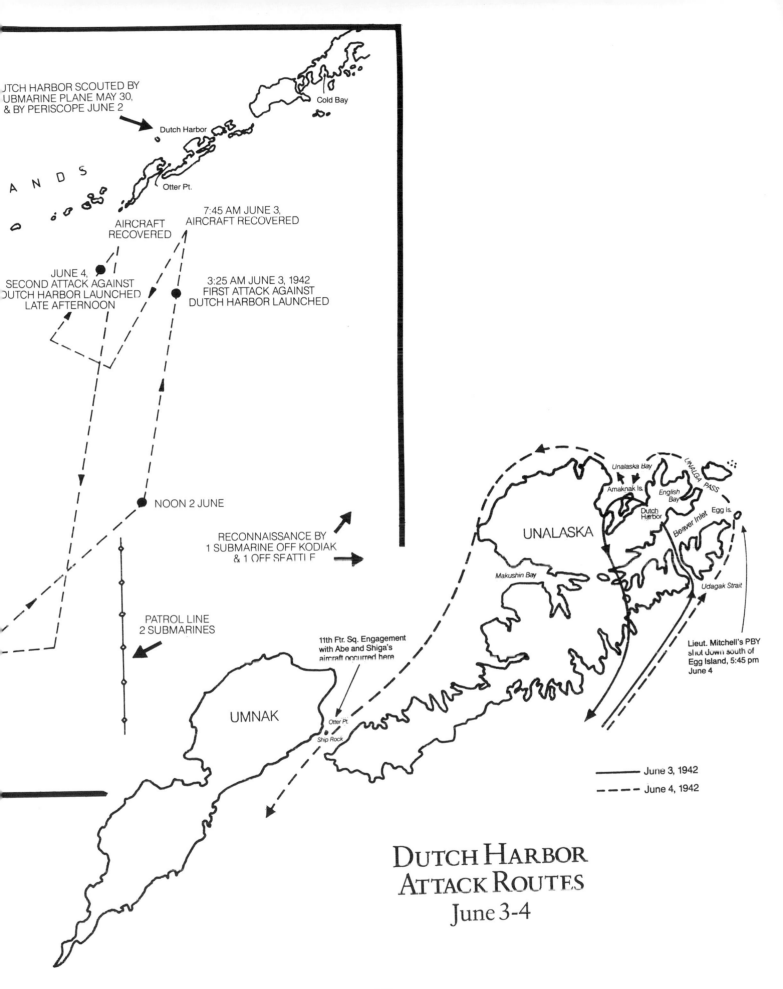

DUTCH HARBOR SCOUTED BY
SUBMARINE PLANE MAY 30,
& BY PERISCOPE JUNE 2

Cold Bay

Dutch Harbor

Otter Pt.

ANDS

AIRCRAFT
RECOVERED

7:45 AM JUNE 3,
AIRCRAFT RECOVERED

JUNE 4,
SECOND ATTACK AGAINST
DUTCH HARBOR LAUNCHED
LATE AFTERNOON

3:25 AM JUNE 3, 1942
FIRST ATTACK AGAINST
DUTCH HARBOR LAUNCHED

NOON 2 JUNE

RECONNAISSANCE BY
1 SUBMARINE OFF KODIAK
& 1 OFF SEATTLE

PATROL LINE
2 SUBMARINES

11th Ftr. Sq. Engagement
with Abe and Shiga's
aircraft occurred here

UMNAK

Otter Pt.

Ship Rock

Unalaska Bay

Amaknak Is.

English Bay

Dutch Harbor

UNALGA PASS

Egg Is.

Beaver Inlet

UNALASKA

Makushin Bay

Udagak Strait

Lieut. Mitchell's PBY
shot down south of
Egg Island, 5:45 pm
June 4

_____ June 3, 1942

_ _ _ _ June 4, 1942

DUTCH HARBOR
ATTACK ROUTES
June 3-4

they were going until they were at sea. When the ship docked at Dutch Harbor late on the evening of June 2, it was dark. The battalion commander requested the disembarkation be delayed until the next day; however, the port commander ordered the ship to be unloaded immediately and cleared from the dock. Otis Boise found out the reason shortly afterwards when a major from another infantry unit arrived to brief the battalion officers that the Japanese were expected to attack Dutch Harbor the next morning. He cautioned: "If you hear the anti-aircraft guns going off around six'clock in the morning, that's not reveille."[5]

Lieutenant Samejima's force, accompanied by the Zeros, was the first to arrived at Dutch Harbor. Lieutenant Yamagami's force arrived ten minutes later, at 5:55 AM. They found clear skies and a ceiling of ten thousand feet. Below, the small, compact base, surrounded on three sides by mountains, was spread out, an inviting if unknown target. The radar operator aboard the *Gillis*, moored alongside the Ballyhoo dock, detected Samejima's first wave of attackers coming in at nine thousand feet and sounded the alarm. It was 5:45 AM. The scream of the air raid siren sent men rushing for their gun positions and for cover. The captain of the *Gillis*, Lieutenant Commander Norman F. Garton, immediately ordered the crew to get the ship underway. The captains of the other vessels in the harbor, the destroyers *King* and *Talbot*, the submarine S-27, the Coast Guard cutter *Onondaga* and the transports *President Fillmore* and *Morlen* joined in the effort to get out of harms way. The only immobile vessel was the old *Northwestern*. All the vessels were still in Unalaska Bay when the Japanese began their attack five minutes later.[6]

The radio operator at Dutch Harbor tapped out a hurried message, "about to be bombed." Admiral Theobald's radio operator picked it up as did the radio operators at Kodiak and Cold Bay. Theobald, sticking to the doctrine of radio silence, did nothing. Colonel Eareckson, at Cold Bay, immediately ordered the P-40 pilots to scramble. Within minutes they were airborne, heading towards the embattled base. To the east, at Otter Point, Major Chennault's P-40 pilots went about their morning business, unaware of what was taking place at Dutch Harbor. The jerry-rigged communications system that had been hastily installed between the Navy base and the forward Army air field had failed.[7]

Dean Freiday was one of the Navy photographers who had been sent to various vantage points overlooking Dutch Harbor to record the attack. He had moved to an Army position on Sheep Ranch Hill, overlooking Dutch Harbor. After the early morning alert, he had gone back to sleep. He was awakened by the drone of aircraft engines. He and the Army troops looked up to see Samejima's bombers coming in over the far end of Unalaska Valley. "Just as everyone had assumed that they were a patrol from Otter Point," Freiday later recalled, "the first plane peeled off toward Fort Mears . . . bugles sounded up and down Unalaska Valley; and men scurried into trenches and foxholes." The anti-aircraft artillery battery on nearby Battery Hill, behind Unalaska, opened up. After the initial shock of being under attack, Freiday grabbed his camera and began taking pictures.[8]

To Navy weatherman Paul Carrigan the first wave of four Kates appeared as distant specks as they flew northwest past Pyramid Peak. Slowly, the perfect diamond formation took on the shape of "black crosses against a

Fort Mears was hit the hardest during the Japanese attack. The photograph, one of a series, was taken from near the Army water tank on the hill behind the garrison during the first day attack. Twenty-five of the thirty-five men killed on the ground during the attack died when the bombs exploded in the densely packed area. The greatest material loss, a radar set, occurred at Fort Mears. USN photo

The photograph was taken by the Japanese. Two Kate horizontal bombers fly formation in the foreground while Fort Mears burns below. Japanese photo via Larry Golden

Another closer, lower-level view of Dutch Harbor that was taken by the Japanese. The seaplane ramp can seen in the lower right hand corner, while a Kate bomber is barely visible in the upper right hand corner. The photographs and the information that the pilots brought back allowed the next day's attack to be planned with more precision.
Japanese photo via Larry Golden

The Dutch Harbor Naval Operating Base in March 1942. One of the original North American Commercial buildings is in the foreground. Navy barracks are behind it. The barracks ship Northwestern *can be seen at the far right. Behind it is the reinforced concrete power house, and to the left of the power house is "Power House Hill." The area, which contained an antenna field, a camouflaged fuel storage area and barracks, was hard hit during first day attack. An Army and a Marine private and Navy sailor were killed. The hill was renamed "Suicide Hill." During the second day attack, the* Northwestern *was hit and the adjacent warehouse (long building next to the ship's stern) was set afire by the burning ship.* USN photo

A Navy photographer took the photograph of one of the 550-pound bombs exploding near the antenna field on the slope of "Suicide Hill" from a bomb shelter at the seaplane ramp. The uncompleted PBY hangar and a SOC-1 Seagull can be seen in the foreground. The Seagull was removed before the next day's attack.
USN photo via AAHM

One of the bombs dropped in the "Suicide Hill" area destroyed a truck and killed its Army driver. To the left of the truck is one of the shelters that had been built at the direction of Commander Updegraff and his deputy, Lieutenant Commander Carson. Thanks to their diligence, many lives were saved. USN photo

The only brick building in the Aleutian Islands, the Navy prewar communications station apartment building, escaped the bombing attack with a near miss. The building, although in bad repair because of cheap construction practices and the ravages of time, still stands.
USN photo

background of grey sky," nine thousand feet above Dutch Harbor, as they headed at two hundred miles per hour towards their target.[9]

The crews of every anti-aircraft gun began blasting away at the bombers. Sixteen bombs came screaming down on Fort Mears. Two landed in the nearby bay. The rest struck home in the congested Army area. Two barracks, and two warehouses were destroyed and eight other structures damaged. Twenty-five men, seventeen from Otis Boise's battalion and eight from the 151st Engineer Combat Regiment died. Twenty-five others were wounded. The men who arrived aboard the *President Fillmore* had not been notified to go to their shelters when the alert came. Fortunately, most of the other 6,282 soldiers at Dutch Harbor had gotten the word and were safely in defensive positions. The only other serious loss was a SCR-271 fixed, long range aircraft warning radar set, intended for Cape Winslow on the north side of Unalaska Island, which was destroyed in the attack.

The bombers continued on north past Mount Ballyhoo. The men at Dutch Harbor fought back. Tracers from the 20mm and 37mm anti-aircraft guns laced the sky and puffs of exploding flack from the three inch guns aboard the ships in the harbor appeared below Samejima's bombers. The Army gunners aboard the *President Fillmore*, who had set their 37mm anti-aircraft guns up on the deck, fired so fast that the cargo ship appeared to be on fire.

The first wave was followed by a second wave of three Kates, which appeared over Mount Ballyhoo from the north, then circled around to the west, turned north and aimed for the perfectly aligned barracks at Fort Mears. In the confusion of battle and not knowing the layout of their target, the bomber pilots overshot their mark, and the six bombs that were observed being dropped landed in an open area beyond the barracks. One Army man was killed; no other damage was done.

Three more Kates arrived for a third attack, this time heading on a southwesterly course across Unalaska Bay toward the prewar Navy radio stations. A Navy photographer pointed his camera skyward and snapped a photograph of the perfectly aligned formation of three Kates. High above, Lieutenant Samejima and the other two pilots looked down at the tall radio antennas and the nearby communications building below. They and the wooden fuel storage tanks were the only military facilities that the Japanese had any certain knowledge of that day. One bomb exploded on the hard ground near the station, shattering widows, peppering the brick front of the station apartment building with fragments and severing a transmitter antenna. Another bomb destroyed a nearby Quonset Hut. A third bomb hit a trench shelter, killing George P. Deal, a Siems-Drake worker and the only civilian to die in the Dutch Harbor attacks. The other bombs exploded harmlessly in the vacant soft ground near the radio station.

The pilots of the fourth and final wave of Kates aimed for the Naval facilities on Power House Hill, which contained the radio antenna of the reception station, camouflaged wooden fuel tanks, and Navy barracks. Again, they overshot their targets. One bomb came crashing down near a Navy pill box, killing one man, who was outside, and wounding another who was standing just inside the shelter. A second bomb exploded on the side of a road. It destroyed an Army one-and-a-half ton truck and killed its driver. Another bomb collapsed a trench on a Marine private, Andy Corbin. He was among the first of the few Marines who served in the Aleutians to die in action. The other bombs exploded harmlessly in the soft, vacant muskeg. Power House Hill was later renamed Suicide Hill because of the casualties that occurred there. It could have been worse, except that the Navy men had taken shelter.[10]

While Kate pilots made their circling attacks, the Zero pilots had been making low level strafing runs against anti-aircraft artillery positions and other targets of opportunity. Thomas P. O'Neal, a young Army enlisted man who had arrived at Dutch Harbor in August 1941 with the 206th Coastal Artillery Regiment, Arkansas National Guard, was manning an observation position at the east end of Unalaska Valley when the first wave of Zeros came roaring in at low level. He had just relieved another man when he heard the roar of an aircraft engine and then the rattle of machine gun fire. Suddenly he realized he was being fired at. The Zero pilot came in so low that he could not depress his fire and the machine gun slugs passed over O'Neal's head. Remembering forty years later, O'Neal had seen the plane pass "so close I could plainly see the pilot in the cockpit with what appeared to be a smile on his face." O'Neal grabbed his rifle and began firing at the Zero, which by then was out of range. Elsewhere, his unit's 37mm anti-aircraft guns had gone into action.[11]

Two Zero pilots spotted Ensign Jack Litsey's PBY on the water near the ramp to the parking area. The VP-41 aviator had been warming up the engines on his PBY in preparation for making a mail run to Kodiak when the first Japanese aircraft arrived overhead. His and Marshall Freerks' Catalina crews were the only ones present at Dutch Harbor that morning. The other crews had taken their Catalinas out of harm's way to nearby coves. Freerks and his crew had just returned and were beginning to rest from a grueling overnight patrol.

Litsey and his copilot, reacting to the Japanese attack, had pushed the throttles full forward and were heading their lumbering PBY across the bay for a takeoff when the Zero pilots struck. As Litsey's radio operator, Martin Zeller, sent out a message that they were under attack, another crew member placed his hand on Zeller's shoulder and leaned forward. A machine gun bullet from one of the attacking Zeros tore through the observers hand and into the radioman's back, killing him instantly. Other machine gun and cannon slugs ripped into the PBY. Aviation Machinists Mate Second Class Rolland Geller died, and a passenger, Aviation Machinists Mate Third Class Bert Brown was seriously wounded. Litsey and his copilot, Aviation Pilot First Class Merlyn B. Dawson, ran the flaming PBY up onto the sand spit outside the harbor. Brown dived through an open blister hatch into the water and drowned. Dawson was reported missing in action. The others made it to safety before the Catalina blew up. The two Zero pilots returned to strafing the Army and Navy facilities at Dutch Harbor.[12]

By 6:35 AM, the Kate bomber pilots had completed their work. Lieutenants Samejima and Yamagami gathered their forces, and headed southeast across the island, then west along the coast before turning south. Admiral Kakuta had brought his carrier to within 130 miles of Dutch Harbor. Lieutenant Kobyashi had departed the scene shortly before with his Zeros. One of the Kate crews spotted Commander Craig's destroyers in Makushin Bay in the far distance as the Japanese flew south across the mountains. The news was reported to Admiral Kakuta, who decided to launch another attack with the *Junyo's* aircraft.[13]

Lieutenants Samejima and Yamagami and their men continued on in steadily deteriorating weather. It was impossible to keep in formation, and the pilots broke up into smaller groups. Their fuel indicators steadily moved toward the empty mark. Below, the cold, bleak and grey North Pacific waters heaved. Admiral Kakuta's fleet maintained radio silence. The navigators aboard the Kates had to find the carriers by dead reckoning. The radio operators could only stare at their silent sets and the grey skies and uninviting waters below. Suddenly, the carriers appeared out of the mist, and one by one the Kate bombers slammed onto the carrier deck and came to an abrupt halt as their arresting hooks connected with the cables across the deck. By 7:45 AM all the pilots and their crews had arrived safely home.[14]

The Search

Lieutenant Jean C. Cusick and his eight man VP-41 crew had taken off from Otter Point at 3:00 AM June 3 on a patrol over the North Pacific. Shortly before 4:47 AM, Lieutenant Shiga's Zero pilots, who were returning to the *Junyo*, spotted the lumbering PBY as it headed through the heavy overcast, squalls and light rain near

Admiral Kakuta's carrier task force. Suddenly, the Catalina's right engine went dead, the wing caught fire and the radio was destroyed under the hail of machine gun and cannon fire. A tracer bullet ripped through Cusick's arm. The attack caught the PBY crew by surprise. Several other Zero pilots made passes at the crippled amphibian as Cusick and Aviation Pilot First Class Clark W. Morrison brought the PBY down for a landing in the choppy sea. The crew did not have time to secure the bow and tunnel hatches in the excitement of the attack, and the burning Catalina immediately began sinking as water poured through the openings.

Ensign M. Wylie Hunt, the navigator, launched a small two man raft and assisted Cusick into it. Two other crew members, Carl Creamer and Joe Brown, joined them. The plane captain, Aircraft Machinist Mate Second Class Burdette B. Siler, Morrison, and the rest of the crew deployed the seven man raft. It was riddled with bullet holes. Morrison and Siler swam over to where Hunt and the three others were. After holding on to the side of the overcrowded raft for a few minutes, Siler swam back to the larger raft and attempted to make it seaworthy. Hunt and his group drifted away. Siler and the others were never seen again. Morrison hung on to the side of the bobbing raft for about an hour, before he was overcome by the cold, icy waters. Cusick, weakened by his wound, died shortly afterward. Hunt, Creamer and Brown continued to drift alone, waiting to die.[15]

As the three lonely men awaited their fate, Lieutenant Lucius D. Campbell and his crew from VP-42 continued to search for the Japanese. They had taken off from near the old whaling station on Akutan Island in the afternoon to look for the overdue Cusick and the Japanese. The radar operator first sighted the Japanese ships on his scope. Shortly afterward, the blip of a fast approaching plane appeared on the scope. Campbell and his crew next sighted the Japanese carriers and their escorts through a patch in the fog as Admiral Kakuta was preparing to recover his aircraft from the aborted second raid of the day. The radio operator tapped out a position report, giving the location, disposition, course and speed of the Japanese ships below. Unfortunately, the transmission that reached Dutch Harbor was garbled. Campbell and his crew had no way of knowing that their message had not been received. Those at Dutch Harbor and elsewhere remained in the dark as to the location of the Japanese fleet that had launched the attack that morning.

After getting the message off, Campbell headed his PBY for the nearest cloud cover. They never made it. Two of Admiral Kakuta's Zero pilots, on combat air patrol, came slashing in. The attack wounded a gunner, cut the control cables to the rudder, damaged the ailerons, punctured the gas tanks and made a sieve of the rest of the amphibian. Despite the fact Campbell and his copilot had no rudder control and limited control of the ailerons, they were able, through skill and determination, to maintain control over the lumbering aircraft. Somehow they managed to evade the Japanese fighters and continued to trail the ships below. After making four more visual contacts to gain additional information, Campbell decided to turn and head for their temporary base at Akutan Harbor. There was less than a half hour of fuel left in the leaking gasoline tanks.

Campbell and his crew made it to within forty miles of Akutan Island before the engines quit, out of gas. Again he and his copilot performed miracles, letting down from five thousand feet through a solid overcast on instruments to make a dead stick landing on the cold grey seas. For the next forty-five minutes Campbell and his crew fought to keep the PBY afloat. Water continued to pour in through the holes in the hull despite efforts to plug them with rags. Bailing efforts could not keep ahead of the rising water and the stricken Catalina slowly settled into the seas. The radio operator managed to repair his radio, enough to send off an SOS and another Japanese position report.

The radio operator aboard the Coast Guard Cutter *Nemaha* received the SOS signal. The cutter arrived in time to rescue Lieutenant Campbell and his men from the sinking PBY. The skipper of the cutter and Campbell assumed that Dutch Harbor had received the Japanese position reports, and for the next three days the *Nemaha* proceeded about her business of patrolling her assigned area while maintaining radio silence. It was not until the cutter put into Sand Point that Campbell learned that both of his radio transmissions had been garbled.[16]

Elsewhere, the PBY crews of VP-41 and VP-42 continued to search in their assigned sectors. Lieutenant Kirmsie's crew from VP-41 spotted a flight of Zeros. Kirmsie managed to duck into a cloud and evade the fighters. Ensign William R. Doerr from VP-41 was returning to Umnak Island when he spotted a Zero. He immediately headed into a cloud, but when his Catalina emerged shortly afterward, the crew was shocked to see that they were flying formation with the enemy fighter. Recovering, the gunners blasted away at the Zero, whose pilot was equally surprised. Doerr and his crew later reported that the Zero had been hit and was last seen heading toward the sea trailing smoke. However, post war records failed to substantiate the claim. It had been a hard day for Patrol Air Wing Four. Three Catalinas had been lost, and worse, eight men had died, one was missing in action and three others were prisoners of war; and the worst was yet to come.[17]

So far the Eleventh Air Force had not been bloodied. Captain Owen Meals had led six B-26s from Umnak on a fruitless search for the Japanese. On landing, one of the wheels of his bomber slid off the wet steel runway matting into the mud. The landing gear collapsed, and a torpedo which had been slung under the Marauder broke free and skidded down the runway. Fortunately, it did not explode. Meals and his crew climbed unharmed from the bomber.[18] Those at Dutch Harbor braced themselves for another attack. Thomas O'Neal recalled:

> It's hard to remember after forty years all the thoughts that we had that day, but I recall we all knew that was only the first attack and there would be more to follow. I know I felt they would be back and the next time it would not only be with aircraft but with ground troops. If they came with ground forces, I felt they would have the force to do the job and our goose would be cooked. There was little doubt in most of our minds that we would be out-numbered, out-gunned and it had been proven that day they had control of the sky.[19]

At 10:45 AM, the pilots of the second attack of the day began taking off from the carriers. Admiral Kakuta and Commander Okumiya decided to commit the bulk of their forces against the destroyers sighted earlier in Makushin Bay. By 11:45 AM the last of the fifteen Kates, seventeen Vals and fifteen Zeros had cleared the carrier decks and were heading northward. The admiral had also decided to launch the four Nakajima E8N2 Dave two-seat reconnaissance float planes from his two cruisers on a scouting mission.

The carrier pilots encountered increasingly deteriorating weather and decided to turn back after flying half way to their target. The Dave pilots continue on. Two headed for the western end of Unalaska Island.[20] They ran into a patrol of P-40s from the 11th Fighter Squadron. Lieutenant John B. Murphy and his wing man, Lieutenant Jacob Dixon, were the first to spot the two Daves. They pulled out of the formation and headed for the surprised Japanese. Murphy pressed down on the gun button on his control stick and a short burst of fifty caliber machine gun slugs tore into one of the Daves. It crashed into the water off the end of the runway at Otter Point. The pilot of the other Dave escaped into a cloud before the American pilots had a chance to intercept him. Murphy and Dixon had drawn the first Japanese blood of the day. They were given joint credit for shooting the Dave down in full view of the personnel on the airfield below.[21]

Letters to Write

Admiral Kakuta moved his carrier task force to within 100 miles to recover his aircraft. By late afternoon all except the Dave, downed by Murphy and Dixon, and another cruiser scout plane which cracked up on landing on the sea, had made it safely back. The crew of the scout plane was picked up from the ocean. Visibility remained poor and Kakuta's weather officer predicted the weather at Dutch Harbor would be even worse the next day. The admiral turned his task force southwest and then turned northwest in order to be in position the next day to conduct the planned air attack against what was believed to be military installations on Adak Islands. An air reconnaissance was also planned for Atka Island.

By sunrise on the morning of June 4, Admiral Kakuta's carrier force had reached a point 250 miles southeast of Adak. By then the wind velocity had increased from twenty-five to thirty knots. Because of the sea conditions, the speed of the ships had been reduced to nine knots. The admiral and his staff realized that they would not be able to reach the launch point by the scheduled time. Even if they did, the heaving seas and high winds would make the launch and recovery of the aircraft a hazardous undertaking. However, the weather to the east had cleared and Dutch Harbor offered a better option. Kakuta decided to make a ninety degree course change and head northeast for another attack.[22]

By 11:54 AM on the 4th, Admiral Kakuta's carriers had approached close enough to their launch point southwest of Dutch Harbor for two Kates to be flown off from the *Ryujo* on a weather reconnaissance mission. They returned at 2:50 PM. A second reconnaissance mission consisting of two Kates under the leadership of Lieutenant Samejima was dispatched from the *Ryujo* at 2:44 PM. After finding the weather conditions over Dutch Harbor marginal, they returned to their carrier, landing at 6:05 PM. Admiral Kakuta, after considering the pros and cons, decided to go ahead with the attack. The aircrews were chosen with care. Only the most experienced were selected. The eleven Zeroes, nine Kates and eleven Vals began rumbling down the decks of the *Junyo* and *Ryujo* as Lieutenant Samejima and his flight crew were returning.[23]

This time, the Japanese had considerably more knowledge of the military installations from photographs taken the previous day and the reconnaissance missions. They came in from the southwest, paralleled the east coast of Unalaska, then turned northwest across Beaver Inlet, flew over Unalga Pass, before heading southwest towards their target. Ensign Albert E. Mitchell, VP-42, and his crew were the first to sight the approaching Japanese, who also saw the lumbering PBY. Mitchell, who had been ordered to fly the mail in his mechanically unsound PBY from Cold Bay to Dutch Harbor, arrived just in time to be pounced on by Kobayashi's fighter pilots. They went in for the kill. Army observers on Fisherman's Point near English Bay watched helplessly as the Catalina hit the waters to the south, off Egg Island, in flames. Several survivors crawled into a raft, only to be strafed

Lieutenant Zenji Abe, leader of the dive bomber attack on Dutch Harbor, in the hangar deck of the Junyo. *He survived the war and retired as a colonel in the Japanese Self Defense Force.* Abe collection

by the Zero pilots. All died.[24]

The observers on Fisherman's Point noted the time, 5:37 PM, as the Japanese continued across Beaver Inlet. Other Army observation posts at Priest's Rock and Eider Point submitted reports at 5:45 PM on the approaching Japanese. At 5:52 PM, the observation post on the top of Mount Ballyhoo called in to say that the Japanese were circling overhead. Seven of the Zeros and Lieutenant Abe's dive bombers headed south, close to the west slope of Mount Ballyhoo, before passing out of sight through the mist in the clouds above.[25]

The cloud ceiling hung at about six thousand feet. There was no turning back for Abe this time. Admiral Kakuta had been adamant that the more accurate dive bombers carry out their attacks regardless of the weather at Dutch Harbor. He had purposely pointed out that the Kate aircrews had succeeded in striking their targets the previous day. He expected the same of the Val crews. Abe ordered his pilots to follow him in a single file. They arrived over Dutch Harbor to find the base covered with clouds. Abe circled, looking for a hole in the clouds. Seeing one, he tilted the nose of his aircraft in a fifty degree angle and dove towards the hole and the target below. The other Val pilots followed him down, each looking for his assigned target. The time was 5:55 PM; the second attack on Dutch Harbor was on.[26]

The Junyo's dive bomber pilots on the eve of the first day attack on Dutch Harbor.
Abe collection

The anti-aircraft guns opened up as Abe's Vals came plunging down through the hole in the overcast. At between 1,000 and 1,500 feet, the pilots pulled their release handles, and the 550-pound bombs went screaming down. This time the damage done by the more accurate dive bombers was more extensive than the previous days attack. The four new steel fuel oil tanks, which had been filled three days prior, erupted in flames as their 22,000 barrels of fuel burned out of control. An adjacent steel diesel fuel tank was also hit. Its contents of 15,102 barrels were consumed in flames. The heavy clouds of smoke rising from the burning fuel gave the impression of total destruction.

Another 550-pound bomb clanged into the forward port side deck of the *Northwestern*, punched through and exploded, setting it and an adjacent warehouse on fire. The 336-foot ship survived the attack largely due to the efforts of Marine Major C.P. Groves and Siems-Drake Fire Chief Harold J. Davis, who directed the effort to bring the fire under control. Three days later the *Northwestern's* boilers were back in commission, supplying steam to the base.[27] Later, the Navy, intending to send her to Seattle to be cut up for scrap, had the *Northwestern* towed to an anchorage in Captains Bay. Since the project was given a low priority, the old ship remained anchored in the bay until a storm cast her loose. She drifted to the head of the bay where she foundered. The remains of the *Northwestern* are still visible today.[28]

Three of the dive bomber pilots headed for the Naval Air Station pier. One bomb hit the sea side of the southeast corner of the pier, splintering the deck and shearing off piling without exploding. The other two bombs exploded harmlessly in the water. Another Val pilot, apparently disoriented from the main attack on the military facilities at Dutch Harbor, dropped his bomb on the Bureau of Indian Affairs hospital at Unalaska. The nurses' wing was demolished. Fortunately it was empty and no one was hurt.

The anti-aircraft guns blazed away in defiance at Abe's bombers and the Zero fighters that were making strafing attacks. Two Zero pilots went after the Army transport, *Fillmore*, at the end of Ballyhoo spit. The ship's gunners lashed out at their tormentors, forcing them to switch their attack on the nearby *Gillis*. The seaplane tender gunners opened with everything they had including the three inch deck gun. Altogether, the *Gillis'* gunners expended seventy five rounds of three inch and two thousand rounds of twenty millimeter cannon and fifty caliber machine gun rounds at the attackers, claiming one, unconfirmed, shot down.

Lieutenant Yamagami's Kates next went into the attack as Abe's dive bombers withdrew and the Zero pilots continued their strafing attacks against the anti-aircraft positions. The first flight was sighted at 6:21 PM, approaching from the northeast, flying high over the broken clouds and the smoke pouring from fuel storage tanks hit by Abe's dive bombers. They first headed for the fuel tanks on Power House Hill. The bombs missed their target. One, however, made a direct hit on a 37mm anti-aircraft gun position on the slopes of Mount Ballyhoo, overlooking the base. Two Army gunners died in the explosion and two others were seriously injured. The remaining dazed and slightly wounded members of the crew were dug out of the collapsed position. The Kate pilot continued on, dropping six bombs, apparently intended for the Naval Air Station. Five landed in the harbor between the station and the

This photo was taken from the shore bluff near the water inlet on Water Supply Lake shortly after Abe's pilots completed their dive bombing attacks against the fuel storage tanks. The old communications station and the apartment building can be seen outlined by the smoke from the burning fuel.

This photograph, one of a series, was taken from the small hill with the water tower near the Navy base. It shows one of Abe's dive bombers pulling out of a dive after dropping a 550-pound bomb on the fuel tank farm. One of the antennas from the old Navy radio station can be seen in the foreground. Note the stacked construction material and the personnel in defensive positions. USN photo

A Navy photographer snapped a series of photographs of Abe's dive bombers attacking the Navy base and dock area from a vantage point on the slope of Mount Ballyhoo above the seaplane ramp. In the first, a 550-pound explodes harmlessly on the slopes of Power House Hill. Smoke from anti-aircraft fire can be seen in the distance. The darker smoke to the left is from remnants of the fires at Fort Mears. The second photograph shows the near misses of the dock area. The third was taken shortly after the Northwestern was hit. The fourth shows the fire spreading to the nearby warehouse. The fuel tanks burn in the distance. USN photos

One of Abe's dive bomber pilots, according to Henry Swanson, an old Aleutian hand, was attempting to avoid antiaircraft fire when he inadvertently dropped his bomb on Bureau of Indian Affairs hospital in Unalaska. It was the only one to strike the civilian community. Fortunately, no was harmed. Martha Tutiakoff, a worker there, and the other women of Unalaska helped care for the wounded at Dutch Harbor until they could be evacuated to Seattle. USN photo

The Northwestern stranded (according to a postcard caption) at low tide on Eagle River Flats near Anchorage prior to the war. The former passenger and freight ship was launched in 1889 and served with the Alaska Steamship Company from 1906 to 1937, when she was retired due to old age. She was scheduled to be broken up for scrap at Seattle when the Seims-Drake-Puget-Sound, a joint venture of three construction firms, bought her for use as a barracks ship and power plant for their construction project at Dutch Harbor. It was a common practice. Rather than build temporary housing facilities, construction companies brought in old ships. The City of Baltimore and the Chesapeake Bay provided housing at Sitka while the Yale served the same purpose at Kodiak. At Dutch Harbor, the beach was dug away, the Northwestern was then pulled into the cavity and a berm of gravel was dumped on the outboard side to hold her firmly in place. She was capable of accommodating 280 workers and supplying power with her 200kw generator. Paul L. Earl collection

Another view of the burning Northwestern. The seaplane ramp and the lower slopes of Mount Ballyhoo can be seen in the distance. The Japanese, following their attack, publicly announced that they had destroyed a large transport, set afire a group of fuel tanks, shot down fourteen aircraft, and destroyed a base from which attacks could have been launched against them. The news was carried in the June 18, 1942 edition of the Anchorage Daily Times. USN photo

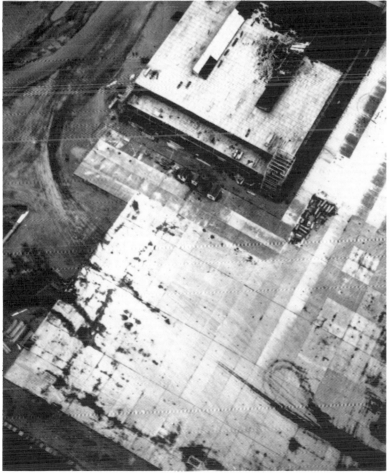

A number of bombs, dropped by the Kate pilots and apparently intended for the Naval air facilities, landed in the harbor instead. A ship, probably the Gillis, *can be seen in the distance.* USN photo

Another bomb, probably a 150-pounder by the amount of damage it inflicted, exploded on the roof of the uncompleted seaplane hangar. USN photo

One of the Navy's anti-aircraft positions on the slopes of Mount Ballyhoo took a direct hit from a bomb dropped by a Kate horizontal bomber. The commander of the battery of 20mm guns, Lieut Kenneth Greiner and three of his men were killed. The other nearby gun crews continued to fire at their attackers. The road that ran near the position was later named in honor of Lieutenant Greiner. USN photo

sandspit. Another blew a fifty-foot diameter hole in the roof of the uncompleted PBY hangar, showering debris and fragments on Lieutenant Charles Perkins' PBY, which had been pulled in for repair after being damaged in an encounter with Admiral Kakuta's force earlier that day. Other than torn fabric on the wing and tail control surfaces and several holes in the hull, the Catalina emerged from the blast intact. The Kate pilots turned west over the harbor and disappeared over Mount Ballyhoo, flying on a course that took them along the north coast of Unalaska Island.

The next flight of five Kates was sighted four minutes after the first. It made its approach from the northwest, delivering an attack against the ammunition storage area on the south slope of Mount Ballyhoo. Ten bombs were dropped. Nine exploded harmlessly on the open ground along the access road. One made a direct hit on a Navy 20mm anti-aircraft gun position, killing the battery officer, Lieutenant Kenneth Greiner and three of the gun's crew. A nearby road was later named after the slain officer.

It was the last in the succession of attacks that the Dutch Harbor personnel had endured during the two day period. Reports from various observation points continued to come in as the Japanese flyers regrouped for their flight back to the carriers. The final report came in at 7:55PM from Mount Ballyhoo. The last of the Japanese planes could be seen disappearing south across the middle of Unalaska Island.[29]

Lieutenant Abe, according to prearranged plans, led his eleven Vals westward at 3,300 feet above the Bering Sea. They flew along the north coast of Unalaska to a rendezvous with their Zero escorts from the *Junyo* over Ship Rock, a prominent landmark, rising out of the waters of Umnak Pass, about three miles east of the Otter Point airbase. The Japanese had code named the place, appro-

priately enough, "Zero West." As he approached the area, Abe sighted what he thought were the Zeros high above his Vals. Instead, they were Chennault's P-40s. Lieutenant Shiga's Zeros arrived about the same time. The Japanese were still unaware that the Americans had built an air base at Otter Point.[30]

Because of the faulty communications link with Dutch Harbor, the men at Otter Point were still in the dark. Nevertheless, the base had been in an high state of alert since the previous day. The men were positive that the Japanese were going to land troops on the island. There were few defenses. The large guns had not been set up. The pilots of the 11th Fighter Squadron provided the only real defense. Jack Chennault had sent part of his P-40s up on a combat air patrol. Others were held in readiness on the ground when the unsuspecting Japanese arrived on the scene. The Zero pilots spotted Capt Jack L. Marks' B-17B returning to Otter Point and went after it. Marks yelled that he was being attacked and took evasive action. Chennault's airborne pilots bore in against the surprised Japanese while the others on the ground took off and climbed towards the air battle that was developing in clear view of the ground personnel below.

Altogether, eight P-40s were committed to the swirling dogfight. Lieutenants Lester M. Chancellor, James A. Dale and Herbert C. White each singled out one of Abe's Vals. Two tumbled out of the sky into the waters below. Two others were so severely damaged they could not make it back to their carrier. Lieutenant John J. Cape Jr. went after one of the Zeros, blasting it out of the skies. While he was concentrating on his prey, another Zero pilot slipped in behind the young lieutenant, who made the mistake of trying to dog fight with his more agile foe.[31] Sergeant John R. Melter, from his vantage point in the 11th Fighter Squadron's maintenance area, watched as John Cape's P-40 came "straight down out of a cloud and went

The airbase at Otter Point was later renamed Cape Field. The aerial photograph showing a winter scene was taken after the field had been expanded from one to three runways. Ship Rock, which Lieutenant Abe use as an assembly point for his dive bombers, can be seen in the upper right corner.
AAF photo

straight into the bay."[32] Lieutenant Cape's fighter slipped beneath the waves without a trace. Those in authority, in keeping with the tradition of honoring their fallen air heros, named the airbase at Otter Point in his honor.

Another of Lieutenant Shiga's Zero pilots went after Lieutenant Winfield E. McIntyre. The young pilot did not stand a chance against the more maneuverable Zero, whose pilot shattered the heavier and less agile P-40 with cannon and machine gun fire. McIntyre managed to dive away from his attacker and head for land, where he survived a high speed crash landing. The crew of a nearby PBY spotted McIntyre on a beach waving his parachute, landed and sent a rubber boat ashore. Within hours the lieutenant was safely back at the airbase being treated for a bad gash on his forehead and shock.

The whole action had lasted only a few minutes and had earned the 11th Fighter Squadron the title of "The Aleutian Tigers." General Buckner formally praised Chennault and his men, stating: "The enemy's next move is unknown, but whatever it is I am sure that each of you will meet it with the same firm resolution and unflinching devotion to duty which you have already displayed."[33]

Shortly afterwards, one of the squadron's enlisted men, Edward Lange, with assistance from Gerlad Webber, designed a squadron emblem, which featured a Bengal tiger. The emblem was painted on the noses of the P-40s, thereby insuring a visual immortality for the 11th Fighter Squadron.[34]

Abe, his own airplane riddled with some twenty bullet holes to include a large one in the wing and a damaged hydraulic system, led the surviving members of his squadron south towards the *Junyo*. The pilots of the two damaged Vals, with all hope lost of reaching the *Junyo*, shouted "Banzai to the Emperor" as they headed for the cold waters of the North Pacific below. After a harrowing experience landing his Val, Abe reported his losses to his superiors and went below to write letters of condolences to the next of kin of his fallen air warriors.[35]

For Abe and the rest, the return flight back to their carriers had been fought with the same gut wrenching feelings of the previous day as they groped their way through terrible Aleutian weather towards the safety of their carriers, heaving about in the swells of the North Pacific. Lieutenant Abe lost yet another of his Vals, when petty officer Okada and his navigator Sugie, hopelessly lost, disappeared. Radio operators at Dutch Harbor listened as they called several times, reporting that their dive bomber was running out of fuel and asking for directions.[36]

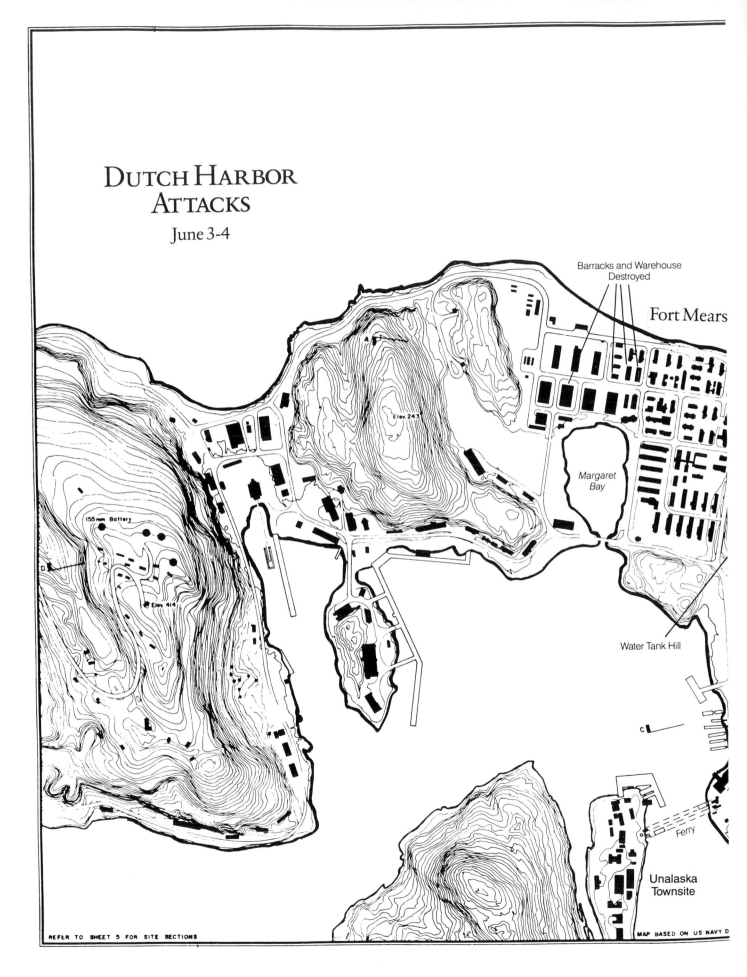

DUTCH HARBOR
ATTACKS
June 3-4

Barracks and Warehouse Destroyed

Fort Mears

Elev. 243

155mm Battery

D

Elev. 414

Margaret Bay

Water Tank Hill

C

Ferry

Unalaska Townsite

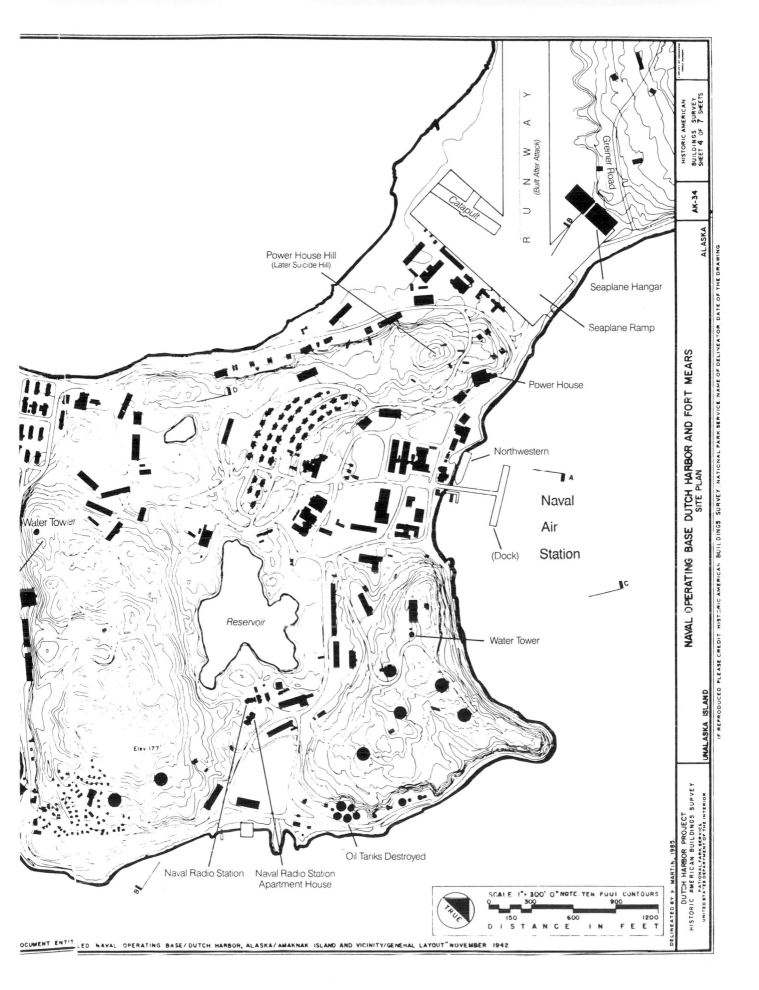

Power House Hill
(Later Suicide Hill)

Catapult

R U N W A Y
(Built After Attack)

Greiner Road

Seaplane Hangar

Seaplane Ramp

Power House

Northwestern

Naval

Air

(Dock)   Station

Water Tower

Reservoir

Water Tower

Elev 177'

Oil Tanks Destroyed

Naval Radio Station   Naval Radio Station
Apartment House

SCALE 1" = 300' 0" NOTE: TEN FOOT CONTOURS
0   300   900
150   600   1200
D I S T A N C E   I N   F E E T

TRUE

DUTCH HARBOR PROJECT
HISTORIC AMERICAN BUILDINGS SURVEY
NATIONAL PARK SERVICE
UNITED STATES DEPARTMENT OF THE INTERIOR

NAVAL OPERATING BASE DUTCH HARBOR AND FORT MEARS
SITE PLAN

UNALASKA ISLAND   ALASKA

AK-34

HISTORIC AMERICAN
BUILDINGS SURVEY
SHEET 4 OF 7 SHEETS

IF REPRODUCED PLEASE CREDIT HISTORIC AMERICAN BUILDINGS SURVEY, NATIONAL PARK SERVICE, NATIONAL PARK SERVICE, NAME OF DELINEATOR, DATE OF THE DRAWING

DELINEATED BY P. MARTIN, 1985.

DOCUMENT ENTITLED "NAVAL OPERATING BASE/DUTCH HARBOR, ALASKA/AMAKNAK ISLAND AND VICINITY/GENERAL LAYOUT" NOVEMBER 1942

Those aboard the *Junyo* heard the calls for help and broke radio silence in an attempt to guide the lost crew back to safety. However, the radio receiver aboard the dive bomber had been apparently damaged in the tangle with Chennault's fighters. Okada and Sugie disappeared somewhere over the North Pacific without a trace, a common experience in the years ahead for those American, Canadian and Japanese who fought above the Aleutians.[37]

Lieutenant Shiga's Zero pilots, after disengaging from the dog fight with the 11th Fighter Squadron pilots over Umnak Pass, headed for the *Junyo*. On the way back, they encountered the seaplane tender *Williamson* which had been searching for one of the lost PBYs south of Umnak. As the Zero pilots began to make their pass at the *Williamson*, one of Commander Lake's S boats popped to the surface between them and the seaplane tender. The Zero pilots went after the submarine, whose commander promptly ordered a crash dive. The Japanese then turned their attention on the *Williamson*, making several strafing attacks, before breaking off contact. The seaplane tender suffered eleven casualties.[38]

Pilots of the 11th Fighter Squadron scrambled from their alert facility at Otter Point. AAF photo

Pilots of the 11th Fighter Squadron as they appeared in a September 28, 1942 Life magazine article. From left to right: Lieuts Francis D. Barnard, Mike J. Buku, Willie E. Brinkman, James A. Dale and Maurice S. Feltz. Life photo

The Brave American Pilot

While the battle swirled around Dutch Harbor and over Umnak Pass, another one had been fought over the cold, bleak North Pacific. Lieutenant Marshall C. Freerks and his VP-42 crew, returning from an overnight patrol, were the first to sight Admiral Kakuta's carrier force as it made the run-in for the second day's attack. The contact was made by radar at 6:50AM while the Japanese were 210 miles southwest of Dutch Harbor and still heading towards Adak. Freerks' radio operator sent a description of the Japanese force to include the local weather, visibility and sea conditions. It set in motion a day-long unsuccessful attempt to sink the carriers and their escorts.

Freerks shadowed Admiral Kakuta's ships for an hour, dodging in and out of the clouds to keep from being detected, before a shortage of fuel forced his return to Otter Point. Before leaving, he attempted to bomb the Japanese, but was driven off by anti-aircraft fire. Fortunately, the weather had prevented the Japanese from launching their Zeros.

Curtiss P-40E Warhawk, 11th Fighter Squadron. The distinctive Bengal tiger's head painted on the nose of the fighter has made it a favored of aircraft modelers. The design was adopted shortly after the Japanese attack on Dutch Harbor. AAF photo

Lieutenant Eugene W. Stockstill, VP-42, and his seven man crew arrived from Cold Bay on the scene shortly after Freerks had departed. By then Admiral Kakuta had managed to launch his combat air patrol. The Zero pilots spotted Stockstill's Catalina and shot it down in flames with the loss of all eight aboard.[39]

Lieutenant Charles Perkins, VP-42, was the next to arrive. Hearing Freerks report, he took off from Dutch Harbor with a torpedo under one wing and bombs under the other and headed for Kakuta's carriers. He was joined shortly afterwards by Ensign James T. Hildebrand from VP-41. By the time Perkins and his crew sighted the carriers at 11:00AM, Admiral Kakuta's force had turned northeast and were within 165 miles of Dutch Harbor, and was preparing to launch the first two weather reconnaissance aircraft.

12:20PM, the bombers became separated in the fog and Eareckson ordered the pilots to land at Otter Point. Captains George Thornborough and Henry S. Taylor, either not hearing the order or ignoring it, continued on. Their perseverance was rewarded. Ahead, the Japanese ships loomed out of the mist.[41]

Both B-26s were armed with torpedoes. The plan for equipping the army bomber with the navy weapon had originated during informal discussions between army and navy officers at Kodiak. Captain Gehres learned of it and passed the idea to Admiral Theobald. Both the admiral and General Butler agreed to give it a try, even though the bombers were not equipped with torpedo directors that were used to compute the proper launch time. The navy experts instructed the B-26s crews on how to launch the sophisticated weapon, being careful to note that the tor-

B-26, 73rd Bombardment Squadron, at Cold Bay with a torpedo slung under its belly in anticipation of the Japanese attack on Dutch Harbor. USN photo

Perkins remained in the vicinity of the Japanese for two hours, sending out position reports to Colonel Eareckson's bomber pilots who were converging on the area. Finally, with fuel running low, Perkins headed towards one of the cruisers with the intention of launching his torpedo. The Japanese put up an intense anti-aircraft barrage, knocking out one of the PBY engines and forcing Perkins to drop his torpedo and bombs and limp back to Dutch Harbor. Ensign Hildebrand and his crew remained in the area and were never heard from again.[40]

While the PBY crews continued to shadow the Japanese, five of Captain Meals' B-26s from the 77th Bombardment Squadron had taken off from Otter Point, heading towards the reported sighting. After a fruitless search, hampered by fog and clouds, Captain Meals called a halt to the effort and returned to Otter Point, landing there at 1:55PM. In the interim, Colonel Eareckson, never the one to remain behind in the rear area when there was action going on, had led five B-26s from the 73rd Bombardment Squadron out of Cold Bay. Departing at

Dean Mendenhall, 73rd Bombardment Squadron, poses beside a torpedo that has been slung under a B-26. The aerial weapon barely cleared the ground. Lieutenant Mendenhall was killed October 16, 1942, during an attack on two Japanese destroyers. Raiford L. Perry photo

pedo had to run for a certain distance through the water in order to arm itself. In the absence of the directors, the Navy provided the bomber pilots with plotting boards with the necessary calculations entered on them. Makeshift adapters were rigged under the bellies of the B-26s to hold the 2,000-pound torpedoes which cleared the ground by six inches.

There were twenty-four torpedoes stored on the *Casco*. Half were sent to Otter Point and the rest retained at Cold Bay. Those destined for Otter Point were hoisted out of the *Casco's* hold, loaded on whaleboats and then taken to PBYs, where they were slung under the wings and flown to the forward base.[42]

The normal method of delivering a torpedo attack required a low-level approach by a trained crew, a hazardous undertaking even under ideal conditions when there were fighters to provide protection. Taylor and Thornborough were about to test the theory without any fighter protection, under marginal weather condition and in the face of intense enemy opposition.

Taylor, who had become separated from Thornborough, burst out of a squall and nearly ran into one of the carriers as his B-26 rushed along under a one hundred foot ceiling. Turning, he headed for one of the Japanese ships. A small anti aircraft round smashed into the nose of his bomber, wounding the bombardier, Lieutenant Vern Peterson. Taylor flew into the safety of the clouds while the copilot pulled Peterson from the exposed nose position. Taylor made another torpedo approach, only to have his bomber hit again. Lining up for yet a third attempt, he and his crew were attacked by several Zero pilots who manage to riddle the bomber further before Taylor could reach the safety of the clouds. Giving up any hope of launching his torpedo, Taylor dropped it and headed his damaged bomber for Otter Point.[43]

Thornborough, in the meantime, had attempted two torpedo runs at the carriers. Each time the Japanese turned them towards the approaching B-26. Frustrated by the narrow frontal target he was being presented with, Thornborough decided to make a conventional diving attack and drop the torpedo like a bomb. The Navy personnel at Cold Bay had instructed him that the weapon had to make a run through the water for the impeller on the nose to make a required number of revolutions to arm the warhead. The captain headed his bomber in a high speed dive towards the *Ryujo* with the hope the wind would turn the impeller and arm the torpedo. Commander Okumiya and the others aboard looked in wonder as the "brave American pilot" bore down on their carrier. They watched as the torpedo separated from the bomber and came hurtling at the carrier only to flash across the deck and into the ocean on the opposite side without exploding.

On arrival back at Cold Bay, Thornborough went to the command post where he found Lieutenant Commander Russell. He gave Russell the first detailed briefing that the Americans had received up until that time on the strength and dispositions of Admiral Kakuta's task force. He then ordered his bomber loaded with 500-pound armor piercing bombs; and despite a lowering ceiling, headed out again to try to find the Japanese.[44] Later that night, the air field control tower operator at Cold Bay heard him report that he was "over the station at 9,000 feet on top." The darkened field by now was covered by the overcast. Efforts to assist him failed and Thornborough disappeared. The body of his radio operator, still strapped to his seat, was found a month later on a beach about 90 miles north of Cold Bay on the Alaska Peninsula. Russell flew in a burial party. The rest of the crew and their bomber were never found. Captain Thornborough was posthumously awarded the Distinguished Service Cross and the airfield at Cold Bay was named in his honor.[45] Russell later remembered him as "brave and intelligent pilot and a good fighting man."[46]

Captain Donald Dunlop next went looking for the elusive Japanese with five B-17Es and the LB-30. The 36th Bombardment Squadron bombers had been moved forward from Kodiak to Cold Bay following the first attack on Dutch Harbor. They searched from 3:45 to 7:45 PM without any success before returning to Cold Bay.

Lieutenant Thomas F. Mansfield, the pilot of the sixth B-17E, late in getting off due to mechanical problems, was still at Cold Bay when Captain Thornborough landed after the unsuccessful torpedo attack. Armed with the latest intelligence on the location of the Japanese, he took off in the late afternoon. While en route to the target, Mansfield was joined by Captain Marks, who had taken off from Otter Point in the B-17B in search of the Japanese.

Together, they went looking for Admiral Kakuta's force, which they found. Marks made his bomb run at 900 feet. His bombardier, Sergeant Hunter dropped a 2,000 and a 1,000 bomb through the overcast. The blast struck the B-17B with a wallop, shaking its crew up. Mansfield, whose B-17E was equipped with radar, elected to use it to drop his bombs. He then informed Marks that he was descending for a bomb damage assessment. After reporting seeing Kakuta's fleet and noting that a cruiser and carrier were burning, Mansfield and his crew disappeared. They were shot down by gunners aboard the *Takao*. One of Mansfield's men survived the crash and was taken prisoner. Marks returned to Otter Point.[47]

Owen Meals was about to lead his B-26s on another search, when Lieutenants Abe and Shiga appeared over Umnak Pass with their Vals and Zeros. "We rolled our planes back into their protective revetments as fast as we could get them there while our fighters took off after the Japs," Meals later recalled. By now, Admiral Kakuta had

Owen "Jack" Meals at the August 1980 Eleventh Air Force reunion at Elmendorf AFB. USAF photo

moved his carriers to a location about 90 miles south of Umnak to recover his aircraft. Shortly after Abe and Shiga had departed, Meals' medium bombers began thundering down the runway at Otter Point, heading towards Captain Marks' last position report. One B-26 with a flat tire never got off the ground and another developed engine trouble and had to turn back. "That," Meals later recalled, "left me with three planes . . . I directed them to fan out to cover as broad an area as possible. We left Umnak at 2030 (8:30 PM), and, while it was still light, we knew that it wouldn't be long before dark."[48]

Twenty-five minutes later Owen Meals crews found Kakuta's task force. He was flying south at three to five hundred feet above the surface of the ocean when:

> . . . all of sudden in front of me I saw the outline of a large vessel. We came onto it so unexpectedly that the Japs must have been as surprised as we were. Poor visibility and the dull light prevented me from identifying the ship's type. And there wasn't much time for that anyway. I flashed the news over the radio to the other two planes piloted by Capt Kenneth W. Northamer and Lieut Brady Golden. I could just make out one of my 26s in the far distance. The other was completely out of sight. We squared away to make our torpedo run. I swept in low and my co-pilot, Lieutenant Patch, released the torpedo. We climbed into the overcast fast to get out of range of the Jap AA fire. But before the ship was gone from our view, my rear gunner saw the torpedo strike the port bow, about a third of the way back in the ship and saw a large explosion as flame and water shot high into the air. The gunners said they also spotted some bursts of AA fire but none of them were very close. By this time Captain Northamer had rushed back after picking up my radio call. It was his plane that I had discerned in the distance. He went in for his torpedo attack and was close enough before pulling away to identify the ship as a Jap cruiser. His torpedo was believed to have exploded in the stern. We returned our own separate ways to Umnak. When we got there we learned that Lieutenant Golden had never located the cruiser.[49]

Dutch Harbor, A Small Affair

The attack marked the end of the Dutch Harbor raid. Compared to other World War II events it had been a small affair, a side show that contributed little to the strategic course of the war. Admiral Yamamoto's scheme to draw Admiral Nimitz's forces away from the main battle area around Midway had failed. Whether or not Admiral Kakuta's carriers would have turned the battle in the Japanese favor if they had been at Midway as some have contended is a matter of historic speculation.

Likewise, the value of the airfield at Otter Point to the air defense of Dutch Harbor was also doubtful. In the final analysis, it had failed in its intended purpose of protecting Dutch Harbor against an air attack. Commander Foster was right. The fields at Cold Bay and Otter Point were simply too far away for adequate point air defense. Without early warning radar it was hopeless. Admiral Kakuta's pilots had hit and departed their targets before General Butler's fighter pilots could react. The fact that the Japanese had lost aircraft was due to their unfortunate decision to use Ship Rock as an assembly point. They would have gotten away with only minimum losses if they had known of the existence of the Otter Point airfield.

General Butler and others believed the discovery of the field had prevented the Japanese from launching more attacks against Dutch Harbor. Contemporary authors also gave much importance to the fact that the airfield stopped the Japanese from advancing farther eastward. A May 1943 *Readers Digest* article , "Report on the Aleutians," declared:

> Little short of a miracle kept the Japs out of Alaska last June. They were not aiming at the Aleutian Islands; they were heading for the North American mainland . . . Between them and the mainland was Dutch Harbor, the only semblance of a fortified port we had in that whole 1000-mile chain . . . Then the incredible happened. From behind them, out of nowhere, they were attacked by American army land-based fighting planes . . . By that slim margin we saved Alaska.[50]

It was good for morale and popular consumption, but it had no basis in fact. Otter Point did play two vital roles. It contributed to the Japanese decision not to temporarily occupy Adak since it was within easy bombing distance of the American field, and it provided a base from which the Americans could launch their counter offensive.[51]

There had been problems. Communications had been poor. It was not geared to the high speed, high volume of traffic required in modern warfare. There was lack of radios, cryptographic equipment and trained operators. Weather forecasting had been inadequate. The air units had been required to operate from marginally prepared

A PBY lands on the air field the Navy built on Amaknak. The field is still in use today as Unalaska Airport.

bases. Logistic support was poor. All these deficiencies were later corrected. Communications were improved, additional weather personnel were obtained and reporting and forecasting detachments were established at key locations, air field support facilities were greatly expanded and a service command activated to provide better logistic support.[52]

Thanks to the prior warning, the foresight of Commander Updegraff and the determination of his chief of staff, Lieutenant Commander Thomas, the damage inflicted at Dutch Harbor was not great. Thirty-five men were killed in the bombing attacks, twenty-five of whom died from the first string of bombs dropped by Samejima's Kates that landed in the congested Fort Mears area. Had the young men been under cover and not scrambling out of their barracks when the attack began, they probably would have lived to tell their grandchildren of their experiences. Twenty-eight men were wounded in the bombing attack.

With the exception of the loss of the SCR-271 radar, the material damages were insignificant. New fuel storage tanks were built and more fuel was brought in to replace the fuel that had been consumed in flames. The loss of the barracks and other structures at Fort Mears did not harm the Army at all, since the garrison was dispersed to defensive positions around Dutch Harbor after the attack. Likewise the loss or damage to the Navy facilities were of no importance and could be easily replaced or repaired. Other than the sentimental impact, the damages sustained by the *Northwestern* did not affect the operations at Dutch Harbor in the least.[53]

The air losses, particularly those of Patrol Wing Four, were more severe. The Eleventh Air Force lost seventeen bomber crew members and one fighter pilot. Two men were wounded. Aircraft losses included a B-17, a B-26 and two P-40s. Another B-26 was damaged. Elsewhere, one of the LB-30s cracked up while trying to land at Kodiak.[54]

Captain Gehres had ordered his PBY crews to remain with Admiral Kakuta's fleet once they had made contact, so that they could continue to call in position reports. This, in true Navy tradition, they did, but not without cost. Admiral Kakuta's Zero pilots shot down four of the six Catalinas that had come within sight of his carriers. Marshall Freerks was lucky. The Japanese pilots had been temporarily prevented from taking off because of the weather. Perkins somehow had managed to stay out of sight of the Japanese. One PBY crew, Hildebrand's, disappeared without a trace. The Japanese fighter pilots accounted for two more PBYs during their attacks on Dutch Harbor. Patrol Air Wing Four lost twenty-three killed in action, three prisoners of war and ten missing in action within a two day period of intense action. Two men were wounded. Six PBYs were lost and one was damaged.[55] After forty-eight hours of continuous operations in terrible weather, the surviving crews were at the limit of their endurance, yet there was more to come.[56]

General Butler in his report to General Arnold two days after the attack on Dutch Harbor noted that Captain Marks had scored a hit on one of Kakuta's ships with a thousand pound bomb, and that Captain Meals had succeeded in torpedoing one of the cruisers.[57] The score was later inflated to include the sinking of a heavy cruiser by Captain Meals, which he denied, attributing it to "some overzealous intelligence reporting outside the squadron."[58]

A World War II documentary film, *Report from the Aleutians*, went even further with the claims. John Huston, the narrator, describes at the beginning of the film how the Japanese were prevented from invading Dutch Harbor by ". . . land based planes from secret airbases," which, "swarmed down, seemingly out of nowhere, to knock out two troop filled transports, three heavy cruisers, two destroyers and one aircraft carrier."[59]

Notwithstanding the American claims, none of the Japanese ships were hit. The Japanese did admit to the loss of one Zero, one Kate, five Vals and two Daves. The crews of the Kate and one of the Daves were saved. Lieutenant Shiga's pilots claimed they shot down six P-40s near Otter Point.[60] Exaggerated claims were not uncommon for both sides during the war. Under the circumstances at Dutch Harbor it was understandable. Communications were poor and it was the first introduction to the confusion of combat for the American crews who had to fly under appalling weather conditions. Many of the Japanese air crews were already hardened combat veterans, but this was also their first experience at northern operations.

Although the losses on both sides could be considered insignificant, the loss of one of the Zeros, flown by Petty Officer Tadayoshi Koga from the *Ryujo*, was to have considerable repercussions. How it was shot down is a matter of conjecture and what it was later used for has been inaccurately represented in a popular history of the Aleutian Campaign.

In one account, championed by Admiral Russell, Aviation Machinist Mate First Class Wheeler H. Rawls aboard Lieutenant Mitchell's PBY managed to hit Koga's Zero with a slug from his fifty caliber machine gun before the Catalina crashed into the sea. According to Brian Garfield in *The Thousand Mile War*, first published in 1969, the bullet severed the indicator line to the oil pressure gauge. When he saw the pressure gauge reading zero, according to Garfield, the alarmed Koga headed towards nearby Akutan Island. Where, according to prearranged plans,

The right landing gear collapsed on the LB-30 as Lieutenant Frederick C. Andrews was landing at Kodiak on June 5. The bomber slid off the runway and into nearby Chiniak Bay. Incredibly, no one was hurt. Walter Szczyrbek collection

he was to land his fighter, and after destroying it, walk to the beach where he could be picked up by one of Admiral Yamasaki's submarines. A submarine had been stationed off the island to recover downed aircrews. Koga made it to the designated landing area on the south coast of the island. Looking down he saw what must have appeared to him a grassy field. Apparently not seeing the glint of water beneath the tall blades of muskeg grass, he lowered his landing gear and proceeded to land. The landing gear dug into the marshy bog, and Koga's Zero flipped over on its back, breaking the young pilot's neck.[61]

According to Kunio Yamigada, the Japanese author of the book *Zerosen Monyu* (Zero Fighter in Flames), published in 1984, Koga's Zero was damaged by ground fire while strafing two PBYs at Dutch Harbor. With the exception of Perkins' damaged amphibian, there were no PBYs at harbor at the time. Captain Gehres had ordered the dispersal of his aircraft out of the Dutch Harbor area in anticipation of the attack. However, the damaging of Koga's fighter by ground fire seems the most plausible account, particularly in view of the timing of the attack on Mitchell's PBY, which occurred as the Japanese were approaching Dutch Harbor for their attack, and the evidence of a photograph that was taken at Dutch Harbor which shows a Japanese aircraft streaming smoke or oil.

In Yamigada's account, Petty Officer Tsuguo Shikada, one of the Zero pilots engaged in the second day's attack and a friend of Koga, was part of a three plane formation with him that observed oil and smoke spewing from the fighter pilot's plane. Koga's plane was losing altitude as Shikada flew alongside of him. From Koga's hand signals, Shikada discerned that he was having trouble with his fuel system. The Zero pilots proceeded towards the southern end of Akutan Island which had been selected as the assembly area for the *Ryujo* pilots. Shikada caught the glimpse of water just as Koga was about to land on a flat grassy area near the beach. It was too late.[62]

Koga had apparently attempted a normal wheels down, flaps-down, power-off stall landing. The Zero skidded along for a short distance, during which the landing gear, flaps and belly tank were torn off. The fighter then flipped over and continued to slide for a few more yards, with further damage occurring to the wing tips, vertical stabilizer and trailing edge of the rudder. It came to a rest with the fuselage and engine half buried in knee-deep mud and water. Shikada and another Zero pilot, circling overhead, looked down in horror. Nobody moved below. The normal practice called for the plane to be destroyed to keep it from falling into enemy hands.[63] Shikada had enough ammunition for the job, but he was uncertain if Koga was still alive. Afraid that he would be killing an old friend, he could not bring himself to strafe the Zero below. His companion came to the same conclusion. With their fuel running low, they turned and headed back to the *Ryujo*.[64]

On July 10, Lieutenant William Thies from VP-41 and his crew found Koga's Zero. They had been out all night on patrol in the Arctic twilight and had been become temporarily lost. The navigator managed to get a fix with his sexton when the sun came out. They were 240 miles off course. Thies and his crew headed north with the idea of sighting the Aleutians and then working their way back to Dutch Harbor. They located the Shumagin Islands and turned west. Since the day was clear, Thies elected to fly over the islands. As they were heading back to Dutch Har-

Lieutenant William Thies, left and Captain Gehres, right.
USN photo

bor, Thies' enlisted copilot, George Raptist, who had become airsick in the rough North Pacific air, went back to the port waist observation position to vomit. He looked down and saw Koga's Zero.

Lieutenant Thies had a hard time convincing Commander Foley of his find and that a ground party should be sent back to Akutan Island to investigate the crash site. Thies rightly believed that the Zero would provide vital information. Foley relented, and the next day, the 11th, Thies gathered a well armed party and headed for Akutan in YP-151, one of Squeaky Anderson's "Yippy" boats.[65] The party found the badly decomposed body of Koga still strapped into the cockpit with his head and shoulders submerged in the water. Koga, unable to free himself, had apparently drowned. There was also evidence that he had banged his head against an object on landing.

Thies and his party had to cut through the side of the cockpit in order to remove Koga's body. After retrieving documents, examining his flight suit and taking photographs, they buried Koga in a nearby piece of high ground. Thies and his party examined the plane in detail and determined that it could be salvaged, repaired and flown. They also removed one of the 20 mm cannons, the gun sight and several other small items of equipment before returning to Dutch Harbor. A salvage party was dispatched to Akutan on July 12 to recover the Zero. After considerable difficulty, the party managed to remove the engine, but was unable to transport it back to beach. A third party under the leadership of Mr Jerry Lund, an experienced rigger with Siems-Drake, returned on July 15 with a medium size bulldozer, which they used to carve a road through a stream bed to the crash site. Tripods were rigged and the engine and the upside down Zero were loaded aboard sleds, which the bulldozer pulled back to the beach. The sleds were then hauled through the surf and

hoisted aboard a barge, which was towed back to Dutch Harbor, where it arrived on the 18th.

Koga's Zero was cleaned and subjected to further examination at Dutch Harbor. Other than the damages that occurred during the landing and those resulting from the need to remove Koga, the only other damages that were found were a number of bullet holes the size of a fifty caliber round. The rounds had punctured the upper and lower surfaces of the Zero. One had passed through the fuselage tail cone, tail wheel bracket and the solid rubber tire. Another had hit the plywood belly tank from below. The round that did the damage had gone through the underside of the cowling near the oil cooler, severing the oil return line. Most of the 15.3 gallons of oil aboard the Zero had leaked out. However, it was not enough to damage the 925-horsepower Nakajima-manufactured Sakae engine. Other than some rust on several of the fourteen cylinders due to its emersion in the water, the radial engine was in a good state of repair.[66]

The Akutan Zero, as it was popularly referred to later, was a Type O, Model 21 (AM6M2) that had come off the Mitsubishi assembly line on February 19, 1942. It was the first intact model of its type to be shipped to the United States. Another captured by the Chinese and turned over to the Americans in China did not reach the United States until much later. The Akutan Zero arrived at the San Diego Naval Air Station on August 12, 1942. There it was repaired, and by September 25 it was ready for flight testing.[67]

Despite the account given in *The Thousand Mile War* and later repeated in other books, Koga's Zero was not used in the design and development of the Grumman F6F Hellcat. No one "rushed to their designer boards," following the capture of the Zero. The Hellcat prototype, based on the design of the Grumman F4F Wildcat, which it resembled, and the experience gained during the first six months of war, was first flown June 26, 1942. The contract for the new fighter had been let in June the previous year. The prototype's Wright R-2600-16 engine proved too weak, and the 2000 horsepower Pratt and Whitney R-2000-10W was substituted. It was flown again July 30 and accepted by the Navy shortly afterwards. The first production model was ready by October 3, 1942, and by March 1943, the first group of Hellcats were operational aboard the new carrier *Essex*. The remarkable fighter was more than a match for the Zero.[68]

What the Zero was used for was to develop tactics to counter its strengths and take advantage of its weaknesses. The Americans learned from the Akutan Zero and the reports forwarded on the one captured in China that the Japanese had developed an exceptionally well constructed fighter of remarkable grace and agility. They also learned that the thirty-three year old designer of the Zero, Jiro

Horikoshi, had produced a fighter that was fragile and lacked armor plating and self-sealing fuel tanks. It was a deliberate trade-off to achieve superior maneuverability and range by keeping the fighter as light-weight as possible.

While at San Diego, the Zero was flown by Lieutenant Melville Hoffman in carefully planned test flight engagements against the Navy's Grumman F4F-4 Wildcat and Vought F4U-1 Corsair and the Army's Lockheed P-38F Lightning, Bell P-39D-1 Airacobra and North America P-51A Mustang. Plans were made to fly it against the Curtiss P-40F Warhawk, but were not completed due to technical difficulties. The results of the tests varied according to the capabilities of the American fighters. The Wildcat proved to be the poorest performer against the Zero while the Corsair was able to hold its own in almost all aspects. The Lightning proved to be a good performer against the Zero while the Airacobra, although capable at altitudes below 10,000 feet, was inferior at higher altitudes. The results against the early model P-51 were mixed, with the Zero enjoying most of the advantages.

The Zero, because of its lightness, low wing loading and large ailerons, was more maneuverable than the American fighters and had a better zoom climb capability. Its ma-

jor weaknesses were its poor diving abilities, sluggish response to controls at speeds above 300 miles per hour, lack of armor plating and self-sealing tanks and lack of robustness. The results of the tests to include recommendations were compiled into two classified intelligence reports. The Navy report was distributed to its flying units in early November 1942. The Army made its report available a month later. Both Services warned its pilots to: "Never attempt to dog fight the Zero. Never maneuver with the Zero at speeds below 300 miles per hour indicated unless directly behind it. (and) Never follow a Zero in a climb at slow speeds."[69]

Following the evaluations, the Akutan Zero remained at San Diego for a while. It was the subject of a twenty minute training film, "Recognition of the Japanese Zero Fighter," released by the Office of War Information. "Dedicated to the flyers who are helping make the total number of Zeros . . . Zero," it was narrated by a Hollywood actor turned Army Air Forces captain, Ronald Reagan. The Zero was flown to the Anacostia Naval Air Station, Maryland. Later it was returned to San Diego where it was used to familiarize new pilots being assigned to the Pacific. Koga's Zero was destroyed in February 1945, when another plane accidentally taxied into it.[70]

A recovery crew swarms over Koga's Zero. The nineteen year old enlisted fighter pilot apparently drowned when his plane flipped over in the water logged muskeg. The soft marshy surface prevented serious damage to the Zero. Except for a bent propellor, separated landing gear and flaps, damaged wing tips and a battered vertical stabilizer, the fighter was in good shape. The plywood drop fuel tank was torn from the Zero as it slid across the marsh. USN photo by Art Bowman

One of the holes made by a .50 caliber machine gun round can be seen in the tail cone just under the extended tail wheel. The round that did the damage severed the oil return line under the engine. The Zero was painted light grey with a yellow band around the fuselage located immediately behind the national insignia. A stenciled data plate can be seen just forward of the horizontal stabilizer. The nose cowling was painted black. The propeller and spinner were natural metal. Koga's decomposed body can be seen just behind the wing tip. The son of a carpenter from a small village on Kyushu Island, Koga was three months from his twentieth birthday when killed. The Americans buried him near the crash site. Jim Rearden of Homer, Alaska, who is an authority on the Akutan Zero and the author of the book, Cracking the Zero Mystery, found Koga's grave but not the body which had been removed, probably by a grave registration unit after the war. USN photo by Art Bowman

When Jiro Horikoshi saw the Imperial Japanese Navy's technical requirements in 1937 for its proposed new carrier fighter, he became depressed. The Navy wanted a plane with a maximum speed of 310-miles per hour that was highly maneuverable and had an endurance of an hour and a half at full power. All of this was to be achieved with an engine of less than a thousand horsepower. The Japanese, with a paucity of resources, did not have access to the advanced metal alloys that America and other Western nations were using to build engines of incredible power. Horikoshi designed a fighter that met the Navy's specifications by eliminating weight whenever possible, ignoring standard stress factors where feasible, eliminating armor plating and self-sealing fuel tanks, building the wing as a single unit, and using the light weight "extra super duralumin" developed by Sumitomo Metals for the wing spar. The 950-horsepower Sakae engine shown in the photo is from Koga's Zero. USN photo

The cockpit of Koga's Zero. Like the rest of the fighter, it was straightforward and simple. The charging handles of the two cowl mounted 7.7mm machine guns which Japanese pilots preferred for close in engagement can be seen on either side. The two wing mounted 20mm cannons provided formidable hitting power. USN photo

The Akutan Zero in U.S. markings. Horikoshi designed a clean aircraft with flush rivets and few protruding parts to spoil the air flow. The raised canopy provided excellent all-round visibility. The feature was later adopted by the Americans on their fighters.
USN photo

All Is Lost

While the battle had swirled around Dutch Harbor, Wylie Hunt and his two companions had undergone their lonely ordeal. They had been adrift for about five hours after Lieutenant Cusick died when the Japanese heavy cruiser *Takao* appeared around noon and steamed over to where they were. Brown was so weakened from the ordeal that the Japanese had to pull him aboard with a rope. Hunt and Creamer managed to make their way up a steel ladder which the Japanese lowered.

As soon as they were aboard, they were given a hot bath, fed, clothed and examined by a doctor. They were then issued bedding and taken to a compartment below decks in which a divider had been set up. Hunt was confined to one section and the enlisted men to the other under the supervision of a guard. After about an hour, three Japanese officers came in and began to question him. They were particularly interested to know how many ships and planes there were in the Dutch Harbor area and their dispositions. Hunt pleaded ignorance. After about three hours, the Japanese gave up and allowed him to go to sleep. They returned later that evening for another session similar to the one in the afternoon.

The questioning continued the following day, the 4th, with Hunt again claiming ignorance. He was left alone on the third day until about noon, when according to Hunt:

> . . . a Japanese lieutenant commander aviator came down and began asking me questions. He told me that he was from one of the aircraft carriers and that he had participated in both of the attacks upon Dutch Harbor. I gathered from his conversation that he had been on the flight which was jumped by Army fighters over Umnak. He appeared to be enraged over this. He started out by cuffing me about the head several times with his fist and striking me with a stick he carried. [71]

This was the first time Wylie Hunt had been mistreated since his capture three days before. The Japanese officer continued his questioning for another thirty minutes before leaving. Shortly afterwards, several ship officers arrived. Brown and Creamer were taken away and Hunt was tied to a chair and questioned further on how many fighters there were in the Dutch Harbor area and where they were based. He was also asked to provide particulars on the U.S. Navy forces in the area. When Hunt, out of ignorance, refused to answer, the Japanese threatened to kill him. Finally, he was blindfolded and taken up to the deck where a weight was tied around his waist. Hunt was then led to a platform and the blindfold was removed. The young lieutenant looked down at the cold waters below and made his peace with God.

The Japanese threatened to push him overboard if he did not answer their questions. Hunt asked for a priest. The Japanese, after some deliberation, decided he was telling the truth. For the rest of the voyage back to Ominato, Hunt was treated with consideration. After arriving at the base on June 25, he and the others were put aboard a train and sent into captivity that was to last until the end of the war. [72]

Hunt was more fortunate than the young Navy pilot and his enlisted crew member from the carrier *Enterprise*, whose Devastator torpedo bomber had been shot down during the attacks against the Japanese carriers near Midway on the morning of the 4th. The Japanese had pulled them from the water and treated them with kindness. They had questioned the pilot at length, and unlike Hunt he had spoken freely. A few days later the captain of the ship, who had been ordered to proceed to the Aleutians to support the landings at Attu and Kiska, decided the two Americans should die. Weights were tied to them, and they were thrown into the sea. [73]

The two had been part of an epic battle that decided the course of the war in the Pacific. Admiral Nimitz had three advantages over Admiral Yamamoto's force at Midway. His cryptanalysis had given him the vital intelligence needed so that he could deploy his carriers to ambush Admiral Nagumo's carriers before Admiral Yamamoto's powerful battleship force could be brought to bear. Second, he had Midway from which he could launch his PBYs to search for the approaching Japanese and the Army Air Forces bombers to strike the ships. Third, he had radar ashore and on the ships. Both sides had an abundance of brave young men.

Admiral Nimitz ordered Admirals Fletcher and Spruance to position their forces 700 hundred miles northeast of Midway. After issuing similar instructions that he had given Admiral Theobald about not engaging a superior enemy unless there was an assurance of success, Admiral Nimitz turned the tactical operations over to his two commanders.

The battle began on the morning of June 3 when Ensign Jack Reid and his PBY crew spotted the Midway Occupation Force. Navy Captain Cyril Simard, the commander at Midway, immediately dispatched nine B-17s. The crews found the Japanese and dropped their bombs from a high altitude, claiming two battle or heavy cruisers and two transport sunk. In fact they hit nothing. Early the next morning, the 4th, the crews of four Catalinas from Midway, armed with torpedoes and guided by their radars, relocated the Midway Occupation Force. This time they succeeded in scoring a hit on the oiler *Akebono Maru*, forcing the ship out of formation.

Admiral Nagumo to the north had already begun his attack on Midway. The 108 Japanese aircraft arrived over the small atoll at 6:50 AM. The Americans, forewarned by radar, launched an interceptor force of six Wildcats and twenty Brewster F2A Buffalos. The Zero pilots slaughtered the clumsy Buffalos and their hapless Marine pilots. Nine of the twenty-six planes survived the encounter. The Japanese Kate and Val pilots, after inflicting considerable damage, departed at 7:10 AM. Their commander, Lieutenant Joichi Tomonaga, signaled ahead that another attack was needed, setting in motion a series of events that would lead to disaster for the Japanese.

The events were beginning to built as Tomonaga's force was returning to their carriers. A PBY crew had spotted the carriers earlier, and Midway's full complement of fifteen B-17s, four B-26s and six Avenger torpedo bombers were launched. In the ensuing attack, two of the Marauders and four of the Avengers were shot down. The B-17 crews dropped their bombs from twenty thousand feet, erroneously claiming four hits on the carriers. Tomonaga's request and the bomber attack convinced Admiral Nagumo that another air strike was needed to soften up Midway before the assault troops could be landed. At 7:15, Admiral Nagumo ordered the Kates and Vals that were being held in readiness on the carrier decks for a strike against a surface force lowered to the hangar deck so that their maintenance crews could remove the torpedoes and armor piercing bombs and replace them with general purpose bombs.

So far, Nagumo was unaware of the approaching American carriers. At 7:28, the pilot of a spotter plane from the cruiser *Tone* reported the presence of the American ships. However, the report was frustratingly vague. While Admiral Nagumo waited for more precise information, he issued orders at 7:45 that the removal of the torpedoes from the Kates be halted. The spotter pilot reported in at 8:20 that the American force contained an aircraft carrier. Shortly afterwards he reported Americans planes heading towards the carriers. At the same time, eleven Marine Vindicator dive bombers arrived from Midway for another attack. The Japanese easily beat them off, but their presence further rattled Nagumo. Trained to wage a close in engagement of battleships and cruisers, the admiral was unfamiliar with the spatial and timing complexities of fighting a carrier war over great distances. First believing that he would have to commit his forces on another air strike against land targets, Nagumo now had to rapidly readjust to the fact that an American carrier force was bearing down on him.

Lieutenant Tomonaga's force returned and landed on their carriers between 8:40 and 9:00. The mechanics worked feverishly to refuel and rearm them for a sea engagement. By this time the hangar decks were a scene of organized chaos with unsecured ordnance and fuel lines lying about. It was a setting for a disaster.

Admiral Spruance was the first to launch his aircraft. Beginning at 7:05 AM, sixty-nine Douglas SBD-3 Dauntless dive bombers, twenty-nine Douglas TBD-1 Devastator torpedo-bombers and their escort of twenty Wildcats began rumbling down the decks of the *Enterprise* and *Hornet*. News of the Midway attack had prompted Admiral Spruance to launch his aircraft while his force was still 175 miles away from the Japanese, even though it meant the possibility that many would run out of fuel and have to ditch in the ocean. He figured correctly that Admiral Nagumo would be refueling and rearming his Midway strike force when the American dive bombers and torpedo-bombers arrived. He committed virtually every strike aircraft he had in the hopes their coordinated attacks would overwhelm the Japanese defenses.

The American carrier pilots were briefed that they could expect to sight the Japanese by 9:20 AM. At 9:05 Admiral Nagumo, anticipating the American attack, ordered a ninety degree course change which put him on a north-easterly instead of a south-easterly heading. The dive bombers and fighters from the *Hornet* reached the intercept point, and finding nothing, the air group commander decided the Japanese were heading towards Midway. He turned south towards the island over a hundred miles away. Five of the thirty-seven dive bombers and all twelve fighters ran out of fuel and their pilots had to ditch in the ocean.

The *Hornet's* torpedo-bombers under the command of Lieutenant Commander John Waldron, which had become separated from the rest of the carrier air group, reached the intercept point. Commander Waldron decided to turn north instead of south. His decision took his squadron, Torpedo 8, directly towards the Japanese carriers and into the pages of history. In the ensuing attack, all of the fifteen Devastators were shot down and only one man, Ensign George Gay, remained alive from the thirty aircrews committed to the battle. Commander Waldron certainly did not have any illusions about the ability of his old and slow bombers to survive without fighter escorts against the combined Japanese fighter and anti-aircraft defense system. The night before he had written:

> I actually believe that under these conditions we are the best in the world. My greatest hope is that we encounter a favorable tactical situation, but if we don't, and the worst comes to the worst, I want each of us to do his utmost to destroy our enemies. If there is only one plane left to make the final run-in, I want that man to go in and get a hit. May God be with us.[74]

Waldron and his men proved to the Japanese that Americans were just as willing to die as they were for a cause.

The Devastators from the *Enterprise's* torpedo-bomber squadron, Torpedo 6, were the next to arrive. Their leader, Lieutenant Commander Eugene E. Lindsey, like Commander Waldron, had turned north. Shortly after 9:36 AM he spotted the Japanese and ordered an attack without the benefit of fighter protection. Only four of the fourteen survived the attack. No hits were scored.

Admiral Fletcher aboard the *Yorktown*, fearing the presence of a Japanese carrier nearby, had held back from launching his aircraft until 8:30. When he did, it was only a partial complement. The Devastator pilots of Torpedo 3 led by Lieutenant Commander Lance E. Massey, sighted Nagumo's carriers at around 10:00 AM. Like their comrades in arms from the other carriers, the squadron suffered grievously. Seven of the twelve went down and the Japanese ships plowed ahead unharmed. Counting those from Midway, the Americans had sent eighty-three aircraft in seven attacks against Admiral Nagumo's force. Thirty-seven had been destroyed and not one Japanese ship or plane had been harmed. However, the attacks had scattered the Japanese ships, forcing them out of their self-protecting boxes.

It was at this point, with the Japanese frantically rearm-ing their bombers and the Zeros still at the lower altitudes following the torpedo-bomber attacks, that Lieutenant Commander Wade McClusky, a 1926 Annapolis graduate and commander of the *Enterprise* air group, arrived over the Japanese carriers with thirty-seven Dauntless dive bombers from Bombing 6 and Scouting 6. Commander McClusky, like the others, had been thrown off by Nagumo's course change. However, he decided to extend the search even though the bombers were running dangerously low on fuel. By chance he had spotted the Japanese destroyer *Araski* as it hurried to join Nagumo's force after lagging behind to drop depth charges on the American submarine *Nautilus*. Playing a hunch, McClusky decided to fly the course of the destroyer. At 10:20 AM, he spotted three of the four large Japanese carriers. At the same time, Lieutenant Commander Maxwell Leslie arrived with Bombing 3 from the *Yorktown*. The tactical conditions were perfect. Below, the Japanese who had been preoccupied with the torpedo-bomber attacks, looked up in horror as the American dive bombers tilted over into a seventy degree dive from 14,500 feet and came hurtling down.

Very rarely has the course of a war been changed in so short of a period of time. McClusky and Leslie and their pilots started their attack at 10:25 AM. The *Enterprise* pilots went after *Akagi* and *Kaga* while the *Yorktown's* pilots concentrated on the *Soryu*. By 10:30 AM the three carriers were in flaming ruins. The 500- and 1,000-pound bombs exploded on the crowded decks amid parked aircraft or smashed through to explode in the bowels of the ship and among the aircraft and the unsecured bombs and torpedoes in the hangar decks. The explosions set off a chain reaction of detonating torpedoes and bombs and flaming gasoline. All three carriers sank shortly afterwards. The *Soryu* was finished off in a torpedo attack by the *Nautilus*. When McClusky landed on his carrier, he had only two gallons of gas left in his fuel tanks.

The Japanese, although gravely wounded, still had the *Hiryu*. Admiral Nagumo ordered an attack against the Americans. The first wave, consisting of Vals and Zeros, departed at 11:00 AM followed by a second wave of Kates at 1:31PM. The first wave arrived over the *Yorktown* at noon. Three Val pilots succeeded in dropping their bombs on the carrier. The second wave attacked shortly afterwards. Two torpedoes slammed into the side of the *Yorktown*. The captain ordered the ship abandoned. The carrier was subsequently sunk by a Japanese submarine as a salvage party tried to make her seaworthy for the trip back to Pearl Harbor.

The final carrier battle was played out when twenty-four dive bombers from the *Enterprise* found the *Hiryu* at 5:00 PM and sent her to the bottom. Admiral Yamamoto ordered the Midway operations cancelled during the early morning hours of the 5th. This was not the end of the Japanese ordeal. The cruisers *Mikuma* and *Mogami* with the Midway Occupation Force were damaged in a collision. They were found early on the 5th by aircraft from Midway as they attempted to limp away. Attacks were launched and on the 6th, the *Mikuma* was so severely damaged that she had to be abandoned. The *Mogami* managed to escape her tormentors, but not before further damage was inflicted on her.

In addition to the ships, the Japanese lost all the aircraft on the four carriers, about two hundred and fifty, and ninety pilots. Considering the fact that they were only training a hundred pilots a year and there were fifteen hundred in service, the loss was severe.[75] Although the Japanese could build more carriers to replaced those lost at Midway, they could never keep up with the industrial might of the United States. The Japanese started the war with twelve carriers. They produced thirteen more of varying tonnage, many of which were conversions from other vessels. Four others were still under construction at the end of the war. The Americans began the war with seven carriers, one of which was a small escort carrier. By the end of the war, seventeen large Essex class and nine light Independence class carriers had joined the fleet. The Americans also produced seventy-five escort carriers, a light-weight but versatile warship.[76]

The day following the epic battle of Midway was a despondent one for the Japanese. Admiral Yamamoto "sat sipping rice gruel helplessly on the forward bridge" of his command ship, the *Yamato*. All had been lost. Within one day, within a space of five minutes, his chance at achieving perhaps the greatest naval victory in history had been snatched away from him. The slow, cruel decline of his navy had begun.[77]

Shortly afterwards, Admiral Yamamoto went below to his cabin in brooding silence. American radio operators monitoring the Japanese transmissions notice a sudden surge in messages between Admiral Hosogaya's Northern Force and Admiral Yamamoto's Main Body. Hosogaya, after some initial hesitation, wanted to continue with the occupation plans. He argued that it would prevent the Americans from using the islands as an invasion route to Japan. Yamamoto, finally on the afternoon of June 5, reluctantly gave his consent.[78] The occupation, would after all, divert the Japanese public's attention away from the disaster at Midway, which the Japanese military did everything possible to hide. Captain Hideo Hiraido, Chief of the Navy Press, ventured the idea that "the enormous success in the Aleutians was made possible by the diversion of Midway." On June 10, the Tokyo radio, with the musical accompaniment of the "Navy March," announced that another great victory had been achieved. Two American carriers had been sunk, heavy damage had been inflicted on Midway and the Aleutian Islands had been occupied.[79]

"The Japanese did many foolish things during the war, but never, so far as we know, did they seriously contemplate anything so idiotic as invading the United States via the Aleutians-yet they thought we were foolish enough to try the reverse."[80] Suddenly, according to Samuel Eliot Morison, who wrote the acidic comment on the folly of the Japanese, Americans were faced with the prospect of an enemy lodgment on a remote, strategically worthless piece of North American soil. The President, the Joint Chiefs of Staff and the public could not ignore the fact that the Territory of Alaska had been invaded. They were about to prove that the Japanese did not have a monopoly on foolishness.

The Kiska Weather Detachment. Front row, from left to right: Ships Cook Third Class J.C. McCandless, Radioman Third Class R. Christensen, Aerographers Mate Third Class W.M. Winfrey, Seaman Second Class G.T. Palmer, Aerographers Mate Second Class W.I. Gaffney. Second row, from left to right: Aerographers Mate Second Class J.L. Turner, Chief Pharmacy Mate R.L. Copperfield, Aerographers Mate First Class William C. House, Lieut Mull, Radioman Second Class L.L. Eccles, Chief Pharmacy Mate L. Yaconelli and Radioman Third Class M.L. Courtney. Lieutenant Mull and Chief Yaconelli were from the Casco. *The dog, Explosion, had been given to the men earlier by Ensign William C. Jones, a radio technician who helped set up the radio. The dog got her name from the fact that she had been born the night that a small, nearby dynamite storage shack at Dutch Harbor exploded. When the Americans and Canadians reoccupied the island a year later, she was there to greet them. The photograph was taken just prior to the departure of the* Casco.
Howard W. Curtis collection

The Navy weather and radio station at Kiska Harbor where William House and his companions kept their lonely vigil. The PBYs in the harbor were probably flown by Russell and Coleman during their visit to the station in late May. North Head where the Japanese established a major defensive system is clearly visible. The two ranch-style houses and the generator shed between them that provided power and heat were built by a Seabee unit. The other buildings belonged to fox trappers. A number of buildings were maintained around the island for supporting the harvesting of the foxes that had been artificially introduced to Kiska and other Aleutian Islands as one of the means of providing an economy for the island inhabitants. The last trappers, a man and his daughter, left the island around April 1942. USN photo

5

A TIME FOR COURAGE

· · · · · · · · · · · ·

A Journey of Sorrow

Admiral Hosogaya's chief of staff, Captain Tasuku Nakazawa, sensed that something had gone terribly wrong. After recovering his Dutch Harbor attack force, the commander of the Northern Force decided to wait for further developments. The message of the defeat at Midway came during the early morning hours of the 5th.

Admiral Hosogaya signaled Admiral Yamamoto at 8:00 AM and suggested the Aleutian Island occupation be cancelled. Admiral Yamamoto, suffering from nervous exhaustion and a stomach ailment, was even more against the operation. Several hours later, Rear Admiral Matome Ugaki, Admiral Yamamoto's chief of staff, queried Hosogaya on his ability to continue with the original plans if reinforcements were sent to him.

The commander of the Northern Force now had second thoughts and was convinced the occupation, except for the Adak landing, should proceed as scheduled. He and his staff were concerned that the island was too close to the American airbase at Otter Point. In the interim, Hosogaya had ordered Rear Admiral Sentaro Omori's Adak-Attu Invasion Force, which had been holding 225 miles southwest of Adak, to proceed to Attu. At 12:59 PM, Admiral Yamamoto, at the urging of his staff and Admiral Hosogaya, relented and directed that both Attu and Kiska be occupied. Admiral Kakuta headed his carrier task force west in support of the landings, and Admiral Yamamoto dispatched additional ships including two battleships and the light carrier *Zuiho* north to support the effort.[1]

Lieutenant Commander Nifumi Mukai's elite five hundred man Maizuru Third Special Landing Force waded ashore from their landing craft at Reynard Cove on Kiska at 10:27 PM on the 6th. The force split into three groups and proceeded south towards Kiska Harbor. Several of the landing craft also moved along the coast towards the harbor.[2] The first indication that the Japanese had landed, according to William House, occurred at 2:14 AM on the 7th when "the Jap landing force came around North Head and opened fire." Japanese 13mm machine gun slugs ripped through the walls of the building they were living in, wounding one man. House and another man remained behind to burn the code books while the rest headed for the safety of the hills behind the weather station.

House and his men had sat out their lonely vigil in the weather station while Admiral Kakuta's airmen struck Dutch Harbor. The station consisted of a group of three buildings (barracks, radio hut and power plant) connected by a boardwalk and located some three hundred yards from the beach. House fully expected they would be the next target; and he had his weathermen establish caches in the ravines behind their camp with orders that if the Japanese landed they were to take to the hills. Without any means of defending themselves, it was all they could have done.

After burning the code books, House and his companion raced to join the others as Commander Mukai's men appeared over the ridge-line from the northeast. The Japanese found the caches and succeeded in capturing all but five of the men. Four surrendered ten days later. William House eluded capture.

House remained in the vicinity of the Japanese for a few days, and then headed for the opposite side of the island where he hid out for forty-nine days, subsisting on tundra grass, shellfish and angle worms. From his lonely outpost he watched the American aircraft strike back at the Japanese. Finally, realizing that it would be a long time before his countrymen would return in force, and after fainting from malnutrition and knowing that he was slowly dying of starvation and exposure, William House made his peace and walked into the Japanese camp on July 28. His weight had dropped to eighty pounds and his thighs had shrunk to the size of a child's arm.

The Japanese, who had already evacuated the other American prisoners of war, kept House at Kiska until September 20 when he was put aboard the *Osada Maru* with the Aleuts from Attu and sent to Japan where he remained until the end of the war. The Japanese treated

House with kindness while he was on Kiska, giving him odd jobs to do around the camp they were establishing. His treatment as a slave laborer in the steel mills of Yokohama and Kamaishi was less kind.[3]

The labor troops and their equipment were landed the next day. They began building garrison and defense facilities. The two armed troop transports, the heavy cruiser *Asahama*, the light cruisers *Kiso* and *Tama*, three auxiliary vessels, four destroyers and four transports including the *Nissan Maru* remained anchored in the harbor. In the days ahead, other ships arrived, bringing in more men, equipment and supplies. The Japanese dug in and began installing an elaborate anti-aircraft and coastal defense system to protect their newly acquired possession on the North American continent.[4]

Admiral Omori's Attu invasion force reached its destination during the early morning hours of June 7. The landing commenced at 3:00 AM. Major Masatoshi Hotzumi, the Army commander of the Army North Sea Detachment, consisting of the 301st Independent Infantry Battalion, the 301st Independent Engineer Company and a service unit, decided to take his force of 1,143 men ashore at Holtz Bay. Due to darkness, fog and lack of suitable maps, part of the force became lost and finally ended up in the pass to Massacre Valley. The others pushed overland through the snow across the pass into Chichagof Harbor where they surprised the villagers who were preparing for Sunday church services.[5]

According to Etta Jones, the villagers had been expecting evacuation from the island, and initially they mistook the ships outside the harbor as American. The first inkling that the Japanese had arrived was when one of the villagers spotted the float reconnaissance plane from the light cruiser *Abukuma*, the occupation force flag ship, flying overhead. Shortly afterwards, the quiet valley behind the village resounded with the crack of rifle fire and loud unintelligible shouting as Major Hotzumi's men swept down on the defenseless village.

Etta Jones looked out of her window to see a sight that left her cold with fear. Wildly shouting Japanese were pouring over the hill crests that surrounded the village. Her husband, Charles Foster, began sending out a message to Dutch Harbor on his radio. Bullets thudded against the houses and one of the Aleuts was wounded. The Japanese quickly rounded up the forty-two Aleuts and the Joneses. A Japanese officer questioned the couple at length, giving them the impression he believed they were American agents in contact with the Russians on the Kamchatka Peninsula.

They were separated from the rest of the villagers and moved to another house. The next morning, according to Etta Jones, the Japanese took Charles Foster away for further questioning. That was the last time Etta saw him alive. One of the village women told her that they had buried her husband near the church. A week later the Japanese put her aboard a transport and sent her to Yokohama where she was interned for the rest of war with a group of Australian nurses. She was treated well and was freed at the end of the war and flown to San Francisco. Etta Jones was sixty-five years old at the time.[6]

How Charles Foster Jones died is debatable, but in all likelihood it was by his own hand as claimed by the Japanese and confirmed by several of the surviving Attuans. According to their account, the couple were confined in a hut where they attempted to commit suicide by slashing their wrists. Charles Foster was successful but Etta recovered. After the war Charles Foster's body was disinterred and reburied on August 8, 1948 in Plot A, Grave 2, Fort Richardson Cemetery near Anchorage.[7]

The Japanese established their headquarters in the village and began building fortified positions around Chichagof Harbor. A small detachment was also sent to

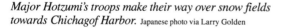

Major Hotzumi's troops make their way over snow fields towards Chichagof Harbor. Japanese photo via Larry Golden

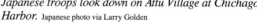

Japanese troops look down on Attu Village at Chichagof Harbor. Japanese photo via Larry Golden

Charles Foster and Etta Jones during younger and happier times.
Hanna Call Collection, Alaska and Polar Regions Dept, U of Alaska, Fairbanks

Kawanishi E7K2 Navy Type 94, Allied code name Alf, at Chichagof Harbor. It was probably this reconnaissance float plane that flew over the Aleut village during the early morning landing of the Japanese.
Japanese photo via Larry Golden

Sarana Bay. When the Japanese learned in late August that the Americans were planning to occupy Adak, they decided to move the Attu garrison to bolster the defenses of Kiska. They also decided to take the Attuans and their personal belongings with them. On September 17, the Attuans boarded the *Yoko Maru*, leaving a place that their ancestors had inhabited for three thousand years. They arrived at Kiska on the 19th where they were transferred to the *Osada Maru* to begin a journey of sorrow.

By now their number had been reduced by two with the death of the old chief from natural causes at Attu and the death of a woman during the trip to Kiska. The remaining forty were taken to an internment camp near Otaru City, Hokkaido. Professor Henry Stewart, an archaeologist at Waseda University, Tokyo, in his research of the Attuans in Japan, claims they were treated with kindness and their high mortality rate was due to tuberculosis contracted before their internment. The film, *Alaska at War*, paints a similar picture.[8] However, the account given in the three appendices to Ethel Ross Oliver's *Journal of an Aleutian Year*, portrays a darker story, one of mistreatment and death by neglect and the ravages of starvation. An appendix, prepared by Mrs. Oliver dur-

ing her 1946-47 stay on Atka Island as a school teacher, lists the names of nineteen who died in Japan including three of four infants born in captivity. Two died of tuberculosis, four of beriberi, two of starvation, two of food poisoning from eating rotten garbage, two of pneumonia and the rest from various other causes of privation.[9]

Only twenty-four of the original forty-two Attuans who watched Major Hotzumi's men sweep down from the hills that Sunday morning were alive at the war's end. They could not go home again, for their village, their church, their homes and their way of life had been destroyed by a war that ended so many dreams and hopes. The bureaucrats in their mindless deliberations decided it would be too expensive and difficult to rebuild a new life for them on the island. Instead, those who were not sent to boarding schools to complete their education or were too sick to proceed further, were resettled on the island of Atka among their ancestral enemies. They, like the other Aleuts caught up in the war in the Aleutians, were to suffer a far greater proportion of casualties in terms of life and human privation than those actually engaged in combat, a tragedy of the innocent that is so common in modern warfare.

Attu Village as it looked prior to the Japanese occupation.
National Archives

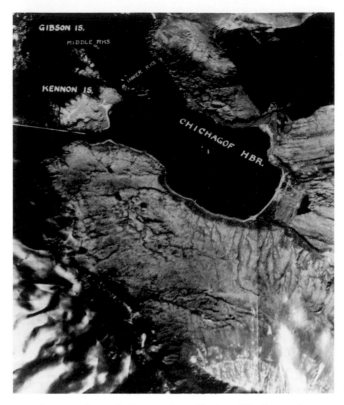

The vertical aerial photograph on Chichagof Harbor and Attu Village was taken August 6, 1942. AAF photo

The oblique aerial photograph of Attu Village was taken September 28, 1942, shortly after the Japanese evacuated the Aleuts from the village. The circular and rectangular mounds of earth that surround the village show where the Japanese set up their tents. The smoke rising from the village is the result of bombs that were dropped from the LB-30 and B-24 that were flown on a raid against suspected Japanese positions in Chichagof Harbor that day. AAF photo

Sunday, I Think

For a short period of time following Admiral Kakuta's withdrawal from the eastern Aleutian area there was silence and confusion as the Americans searched for his fleet over the cold, grey waste of the Bering Sea and North Pacific. General Butler ordered the 54th Fighter Squadron to deploy its P-38Es forward on the 5th in anticipation that the Japanese were planning another strike. The squadron headquarters and one flight were held in readiness at Elmendorf Field, another flight was sent to Thornborough Field and the third to Cape Field.

The squadron personnel were still green and the P-38 unproven in battle. One of the flights, en route to Cape Field, spotted a ship below and promptly attacked it. It turned out to be Russian. Fortunately, no one was hurt. On landing at the forward field, one of the pilots accidentally pressed the gun button on his control yoke and sent a stream of 50 caliber and 20mm rounds down the runway. General Butler in his report to General Arnold noted that the squadron had been ". . . pretty wild for a couple of days, and chased friend and foe alike." However, he believed it was settling down into a "first class organization."[10]

Attu Village burns from the results of a later raid. The village was completely destroyed and, except for a small marker, all traces have completely vanished, the legacy of war and the relentless Aleutian environment. AAF photo

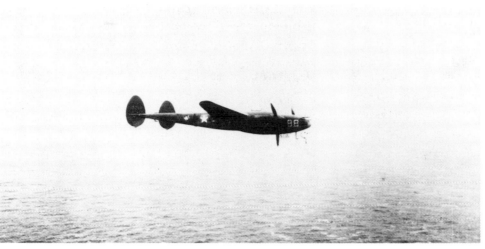

The P-38 Lightning was first introduced into combat during the Aleutian Campaign. The 54th Fighter Squadron was initially equipped with the P-38E. Its two 1,325 horsepower Allison V-1710-49 liquid cooled engines gave it a margin of safety over the icy expanses of the North Pacific and Bering Sea. With a maximum load of fuel it had a range between 1,500 and 2,000 miles. It was the only fighter that was suited for the long distance flying required during the Aleutian Campaign. AAF photo

Stan Long, one of the Aleutian Warriors, and his P-38E. The Japanese flag under the canopy denotes the Kawanishi H6K4 "Mavis" flying boat he was credited with shooting down August 4, 1942. AAF photo

Men of the 54th Fighter Squadron. From left to right: Capt Arthur P. Hustead, Capt Robert L. McDonald, Capt Morgan A. Giffin, Capt Howard W. Millard, Lieut Herbert Hasenfus and Lieut Stanley A. Long. US Army Military History Institute

The squadron did settle down to become a first class organization, but at a terrible price. The P-38E was a new aircraft, unproven in battle. The 54th Fighter Squadron was to put them to their first operational test. The big, twin boom fighter, originally designed to intercept bombers at high altitudes, had two important advantages over the single engine fighters in the Aleutian theater. It had two engines and it possessed the range needed to operate over the vast watery expanses of the North Pacific and Bering Sea. As a result, the Lightning pilots drew the most difficult fighter missions of the campaign and suffered the most casualties. Half of the thirty original pilots were dead within a year. Stan Long, a survivor and retired Air Force colonel, remembered:

None of the pilots sent to Alaska were highly qualified. We were just out of flight school with practically no gunnery training and, most important of all, no instrument training with the exception of a few hours in a Link trainer. Our planes only had the needle, ball and airspeed indicators which was barely enough to permit us to fly through a fifty-foot overcast, let alone make an instrument landing penetration. In the Aleutians where we were to be based, there were no navigation aids or facilities for instrument landings available even if we had possessed the equipment in our planes or had the proper training to utilize it. So it is not surprising that our attrition rate was very high, and those that survived were just damned lucky.[11]

The weather, the long missions and the uncertainty of survival in the hostile skies over the Aleutians quickly aged men and stripped away the innocence of youth. A day off from the ordeal was a welcome relief for many, who like the bomber crew above waiting in the early morning hours for the start of a mission, committed their lives to battle in a strange and frightening place.
AAF photo

The squadron suffered its first major casualties when a C-53 crashed north of Cold Bay while en route to Cape Field. Four pilots and six enlisted men, who were passengers, died. Their bodies washed ashore and their squadron mates buried them in the high ground above the shoreline.[12] The squadron continued to soldier on, and in time, the long, hard hours spent by the ground crews and the courage and perseverance of the pilots paid off.[13]

False sightings of Admiral Kakuta's fleet continued to come in. On the 5th, Captain Marks saw what he believed was a Japanese cruiser near Umnak Island. Other bombers were launched. The cruiser turned out to be a rock. The next day, Colonel Eareckson dispatched his five operational B-17s along with the LB-30 Liberator from Thornborough Field at 4:00 AM to help Patrol Air Wing Four look for the Japanese fleet.

The bomber crews flew until 1:00 PM without seeing anything. They then landed at Cape Field where one of the B-17s promptly got stuck in the mud. Another weather front had moved in, bringing with it rain and misery. The men were hungry and tired; and, according to Billy Wheeler, "felt like offering half interest in hell to anyone who could produce food."[14] After waiting in vain for two hours for promised sandwiches to be delivered, the crews of three of the B-17s decided to return to Cold Bay. They left their helpless squadron mates with their mired bomber behind to figure out for themselves how they were to get home. Eareckson gave his exhausted bomber crews the next day off. Wheeler noted on the 7th in his diary that "morale is high but the energy reserve is low."[15]

The next day, the 8th, the men of the 36th Bomber Squadron were in the air again. The ground crews, work-

ing in the open on the wind-swept ramp at Thornborough Field, had repaired and serviced the big bombers in time for what turned out to be another wild goose chase after the illusive Japanese. A patrolling PBY crew over the Bering Sea spotted on the radar scope what they thought was the Japanese fleet. In actuality, it was the Pribilof Islands. In what was later jokingly referred to as the "battle of the Pribilofs," Eareckson ordered an attack by six B-17s. It almost turned into a tragedy.

Captain Cone and his bomber squadron had been in the air since 8:00 AM that morning on patrol and had just landed at Cape Field when the order came through. They took off at 2:00 PM and arrived over the scene of the radar sighting to find nothing but the rocky shoreline of the Pribilofs and the eternal icy waste of the Bering Sea. Low on gas, Cone and his men turned and headed back to Cape Field. The ceiling there was down to six hundred feet and the short nightfall of the summer months in the Aleutians was about to occur. None of the crews had ever made a night landing on an Aleutian airfield. Captain Cone ordered his pilots to spread out in a line abreast formation and begin looking for a hole in the overcast below.[16]

Billy Wheeler, copilot of one of the bombers, looked out. The scene was breathtaking, for the sun was setting and "every cloud was a blaze of beautiful color." The time was 11:30 PM. Below on Cape Field it was dark and raining. Fortunately, the men in the bombers could make out the land below through the cloud layer by its darker shading against the sea. They circled and one by one, the pilots began letting down. Once into the clouds, Wheeler remembered, the twilight "turned to insidious dark." Below, the men on the field did everything they could to bring Cone and his men to a safe landing. Emergency flares were lit to outline the runway and a spotlight was turned on at one end to guide the them in. The light did more harm then good since it blinded them. Somehow, they groped their way down to a safe landing on the slick, steel runway. The whole operation took fifty nerve-racking minutes. The men were exhausted.[17]

Captain Gehres' PBY crews from VP-41 and VP-42 were also exhausted. There had been no letup in patrols since the Dutch Harbor attack as they searched the Bering Sea and North Pacific for Admiral Kakuta's carriers. The crew of one Catalina spotted the Japanese task force on the morning of the 6th and was promptly chased away by the Zero combat air patrol. It was the last reported visual sighting of the Japanese aircraft carriers. Another crew returning from a patrol sighted a submarine and dropped several bombs near it without any observed results. On the 7th, a crew from VP-41 reported that it had been attacked by a "single-engine plane maneuvering like a fighter."[18]

Relief for two Catalina squadrons finally arrived in the form of twelve PBY-5 seaplanes from VP-43. The squadron, commanded by Lieutenant Commander C.B. "Doc" Jones, had received their orders on June 6 to deploy north and join Patrol Air Wing Four while they were stationed at North Island Naval Air Station near San Diego. Carl Amme remembered that they held a farewell party in the Del Coronado Hotel that night, and left the next morning for Kodiak, which they reached on the 9th after stops at Tongue Point Naval Station near Astoria, Oregon and Sitka.[19]

On June 10, Machinist Leland I. Davis, one of VP-43's warrant officer pilots, spotted and attacked a submarine south of Tanaga Island. The crew observed several bomb hits near its hull and later submitted claims that the submarine had been sunk.[20] It was believed to be the submarine that had remained behind to recover Tadayoshi Koga. A review of Japanese records after the war failed to substantiate its sinking.[21]

Elsewhere, William House failed to make his report on the 7th as scheduled.[22] *The Anchorage Daily Times* later carried an article stating that Charles Foster Jones had notified Ralph Magee, an Indian Service schoolteacher on Atka, by radio that "he had a hunch the Japanese would invade and he was assembling the natives and had a rifle and shotgun to repel the attack."[23] That was the last that was heard from the Americans on the island, which along with Kiska had by now become Japanese property.

Colonel Eareckson submitted his report to General Butler, dating it, "Sunday, I think," and noting: "Tactical operations for today: No hits, no runs, no errors."[24] If it was Sunday, then it was the 7th and the Japanese had already landed on Attu and Kiska, establishing a enemy lodgement on North America soil, the first since the War of 1812.

Following Dutch Harbor, Admiral Kakuta's reinforced carrier task force had remained in the North Pacific south of Kiska, supporting the landing of additional troops, equipment and supplies at Kiska where the Japanese were planning to establish their major base in the Aleutians. The smaller Attu garrison was similarly reinforced, but to a much lesser extent. A small, temporary tent camp was established on Agattu. The Japanese high command was concerned that the United States Pacific Fleet would intervene in "this token occupation of American soil." Admiral Kakuta's force returned briefly to Ominato for replenishment in late June. When he headed back into the North Pacific again on June 29, Admiral Kakuta's three carriers had been joined by a fourth, the *Zuikaku*. The Japanese carrier task force remained in position south of Kiska until July 6 in anticipation that the Americans would engage them in battle. By then the Japanese had become convinced that Admiral Nimitz was not going to accept a carrier duel in the fog-shrouded waste of the North Pacific.[25]

Admiral Nimitz had already given up any idea of sending additional forces north. He was aware, through radio intercepts, that a large Japanese naval force was operating in the North Pacific and that troops had been landed at Attu and Kiska. The reports, however, were uncertain since the Japanese had changed their code again; and all his intelligence staff could get was the volume and direction of the radio communications. Initially, the Japanese were suspected of being in the Bering Sea and heading for another attack on Dutch Harbor. Admiral Theobald, still at sea literally and figuratively, thought the Japanese were planning to invade the mainland and asked for reinforcements.

Admiral Nimitz's staff began making plans to send the *Enterprise* and the *Hornet*, the only two American carriers in the Pacific, along with six cruisers and ten destroyers, north to engage Admiral Kakuta's force. Orders were issued to Admiral Spruance to head north with the task force. Admiral Theobald returned to Kodiak on June 8 for a short period to confer with his commanders and plan the destruction of Admiral Kakuta's force. He then headed back to sea only to learn, on the 10th, that Admiral Nimitz had decided not to commit his carriers. By then, Admiral Theobald had confirmation that the Japanese had occupied Kiska and that he was now faced with the embarrassing problem of trying to dislodge them with only limited forces.[26]

Another weather front moved in and obscured the Aleutians under a blanket of clouds, preventing the daily morning air reconnaissance flights from being flown on the 6th and 7th. On the morning of the 8th, Captain Robert E. "Pappy" Speer and his copilot, Lieutenant Frederick Ramputi

The crew of LB-30, "Tough Boy," at Cape Field, June 1942. The caption on the nose describes Tojo before and after Pearl Harbor. The crew, not the one who discovered the Japanese on Kiska, are from left to right, front row: waist gunner (?); Sgt Fraley, radio operator; waist gunner (?); TSgt Billy S. Johnson, flight engineer; tail gunner (?); rear row: Lieut Fred Ramputi, pilot, left and Lieut Jim Hart, copilot, right. "Tough Boy," tail number AL-613, according to Fred Ramputi, had a history that could probably match any other Liberator in the Pacific. The bomber, like the other two LB-30s sent to Alaska, was manufactured at the Consolidated's San Diego plant for the British. However, it was transferred the Army Air Forces immediately after Pearl Harbor. It was assigned to the Eleventh Air Force in February 1942. "Tough Boy" survived the war in the Aleutians and was condemned for salvage in September 1943. However, the LB-30 received a reprieve, and was converted into a transport and assigned to the Pacific Wing, Air Transport Command in February 1944. Fred Ramputi saw "Tough Boy," on Guam in 1945. The old Liberator survived the war and ended up on January 10, 1946, in the hands of the Reconstruction Finance Corp at Kingman, Arizona, where no doubt the old warrior was turned into aluminum ingots. Of the other two LB-30s assigned to the Eleventh Air Force, AL-622 was destroyed in a crash at Kodiak June 5, 1942, and AL-620 was dropped from the inventory by condemnation October 30, 1943, while still assigned to the Eleventh Air Force. Fred Ramputi collection

headed down the islands from Otter Point in the LB-30. Four PBYs from Patrol Wing Four also took off on patrol that morning.

The two bomber pilots arrived over Kiska Harbor at 1:00 PM. Speer decided to drop down to two hundred feet and circle the harbor in order to determine if William House and his men were safe. They promptly sighted what they thought were American ships. Speer flashed a recognition signal only to be greeted by a return signal he did not recognize and a burst of gunfire. He pulled back up into the clouds, handed his radio operator, Sergeant Lester A. Smith, a message to encode and send back to Cape Field; and then headed back to the base.

On the way back Speer passed Lieutenant Milton R. Dahl and his crew from VP-41 heading in the opposite direction. Shortly afterwards he heard Dahl report that there

were two transports at the harbor entrance and two more along with two destroyers in the harbor. The Japanese began shooting at the PBY; and Dahl, after remaining over the harbor to confirm the sighting, left for Attu. On the way, the crew spotted a Japanese cruiser and a destroyer headed for Kiska. Until then Speer had not been certain of the identity of the ships. He arrived back at Cape Field to find that his and Dahl's messages had gotten through. Dahl reached Attu and confirmed the presence of Major Hotzumi's force on the island. Shortly afterwards, Lieutenant William J. Bowers, in another PBY, reported the presence of the Japanese on the two islands.[27]

The Japanese had already announced their presence on the islands before Speer and Dahl arrived on the scene. Newsreel teams and reporters had been present to cover the landings. It made great propaganda. Tokyo Rose broadcast the news and Radio Berlin noted it in one of its commentaries. *The New York Times*, in the absence of

Japanese destroyers and transports in Kiska Harbor, June 1942. Japanese photo via Larry Golden

military confirmation, speculated on the truth of the reports. The American public remained ignorant. The military, hiding behind its veil of secrecy and censorship, was noncommittal, a condition that remained unchanged during the war.[28]

John Driscoll, a correspondent for the *New York Herald Tribune*, would later comment:

> In view of the mounting importance of Alaska, to which all sections of the U.S. have contributed, it is about time that the public receive more information and some reassurance about what goes on there. Until now there has been less information available from Alaska than any other of our fighting fronts.[29]

While other theaters of operation in the Pacific were more free with their information (Admiral Nimitz and General MacArthur held frequent press conferences), General DeWitt and the Western Defense Command shielded Alaska's military operations from the public with a zeal that on occasion was absurd.[30] The Navy finally issued a news release on June 12. Down-playing the occupation of the two islands, the Navy noted that the "Japanese have made landings on a small scale on Attu Island, at the extreme tip of the Aleutian archipelago and that Japanese ships have been reported in the harbor of Kiska." To further soothe public morale, the release went on to say that "continuing Army and Navy aircraft attacks have forced them to retire from the populated regions of the islands."[31]

The next day, Bob Atwood's *The Anchorage Daily Times* featured the story under the headline "Alaska War Continues." It quoted the Navy news release and went on to state that "qualified Navy and Army sources" had said there was nothing to be concerned about. The paper also noted that Al Jolson had arrived on the 12th to entertain the troops.[32]

The Joint Chiefs of Staff (Generals Marshall and Arnold and Admiral King) were concerned. Suddenly, the Japanese had established a lodgement twenty-two hundred air miles from Seattle. General Marshall, although not unduly troubled by the Japanese occupation of the remote islands, immediately ordered reinforcements rushed to Alaska. General Arnold reluctantly agreed to send additional air units.[33] Admiral King left the decision up to Admiral Nimitz since it was his theater of operations. The Commander-in-Chief, Pacific, immediately ordered eight Fleet submarines into the North Pacific to reinforce the prewar S class submarines that had been patrolling the frigid waters around the Aleutians. He also directed Admiral Theobald to launch a bombing attack to drive the Japanese out of Kiska before they could consolidate their position.[34] The Joint Chiefs of Staff began preparing an estimate of the situation to determine an appropriate response to the lodgement.

The estimate was completed June 13. The Joint Chiefs of Staff speculated that the Japanese landings in the Aleutians had been intended to support future operations against the Soviet Union. They figured that the Japanese would launch attacks to seize Petropavlovsk and other Siberian bases in conjunction with a planned German offensive on the eastern front. They believed the occupation of Attu and Kiska had been intended as a preliminary step for cutting the lines of communication between the United States and the Soviet Union.

The Joint Chiefs of Staff estimated that the next move of the Japanese would be to occupy St. Lawrence Island and Nome in order to support their Siberian operations. The Nome garrison at the time consisted of about two hundred men, five trench mortars and six 30-caliber machine guns. There was no military garrison on St. Lawrence.[35]

Marshall, King and Arnold met on June 15. Time was critical; and they felt that immediate offensive actions were required. They ordered the reinforcement of the Nome garrison. No mention was made of St. Lawrence Island. They further directed that additional bombers be sent to Alaska to support the attacks against Kiska and to patrol the Aleutian and Bering Sea areas. The possibility of involving the Soviet Union in the war against Japan was discussed and a recommendation was made to the President that discussions be held with the Russians. Finally, they decided that the Japanese garrisons in the Aleutians had to be destroyed.[36]

A Heart-breaking Operation

Admiral Theobald, on June 11, launched what was later to become known as the "Kiska Blitz." It was a hurried and extemporaneous operation that accomplished little material damage but did put the Japanese on notice that their incursion on American soil would not be tolerated. The straight line distance between Cape Field and Kiska was 617 miles. The actual distance flown could be considerably longer depending on the mission that was planned. The weather, as usual, remained terrible. Not much was known about the Japanese. For the men of the Eleventh Air Force and Patrol Wing Four, it was a time for courage.

On June 7, Captain Jack F. Todd was ordered to lead five B-24D Liberators and their crews drawn from the 21st, 27th, 38th and 392nd Bombardment Squadrons, 30th Bombardment Group, March Field to Alaska for two weeks of temporary duty. Todd and his men left at 5:00 PM the same day, stopping briefly at the Sacramento Air Depot, Spokane and Edmonton on the now very familiar route to Alaska. They arrived at Ladd Field on the 9th. The next day they landed at Thornborough Field at 9:30PM.

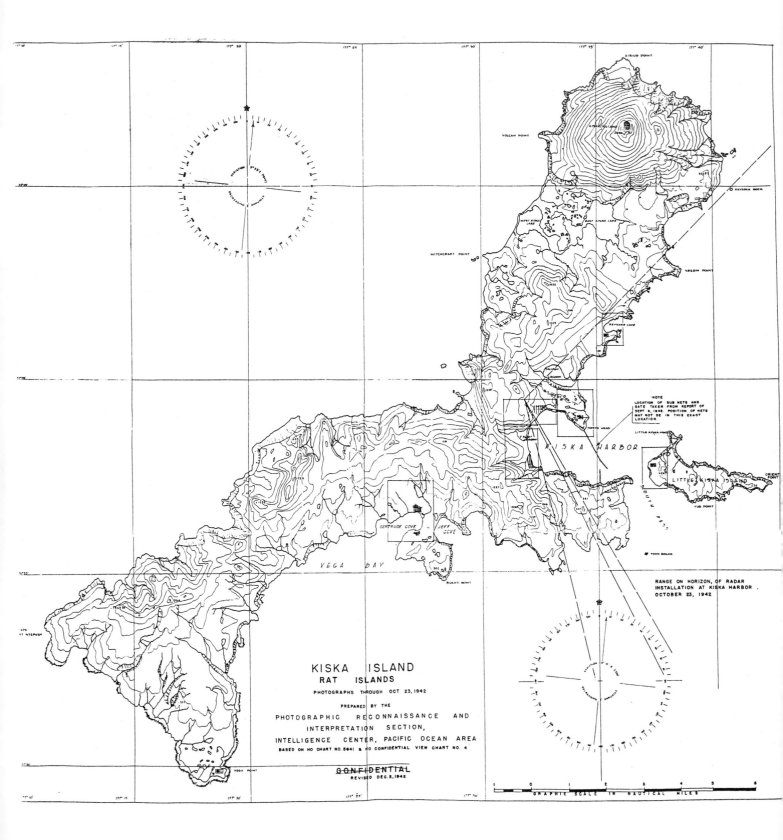

KISKA ISLAND
RAT ISLANDS
PHOTOGRAPHS THROUGH OCT 23, 1942

PREPARED BY THE

PHOTOGRAPHIC RECONNAISSANCE AND
INTERPRETATION SECTION,
INTELLIGENCE CENTER, PACIFIC OCEAN AREA
BASED ON HO CHART NO. 5641 & HO CONFIDENTIAL VIEW CHART NO. 4

CONFIDENTIAL
REVISED DEC. 2, 1942

Colonel Eareckson greeted and gave them a quick briefing. Their baggage was unloaded and the bombers serviced while Todd and his men managed to get a quick three hours sleep. The next morning at 9:00 AM, with Lieutenant Clark A. Hood, an experienced VP-42 navigator aboard for assistance, Captain Todd taxied his big bomber onto the runway and pushed the throttles forward. The Liberator thundered down the runway, followed by three others from the 30th Bombardment Group. Eareckson also sent Captains Speer and Ramputi along in their LB-30 to help guide the newcomers to their target. The first of many bomber missions against Kiska had been launched.[37]

After stopping at Cape Field to fill the gas tanks and load bombs, Captain Todd led the formation of bombers on a course that paralleled the south side of the islands. They reached Kiska and flew around it to make the bomb run on the harbor from the west over the hills behind where the Japanese were establishing their camp. Captain Richard G. Lycan, one of the B-24 pilots, looked down to see what appeared to him to be a quarter of the Japanese navy in the harbor and the flashes of the guns below. Eareckson's briefing had been very sketchy. Lycan recalled that "We knew the enemy was at Kiska, but we didn't know much else." They were not prepared for the intensity of the anti-aircraft fire that greeted them.[38]

The Japanese had already begun installing an impressive array of anti-aircraft weapons on Kiska. Four dual purpose 120mm guns were in place near the end of North Head. Batteries of 13mm, 20mm, 25mm and 75mm guns were being installed around the harbor and on Little Kiska. Additionally, the ships in the harbor were equipped with a large number of guns. They were waiting for the first American attack.[39]

The ceiling was at around two thousand feet with tops that reached three to four thousand feet. Todd decided to make a straight-in approach under the clouds. The bombers flew in a tight formation. Captain Speer had warned Todd earlier about making a low level approach, but the captain "apparently had no respect for Japanese anti-aircraft." "All I remembered," Richard Lycan later recalled, "was a big puff of orange color flame and a sensation of light, then Jack fell off on his right wing and I didn't see him after that." An anti-aircraft round had exploded against the right wing near the fuselage of Todd's aircraft. The bomber disintegrated, and pieces fell on and tumbled down the hillside near Trout Lagoon. Two other nearby bombers were hit by fragments from Todd's exploding B-24.

Lycan's bombardier, concentrating on his bomb sight, saw the glare, and thought his plane had been hit. Not looking up, he continued to concentrate on the bomb run while Lycan, in a daze, flew on course for another thirty-five to forty seconds before heading for the protection of a cloud. Speer and Ramputi in the LB-30, on seeing Todd's bomber explode, pulled their bomber around in a hundred and eighty degree turn. The tail gunner, Lester Smith, recalled counting at least seventeen flack bursts where the bomber would have been had the two pilots continued on their original course. The other bomber pilots also took diversionary actions and climbed to eighteen thousand feet before dropping their bombs. No hits were reported. The Japanese had drawn the first blood.[40]

Colonel Eareckson decided to lead the next mission. This time the tactics would be different. Instead of flying in formation, the B-17Es from the 36th Bombardment Squadron would go in separately below the cloud level through the passes behind the Japanese positions. Hopefully, the attack would surprise the Japanese before they could bring their anti-aircraft to bear. The squadron's

A Japanese film crew was present when Jack Todd's bombers arrived over Kiska. One cameraman filmed Todd's B-24 as it exploded and crashed against the hill slope overlooking Trout Lagoon to the south. The LB-30 flown by Speer and Ramputi is visible to the left, above the point where the anti-aircraft shell exploded the right wing of Todd's bomber. The Kimikawa Maru *can be seen in the foreground.*
Japanese photo via Admiral Russell

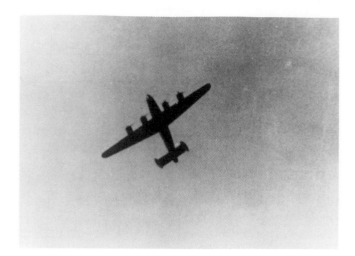

Japanese photo of one of the B-24s over Kiska during the blitz. The Japanese initially mistook the bomber for a four engine flying boat. Japanese photo via Larry Golden

The Kimikawa Maru *receives a near miss.*
Japanese photo via Larry Golden

Bombs being loaded aboard one of the B-24s. AAF photo

five bombers lifted off from the runway at Cape Field at 3:00 on the 11th. Colonel Eareckson led the first element and Captain Cone the second. The attack, as planned, caught the Japanese by surprise.

The 500-pound bombs fell down among the Japanese ships in the harbor. Eareckson, Cone and the others were sure that they had scored hits on at least three ships. Aerial photographs taken later proved otherwise.[41]

Eareckson's bomber crews went after the Japanese on Kiska the next day, the 12th. This time he led six B-17s and a B-24 on a low level strike. The crews reported hitting

and severely damaging a cruiser and setting a destroyer on fire. The reports were wrong. On the 13th, the crew of the LB-30 flew a weather reconnaissance mission and for the third straight day, Eareckson headed out from Cape Field, this time with five B-17s and three B-24s. Two of the bombers turned back and the rest bombed through the clouds without observing the results.

The 14th was more of the same, except that Eareckson led his bombers in at seven hundred feet, the lowest altitude yet. Three B-17s and four B-24s were committed. One of the engines on Captain Cone's Fortress was shot out and the hydraulic system on Captain Dunlap's B-17 punctured. It took him almost ten minutes to convince the control tower on return to Cape Field that his brakes were not working. Somehow he managed to land the plane on the steel matting. Eareckson and his crews submitted claims for hitting two cruisers and shooting down a Japanese float plane. None of the claims could be substantiated.[42]

A mission was planned for the next day, but then it was cancelled due to weather. The Eleventh Air Force had settled into a routine described by Billy Wheeler as "another day another mission—the damned war seems to be getting into a rut."[43] The "Kiska Blitz" for Eareckson's bomber command was winding down. General Butler noted to General Arnold that it had been:

> … a heart-breaking operation since the flights take about ten hours at the cruising speed which they are forced to use because of the distance and when they arrive, the target may be totally obscured or the ceiling may be so low that attacks are almost suicidal. There are few relief crews for the heavy bombers and the crews available are readily becoming completely exhausted. Without reinforcement, we cannot keep up the fight at this rate for very long, as we will have neither men nor ships fit to continue into battle.[44]

PBY-5A Catalina from Patrol Air Wing Four with under-wing ordnance. USN photo via AAHM

Colonel Eareckson's bombers had flown five missions. Ten men had died, one bomber had been destroyed and two others damaged. Despite the claims, which even General Butler admitted to General Arnold were exaggerated, none of the Japanese ships had been hit. Counting the losses at Dutch Harbor, it had not been a good month. The score so far was all in favor of the Japanese.[45]

Captain Gehres' crews achieved slightly better results. The Consolidated PBY Catalina, first operational in 1936, had been designed for long-range maritime reconnaissance. Powered by two twelve hundred horse-power Pratt and Whitney R-1830-82 Twin Wasp radials, it was slow and not very maneuverable; but it and its crew of seven to nine men could stay in the air for a long time, up to twenty-four hours or about nineteen hundred miles. It contained a small galley and bunks for the comfort of the crew on the long patrols.

The hundred and four foot wings had hard points from which four thousand pounds of bombs, depth charges or torpedoes could be hung. Bombs and depth charges were the weapons of choice in the Aleutian Islands since torpedo runs were considered suicidal. Armed with two 30- and two 50-caliber machine guns in addition to its under-wing stores, the Catalina was capable of offensive operations against submarines and unarmed or lightly armed merchantmen. The PBY was not designed to go against heavily armed warships or shore based anti-aircraft positions. Captain Gehres thought otherwise. On the 10th, he ordered the *Gillis* into Nazan Bay, Atka where it could support operations against Japanese shipping in Kiska Harbor.

The newly arrived VP-43 was augmented with crews from VP-41 and VP-42. Captain Gehres had ordered the two squadrons, which were still scattered at various locations on the Alaska Peninsula and the eastern Aleutians, to help out with the attacks against the Japanese when not conducting their normal patrols. The crews of the two squadrons, on completion of their patrols, had standing orders to proceed to Kiska and drop their bombs before returning to their home bases. Commander Jones and VP-43 moved to Nazan Bay.

Carl Amme, later to retire as a navy captain, remembered taking off with several other PBY crews from Cold Bay at midnight and immediately running into instrument flying conditions. They finally emerged above the cloud cover only to encounter icing conditions. Amme and the others managed to remain together as they headed for Atka. When they arrived there they had been without sleep for twenty-eight hours. North Island (and another life) was four days behind them. Amme and the others went to bed at 8:30. By the time they woke at 2:30PM, the first PBY mission against the Japanese on Kiska had been flown. Their turn would come.

While Jack Todd was leading his attack, Commander "Doc" Jones had launched his first mission against Kiska,

The PBY-5 seaplanes from VP-43, similar to this one at Dutch Harbor, operated from the seaplane tender Gillis *in Nazan Bay, Atka Island. The Catalina crews lived aboard the ship during the Kiska Blitz.*

USN photo via AAHM

A Japanese photographer took this photograph of a PBY on a low level flight over Kiska. Japanese photo via Larry Golden

Other photographs were taken of Machinist Davis' PBY, as the Japanese anti-aircraft gunners found their range, and blew the flying boat from the skies near where Captain Todd and his crew had lost their lives. Japanese photos via Larry Golden

some 360 miles from Nazan Bay. The Japanese gunners found the range of one of his PBYs flown by Ensign James O. Clark, as it pounded over the harbor and tore it apart. The plane captain, Aviation Machinist Mate First Class W. H. Lansing and the second radioman, Seaman Second Class Ellis J. Keith, were killed and another man critically wounded. The port engine and aileron were rendered useless and the rest of the seaplane riddled with cannon fire. Ensign Clark and his copilot managed to get their damaged plane back to Nazan Bay where it promptly sank upon landing near the *Gillis*.

The attacks continued the next day as the Catalina crews flew back and forth between the *Gillis* and Kiska Harbor in an attempt to keep the pressure on the Japanese. The pilots used the cloud cover as much as possible to hide their approach before dropping down surreptitiously to deliver their bombs against whatever target popped into view. The Japanese gunners soon learned to register their guns on the bottom of the grey overcast and cut loose on anything that came into view. After dropping their bombs, the pilots then did the best they could to fly their lumbering Catalinas out of harms way while the gunners returned the fire streaming up at them from the shore positions and the ships in the harbor. It was not a very accurate and certainly not a very safe means for delivering ordnance against a target. However, Commander Jones and his men were professionals and they did their jobs.[46]

One contemporary author, in typical media hype of the day, referred to Patrol Air Wing Four as the "PBY Interceptor Command," the attacks as the "Kiska Shuttle Service,"

Other crews were put up by Ralph and Ruby Magee in their home in Atka Village. When Comdr Norman Garton withdrew the Gillis, Atka Village was burned to prevent it from being used by the Japanese who were expected to land there. The Russian Orthodox Church and its priceless records went up in the inferno. Paul Earle collection

and Dutch Harbor as "PBY Elimination Base." He described the Catalina crews attacking like dive bombers through the overcast at three hundred miles an hour, dropping their "bombs by seaman's eyes bombsight" and making "four handed pull outs." According to his account, direct hits were scored on three cruisers, a large transport, and near misses on two cruisers, a destroyer and a transport. He went on to say the PBY crews had dropped sixty-five thousand tons of bombs in a ceaseless three day attack.[47]

The actual results were considerably less. The official history of Patrol Air Wing Four states that the damages done at Kiska were "never accurately determined."[48] Post war records show that the *Hibiki* was the only casualty. Several bombs exploded in the water near the bow of the destroyer and severely damaged her. The crew managed to get her back to Ominato.[49]

The last casualty occurred on the 14th. Machinist Leland Davis, an old, experienced Navy warrant officer pilot and his five man crew headed into the flack filled skies over Kiska. Below, a Japanese cameraman pointed his camera skyward as puffs of exploding anti-aircraft shell appeared around him. Suddenly, the PBY came apart in a violent explosion. Pieces of burning metal fluttered down on the hillside below.[50]

Captain Gehres had committed approximately twenty of his PBYs to the attack. Most were from VP-43. The men had flown almost continuously and were exhausted. One plane had been lost and many others returned with holes in them. Seven men had been killed and two more wounded. In return, one Japanese destroyer had been severely damaged, the total fruit of their dangerous labors. The "Kiska Blitz" was over and the Japanese remained in control.

While the attacks did little material damage, Commander Mukai later stated they did interfere considerably with the Japanese efforts to develop their support base and

The Kawanishi H6K, Allied code name Mavis, was one of Japan's finest long range reconnaissance aircraft. The seaplanes carried a crew of nine, had a range of 3,779 miles and could carry a bomb load of 2,200 pounds. Its major weaknesses were light armament and lack of armor plating and self sealing fuel tanks. The Mavis was not a success in the Aleutians. Operations in the swells of Kiska Harbor were difficult and the big four engine aircraft proved to be an inviting target for the air attacks and naval bombardment. AAF photo

defense system. It also forced the Japanese to withdraw their ships from Kiska Harbor.[51]

Commander Norman Garton, captain of the *Gillis*, called it quits. The PBY crews were exhausted and their planes worn out and battle damaged. Garton's own men were near the end of their endurance after days of ceaseless activity. They had gone through the stores of gasoline and ammunition. There was nothing else that could be done but to pull out of Nazan Bay and head for Dutch Harbor.[52]

As an added incentive, a Japanese single engine float reconnaissance plane from Kiska was spotted circling overhead. By now the Japanese were starting to bring in float planes. Commander Sukemitsu Ito, commander of the Yokohama based Toko Seaplane Squadron, arrived at Kiska on June 7 from Paramushiro with his six large four-engine Kawanishi H6K4 long-range naval seaplanes. His crews availed themselves of the PBY buoys that the Americans had left behind. Their supplies arrived shortly afterwards aboard the *Kimitsu Maru*.

Originally, the Japanese intended to use the seaplanes for long-range patrols between Kiska and Midway. They now decided to put them to use in the Aleutians, and Commander Ito's men began flying patrols to the east. However, fog interfered with their observations.[53] Commander Garton was aware of their presence from reports of the PBY crews who claimed, erroneously, to have sunk several. It was only a matter of time before they would arrive and bomb his ship.

The seaplane tender *Hulbert* arrived at Atka on June 13, and took aboard sixty-one Aleuts and Ralph and Ruby Magee, the two Indian Service school teachers on the island. Two PBYs were sent back two days later to pick up twenty-two others who had been away from the village when the *Hulbert* arrived. The village was burned to prevent its use by the Japanese who were expected to arrive at any moment. Lieutenant Thies was dispatched to pickup the weather team at Kanaga. He landed on the water near the station. The five grateful men, after setting fire to the station, clambered aboard the amphibian.[54]

The Japanese now owned the western Aleutians. Commander Ito's Mavis crews arrived over the village of Atka and found only burned out ruins. They dropped their bombs anyway.[55]

It Killed At An Alarming Rate

The Americans settled in for the campaign to oust the Japanese from the Aleutians. Patrol Air Wing Four was attached to the Eleventh Air Force on June 15, and assigned the responsibility for watching out for Japanese movements in the Aleutian Island area and reporting them so that the Eleventh Air Force's bombers could conduct strike

The Dutch Harbor airfield later in the war. USN photo

missions. The wing was also responsible for protecting Allied shipping and for search and rescue. Finally, the wing gained nine more Catalinas with the arrival of VP-51 at Kodiak on June 11th.[56]

Dutch Harbor became a major support base in the eastern Aleutians. The SeaBees took over the construction from Siems-Drake-Puget-Sound. One of their first projects was to build a runway. There was not much room, but they succeeded in carving one out of the lower slopes of Mount Ballyhoo. Some three thousand feet long by three hundred feet wide, it ran across the narrowest part of Amaknak Island and took up part of the seaplane ramp. The catapult and arresting system that had been hastily installed was removed.

Even then, the runway was still not suitable for handling a large number of aircraft. Lightly loaded PBYs were able to use it as well as fighters in an emergency. Four P-38 pilots from the 54th Fighter Squadron decided to test their skills. The first two did not bother to clear the end of the runway before the second pair set down behind them. All came to safe stops, turned around and took off for Cape Field.[57]

Cape Field at Otter Point became the Eleventh Air Force's major forward operating base for the air offensive that was now launched against Kiska. Talley's engineers moved in and began building additional runways, taxiways and hardstands. Pacific huts and Quonset huts replaced the tents. The living became easier. General Butler moved his fighter and bomber squadrons and their support units forward; and on July 20, he moved Colonel Davis and the advance headquarters of the Eleventh Air Force to Cape Field.

General DeWitt promised additional flying units from his command, and RCAF Wing Commander McGregor at Elmendorf Field was wondering if his Canadian pilots would be sent to the Aleutians.

Cape Field became a rear base as the war moved westward in the Aleutians. AAF photo

Nome Field, located 580 air miles from Anchorage, was built by the Civil Aviation Administration on the southern shore of the Seward Peninsula. The field was used as a base from which bombers flew patrols over the Bering Sea. The 36th Bombardment Squadron deployed part of its limited bomber force there following the Japanese attack on Dutch Harbor. The 404th Bombardment Squadron relieved the 36th Bombardment Squadron in mid-July 1942, and remained at Nome until mid-August 1942, when it was relieved in turn by Number 8 Bomber Reconnaissance Squadron, RCAF, which remained there until December 1943. The field was later named Marks Field in honor of Major Jack Marks. The photograph shows the field as it looked in winter. The Gold Rush town of Nome can be seen to the right. AAF photo

It was the enlisted men, in the words of Wilton Sass, who were "the heart" of the effort that kept the Eleventh Air Force going. Men such as Howard D. Nelson, bending over an Allison engine, Harold R. Green, center, and August W. Heine, worked long hours, often under deplorable conditions in order to keep aircraft operational and the pressure on the Japanese. They were the real warriors in the Aleutians.
Howard Nelson collection

Men repair a P-40E from the 11th Fighter Squadron at Cape Field. AAF photo

When the P-39s from the 54th Fighter Group arrived on temporary duty, the mechanics from the other units helped with the maintenance. The photograph above was taken by Less Spoonts at Adak. Less Spoonts collection

Elsewhere, Operation Bingo got underway in response to the Joint Chiefs of Staff directive to reinforce the Nome garrison. In what became America's first massive tactical airlift of the war, every plane capable of carrying cargo and passengers that Generals Buckner and Butler could lay their hands on, was rounded up and committed to the effort. The fifteen military transports and the bombers that were pressed into service were augmented by forty civilian transports. They included modern DC-3s and antiquated Ford Tri-motors among their ranks. Passengers aboard commercial airlines suddenly found their travel plans disrupted as the military confiscated the planes and their crews and sent them north to support the airlift effort. Four of Commander Russell's twelve PBYs and the bombers that could be spared from Colonel Eareckson's command were committed to patrolling the Bering Sea in support of the airlift operations.[58]

The airlift began June 21. When it tapered off in mid-July, the combined force of military and civilian transports had flown 218 trips and airlifted 2,035 troops and over 883,000 pounds of cargo and equipment into the small Gold Rush town within an eighteen day period. Heavy equipment, fuel and other bulk cargo was shipped in by sea from Seward.[59]

By then, any idea of Germany and Japan joining forces to attack Siberian Russia had faded. Both already had their hands full and Japan had no interest in taking on another enemy. The neutrality treaty remained in force. The Russians were equally unwilling to take sides with the Americans against the Japanese despite efforts by President Roosevelt to convince Vlachyslav Molotov during the Soviet Commissar for Foreign Affairs' visit to Washington in the summer of 1942 that American bases were needed in Siberia. Without the bases, General Buckner had little hope of realizing his dream of launching an offensive against Japan from the north. However, before anything could be done, the Americans had to get rid of the Japanese in the Aleutians.[60]

Kiska, however, was still out of reach of all but the heavy bombers and Captain Jackson's P-38s. Even then, the B-17s and B-24s could only carry half their loads in order to complete the straight line, 1,234-mile round trip. Worse yet, until the Navy could finish the field at Dutch Harbor, the only alternate one in the event of bad weather was Thornborough Field 243 miles to the east.[61]

Eareckson's command, the 28th Composite Group, settled into a routine. A weather reconnaissance bomber was dispatched early each morning to determine if there was enough visibility at the intended target. If there was, the bombers were launched. Following the last mission of the "Kiska Blitz" on the 14th, Eareckson's bomber crews sat out the next three days in enforced idleness. The targets at Kiska were obscured by clouds. Billy Wheeler noted in his diary:

> No missions flown . . . Relaxed and fished . . . considerable conjecture among the local warriors about the Jap need for such a God-forsaken hole. The general consensus of opinion seems to be that they need a submarine operating base. They could raid Lend Lease shipping.[62]

While the air crews struggled with their gnawing fear of the uncertainties of the enemy and the weather, the ground crews fought their own battles to overcome the primitive conditions and inadequate facilities. Most of the work was done outdoors in the cruel elements of the Aleutians. Men struggled to change engines and hang bombs with limited tools in cold drizzling rain, their hands numbed with cold, their bodies worn with fatigue; but always fighting to stay alert with the consciousness that the lives of those who flew into battle depended on their skill and their perseverance.

Years afterwards, Albert Aiken remembered they were the "finest group of enlisted men," he had served with in his twenty-six years as an Air Force pilot; and they deserved the "best medals that could be given."[63]

Eareckson's bombers finally made it off the runway at Cape Field on the 18th. This time the crews of three B-17s and the LB-30 from the 36th Bombardment Squadron and four B-24s from the composite squadron of the 30th Bombardment Group succeeded in drawing their first blood. The plan called for the LB-30 to scout ahead and report the weather. The B-17s were to go in next followed by the B-24 an hour later.

The *Nissan Maru* had arrived with the occupation force, carrying a load of coal, fuel oil and gasoline. Captain Cone led the B-17s in at fourteen thousand feet to avoid the smaller anti-aircraft guns. The skies over Kiska were clear. The bombardiers picked their targets and dropped their bombs independently of each other. Master Sergeant Alpha G. Story, Cone's bombardier aimed for the *Nissan Maru* in the center of the harbor. One of his bombs struck home in the mid-section and bridge areas, setting the 6,537 ton transport afire.

In addition to the *Nissan Maru*, Cone's bomber pilots filed reports which claimed that another transport had been hit and two possible float planes shot down.[64] The Japanese admitted to the sinking of the *Nissan Maru*, but not to the rest.[65] William House on Kiska recalled that the bow of the transport was still above the water when he surrendered to the Japanese in July. When he left in September, the *Nissan Maru* had settled to the bottom of the harbor with only its mast protruding from the waters.[66]

The B-24 crews arrived over Kiska shortly after Captain Cone's force had departed. They went in at low level but did not score any hits. On the way back, the B-24 flown by Captain Ira F. Wintermute ran out of gas over the Bering Sea one hundred miles from Cape Field. Captain Wintermute and his copilot managed to ditch the bomber, which broke apart and sank within five minutes. Two of the crew, Lieutenant Horace T. Freeman Jr. and Private Brooke C. Quattlebaur, were trapped in the B-24 and died. The rest of the crew clambered into a life raft. They were picked up by a patrolling PBY the next day.[67]

The bomber attacks continued. Seven more missions were planned during June of which two were successful. One flown on the 25th involved the use of incendiaries for the first time. The gunners reported seeing smoke, but photographs that were taken later failed to confirm any

The photograph of the burning Nissan Maru *was taken several days later. The 474-foot long, 58-foot wide ship, commissioned in 1938, later sank in the harbor where she remains today. Other Japanese ships can be seen in the harbor.*
AAF photo

KISKA HARBOR

The Japanese also photographed the burning transport.
Japanese photo via Larry Golden

damages.[68]

Distance and weather continued to be the major inhibitors, and the Japanese were establishing an impressive anti-aircraft system that hindered precision bombing. In order to keep the pressure on, the bomber crews began using Kiska volcano as a reference point to fly a time-distance course to a point above the overcast where the bombardier released his bombs, hoping to hit something. Admiral Theobald called a halt to the practice. Crew lives were being needlessly jeopardized for uncertain results and bombs were being wasted.[69]

The persistent, unrelenting, terrible weather, however, was the number one foe in the Aleutians. At best, it made lives miserable and at worst it killed at an alarming rate. The official Army Air Forces history summed it up, stating:

> It was weather, in the last analysis, that relegated Alaska and the Aleutians to a relatively inactive theater. No strategic offensive was attempted by either side. The tempo of operations in the Aleutians was much slower because of it. Aircraft and military reputations were lost, honors and promotions slow to come by.[70]

The first mission was flown against Attu, some 778 miles from Cape Field, on July 2. The crew of the B-17 weather ship reached the island and noted the presence of the Japanese. They then flew on to nearby Agattu where they spotted Japanese ships in McDonald Bay.[71] The crews of the seven following B-24s arrived over Attu, but could not find their targets. They then proceeded to Agattu where they dropped their bombs. The *Kamikawa Maru*, *Kimikawa Maru* and the oil tanker *Fujisan Maru* were damaged by near misses. The six destroyers which had also taken refuge there from the bombing attacks on Kiska Har-

bor were not harmed. Several persons on the bridge of the *Kimikawa Maru* were killed and a number of others were wounded.[72]

The air battle continued on into July and settled down into a routine that demanded administrative and logistical support in ever increasing volumes. General Butler had realized the need for a centralized administrative and logistical system shortly after assuming command. He recommended a service command be established to support his many and widely separated bases and fields. The support that was being provided was fragmented, coming from many sources, and poorly coordinated. Somehow the Eleventh Air Force made it through Dutch Harbor and the initial build up in the Aleutians.

With the air campaign underway and other units beginning to arrive, the support system was beginning to unravel. To solve the problem, the XI Service Command was established June 21 at Elmendorf Field as a provisional command. Colonel Robert V. Egnico assumed command shortly afterwards; and on July 18, 1942, the command became a permanent organization with the responsibility of providing logistical support to the assigned and attached units of the Eleventh Air Force. An air depot was formed at Elmendorf and the field became the air administrative and logistical support hub of Alaska for the remainder of the war.[73]

The XI Bomber Command was formed July 1 as a provisional organization for command and control over tactical operations. The 28th Composite Group was retained to provide administrative and logistical support. Colonel Eareckson assumed command over both. He had less than fifteen heavy bombers at his disposal to use against Kiska; and part of that force, from the 36th Bombardment Squadron, had been sent to Nome. The shorter

Captain Ira Wintermute, holding map, briefs another B-24 crew. In addition to surviving the ditching in the Bering Sea, a month later he was forced to bail out when his bomber was hit by anti-aircraft fire over Kiska. When this photograph was taken in September 1942, he was still going strong. AAF photo

One of the methods used to bomb the Japanese in Kiska Harbor when it was covered with clouds, was to use Kiska Volcano as a reference and then fly a time-distance route from it as this B-24 is doing. It was not a very effective means of bombing, but in the absence of anything better it was the only method available until an improved airborne radar provided a more precision method of bombing through the overcast. AAF photo

range B-26s of the 73rd and 77th Bombardment Squadron and the A-29s of the 406th Bombardment Squadron were committed to flying anti submarine patrols and training missions until a base could be developed closer to Kiska.[74]

However, a buildup of forces to drive the Japanese from the Aleutians had begun. The 404th Bombardment Squadron was alerted in mid-June to deploy to Alaska. The squadron had been activated as the 14th Reconnaissance Squadron on January 15, 1941, at Miami Municipal Airport. It moved to MacDill Field, Florida on June 11, 1941, and to Barksdale Field February 1942; and on April 21, it was redesignated the 404th Bombardment Squadron (Heavy). Up until its deployment to Alaska, the squadron's B-24Ds had been employed in flying anti-submarine patrols over the Gulf of Mexico. Major Robert C. Orth, who led the squadron to Alaska, had assumed command on April 10, 1942.

The deployment of the air echelon began on June 21 when Major Orth led his eight Liberators on a flight that took them by way of Scott Field, Illinois; Saint Paul, Minnesota; Hill Field, Utah; Ephrata and Geiger Field, Washington and then across the border and up the Northwest Staging Route to Ladd Field and Nome. For some unexplained reason, according to the squadron historian, the B-24s were painted desert pink during their stop at Saint Paul. This led to rumors that the 404th was destined for North Africa, and gave the squadron its nickname, "The Pink Elephant." The bombers were repainted olive drab at Geiger Field.

Major Orth and his B-24s arrived at Ladd Field on July 12. From there they flew on to Nome where they conducted their first patrol over the Bering Sea six days later. Before they left for the Aleutians on August 21, the bomber crews had flown thirty-nine missions. Their arrival at Nome allowed Captain Cone's B-17 and Commander Russell's PBY crews to return to the air battle that was raging over the Aleutian Islands.

While Major Orth's bomber crews were engaged in the

Major Robert C. Orth, Commander, 404th Bombardment Squadron in his office. The white splotches on the scheduling board behind him are the results of a censor's clumsy attempt to erase information on the photograph negative.
AAF photo via AAHM

tedious business of patrolling the icy waste of the Bering Sea for a non-existent enemy, the rest of the squadron began its movement to Alaska. The ground echelon had remained at Barksdale Field until July 25 when it was moved to Will Rogers Field, Oklahoma. There it was split in half. One half, under the command of Lieutenant Louis C. Blau, was ordered to Alaska. Colonel F. C. Robison, the Commander of the 44th Bombardment Group, the 404th's parent unit, gave the men a pep talk, noting that their duty in Alaska would be only three months, and that they would be returned in time for the group's planned deployment to England.[75]

It never happened; the 404th Bombardment Squadron remained in Alaska for the duration of the war. The 44th Bombardment Group and the other squadrons went to England as planned. While there it covered itself in glory, winning two Distinguished Unit Citations, one of which was for the famous low level raid on the Ploesti oil fields in Romania.[76]

Lieutenant Blau and his men left Will Rogers Field on August 14 for Fort Lewis near Seattle. They remained there until September 10 when they boarded the S.S. *Otsego* at the Port of Seattle for the trip north. It was during this period that Sergeant J.B. Nunn designed the squadron emblem that featured an elephant with machine guns for tusks. The *Otsego* arrived off the Anchorage dock the late afternoon of September 21 where it ran aground and began listing badly. The *Otsego*'s captain ordered the ship abandoned and the men of the 404th finished their voyage to Alaska in lifeboats. Shortly afterwards they boarded another transport to rejoin the squadron at Cape Field.[77]

Additional fighters were also sent to Alaska. The 54th

Fighter Group had been activated at Hamilton Field, California on January 15, 1941. Like many of the units activated in the wake of the outbreak of war in Europe, the group, under the command of Lieutenant Colonel Phineas K. Morrill, trained for tactical operations until Pearl Harbor. By then the group had been shifted to Paine Field. With the United States entry into World War II, the group's P-40s were exchanged for P-39D Airacobras, and it was assigned the mission of providing fighter defense of the Northwest. In late January 1942, the 54th Fighter Group was moved to Harding Field, Louisiana and was assigned to the Ninth Air Force. It was reassigned to the Third Air Force in April for the duration of the war.

In late May, Colonel Morrill led his group back west to California to participate in training maneuvers with the IV Fighter Command. Shortly after their arrival, Morrill was ordered to deploy his group to Alaska for temporary duty with Colonel Sillin's XI Fighter Command.

The squadron emblem of the 404th Bombardment Squadron on the side of one of the squadron's B-24s. It was approved November 1942. AAF photo

Lieutenant Les Spoonts was assigned to the 57th Fighter Squadron, one of the three squadrons belonging to the 54th Fighter Group. The others were the 42nd and 56th Fighter Squadrons. Spoonts remembered his squadron was operating from Lindbergh Field, San Diego when the Japanese struck Dutch Harbor. The 42nd was at the Ontario Airport and the 56th at the Orange County Airport near Santa Ana. The 54th Fighter Group began its deployment from the three locations. The 42nd Fighter Squadron, under the command of Major Wilber G. Miller, was the first to leave, departing on June 8 for Kodiak. The squadron, less its ground personnel, arrived on the 12th to reinforce the 18th Fighter Squadron's P-40s and the Navy's Wildcats in providing air defense of Fort Greely and the Kodiak Naval Base. The 56th and 57th Fighter Squadrons departed on June 12 along with the group headquarters and remainder of the 42nd Fighter Squadron. For

P-39D Airacobra, 57th Fighter Squadron, Kodiak Naval Station, June 1942.

Spoonts and the others, their destination for a time had been a mystery.[78]

All they knew was that they had received orders to move on a moments notice. Spoonts later recalled:

> We had been there [San Diego] a week to ten days and needed to get some laundry done, but we were afraid to take it into town. Then one day, sure enough, they came in and said load em up, we're leaving as soon as we can get you in the airplane and get it going. We had our B-4 bags that went in the gooney birds [the C-47s that were used to transport the mechanics, equipment and other cargo for the group], and I had a laundry bag that I stuffed over the engine behind my head. That was it. We didn't have any Class A uniforms, and it was all summer clothing. This was 12 June. We took off.[79]

Les Spoonts and the other members of the 57th Fighter Squadron still did not know what their final destination was going to be until they arrived at Geiger Field, Washington to join the 56th Fighter Squadron. Spoonts recalled that they thought they were returning to Harding Field. When they landed at Geiger, they were met by Lieutenant Colonel Charles M. McCorkle, the Deputy Commander, 54th Fighter Group, who informed them that they were going to Alaska.

The group headquarters section and the ground personnel of the three fighter squadrons were transported to their destinations in Alaska by a combination of military and civilian transports. Colonels Morrill and McCorkle, the pilots of the two squadrons, along with other pilots detailed from the 54th Fighter Group departed for Alaska in thirty eight P-39s. Altogether, three hundred and twelve men, their luggage and the group's equipment were moved north during June. It was the first deployment of an air unit to Alaska to be conducted entirely by air.[80]

The route of the P-39 pilots took them to Great Falls, Montana, where Spoonts remembered a large crowd greeting them and being served coffee and doughnuts by the Red Cross. Edmonton was a great place but Fort Nelson was a gravel strip in the wilderness. Spoonts and the other pilots had to refuel their aircraft by hand pumps from a stack of fifty-five gallon barrels. Take offs proved difficult and slow due to the need to wait for the dust to settle between each one.

After leaving Fort Nelson, the P-39 flight encountered the mountains of northern British Columbia. "The last sign of civilization," Spoonts remembered, "was a Hudson Bay trading post on the edge of a lake on the edge of a prairie." The maps the pilots carried still contained errors and had blank spaces on them. The mountains below were still covered in snow and there were very few places to land in an emergency. Compared to the other fields on the Northwest Staging Route, Watson Lake was "a deluxe airport" with fuel pits and long gas hoses. The airfield at Whitehorse was crowded with aircraft, mostly civilian.

The two squadrons arrived at Ladd Field on June 20. Colonel McCorkle led the 56th Fighter Squadron on to Nome before preceding to Elmendorf Field. The squadron under the command of Captain William P. Litton, provided air defense for the garrison there. It remained there until October 20 when it was transferred to Elmendorf.

The next morning, Colonel Morrill led the 57th Fighter Squadron, commanded by Captain Ward W. Harker, on the final leg to Elmendorf Field. Spoonts and one other pilot remained behind with mechanical problems. They took off only to run into a rain storm. Instead of turning back, they decided to find their way around it. They landed at Elmendorf Field, expecting to find the others. Instead, they were greeted by several of the squadron mechanics who had arrived earlier in a C-47. It was not until the next day, when the rest of the squadron arrived, that the two P-39 pilots learned the others had decided to turn back. "So here," Spoonts recalled, "we had two second lieutenants who had flown around the storm, while all the brass had sat it out."[81]

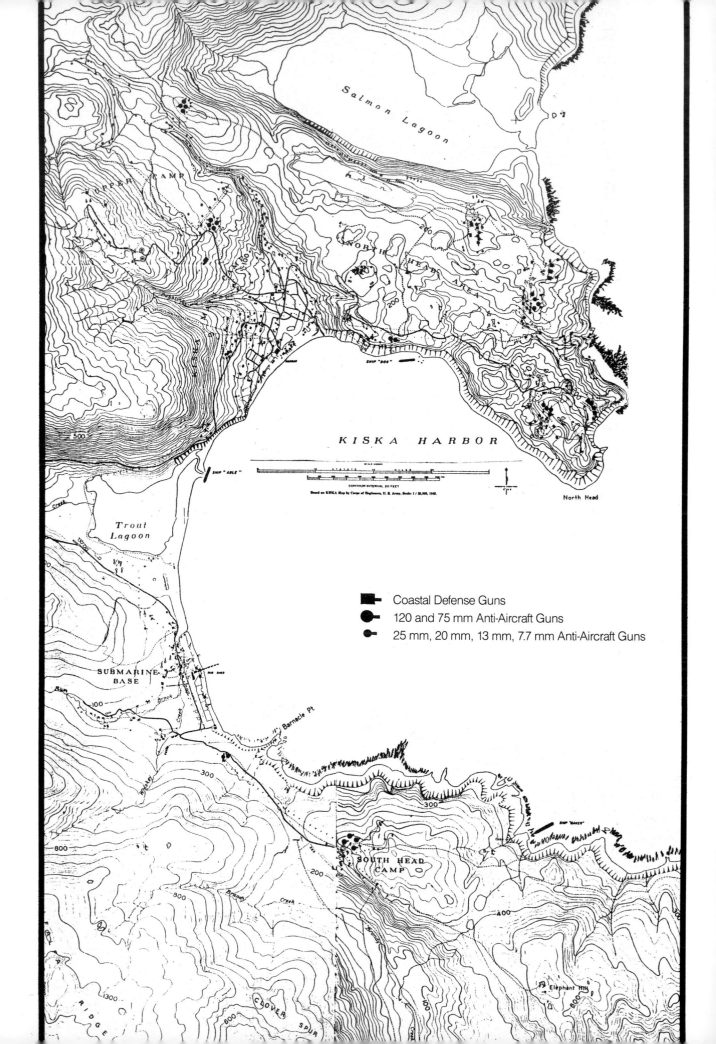

Salmon Lagoon

KISKA HARBOR

Trout Lagoon

North Head

Coastal Defense Guns

120 and 75 mm Anti-Aircraft Guns

25 mm, 20 mm, 13 mm, 7.7 mm Anti-Aircraft Guns

SUBMARINE BASE

Barnacle Pt.

SOUTH HEAD CAMP

The 57th Fighter Squadron remained at Elmendorf Field until September 30 when it relieved the 42nd Fighter Squadron, which had been deployed to the newly constructed airfield at Adak.[82]

The Enemy on Kiska

Until a base could be established closer to Kiska, the burden of the air battle fell on the crews of the four engine bombers. July proved to be a hard month, as Colonel Eareckson continued to keep up the pressure with the few B-17s and B-24s at his disposal. Eleven missions committed against Kiska and Attu succeeded in reaching their targets. Bombs were dropped without any determined results. Other missions were turned back or cancelled because of the weather.[83]

The Japanese continued to reinforce their defense on Kiska. In mid-June they began bringing in the Nakajima A6M2-N float fighter, code named Rufe by the Americans. The Imperial Japanese Navy had wanted a float fighter that could protect its forces in the absence of aircraft carriers and landing fields. The Nakajima company was assigned the responsibility for developing it because of their experience with float aircraft. Their designers developed a fighter that was closely patterned after the A6M2 Zero. Production of the Rufe was begun in April 1942. Although the large, heavy central float and the two smaller mid-wing floats reduced its top speed to two hundred and seventy-one miles per hour, it was still a very nimble fighter.[84]

Lieutenant Jack Litsey, VP-41, whose PBY had been destroyed by Zeros during the first attack on Dutch Harbor, fell victim to another fighter attack, this time by a Rufe pilot from Kiska. The attack occurred on June 25 while Litsey was conducting a reconnaissance and photographic mission over Kiska. One man, Aircraft Machinist Mate Second Class Austin W. Crosby, was killed before Litsey could maneuver his lumbering Catalina out of harms way.[85]

On July 17, another Rufe pilot shot down Jack Marks' B-17E over Kiska Harbor. They had been part of a mission of three B-17s and seven B-24s sent out from Cape Field to bomb and take photographs of Japanese installations and shipping at Kiska. The B-17s were making their bomb runs over the harbor at fifteen thousand feet when the Japanese attacked. The three bomber crews broke formation and began taking evasive actions. The Rufe pilots concentrated on Marks' bomber, the leader of the formation. The B-17's right engine burst into flames and the Fortress, out of control, crashed into the waters below and sank to the bottom of the harbor.[86]

The 36th Bombardment Squadron's RB-17B, Old Seventy, was lost the next day. Major Marvin E. Waslseth and his crew of five had taken the ex-Cold Weather Test Detachment aircraft on a photo reconnaissance mission over Kiska and were returning to Cape Field when it disappeared. A search was launched and several days later the burned wreckage of the bomber was found on Cape Udak on the southwest end of Umnak Island. Major Waslseth had apparently tried to fly the coastline of the island and had crashed against the side of the cape twenty feet beneath its top. The bodies were buried near Nikolski village. Billy Wheeler's diary entry for the day noted: "These were the only burials in the squadron-bodies are rarely found in our job."[87]

The surf conditions in Kiska Harbor took a heavy toll on Japanese float planes. The photograph is of two Nakajima A6M2-N float fighters. Japanese photos via Larry Golden

The bombing missions continued on into July and August. Very little material damage was achieved, but the offensive campaign that the Americans had launched helped convince the Japanese that they should hang on to the two remote islands. Admiral Hosogaya's intelligence staff now thought the Americans had established bases on Atka and Adak. The commander of the Fifth Fleet, who had been planning to evacuate Attu and Kiska at the onset of winter as specified in the original plans, decided to dig in instead. The Imperial General Headquarters concurred and on June 23 issued a directive that Attu and Kiska would be held. Reinforcements were brought in.

Major Hotzumi's North Sea Detachment was reinforced with the arrival of the 32nd Independent Field Anti-Aircraft Battery. However, it was on Kiska that the Japanese concentrated their main effort. They believed the occupation and fortification of Kiska would prevent the United States from advancing along the Aleutian Chain and establishing bases from which attacks could be launched against their home islands. Additionally, there was the psychological advantage of having their flag on North American soil. It was in the final analysis a good diversion that would tie down, with a minimum force, a large number of Americans and Canadians who could have been employed to advantage elsewhere.[88]

The description on the bottom of the oblique aerial photograph of Kiska states that it was taken at 1:30PM on October 31, 1942, from an elevation of 9,000 feet. Little Kiska is in the foreground. Above it is South Head. The flat triangular area where South Heads bends into the main body of Kiska was where the Japanese built their midget submarine base. To the right of it is Trout Lagoon. The main camp area was located where North Head begins. To the right of North Head is Salmon Lagoon. AAF photo

The occupation force was designated the 5th Garrison Force. Twelve hundred more personnel arrived in late June. Navy Captain Teshimi Sato replaced Commander Mukai as the commander of the Kiska garrison on June 30. On August 25, Major Hotzumi was alerted to move his force from Attu to Kiska. The move was made in mid September. A communications detachment was left behind at Attu to await the arrival of another garrison force, and Major Hotzumi and his Army North Sea Detachment moved into the Gertrude Cove area, southwest of Kiska Harbor.

Unlike Attu, which was later garrisoned entirely by the army, Kiska had a mixed force of army and navy units. The entire garrison was redesignated the 51st Base Force and placed under the command of Admiral Hosogaya's Fifth Fleet. Rear Admiral Katsuzo Akiyama arrived at the end of September with approximately two hundred communications personnel and replaced Captain Sato as the base force commander. An additional Army infantry battalion was brought in during November to reinforce the units at Gertrude Cove and the North Sea Detachment was upgraded to a garrison force. Major General Toichiro Mineki assumed command of the garrison, which was reinforced with an additional five hundred and seventy more Army men in late December.

The naval force continued to occupy the areas around Kiska Harbor. A road was built between the army and navy camps. By the end of the year, the Japanese had built up a force of over five thousand on the island.[89]

They occupied an island that is twenty-five miles long and eight miles wide at its broadest point and less than two miles at its narrowest. Kiska is located on the same latitude as London, England and the same longitude as New Zealand. It is completely devoid of trees, wind swept, hilly and bleak. The 3,996-foot Kiska Volcano on the north end dominates the rest of the island.

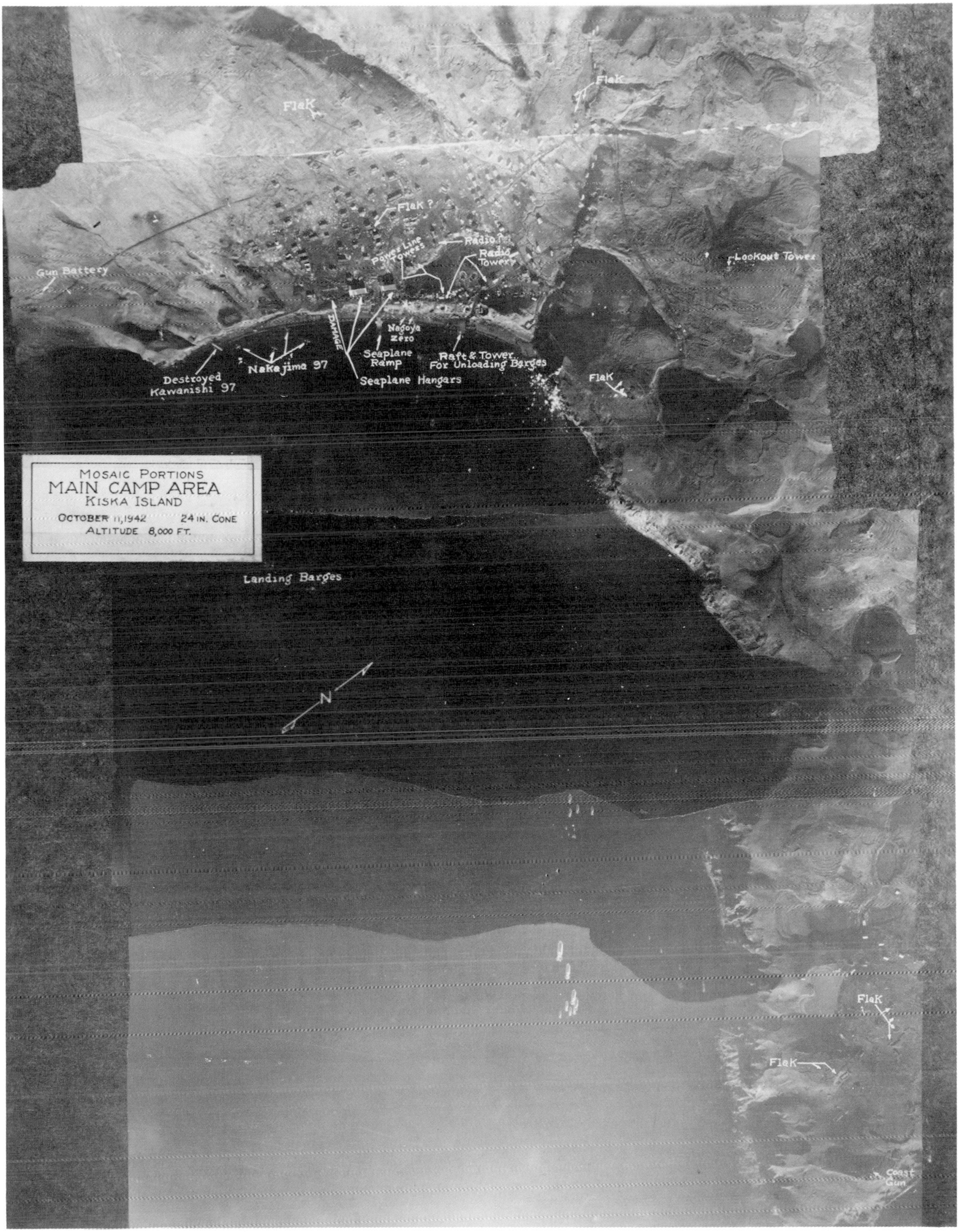
Flak
Flak
Flak ?
Power Line Towers
Radio ?
Radio Tower
Lookout Tower
Gun Battery
Damage
Nagoya Zero
Seaplane Ramp
Raft & Tower For Unloading Barges
Destroyed Kawanishi 97
Nakajima 97
Seaplane Hangars
Flak
MOSAIC PORTIONS
MAIN CAMP AREA
KISKA ISLAND
OCTOBER 11,1942 24 IN. CONE
ALTITUDE 8,000 FT.
Landing Barges
N
Flak
Flak
Coast Gun

Aerial view of the main camp. Note the falling bombs in the foreground. AAF photo

Rear Admiral Katsuzo Akiyama, commander on Kiska Island. For over a year his garrison tied down Allied forces that could have been used to better advantage elsewhere. It was one of the better investments the Japanese made during the war. Japanese photo via Larry Golden

Two of the four dual purpose 120mm guns the Japanese installed on Kiska. The guns, capable of anti-aircraft and coastal defense, were located on North Head. They were poorly camouflaged and easily seen from the air. The thin splinter shield did not offer adequate protection. The Japanese removed all the data plates and not much was known about them. Three were still there in 1990. Frank Rosse collection

The super-abundance of precipitation fosters a lush growth of tall, thick, fibrous grass along the lower slopes. The grass is considerably shorter at higher elevations, which consist of a series of ridge lines and hill masses. The low levels are boggy and the numerous small streams have cut deep, steep-sided gullies.

It was on this lonely, isolated island that the Japanese, for a brief period of time, established the farthest outpost of their empire. They began turning the island into a bastion.

More anti-aircraft artillery guns were installed. When the Americans and Canadians reoccupied the island a year later, they found four 120mm dual purpose guns, twenty-two 75mm dual purpose guns and an assortment of forty-three smaller pieces ranging from single barrel 13mm to twin barrel 25mm guns. The largest concentration was on North Head. Other positions were sited around the main camp and the north-central area behind it, the submarine base in Kiska Harbor, South Head, Gertrude Cove and on Little Kiska. The anti-aircraft guns were grouped into batteries, each with a central fire direction center. They were revetted to protect them against blasts from exploding ordnance and the ever persistent wind. A telephone communications system connected the batteries to a central command center—a reinforced concrete bunker that was dug into the ground and covered with a thick layer of dirt. The center was located in the main camp area. The lines were strung from cables connected to the numerous telephone poles that dotted the landscape.[90]

A radar was sited a short distance from the main camp area on a hill about five hundred feet above sea level. It had a range of about forty miles. Part of its coverage was masked by a high ridge of hills to the southwest and Kiska

One of the 120mm guns as it looked in September 1989. The guns were an inviting target. Little Kiska can be seen in the distance. author photo

Volcano to the north, limiting its coverage to the approaches from northeast, east and southeast.[91]

The sixty-nine anti-aircraft pieces were grouped in an area of about five square miles and provided protection for thirty-three principal targets. Colonel Jean K. Fogle's Eleventh Air Force intelligence staff soon figured out their capabilities and limitations after debriefing the bomber crews and studying the numerous aerial photographs that were taken.

The Japanese gunners depended on visual and optical range finders to sight their guns. Since the Japanese did not have proximity fuses, the larger caliber rounds had to be manually set to explode at predetermined altitudes. The smaller caliber rounds had to strike their targets in order to be effective. Secondly, with a few exceptions, the Japanese did not relocate their guns once they had emplaced them. Using this information, the bomber crews were able to plan their bomb runs so as to avoid the

The 25mm twin-barrel Navy anti-aircraft gun was highly effective against low flying aircraft. Ten positions were found on Kiska. The guns were generally mounted in revetments. A dugout was constructed near all the gun positions on Kiska where the crews could quickly take shelter. This gun was hastily abandoned by the Japanese who left its shells scattered about. USA photo

The dual purpose 75mm gun was the predominant type of ordnance on Kiska. Most of the 22 guns were sited in four gun batteries and controlled from a fire direction center. The gun could be traversed 360 degrees and elevated 85 degrees. Mounted on a trailer, as shown in the photograph taken during the winter at Kiska, it could be moved to where it was needed the most. However, with few exceptions, the Japanese on Kiska sited the guns in permanent positions. Revetments were build to protect the crew and their guns against bomb blast. The Japanese seldom moved them and American intelligence personnel took advantage of the fact to brief bomber crews on how to avoid their fire. Frank Rosse collection

The crew of a 25mm twin-barrel anti-aircraft gun. The Japanese in the Aleutians were also fond of dogs.
Japanese photo via Larry Golden

A battery of four 75mm guns survives on North Head, frozen in time from a period when they once sent death streaking skyward. Kiska, because of its remoteness, is one of the few battlegrounds on which the original instruments of death remain. However, time, weather and man are slowly destroying the remnants of what was once a center of human conflict, tragedy and triumph. The photo was taken in September 1989, by Susan Morton, an archeologist with the Alaska Region, National Park Service. Susan Morton photo

Almost all of the small bore anti-aircraft guns were removed after the Americans and Canadians occupied the island. This 25mm twin-barrel gun remains, part of a battery on North Head. Susan Morton photo

The Allies found fifteen single barrel 20mm guns on Kiska. Four had been removed from aircraft. Usually, they were set up individually or in batteries and were located so as to protect the 75mm guns. USA photo

Fourteen 13mm twin barrel and four single barrel anti-aircraft machine guns were found in revetted positions near Japanese facilities. USA photo

heaviest concentration of fire. As a result, of the 601 missions totaling 3,609 sorties flown against Kiska between June 11, 1942 and August 14, 1943, 15 aircraft were lost to anti-aircraft fire for an operational loss rate of less than one half of one percent of the sorties flown. (A mission is a flight by a group of planes, a sortie is one trip by one plane.)[92]

Six more were lost to Rufe fighters that contributed to the air defense of the island.[93] In addition to the Rufes, the Japanese brought in other float planes. The seaplane tender *Kimikawa Maru* arrived a few days after Commander Mukai's force had landed. Six Aichi E13A1 Jake three seat, twin float reconnaissance aircraft were off-loaded to support the forces ashore. Shortly afterwards, Captain Tarohachi Shinoda came into the harbor with the *Kamikawa Maru* and several other vessels. The force had been detached from a group of auxiliary vessels following the defeat at Midway and sent north with additional float planes for Kiska. Fourteen Nakajima E8N2 Dave two seat, single float reconnaissance biplanes and four Mitsubishi F1M2 Pete two seat, single float monoplanes were lowered over the side.

Supplies and spare parts for the aircraft were brought ashore and construction of a seaplane ramp and three hangars was begun at the main camp. A row of buoys was laid just off shore. The float planes were moored at the buoys during calm weather and were dragged ashore or flown over to Salmon Lagoon during rough weather. Wheeled cradles pulled by an Allis-Chalmers tractor were used to move the planes from the water to the hangars for maintenance. Salmon Lagoon was also used on occasion as a maintenance area.[94]

The reconnaissance aircraft were organized into the 51st Base Air Unit under the command of Commander Nobukichi Takahashi and employed in flying reconnaissance and anti-submarine patrols. They also had a limited capability for carrying bombs. There were forty pilots and twenty crew members and seventy support personnel assigned to the reconnaissance aircraft. The Rufes, which were used for fighter protection, were organized into the 452nd Naval Air Group and subordinate to the 51st Base Air Unit.

The *Kimikawa Maru* was withdrawn shortly after her arrival at Kiska and used to patrol the waters around the other nearby islands. Captain Shinoda departed with the *Kamikawa Maru* around June 19 to avoid the American bombing. He took the seaplane tender to McDonald Bay, Agattu Island where his and the other Japanese ships were attacked by the B-24 crews on July 2. Captain Shinoda next moved his ship to Attu, but fog prevented him from finding an anchorage. He then headed back to the vicinity of Kiska where he remained until the end of July before being ordered to return to Japan.

The seaplane base area at the main camp. The American weather station can be seen in the lower right hand corner of the photograph. AAF photo

Of the original twenty-four float reconnaissance planes that had been left behind at Kiska, only two were operational by the end of September. Over half were destroyed during storms. The remainder were lost to bomber attacks. The twelve original Rufes suffered a similar fate. The Japanese shipped in crated replacements aboard transports. They were usually off-loaded at Attu, reassembled and flown the remaining distance. A navigational radio aid was erected near the tip of South Head to help guide the pilots to their destination. Occasionally, when the circumstances were right and the weather good, the transports brought the aircraft directly to Kiska. The pilots of the Eleventh Air Force and the weather, however, continued to take a heavy toll, and the number of float fighter and reconnaissance aircraft that the Japanese were able to maintain at Kiska seldom exceeded fourteen.

Usually, it was a much lower figure.[95]

Commander Ito's Mavis flying boats also did not fare well due to the weather and the American bombing attacks. Shortly after their arrival, Ito committed his aircraft to flying long range patrols to the east and southeast. The *Kamitsu Maru* arrived with a load of gasoline in drums and other supplies for the four engine flying boats. The cargo was off-loaded and stored behind the beach at the main camp and the cargo ship returned to Japan for another load. The patrols proved difficult due to the prevalence of fog. Three of the Mavises, according to Commander Ito, were lost to U.S. Naval bombardment on August 7. Another disappeared on a flight and the crew of another was forced to land on the ocean due to weather. The Mavis sank, but the crew was saved.

Although a replacement for one of the lost flying boats

The Aichi E13A1 Jake twin float reconnaissance plane was one of several types of aircraft the Japanese used on Kiska. It also was used for search and rescue, as a transport aircraft and in a limited attack role. Its 1,298 range proved useful in the Aleutians. It was armed with one light machine gun and could carry 551 pounds of bombs. The Jake accommodated a crew of three. The photographs shows how the Japanese shipped their aircraft to Kiska. Japanese photos vie Larry Golden

Japanese float plane pilots being briefed on the beach at Kiska. A Jake can be seen in the background.
Japanese photo via Larry Golden

The photograph found at Attu has appeared in several publications. It perhaps best represents the human element of the war in the Aleutians. It shows the pilots who fought against overwhelming odds under deplorable conditions and their ground crew who maintain their aircraft under very spartan conditions. The ground crew is dressed in rubber hip waders and gloves needed for handling the float aircraft in the icy waters. Japanese photo

One method the Japanese used to replace their aircraft losses at Kiska was to ship them to Attu where they were flown the rest of the way to Kiska. The aerial photo, taken November 7, 1942, at Holtz Bay, shows four Rufes in a cove at Attu. AAF photo

was sent to Kiska, Ito decided to call it quits after little more than two months in the Aleutians. He departed with the three remaining Mavises on August 17. In his post-war interrogation report, Ito made no mention of losing any of his aircraft in an aerial engagement with the Americans.[96]

The Japanese also established a coastal defense system to cover the entrance into Kiska Harbor. Two batteries of coastal defense guns, one consisting of four navy 4.7-inch guns and the other of three navy 6-inch guns were sited on the tip of North Head. Two of the 4.7-inch guns (Model 1905) were manufactured by the British firm of Armstrong Whitworth and Co. The other two were Japanese copies from the Kure Naval Arsenal. One of the 6-inch guns (Model 1900) was made by Armstrong Whitworth and the other two by the Kure Naval Arsenal. Three more 6-inch guns were located on Little Kiska. One, a Model 1898, was manufactured by Sir Armstrong Mitchell. The others

came from the Kure Naval Arsenal. Except for a few minor differences, the British and Japanese versions of the guns were identical in appearance and operation.

The guns were situated so as to cover the main approach into Kiska Harbor. The Japanese also installed four 76mm naval guns (Model 1898), manufactured by the British Yasu Manufacturing Co, which probably had been removed from the beached transport ships at Kiska. Two of the guns were located at the submarine base and were well protected and camouflaged by covered revetments. They covered the narrow approach into the harbor between Little Kiska and South Head. The other two were located on the high ground behind the main camp and were sited to cover the low ground at the inner end of Salmon Lagoon. Two old coastal defense guns were located at Gertrude Cove. Compared to the other occupied areas on the island, Gertrude Cove was lightly defended.

The 120mm and 75mm dual purpose guns were also

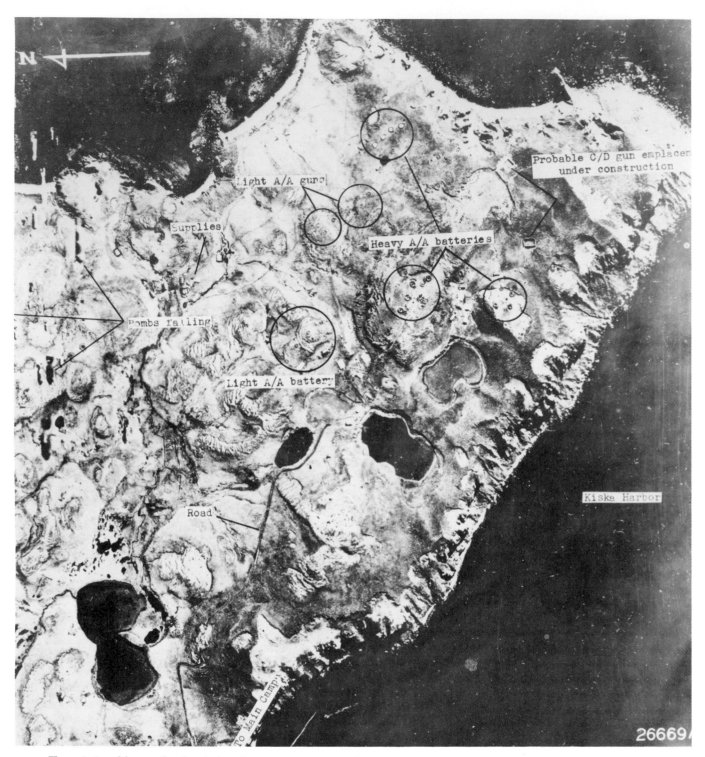

The majority of the costal and anti-aircraft guns were concentrated on North Head, which guarded the approach into Kiska Harbor. The location of the four dual purpose 120mm guns is marked in the circle in the upper part of the aerial photograph. The three 6 inch costal defense guns, hidden by camouflage and not visible, were located directly north of the 120mm guns. The four 4.7 inch guns were sited on the bluff near the tip of the head to the south of the dual purpose guns. A battery of four 75mm dual purpose guns was located a short distance away to the west. In addition to these guns, Eleventh Air Force intelligence personnel noted two twin barrel 25mm, two single barrel 20mm, five 13mm twin barrel, four 13mm single barrel and twenty-six to thirty-one 7.7mm guns on North Head. AAF photo

The Japanese had four types of coastal defense guns on Kiska. The largest was the Navy 6-inch gun. Three were located on North Head and three on Little Kiska. Despite a popular story, none of the guns on Kiska came from Singapore. Frank Rosse collection

The next largest size costal defense gun was the 4.7-inch gun. Like the 6-inch gun, they were manufactured at the turn of the century and badly worn. The Japanese had four on North Head. When this photograph was taken in September 1989, three of the guns were still in place.
Author's photo

Four 76mm Naval guns were found on Kiska that had apparently been removed from damaged Japanese transports and installed in costal defense positions. The guns, unlike the larger guns, were mounted in covered revetments and well camouflaged. Two old 75mm guns were also found at the Army camp in the Gertrude Cove area. USA photo

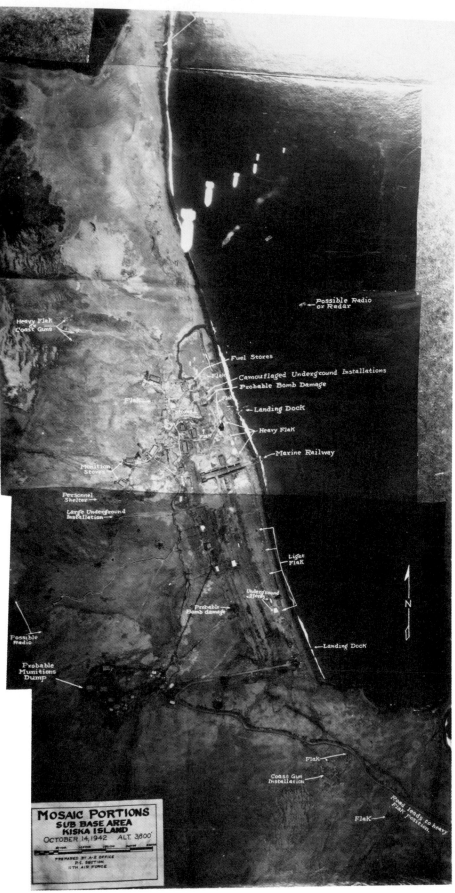

Labels on photo:

Possible Radio or Radar

Heavy Flak Coast Guns

Fuel Stores
Camouflaged Underground Installations
Probable Bomb Damage

Landing Dock

Heavy Flak

Marine Railway

Munition Stores

Personnel Shelter

Large Underground Installation

Light Flak

Underground Stores

Probable Bomb damage

Possible Radio

Probable Munitions Dump

Landing Dock

Flak

Coast Gun Installation

Flak

Road leads to heavy Flak Position.

N

MOSAIC PORTIONS
SUB BASE AREA
KISKA ISLAND
OCTOBER 14, 1942   ALT. 3800'

PREPARED BY A-2 OFFICE
P-I SECTION
11TH AIR FORCE

A mosaic of the midget sub-marine area. AAF photo

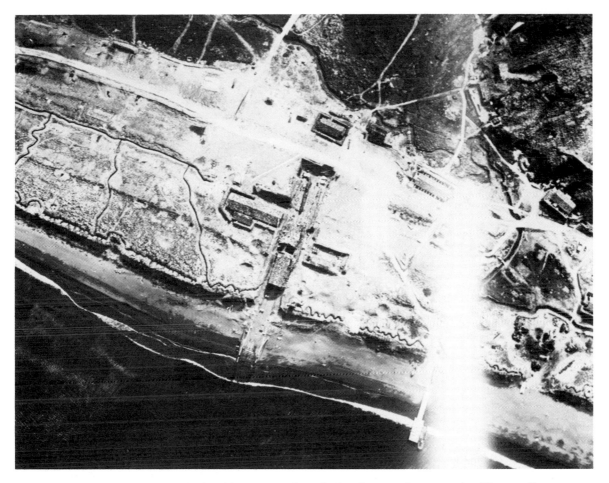

A closer view of the submarine shed and the marine rail way leading from it to the waters edge. The wavy lines were trenches. AAF photo

used for coastal defense. The whole system was primitive by American standards. Although, collectively the guns could produce a formidable amount of fire power, their range was short and they were badly worn with age. None were adequately protected against counter fire. Only the 6 inch guns had splinter shields and except for the 76mm guns, the camouflage was poor. The Japanese depended on optical range-finders to determine distances. There was no radar. Night illumination was provided by two 150cm search lights, one on each side of the 4.7 inch battery. A 98cm searchlight was located on Little Kiska and a second was sited on the high ground behind the main camp. In short, they could not have withstood the modern ordnance and fire direction systems found aboard American war ships.[97]

The Japanese also shipped in one hundred men and six Class A midget submarines to Kiska from the Special Submarine Base Force in June for harbor defense. Two hundred construction personnel arrived with the force to begin building a submarine base on the south side of Kiska Harbor near Trout Lagoon. The base, when finished, consisted of a marine railway that ran from the water to a roofed submarine shed to house the submarines while

they were being serviced and repaired, a machine and battery repair shop, a marine equipment storage building, an acid storage building and a powerhouse.[98]

The submarines were of the same design as those that had unsuccessfully participated in the attack on Pearl Harbor. They displaced forty-six tons, were seventy-eight and a half feet long with a beam of six feet and employed a crew of two. Power was provided by a series of twelve volt storage batteries located on racks that filled most of the interior of the submarine. They ran a 600-horsepower engine that drove twin counter rotating propellers. The submarines were capable of making twenty-three knots on the surface and eighteen submerged. Their operating radius was eighty miles at six knots. They were armed with two bow mounted 18-inch torpedoes.[99]

The Japanese settled down on Kiska, which they renamed Miokoda Island, for a long stay. Wooden barracks were constructed, revetted with high, thick berms of dirt and camouflaged. They were heated by small cast iron stoves that burned coal and charcoal. Bath houses and latrine facilities were built. A water system was established. Power plants were installed at the main camp, on North Head, and at the submarine base and an electrical

One of the badly damaged midget submarines the Allies found at Kiska after they landed in August 1943. USA photo

The same submarine and area as they looked in September 1989. author's photo

The Japanese main camp area and the extensive effort they made to camouflage and protect their facilities against air attacks. USA photo

distribution system was set up to carry the current to the buildings in the area. The conditions in the Army camp at Gertrude Cove were more austere, but still comfortable.[100]

An elaborate tunnel and underground shelter system to include two underground hospitals was built. Many were equipped with electric lights, and the larger shelters were stocked with supplies. One shelter near the officers' quarters in the main camp was later found supplied with saké and a record player and a supply of American, French and Japanese records.[101]

The Japanese ate well. When the Americans and Canadians reoccupied the island, they found stores of canned fish of various types; sacked rice and wheat and other staples; a variety of dried, pickled and canned vegetables and fruits; various spices; and a plentiful supply of tea, cider, beer, saké and gin. There was no central storage area and each unit had its own mess facility. Clothing appeared not to have been a problem. The Japanese were equipped with warm and waterproof garments. Except for the bombing, Admiral Akiyama's force on Kiska fared as well, if not better, than their American and Canadian opposites.[102]

The Japanese made certain, to the embarrassment of the Americans, that their presence on Kiska was well publicized. Reporters were sent to the island and they filed

A Japanese barrack. USA photo

An age old military custom, calisthenics in the morning at Kiska. Japanese photo via Larry Golden

stories, describing in glowing terms the activities of the Japanese occupation troops and the apparent inability of the Americans to do anything about the situation. One account, broadcast by Radio Tokyo in late July noted:

> Forty days have passed by since the Navy took over this island. The process of transformation from what was once known as Kiska Island to that of Miokoda has been one of amazing rapidity. Each day the scene takes on new shape. Each morning I notice a number of new houses that spring up like mushrooms on the mountain side. New roads extend between rows of new buildings. It is amazing. Miokoda Island is truly growing like a child.[103]

The Japanese apparently found conditions on Kiska pleasant. The cold was not too severe, the mountains covered with lilies and violets and the streams full of salmon and trout. Their only annoyance was the American bombers; but the Tokyo broadcast noted that the American bomber crews, which the Japanese on Kiska referred to as "Roosevelt regulars," were not very accurate. The Japanese were scornful of their practice of blindly bombing through the clouds from high altitudes, a practice that proved to be wasteful.[104]

The relief map, built up from clay, and the aerial photo taken by an F-5 (photo-reconnaissance version of the P-38) on June 10, 1943, illustrates the rugged conditions found on Kiska Island. USA photo

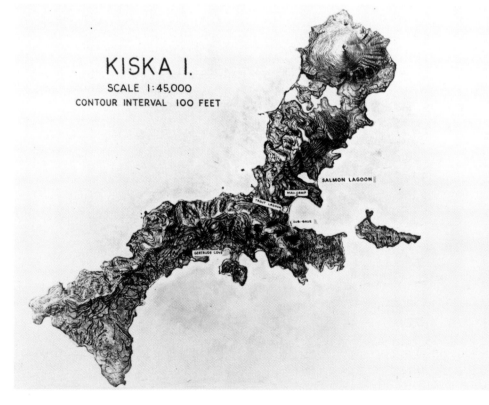

KISKA I.

SCALE 1:45,000
CONTOUR INTERVAL 100 FEET

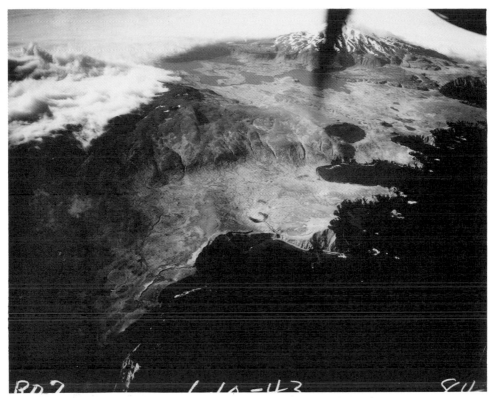

An Abomination

With the Japanese firmly planted on Kiska and Attu, it became a military necessity to remove all civilians from the other threatened islands. At the time there were approximately nine hundred Aleuts and a small number of Alaska Indian Service teachers and other government agents living in eight villages (Attu included) in the chain and on the two islands in the Pribilofs.

The idea of their removal had been discussed even before the Japanese came. Acting Territorial Governor E. L. "Bob" Bartlett called a meeting of other government officials three months prior to the occupation of the western islands to discuss the possibility of evacuating Alaskan Natives from their homes. All agreed that, except for those located at Unalaska where the large number of military personnel at Dutch Harbor threatened a social disruption, it would be an unwise move.[105]

The military also opposed the idea of removing the Aleuts from the islands. Rear Admiral Charles S. Freeman, Commandant, 13th Naval District felt the Aleuts should not be evacuated unless their lives were threatened. General Buckner was more adamant, stating that it would "be a great mistake," and:

> . . . in effect, that evacuating them was pretty close to destroying them; that they now live under conditions suitable to them; and that if they were removed they would be subject to the deterioration of contact with the white man, would likely fall prey to drink and disease, and probably would never get back to their historic habitat.[106]

Unfortunately, the events of the Japanese occupation drove a decision process, that while logical in its purpose, was fatally flawed in its execution. The loss of Attu Village and its inhabitants was a forewarning of things to come. Atka and the Pribilofs were the next potential targets. The possibility existed that they would become a battleground. Generals DeWitt and Buckner and the others in authority were convinced the Japanese were planning further offensive operations. In the context of the times, the decision to remove all non-combatants to a safer location conformed to standard military doctrine and was therefore justified. How the evacuations were conducted and what happened later was not justifiable.

The *Delarof*, "a huge ugly, gray, grimy combination freight and passenger ship," arrived at St. Paul in the Pribilofs on the afternoon of June 15. The inhabitants, with very little warning and allowed only one suitcase and a bedroll per person, were quickly herded aboard. The ship then headed for St. George where the people on that island were handled in a similar manner. The *Delarof* next steamed for Dutch Harbor with four hundred and seventy-seven Aleuts and twenty-two whites aboard. A few communications personnel were left behind to await a military garrison that was planned for the islands.

The transport reached Dutch Harbor on June 17, where it took aboard the eighty-three Atkans and the Magees who had just arrived at the naval base. No one, including Captain Downey, the master of the *Delarof*, knew what their final destination was to be. The local military and civilian authorities had been debating the problem while

A last look homeward. Only half of the Aleuts returned to the Aleutians after being allowed back. Of the eight prewar villages, Attu, Biorka, Kashega and Makushin ceased to exist. USA photos

he was in the process of picking up the group from the Pribilofs. Various locations were discussed, including Port Graham on the Kenai Peninsula and Marysville in Washington State.

The villagers at Unalaska expressed a desire, that if they had to be evacuated, they wanted to be relocated to villages on the Alaska Peninsula where conditions were very similar to those in the Aleutians. It was the most intelligent solution then and even more so given the tragedy of future events, but no one in authority listened.

The matter was settled, in typical bureaucratic fashion, by the Bureau of Indians Affairs office in Washington D.C., who directed the Aleuts be taken to southeastern Alaska and housed in abandoned canneries there. The Pribilof group were put ashore at Funter Bay on Admiralty Island near Juneau on June 22, after an arduous voyage made difficult by being crammed into the hold of the *Delarof* with very limited sanitary facilities. The ship then proceeded on to Killisnoo near Angoon where the Atka group was disembarked.

The matter of the evacuation of the Aleuts for the moment seemed settled. However, the Navy felt uneasy about the presence of the Aleuts in the eastern Aleutians. The non-essential civilians placed a strain on the supply system, and there was a general fear that the Japanese were planning to advance up the island chain. The tone had been set by the school teacher at Nikolski who had requested evacuation of her village because of the fear of a Japanese attack and the limited food supplies.

As a result, one hundred and fifty-nine Aleuts from Akutan Village on Akutan Island, Nikolski on Umnak Island and Biorka, Kashega and Makushin on Unalaska Island were relocated to Ward Cove near Ketchikan in mid July. The second transport of the Aleuts from the eastern Aleutians was completed on July 26, when one hundred and ten Aleuts from Unalaska were deposited at Burnett Inlet on Etolin Island.[107]

They were out-of-the-way places, abandoned canneries, gold mines and Civilian Conservation Corps camps; no longer useful for commercial purposes; dilapidated, unsanitary, and ill equipped for their intended use as temporary quarters for the Aleuts who were crowded into them without regard for privacy or common decency. It was an abomination. Territorial Governor Gruening in a September 20, 1943, letter to the territorial Attorney General's office complained that the conditions he found at one of the camps were: "Shocking . . . I have no language at my command which can adequately describe what I saw; if I had I am confident you would not believe my statements."[108]

Funter Bay was the worst of the lot. An estimated forty of the four hundred and seventy-seven Aleuts kept in the two camps there died, the victims of influenza, measles, pneumonia and tuberculosis.[109] The Aleutian/Pribilof Islands Association compiled an incomplete tabulation of sixty-three names of those who died in the relocation camps. The actual figure was probably considerably higher.

The Aleuts were kept in the relocation camps until near the end of war despite the fact the Japanese threat to the islands had long since evaporated. For some yet to be explained reason, the military had been reluctant to allow them back. When the Aleuts did return during 1944 and 1945, they found their homes vandalized and their personal belongings stolen by military personnel. Both the military and the civilian authorities who were responsible for their plight, made an effort to compensate the Aleuts. However, it was not enough and nothing could make up for the personal loss of such items as religious icons and other precious family items.[110]

What had been done was mindless and cruel. There were strong undertones of racism as reflected in a 1942 Army intelligence report which described the Aleuts as a "turbercular (sic), venereal, mentally undeveloped people, whose manner of life is a reflection of the hard, restrictive environment to which they are subjected."[111] There was also bureaucratic insensitivity resulting from a long tradition of paternalism and a feeling that the Aleuts were wards of the state; and, as a small, isolated minority, did not matter in the scheme of larger events[112].

The evacuation of loyal American citizens, their shameful treatment in the relocation camps and the destruction of their property by unthinking military personnel remains the worst legacy of the war that was fought in the Aleutians. Philemon Tutiakoff, former chairman of the Aleutian-Pribilof Islands Association, and one of the evacuees, noted over forty years later: "There are no words that describe the devastating consequences my people have experienced." It would take years for the injustice to be corrected.[113]

A Sorry Affair

General Arnold sensed something was wrong with the way the Eleventh Air Force was being handled. A non-believer in the formalities of large, structured staff organizations and a chronic disregarder of the staff study and other bureaucratic methods for arriving at a common, no fault decision, the impatient, get it done now, Army Air Forces' Chief of Staff often acted impetuously and without apparent rational reason.

Brigadier General Lawrence Kuter, a rising star on Arnold's staff, was en route to give a speech to the Midland, Texas, Chamber of Commerce in mid-June 1942, when General Arnold called him, told him his speech plans were being cancelled, and directed him to fly to Alaska and "fix things." Kuter had been provided a Lockheed C-56 Loadstar for the trip from Bolling Field to Midland. After finding a copilot who was familiar with Alaska and gathering maps, spare parts for the small transport and suitable clothes, Kuter headed north, still not knowing why his schedule had been abruptly changed.

He had never met Admiral Theobald and the last time he had seen General Buckner was when he was a cadet at West Point and the then Major Buckner had given him ten demerits. General Butler greeted Kuter at Ladd Field. The first thing the Commander, Eleventh Air Force said was: "Why were you sent up here?" Admiral Theobald showed "obvious concern" over the general's visit. Buckner was equally worried over why General Arnold had suddenly dispatched one of his young generals to Alaska.

When General Kuter met with the three commanders at Elmendorf Field, he could only tell them that General Arnold had sent him to Alaska to gather information on air operations. He then flew on to Cape Field to meet with Colonel Eareckson.

Before returning to Washington, General Kuter stopped at the Presidio where he met with General DeWitt and his staff. "It became grimly amusing," Kuter later recalled, "to hear successive intelligence staffs up the chain of command each add its own factor to the lower level's evaluation of the seriousness of the enemy threat." The Western Defense Command's intelligence staff, from its vantage point in sunny California and two thousand miles away from the action, estimated that the Japanese had a fifteen thousand man division in the Aleutians and were about to invade the West Coast.[114]

General Buckner was not at all happy with the surprise visit. According to him, Kuter had expressed the opinion that the "higher ups who made decisions in Washington" regarded Alaska as a theater of "very little importance."[115] He was right so far as General Arnold was concerned. The Army Air Forces' Chief of Staff looked upon Alaska as a nuisance, a place that could "in no sense be classed as an air theater." He openly wondered why the Japanese with less than fifty aircraft were able to contain the more than the two hundred and fifteen [his figures] possessed by the Eleventh Air Force. He felt that any more commitments "would be a wasteful diversion from other theaters which are air theaters," and that the Navy should take care of the problem and leave him to employ his aircraft to better advantage elsewhere.[116]

While Kuter was en route to Cape Field, General Buckner telephoned General DeWitt who in turn sent an "eyes only" message on June 23 to General Marshall. He expressed his and Buckner's concern that Kuter's possible negative report would have the tendency to "undermine the splendid morale and achievements of all units of Alaska Defense Command, especially air units which have been operating under most adverse and difficult conditions."[117] General Marshall quickly reassured General DeWitt that the trip had been made at his request "in order that somebody from the War Department should actually see conditions in Alaska and hear you and your officers state your situation and requirements . . ."[118]

Although General Marshall disavowed any intentions of slighting Alaska, the new theater of operations had been shoved to the back of the priority list. Generals DeWitt and Buckner were in the process of preparing plans to retake the two Aleutian Islands when General Kuter arrived on the scene and dashed their hopes.

The Joint Chiefs of Staff felt that although the possibility looked promising on a map, the weather and terrain were too difficult to overcome. There were other priorities. At the top of the list was the planned invasion of North Africa

The C-53 Skytrooper, a passenger version of the Douglas DC-3, was also used in Alaska. The transport, intended to carry paratroopers and other passengers, differed from the C-47 cargo version of the DC-3, in that it lacked the large side cargo door and its floor was not reinforced to handle heavy loads. USA photo

and the operations that were getting underway to retake the Solomon Islands and New Guinea from the Japanese. In short, despite their parochial views, and public concern about American soil being occupied, the Alaskan commanders would have to go it alone for the rest of 1942. Additionally, other than the 54th Troop Carrier Squadron, no new air units were programmed for Alaska.[119]

General Kuter's visit did have one positive outcome. Colonel Eareckson met Kuter at Cape Field and impressed him with the seriousness of the lonely little war that was being fought in the Aleutians. Years later, General Kuter recalled:

> Colonel William O. "Wild Bill" Eareckson, in command of B-24s based at a muddy, rain-blown field in the Aleutians, was flying a mission as a tail gunner when I landed at Umnak, because his tail gunners were not trained for low-level, bad weather operations. On his return to base, he went into a muddy mess tent and made biscuits, because his cooks didn't know how. He got better cooks and trained gunners.[120]

Thanks to the persistent efforts of Generals Buckner and DeWitt, the support of General Marshall and the public knowledge that American soil had been violated, Alaska did receive more personnel. The Eleventh Air Force's strength increased from 4,489 on first day of the Dutch Harbor attack to 7,717 on 30 August 1942, when Adak Island was occupied. It would climb to 11,654 by the time of the occupation of Amchitka Island in January 1943, and further increase to 14,824 by May 11, 1943, the day the 7th Infantry Division landed on Attu.[121]

Chuck Pinney was among the group of additional pilots who arrived immediately after the attack on Dutch Har-

bor. He recalled that he had graduated from flight school and received his commission on May 20, 1942. He was ordered to Alaska after a brief tour with the 48th Bombardment Squadron at Bakersfield, California. He was among a group of about thirty-six new pilots sent north who were: "fresh out of flying school, no identification cards, no dog tags, no shot records, no instrument cards," and "just fill ins."[122]

Many went to the hard-pressed 42nd Troop Carrier Squadron, which was struggling to keep up with all the transport requirements being placed on it. Ever since the Japanese attack on Dutch Harbor, every pilot in the squadron had been averaging over two hundred hours a month in the air. Their pressure was relieved somewhat when several ferry crews arrived with additional aircraft. They were detained to help out with the missions despite the objections from their higher headquarters. The replacement pilots that arrived with Pinney were a godsend.

The 42nd Troop Carrier Squadron, based at Elmendorf Field, was the only air transport squadron in Alaska. It was equipped with thirteen C-47s and C-53, and committed to flying personnel and high priority cargo throughout the territory. The crews lived like gypsies, moving from place to place dictated by their mission requirements, and spending the night at the most convenient place, which often turned out to be in their aircraft or camped out under the wings. Richard L. Hampton, a former sergeant and aerial engineer, described a night spent at Port Heiden on the Alaska Peninsula:

> We tied our two-motored transport plane securely so the wind wouldn't blow it away. We went to sleep in a nearby tent. About midnight, we heard noises. The wind had changed and was starting to blow in the opposite direction. By the time we got our clothes on and got to the plane, the wind was blowing 90-miles per hour and had torn the tail surface loose, and the inner bracing and the riveting were shearing fast. We spent the next two hours driving four-by-fours in the mud to tie the plane to, and then returning to our tent, we found the wind had blown it down.[123]

The rest of the pilots who arrived with Pinney were assigned to the 73rd and 77th Bombardment Squadrons which were at the time engaged in flying training and anti-submarine patrol missions. Many of the two squadrons' original and more experienced pilots had moved into staff positions in the Eleventh Air Force and XI Bombardment Command headquarters.

Pinney was assigned to the 77th Bombardment Squadron and learned to fly the B-26, which he found to be a sturdy aircraft with the flight characteristics of a rock. After completing his transition training, Lieutenant Pinney was given the job of flying the squadron's old B-18 on "morale" resupply missions. The experience proved pleasant, and Chuck Pinney got to see a lot of Alaska and meet

The 42nd Troop Carrier Squadron was based at Elmendorf Field and flew missions throughout Alaska, transporting high priority cargo and passengers. The squadron flew C-47 Skytrains, one of which is shown in the photograph taken at Elmendorf Field. The B-24 was assigned to one of the bomber squadrons and was probably back for depot level repair. The A-29, between the two, was flown by the 406th Bombardment Squadron. USA photo

Another C-53, at Adak, code named Longview, November 4, 1943. USA photo

people that he would not have ordinarily met as a B-26 pilot. It ended, however, with the occupation of Adak and the deployment of the 77th Bombardment Squadron there. Pinney, like the other medium bomber pilots, began flying combat missions.

The fact that General Buckner and Admiral Theobald were not getting along and that there was a lack of unity of command became readily apparent to those around them and to those who were engaged in the deadly day-to-day conduct of the war. Admiral Russell remembered he and the other commanders, army and navy, continued to work together despite the difficulties that were occurring at the higher headquarters.[124]

Nevertheless, the problems persisted and they affected operations down to the lowest levels. Worst yet, lives were lost and men suffered while Buckner and Theobald squabbled and DeWitt continued to cling to his military fiefdom. Word of the Alaska problems reached the halls of Congress, and Senator Albert B. "Happy" Chandler, a Democrat from Kentucky and Chairman, Subcommittee to Investigate Military Establishments decided to head to Alaska and find out what was going on.

Senator Chandler and his group stopped at San Francisco where he met with General DeWitt and held a press conference. His comments were picked up by the Associated Press; and *The Anchorage Daily Times*, in its August 7, 1942, edition quoted Senator Chandler as saying:

> . . . whatever it takes, we must get those fellows off those islands. . . . This is no junket or lark. We're not sure what our itinerary will be, but we're going up there to find out what's going on. We want to find out how the inland highway is progressing, all about the morale of the civilians and troops. The people all over the country are more alarmed over the Aleutian situation than about any other phase of the war.[125]

The senatorial party (Senators Chandler, Mon C. Wallgren and Rufus H. Holman and special consultant George W. Malone) arrived in the territory August 10. When they departed thirteen days later, they had traveled approximately eight thousand miles, and had visited Elmendorf Field, Ladd Field, Marks Field, Kodiak Naval Base, Thornborough Field, Cape Field, Sitka Naval Base, Juneau, Edmonton and Whitehorse in Canada and had flown the route of the Alaska Highway, then under construction.[126]

When the party visited Cape Field, the sun was shin-

Charles "Chuck" Pinney, seated to the left during a formal dinner with Canadian pilots, was one of the young air warriors sent to the Aleutians shortly after the Japanese struck Dutch Harbor. Retired from the Air Force, he and his wife live in Manitou Springs, Colorado. Colonel Pinney was the key mover behind the highly successful 1980 Eleventh Air Force reunion and remains a tireless worker in preserving its heritage and keeping its memory alive. Pinney collection

ing for the first time in weeks. One of the senators allegedly remarked later: "This so-called one-way weather seems to favor the Japs but not us." The comment gave rise to the expression "senatorial weather."[127] Senator Chandler, on return to San Francisco, publicly noted the "situation was serious but encouraging," and stated he "felt a lot better than when he left for Alaska." He was "alarmed that the military had not given full consideration to Japanese in the Aleutians."[128]

The Chandler Committee filed its report shortly after it returned to Washington. The committee listed the lack of unity of command as its number one finding. The other findings involved the recognition of Alaska's strategic location, the use of the territory to launch an offensive against Japan, and the need to drive the Japanese from the western Aleutians. The committee, on September 1, recommended to the President that a separate unified command be established in Alaska. The other recommendations in order of importance were: sending more forces to Alaska, providing additional heavy equipment, and improving the methods for unloading ships.[129] President Roosevelt sent the report to the Joint Chiefs of Staff for their review and comments.

The Chiefs submitted their comments to the President on October 9. While they agreed with the need to send more forces and equipment to Alaska, they found that the existing command arrangement was satisfactory and recommended no changes be made. The President agreed and notified Senator Chandler of his decision four days later.[130]

Senator Chandler's visit was followed by one from Colonel H. W. Shelmire from General Arnold's staff who arrived in mid September on a detailed fact-finding trip of Alaska's bases. While finding conditions generally satisfactory elsewhere, he described Fort Richardson, headquarters of the Alaska Defense Command, as "the dirtiest post I have ever seen," and noted that the morale was low, officers were quarreling and everyone was "glum and discontented."

Because of the confused command arrangement, "the whole situation in Alaska," Colonel Shelmire reported, "is seething with discontent." He recommended that the Alaska Defense Command be "divorced entirely from the Western Defense Command and the Navy," and made a separate theater of operations and placed under an Army Air Forces general.

The choice, he believed, was the most logical, since the Eleventh Air Force was the only military organization that was actively fighting the Japanese. The ground units were, for the most part, engaged in garrison duty and static defense. He did not mention the considerable contributions being made by the navy.[131]

Of the Services, the navy, because of its ability to control the sea approaches, was in the best position to defend the territory and drive the Japanese from the Aleutian Islands.

Because of the stepped up naval activities in Alaskan waters, the Pacific Naval Coastal Frontier, responsible for the defense of the sea approaches to the western United States, had been divided in July 1941, into the Pacific Southern Naval Coastal Frontier and the Pacific Northern Naval Coastal Frontier. The latter was responsible for the area from Washington State north to Alaska.

Rear Admiral Charles S. Freeman, Commandant of the 13th Naval District, headquartered in Seattle, became Commander, Northern Naval Coastal Frontier as an additional duty. Captain Parker, in addition to his duties as Commander, Alaskan Sector, assumed the responsibilities as Deputy Commander, Northern Naval Coastal Frontier. In January 1942, all naval coastal frontiers became sea frontiers.

All the organizational changes added to the layering of commands in Alaska. Captain Parker, as Commander, Alaskan Sector, 13th Naval District and Deputy Commander, Northern Sea Frontier was responsible for the coastal off-shore defense of Alaska and protecting the convoys plying between the west coast and Alaskan ports. Like Buckner, Parker was also responsible for supporting Admiral Theobald in his efforts to drive the Japanese off the Aleutian Islands and from the North Pacific. Admiral Theobald's other naval forces came from those allocated by Admiral Nimitz to the North Pacific.[132]

On June 26, 1942, Rear Admiral John W. Reeves replaced Captain Parker. The admiral was not a happy man. Two weeks prior he had written to Admiral Freeman to describe the lack of coordination between Buckner and Theobald, commenting that it was "one of the worst managed affairs I have ever seen."[133]

The relations between General Buckner and Admiral Theobald continued to deteriorate. They finally erupted in a dispute over which Aleutian island should be occupied. Generals DeWitt and Buckner had pressed for a base that was closer to Kiska and Attu ever since the Japanese had occupied the two islands.

Admiral Theobald fully agreed with the idea. However, the two generals and the admiral differed on which islands the base should be built. DeWitt and Buckner opted for Tanaga Island which had enough flat areas for an airfield and was 160 miles east of Kiska. Its major drawback was a lack of natural harbor. Theobald wanted to occupy Adak Island, 60 miles east of Tanaga. It had an excellent natural harbor, Kuluk Bay, but unfortunately there were very few flat areas where an air base could be constructed.

Admiral Theobald was also concerned about the rough sea conditions around Tanaga Island and the lack of a suitable anchorage. Additionally, he had very few ships

at his disposal and none could be expected from Admiral Nimitz. Despite these considerations, Generals DeWitt and Buckner remained adamant for Tanaga.

Reaching an impasse, the three commanders referred the matter to the Joint Chiefs of Staff for a decision. The Chiefs opted for Tanaga Island. Admiral Theobald, refusing to give in, had his staff gather additional information on why Tanaga was not suitable from the Navy's point of view. On August 4, he sent a message to Admiral King, asking for his support in reversing the Joint Chiefs of Staff decision. Admiral King sided with Theobald and was able to convince his fellow members on the Joint Chiefs, Generals Marshall and Arnold, to change their minds. Theobald's maneuvering put him on a collision course with the angry Buckner.[134]

Admiral Theobald, with expensive and scarce ships and their crews to protect, was being cautious. He fully realized Admirals King and Nimitz took a dim view of any naval officer who squandered his resources needlessly. Buckner, smarting over the rebuke of his idea, and realizing he was in a supporting role with no real final authority over the operations in the Aleutians, continued to exert the force of his personality whenever the opportunity presented itself. He firmly believed that Admiral Theobald was afraid to use his ships for offensive operations.[135]

The relations took a definite turn for the worse during an August 18 meeting at the admiral's Kodiak headquarters to discuss the planned landing on Adak. Buckner, still seething over Theobald's end run to reverse the Joint Chiefs of Staff decision on Tanaga, began pressing the admiral on the issue; and in the words of Theobald, ". . . commenced to intersperse his remarks with observations which were in reality an attack on me . . . making it clear

The formal photograph of Buckner was taken after he was promoted to lieutenant general. General Buckner remained in Alaska until June 1944, when he was assigned as the Commander, US Tenth Army. He led it during the last operation of the war in the Pacific, the taking of Okinawa. He was again threatened with relief, this time by Admiral Nimitz for his lack of aggressiveness. General Buckner was killed in battle on June 18, 1945, when he was hit by a piece of shrapnel in the heart while at a forward command post. He was one of two three star generals to die in battle. Lieutenant General Lesley J. McNair, Commander, Army Ground Forces, was killed during the breakout operations from the Normandy beachhead. USA photo

The promising career of Admiral Theobald was shattered in Alaska. Brilliant, but overcautious, the admiral was saddled with a convoluted command arrangement and an impatient General Buckner who had seen his forces stripped away from him and placed under the operational control of the Navy. The clash of personalities provided a classic example of how the egos of those in charge let to the hampering of operations and the suffering of others. The problem is probably best illustrated by the epitaph the Germans left on the memorial to their war dead at El-Alamein, "The price of pride is high, and paid by the young." Admiral King, while ruthless in weeding out those who did not measure up, also found them honorable jobs befitting their rank and experience. Admiral Theobald became the Commandant, First Naval District, Boston Naval Yard, where this photograph was taken. USN photo

that, in his opinion, my recommendations were prompted by my unwillingness to accept necessary and proper wartime risks."[136]

Admiral Theobald objected to Buckner's insinuations, and the general backed off. The conference proceeded as scheduled. However, as he was about to leave, the Commander, Alaska Defense Command pulled a slip of paper and began to read a poem that he had composed to those present at the conference.

> In far Alaska's ice spray, I stand beside by my binnacle
> And scan the waters through the fog for fear some rocky pinnacle
> Projecting from unfathomed depths may break my hull asunder and
> place my name upon the list of those who made a blunder.
>
> Volcanic peaks beneath the waves are likely any morning
> To smash my ships to tiny bits without the slightest warning.
> I dread the toll from reef and shoal that rip off keel and rudder
> And send our bones to Davy Jones—the prospect makes me shudder.
>
> The Bering Sea is not for me nor my fleet Headquarters.
> In mortal dread I look ahead in wild Aleutian waters
> Where hidden reefs and williwaws and terrifying critters
> Unnerve me quite with woeful fright and give me fits and jitters.[137]

The day after the conference, Admiral Theobald, seething with anger, fired off a letter with an attached copy of the poem to Admiral King to express his official displeasure over Buckner's affront.[138] The following day, he sent a personal note to General Buckner full of nineteenth-century politesse and disavowing all future social relationships except those necessary for the conduct of official business.[139]

Buckner responded on August 6, expressing his surprise that the admiral would be offended by his remarks and the poem. He went on to explain that he had made the remarks and read the poem only "with the view towards introducing a touch of levity into an otherwise ponderous discussion," and with the "thought we might indulge in a good laugh over them." He went on to explain that it was only his intention to "smoke out" the admiral and no feelings of ill will were meant. The general ended his letter, stating that they had serious business to attend to and now that they had "mutually smoked each other out," he hoped the "smoke would blow away with sufficient promptness to give us an unobstructed view of the Japs."[140]

The admiral was not amused and neither was General Marshall when Theobald's letter with the attached copy of the poem and a note from Admiral King landed on his desk. Buckner, in the words of Forrest C. Pogue, General Marshall's biographer, had violated one of the Army Chief of Staff's "unswerving tenets—the necessity of cooperating with other services in outlying bases and distant theaters of operations." The impetuous Commander, Alaska Defense Command was in far more serious trouble than he thought.[141]

On September 3, General Marshall, who had also received a formal letter from Admiral Freeman, complaining of General Buckner's conduct, wrote to General DeWitt, stating that he planned to relieve Buckner and replace him with an Army Air Forces general. The conditions in Alaska, Marshall felt, had "reached a point where there appears to be no other cure but a complete change."[142]

Additionally, General Marshall had come to the conclusion that the Alaska Defense Command should be a separate command under an Army Air Forces general. General Arnold recommended Major General George H. Brett as a candidate.[143]

The Army Chief of Staff, at the same time, informed Admiral King of his decision and that in addition to Buckner he was also going to replace General Butler. By then Buckner's poem had made it all the way up to the Secretary of War Henry L. Stimson. It had been circulated in Alaska. General Brehon Sommervell, Commander, Army Service Forces, had brought a copy back from his trip there.[144]

Generals Marshall and DeWitt were close friends of

long service together. DeWitt was one of the few generals who called General Marshall by his first name, something not even the President did. He was Marshall's senior in service and age and had been a final contender for the general's job. However, he lacked operational experience and had been passed over by the President who selected General Marshall over the heads of thirty-three general officers. If DeWitt had been chosen, it would have been an entirely different war for America.

DeWitt was one of three Spanish American war veterans who had achieved general rank and was still on active duty when the war began. He had enlisted in the Army while a sophomore at Princeton, received a commission and became a logistician. He was a classmate of Marshall at Fort Leavenworth and served as the Chief of Logistics on General John Pershing's staff during World War I while Marshall had been the Chief of Operations. Of medium height and mild manner, DeWitt gave the appearance of a "push over." He was anything but; those who knew him better found him obdurate. General Marshall tended to accept his old friend's decisions without question.[145]

General DeWitt replied on September 5. He was not surprised at the decision to relieve General Butler since the Commander, Eleventh Air Force had not been responsive to Admiral Theobald's requirements. DeWitt was also personally angry with the Eleventh Air Force commander for going over his head to General Arnold's staff on occasion, and at one point had threatened to relieve him of command. He felt otherwise about the Commander, Alaska Defense Command who had been sent to Alaska to build its defenses. This, he had accomplished in a outstanding manner. General DeWitt described his subordinate as a "fine, efficient, energetic" officer who had brought his command to a "high pitch in morale and fighting spirit."[146]

He went on to carefully point out in his five page rambling letter that it had been at his direction that General Buckner had tried to persuade Admiral Theobald at Kodiak to change his decision about landing at Adak. However, he felt that Buckner had been too aggressive and in the final analysis should be relieved as soon as the occupation of Adak was completed. As for creating a separate command in Alaska, General DeWitt ended his letter, stating, he had "thought a great deal about it" and believed "it unwise."[147]

Shortly after his letter to General Marshall, DeWitt met with Admirals King and Nimitz during their early September conference in San Francisco to discuss future strategy in the Pacific. One of the topics they covered was the unsatisfactory personal relationships between Buckner, Butler and Theobald. King and Nimitz supported the admiral, but contended that if relations did not improve between the two commanders, changes would have to be made.[148]

On September 8, General DeWitt informed General Marshall that he agreed the situation in Alaska was "certainly deplorable;" and that he had no doubt that the Commander, Alaska Defense Command would have to be relieved; and that he was planning to go to Alaska to look into the matter first hand.[149]

General DeWitt visited Alaska as promised and met with General Buckner on September 16. Buckner admitted to reading the poem and being aggressive in his opposition to Theobald's decision on Adak, but disavowed any thought of questioning the admiral's courage.

The Commander, Western Defense Command conferred with Admiral Theobald three days later at Kodiak. The admiral stated that Buckner's aggressive attitude had offended him; but acknowledged the general had been a victim of circumstances in his support of General DeWitt's desires to occupy Tanaga instead of Adak. He recommended to DeWitt that Buckner should not be relieved. Admiral Theobald then asked General DeWitt to invite General Buckner, who had been kept waiting in the outer office, into his office. The two shook hands and promised to cooperate.

General DeWitt, based on Admiral Theobald's recommendation and the pledge by the two commanders to get along together, recommended to the Army Chief of Staff on September 23 that Buckner remain in place.[150] General Marshall was very reluctant to accept his old friend's recommendation. He still believed that Buckner and Butler should be transferred after the garrison had been established on Adak and that Theobald should be replaced at a later date. He attached DeWitt's letter to a memo and sent it to Admiral King for his comment. The admiral supported DeWitt and suggested that "a wait and see attitude [was] in order."[151]

General Marshall informed General DeWitt on October 2 of the decision not to make any changes in the near future. However, he also noted there was "no escaping the fact that Buckner's reasons were based on a lack of faith in Theobald's willingness to engage the enemy except under conditions so favorable to us that they were unlikely to develop."[152] The whole sorry affair, for the moment, had been ended.

A Dismal Failure

While their seniors squabbled, the men of the Eleventh Air Force and Patrol Air Wing Four continued to hammer away at the Japanese on Kiska and occasionally Attu. They and the crews of the submarines prowling the approaches to Kiska were the only ones carrying the war to the Japanese. The submarines were more successful. On July 5, the crew of one of the newly arrived fleet sub-

The Japanese beached the Kano Maru in Kiska Harbor off the shore of South Head after Commander Abele from the USS Grunion put a torpedo into the 8,572-ton ship. The photograph was taken following the occupation of the island by the Americans and Canadians. The landing barges tied along side are Japanese. The 477-foot, diesel engine powered cargo ship built at the Sogaro shipyard in 1934, was in a good state of repair despite the damages suffered from the torpedo and later bomber attacks. She was salvaged after the war.

Frank Rosse Collection

marines, the USS *Triton*, under the command of Lieutenant Commander Charles C. Kirkpatrick, sent a torpedo into the *Nenohi* off Agattu Island. The Japanese destroyer capsized in two minutes. Five men survived.

That same day, Lieutenant Commander Howard W. Gilmore and the crew of the USS *Growler* intercepted a convoy outside of Kiska bringing in reinforcements and sank the *Arare* and severely damaged two other destroyers. Ten days later, Lieutenant Commander Mannert L. Abele and the crew of the newly commissioned USS *Grunion* sank two 300-ton patrol boats (Sub-chaser No. 25 and Sub-chaser No 27) in Kiska Harbor and damaged the transport *Kano Maru*. The *Grunion* disappeared on July 30, after Commander Abele reported he was attacking a Japanese ship.

Up until this point the navy had not used its surface ships against Kiska. In mid-July, Admiral Nimitz dispatched a task force of five cruisers, five destroyers and three minesweepers, under the command of Rear Admiral William W. "Poco" Smith, north. On July 19, Admiral Theobald went aboard the cruiser *Indianapolis*, and took the task force west out of Kodiak Harbor into the summer fog of the North Pacific.

The American public and press were complaining about the Japanese lodgement on American soil. Admiral King was urging Admiral Nimitz to do something about it and the Commander in Chief, Pacific Command had put the pressure on Admiral Theobald, who now had been equipped with the impressive title of Commander, North Pacific, to be more aggressive. All Theobald could do was complain about Eareckson's inaccurate high altitude bomber attacks. However, with Admiral Smith's ships, he had at his disposal the means of causing the Japanese on

Kiska considerable grief. Admiral Nimitz also hoped the naval bombardment of Kiska would divert the Japanese attention away from the southern Solomon Islands where he was planning to go on the offensive.[153]

In preparation for the bombardment, Colonel Eareckson was ordered to step up his bomber attacks from Cape Field and Captain Gehres to deploy his PBYs to Nazan Bay, Atka and Kuluk Bay, Adak. Patrol Air Wing Four was assigned three missions: conduct patrols over the waters near Kiska, fly protective screening missions over Theobald's task force as it approached Kiska, and harass the Japanese on Kiska.

To support the operation, Captain Gehres and his staff moved to Dutch Harbor on July 19, and the *Casco* was dispatched to Nazan Bay and the *Gillis* to Kuluk Bay. The two seaplane tenders arrived at their destinations on the 19th. The operations got off to a bad start the next day. Lieutenant Roy Green and his Catalina crew from VP-43 crashed while taking off and everybody on board was killed. Finally, three of Commander Ito's flying boats bombed the *Gillis*. Although the *Gillis* was not damaged, Gehres decided to pull it back from its exposed forward position.[154]

Admiral Theobald and his ships reached Kiska on the night of July 21. The island was obscured by fog, and for the next six days the task force steamed around the area waiting for the opportunity to move in and bombard the Japanese shipping and installations in Kiska Harbor. Two of the minesweepers ran into each other and a third was rammed by a destroyer in the rough seas. Finally, Theobald gave up and returned to Kodiak, never to go to sea again.[155]

The same fog that plagued Admiral Theobald also kept

the Eleventh Air Force grounded. One mission of three B-17s got through on July 20. Two Rufe pilots made a head on pass at the bomber flown by Fred Ramputi, knocking out the number three engine and wounding the bombardier. Another mission of two B-17s and eight B-24s, a big one by Aleutian standards, was dispatched from Cape Field two days later. Eight reached Kiska to find it obscured by fog. The crew of one dropped their bombs through the overcast, then turned with the rest and headed for Cape Field. One B-24, flown by Lieutenant Edwin P. Heald and his eight man crew disappeared, the apparent victim of Japanese gun fire.

No more missions were flown until July 29, when nine bombers were sent against the islands with equally dismal results. Weather prevented any more missions from being flown during the last two days of July.[156]

The results achieved by Captain Gehres' Patrol Air Wing Four were equally lackluster. A mission of four PBYs was dispatched against Kiska on July 27 followed by two more the next day. The crews reported bomb hits on several buildings.

Any gains that might have been achieved were offset on July 30 when Lieutenant David A. Brough from VP-42, flying low and slow, suddenly spotted the *Gillis* and *Williamson*, and made a "hot landing," on what he thought was the smooth waters of Nazan Bay. He did not realize the two tenders were underway and well out to sea. The Catalina smashed into the waves and sank. Three men were pulled from the icy waters.[157]

The first attempt to blast the Japanese on Kiska with naval gun fire had been a dismal failure. Had Theobald pressed on, he might have achieved success since Kiska Harbor was full of Japanese ships bringing in rein-

forcements, equipment and supplies. The weather and the Japanese abetted by Theobald's timidity had won the first round. The Commander, North Pacific turned the responsibility for the second strike against Kiska over to Admiral Smith and retired to his office on Kodiak. Admiral Smith steamed out of Kodiak on August 3 with his task force less the three crippled minesweepers and headed for another go at Kiska.[158]

At the same time, someone took mercy on Commander Russell's worn-out squadron and ordered it back to Sand Point Naval Air Station for a rest. Another Catalina squadron, VP-62, had arrived July 24 as a replacement for VP-42 with eight PBY-5As. It was followed by the seaplane tenders *Teal* two days later and the destroyer *Kane* shortly afterwards. Commander Jones moved to Nazan Bay with his squadron, VP-43, and the *Kane* joined the *Casco* there in support of Admiral Smith's task force. They were promptly attacked by three of Commander Ito's Mavises. No damage was inflicted.[159]

By August 7, the opening day of the Guadalcanal Campaign far to the south, Admiral Smith's task force, with the PBY crews scouting ahead, had moved into position off the southeast end of Kiska. The fog had finally cleared and the task force was treated to the scene of the barren mountains of Kiska against the gray overcast Aleutian sky. Rather than risk his ships in bombarding the

The aerial photograph was taken of the seaplane base, Kiska Harbor, on September 28, 1942. The damaged Mavis flying boat can be seen in the lower left hand corner. The other aircraft are single pontoon Rufe fighters and twin pontoon Jake reconnaissance planes. The seaplane ramp and hangars are visible in the upper left hand corner. USA photo

Japanese from the mouth of Kiska Harbor, Admiral Smith decided to lob his shells over South Head at a distance of 14,500 yards for the destroyers and 19,500 for the cruisers. Since he could not see his targets, he catapulted his Curtiss Seagull spotting aircraft off the cruisers to circle over Kiska Harbor and direct the fire.

The slow moving biplanes were promptly pounced on by the Japanese Rufe float fighters, and their pilots were forced to duck into the low hanging clouds to escape the fusillade of cannon and machine gun fire, thereby negating their value of forward spotters for the ships. Other Japanese float plane pilots headed for the American ships. One strafed and dropped a bomb near the destroyer *Case*, while the crew of a Mavis circled overhead, dropping bombs through the overcast.

Admiral Smith called its quits after firing off 631 rounds of 8-inch, 3,534 rounds of 6-inch and 2,620 rounds of 5-inch shells during the hour and a half bombardment. Recovering his spotter aircraft, he headed back to Kodiak.

The Seagulls had taken a beating. Ensign Ralph J. Sagesser from the *Indianapolis* had been shot down and a Rufe pilot had scored hits on the upper wing of the cruiser's other spotter float plane flown by Lieutenant Robert A. O'Neill. Another Seagull from the cruiser *Louisville* had fifty-five bullet holes in it and its pilot, Lieutenant John R. Brown, had been wounded in the right foot. Lieutenant George C. Duncan also barely made it back to the *Louisville* with thirty-five bullet holes in his aircraft. The two pilots from the *St. Louis* were not able to find their cruiser, but fortunately had enough gas to make it to Cape Field.[160]

Without the benefit of accurate information from the spotter aircraft, Admiral Smith's gunners had fired blindly at their targets. According to Japanese accounts, the damage inflicted had been minimal. Two men were killed. Additional casualties had been averted from the shells that "came like rain" because of the shelters that had been constructed. Most of the shells fell in the main camp area and beyond it. The north end of the barracks area was destroyed. Commander Ito claimed that three of his Mavises had been destroyed. An aerial photo taken shortly after the attack showed one of the flying boats partly submerged just off the beach near the seaplane base.[161] Admiral Nimitz called it a qualified success, noting:

> . . . coming simultaneously with our movement into the Solomons, this action to the north, in addition to damage caused, probably had some diversionary effect, as there appeared to be considerable delay in the movement of the majority of the Japanese carriers and other heavy units to the South Pacific.[162]

Eareckson's bombers had been scheduled to fly a mission on August 7 in support of the Kiska bombardment. Three B-24s were dispatched, but returned when their crews found their targets obscured by the overcast. Four more were sent out. The crew of one turned back to Cape Field with mechanical problems, and the other crews found the conditions at Kiska unchanged and also returned with their bomb loads. Elsewhere, a B-24 and a LB-30 mission was flown in support of P-38s which were providing air cover over Nazan Bay for the seaplane tenders.[163]

The next day, the Eleventh Air Force bomber crews tried again, only to be frustrated by the weather. However, six PBYs from VP-41 and VP-51 managed to slip into Kiska Harbor under the low overcast and unload their bombs on the Japanese. One hit the *Kano Maru*, finishing off the job begun by the crew of the *Grunion* the previous month. The Japanese had beached the 477-foot long transport midway down South Head in Kiska Harbor.[164]

The success of finishing off the *Kano Maru* was offset by the loss of two Catalinas elsewhere that were conducting a search for a missing Catalina from VP-41. One from VP-41 flown by Lieutenant Julius A. Raven and his seven man crew disappeared without a trace. Ensign Fergus F. Kelly from the recently arrived VP-62 crashed into the side of Makushin Mountain on Unalaska Island. All six aboard died, including Commander Malcolm P. Hanson, from the Navy Bureau of Aeronautics. The missing Catalina, out of gas, was found bobbing on the ocean southwest of Umnak.[165]

Other than the sinking of the *Nissan Maru*, scoring near misses against several other ships, destroying a few facilities on Kiska and Attu, killing a small number of Japanese, possibly shooting down several planes, and generally disrupting the Japanese routine, Colonel Eareckson's provisional XI Bomber Command had not turned in an impressive record since Admiral Kakuta's airmen had struck Dutch Harbor. Three bombers had been shot down over Kiska, two others had been lost en route back from the island and six, mostly the medium bombers, had been destroyed in accidents.

The losses were heavy considering the fact that Colonel Eareckson had precious few planes for the business of carrying the war to the Japanese, a condition that did not change much during the months ahead. Someone had jested that the only reason the Eleventh Air Force had only one wing in its emblem versus the two in the emblems of most of the other air forces was that it had so few aircraft.

In early August, the Eleventh Air Force had two hundred and twenty-six aircraft of which two hundred and twelve were classified as combat aircraft. The figures were misleading since one hundred and eleven were single engine fighters, and forty-seven, including the A-29s, were medium bombers. The medium bombers were useless for offensive operations against Kiska because of their

The B-24D bore the brunt of the bomber offensive against the Japanese in the Aleutians during 1942. It had the range and the weight carrying capacity to reach the targets. Here, a crew prepares to board their revetted Liberator for another mission. USA photo

The B-17E, although it achieved fame in the European Theater because of it ability to absorb punishment and for its grace and beauty, did not meet the operational requirements of the Pacific where bombers of longer range and greater bomb load capacity were required. The Flying Fortress as a bomber was withdrawn from the Pacific in early 1943, in favor of the less graceful slab sided B-24s. The B-17s did not stand up well to Aleutian duty, and by late 1942 were being used primarily for weather reconnaissance and as a photo ship to verify bombing results. USA photo

Another aircraft that was heavily committed during the Aleutian Campaign was the P-38 Lighting. The twin engine fighter made its operational debut in the Aleutian Islands. USA photo

limited range. The Canadians contributed another twenty-two fighters, which also suffered range limitations. This left twenty-three bombers (six B-17s, fifteen B-24s and two LB-30s) and twenty-one P-38s to carry the war to the Japanese. However, these numbers were further reduced by maintenance problems.

The Eleventh Air Force averaged three B-17s and twelve B-24s in commission during the first week of August. The mechanics also managed to keep the LB-30 "Tough Boy" and an average of nineteen P-38s mission ready. With the exception of the B-17s, it was not a bad in-commission rate considering the conditions the mechanics had to work under.[166]

Eareckson's heavy bomber crews and the P-38 pilots were the only ones seeing any action. The medium bomber crews and P-40 pilots had to bide their time until a field could be built closer to Kiska. The Canadians were particularly anxious to get into the action. They refused to see themselves becoming rear echelon forces to the Americans. Wing Commander McGregor wanted to move part of his force forward to Cape Field where they would have a chance of fighting the Japanese instead of the boredom of Elmendorf Field.

He received a warning order on June 27 to send part of X Wing to Nome, only to have it cancelled a few days later. Instead, American squadrons were sent. McGregor had already formed the opinion that General Butler regarded the Canadians as convenient rear-area forces, and the Nome incident seemed to confirm it. On July 4 the top RCAF brass arrived in the form of Minister of National Defense for Air, C. G. Power, Air Marshal L. S. Breadner, Chief of the Air Staff and Air Commodore Stevenson, Commander of the Western Air Command. McGregor discussed his concerns with them and they discussed them with Generals Buckner and Butler.

Two days later Butler ordered all of Number 111 Fighter Squadron's pilots and selected members of its ground crews sent to Cape Field to relieve an equivalent number of 11th Fighter Squadron personnel. McGregor planned to conduct the relief in two phases. On July 13, he began the first phase when, acting as an observer, he and a group of six pilots took off in their P-40s and headed for Naknek and Thornborough Fields and finally Cape Field, their destination. Transports followed with the ground crew and additional pilots and support staff.

It was an unlucky flight from the start. One P-40 was lost and another damaged on the first leg of the flight. Replacements were brought forward. Bad weather further delayed them at Naknek and Thornborough. They finally made it off the latter field on the 16th.

Shortly after passing Dutch Harbor, they ran into more bad weather. McGregor ordered them to turn back. As they followed him into the turn, the pilots lost contact.

Number 111 Fighter Squadron was the first RCAF squadron to be deployed to the Aleutians. The squadron operated from Cape Field until mid October 1942, when it was moved to Kodiak. However, as in the case of the American squadrons, elements were rotated to the forward fields where they flew combat mission over Kiska. The first photograph shows Canadian pilots under camouflage nets at Kodiak preparing for deployment to Amchitka in early 1943. The second is of a group of squadron pilots at Amchitka. Canadian Forces photos

Pilots of Number 111 Fighter Squadron at Kodiak, from left to right: Warrant Officer F.R.F. Skelly, Flight Lieutenant R. Lynch and Warrant Officer G.R. Weber. Canadian Forces photo

Number 8 Bomber Reconnaissance Squadron Bolingbroke at Marks Field during the Winter of 1942-43. The aircraft in the distance is a B-25.

J.A. Hill collection, National Defense Headquarters

Curtiss P-40K Warhawks assigned to Number 111 Fighter Squadron at Kodiak. Note the American registration on the tail. They had been originally intended for American squadrons in Alaska, but were diverted to the Canadians. The RCAF was normally equipped with the Curtiss Kitthawk Mk.1, the export version of the P-40. Canadian Forces photo

Five crashed in the fog. Included among those killed was Squadron Leader J. W. Kerwin who had assumed command from Squadron Leader Nesbitt four weeks prior. McGregor barely missed a rocky ledge. He circled for half an hour looking for the missing pilots. One other pilot, Pilot Officer O. J. Eskil, answered his radio call. Eskil continued on to Cape Field while McGregor returned to Thornborough Field to organize a rescue effort. The transports made it safely to Cape Field.

Wing Commander McGregor and the acting squadron commander, Flight Lieutenant H. T. Mitchell, met with General Butler and Major Chennault to decide the next step. They agreed that in the interim, until more P-40s could be obtained, the survivors of Number 111 Squadron would be formed into a flight of the 11th Fighter Squadron and fly P-40s on loan from the American squadron. This was accomplished on July 23, and the next day the Canadians began flying defensive air patrols and practicing their air-to-air and ground attack skills.

The Canadians, like their American counterparts, found conditions at Cape Field primitive. They lived in five-man tents which they learned to dig into the ground to avoid the effects of the weather. Wooden floors soon made their appearance, and the Canadians became adept at the art of homemade furniture. They developed an excellent relationship with the Americans. Eventually, as more pilots and replacement aircraft arrived, Number 111 Squadron assumed its old identity.

Squadron Leader Kenneth A. Boomer replaced Flight Lieutenant Mitchell as squadron commander on August 20. Since Canada's allotment of P-40s was limited, a shipment of new P-40Ks intended for the XI Fighter Command was diverted to the squadron, quietly bypassing the bureaucratic channels in Washington DC. The 11th Fighter Squadron continued to fly P-40Es until the end of the year.

Number 8 Bomber Reconnaissance Squadron also escaped the confines of Elmendorf Field. On July 12, the squadron commander, Squadron Leader Charles Willis, was ordered to send three of his Bolingbrokes to Marks Field. A small ground party left by transport the next day. The Bolingbrokes, after a weather delay, arrived several days later. They were put to work flying patrols southward towards Nunivak Island, then returning by way of Stuart Island and Norton Sound. The first patrol was flown on July 19, one day after the first patrol by the 404th Bombardment Squadron. The Canadian squadron assumed the entire responsibility for flying patrols over the Bering Sea and Norton Sound when the 404th was withdrawn for Aleutian service.[167]

So far, Eareckson's bomber crews had been the only ones in the Eleventh Air Force to see action against the Japanese on Kiska. Up until Captain Gehres decided to send his seaplane tenders to Nazan Bay, the 54th Fighter Squadron had contented itself with flying training missions and helping protect Cape Field against a possible Japanese attack. When Commander Ito's crews began attacking the seaplane tenders, the P-38 pilots were ordered to begin flying combat air patrols over Nazan Bay.

The first patrol was flown on the morning of August 4. Colonel Eareckson provided a bomber to escort each flight of two Lightnings. It was deviation from the normal practice where fighters provided the escort. However, in the Aleutians things were different. The P-38s were not equipped then for long range navigation over water and the pilots had only a rudimentary training in instrument flight. The better equipped bombers and their navigators provided the necessary support. The first two missions were flown without incident. The fighter pilots arrived over Nazan Bay, circled around until their fuel ran low and then headed for home as their relief arrived.

The third flight of the day was the one that made history for the twin engine fighter. Lieutenants Kenneth Ambrose and Stanley Long were among the first complement of P-38 pilots to arrive with the 54th Fighter Squadron in Alaska. They were also the first Lightning pilots to score an aerial victory during the war. Lieutenant Major H. McWilliams led the two in his B-17. On reaching the orbit point over Nazan Bay, he flew on ahead towards Kiska while Ambrose and Long began circling over the two seaplane tenders anchored in the bay below. Shortly afterward, McWilliams spotted three of Ito's seaplanes heading towards Atka.

He immediately notified Ambrose and Long who climbed to 22,000 feet to be in a better position to intercept the Mavises. Long was the first to spot the Japanese as they flew along the south coast of Atka in a V formation at 7,000 feet towards Nazan Bay.

The Japanese also spotted the two P-38s barrelling down towards them. They turned west, broke formation, and headed for the only cover available, the sea fog which extended up to 1,500 feet from the frigid waters below. The two P-38 pilots dived in hot pursuit. Ambrose and Long quickly caught up with the lumbering four engine seaplanes, circled around, picked out their targets, and began attacking from the front and sides to avoid the tail mounted 20mm cannon.[168]

Stan Long was the first to attack, firing at both seaplanes at close range. The canopy of one the Mavises disintegrated. The two Lightning pilots then climbed for altitude and Lieutenant Ambrose, after congratulating Long, instructed him: "Lets concentrate on the outside one." On the second pass, Ambrose succeeded in setting the left wing of one of the Japanese aircraft afire. The big seaplane was observed heading out of control into the overcast. The other escaped.

The two fighter pilots headed towards Kiska in hopes

The painting, showing the first aerial victory by a P-38, was commission for Colonel Stan Long by his daughter.
Stan Long collection

Colonel Jack Chennault, right, was on hand to greet Lieut Kenneth Ambrose, left, after his return to Cape Field. USA photo

Lieutenant Long's P-38E Lightning. USA photo

of spotting another Mavis. After flying 150 miles, they spotted another seaplane emerging from a cloud. The Japanese crew spotted the two Lightnings and tried frantically to evade them. Ambrose made a head on pass and then Long came in from the side and raked the Mavis from the nose to tail with machine gun and cannon fire. The seaplane disappeared into the clouds. Ambrose and Long were each given official credit for shooting down a Mavis.[169] Years later, Stan Long remembered:

Upon first contact with the bomber it was hard to believe what I was seeing and still unbelievable even when the huge red rising sun of Japan was spotted on the plane, but reality came back to me soon, and I realized that this was the enemy, and so the shooting started. Upon return and landing back at Umnak, someone said that I didn't close my shell ejection door, and as a result I had ejected all of the machine gun casings and that I should have saved them for the war effort. I really couldn't have cared less. I was more interested in getting some strength back into my weakened legs, so that I could stand up after all the excitement.[170]

It was the first P-38 aerial victory of the war.[171] The two pilots were greeted in triumph on landing at Cape Field. One of the 54th Fighter Squadron historians, Sergeant Abernathy, provided a vivid account:

At 1:00 PM, a B-17 with two P-38s buzzed low over the field. We figured something was up . . . Ambrose came taxing down the strip about 50mph, piled into the revetment, spun it around, gunned both engines and before the props had stopped he had thrown the canopy back and had two fingers up and was hollering . . . 'We got two of them!' Then all the quys nearby came piling over and we proceeded to go wild, it being our first engagement with the enemy.[172]

Lieutenants Long, left, and George Laven, right. Lieutenant Laven shared half credit for shooting down a Jake and credit and a half for two Rufes. He and Lieut. Victor E. Walton also shared in the honor of making what was then billed as the longest fighter mission of the war when they flew an eight hour, over twelve hundred mile round trip from Cape Field to strafe Japanese on Kiska. USA photo

The encounter marked the end of the last serious Japanese attempt at an air offensive in the Aleutian Islands. On August 17, Commander Ito and the survivors of the Toko Seaplane Squadron departed for Paramushiro. The Japanese were left with only their single engine float planes, which had a very limited offensive capability.[173]

The 54th Fighter Squadron continued to deploy its P-38s over Nazan Bay until the naval bombardment of Kiska was completed. The next day, the 8th, the P-38s were used in an escort mission for the first time when eight of the Lightnings accompanied Eareckson's bombers to Kiska, only to be turned back by the weather.[174]

Patrol Air Wing Four, following the naval bombardment of Kiska, returned to its normal operations. The two seaplane tenders were withdrawn from Nazan Bay, and Captain Gehres and his staff moved back to Kodiak to begin planning for the occupation of Adak Island. The Navy, in keeping with its policy of rotating its units in order to provide some relief from the rigors of Aleutian flying, returned VP-41 and VP-51 to the states during the last half of August. They were replaced by VP-61, which arrived August 19 with eight PBY-5 flying boats. Shortly afterwards, the squadron moved to Sand Point in the Shumagin Islands. On August 22, Commander Russell and the veteran VP-42 returned after a much needed rest to their old haunts at Dutch Harbor.[175]

Colonel Eareckson and his men continued their deadly routine. For them there was no rotational policy. They were in it for the duration, even those who had been told that they were being sent to the Aleutians for a short stay of temporary duty.

The men of the 30th Bombardment Group who had arrived shortly after the bombing of Dutch Harbor and were formed into the 27th and 38th Provisional Bombardment Squadrons, discovered in mid-August that their stay was going to be permanent. They and their B-24s were consolidated and became the 21st Bombardment Squadron under the command of Major Ansley Watson. The first contingent of the ground crew of the 21st, which had been left behind at March Field, arrived at Cape Field August 24 followed by the last group of seven officers and one hundred and forty-eight enlisted men on September 3, bringing the squadron up to full strength.[176]

The air echelon of the 404th Bombardment Squadron, their duties at Marks Field completed, arrived at Cape Field on August 24, followed shortly afterwards by the ground echelon to begin what their historian described as "a grim battle against two deadly enemies—the Japanese on Kiska and Attu and the weather."[177] The squadron while on duty at Marks Field had flown thirty-nine patrol missions and lost one B-24 in an accident. It prepared the "Pink Elephants" for what they were about to face in the Aleutians.[178]

Crew members of one of the bombers from the 30th Bombardment Group that deployed to Alaska. From left to right, back row: Sergeant "Jumping Indian" Ivaing, unknown, Capt Moore, Lieut Mathey, Sergeant Palet Smith and TSgt Roy Anesi; front row: Sgt Lowry, unknown, Richard Beavers, Lieut Shinley. Roy Anesi collection

"Wee Willie" was the squadron emblem designed by the Disney studios for the 21st Bombardment Squadron based on a concept by Sergeant Don Cooley. USA photo

Their arrival gave Colonel Eareckson two squadrons of B-24s and a squadron of B-17s to use against the Japanese. The medium bomber squadrons, for the time being, remained out of the action because of their limited range. Following the naval bombardment of Kiska, the provisional XI Bombardment Command operations settled down into a routine of the commitment of a small number of bombers for uncertain results. Death continued to stalk the command.

On August 10, five B-17s and three B-24s thundered down the runway at Cape Field on a another mission against Kiska. Captain Ira F. Wintermute, who had been forced to ditch his B-24 during the June 18 mission, ran into trouble again. His bomber was hit by anti-aircraft fire, and then a couple of Rufe pilots chased him. Breaking free and with two dead engines, he and his copilot nursed their crippled bomber towards Cape Field as Lieutenant Paul A. Perkins, the navigator, kept repeating, "we'll make it—

we'll make it." Then a fire broke out.

Captain Wintermute managed to reach Semisopochnoi Island, forty miles due east of Kiska. He ordered the crew to bail out. Lieutenant Perkins and Staff Sergeant Cliffort R. Brockman landed in the water 300 yards offshore and drowned. Master Sergeant Eugene W. Latham's parachute caught on one of the propellers and he was dragged down with the bomber. The other crew members landed safely and constructed shelters out of their parachutes. The next day, a PBY flew over and dropped supplies, and on August 13, Lieutenant G. W. Smith from VP-43 made a daring landing on the open sea and recovered the six survivors.[179]

The Aleutian weather prevailed during the rest of the month. More missions were cancelled or aborted than those that succeeded in reaching Kiska. On August 24, Colonel Eareckson planned a photo mission for the 404th Bombardment Squadron to introduce it into combat in the

Aleutians. It was cancelled.[180]

Tragedy struck again on August 28, as Admiral Theobald was preparing to land forces on Adak. Colonel Eareckson led three B-17s on a bombing mission against Kiska. The flight was late in getting off and during the return flight it ran into darkness and rain. The crew of the first bomber landed safely in the heavy rain followed by Colonel Eareckson thirty minutes later. The third bomber flown by Lieutenant Albert J. Wilsey, who had been flying formation with Colonel Eareckson, disappeared during a turn in the darkness. Lieutenant Wilsey and his crew apparently became disorientated and flew off in another direction. The last anyone heard of him was a radio report that he had an hour of fuel left.[181]

Elsewhere that day, all the available B-24s had been committed to flying support for an amphibious force that was approaching Adak Island. Admiral Theobald had taken the first real step in driving the Japanese from the Aleutians.

During the night of August 12-13, the venerable U.S. Army transport Saint Mihiel and the USS Franklin Bell pulled away from the piers at Oakland, California and headed for Kodiak under the escort of a lone destroyer. Loaded aboard were the combat troops intended for the occupation of Adak under the command of Brigadier General Eugene M. Landrum. They were followed the next day by two chartered freighters, the Thomas Jefferson and Stanley Griffith, carrying equipment and supplies.

Eleven days later the merchant ship Branch departed Cold Bay with additional occupation troops and part of the 807th Engineer Aviation Battalion. It joined the four transports, which after stopping at Kodiak, had headed into the Bering Sea. The convoy turned south for the final run into Adak under the protection of the cruisers Nashville and St. Louis and the destroyers Brooks, Dent and Kane while the cruisers Indianapolis, Louisville and Honolulu and the destroyers Gridley, McCall and Reid maintained a watch nearby as the covering force. The Canadians also sent the auxiliary cruisers Prince David, Prince Henry and Prince Robert and the corvettes Dawson and Vancouver into the North Pacific to support the landing.[182]

While General Landrum's occupation force headed towards Adak, the men of the Eleventh Air Force and Patrol Air Wing Four continued to battle the elements and occasionally the Japanese.

The week prior to the landing had not been a good one for the patrol wing. It began with the disappearance of a Catalina on a routine flight from Cold Bay to Kodiak on August 25. Two days later, the newly arrived seaplane tender Avocet struck a reef near Whale Island. The crew of the severely damaged ship managed to get her back to Kodiak.

Elsewhere, near Amlia Island, the Williamson was severely damaged when the wing of a PBY from V-43 it was towing in heavy seas at night broke off. The depth charge that was attached to the wing fell free and exploded under the seaplane tender. The ship's captain ordered the searchlights turned on so that rescue operations could be conducted. Three men turned up missing from the PBY and a sailor aboard the seaplane tender was killed. The next day, the 27th, the crew of another PBY tangled with a Japanese float plane pilot near Amchitka. They managed to escape unharmed.[183]

On August 29, a patrolling PBY crew spotted what they thought was a Japanese task force of three cruisers and four destroyers northwest of Umnak. Eareckson's bombers were alerted, but the sighting proved false. In any case, no missions could be flown that day. Another Aleutian storm had blown in.[184]

Early the next morning, in the middle of the storm, Brigadier General Eugene Landrum began landing his forces on the beaches of Kuluk Bay. The landing of personnel and equipment continued throughout the day until 8:00 PM when it was halted due to rough weather.

The following day, a fleet of five tugs, six powered and two towed barges, two 100-ton fishing scows, a towed schooner and the yacht Cavanugh arrived under the escort of the five Royal Canadian Navy warships. It contained the rest of the 807th Engineer Aviation Battalion and the heavy equipment they needed to carve a base and air field out of the until then uninhabited island.[185]

America and her Canadian allies were now on the offensive in the North Pacific, while in the South Pacific a struggle of epic proportions that would decide the course of the war in the Pacific was being fought in the disease ridden jungles and the surrounding waters of an obscure island that would become a household word.

The Butcher's Bill Had Been Unendurable

Ten great air and sea battles were fought between Pearl Harbor and the end of 1942. The Japanese won five starting with the sinking of the British battleship Prince of Wales and the battle cruiser Repulse. Two were stand-offs: Coral Sea and the Eastern Solomons. However, of the three the Allies won, two were decisive. The balance of power in the Pacific lost at Pearl Harbor was restored at Midway, and the Americans won the four day sea Battle of Guadalcanal, which marked the end of the Japanese offensive capability in the Pacific.

Following the fragile degree of superiority that was achieved after Midway, American planners decided to go on the offensive by initiating operations in the southern

Solomon Islands and on New Guinea. Vice Admiral Robert L. Ghormely, commanding the South Pacific Area, was assigned the mission of seizing the small island of Tulagi where the Japanese had built a seaplane base and the larger island of Guadalcanal where they were constructing an airfield. General Douglas MacArthur was given the responsibility for taking the rest of the Solomons and clearing the Japanese from New Guinea. The objectives of the operations were to isolate the Japanese military bastion at Rabaul on New Britain Island and secure the vital supply line between America and Australia.

The reinforced 1st Marine Division began its amphibious assault, the first of the war, against Tulagi and Guadalcanal on August 7. For the next six months, the Americans and Japanese fought a war of attrition, one that would divert resources and attention away from the Aleutian Islands. While Major General Alexander A. Vandegrift and his Marines earned glory and fame, fighting a tenacious enemy and the disease ridden jungles of Guadalcanal, the American and Japanese fought six naval and air battles.

The battle for Guadalcanal became a "meeting engagement," a phrase used by military tacticians to describe chance encounters of opposing forces that erupt into pitched battles. Each side sought to bring in reinforcements and resupply their forces on the island. The result was a series of sudden, hard fought and violent engagements. The Japanese Navy, because of its superior night fighting capabilities, ruled the waters around Guadalcanal by night. The Americans, who obtained air superiority, controlled the area by day. Each struggled mightily to gain an advantage over the other.[186]

Forty-eight hours after the Marines had landed, a Japanese cruiser force tore into the invasion force in a night engagement off Salvo Island near the landing beaches. It resulted in the sinking of four American cruisers, and the damaging of another and a destroyer. Two Japanese cruisers were damaged. The American transports were not harmed.

On August 10, Admiral Fletcher withdrew his aircraft carriers to safer waters. Shortly afterwards the rest of the naval supporting force including the transports which were still in the process of being unloaded were also withdrawn, leaving the Marines with enough ammunition for four days of heavy fighting and a thirty day food supply.

Admiral Yamamoto began sending ships and troops to Guadalcanal to drive the Americans out. A convoy of transports, protected by warships was dispatched from Rabaul on August 19. One of Admiral Fletcher's reconnaissance aircraft spotted it. A Japanese reconnaissance plane also spotted the Americans.

The Battle of the Eastern Solomons fought on August 24 some 200 miles east of Guadalcanal was in-conclusive. The Japanese struck the carrier task force commanded by Rear Admiral Thomas C. Kinkaid and damaged the *Enterprise*. In return, pilots from the *Saratoga* found the *Ryujo*, veteran of the Dutch Harbor attack, and sank her. The Japanese transports turned back. Admiral Fletcher also decided to vacate the scene.[187]

The I-26, after completing her Aleutian duties, had been ordered south. On August 31 the captain of the I-26 sent a spread of six torpedoes toward the *Saratoga* as it was patrolling southeast of Guadalcanal. One hit home, putting the aircraft carrier out of commission for another extended period of time. Admiral Fletcher was aboard as the task force commander.

There were some in the senior Naval ranks, principal of which was Admiral King, who regarded Admiral Fletcher's reputation for hard luck to be the result of ineptitude. He had lost two carriers under his command and two others had been damaged. Since Fletcher had been slightly wounded in the attack, Admiral Nimitz placed him on leave. On completion of his leave, Admiral Fletcher asked to be returned to sea duty.

Instead, Admiral King him sent him to a shore billet at Seattle where he replaced Admiral Freeman as Commander, 13th Naval District and Northern Naval Sea Frontier. His responsibilities included Alaska and the North Pacific. He would remain in that position for the rest of the war.[188]

The connections between Alaska and the battles that were raging in the southern Solomon Islands area continued. On September 15, the commander of the I-19, the same submarine that had been used to scout Dutch Harbor, launched six torpedoes at the escorts of a convoy bringing in Marine reinforcements to Guadalcanal.

Three struck home in what was probably the most effective torpedo salvo of the war. One hit the small carrier *Wasp*, fatally damaging her so that she had to be sunk later. Another tore a thirty by eighteen foot hole in the hull of the new battleship *North Carolina*, putting her out of commission for several months. The third slammed into the destroyer *O'Brien*, sending her to the bottom.[189]

The Japanese continued to bring in reinforcements, using destroyer transports to land them at night at Cape Esperance on the northwest tip of Guadalcanal. In order to stop the flow of reinforcements and protect the landing of the Army's American Division, a small cruiser force under the command of Rear Admiral Norman Scott was sent into the area. In the resulting night Battle of Cape Esperance, fought October 11, the Japanese lost a cruiser and a destroyer. One of Admiral Scott's destroyers was sunk. The next eye-gouging came on October 26-27 during the Battle of Santa Cruz.

The Japanese efforts to reinforce their garrison with piecemeal commitment of forces continued to meet with failure while the Americans, despite the submarine threat and the almost nightly harassing air and sea attacks against Henderson Field, were able to bring in larger number of reinforcements and keep the men on Guadalcanal resupplied.

The war of attrition continued as the Japanese battered themselves against the American defenses. Admiral Yamamoto realized that his "Tokyo Express" operation was not working. The Marines were slaughtering the Japanese troops that were being thrown against them in piecemeal attacks. And, as always, the American logistics and supply system was proving to be far superior to anything the Japanese had to offer.

Yet the battle for Guadalcanal continued. By mid-October, Admiral Nimitz decided to relieve his old friend, Admiral Ghormley, who although an excellent and conscientious Naval officer with a long record of achievements, lacked the personal qualities needed to inspire men engaged in battle. As a replacement, he sent Admiral Halsey, an officer with a reputation for aggressive actions.[190]

When Halsey arrived at the South Pacific Force headquarters and logistics base at Noumea on French-controlled New Caledonia Island, Admiral Yamamoto had already set in motion his plans for driving the Marines from Guadalcanal.

On October 11, the mightiest Japanese naval force to be committed to battle since Midway, steamed out of Truk in support of a planned major reinforcement and resupply effort of Guadalcanal that was being assembled in the Rabaul-Shortland area. It included two battleships, three heavy and one light aircraft carriers, nine cruisers and twenty-eight destroyers. To counter this force, Admiral Halsey dispatched two carrier groups built around the *Enterprise* and the *Hornet*.

In the resulting Battle of Santa Cruz, fought October 25-26, flyers from Admiral Kinkaid's *Enterprise* group mauled the Japanese carrier *Shokaku*, putting the veteran of Pearl Harbor and the Coral Sea out of commission for nine months. In return, Japanese pilots from the *Shokaku* and her sister carrier *Zuikaku* savaged the *Hornet* so badly with four bomb and two torpedo hits and the suicide crash of two bomb laden Vals that the veteran of the Doolittle raid had to be taken under tow.

She was being slowly pulled from the battle area, when Japanese Kate and Val pilots from the *Junyo* caught up with her and put a torpedo into her aft engine room and scored hits on her flight and hangar decks with two bombs. This time the *Hornet* was too crippled to continue. Rear Admiral George P. Murray, leader of the task force, ordered the carrier sunk. Destroyers moved in and sent nine torpedoes slamming into the side of the *Hornet*, which still refused to sink. Since the Japanese were fast advancing, Admiral Murray decided to abandon the *Hornet*, now a flaming hulk. The Japanese, on arriving, sent two more torpedoes into her. Finally, the gallant ship slid below the waves.

The sinking of the *Hornet* left the United States with only one carrier in the Pacific, Admiral Kinkaid's *Enterprise*, which had been damaged by two bomb hits. The Japanese had given the Americans a severe beating.[191]

Between the 2nd and the 10th of November, the Tokyo Express sent sixty-five destroyer loads of supplies down The Slot. On November 10, Australian coast watchers on Bougainville Island further up the Solomons reported that there were sixty-one Japanese ships heading towards the southern Solomons. They were part of a force commanded by Vice Admiral Nobutake Kondo, whose mission it was to implement Admiral Yamamoto's plans.

It was a powerful armada, containing five battleships, the *Junyo* and the light carrier *Hiyo*, ten cruisers, forty-five destroyers, thirteen submarines and eleven transports carrying 10,000 Army troops of the Hiroshima Division and 3,500 special naval attack troops. Arrayed against the Japanese, was a force of two battleships, the hastily repaired *Enterprise*, eight cruisers and twenty-four destroyers. Admiral Halsey was using part of the force to protect seven transports bringing in Marine aviation personnel and replacements from Noumea. The *Enterprise*, the battleships and eight destroyers were still in the harbor at Noumea. With the two forces converging on Guadalcanal, a meeting engagement of large proportions was in the making.

The Japanese plans called for a raiding group of two battleships, a cruiser and fourteen destroyers under the command of Vice Admiral Hiroake Abe to bombard Henderson Field. Admiral Kondo took the bulk of his force 150 miles north of Savo Island to protect the two carriers, whose aircraft were to support the troop landings, scheduled for November 14.

During November 11 and 12, the Japanese initiated air attacks against the American transports unloading personnel and supplies at Lunga Point near Henderson Field. Although most of their aircraft were shot down, the Japanese managed to damage three transports, a cruiser and a destroyer. With the approach of Admiral Kondo's bombardment force, the transports were withdrawn after 90 percent of the unloading had been completed.

Admiral Abe's force of two battleships, one cruiser and fifteen destroyers steamed into position the night of the 12th to begin their bombardment of Henderson Field. They were met by Rear Admiral Daniel J. Callaghan's five cruisers and eight destroyers. In the ensuing 34-minute night battle that began at 1:24 AM on the 13th, Admiral Callaghan's forces became separated, resulting in a melee of individual engagements as the opposing warships

force on August 30, prevented any missions from being flown over Kuluk Bay that day. Instead, Butler sent five B-24s against Kiska. They were turned back because of an overcast over the island. The P-38 pilots flew patrol missions between Great Sitkin and Little Tanaga Islands.

The weather remained bad the next day and two B-24s were committed to a patrol over Tanaga Island. The planned mission for the next day was scrubbed, and on September 2 the weather finally cleared over Kuluk Bay to permit the flying of a combat air patrol. Six missions consisting of two P-38s and a bomber were committed. Six more similar missions were flown the next day. The flights were scheduled to take off at two-hour intervals, fly cover for unloading operations at Kuluk Bay 384 miles from Cape Field and then proceed to Kiska.

Five of the missions were turned back by low ceilings and rain. The one flown by Lieutenants George Laven Jr. and Victor E. Walton succeeded in reaching Kiska. It was the first P-38 strike mission against the Japanese on the island and was billed at the time as the longest fighter mission of the war.

While their B-24 escort orbited over Segula Island 25 miles east of Kiska, the two fighter pilots streaked in at low level and made their approach from the northwest at five hundred feet, flying over the saddle behind the Japanese main camp. Lieutenant Laven headed for the beached Mavis, his assigned target. The Americans were not aware that Commander Ito had withdrawn his seaplanes and the Mavis they left behind had been damaged in the August 7 naval bombardment.

Laven came in too high to be certain that any of his machinegun and cannon rounds had struck the Mavis. He then headed for the main camp area, banked his twin-engine fighter in a tight turn to the right, and sped towards his number two target, the fortified installations on North Head.

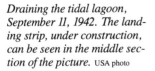

Draining the tidal lagoon, September 11, 1942. The landing strip, under construction, can be seen in the middle section of the picture. USA photo

Photograph of Adak late in the war. The dike and canal around the field can be seen. Sweeper Cove to the left was dredged and docks built to service the ships.
FFA collection, Anchorage Museum of History and Art

Adak Field as it looked in mid-September. Louis Blau collection

As he roared in, he surprised a group of Japanese lined up waiting to be fed at a kitchen. The stunned Japanese scattered and crumpled in all directions before the on-slaught of the Lightnings' concentrated fire. Laven continued on, spotting a submarine net tender just off North Head. He opened fire on it, having the satisfaction of seeing several crew members fall in a heap on the deck and two others jump into the water. The Japanese had fired back as Laven was making his attacks. Several rounds hit the fighter along the leading edge of the wings. One round went through the horizontal stabilizer, severing a control cable.

Lieutenant Walton followed Laven in the attack. After strafing the main camp and seaplane areas, he made a right turn and went after the Mavis. He had the satisfaction of seeing his machine gun and cannon rounds strike the seaplane. He then swung in behind Laven who was heading west through a valley. En route he strafed a group of Japanese huts. Walton's plane was hit by ground fire which damaged one of the ailerons.

Despite the damage to their aircraft, the two fighter pilots made it safely back to Cape Field. They had less than twenty gallons of gas left in their fuel tanks and had been in the air for eight hours.[197] Billy Wheeler quipped: "Those pea shooters are a bunch of blood-thirsty sons of guns."[198]

Another pilot from the 54th Fighter Squadron became separated from his bomber escort 300 miles from Cape Field. The P-38s at the time were equipped with only a rudimentary navigation system consisting of an altimeter, turn and bank indicator, airspeed indicator, compass and a clock. The pilot, whose name unfortunately was omitted from the histories, found himself in fog so thick that he could not see the wing tips. Climbing above the fog, he flew alone for two hours, occasionally letting down to as low as 100 feet, hoping for better visibility, before climbing back up into the clear. Finally, he found a hole in the overcast, and on letting down, spotted a land-mark which he recognized and made it safely back to Cape Field. Someone remarked that "the boys told him to log five minutes of time for himself and give the rest of the time to Jesus."[199]

Colonel Eareckson's bomber crews and Major Jackson's P-38 pilots continued to fly missions along the Aleutian Islands, keeping the pressure on the Japanese while the build up of forces on Adak continued. The crew of a B-24 on a mission over Tanaga on September 6 submitted a claim for the sinking of a Japanese mine layer. The next day three B-24s reached Kiska where they were attacked by three float fighters. A victory claim was submitted against one of the Rufes. For the next six days, the bomber crews continued to fly missions, several of which were disrupted by weather, down the Aleutian Chain as far as

Like all advance fields during the initial phases, the living conditions were primitive. USA photo

With time, the conditions improved. The photograph of a headquarters area was taken in October 1943. USA photo

Another version, this one is a drawing of a pilot's quarters. The quarters were heated by oil or coal burning stoves. Because of the weather, the occupants sometimes spent days on end in their quarters, subsisting on food scrounged, purchased or sent to them; venturing out only to answer the call of nature. Informal contests were held to see who could get in the most "sack time." USA photo of a drawing by Bud Shuoly

Living interior of one of the Pacific huts on Adak. USA photo

Men also used their idle hours to read and to write letters. The photographer caught Lieuts George W. Morgan and Lloyd W. Ward busy with their mail. USA photo

Attu, looking for any sign of the Japanese plans to interfere with the operations on Adak.

On September 13, two P-38s were dispatched with the LB-30 "Tough Boy" on an anti-submarine sweep and intelligence collection mission against Kiska for the mission that was planned for the next day. One of the Lightning pilots, Lieutenant Herbert Hasenfus, encouraged by the apparent lack of air opposition, decided to make a strafing run on a small ship outside Kiska Harbor.

He reduced his speed and was preparing to make the attack when two Rufes came barreling at him head on. Hasenfus slammed the throttle forward, but before he could get his speed up, the lead Rufe pilot sent a burst of fire into his P-38, knocking out an engine and ruining the hydraulic system. Hasenfus ducked into the overcast and managed to fly his badly damaged fighter back to Adak on one engine where he made a belly landing on the runway in front of one of John Huston's cameramen, who recorded it for a scene in *Report From the Aleutians*. The lieutenant emerged from his fighter unharmed.

Lieutenant Frederick E. McCoy, the other P-38 pilot, engaged in a head-on attack against another Rufe pilot. He was able to send a burst of machine gun and cannon fire into the belly of the Rufe as the pilot pulled up to avoid a collision. The crew of the LB-30 confirmed the kill, the first against a Japanese float fighter in the Aleutians. McCoy and the LB-30 crew returned safely to Adak.[200]

The gruelling long-range missions over the icy expanse of Aleutian waters took their toll on the 54th Fighter Squadron. By mid-September only sixteen pilots were fit to fly. Ground crews were having to lift numb and exhausted pilots from their cockpits. The constant specter of death and the physically and mentally exhausting seven- and eight-hour missions in marginal weather conditions, watching the fuel indicator needle steadily move towards empty, were rapidly aging what once used to be young and carefree boys. Pilots complained of severe headaches, backaches and nervous apprehension.[201]

Death stalked the 54th Fighter Squadron. Lieutenant Carl Middleton was the first to die, when he entered the clouds shortly after taking off from Cape Field on June 27, became disoriented and spun in. Funeral services were held two days later. The squadron historian noted:

> Buried "Spider" today in this dreary, uncivilized little island. The funeral was impressive but superficial. The wind howling over the tundra was the funeral march and the sting of the rain helped bring tears. He lay in a plain pine box coffin and the Chaplain raised his voice over the howl of the elements in prayer for the soul. He placed a small flower on the coffin and the wind flung it back to earth. We all saluted our comrade as an infantry squad fired three volleys over his grave and that was the last chapter in the life of Lieutenant Carl Middleton.[202]

Ground crews prepare their P-38s for another mission at Adak during early 1943. USA photo

Men of the 54th Fighter Squadron do their laundry.
Stan Long collection

Lieutenants Howard W. Millard, left, and Robert L. McDonald, right, celebrate just prior to leaving the Aleutians for home. They were the survivors of the original 54th Fighter Squadron pilots sent to the Aleutian Campaign.
Lyle Bean collection

The 54th Fighter Squadron converted to P-38Gs in 1943, as shown in this scene at Adak. The aircraft in the foreground is an F-5A, photo-reconnaissance version of the Lightning modified from an P-38F airframe. USA photo

Another view of P-38Gs at Adak. The 54th Fighter Squadron was equipped with twenty-four of the two hundred and ten P-38Es that Lockheed built and delivered to the Army Air Forces between October 1941 and February 1942, before upgrading to newer models. The G model had a greater fuel capacity and more powerful engine. USA photo

The 54th Fighter Squadron was originally equipped with the Republic P-43A Lancer. Two of the fighters were sent to Alaska. Like the obsolete P-36s that arrived with the 18th Fighter Squadron, they were not committed to the Aleutians, but used instead for pilot proficiency. Lyle Bean, one of the original pilots with the 54th, recalled that "it was fun to fly but not very desirable for combat." Lyle Bean collection

The squadron lost ten more men, four pilots and six enlisted men, on July 5, when the C-53 they were riding in as passengers crashed 40 miles north of Thornborough Field. Another pilot died on July 21 when a flight of four P-38s led by Major Jackson were suddenly confronted by a mountain while flying under a one hundred foot overcast. Jackson and two others managed to avoid it. The fourth Lightning flown by Lieutenant Lawrence I. Stoland crashed into the mountainside. Two other P-38 pilots were forced to land in the water that month. Both were rescued.[203]

While General Butler's bomber crews and fighter pilots wagered their lives against the Aleutian weather in support of the Adak landing, Captain Gehres' PBY crews continued to fly patrols over the Aleutian waters, searching for any sign of the Japanese who might interfere with the Adak operations. To support them, Gehres sent the *Casco* and *Gillis* to Nazan Bay and the *Teal* to Kuluk Bay.[204]

The Japanese had also been carrying out their own naval operations while the Americans were landing troops on Adak. Beginning on August 27, they began transferring their Attu garrison to Kiska. Admiral Hosogaya committed a small number of his warships to the effort to include the submarine RO-61 which was sent ahead to screen the operation. The captain of the submarine, Commander Tokutomi, slipped into Nazan Bay on August 29 during a moderate gale. When he raised his periscope, he was greeted by the sight of the two seaplane tenders and the destroyer *Reid*.[205]

Colonel Talley and Lieutenant Colonel Leon B. DeLong, a former Morrison-Knudson engineer who had been given a direct commission, arrived about the same time as Commander Tokutomi. They had hitched a ride with Captain Gehres in a PBY and were intending to go to Adak when the weather forced them to divert to Nazan Bay. Commander Willis E. Cleaves invited the two army colonels and Captain Gehres to stay aboard his tender until the weather at Adak cleared.

That night as they sat down for dinner in the wardroom, Talley could not help but notice the luxurious surroundings and the fact that there was a mess attendant standing behind every two officers. The engineer colonel, used to army's more austere living conditions, remarked, "You know the trouble here in the war is that we're trying to win it with creases in our trousers." After receiving a noncommittal reply from his host, Talley went on to say, "You know, before this war is over we're all going to be down in the mud and we're going to be glad to get down in it for our own protection before we're through."

Gehres, who had been silent up to that point, asked the colonel, "Talley how badly do you want to go to Adak?" Shortly after dinner, Talley and DeLong departed for Adak aboard the *Reid*.[206]

When Commander Tokutomi raised his periscope the next night, August 30, the *Reid* was gone and the two tenders were silhouetted against the sky. He promptly launched two torpedoes and hightailed it out of the confines of the harbor. One torpedo missed its target and ran up on the nearby beach without exploding. The other slammed into the port side of the *Casco*. Two men were killed, three disappeared and three were wounded in the explosion which made a shambles of the engine room. Commander Cleaves managed to beach the stricken seaplane tender and send out a distress call.[207]

Radio operators at Dutch Harbor and Kuluk Bay picked up the signal. Lieutenant Carl Amme at Dutch Harbor and Lieutenant Sammy Coleman at Kuluk Bay took off for the scene in their PBYs. Amme rounded up several doctors and first-aid supplies and departed during the early morning hours of August 31. He arrived over Nazan Bay to find it covered in fog. He then headed west towards Adak in

search of a sheltered area where he could land his PBY and wait for the fog to clear. En route, the wind shifted towards Atka; and Amme decided to turn back, hoping to find that the fog had cleared over the bay. As they passed the north side of Atka Island, his copilot, Arne Havu, noted the skies had cleared from Korovin Volcano to about one hundred yards offshore. Havu looked down and spotted Coldman's PBY and then he saw the RO-61's conning tower.

Lieutenant Coleman's copilot, Phil Anderson, also sighted the submarine. Amme made a tight 180-degree turn and headed for the RO-61 at five hundred feet while Coleman was commencing his bomb run. Two of Coleman's depth charges straddled the submarine, followed shortly afterwards by the depth charges from Amme's PBY. By the time Amme turned to make another attack, the RO-61 had disappeared below the waves. Coleman, running low on fuel, headed back to Kuluk Bay. Amme remained in the area and spotted an oil slick east of where the depth charges had been dropped. The slick moved eastward and then turned ninety degrees to the north about a mile off Korovin Volcano as the captain of the RO-61 tried to distance his submarine from the scene of the attack.

Amme spotted the destroyer *Reid*, ten miles away, and directed it to the location of the oil slick. After dropping smoke bombs ahead of the slick to mark the submarine's position for the crew of the *Reid*, Amme headed for Nazan Bay to deliver the doctors and their supplies to the *Casco*. The captain of the *Reid*, Lieutenant Commander Harry H. McIlhenney, raced his warship to the spot of the last smoke bomb, and the crew unloaded a barrage of depth charges. Another PBY flown by Lieutenant Sorenson arrived on the scene. Sorenson dropped his depth charges just ahead of the moving oil slick.

The RO-61 popped to the surface so close to the *Reid*, that its surprised crew had trouble depressing their guns. The crew of the 40mm gun on the fantail managed to bring their weapon to bear on the submarine while Commander McIlhenney swung the destroyer around. The submarine sank under the hale of fire. Five crew members were plucked from the ocean. They were taken to Dutch Harbor, where they were held for a brief period, questioned and then transported to a prisoner of war camp in the states.[208]

Commander McIlhenney sent a signal to Commander Cleaves aboard the *Casco*, stating: "Got sub that got you. Have five survivors for proof."[209]

A Max Effort

The occupation of Adak and the construction of the airstrip on the water-soaked lagoon at the head of Kuluk

B-24D Liberators lined up at Adak shortly after the first major raid from the island against the Japanese.
Stan Long collection

The B-24D Liberator was the heavy bomber of choice in the Aleutian Campaign because of its range and load carrying capability. The white circle is where the censors retouched the photograph to hide the squadron emblem. USA photos

Bay was a remarkable operational and engineering achievement. Within seventeen days of the landing, General Butler launched his first major strike against Admiral Akiyama's forces on Kiska. By Aleutian standards, it was a "max effort," although hardly on the scale of the thousand plane raids of the European theater.

The stillness of the morning erupted into a roar of engines, spoiling the tranquility of the ravens that inhabited the once peaceful island. One by one, beginning at 7:00 AM, twelve of Eareckson's B-24s and a B-17 camera plane taxied into position and thundered down the steel runway in a spray of water. The pilots pulled back on the control wheels and the B-24s, each laden with four thousand pounds of bombs, lifted from the runway and began the slow climb for altitude.

Immediately after the last bomber had departed the end of the runway, the fighters began taking off. Colonel Phineas T. Morrill, who had replaced Colonel Sillin eight days earlier as the Commander of the XI Fighter Command, led the fourteen P-38s; and Lieutenant Colonel Charles M. McCorkle, who had moved to the position formally occupied by Morrill as the Commander, 54th Fighter Group, the fourteen P-39s. The two colonels did

not want to miss what was to be the first major air attack on a North American target. By 8:00 AM, Adak had returned to normal.

The plan called for the fighters to go in first, the P-39s suppressing the anti-aircraft defenses along the south side of the harbor and the P-38s attacking the defenses on the north side and defending the bombers against the Japanese float fighters. Eareckson's bomber crews would then make a low-level attack from the east against the Japanese shipping in the harbor and the installations on the land.

The bomber crews had not flown a low-level mission since June 18, when the provisional XI Bomber Command switched to making high-altitude bomb runs of 18,000 to 20,000 feet to avoid the lethal light and medium anti-aircraft guns. To prepare them for the Kiska raid, Colonel Eareckson had put them through a two-week training program of making low-level approaches against targets set up on Umnak Island.[210]

The bombers and fighters flew in formation to Segula Island. While the bombers orbited near the island, the fighters sped ahead to soften up the Japanese defenses.

Colonel McCorkle led his P-39 pilots across Little Kiska at 9:25 AM in a strafing attack. The Airacobra

The series of photographs were taken during a low-level attack on the main camp at Kiska on December 20, 1942. They illustrate how low the bombers had been flown on the September 14 "max effort" raid. Until then, the bomber crews had flown their missions at high altitudes to avoid the light and medium altitude anti aircraft fire. With the introduction of fighter escorts to suppress the Japanese anti-aircraft gunners, Colonel Eareckson's bomber crews began flying low-level missions as a matter of routine.

USA photos

pilots then proceeded to attack the anti-aircraft positions on South Head, before turning north to hit the positions in the submarine and main camp areas and on North Head. The Rufe pilots rose to challenge McCorkle's pilots as they swept in at low-level. Two were shot down by Lieutenant Gene L. Arth and his wing-man, Wintow E. Matthews. In addition to the Japanese planes, Colonel McCorkle reported that the positions on Little Kiska had been devastated, three submarines damaged, a four engine flying boat destroyed, four anti-aircraft positions strafed, about four hundred Japanese killed or wounded and their camps partially destroyed.

The P-38s followed close on the heels of the P-39 pilots by attacking positions on North Head, before turning to deal with the Rufe pilots. Major Jackson and Lieutenant Dewey E. Crowe collided in an attempt to shoot down a Rufe off North Head. Both fighters crashed into the ocean. There were no survivors. The 54th Fighter Squadron submitted claims, unsubstantiated later, for shooting down three Japanese aircraft. Lieutenants Richard B. Gardner and Hawley P. Mills were each credited with shooting down a Rufe and Lieutenant Laven was given credit for a "cruiser-type biplane."[211]

Colonel Eareckson led the first flight of six bombers, all from the 404th Bombardment Squadron, on a low-level approach against the shipping in the harbor. The crews, as they skimmed over Little Kiska and headed west across the harbor at two hundred feet, saw the flames and smoke from fires started by the fighter attacks. One B-24, flown by Lieutenant Andrews, peeled off to the left and went after several tenders that had been spotted at the end of South Head. The others roared into the harbor, dropping bombs on their targets, the three large cargo ships that had been spotted by the reconnaissance flight the previous day.

After his flight had unloaded its bombs, Colonel Eareckson then led them on a circling attack against other shipping in the harbor, before following the other bombers from the first wave west across the island.

Major Ansley Watson led the second wave of six B-24s from the 21st Bombardment Squadron. The 36th Bombardment Squadron provided the crew for one of the bombers. The bombers thundered across the harbor at low-level on the heels of the first wave. The bombardier's targets were the main camp and submarine base. Numerous hits on Japanese installations were claimed. The bombers continued on over the island. The B-17 with an escort of two P-39s flew over shortly afterwards to take photographs and assess the damage.

The intelligence staff of the Eleventh Air Force, after assessing the bomb damage, claimed hits on a large transport and several small barges, two mine layers and several other small vessels sunk, the destruction of a four-engine flying boat and five other Japanese aircraft and extensive damage to the ground installations. There were no American losses other than the two P-38s.[212]

The raid had achieved its purpose. With the base on Adak, the Americans were now within effective striking distance of Kiska. More missions could be flown and heavier bomb loads carried. The Japanese were in reach of the single engine fighters, although Colonel McCorkle cautioned that because of their limited range they should be employed only under optimum weather conditions. However, the lethal punch of the Airacobra's 37mm cannon, two fifty and four thirty caliber machine guns proved an ideal flack suppression weapon as did the concentrated fire power of the Lightning. None of the bombers sustained serious damage.[213]

Commander Mukai, after the war, admitted that following the September 14 raid the damage done by bombing became more severe. The Japanese radar was unable to detect the approach of aircraft because of the switch to low-level tactics and there was less time to prepare for the attacks. The raids forced the Japanese to limit the time spent by their ships in the harbor and eventually to rely on submarines for resupply. The raids inflicted great damage on buildings and aircraft, although few men were killed because of the fortifications that had been built. The Japanese began emphasizing anti-aircraft drills and beefing up their fortifications.[214]

Before Spring Comes

The September 14th raid served notice to the Japanese that their situation was becoming untenable. Since August, Eareckson's bomber crews had been dropping psychological warfare leaflets along with the bombs. One, in the shape of a Kiri leaf, prophesied: "Before spring comes again, the raining bombs from the skies, just like the Kiri leaves fluttering to the ground, will bring sad fate and misfortune to the Japanese."[215]

With the occupation of Adak, Patrol Air Wing Four extended its patrols over the sea approaches between the Aleutians and Kurile Islands in search of Japanese shipping, while the Eleventh Air Force concentrated on keeping the pressure on Attu and Kiska. The Canadians assumed more responsibility for flying anti-submarine patrols over the Bering Sea and Gulf of Alaska. Squadron Leader Willis' Number 8 Bomber Reconnaissance Squadron, based at Elmendorf Field, flew patrols over the Bering Sea from Nome and the Gulf of Alaska from Kodiak. It was assigned to X Wing at Elmendorf Field, commanded by Group Commander McGregor.

Number 115 Fighter Squadron was redesignated a bomber reconnaissance squadron June 22, and continued its anti-submarine patrols from Annette Island with its

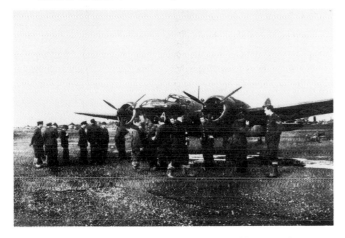

Number 8 Bomber Reconnaissance Squadron was equipped with the Bristol Bolingbroke Mk.IV during its stay in Alaska. The Bolingbroke was the Canadian version of the Bristol Blenheim three-seat light bomber in service from 1937 to 1944. It could carry a one thousand pound bomb load. The Canadians employed the Bolingbrokes as an anti-submarine aircraft in Alaska despite the fact that parts were hard to come by and maintenance was difficult. The photograph was taken at Yakutat. Canadian Forces photo

Bolingbrokes and their crews at Marks Field, Nome, late Summer 1942. Mr J.A. Hill collection via National Defense Headquarters

Captain Jim McCall was stationed at Naknek from June 20 until November 18, when it was relocated to Thornborough Field where it operated until May 1, 1943, flying shipping escort, patrols and other special missions. Captain M.F. Itz, the squadron's operations officer, commanded a detachment of A-29s at Yakutat from June 21, 1942 until July 22, 1943. Major Courtney established another detachment of Hudsons at Kodiak February 3, 1943. It remained there until July 22, when it, along with the other detachments, was withdrawn to support the planned amphibious assault on Kiska.

By then, the 406th Bombardment Squadron had been brought up to full strength with the arrival of the rest of the squadron from Paine Field in November 1942. The squadron had also converted to B-25s beginning in February 1943. Members were sent on detached duty to the Aleutians to fly combat missions with the other medium bomber squadrons. The men of the 406th Bombardment Squadron had become seasoned veterans of the unforgiving Alaskan flying environment.[217]

The patrols soon became superfluous as the threat of Japanese submarine activity in the eastern Pacific diminished in the face of the Allied onslaught and the failure of the Japanese to realize the importance of using their long-range submarines as commerce raiders, a lesson that was not lost on the Americans. Reports from the patrols soon became a monotonous "negative" as the Canadian and American crews searched in vain for any sign of the Japanese.[218]

Morale in the Eleventh Air Force went up after the September 14th raid. A turning point in the air war in the Aleutians had been reached. General Butler now had a

Bolingbrokes were assigned to Number 115 Bomber Reconnaissance Squadron, shown here with a Curtiss Kittyhawk from Number 118 Fighter Squadron at the RCAF base on Annette Island in southeastern Alaska. Canadian Forces photo

Bristol Bolingbrokes. Number 118 Fighter Squadron also continued to serve at the RCAF base on Annette Island, providing air defense of British Columbia and southeastern Alaska with its P-40s. Both were assigned to Y Wing at Annette Island under the command of Wing Commander A.D. Nesbitt. The three RCAF squadrons remained at their necessary but tedious and dangerous duties for the remainder of the Aleutian Campaign.[216]

Major Courtney's 406th Bombardment Squadron also continued to fly anti-submarine patrols from Yakutat and Naknek. Shortly after the squadron's arrival Courtney was directed to send detachments with two B-18s to Nome and Naknek for patrols over the Bering Sea. The detachment at Nome remained there from June 20 to July 20 when it was relieved by the 404th Bombardment Squadron. A detachment of A-29s and B-18s under the command of

Major Douglas Courtney and Capt M.F. Itz.
Douglas Courtney collection

effective means of striking the Japanese. No longer would Colonel Eareckson's bombers have to go in at high altitude to avoid the anti-aircraft and the defending fighters; no longer would they have to scatter their bombs through the clouds and mist; and no longer would they have to face the grueling 1,234-mile round trip flights between Cape Field and their targets. With an escort of fighters to suppress flak and fighters, they could go in   lower altitudes with greater bombing accuracy.

General Butler began to build up his forces on Adak. Major Meals was notified in early September to deploy the entire 77th Bombardment Squadron from Elmendorf Field to Adak, and the 73rd Bombardment Squadron was ordered to send its B-26s to the advance base where they would be supported by the 77th's ground personnel.[219] Colonel Chennault also received orders to deploy P-40s from the 11th Fighter Squadron at Cape Field to Adak. The Canadian pilots from Number 111 Fighter Squadron were included in the air echelon which arrived at Adak in late September.

The buildup of fighter forces needed to support the bomber offensive in the Aleutians continued. The 343rd Fighter Group was activated 11 September and assigned to the XI Fighter Command. The latter organization had been activated March 15, 1942, as a fighter interceptor command and then redesignated a fighter command in May. It controlled the fighter, air warning radar and other combat support squadrons. The three fighter squadrons, 11th, 18th and 54th, were split from the command and assigned to the new group.

Initially, the group headquarters was located at Elmendorf Field, but as the war in the Aleutians progressed, it was moved to Adak, then to Amchitka and finally to Alexei Point on Attu following the recapture of the island. Colonel Chennault was assigned as the group's first commander. He established an advance headquarters at Adak.[220]

The buildup of the fighter strength in the Eleventh Air Force was completed with the activation of the 344th Fighter Squadron on October 2 at Elmendorf Field and its assignment to the 343rd Fighter Group. Captain Elmer E. Booth, one of the original pilots from the 18th Fighter Squadron, assumed command of the new squadron, whose mission it was to provide rear security.

The squadron was made up of transfers from the other fighter squadrons, and for a while it was known as the "eight ball outfit." The squadron adjutants, honoring an old military tradition, used the opportunity to unload their undesirables. One made a particularly conscious effort to get rid of his problems only to find himself on orders to the 344th Fighter Squadron.

However, there were enough good men who either volunteered or were transferred to the new squadron to make it an effective organization. Many of the pilots were Aleutian combat veterans and several had been among the first group to deploy to Alaska with the 18th and 11th Fighter Squadrons. More importantly, the squadron had a core of seasoned and dedicated enlisted men who held it together. One, Master Sergeant Bailey E. Choats, an Old Army NCO, and line chief for the squadron, became a legend for his authoritative roar and his superlative handling of the aircraft maintenance section.[221]

The buildup of the Eleventh Air Force was completed with the arrival of the 54th Troop Carrier Squadron November 19, 1942. The squadron had been activated under the command of Captain William G. Harley at Hamilton Field, California June 1, 1942. From there it was transferred to Bowman Field, Kentucky, and then to Florence Field, South Carolina, where it received orders to deploy to Alaska.

With the exception of Harley, who was promoted to major shortly after assuming command of the squadron, all the pilots were recent graduates of flight school and most of the other members of the 54th were new to the Army Air Forces. They spent their first months training and getting organized as a squadron. The first six C-47s arrived, and the 54th Troop Carrier Squadron began to take shape. In early October it was brought up to full strength with thirteen C-47s, and preparations were made for its deployment to Alaska.

The ground echelon departed Florence Field October 17 by rail for Seattle where they were issued winter clothing and equipment and boarded a transport for Alaska. They arrived at Elmendorf Field on November 15. The air echelon departed on October 15 in their new C-47s, stopping at Hill Field, Utah, where their aircraft were winterized. They then headed for Great Falls and the beginning of the Northwest Staging Route for Alaska.

En route, Major Harley and his men ran into bad weather. Both Great Falls and Hill Field were closed, and

Douglas C-47 Skytrains, 54th Troop Carrier Squadron.
USA photos

the only alternative was to land all thirteen C-47s in a large cow pasture near Whitehall, Montana. They remained there for two days until the weather lifted. After spending additional time at Great Falls for further aircraft winterization and issuance of cold weather clothing and equipment, the air echelon departed for Elmendorf Field, arriving there November 19 without any serious incidents.[222]

The 54th Troop Carrier Squadron and the 42nd Troop Carrier Squadron were assigned to the XI Service Command. Based out of Elmendorf Field, both squadrons flew regular shuttles, transporting high priority cargo and passengers between Alaskan bases. The Navy Air Transport Command also sent aircraft to Alaska to support its operations in the Aleutians.

Both services also depended on commercial air carriers under contract to augment their airlift capabilities. They ranged from the large airlines (Pan American, Northwest Airlines and United Airlines), who were used primarily for transporting passengers and cargo between the states and Alaska, to the small Alaska bush pilot operators who provided much of the local services.[223]

Robert "Bob" Reeve was one of the few pilots who would risk flying the Aleutians. In November 1942, he signed a contract with the Alaska Communications System, or ACS as it was commonly referred to, and became one of the few civilian flyers in Alaska who regularly flew in a combat zone. The military issued him an identification card which stated he was a captain. It was insurance in the event the Japanese captured him.

Reeve's job required him to carry high priority cargo and passengers for the ACS. Reeve, who had earned the name "The Glacier Pilot," for pioneering the use of glaciers as landing fields, quickly adapted to the Aleutian flying conditions and became a familiar sight up and down the chain. He survived on skill and determination and

Bob Reeve, with his earnings from delivering supplies and equipment to the air field construction site at Northway near the Canadian border, purchased another Boeing 80A, the "Black Mariah." He used this transport, his other Boeing 80A, "The Yellow Peril," and his Fairchild 71 for his Aleutian operations. He lost the "Black Mariah" to a forced landing near Cold Bay. Reeve was flying a load of equipment and radar personnel to Amchitka when the weather turned sour. Reeve recalled, "I found myself one thousand feet on top of the fog, had one half-hour of gas, it was midnight, no moon, blacker than hell, and I had no place to go. I was in just about the worst fix of my life." He remembered from previous flights that clear areas were created in the fog from the temperature differences in streams flowing into the ocean. He found a clear area and set the plane down in the water just off shore. Everyone survived the ditching, but the Boeing 80A was a loss. The "Yellow Peril" survived the war and was later acquired by the Boeing Museum of Flight and restored. The photograph of Bob Reeve and his son Richard, the "Yellow Peril" and the Fairchild was taken at Merrill Field during the war. Reeve collection

developed a detailed knowledge of Aleutian flying.

He remained at the job until the end of the war; and then, based of his wartime experiences decided to form an airline to service the islands. Reeve purchased several surplus C-47s, and Reeve Aleutian Airways became a going concern. For years it provided the only air passenger and service in the islands, its aircrews noted for their skill and safety record.[224]

To oversee the stepped-up air offensive in the Aleutians, General Butler established an advance headquarters at Adak under the supervision of Colonel William M. Prince. Colonel Davis continued his duties as the Eleventh Air Force chief of staff from Cape Field, and spent most of his time shuttling between Adak and Kodiak, solving the various operational and administrative problems of a large organization engaged in combat.

Colonel Eareckson, like a Viking warrior, personally led his men into battle, flying virtually every mission planned against the Japanese while his deputy Lieutenant Colonel Jack Donohew tended to the running of the bomber command. Eareckson maintained a lean headquarters at Adak, keeping his operations and intelligence staff there while his administrative and logistics staff remained behind at Elmendorf Field to make certain that the bombers had enough bombs and gas and the paperwork was taken care of.

General Butler remained at Kodiak where he tried to get along with Admiral Theobald and keep from being ignored in the scheme of things. Although still officially located at Elmendorf Field, Butler's headquarters for all intents and purposes operated from Kodiak where it was in a better position to coordinate operations with Admiral Theobald and his staff who had the ultimate responsibility in Alaska for driving the Japanese from the Aleutians. General Buckner, much to his chagrin, continued to play a supporting role from the Alaska Defense Command headquarters at Fort Richardson.[225]

The Eleventh Air Force had settled into an organizational structure, that with a few minor changes, was to remain unchanged for the remainder of the Aleutian Campaign.

A new mission statement was issued November 1, which also remained unchanged for the duration. It required the bomber squadrons to isolate Kiska and Attu and destroy all vessels approaching the two islands. The fighter squadrons were responsible for protecting the bombers and striking specific targets on the islands. The Eleventh Air Force was also responsible for standing alert against a possible Japanese attack and conducting patrols. The latter duty was performed by Fleet Air Wing Four, the RCAF and the 406th Bombardment Squadron.

The aircraft strength of the two B-24D squadrons remained at around ten bombers each. The 36th Bombardment Squadron possessed eleven B-17Es and a LB-30. Each of the two medium bomber squadrons were equipped with around ten B-26As.[226] The Western Defense Command promised Butler newer, winterized B-17Es and B-24Ds as replacements for the ones sent to Alaska in June. The Command also promised to send more capable B-25s to Alaska in exchange for the B-26s. Billy Wheeler noted in the September 27 entry to his diary:

> Squadron is receiving some new ships — thank God! However, our pleasure in receiving them is tempered by the fact that they have been used as training ships in the states. It is almost unbelievable to men who have been in combat that the powers that be should send old ships to fight the war.[227]

The Hostile Skies

Following the September 14 raid, the weather turned sour, reducing the number of raids that could be flown against Kiska for the remainder of the month. Instead, Colonel Eareckson committed his bombers to flying normal reconnaissance missions over Attu and Kiska and in support of a reconnaissance party that was investigating the possibility of using Amchitka Island as the next forward base. The abandoned Aleut village on Amchitka was destroyed September 21 in a fire bombing attack to prevent its possible use by the Japanese. Two days later Eareckson with two P-38s as escorts flew over the island in a B-17 while a PBY landed and reconnaissance party

Attu Village before the war. Nothing of it remains today except memories. Dept of Commerce photo

The oblique, aerial photograph of Chichagof Harbor was taken on September 21, 1942, according to the legend at the bottom. The numbers are the work of a photo interpreter to point out various items of interest. One, two and nine are Attu Village. USA photo

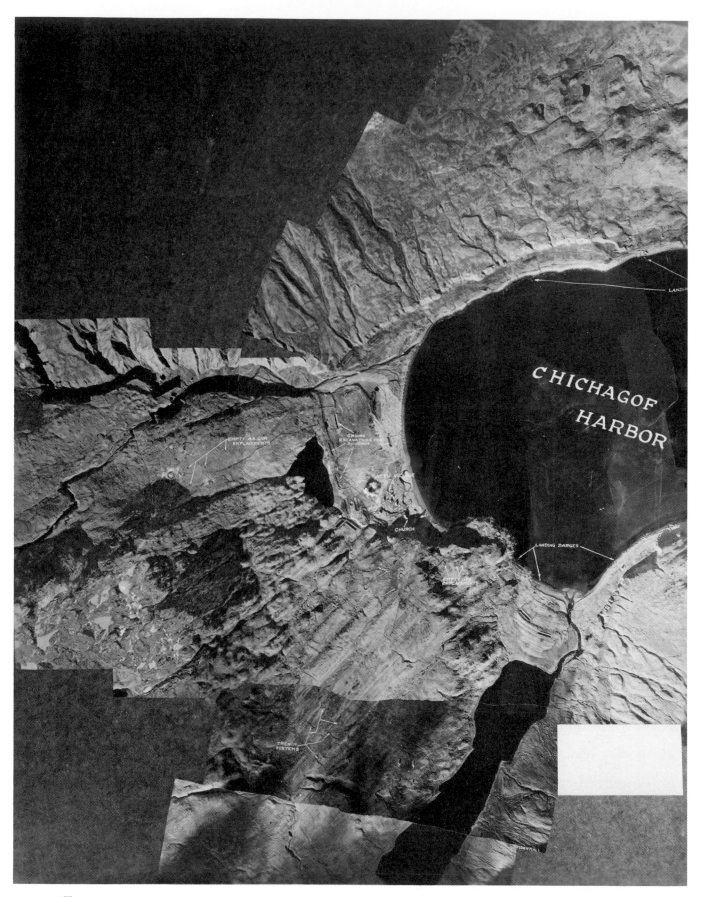

CHICHAGOF
HARBOR

The mosaic, made up from vertical aerial photographs taken at an altitude of five thousand feet, shows Attu Village, a bomb burst near it, and empty Japanese building and gun revetments. USA photo

paddled ashore in a rubber boat to investigate the island. The party, led by Lieutenant Colonel William J. Verbeck, Colonel Castner's assistant, determined that the island was unsuitable for base construction. They were picked up by another PBY on the 25th.[228]

On September 23, Major Donald Dunlap took off from Cape Field at 7:00 AM and headed down the Aleutian Chain on a reconnaissance of the Semichi Islands, Agattu and Attu. On reaching Attu at 10:00 AM, he circled his bomber over Chichagof Harbor, while his crew searched in vain for any presence of the Japanese. All they observed were empty anti-aircraft positions and traces of places where tents were once pitched. The Japanese had completed the transfer of the Attu garrison to Kiska seven days earlier.[229]

A crew in the LB-30 returned on the 28th to bomb and destroy Attu Village. They reported that all the houses except the church had been destroyed. Fred Ramputi flew over the burned-out village the next day and confirmed that the church and one other building were still standing, five other buildings were partially destroyed and the remainder of the village had burned to the ground.[230]

The business of obliterating the small village was finished on October 15 when a B-24 arrived overhead. The bombardier, Lieutenant Sam Newman, a devout Catholic, kneeling over his bombsight, watched as the church slowly moved into view. The incendiaries burst and Attu Village became history.[231]

A mission similar to the one flown on September 14 was planned for the 22nd. Twelve bombers with an escort of fifteen P-39s and twenty P-40s, twelve from the 11th Fighter Squadron and eight from the 18th Fighter Squadron were launched. The P-40s from the two squadrons had been deployed forward to the island from their bases at Cape Field and Kodiak.

It was a common practice during the Aleutian Campaign to send aircrews and their aircraft on temporary duty to the forward bases. Sometimes they flew as a unit and other times they were integrated into another unit. It gave them the opportunity to escape the tedium of rear area duty which consisted mostly of standing alert, flying patrols, training and hassling with paperwork. It also gave them the chance to engage in combat, and perhaps earn a medal or two.

Lieutenant Aiken from the 18th Fighter Squadron was among the Warhawk pilots sent forward. The mission was planned similarly to the one flown on the 14th, except that the P-40s were scheduled to come in behind the bombers. The whole operation was cancelled when the P-39 pilots encountering rain squalls and lowering ceilings, turned back. Colonel Eareckson, who was leading the bombers, decided to scrub the mission.[232]

The pilots from the 11th and 18th Fighter Squadrons continued on under a 200-foot ceiling. The two groups of planes met head on.

Aiken recalled that it "was the maddest scramble for safe air space that I ever experienced in my life." Lieutenant Aiken managed to get his flight turned around and began climbing through the clouds for the clear sky above to avoid the crowd of planes below. When he and his flight emerged on top, Lieutenant John A. Berntson was missing. The young 18th Fighter Squadron pilot apparently had become disoriented and spun into the water below. He was the squadron's first casualty in the Aleutian Campaign.[233]

The next day was clear over Kiska and three bombers from the 21st Bombardment Squadron were committed to a high altitude attack. Captain Richard Lycan, Lieutenant Thomas F. Bloomfield and Lieutenant Ernest C. Pruett approached their target, a group of vessels

Pilots of the 11th Fighter Squadron. M. Green collection

-223-

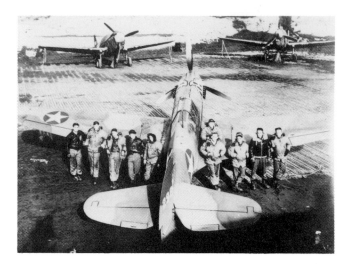

Pilots, 11th Fighter Squadron, Cape Field. USA photos

An unidentified fighter P-40 pilot, Aleutian Islands. USA photo

Armorers load 50 calibre rounds into 11th Fighter Squadron P-40E while the pilot, Lieut James Perryman looks on.
USA photo

anchored near the main camp area, from the southeast at an altitude of eleven thousand feet. The three pilots and their B-24 crews dropped fifteen 500-pound bombs. A number of near misses were noted among the ships which included one large transport, several smaller ones and three destroyers. Hits were also observed on shore installations.[234]

Colonel Eareckson, on September 25, launched a raid of eleven bombers. Colonel Chennault led a composite group of P-40s made up of eight from the 11th Fighter Squadron, six from the 18th Fighter Squadron and four P-40Ks from Number 111 Fighter Squadron. It was the first joint U.S. and Canadian operation of the Aleutian Campaign. Major Wilber G. Miller, Commander, 42nd Fighter Squadron, led eleven P-39s.

Pilots from the 21st Bombardment Squadron, from left to right: Lieut Ernest C. Pruett, Lieut Bockman, Lieut Russell W. Tarvin and unknown. Lieutenant Pruett's bomber crew was credited with crippling the Nozima Maru *and forcing the Japanese to beach her near Trout Lagoon. Lieutenant Tarvin's crew sank the* Montreal Maru *January 5, 1943.*

Larry Reineke collection

The fighters were assigned the mission of suppressing the anti-aircraft guns, protecting the bombers against the fighters and strafing ground targets. The bombers went after shipping in the harbor and the facilities ashore. Lieutenant Pruett's crew was credited with hitting a large transport ship, which was seen listing as the bombers departed. The Japanese beached the *Nozima Maru* near Trout Lagoon where she became a target for subsequent bomber attacks.

Eareckson's bomber crews also reported several near misses on other ships in the harbor and damage to facilities on the shore. About one hundred and fifty Japanese were claimed to have been killed.

The fighter pilots strafed Japanese positions and engaged the Japanese float fighters that had taken off from the harbor.

Two Japanese Rufe pilots went after Lieutenant Aiken and his wing-man who were flying top cover for the strikes. Squadron Leader Boomer spotted them and shot one of the attackers down. Elsewhere, Colonel Chennault bagged a Rufe over North Head who had tried to ram him. All the Americans and Canadians returned safely to Adak.[235]

Another major raid was launched on September 27. A pattern had now been established that would be followed in the months ahead.

Lieutenant Ramputi took off at 7:30 AM in the LB-30 to checkout the weather and take photographs. He reported low ceilings east of Kiska, and ceilings from three to five thousand feet beyond as he continued down the chain past the tiny island of Buldir midway between Kiska and the Near Islands. Oblique photographs were taken of the island. More oblique photographs were shot of the Semichis as Ramputi and his crew flew along the

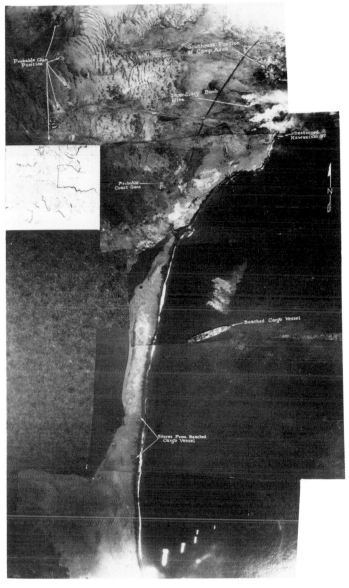

The aerial photograph was taken shortly after the Nozima Maru *was hit. Note the bombs at the bottom of the photograph falling towards the submarine base. The 7,190 ton, 450-foot long transport eventually wound up near a small stream flowing out of Trout Lagoon. The* Nozima Maru *was a modern, diesel powered transport built in 1935 by Mitsubishi Jukogyo Kaishi, Ltd. It was capable of making 19 knots maximum speed.* USA photo

south coast of the group of small islands. They reached Attu at 11:00 AM, found it obscured by clouds, and continued on at ten thousand feet to Agattu, where they took vertical photographs before heading back to Adak. Ramputi and his tired crew landed at 1:30 PM.

The weather ship had completed another day's work. The film was turned over to the photo lab at Elmendorf Field for processing and for use by the photo interpreters.

At 9:30 AM seven B-24s and a B-17 carrying a camera to verify bombing results thundered down the runway at Adak and headed for Kiska. They were escorted by a

The photograph of the Nozima Maru *was taken after Kiska was reoccupied by the Americans and Canadians. The submarine base can be seen in the distance.* Frank Rosse collection

The Nozima Maru *as she looked in September 1989. Most of the ship was cut up for salvage after the war.* Susan Morton photo

mixed group of eleven P-39s, four P-40s and one P-38. Four of the Liberator crews, on reaching Kiska, found the island obscured by clouds that had moved in shortly after Ramputi's report. They decided to turn back. The fighter pilots joined them. The other three bomber crews dropped their bombs through the overcast and headed home.[236]

The next's day effort was more eventful and successful. Seven missions were flown. The LB-30 and a B-17 were dispatched to Attu. Five B-24s and a camera B-17, escorted by seventeen fighters were committed on a bombing and strafing attack against Kiska. The first attack was followed by a second one of five B-24s and a B-17. Two B-26s, in their first Aleutian mission since Dutch Harbor, were committed to search for a Japanese submarine sighted near Nazan Bay. Three B-24s were sent aloft in response to another Patrol Air Wing Four sighting of a Japanese transport east of Attu. Two more B-26s were sent to replace the first two Marauders. Finally, a crew of B-17s

flew a mission over Adak to take aerial photographs needed in a mapping project. It was a busy day.

Colonel Eareckson's bomber crews succeeded in dropping their bombs on shipping in the harbor and on the main camp. A claim was submitted for the sinking of a submarine.[237] The Japanese admitted after the war that the RO-65 had been hit, but claimed her sinking was due to an accident, perhaps from mishandling after the bomb damage.[238]

Major Milton Ashkins, who had assumed command of the 54th Fighter Squadron on September 20, was credited with shooting down a Rufe.[239] Captain Arthur T. Rice, 57th Fighter Squadron, on detached duty with the 42nd Fighter Squadron, shot down two Rufes in a remarkable display of aerial marksmanship. When his machine guns jammed, he used his 37mm cannon. It took four rounds to down the first Japanese float fighter and one to destroy the second.[240]

The 54th Fighter Group also suffered its only combat casualty that day. Major Wilbur G. Miller had just led the 42nd Fighter Squadron on a strafing attack against the Japanese anti-aircraft positions when he saw several Japanese fighters attacking one of the fighters that was flying top cover for the bombers. He sped to the rescue, and in the dog fight that ensued, Miller was shot down by one of the Japanese fighter pilots.[241]

Albert Aiken recalled later that he was engaged in a fight with one Rufe pilot when another attacked him. He quickly broke free from the engagement and dove for the surface of Kiska Harbor. After shaking the two Japanese float fighters, Aiken's found himself in the vicinity of Gertrude Cove where he spotted a P-39. He flew up alongside the fighter and tried to use his radio to contact the pilot only to find that it had been damaged in the engagement with the Japanese. To Aiken, something did not look right. The pilot in the other aircraft was staring straight ahead and the fighter was in a gradual descending turn.

Aiken remembered that after a few seconds of flying formation, he pulled away to check the skies around him before rejoining the silent fighter.

> I followed him in a more loose formation. I couldn't call him, I couldn't say anything, I was just helpless as far he was concerned to communicate. So I just sat there and watched him helplessly fly right into the water. I feel to this day that he was either dead since I couldn't see any damage on his airplane, or he could have been hit and was unconscious . . . I just don't know, but the airplane went in and I never saw it again. It didn't skip or anything, it just went in like a bullet. . . . When I got back to Adak, I learned that it was Major Miller.[242]

Bombs explode in the seaplane area of the main camp, Kiska. USA photo

Lieutenant Aiken continued to fly combat missions until he was sent to the states for advanced fighter training. When he returned, the 18th Fighter Squadron had moved to Amchitka. He remained with the squadron until August 1943, when he received his reassignment orders. His experiences were like that of so many other young men who fought in the hostile skies above the Aleutian Islands.[243]

The only other casualty from the raid occurred when Lieutenant Collier H. Davidson's B-24, "Jap Panic," was hit. Sergeant Henry A. Sarenski, one of the waist gunners, was wounded and the bomber badly damaged with the hydraulics shot out. Davidson made it back to Adak where he landed without the benefit of brakes. The Liberator went hurdling down and then off the runway before coming to a stop. No one was hurt, but "Jap Panic" was, in the official jargon, "damaged beyond repair."

Consigned to the junk yard "Jap Panic," tail number 41-11802, like the other broken aircraft in the Aleutians became a supplier of parts. The first opportunity came in early December when another B-24 returned from Kiska with the leading edge of a wing spar damaged and the de-icer boot full of holes.

Master Sergeant R. M. Brosius organized his mechan-

Major Milton Ashkins, left, and pilots of the 54th Fighter Squadron. USA photo

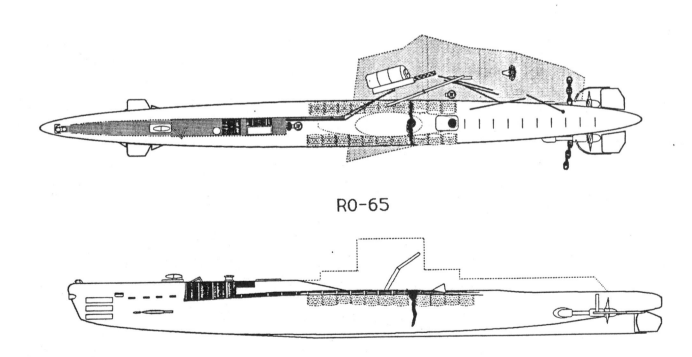

RO-65

RO-65
USS SAFEGUARD, MDSU1 & NPS
9/89

During September 1989, the National Park Service with the cooperation of the U.S. Third Fleet conducted project Seamark to locate and document submerged objects in Kiska Harbor. The Navy provided the U.S.S. Safeguard (ARS-50), a towing and salvage vessel. Sonar scans were made of the harbor bottom to pinpoint and document objects. Diving teams from the National Park Service Submerged Cultural Resources Unit, Santa Fe, New Mexico; U.S. Navy Mobile Diving and Salvage Team One, Pearl Harbor; and the Safeguard explored and further documented the larger objects located beneath the surface of Kiska Harbor. One of the objects was the RO-65. The drawings of the sunken submarine were made by Lieutenant Paul Currivan, Executive Officer, Mobile Diving and Salvage Unit One on his Apple Computer based on information provided him by the divers. Similar drawings were made of the Nissan Maru. A remote control underwater video camera was also used, and a video recording of what possibly could have been Jack Marks' B-17 was made. However, limited time and other priorities prevented a diving team from being sent down for verification.

Major Arthur T. Rice, as Commander, 11th Fighter Squadron.
USA photo

ics and they began an all night tedious process of removing a spar and de-icer boot from "Jap Panic" and installing them on the damaged bomber. One of the two drills they were using to make the repairs broke shortly after they started work. They managed to keep the other in repair, and ten hours later the bomber was back in operation.

The old bomber continued to yield up parts. Engines were removed and installed in other B-24s. Her wiring system was used to repair another Liberator. Gradually, she was stripped of all usable parts. The bomber and the other aircraft that were damaged beyond repair provided a valuable source of parts and provided credibility to the gag that aircraft were kept aloft over the Aleutians by bare hands, the help of God and a few wrecks.[244]

Only one mission was flown on September 29, the last Aleutian flight for the LB-30 "Tough Boy." Fred Ramputi headed on down the Aleutian Chain on a weather reconnaissance. The crew sighted a Japanese freighter near Attu and dropped several bombs without achieving any hits. The other missions were cancelled due to weather.[245] The next day, Eareckson led nine of his B-24s on what by now become a routine raid against Kiska. Again, one of the 36th Bombardment Squadron's B-17s was sent along as the camera aircraft to take photographs of the results.

The B-17 was flying at an altitude of twenty-eight thousand feet over Kiska when the supercharger on the number two engine blew up. A piece of turbine wheel smashed into the ball turret, wounding Private Nuel D. Curtis. The bomber pilots immediately descended to a lower altitude and headed back to Adak while the crew tried unsuccessfully to remove the young gunner from the jammed turret. He died two hours after the bomber landed at Adak.[246]

The Eleventh Air Force learned by doing. There were no examples to follow. Unlike the Eighth Air Force, it could not draw on the experiences of the Royal Air Force. Most of its effort was against Kiska whose features soon became familiar to the Eleventh Air Force air crews. Occasional missions were flown against the more distant Attu which was regarded as of secondary importance. The tiny Eleventh Air Force essentially became a one target air force.

Instead of the complex missions flown elsewhere with bomb loads that varied according to the target, Eareckson's bomber command settled on a bomb load of general purpose bombs, usually equipped with delayed fuses and dropped at low-level.

Occasionally, napalm bombs, consisting of practice bombs filled with gasoline in which strips of rubber had been dissolved and a detonator attached, were dropped along with the general purpose bombs. The bombs were prepared by the 390th Chemical Company (Air Bomb), commanded by Captain Earl H. Beistline.[247]

The photograph of wrecked P-38s and Jap Panic (41-11802), seen in the background, was taken by Les Spoonts in late 1942 at Adak. Aircraft that were damaged beyond repair were used as a source of parts for others. Les Spoonts collection

B-24 damaged by anti-aircraft over Kiska. Larry Reineke collection

The effects of Aleutian flying can be clearly seen on the faces of these fighter pilots from the 54th Fighter Group. Les Spoonts collection

B-24 under repair at Adak. The two men on the ground are wearing Eddie Bauer quilted down jackets that were issued to Eleventh Air Force personnel. USA photo

Staff officers, 404th Bombardment Squadron, plan another mission. Berthram Hoak collection

Lieutenants Reinhard A. Ryder, Glynn Lowrey and Paul E. Perkins, 21st Bombardment Squadron, waiting to go out on another mission. USA photo

Don't Let Us Stay Up In This Place

John Huston's crew finished the filming of "Report From the Aleutians" and went home. The film was released the next year. It portrayed conditions in the Aleutians as being almost idyllic. Huston later admitted the film had been made for propaganda purposes to show the folks back home that the Americans were on the offensive in the Aleutians and that morale there was "first rate."

Bomber crews, 404th Bombardment Squadron, waiting for the return of their comrades. Louis Blau collection

It omitted the shock and terror of combat and the corrosive effect on the minds of men forced to endure unnatural hardships and isolation. Huston's second war documentary, "Battle of San Pietro," more than made up for the realities of war left out in "Report From the Aleutians."

Morale was not "first rate" in the Aleutians. Mail was slow in arriving, the food was bad and the living conditions left a lot to be desired. The Aleutian weather added to the misery. The units that had been rushed to Alaska in response to the Japanese thrust into islands suffered the most. Promotions, pay and other personnel actions were still controlled by their parent units in the states. Commanders of the units on attached duty vented their frustrations when they saw less qualified men from assigned squadrons being promoted while their men were frozen in grade.

Most of the men sent to Alaska on temporary duty had arrived without proper training and with little to prepare them for the conditions they had to face. They began to think of themselves as forgotten men. One squadron commander, in a letter to a Fourth Air Force friend, summed it up:

> Since I arrived the target hasn't been visible. The weather is getting worse. The thing we can't understand is why we continue to send our men out into this God awful stuff against a target which can't be seen one tenth of the time and if hit, isn't worth the gas burned up to get to it . . . I think everyone would like to have us remain in Alaska permanently . . . God forbid. Don't let us stay up in this place.[248]

Word of the problems reached General Arnold, who sent a stinging rebuke to General Butler, noting:

> I have received reports concerning long periods during which personnel have not been paid; personnel leaving the United States on flying status as members of combat crews, and upon arriving in Alaska being taken off flying status; promotions which should be made and have not; combat crews being retained out in the Aleutians in the combat theatre for many months, when six weeks is about the maximum that anybody should be kept on operating status in such difficult operating areas.[249]

General Arnold sent an Inspector General team to find out what was wrong so that corrective actions could be taken. They found six bomber squadrons, some incomplete, and one headquarters group squadron scattered over a twelve-hundred-mile area from Elmendorf Field to Adak. Three of them had been sent to Alaska with the expectation they would be returned to the states within a few weeks when the emergency was over. Instead, they were held over.

The men were beginning to wonder if they were ever going to be sent home. One remarked to the inspectors: "Now we feel that only being shot down can get us out of here. It is just like having an undated death warrant."[250]

Despite the constant specter of death, Eareckson's men continued to fly the missions. They had become by now seasoned professionals. The inspectors also noted that they were doing excellent work under extremely trying conditions, and that there were numerous instances of apparently unrecognized meritorious performance of duty under fire. They also noted that Colonel Eareckson "repeatedly distinguished himself by his command efficiency under severe difficulties as well as his personal leadership."[251]

Many of the problems noted by the inspection team were corrected in time. The ground personnel for the three squadrons on temporary duty joined their units. A rotational policy was established so that the men could get a break from the rigors of combat. Efforts were made to provide recreational facilities in the Aleutians. However, the conditions still remained primitive, and in comparison, Elmendorf Field was heaven. It was a place of "clean beds, no mud and above all, women."

Fourth Avenue in nearby Anchorage was lined with bars where Scotch cost fifty-five to seventy-five cents a shot. The Lido Club and the Aleutians Gardens offered fine dining, especially after the monotonous fare at the forward bases. There were also establishments for the other basic human need.[252]

The time spent in Anchorage the 11th Fighter Squadron historian noted was a "great morale builder." The leave policy for the squadron was implemented in November and two of its members wound up in jail. The squadron commander had to get them out, and for a long time the two bore the nickname "jailbird."[253]

Days of Glory

Colonel Eareckson stepped up the bombing campaign against Kiska during October. With escort, the raids became more effective. Two missions flown on October 2 and 3 accounted for the largest number of Japanese aircraft shot down during the Aleutian Campaign. Eleven B-24s thundered down the runway at Adak on the 2nd,

Capt. Cecil A. Thomas in his P-39. USA photo

turned west and headed for Kiska. They were accompanied by six P-39s. The bomber crews roared in at low altitude, dropping demolition bombs on two cargo vessels in the harbor and the main camp while the P-39 pilots went after the anti-aircraft positions. Below, the Rufe pilots beat their way across the swells in Kiska Harbor and climbed for altitude in a vain attempt to intercept the bombers.

The Airacobra pilots tore into them. Captain Kenneth E. George and Lieutenant Cecil A. Thomas from the 42nd Fighter Squadron were each credited with a victory, while Lieutenant James R. Burgett III on temporary duty from the 56th Fighter Squadron bagged another float fighter.[254]

The next day six of Eareckson's bombers, escorted by four P-38s and six P-39s, thundered across the harbor at low altitude in a bombing and strafing attack. A hit was scored on the beached *Nozima Maru*. Other bombs exploded in the main camp area. The fighter pilots had a field day. Lieutenants George Laven Jr. and Victor Walton from the 54th Fighter Squadron shared joint credit for knocking a Jake out of the sky while Captains Louis H. Bowman and Pat M. Deberry, 42nd Fighter Squadron, were each credited with a Jake. A fourth Jake was shot out of the ski by Lieutenant Frank A. Beagle on temporary duty to Adak from the 56th Fighter Squadron. Captain Robert L. McDonald send a Rufe pilot to his death with a blast of cannon and machine gun fire from his P-38.[255]

The Japanese pilots, within a two-day period, had lost four of their float fighter and five float reconnaissance aircraft. It was something they could not afford. No Eleventh Air Force planes had been lost.

Staff Sergeant John J. Molinsski, a crew member in the 404th Bombardment Squadron, was the only fatality. The Americans had clearly established air superiority over the Aleutian Islands. The Japanese pilots, worn out by losses and the constant battle against the elements, became less aggressive.

The Japanese had no effective means of responding to the American raids, although they made a feeble attempt. One of their Jakes was observed circling over Adak on October 1 at six thousand feet. The anti-aircraft gunners opened up, but it got away. The next day, at 5:00 AM, another Jake pilot, who now had been dubbed "Good-Time Charlie," flew over and dropped two bombs. Both exploded harmlessly in the muskeg. That constituted the Japanese bombing offensive against the forward base.[256]

The days of glory ended at Cape Field. The last mission against Kiska from the base had been flown on September 13 by Fred Ramputi and crew of "Tough Boy," and Lieutenants Hasenfus and McCoy in their P-38s. Cape Field became just another staging field on the Aleutian Chain for the war against the Japanese that was moving relentlessly westward.

General Butler began building up his forces on Adak and stepping up the pressure against Admiral Akiyama's forces huddled on Kiska. Nine and ten ship bomber missions with sizable fighter escorts became routine. The Japanese Army garrison at Gertrude Cove was added to the target list. The first mission was flown on October 6. It proved productive. The *Borneo Maru*, which was bringing in supplies and equipment for Major Hotzumi's troops, was hit by a bomb, and left burning in the cove.

After being weathered out on the 7th, the missions were resumed on the 8th with increased intensity; and for the next three days the bomber crews went after Japanese shipping, which had been placed at the top of the prior-

A B-24D, 404th Bombardment Squadron, thunders down the runway at Cape Field. With the movement of forces westward, Cape Field became another support base. USA photo

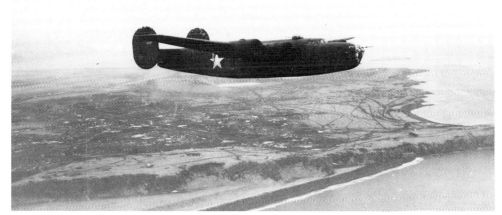

A B-24D over Cape Field.
USA photo

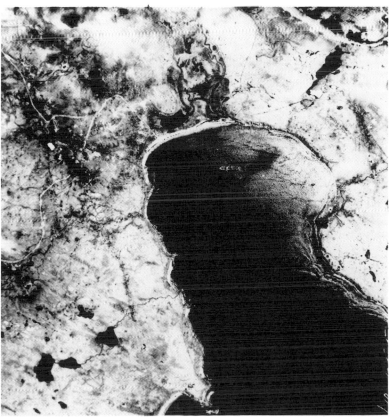

The aerial photograph of Gertrude Cove area and the Borneo Maru, upper center of the cove, was taken shortly after the 5,864-ton ship was disabled. The coal burning ship was built in 1917 at the Kawasaki Kobe shipyard. It was 385 feet long with a beam of 51 feet.
Louis Blau collection

The Borneo Maru *as she looked August 1986.* author's photo

ity list to prevent the Japanese from bringing in reinforcements and supplies. The bomber crews also pounded the Japanese positions ashore with general purpose and fire bombs, while the P-39 and P-38 pilots mercilessly crisscrossed the Japanese positions, strafing them with their deadly cannon and machine guns. Flames and smoke rose from bombed out buildings and men were observed running from them on fire.

The Japanese fought back as best they could, but the Americans had now developed the tactic of coming in from different directions and altitudes to confuse the Japanese gunners into a fine art. After the decimation of early October, the float fighters were no longer a threat; and the Japanese were hesitant to send their float reconnaissance planes aloft to shadow the bombers and provide information on their altitude to gunners below in the face of the American fighters.[257]

After a two-day delay because of weather, another raid was sent against Kiska on the 14th. This one included six B-26s from the 73rd Bombardment Squadron on their first mission against Kiska. The ground echelon of the 77th Bombardment Squadron had arrived at Adak on October 3. Within two days they had set up their camp. The air crews, who were involved in transitioning into B-25s, did not arrive until December 12. In the interim, the aircrews from the 73rd Bombardment Squadron arrived on October 13. General Butler decided to use the more maneuverable medium bomber against Japanese shipping.[258]

For the October 14 raid, Eareckson, in addition to the B-26s, committed nine B-24s and a B-17 camera aircraft. Twelve P-38s were sent along to suppress the anti-aircraft fire and provide air protection. The heavies roared in at low altitude and the bombardiers unloaded fire bombs on the main camp area and 500-pound general purpose bombs on the submarine base while the gunners strafed Japanese positions.

The B-26s, equipped with torpedoes, were sent against shipping in Gertrude Cove. The first three Marauder crews headed in at low-level for the *Borneo Maru*. The torpedoes were released six hundred yards from the beached ship. One hit the water and flipped end over end. Another missed the ship and exploded against the shore. The third disappeared, presumedly stuck on the bottom of the shallow harbor. The second flight of three arrived several hours later. This time, the crews watched in frustration as their torpedoes hit the water and appeared to run "hot and true," only to disappear without striking anything. They had apparently become stuck in the mud on the bottom of the shallow cove.

The whole operation had been a complete failure. The idea of employing the B-26 to drop torpedoes was dropped.[259]

Colonel Eareckson, circling overhead, watched the results. A spent 13mm-round from one of the Japanese anti-aircraft positions punched through the side of the aircraft and fell at his feet. He picked it up and remarked that it was a quick way to pickup a souvenir.[260]

When A Call Was Received

The Eleventh Air Force had not suffered a fatality on a Kiska mission since the accidental death of Private Curtis. The fates were again unkind in a cruel manner on the October 14 raid. Lieutenant Luther B. Stockard felt the rounds tear into the left engine of his P-38. He looked out to see it burst into flames which began to spread to rest of the fighter. While two of his squadron mates, Capt Victor E. Walton and Lieutenant Robert L. McDonald orbited nearby, Stockard bailed out near Little Kiska. For a few minutes he was swinging free under the canopy of his parachute; then he hit the icy waters below.

One of the bombers circled overhead and the crew dropped a life raft. However, the young lieutenant, overcome by cold, could not reach it. A PBY was summoned. Stockard, alone and feeling his life slowly slip away,

Staff Sergeant Ralph Bartholomew, right, and Chief Steward Ira Norman of Centralia, Washington aboard the supply vessel HA-2. Bartholomew collection

waited in vain. He was dead when the Catalina arrived an hour and a half later. Life expectancy in the Aleutians waters was approximately twenty minutes.

General Butler launched an investigation which determined that the rescue procedures that had been established were inadequate. The PBY that was supposed to come to the rescue of downed flyers had been positioned too far away and there had been a breakdown in communications. After the death of Stockard, a PBY was required to accompany the Eleventh Air Force aircraft and stay just outside of the range of anti-aircraft guns while the air strikes were being made. Better communication procedures were also established. The Eleventh Air Force also acquired a number of OA-10s, the Army version of the PBY, for search and rescue work.[261]

The 10th Emergency Rescue Boat Squadron was another unit employed in search and rescue work in the Aleutians. It was a unique organization. Many of its five hundred members were Alaskans who volunteered or had been drafted into the Army. Many were fisherman who followed the compelling but dangerous trade of men and women who go out to sea in small vessels for their livelihood. They were naturals for a job that required skill and courage.

Colonel Davis had originated the idea of forming a crash boat rescue service based on the British and German experiences in the English Channel where both nations had employed small, fast boats to rescue their downed aircrews. He dispatched Lieutenant Gordon R. Donley in December 1941 to Ketchikan, Alaska to begin recruiting and training men for the new unit. Eighteen-year-old Ralph M. Bartholomew, already experienced with the sea and having a thirst for adventure, was among the first to join.

Bartholomew remembered that Donley arrived with a few experienced non-commissioned officers, and

. . . immediately began recruiting young men in Ketchikan who had been raised in the local fishing fleet and had their basic small boat training already. The official name of our organization became the Air Corps Marine Rescue Squadron, later changed to the 924th Quartermaster Boat (Aviation) and then to the 10th Emergency Rescue Boat Squadron.[262]

Donley found room for his embryonic squadron in a bunk house belonging to the New England Fish Company, but had to move out when their accommodations became too small and the fish company wanted its facilities back for the fishing season. The growing squadron then moved into the abandoned Civilian Conservation Corps camp at Ward Lake, only to be booted out when the Aleuts who were evacuated from the Aleutians were moved in. The squadron was then moved to Annette Island.

By then Donley, with the assistance of the U.S. Coast Guard, had instituted a training program for his men. Two twin-screw cabin cruisers, P-30 and P-31, were acquired; and Donley sent Ralph Bartholomew, now a radio operator, and nineteen others to Stockton, California, for further training and to pickup two 104-foot rescue boats, P-114 and P-115, that had been built for the squadron.

They remained at Stockton until just before Thanksgiving, 1942, when they headed back for Alaska in their new crash rescue boats. Bartholomew recalled stopping at San Francisco, where the girl friend of one of the crew members of P-115, Sergeant Don DeSomery, brought a Thanksgiving dinner aboard for the men. The two were later married.

On arrival in Alaska, the P-114 was sent to Adak and the P-115 to Cold Bay. Six more crash rescue boats, P-141 through P-146, arrived shortly afterwards. They were assigned to Umnak, Adak and Amchitka.[263] Eventually the squadron would grow to thirty-seven crash boats and operate from every major base in the Aleutian Islands.

By mid-1944, the 10th Emergency Rescue Boat Squadron had chalked up two hundred and five missions, saved twenty-one persons, assisted one hundred and ninety-four others in distress and recovered eight aircraft

The 104-foot P-115 offshore rescue boat that Ralph Bartholomew went to California to pickup. It was powered by three 650 horse power Hall Scott engines and was capable of cruising at 17 knots with a top speed of 21 knots. It was crewed by three warrant officers and thirteen enlisted men. The 10th Emergency Rescue Boat Squadron was equipped with twenty 104-foot offshore rescue boats, some equipped with two Packard 1350-horse power supercharged engines, and another five 85-foot offshore rescue boats. Inshore rescue was performed with five 42- and one 39-foot inshore rescue boats. The squadron also possessed four 22-foot speed boats, a 85-foot freight and rescue boat and a 155-foot aircraft retriever and freight boat, the HA-2. Bartholomew collection

After the war, the P-115 was sold as surplus and converted into a fishing boat, the Shauna *of Ketchikan.* Bartholomew collection

from the ocean without losing any of its men or boats; a considerable achievement in the storm-lashed waters of the Aleutians, where even today the sinking of larger fishing boats is an all too common occurrence. Major Donley, in complementing his men, stated:

> There has been an abundance of experienced Alaskan personnel to draw from. Without them our program and success would not have been possible.[264]

The 10th Emergency Rescue Boat Squadron was inactivated in early 1946. Its boats were sold as war surplus, several winding up as fishing and charter boats. Many of the squadron's men returned to their former occupations as Alaska fishermen. Some still ply their trade. A number, including Ralph Bartholomew, have become prominent Alaskans.

The squadron had answered its call to duty with honor and dedication. Its men performed almost every conceivable type of rescue, to include climbing mountains and hiking across the tundra. "When a call was received," Bartholomew recalled,

> . . . there wasn't such a thing as checking the weather and planning a trip, we just went out in whatever weather there was. . . . We knew we were a successful operation even though it was sometimes a long period between calls, but those things are hard to quantify. When the P-38s were called on for experimental fighter cover for the B-24s bombing of Paramushiru, they were pushed to the very maximum of endurance. One of their pilots made a comment that put our squadron into perspective, he said: "We knew the chances of being rescued by you guys were slim or none. But one thing we knew for certain was that you would be out there looking, and that made the difference."[265]

A Good Day

Three B-26s were sent out again on October 15 without the benefit of a fighter escort. Their target was the *Borneo Maru*. This time they carried 300-pound bombs with a 4.5-second-delay fuse. The three approached the large cargo ship from the southwest at an altitude of one hundred to one hundred and fifty feet above the surface of Gertrude Cove. The Japanese gunners, unencumbered by the suppressive fire of American fighters, opened up with a barrage.

As Captain Daniel Hawley, pilot of the lead B-26, banked away from the target after dropping his six bombs, his tail gunner, Corporal Flakenstein, saw the right wing of Lieutenant Ralph D. O'Riley's B-26 break off about eight feet from the tip. The Marauder tumbled into the water below. O'Riley, his copilot, Lieutenant John E. Joyce, and the two crew members, Staff Sergeant Edward J. McCallick, Jr. and Corporal William F. Moran were killed.

Corporal Flakenstein also saw three or four bombs from his bomber hit the water. One was seen to explode against the side of the ship aft of the port beam. No bombs were observed to fall from Lieutenant O'Riley's B-26. The bomb release in the second bomber failed to work and none were dropped. The crews of the surviving B-26s reached Adak at 11:40 AM.[266]

October 16 was a good day for the Marauder crews. After months of frustration, they finally scored. The Japanese had sent in the destroyer *Oboro* with supplies for the Kiska garrison. She was escorted by another destroyer, the *Hatsuharu*.[267] One of Gehres' PBY crews spotted the two northwest of Kiska and made an unsuccessful attack.[268]

Word was sent to Adak, and at 2:45 PM, six B-26s from the 73rd Bombardment Squadron began thundering down the runway. Captain Richard Salter led the B-26s on a deck level attack against the two destroyers at 5:40 PM, 20 miles north east of Kiska. Technical Sergeant L. O. Gardner, a bombardier on the B-26 flown by Lieutenant Russell I. Maurer, recalled the attack:

> We were the right wing ship of the lead formation. Captain Salter's plane was in front of us and to our left. While firing into the deck of the smaller destroyer, I saw his plane, like a monstrous black bird, rise over the stern of the destroyer to our left and sow bombs like planting corn, right up the center of the ship from stern to bow. The superstructure started to explode violently, erupting flames. . . . We were almost on our target. . . . Suddenly the other destroyer loomed up in my face . . . I toggled three times. . . . The first hit just forward of the stern, at the water line, and the other hit further forward, on top of the deck.[269]

Sergeant Gardner's bombs destroyed the rudder of the *Hatsuharu* and killed four men and wounded another fourteen. The other medium bombers crews barrelled in at deck level, pulled up and over the ships as the bombs were released. Twenty 300-pound demolition bombs with four-second-delay fuses were dropped. Five, including Gardner's two, hit their targets. The *Oboro* erupted in flames and sank.[270] There were seventeen survivors. The Japanese managed to get the badly damaged *Hatsuharu* back to her port.[271]

Of the six B-26s making the attack, one flown by Lieutenant Jack Penworth was shot down with the loss of all aboard. Those killed in addition to Penworth were Lieutenant Dean W. Mendenhall and Sergeants Morris A. Hancock and Dick Tyron. Captain Salter's bomber was also hit and he and his navigator, Lieutenant James D. Matthews were wounded. Salter, although wounded in the face and hands and with a piece of shrapnel in his leg, managed to bring his crew and plane safely back to Adak. He was sent back to the states to recover from his wounds. Matthews died several days later.[272]

Elsewhere, four P-38s and a B-17 were committed against Kiska. Two Lightnings flown by Captain Laven and Lieutenant Delynn E. Anderson went after the *Nozima Maru* with 500-pound bombs. No hits were observed. Major Ashkins and Lieutenant Lyle A. Bean strafed the main camp area.[273]

A mission of five B-24s was launched the next day against the main camp and the *Nozima Maru*. However, clouds prevented the results from being observed. The weather turned bad for the rest of October and only two missions reached Kiska. One flown by seven B-24 crews on the 23rd with a escort of six P-38s attacked the main camp and submarine base. The skies were unusually clear. The next day, three B-17s were sent against the submarine base. By then the clouds had rolled back in. The island remained obscured for the remainder of the month as winter set in.[274] As the month ended, Billy Wheeler noted:

> The writer knows nothing of interest in tactics that occurred during these eight days. General Buckner made his first visit to Adak on the 28th. Keiser brought Buckner and his aide from Elmendorf. On the 29th the new runway was completed at Longview (code name for Adak) and used for the first time by peashooters. Bomber Command planned a night raid at this time which failed, however, to materialize. The Plan: One heavy bomber to precede the main flight by one minute, dropping incendiary bombs on camp. The main flight was to bomb by use of light afforded by the burning incendiaries. Take-off was scheduled for five hours before sunrise so that the returning bombers could land during the day.[275]

The Japanese, alarmed at the rapid American buildup

of forces on Adak, launched the so-called second invasion of the Aleutians. Lieutenant Colonel Hiroshi Yanekawa came ashore at Holtz Bay on Attu with five hundred men on October 27. More units arrived in the months ahead, and by the time the U.S. 7th Infantry Division landed there, it had grown to approximately twenty-five hundred men. They were not first line troops, but older men and young recruits whose duty it was to build an airfield and establish what defenses they could. The Japanese directed their main effort at Kiska, whose garrison they continued to reinforce until early January 1943.[276]

The movement of Japanese troops to Attu and the reinforcement of Kiska raised concerns for a short period of time that the Japanese were planning a major offensive in the Aleutians. However, the danger soon passed, and Admiral Nimitz, with the battle for Guadalcanal raging, withdrew most of Admiral Theobald's naval forces including the twelve Wildcat fighters at Kodiak. All of the fleet submarines had departed for better hunting grounds to the south, the last two leaving shortly after the occupation of Adak.

By December 1, Theobald's forces had been reduced to the light cruisers *Detroit* and *Raleigh*, four destroyers, a handful of motor torpedo boats and other small craft. Admiral Freeman contributed a few more warships including the venerable *Charleston* from the 13th Naval District. The old S boats remained in the northern waters. The crews lived a miserable existence in the damp and cold confines of their prewar submarines. On October 26, Lieutenant Comdr Robert F. Sellars took the S-31 into the roadstead off Paramushiro and sank the *Kaizan Maru*.

In the absence of ships, Theobald concentrated on consolidating his gains and building up his forces in the North Pacific for the next phase of the operation, the occupation of Amchitka. Auxiliary airfields were built on Adka and Tanaga. A garrison force was dispatched to the Pribilof Islands. A fueling dock, oil tanks and ammunition storage facilities were constructed at Sand Bay at the foot of the 5,740-foot smoking volcano on Great Sitkin Island.[277]

At Adak, Army engineers and SeaBees worked under floodlights to build quarters for fifteen thousand men and to erect hangars, warehouses, piers, radio stations and dry-docks. The base quickly became the major American bastion in the Aleutians and the headquarters for the thrust against the Japanese. The military brass moved in. One high-ranking navy officer ordered a load of fertilizer for his flower bed. A load of manure was dispatched as high priority cargo in a C-47. The Army sergeant who opened the door to the cargo plane was reputed to have said: "Jeez, the war's over! They're sending us horse manure by air mail!"[278]

One of the Family

On November 1, Patrol Air Wing Four was redesignated Fleet Air Wing Four. Captain Gehres continued to lead, demanding the utmost from his men. One of his officers later recalled that he

> "was the toughest, most ornery SOB that I ever encountered during my many years in the Navy, but I respected him. He had a war on his hands, and he would sacrifice people and equipment without a second thought if it meant keeping the upper hand on the enemy."[279]

One of the men who had served under Gehres and had won the respect of all who knew him departed in October. James Russell's promotion to commander came through. He was now too senior to command a squadron; so he was shipped off to a desk job in Washington, D.C., where he served as the Director of Military Requirements in the Bureau of Aeronautics until he was sent to sea again in July 1944, this time aboard carriers. He spent the rest of the war as a participant in the epic sea battles fought by the U.S. Navy over the vast expanses of the western Pacific.[280]

One of Lieut Comdr James Russell's PBY-5s being refuelled by the seaplane tender Williamson *in Alaskan waters, 1941.*
USN photo

Russell and the others who had served during these trying days left behind a legacy of courage and devotion to duty. Their replacements continued to fly the long, exhausting patrols out over the desolate North Pacific and Bering Sea, searching for Japanese shipping. It was tedious but necessary work that required great skill and considerable courage.

They relied on dead reckoning and radar to find their way out and back again. Altimeters, calibrated on barometric pressure, were misleading in the changing weather fronts. Compasses swung widely in the northern latitudes and the turbulence of Aleutian weather. Celestial navigation was out of the question because of the persis-

Secretary of Navy Frank Knox decorates Commander Russell with the Legion of Merit. USN photo

The waist blisters of the Catalinas provided an excellent observation place. It was from this vantage point that George Raptist spotted Koga's Zero on Akutan Island. USN photo

The seaplane tender Gillis *in addition to supporting PBYs also assisted patrol torpedo boats that were sent north to participate in the Aleutian Campaign. They did not stand up well under Aleutian conditions and were withdrawn.* USN photo

tent overcast. Radio navigation could not be used because of Japanese monitoring stations. Clouds obscured landmarks and hid mountains. Incidents of PBYs smashing into mountainsides became all too frequent as their crews searched frantically in the grey mist for a landing site. To be forced down at sea without hope of rescue meant a slow death in the freezing waters. Samuel Eliot Morison paid them this compliment:

> The war was far from over for scouting Catalinas of Patwing 4. Blow high, blow low, thick weather or clear, they had to fly. This meant warming up engines with blowtorches, scraping snow and melting ice off the wings, loading heavy bombs or torpedoes with numbed hands, taking off in the dark, sometimes down-wind with an overloaded plane, and, if the plane was water-based, with frozen spray obscuring the windshield.[281]

Unlike the Eleventh Air Force, Fleet Air Wing Four rotated its squadrons between Aleutian duty and their

The PBY-5 and the amphibious version, the PBY-5A, were the work horses of the Aleutian Campaign. Here, bombs are being loaded aboard a PBY-5A prior to the mission.
USN photo via AAHM

home bases on the West Coast to give the personnel a break from the rigors of northern flying. Oliver S. Glenn arrived with VP-61 on 19 August from Alameda Naval Air Station, California. His squadron was equipped with eight PBY-5 flying boats. It relieved VP-51, which returned to the states. Oliver Glen who served in the Aleutians until August 15, 1943, typifies the men of Fleet Air Wing Four.

His squadron along with VP-62 had been formed at Alameda in April 1942, and intended for duty in the South Atlantic, but were instead diverted to Aleutian duty. Many of the pilots were combat veterans from the early days of the war and had participated in the long retreat from the Philippines down through the Dutch East Indies. The squadron commander, Lieutenant Commander Frank Bruner, like most of the other commanders, was a Navy Academy graduate with extensive seaplane experience.

The enlisted men were some of the best in the Navy, and most of the senior personnel had been in for twelve to fifteen years and were extremely versatile in their trades. The Catalina squadrons, Glenn recalled, "carried complete shop equipment, spares, and enough personnel to build a complete airplane on a deserted island." There were about three hundred men assigned to a squadron. However, because of the nature of Aleutian flying and the need to operate away from the fixed bases for extended periods of time, most of the work-load for maintaining the planes fell on the seaplane tenders. Later, with the retaking of Attu and Kiska, operations shifted back to the land bases.

Glenn remembered that there was not very much socializing between the Navy and Army flight personnel because of the differences in their missions and methods of operations. The two kept to themselves, except for bartering airplane parts for beer or liquor. The PBY and the B-24 shared the Pratt & Whitney R-1830 radial engine in common, and Glenn's squadron was always in need of spare parts. In return, they provided the bomber crews with a supply of beer, which they had obtained from a freighter that had run aground at Nazan Bay with fifty thousand cases. Glenn and the others made frequent trips there until the stock was exhausted.

The PBY squadrons were tight knit units with common interests and a shared purpose. Glenn's squadron was

typical. During its training period at Alameda they partied and attended social functions together. "If anything had happened to us," Glenn recalled, "everyone in the squadron would have felt a loss like one of the family." Fortunately, no one was lost during its stay in the Aleutian Islands.

VP-61 was sent to Sand Point in the Shumagin Islands shortly after its arrival, and then on to Dutch Harbor to cover the Adak landing. Three Catalinas from his squadron along with a similar number from the other squadrons were deployed to Kuluk Bay for three days at a time to fly anti-submarine patrols while the ships were being unloaded.[282]

For the most part, the squadron operated from seaplane tenders. A great deal has been written about the aircraft carrier but not much about the less-glamorous seaplane tender, which was often operated in forward and exposed areas without the benefit of air cover so that the aerial searches could be extended farther out. Such operations became a matter of practice in the Aleutian Islands.

The PBY crews usually slept aboard the tenders. A typical flying day usually began about two to three hours before dawn with the taking care of bodily functions and a quick shower. Breakfast followed. Oliver Glenn remembered that the officers mess even in the forward areas under combat conditions was a formal affair with a prescribed seating arrangement and mess attendants. The officers from the PBY usually sat with the junior officers. When the squadron commander was aboard, he sat next to the captain of the tender.

After breakfast, the PBY crew went out to their aircraft in one of the tender's whale boats. Usually the boat and the plane bobbed up and down two or three feet, and not always in the same direction. Dunkings in the cold water were not an uncommon occurrence when someone misjudged a jump or slipped on an ice-coated surface. The plane captain, the senior enlisted man, was always the first to enter by the port waist hatch, followed by the rest of the crew. The patrol plane commander, commonly referred to as the PPC, was the last to enter.

The auxiliary power plant was started and gear and rations stored. The plane captain took his position in the "tower" between the wing and the hull and on the word of the PPC, started the first engine. The mooring line to the buoy was then cast off and the second engine started. The PPC and his copilot, who could be either an officer or enlisted man, then taxied the PBY in a circle or a figure-eight while the engines warmed up. Since there could be three to four other planes milling around in the dark with radio silence imposed, a great deal of care had to be taken.

The takeoff was made into the wind after the engines had been warmed up and the magnetos and other engine and navigational instruments checked. For the first ten seconds or so the windshield was covered with spray and the directional gyro had to be used to maintain direction until the wind had blown the spray away. After lifting off, a compass heading was taken, and another day's patrol begun.

The patrols varied from short-range harbor patrols to long monotonous affairs enlivened by bad weather and an occasional sighting that sometimes turned out to be Japanese ships. Occasionally, false sightings were made, and there were enough to create the "Royal Order of the Whale Banger," which was awarded to confused PBY pilots who mistook whales for submarines and dropped depth charges on them. One crew reported what they thought was a Japanese fleet and virtually every available Eleventh Air Force bomber was launched. The sighting turned out to be cloud shadows.

Coming home in the evening involved servicing the air-craft. The pilots taxied the PBY up to the stern of the tender and idled the engines as slow as possible. The ships crew used long bamboo poles with padded yokes on the ends that fit around the leading edge of the wings to fend off the plane while a heaving line was thrown up to the ship. A heavy mooring line was then secured to it, the engines were cut and the PBY was pulled up behind the tender for servicing. When that was completed, the line was cast loose, the engines were restarted and the PBY was taxied over to its mooring buoy. The crew then waited for what seemed to them a long time for the whale boat to pick them up. Oliver Glenn remembered:

It was the end of a long anxious day and we wanted to get back aboard ship as soon as possible. We weren't hungry, because we had plenty of food in the plane and an electric hot plate to cook pork chops or steaks and potatoes; we weren't cold because we were dressed adequately and some of the later PBYs had good heaters; we weren't sleepy because we had six full length bunks we could have used. It was just that we wanted to get away from the confines and the responsibilities of the plane. That flying in the fog, rain, poor visibility, lots of mountains, freezing water underneath if you ever went into it, and general tension of combat flying was not something that relaxed you; so you were in a hurry to get back to the ship as soon as possible.[283]

Then the Rains Came

No missions against Kiska were flown during the first six days of November. The first of the winter storms blew in and for the first four days of the month the rains, accompanied by sixty-mile-per-hour winds, fell in torrents day and night. The men on Adak huddled in their tents, played poker and avoided going outside except when necessary. Those who had a private cache of food, shunned the canned rations served in mess tents and dined on "bone chicken with bouillon or consomme and crackers with caviar paste."

And "then," in the words of Billy Wheeler, "the rains came." The dike that had been built around the airfield was breached in several places and the tide swept over the camp area. Tent floors turned into mud as their occupants struggled to dig drainage ditches. The airfield was flooded. Finally, things returned to normal and order was restored.[284]

A mission of six B-24s and two B-26s finally made it off the runway on November 7. The crews fought their way through the weather to their target, the submarine base, and dropped their bombs through the overcast without observing the results. The mission scheduled for the next day was cancelled.[285]

Lieutenant McWilliams from the 36th Bombardment Squadron flew the weather reconnaissance mission. On arrival at Attu, his crew spotted eight Japanese float planes off a small creek on the west arm of Holtz Bay. They appeared to have been washed up by a storm and two were damaged.[286]

A 73rd Bombardment Squadron B-26 on the water-covered ramp at Adak. Chuck Pinney collection

The rain storm inundated the runway and ramp area on Adak. USA photo

A closeup of the photograph taken by Lieutenant McWilliams' B-17 crew on November 7, 1942, shows two damaged Rufe float fighters. The photograph on page 177 shows aircraft in relation to the others. USA photo

The fighter pilots, because of the bad weather, had not flown a mission since October 23. On November 9, based on McWilliams' report and the aerial photographs that were taken, Colonel Chennault committed four of his P-38s on the 880-mile round trip flight from Adak to Attu. Colonel Eareckson sent along a B-17 for navigation support.

"The boys hit the jackpot today," Capt Leo Nocenti, the 54th Fighter Squadron historian later recorded in his history.[287] Captains Arthur E. Hustead and Frances J. Pope and Lieutenants Ralph D. Matthews and Harly S. Tawlks approached from the northeast, flying just off the water at 240-miles per hour. They swept in over the east arm of Holtz Bay, strafed a group of tents, turned right, flashed across the waters and commenced a circling strafing attack on the beached Japanese float planes and tents

ashore. In their post strike mission, they claimed all eight destroyed.[288]

While the P-38 pilots were tearing into the Japanese float planes at Attu, four other Lightning pilots and the crews of two 73rd Bombardment Squadron B-26s went after the beached *Borneo Maru*. No hits were scored. Two of the fighter pilots then proceeded to Kiska Harbor where they strafed Japanese positions before returning to Adak.

Another mission of six B-24s and a B-17 was sent against Kiska the next day. It was turned back by weather. For the next sixteen days, it was much of the same. The Aleutian weather had set in preventing flying, and those missions that managed to get airborne found their targets obscured by clouds. Even the crews of the weather aircraft experienced difficulties as they braved the clouds, snowstorms and extreme icing conditions and turbulence on their lonely trip down the Aleutian Islands.[289]

The Eleventh Air Force, in the words of its historian, Lieutenant Jerry Ransohoff, had been "neutralized by the weather."[290]

Finally, the weather cleared. The *Cherryboune Maru* had departed Paramushiro on November 10 with a load of arms and equipment for the garrison that was being established on Attu. On November 27, at 9:40 AM, Lieutenant Charles W. Craven and his B-24 crew on a weather reconnaissance spotted the single-stack, two-masted cargo ship being unloaded off the west arm of Holtz Bay. The sighting was radioed to Adak.

At 12:12 PM the crews of four B-26s led by Capt John W. Pletcher began taking off from Adak. Four P-38s under the command of Capt Arthur P. Hustead were also dispatched. In what had now become a standard routine,

An aerial photograph taken five days after the 54th Fighter Squadron pilots strafed the Rufes. Note the two bombs in upper right center falling towards the tent area.
USA photo

One of the destroyed Rufes that was found after the Battle of Attu. The Japanese, unable to deliver aircraft to Kiska because of the fear of losing their ships to air and sea strikes, resorted to bringing them as far as Attu where they were flown the remaining distance.
USA photo

The Cherryboune Maru in the west arm of Holtz Bay. USA photo

the fighter pilots went in first to suppress the anti-aircraft fire. After the gunners had been cleared from the deck of the transport, Captain Pletcher led his bombers in a low-level attack against the 4,016-ton transport.

Thirteen 500-pound armor piecing bombs with a four-to five-second delay tail fuse were dropped from an altitude of one hundred feet. Three struck near the bow and one was a near miss. The others exploded harmlessly some distance from the transport. When Captain Pletcher and flight departed the scene at 3:25, the *Cherryboune Maru* was burning.[291] Subsequent weather reconnaissance flights for the remainder of the month reported her still burning and settling in the water at the head of the bay. No other strike missions were flown during November.[292]

The month ended on a sad note. Colonel Davis who had pioneered the formation of the Eleventh Air Force and served as its first commander for a brief period, disappeared on the 28th. He and seven others had taken off in a C-47 from Naknek for Elmendorf Field. A search was launched when he did not arrive at main base. Despite frequent snow storms, it was continued for a month before the effort was given up.

Finally, Davis's C-47 was found in September 1943, on a mountainside near Naknek. It had apparently struck at full power and everyone aboard had been killed instantly. Colonel Davis was given a funeral with full military honors at Fort Richardson. The Eleventh Air Force mourned. Later, the field at Adak was named in his honor.[293]

Lieutenant Kenneth Ambrose disappeared during a ferry flight somewhere over the western Washington the same day that Colonel Davis had disappeared. The rest of the 54th Fighter Squadron, their ranks slowly thinning, but now experienced professionals after five months of combat, continued to carry the burden of fighter operations in the Aleutians with their long-range, twin-engine fighters.[294]

The Aleutian winter weather and the distances that had to be flown over open water had proved to be too much for the single-engine P-39s and P-40s. The last mission of 1942, by P-39s, had been flown against Kiska on October 9. The next mission was not flown until January 4, 1943, when ten P-40s provided escort for a bomber attack against Kiska. However, it was aborted due to weather. Finally, on February 4, following the construction of an airfield on Amchitka, the use of single engine fighters in the air war against the Japanese was resumed.[295]

In the interim, the P-40s were used for local air defense patrols. The 54th Fighter Group departed Alaska in early December for its home base at Harding Field, Louisiana. The P-39s with their heavy fire power had proved useful in strafing missions against Kiska and successful in combat against the Rufes. However, the tricycle landing gear

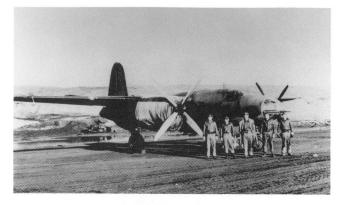

B-26 and crew, 73rd Bombardment Squadron.
John Pletcher collection

The funeral for Colonel Davis was held at Fort Richardson on September 10, 1943. A fly over was conducted including the three B-25s from the 406th Bombardment Squadron. The field at Adak was named Davis Field in his honor.
USA photo

fighter did not standup well to the rugged conditions of the Aleutian forward bases.

Forty-four pilots of the group had participated in nine missions against Kiska between September 14 and October 9, flying seventy-five sorties. Forty-three had been low-level strafing missions and the others had been flown as top cover for bomber attacks. Twenty decorations were awarded for gallantry, including a Distinguished Flying Cross that was awarded to Captain Rice for shooting down two Rufes. Counting Rice's victories, the 54th Fighter Group received official credit for shooting down ten Japanese aircraft. One man, Major Miller, died in battle and another was wounded. One other, Lieutenant Robert J. Neal, was killed in an accident.[296]

The 54th Fighter Group was awarded the Distinguished Unit Citation for its service in the Aleutian Islands. It was well deserved.[297] Unfortunately, through some bureaucratic oversight, the 343rd Fighter Group and its squadrons never received a unit award for the same period despite the fact that it had achieved just as much. It was an injustice.[298]

The air offensive which had been carried out with such vigor during the fall months, and which had slowed down during November, almost ground to a halt during December as the Aleutian winter set in. The month got

The P-39D that Les Spoonts flew to Alaska. The photograph
was taken shortly before the 54th Fighter Group departed
Alaska. Spoonts flew it to San Antonio Air Depot where it was
refurbished and turned over to the training command.
Spoonts collection

H.D. "Papy" Pauling in the cockpit and Harry Krintzman,
maintenance officer, 57th Fighter Squadron. Spoonts collection

A P 39Q was restored at the United States Air Force Museum
to resemble Spoonts' P-39D. It is now on display there.
Spoonts collection

Captain Jim Ingham, 54th Fighter Group, ready to go home.
Spoonts collection

off to a bad start when a PBY crew spotted on the 4th what
they thought were Japanese ships. Eight B-24s, nine B-26
and sixteen P-38s headed for the sighting southeast of
Amchitka Island. There was nothing; the PBY pilot later
admitted that he might have mistaken cloud shadows on
the ocean surface for ships.[299]

The 36th Bombardment Squadron stood down from the
bombing missions against Kiska. The last B-17 mission
had been flown November 11. The Flying Fortress lacked
the range and bomb capacity of the B-24, and there were
too few that were mission ready. At one point the squadron
had been down to two flyable B-17s. The big bomber did
not stand up well to the Aleutian conditions, and by mid-
September it was being used more and more for weather
reconnaissance and photo missions.

During December, the B-17 crews were placed on
ground alert for possible use against Japanese warships

that were suspected of being in the area. At first all the crew except the pilot and navigator had to remain in their aircraft while the latter two were confined to the operations room. The requirement was relaxed, but the crews had to remain in the squadron area. Morale suffered. Billy Wheeler noted in his diary:

> No single factor has as great an effect on morale of the flight personnel as being grounded and at the same time being kept on a continual readiness status. Patience is a virtue that is rarely present to any great extent in the makeup of a flyer, and under circumstances that deny him the opportunity to exercise his skill, he is lost. All men hate inactivity, but the Air Corps is not accustomed to waiting. Men began to vie for the privilege of being champion sack man of the squadron.[300]

Captain Louis Blau, seated, served as the operations officer for the 404th Bombardment Squadron. Following the war, he became a Hollywood lawyer and helped produce 2001, A Space Odyssey *among other films.* Louis Blau collection

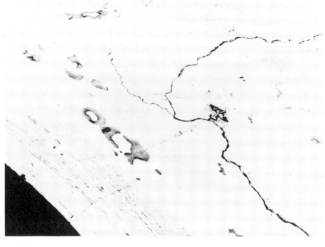

The aerial photograph was taken the day after Andrews and Blau made an emergency landing at Bechevin Bay. The B-24D, 41-2367, is still in the same place. Alan Meader collection

John Andrews and his bomber, July 1983. In 1980, Ted Spencer of the Alaska Historical Aircraft Society succeeded in placing the B-24D on the National Register of Historical Places. During the summer of 1983, he arranged to take John Andrews and Louis Blau back to the airfields they operated from while serving in the Aleutians. John Andrews was also flown back to the crash site. Like Blau, he also became a successful executive after the war. Andrews worked for a manufacturing firm in Boston. Ted Spencer photo

The wreck of the B-24D the day after. The bomber broke in two immediately behind the trailing edge of the wing. Later, the Aleutian wind scattered the aft section of the B-24. The rest, except for the underside, remains in good repair. It would be difficult to remove the old bomber because of its remote location and the fact that its underside was badly damaged from the landing and is corroded after years of exposure to the water logged muskeg. Alan Meader collection

The 21st and 404th Bombardment Squadrons assumed most of the burden of carrying the war to the Japanese. An attempt to bomb Attu and Kiska on the 8th was turned back by weather. The next day, another effort was made against Kiska with equally dismal results.

Captains John Andrews and Louis Blau from the 404th Bombardment Squadron had the weather patrol that day. They had taken off early that morning with two important passengers. Brigadier General William Lynch, General Arnold's Inspector General, was aboard to see first-hand the problems the weather was causing the Eleventh Air Force. He was accompanied by Colonel John V. Hart, who had replaced Colonel Davis as the chief of staff.[301]

The PBY that was sent out to pick up the B-24 crew.
Ted Spencer collection

Andrews and Blau flew their bomber to Attu, circled Holtz Bay where the Japanese were continuing to build up their forces, and then headed back to Adak. They arrived there to find the field obscured by clouds which also hid the other fields as far away as Cold Bay. After three attempts to land at Adak, Andrews and Blau headed for Atka where the weather station there had reported clear conditions. Since the airfield was not ready, the two pilots flew around the north side of the island looking for a place to land. Andrews remembered:

> We were running low on fuel, and nearly out of light, so we decided that we had better land. The question was whether to ditch in one of the bays, or belly in on the land. I was all for putting it on the land because the water was too cold, and I knew we wouldn't last long.[302]

Fortunately, Andrews and Blau spotted a flat area at the head of Bechevin Bay at the northwest end of Atka Island. Everyone crowded to the front of the plane as the two pilots trimmed the bomber and made a low-level approach across the bay. The bomber cleared the beach, hit the soft muskeg and slid inland for about one hundred and fifty yards before coming to a halt. "The noise," Andrews recalled, "was horrendous, followed by a deep silence." General Lynch tapped Andrews on the shoulder, and said, "Let's get out of this damn thing, it might burn."[303]

Except for General Lynch, who had a cracked collar bone, no one else was injured. The B-24 had broken in two just behind the trailing edge of the wing. Andrews decision to move the crew forward had been a wise one.

By then it was getting dark. The crew threw a tarp over one of the wings, ate a meal, pulled out the sleeping bags and went to bed. The next day the crew of a B-24 from the 21st Bombardment Squadron arrived overhead, followed shortly afterwards by another flown by Major Orth. Other planes arrived, and supplies and sleeping bags were dropped. The stranded bomber crew went down to the beach, built a fire and waited. That afternoon, the crew of a PBY landed in the bay and sent a rubber boat to shore to pick up the bomber crew.

After an unsuccessful attempt to take off with the added weight, the Catalina pilots gave up and decided that the bomber crew should be evacuated by one of the seaplane tenders. The *Gillis*, which was nearby, arrived late that night and two whale boats were dispatched to recover Andrews, Blau and the others.

John Andrews' crew, after their ordeal, were given Christmas Leave to return to their homes. The B-24, tail number 41-2367, was left on the islands where it remains today.[304]

The weather cleared enough on the 11th so that the crews of three B-26s and four P-38 pilots could make a low-level attack against the installations in Kiska Harbor. Two missions were planned for the 17th. Only the first, by four B-24s, got through. The weather had turned lousy again.[305]

Major John A. Pickard, one of the original members of the 77th Bombardment Squadron, who had replaced Major Meals as its commander on October 27, led the squadron's aircrews and their new B-25Ds into Adak on December 12. The 77th was committed to its first Kiska mission on the 20th. Four Mitchells along with four B-26s, five B-24s and nine P-38s were sent on a low-level bombing and strafing attack against the submarine base and main camp. With the exception of a direct hit that was reported on an ammunition dump, the mission was uneventful.[306]

It was not until December 26 that another mission could be launched. The crew of the weather reconnaissance flight had reported the previous day that there were eight float planes at Holtz Bay. They had been brought in by the *Kimikawa Maru* on the 25th. Two flights of six B-24s were committed. They were accompanied by nine P-38s. The crews of the Liberators arrived at Holtz Bay to find it obscured by clouds. The crews, after circling for an hour, turned back.

The P-38 pilots, led by Captain Ralph D. Matthews,

pressed on with the attack, flying under the overcast. The Lightning pilots bore in at low-level along the west arm of Holtz Bay, strafing Japanese positions, before crossing over to the east arm to strafe positions there. After exiting the bay, Captain Matthews and Lieutenant Artie L. Kayser decided to make another attack.

It was a mistake. The element of surprise had been lost. The Japanese gunners were alerted. Matthews' fighter erupted into flames and crashed into the water a half-mile from the entrance of the bay, carrying the young pilot to his death. A round severed the fuel line to the right engine of Kayser's P-38.

Another round damaged the left engine. Kayser managed to make it as far as Tanaga before the remaining engine quit. He ditched his fighter one hundred and fifty feet off the west coast of the island and swam to the shore, where he waited from 3:25 PM until he was picked up by a PBY at 5:45 PM.

Other than a bump on the head and a bad case of the chills, Kayser had emerged from his ordeal in good shape—a remarkable achievement considering the time of year and his drenching in the icy Aleutian waters. Kayser had been lucky, but his luck was soon to run out.

The other 54th Fighter Squadron pilots made it safely back to Adak. Lieutenant Earl C. Nedlund managed to fly the distance on one engine. Two machine gun bullets had punched through the right wheel well door, one of which had cut the engine coolant line. The other had hit a wiring cable. Lieutenant Oliver Wayman also made it back to Adak despite being wounded in the attack. The Japanese anti-aircraft gunners at Holtz Bay had been very effective that day.

Elsewhere, a mission of six B-25s and four P-38s sent against Kiska had been turned back by the weather. The results of the December 26 raids were disappointing. The Japanese floatplanes, reported the previous day, had disappeared. They were about to make their reappearance.[307]

The Aleutian winter weather persisted, and it was not until December 30 that Colonels Eareckson and Chennault could launch another mission. This one rivaled the September 14 one in size and complexity. It began when Lieutenant Dewitte H. McIntyre from the 21st Bombardment Squadron taxied his B-24 onto the runway at Adak at 8:45 AM and took off on the daily weather reconnaissance mission. Fifty-two minutes later the first of five B-25Ds from the 77th Bombardment Squadron and four B-26s from the 73rd Bombardment Squadron began thundering down the Adak runway. They were accompanied by fourteen P-38s. The crews of two of the B-25s turned back when their bombers developed mechanical difficulties.

Major Pickard led his three Mitchells in an attack against two large transports that had just arrived in Kiska Harbor. He succeeded in dropping all his bombs without observing any hits. The pilot of the second B-25 dropped one of his bombs with the same results. The remainder were hung up in their racks. Lieutenant Julius Constantine, the pilot of the third bomber was forced to ditch it eight miles off Little Kiska when it was struck by anti-aircraft fire.

Lieutenant Theodore T. Vasataka and his copilot, Lieutenant Baxter D. Thorton, arrived on the scene in their OA-10, but were unable to recover the B-25 crew. The fighter pilot who had been assigned the mission of escorting the rescue aircraft had been forced to break away when the right engine of his P-38 began failing. The OA-10 disappeared after the radio operator sent out a garbled transmission. Its remains and the bodies of the crew were found on the side of Kiska Volcano after the island was occupied. The crew of the B-25 disappeared beneath the waters of the North Pacific.

The crews of the two surviving B-25s and the four B-26s began landing at Adak at 1:08 PM.

The P-38 pilots had been assigned the mission of bombing and strafing the shore installations in coordination with the medium bomber attacks. All but two of the Lightnings carried 500-bombs slung under the wings. The plan called for them to approach their targets in different flights from different directions.

The Japanese Rufes which had been spotted at Holtz Bay on December 25 had arrived safely at Kiska. Their pilots, fresh and spoiling for a fight tore into the P-38 pilots, who expecting no air opposition, were caught by surprise. When they reassembled, Lieutenant Kayser, who had survived the ditching off Tanaga four days before, was missing. Another fighter pilot, Lieutenant John A. Leighton, also could not be accounted for. Several claims for shooting down Rufes were submitted, none of which were later verified. The Japanese fighter pilots had gotten the best of their opponents that day.

The "Fighting 54th" within a period of six months had lost thirteen pilots to combat and accidents.

The second air offensive of the day was launched at 1:46 PM when five B-24s from the 21st Bombardment Squadron lifted off the runway at Adak. Lieutenant Charles J. Paine led "A" flight and Lieutenant Joe B. Baker, Jr., "B" flight. The bombers were loaded with 500-pound general purpose bombs. They were followed at 2:04 PM by four B-25s and four B-26s. The 54th Fighter Squadron, now aware of the presence of Japanese fighters at Kiska, provided an escort of eight P-38s.

The crews of the heavy bombers arrived over Kiska Harbor at 3:45 and dropped their bombs from 7,000 to 8,500 feet. Lieutenant Baker claimed three hits on a large transport, and Lieutenant Irving L. Wadlington, from "B" flight, claimed one hit. The medium bombers arrived next. The crews made a low-level attack against the shipping, dropping their 300-pound bombs without observing their results.[308]

A burst of anti-aircraft fire smashed into the cockpit area of the B-25 flown by Lieutenants Robert L. Debord and David L. McNarney, wounding both and shattering the windshield. In an incredible feat of flying, the two young 77th Bombardment Squadron pilots made it back to Adak. While Debord, who had been hit in the right foot, handled the control wheel and throttles, McNarney, who had lost the use of both hands, coordinated on the rudder pedals.

Another display of an incredible feat of flying that afternoon was demonstrated by Lieutenant C. E. Rodebaugh whose PBY was attacked by four Rufe pilots near Kiska. Without the benefit of cloud cover, Lieutenant Rodebaugh and his copilot used every evasive maneuver in the book to keep their lumbering patrol aircraft from being shot down by the agile fighters. Dropping down to the surface of the water, they hugged the shoreline of Kiska, ducking into a small bay where the faster Rufes could not follow, then flying over a saddle on the island until the Rufe pilots, their fighters apparently low on gas, finally quit their attacks.

All the bombers, many with holes in them, returned safely to Adak from the afternoon attack. One carried a dead tail gunner, Corporal Donald O. Murphy, aboard.[309]

The losses the Eleventh Air Force suffered that day were offset somewhat by the damages inflicted on the *Urajio Maru*. The Japanese beached the old, 350-foot long, 3,110-ton coal burning transport from the shipyards of Liverpool, England, beneath the cliffs of North Head where she remains today, a rusting, badly battered relic of the Japanese plans to extend their empire into the North Pacific.

The *Urajio Maru* and another transport, the *Nichiyu Maru*, had arrived in Kiska Harbor December 29 and 28 respectively with approximately five hundred personnel from the 302rd Independent Engineer Battalion and a cargo of building materials and provisions for the garrison. They were in the process of being unloaded when the American bombers arrived overhead. The *Nichiyu Maru* later made it safely out of the harbor.[310]

The last mission of the year was flown by the crews of six B-24s and nine P-38 pilots. The bomber crews claimed hits on the two Japanese transports and the fighter pilots reported that they had seen several Rufes going down in flames.[311]

In addition to the losses sustained in combat, the winter month of December had been hard on the Eleventh Air Force. On December 25, the engines of a P-38 flown by Lieutenant Thomas Archer quit on takeoff from Adak.

A bomb exploded on the cargo deck behind the bridge area of the Urajio Maru, *buckling the deck area. The Japanese beached her off the shore of North Head. The Americans assigned letters to the beached ships. The* Nozima Maru, *was ship Able;* Kano Maru, *ship Baker; the* Borneo Maru, *ship Charlie; and the* Urajio Maru, *ship Dog.* Frank Rosse collection

A close up of the bomb damage to the Urajio Maru. USA photo

The Urajio Maru *as she looked September 1989. Storms and the sea have worsened the damage done by the bombs.* Author's collection

Lieutenant Archer's P-38 burns. USA photo

The fighter crashed into a parked B-24 from the 21st Bombardment Squadron. Archer died and the bomber was consumed in flames. On December 31, another 21st bomber was destroyed when a P-40 pilot accidentally taxied into it.

The accidents continued to pile up. A P-40 on patrol over Adak caught fire. The pilot bailed out safely. Another P-40 pilot landed in Kuluk Bay short of the runway. He was rescued. The pilot of a third P-40 crashed in the bay and disappeared without a trace. Elsewhere, one of the 406th Bombardment Squadron's A-29s ground-looped at Juneau and was destroyed. The crew escaped unharmed.[312]

Beginning on December 9, 1942, Admirals King and Nimitz held one of their many meetings to discuss strategy in the Pacific. This one was in San Francisco, and with the Guadalcanal operations winding down, they were concerned mainly with the plan for clearing the Japanese from the South Pacific and isolating their bastion at Rabaul.

Admiral Nimitz also brought along a memorandum, "Review of the Aleutian Situation," for discussion, in which he recommended that General Buckner's forces occupy Amchitka Island and build an airfield as the first step in mounting an amphibious operation to retake Kiska. The

Commander-in-Chief, Pacific Command also invited Admiral Kinkaid to attend the conference. He had already decided to replace Admiral Theobald with Kinkaid, who in addition to having proven himself a warrior at Guadalcanal as a carrier task force commander, was more diplomatic and was expected to get along with General Buckner.

Admiral Fletcher in his first visit to Alaska shortly after assuming command of the 13th Naval District and Northern Naval Frontier had noted that the relations between the two commanders was not good. That piled on top of the previous reports and incidents convinced Admiral Nimitz that something had to be done. Admiral King agreed that Theobald had to go, and Kinkaid was given the responsibility for clearing the Aleutians of the embarrassing Japanese presence.[313]

Plans for occupying Amchitka as a preliminary step in driving the Japanese from the Aleutian Islands had been under consideration since the occupation of Adak. The large island, with a good harbor 178 miles west of Adak and 60 miles east of Kiska, provided an ideal place from which air attacks could be launched against Kiska during the breaks in the rapidly changing Aleutian weather.

The only uncertainty at the time was whether or not an airfield could be built there. Although Colonel Verbeck, following his September 23-25 reconnaissance, had reported the island to be unsuitable for base construction, he also acknowledged that he was not qualified to make a final assessment. An engineer was needed for the job.

Colonel Talley had led a reconnaissance party ashore from a PBY at Tanaga on October 22. The party was picked up five days later after Talley had determined that a air field could be built there. Talley's expertise was again requested, this time for Amchitka. The mission was more dangerous because of the closeness of the island to Kiska.

The engineer colonel was more than willing to accept the assignment, since he "wanted to get away from Anchorage, away from headquarters and away from the shadow of the flagpole." However, his trip was repeatedly delayed. Admiral Theobald was not in favor of the idea, since he felt his forces would be too exposed at Amchitka. General DeWitt, siding with him for a change, wanted to occupy Tanaga and had already begun planning to send troops there. However, Admirals Nimitz and King and General Marshall wanted Amchitka taken. The Army Chief of Staff ordered a reconnaissance be made. That settled the matter.

After repeatedly being delayed by transportation difficulties, Theobald was reluctant to risk one of his PBYs. Finally, Colonel Talley and his party, consisting of seven Alaska Scouts for security, Colonel DeLong and Verbeck and three others, were put ashore on December 17. They were picked up two days later, but not until after having hidden from a Japanese float reconnaissance plane that flew over while they were there. The only other signs of Japanese presence was a couple of bore holes where the Japanese had taken soil samples.

Colonel Talley, after examining the Constantine Harbor area, determined that an airfield could be built there within two to three weeks. The Joint Chiefs of Staff issued their directive on December 21. General Buckner's and Admiral Theobald's staffs began serious planning for a joint operation that would render the Japanese garrison on Kiska untenable and pave the way for victory in the north.[314]

Nineteen hundred forty-two had been a hard year for America and her allies, one of men suffering and dying in the steaming jungles of the Pacific, of sailors drowning in shark-infested waters and of airmen going out on missions with little hope of returning.

The Japanese had learned, that when aroused, the Americans would fight with uncommon valor. In turn, the Americans realized they were contending with an enemy who placed honor above suffering and dying and who would fight on against hopeless odds when all reason and logic demanded the ending of the madness.

Colonel Talley and his men on Amchitka. The lead man is an Alaskan Scout. The next is Lieut Col Leon B. DeLong, a former enlisted man in the Marines who went into construction and became an executive with Morrison Knudsen. Talley was able to secure a major's commission for him in the U.S. Army Corps of Engineers. The next is Colonel Talley. The man in the rear was a captain in the Alaska Scouts.
Talley collection

Colonel Talley on the beach at Amchitka later remembered: "A Japanese biplane flew over at about 250 feet altitude while we were there. DeLong and I were together, 50 to 100 feet apart, and our Scouts were around us more or less 300 yards away. We controlled our movements by arm signals, and I told the men if a plane flew over to lie down close to any vegetation, keep head down and double up and not look like a man. I took an excellent picture of the Japanese plane after it passed over, so close you could see the pilot in the photograph.
Talley collection

All over the world that year, the Allies had gone on the offensive. On the night of October 23, Field Marshall Bernard Montgomery launched a massive attack against the weakened German Afrika Korps; and in a twelve-day battle, drove them from El Alamein, a dusty village on the north coast of Egypt located sixty-five miles west of Cairo. The Germans did not stop retreating until they had fled halfway across the breadth of North Africa to Mareth in Tunisia. There they dug in February 1943 to face a combined American and British force coming at them from the west. The Allies had landed on the beaches of western North Africa on November 8, 1942.

The German offensive launched in the summer of 1942 to capture the oil wells in the Russian Caucasus region, ground to a halt in the bitter winter fight for Stalingrad. When it was over, ninety-one thousand enfeebled German soldiers, survivors of the three hundred and thirty thousand trapped in the city, trudged out to a dreadful captivity. Only five thousand lived to see their homeland again.

In the air, the Eighth Air Force launched its first bomber mission on August 17, 1942, when Brigadier General Frank Armstrong led twelve B-17Es on a raid against the railroad marshalling yard at Rouen, France. It was the first that the "Mighty Eighth" would conduct in the years ahead as it grew to a strength of almost two hundred thousand men organized into fifty-seven bomber and fighter groups.

Compared to the titanic struggle that was going on elsewhere, Alaska was a military sideshow, easily overlooked and forgotten among the epic campaigns that were fought in more strategic locations. Where the Eighth Air Force could launch a thousand-plane raid against Germany, a ten-plane bomber raid by the Eleventh Air Force was noteworthy event. At its peak strength of sixteen thousand, the tiny Eleventh could only muster a bomber and a fighter group.

Crowbar

The occupation of Amchitka Island, as implied by the nickname Crowbar, was the first major step taken to force the Japanese out of Kiska. Admiral King and General Marshall agreed that a force should be trained for an amphibious assault on the Japanese bastion. Rear Admiral Francis W. Rockwell, Commander, Amphibious Force, Pacific Fleet was assigned the responsibility for planning the operation. He formed a joint Army and Navy planning staff at his San Diego headquarters and brought in Major General Holland M. Smith, the Marine Corps' amphibious expert, for assistance.

By late December the staff had drawn up a plan which called for the commitment of twenty-seven thousand troops, including the 7th Infantry Division plus a number of other combat units and the attendant support and gar-

rison forces. Transports and landing craft were allocated and a training program developed. Admiral Rockwell indicated the earliest time that the assault could be made was May 1, 1943. The final decision, however, had to wait on the Casablanca Conference.[315]

President Roosevelt, Prime Minister Churchill and their military chiefs met at Casablanca the week of January, 17, 1943, to decide the grand strategy for the next stage of the war. The heart of the discussion centered around the allocation of forces for the war against Germany and Japan. Admiral King pressed for more forces for the Pacific. The British, with only minimum interest in that theater, did not want the Germany first agreement reached by Roosevelt and Churchill in December 1941 overturned.

While the Americans, principally General Marshall, pressed for an invasion of the continent in 1943, the British espoused a strategy of crippling the Germans by stepping up the strategic bomber offensive, sending all possible aid to the Soviets, invading Italy, and eliminating the German submarine threat. The British, with the memories of the Somme, Passchendaele and the other killing fields of World War I very much in their minds, feared the sad carnage would be repeated if the Allies launched an invasion of the continent in 1943. It was in keeping with their historic strategy of avoiding a direct confrontation with a more powerful continental foe while conducting operations, primarily maritime, in peripheral areas where their enemy could not deploy his full strength.

The Americans with a tradition of continental war and an abundance of resources wanted a more decisive and quicker solution. However, Roosevelt and his chiefs relented and agreed to defer their invasion plans until 1944, when the Germans were further weakened and the Allies had built up their forces more. The British in turn softened their stand on the Pacific.

The Americans, primarily Admiral King, wanted to continue the offensive in the Solomon Islands and on New Guinea to isolate Rabaul and insure the protection of the lines of communications to Australia. Second, they wanted to launch another drive across the Central Pacific through the Gilbert, the Marshall and the Caroline Islands aimed at the Japanese main fleet base at Truck in the Carolines. As a subsidiary, the Americans wanted operations in the China-Burma-India Theater stepped up and the Japanese cleared from the Aleutian Islands. The British, while agreeing to the continuance of the Solomon and New Guinea operations and supportive of China Burma India operations, were hesitant about the others.

The strategy for 1943 hinged on the availability of landing craft, which was in short supply; and the British were pressing for a Mediterranean strategy that required an amphibious assault on first Sicily and then Italy, the so called soft underbelly of Europe.

The American and British reached an agreement that continued to place the defeat of Germany first, but recognized the need for a stepped up war against the Japanese. The offensive in the Solomon Islands and on New Guinea would continue. The China-Burma-India Theater was given more priority and the drive across the Central Pacific was deferred until more landing craft could be obtained. The planned operation against Kiska was cancelled.[316]

General Marshall had been concerned all along that the Aleutian operations would send the wrong signal to the British that the United States was willing to withdraw large forces from other more important theaters and commit them against the strategically unimportant islands. He preferred to "make the Aleutians as secure as may be possible," and not take any further offensive operations there for the remainder of 1943, unless the Soviet Union came in on the side of the Americans. The Casablanca conference settled the issue, for a time. Admiral Kinkaid, who had replaced Admiral Theobald, was informed that the ships needed for the Kiska invasion would not be available.[317]

Admiral Theobald had departed for his new assignment as the Commandant, First Naval District, headquarted in Boston, Massachusetts, where he served out his remaining career before retiring in early 1945. No mention was made in his official biography of his service in the Aleutians for which he received no reward or recognition other than a campaign ribbon.[318] Admiral Kinkaid arrived on January 4, 1943, and set up his headquarters at Kodiak. The next day, General Buckner wrote General DeWitt:

> Admiral Kinkaid arrived yesterday and I have just concluded a most enjoyable conference with him. I have been most favorably impressed with him and I am certain that we can work together on our terms with the greatest enthusiasm. Butler has also had a conference with him and came out looking ten years younger and whistling like a bird.[319]

The fifty-four year old Admiral Kinkaid brought with him the experiences of the hard fought sea and air battles in the Solomon Islands and a commitment to offensive operations in the North Pacific. He was by temperament very similar to General Buckner, who had yet to be exposed to the shock of battle. Although not as brilliant as Theobald, he had ranked near the bottom of his 1908 Annapolis class, he made up for it by his decisive actions, his bulldog determination, and his ability to listen to other points of view. He and Buckner got along well together; the bickering stopped and the pace of operations quickened.

Admiral Kinkaid had spent much of his adult life at sea, was a naval ordnance expert, had been exposed to diplomacy as a naval attache, and had acquitted himself well

Rear Admiral Thomas Kinkaid in the Aleutians, 1943.
USN photo

as a carrier task force commander at Guadalcanal despite the fact that he had never had any experience in naval aviation. He was about to embark on another endeavor, the conduct of joint operations, for which he had little training and experience.[320]

As Operation Crowbar got underway, the air offensive was stepped up. Two missions planned for the first week in January were turned back by weather. The third, flown on the 5th, hit the jackpot. A PBY crew spotted the *Kotohira Maru* off Holtz Bay. Three B-25s from the 77th Bombardment Squadron were launched from Adak. The crews succeeded in sending the 6,500 ton freighter and its cargo of provisions, fuel and building materials to the bottom of the ocean.

Lieutenant Russell W. Tarvin's B-24 crew from the 21st Bombardment Squadron spotted a second transport, the *Montreal Maru*, while they were on a weather reconnaissance mission. Tarvin's bombardier, Lieutenant James E. Compton, dropped one of his bombs on the deck. Two others exploded near the ship's hull. The transport, bound for Kiska with elements of the 302nd Infantry Battalion, the 303rd Independent Engineer Battalion and a load of airfield construction material, sank near the Komandorski Islands.[321] General Buckner sent the bomber crew a message, stating: "Congratulations to the crew of the weather ship for turning in the best weather report so far rendered in Alaska."[322]

Aside from those who died in the frigid sea, the loss of the airfield construction materials dealt the Japanese on Kiska a serious blow. The Japanese, after deciding that they were going to remain in the Aleutians, had started construction of an airfield on a ridge adjacent to Salmon Lagoon on Kiska and another at Holtz Bay on Attu. Unlike the Americans, they had very little equipment or construction materials; mostly picks, shovels and push carts. Work was slow. One laborer later remembered that it was like "sweeping the sea with a broom."[323]

The mission planned for January 6 was only partially successful. Six B-24s and six B-25s with an escort of twelve P-38s were sent against Kiska. The pilots of the Lightnings decided to turn back because of the weather. One of the bombers accompanied them back to Adak. The remaining bombers continued on to find six Rufes waiting for them and marginal weather over the target. All the crews except one turned back. The lone B-24 crew, exploiting a hole in the overcast, dropped their bombs on the submarine base before heading for Adak.

The second day's effort met with equally dismal results. The bomber crews reported the Japanese were using smoke pots to obscure the targets and noted that they were in the process of building an airstrip near Salmon Lagoon.[324]

On January 8, another Aleutian storm blew in, putting a halt to all air operations. Colonel Verbeck and his thirty-four Alaska Scouts were the first to go ashore at Amchitka on January 11 followed by the rest of the twenty one hundred man landing force on the next morning.

Brigadier General Lloyd E. Jones' force consisting of the 813th Engineer Aviation Battalion and several other smaller units and their equipment went ashore from four transports during a storm. The landing was protected by a small force of three cruisers, *Indianapolis*, *Raleigh* and *Detroit*, and four destroyers under the command of Rear Admiral Charles H. McMorris.

General Buckner, on the right, visiting the troops as they embark for the landing on Amchitka. USA photo

High seas rolling across Constantine Harbor played havoc with the landing operations, smashing small boats against the beach and scattering supplies. The destroyer *Worden*, from which Colonel Verbeck and his party had been put ashore, was swept onto a pinnacle rock which punctured her hull. Attempts to save her proved fruitless; and her captain, Lieutenant Commander William G. Pogue, ordered abandoned ship. Fourteen men died in the icy waters before they could be rescued. The *Worden* was a complete loss.[325]

The storm increased in intensity the next day as more men, supplies and equipment were landed. Support units for the Eleventh Air Force, including the 464th Air Base Group and a radar detachment, arrived aboard the U.S. Army transport *Middleton*. They were off-loaded without incident. The next day the *Middleton* went aground in the storm, spilling its fuel, which washed up unto the beach and added to the miseries the personnel struggling to unload barges in the pounding surf. The transport U.S.S. *Reardon* was swept onto the rocks and later sank.

The men ashore struggled against the gale force winds which reached thirty-five miles per hour. Despite the problems, kitchens were set up to provide hot meals for the men who toiled to bring up the supplies from the beach as the engineers began to carve out a runway at the head of Constantine Harbor.[326]

Colonel Louis H. Foote's 813th Engineer Aviation Battalion performed another Aleutian construction miracle. Their first priority was to build a four thousand foot long fighter strip. Time was of the essence. Once the Japanese on Kiska learned of the American presence on Amchitka, it would be only a matter of time before they would begin sending their aircraft against the American garrison.

The location that Colonel Talley had picked out for the fighter strip was in a tidal marsh near the head of Constantine Harbor. Foote's engineers threw up a dam, drained the marsh, scraped off the half frozen muck and dumped load after load of gravel and sand from a deposit that soldiers had accidentally found while digging foxholes near the landing strip site. Gradually, Fox Runway took shape.

More engineering units arrived. Colonel Fisher S. Blinn, the Commander, 151st Engineer Regiment, became the resident engineer, responsible for overseeing all the construction on the island. Work was begun on a ten thousand foot long bomber runway on the broad flat area overlooking the harbor. The muskeg was stripped off and sand and gravel fill hauled in, flattened and compressed to form a solid base. An average of twenty thousand cubic feet of feet of fill was brought in daily, with a record of thirty thousand being established during one twenty-four hour period. Marston matting was then laid down.

A seventy by eighty foot wharf, one of the largest in the

The aerial photograph taken by Fleet Air Wing Four crew January 23, shows the lower end of what shortly afterwards became Fox Runway. Talley's engineers were able to drain the tidal marsh and bring in fill to create a fighter strip within weeks. USN photo via Lowell W. Bradford

A second aerial photograph taken February 13 shows the progress that had been made on the fighter strip.
USN photo via Lowell W. Bradford

When this photograph was taken in August 1986, Fox Runway, while worn by the years, still looked usable. In the solitude of the island it's not hard to close your eyes and imagine the sound of powerful engines warming up for another mission. author's photo

Fox runway as it looked shortly after completion. USN photo

The aerial photograph taken of Amchitka in 1946 shows the deserted hardstands where bombers once stood. For a few years the place was the center of the universe for many young men who served on Amchitka. Constantine Harbor and the fighter strip can be seen in the upper left-hand corner. The photograph was probably taken by a crew from the 404th Bombardment Squadron which remained in Alaska on mapping projects until it was inactivated January 4, 1947.

FAA collection, Anchorage Museum of History and Art.

Aleutians, was built. It was protected by a twenty four hundred foot long breakwater. Hangars were erected, a million and a half gallon aviation fuel storage and distribution system was constructed. A five hundred bed hospital went up. Pacific huts dotted the landscape, providing housing and working areas for a garrison of almost fifteen thousand men. Compared to the twenty-one million dollar project, what the Japanese achieved on Kiska paled in comparison. In the final analysis, the war in the Aleutians was won at the front end of a bulldozer and by the determination of engineers, military and civilian.[327]

A Vile Place

The storm that swept in from the west, protecting the Americans from the prying eyes of the Japanese on Kiska, also prevented the Eleventh Air Force from flying any successful missions against Kiska and Attu during the remainder of January. Colonel Donohew, who had replaced Eareckson as the acting commander of the XI Bombardment Command when the latter was sent to Washington DC in early December to brief General Arnold's staff on the lessons learned in the Aleutians and then on to San Diego to assist with the planning for the Kiska invasion, continued to commit his bombers. The results were always the same: terrible weather and aborted missions. The Aleutians were living up to their reputation as a vile place, unsuited to air operations.[328]

In one hideous day, January 18, General Butler lost six of his aircraft and eighteen men. Early that morning, the crew of the weather reconnaissance B-24 reported seeing two Japanese ships in Kiska Harbor. A mission of six B-24s and four B-26s was sent out. Six P-38s were sent along to suppress the anti-aircraft guns and provide fighter protection. The mission got off to a bad start when the crews of two of the B-26s and one of the B-24s turned back for Adak after experiencing mechanical difficulties. The other crews continued on, only to run into bad weather.[329]

The crews of the B-26s and the fighter pilots headed back in time to reach Adak before the weather closed in. However, the Liberator crews were not so fortunate. The historian of the 21st Bombardment Squadron noted in his diary for the day:

> Captain Smith took the weather mission today. Six B-24s took off on a Kiska mission. Lieutenant Tarvin returned 1639 (4:39 PM) with engine trouble. Weather closed in before the others returned. Lieut. Manthe (Frederick L.) landed in semi-light with visibility and ceiling about 00. His plane crashed into two P-38s, tearing them apart and causing various damage to the B-24. Captain Moore proceeded to Cold Bay where he landed about 11 o'clock. The other three crews: Lt. Pruett (Earnest C.), Lt. Bloomfield (Thomas F.) and Lt. Hamilton (Linton D.) are still unreported. Just where they are or where they might be heading we do not know.[330]

Lieutenant Pruett succeeded in landing his B-24D on the west side of Great Sitkin Island. Sergeant Holiel Ascol suffered a serious back injury. The others escaped injury. The crew of a destroyer spotted Pruett and his men the next day and sent a launch ashore to recover them. The B-24s flown by Lieutenants Bloomfield and Hamilton disappeared without a trace.[331]

The accidents continued to mount up during January. The next one occurred on the 21st. The 36th Bombardment Squadron was ordered to deploy its B-17Es from Cape Field to Adak. Seven took off and six made it. In the words of Billy Wheeler, "the weather was uncertain." Two of the Fortress collided during the approach into Adak. The one flown by Lieutenant Major H. McWilliams, who flown the escort B-17 the day Lieutenants Ambrose and Long shot down the two Mavises, disappeared. Fifteen crew members and passengers died.

The pilot of the other B-17E, Lieutenant Brown, managed to land his badly damaged bomber at Adak. It was a considerable flying feat. A large chunk of the vertical fin had been torn off, the rudder rendered useless and the elevator jammed in the level flight position. All that Brown and his crew were left with were the ailerons, trim tabs and the engine throttles. The extent of the damage did not dawn on Brown until he walked around and looked at the bomber's tail after landing.[332]

The Eleventh Air Force also lost two B-25Ds, two A-29s and a P-40E to accidents bringing the total during the month to eleven aircraft. There were no combat losses.[333]

Colonel Chennault sent his fighters aloft, weather permitting, to provide air cover for the troops on Amchitka until the fighter strip could be completed. On occasions, during brief periods of clear weather, the fighter pilots and the bomber escorts were able to remain over Constantine Harbor, providing some reassurance to those below that they were being protected from the Japanese pilots on Kiska.

With all the activity going on at Amchitka, it was only a matter of time before the Japanese would send one of their float planes to check out the situation. On January 24, the men on the ground looked up to see a lone Japanese plane circling overhead. Two more Japanese planes returned the next day. Several small bombs were dropped on the shipping in the harbor without doing any damage. The Japanese were gone before the P-38 pilots and their B-24 escort arrived from Adak to provide air cover.

The Japanese learned to avoid the times that the P-38s were on patrol. Six float plane planes arrived over Constantine Harbor on January 27. Three bombs were dropped and strafing attacks were made. One man was killed and another wounded. The runway was cratered.

P-40s from the 18th Fighter Squadron lined along side of Fox Runway. The tents where Howard Nelson, Wilton Sass and the others lived can been seen in the background. AAF photo

A PBY-5A from Fleet Air Wing Four takes off from the water soaked fighter strip on Amchitka. The weather was so bad that one pilot swore that a discouraged seagull hitched a ride on his wing. USN photo

It was quickly repaired. Nine float planes arrived over Amchitka on February 1. The pilots dropped their bombs in the camp area and strafed several destroyers in the harbor. The attackers were easily driven off without any casualties. On February 13, Captain Morgan A. Giffin, on patrol from the 54th Fighter Squadron and responding to a report from a PBY crew, shot a Jake down off the northwest end of Amchitka.

On February 15, the pilot of a lone Rufe dropped a bomb that exploded near a foxhole, caving it in on its occupants and smothering them to death. The next day Lieutenant Kenneth Saxhaug landed his P-40K on the hastily constructed fighter strip at Amchitka. He was followed by seven more P-40s from the 18th Fighter Squadron and four P-38s from the 54th Fighter Squadron. A C-47 also arrived with personnel and supplies. The two fighter squadrons shifted their operations to Amchitka from Adak and the 11th Fighter Squadron moved forward from Cape Field to Adak. The 344th Fighter Squadron moved into Cape Field in early March.[334]

Wilton Sass, Howard Nelson and the other mechanics from the 18th Fighter Squadron had already arrived at Amchitka. They set up their tents on the slopes overlooking the fighter strip, and began working the long hours required to keep the fighters in good mechanical condition and armed for the fighter-bomber offensive that was launched against Kiska.[335]

The arrival of the fighters put an end to the Japanese limited air offensive. On February 18, Major Clayton J. Larson and Lieutenant Elmer J. Stone, on combat air patrol, intercepted two Rufes over Saint Makarius Bay on the southeast shore of Amchitka Island. The 18th Fighter Squadron pilots were each credited with shooting down a float fighter. One fell into Saint Makarius Bay about

three miles off shore. The other went down off Bird Cape at the southwestern end of the island.[336]

Their Days Were Numbered

The patrols conducted by Fleet Air Wing Four and the bombing attacks by the Eleventh Air Force interfered considerably with the Japanese plans to reinforce and resupply their garrisons on Kiska and Attu. Naval operations, especially submarines, added to their difficulties. Heavy fog and rough seas compounded their problems. As a result, the Japanese admitted after the war that:

> Development of land bases and completion of defensive positions were seriously hampered as a result of these difficulties. Actually, the land bases were never completed. Consequently, enemy planes operated freely, and our forces held only very inadequate defenses against enemy counterattacks. Finally, any continuation of supply transport became impossible. In turn, the food supply became critical. This, combined with the inadequate land defenses, created a most unfavorable position which eventually resulted in the withdrawal from the western Aleutian Archipelago.[337]

Because of the summer and fall air offensive and submarine operations, the Japanese had been forced to withdraw their naval forces from the Aleutian area. Admiral Hosogaya continued to send in transports, most without escorts, to reinforce and resupply the garrisons on Kiska and Attu.

The Japanese made an attempt in November to establish a garrison on Shemya Island where they hoped to take advantage of the island's flat surface to build an air field. Two merchant ships arrived off Shemya early in the month, but the Japanese were unable to off-load them due to rough sea conditions and the lack of a suitable anchorage (the island has no natural harbor). Instead, the personnel from the 303rd Infantry Battalion were put ashore at Attu. Admiral Hosogaya made another attempt in late November. Two transports, escorted by four warships, were dispatched. However, the Japanese returned to their Kuril bases when they encountered unfavorable sea conditions off Shemya. No other attempt was made to occupy the island.

The Japanese efforts to sustain their presence in the Aleutians became increasingly risky. Between November 1, 1942 and February 11, 1943, Admiral Hosogaya dispatched thirty-three ship loads of men and material to the islands. Fourteen failed to reach their destinations. Two (*Montreal Maru* and *Kotohira Maru*) were sunk while en route and the others forced to turn back for various reasons. Two others (*Cherryboune Maru* and Urajio Maru) that made it to their destinations were so badly damaged by bombing attacks that they had to be abandoned. Following the sinking of the *Montreal Maru* and *Kotohira Maru*, the Japanese switched to sending in transports with a speed of twelve knots or more with an escort of warships.[338]

However, Admiral Kinkaid added to their difficulties by dispatching Admiral McMorris and his small force of cruisers and destroyers to cover the approaches to the western Aleutians. On February 18, based on a report by the captain of the S-28 that Japanese shipping was present in Holtz Bay, Admiral McMorris decided to go after them. By the time the American warships arrived, the Japanese had disappeared. Admiral McMorris ordered a naval bombardment of the shore installations at Holtz Bay and Chichagof Harbor. The bursting shells left great, ugly gashes in the snow, but otherwise did little damage.

Admiral McMorris then divided his force and went looking for the Japanese shipping. The force led by Captain Nicholas Vytlacil aboard the *Indianapolis* found the *Akagan Maru* later that evening and sent her to the bottom.[339]

Admiral Hosogaya succeeded in getting a convoy through on March 9. Several weeks later, he dispatched another consisting of three transports escorted by a powerful force of two heavy and three light cruisers and four destroyers, virtually the entire Fifth Fleet. The transports carried troops, their equipment, ammunition and supplies intended for Attu, and the island's new commander, Col. Yasuyo Yamasaki and his staff.[340]

On March 26, the Japanese convoy ran into Admiral McMorris' force of one heavy and one light cruiser and four destroyers 180 miles due west of Attu and 100 miles south of the Komandorski Islands. Despite being outnumbered two to one, McMorris stood his ground. While the transports retired to safer waters, Admiral Hosogaya

pressed the attack. Beginning at 8:00 AM, the two slugged it out for three and a half hours before Admiral Hosogaya, running low on ammunition and fuel and fearing a bomber attack, withdrew his force from the scene of battle.

Admiral McMorris had sent a message to Adak at the start of the engagement requesting air support. Admiral Hosogaya's radio operators intercepted it. The fact that the Americans were no doubt in the process of launching a bomber attack preyed on the Hosogaya's mind. General Butler had in fact ordered an all out attack that turned into a fiasco.

The strike by eleven B-25s on Amchitka, 400 miles from the scene of action, was held up while mechanics frantically installed bomb bay fuel tanks. Eight B-25s and eight P-38s finally got airborne at 1:30 PM, but ran low on gas and had to turn back before reaching the point where Admiral McMorris had reported the last sighting of the transports. The crews dropped their bombs on the Japanese positions in Kiska Harbor before landing at Amchitka.

The planned attack by thirteen B-24s at Adak 150 miles to the east was complicated by the fact that the bombers had been loaded with general purpose bombs for a planned attack on Kiska. While the ground crews removed them, others went to get armor piercing bombs which they found frozen to the ground. Precious time was spent in getting them unstuck, and then a storm blew in. By the time the crews managed to get their Liberators airborne six hours later, Admiral Hosogaya's force was well beyond their range and the only ships they saw were Admiral McMorris's fleet steaming triumphantly for Adak.

Captain Gehres also diverted two of his PBYs from a routine patrol and sent their crews searching for the retiring Japanese. They found two of the transports late in the afternoon; but since the Catalinas were not carrying bombs, there was nothing they could do but send back reports which proved by then to be useless.[341]

The next day, General Arnold sent a stinging personal message to General Butler, demanding: "Why, repeat why six hour delay between takeoff and sighting time?" Butler managed to explain the problem to Arnold's satisfaction, but from then on he kept six B-25s on anti-shipping alert.[342]

The damage inflicted on both sides was minimal. The heavy cruiser *Salt Lake City*, which had just joined Admiral McMorris' force, was hit four times and the destroyer *Baily* twice. Seven men were killed and twenty wounded, thirteen of which did not require hospitalization. The Japanese heavy cruiser *Nachi* was damaged.

Despite being outnumbered and outgunned, Admiral McMorris had achieved a strategic victory. Faced with the combined surface and air blockade, the Japanese gave up trying to send reinforcements and supplies by transports and began using warships. However, after sending in two destroyer loads in early April, they switched to using submarines. Admiral Hosogaya, who had failed to take advantage of his superior force, was placed on the retirement list. The Japanese garrison on Attu, which had received only half of its planned complement of troops, settled in and waited for the inevitable arrival of the Americans. Admiral Akiyama's forces on Kiska continued to dig in and fight back against the incessant Eleventh Air Force bomber and fighter attacks.[343]

Their days were numbered. Admiral Kinkaid, with assault on Kiska postponed indefinitely, proposed on March 3 to Admiral Nimitz that Attu be taken. The aerial photo interpreters had poured over the few photographs that had been brought back from the missions flown over Attu. From all indications, the Japanese had around five hundred personnel on the island, no coastal defense guns and only a handful of anti-aircraft guns in the Holtz Bay and Chichagof Harbor areas. Sarana, Massacre and Temnac Bays appeared deserted.

The only information the intelligence staffs of Admiral Kinkaid and General Buckner had on the Japanese was obtained from visual sightings, aerial photographs and radio intercepts. They were equally ignorant of the terrain and did not fully comprehend the effects of weather. During the seventy-five years that Attu belonged to the Americans before the Japanese occupation, no one had made a detailed study of the interior. As a result, the geodetic survey maps that were made contained little information on the terrain behind the shoreline.

Despite the limited knowledge, Admiral Kinkaid reasoned that the island could be taken with the limited forces that were available. "Seldom," one Army historian noted, "had operations been planned with less knowledge of what the troops would have to face."[344]

Kinkaid proposed that an infantry regiment from the 7th Infantry Division supported by artillery would be sufficient for the ground assault with the transports and warships coming from existing sources already in Alaskan waters and from West Coast ports. General Butler suggested that a small carrier be provided for air support because of the distances that had to be flown from Amchitka. By taking Attu first, Kinkaid correctly reasoned, the much stronger Japanese garrison on Kiska would be isolated and could easily be dealt with later. He also proposed that an airfield be built on Shemya Island to support operations against Kiska.[345]

Admiral Nimitz concurred, and when his chief of staff, Admiral Spruance, left for the Pacific Military Conference in Washington D.C., he took with him Kinkaid's proposal. The Joint Chiefs of Staff had called the conference in the wake of the Casablanca Conference to decide the strategy for the Pacific during the rest of 1943.

Neither the Central nor the North Pacific areas were on the agenda. However, they came up during the course of discussions. Admiral Spruance successfully argued that with the Guadalcanal operations completed, enough shipping and forces could be diverted to the Central Pacific without compromising the planned operations to retake the rest of the Solomon Islands and General MacArthur's plans for clearing the Japanese from New Guinea. He also won approval for an amphibious assault against Attu with a follow on against Kiska. The British gave their approval to modify the Casablanca agreement shortly afterwards.[346]

On March 11, Admiral Nimitz informed Admiral Kinkaid to proceed with the planning to take Attu. An assault date of May 7 was set; and Admiral Rockwell's staff at San Diego temporarily shelved the Kiska plans and began focusing on the mountainous island at the end of the Aleutian Islands, of which little was known and much expected.

The Promised Land

In preparation for the forthcoming invasion of Attu, Admiral Kinkaid moved his and the other headquarters to Adak during March where they would be closer to the action and could better coordinate operations. General Buckner moved in with his staff from Fort Richardson and General Butler and Captain Gehres relocated their headquarters from Kodiak. Promotions came through during the following months. Kinkaid was elevated to vice admiral, Buckner to lieutenant general, Butler to major general and Gehres to commodore. A joint senior officers mess was set up and Admiral Kinkaid introduced the Navy style of good living to the otherwise wind swept, bleak island.[347]

The airfield was named Davis Field in honor of Colonel Davis and the base became the military bastion of the North Pacific. With the arrival of so many senior officers and their staffs and the increased buildup of the base, Adak took on a civilized look. The personnel were housed in Pacific Huts and other amenities of a normal garrison life style began appearing. Billy Wheeler's April 8 entry in his diary noted:

> Adak is practically a garrison post at this writing, no longer the quagmire of which I wrote so piteously September 18. The entire Bomber Command has now moved from the haunts of pleasure and the marts of sin at Elmendorf to this barren and desolate island. We're now living comfortably in Quonset huts and bathing daily in the luxurious Navy shower located next to Major General Butler's quarters. The food has improved with the transfer of mess personnel from Elmendorf. Somewhat outdated Grade B films are

screened nightly in four or five different theaters to which we have access. The new Post PX even peddled Cokes recently—we all sweated out a Coca-Cola line a block long. Cultural note: the installation of electric lights in our snug new latrine has materially strengthened our reading habits.[348]

The idyllic life at Adak for Billy Wheeler and the others was soon to be disrupted. The Joint Chiefs of Staff on March 24 gave their final go ahead for Operation Landcrab, the amphibious assault on Attu. Admiral Nimitz and General DeWitt issued a joint directive April 1, and Admiral Rockwell and his joint staff at San Diego began putting the operation together.[349]

General Buckner, in addition to sending his air expert, Colonel Eareckson, had also dispatched Colonel Castner, Col. William Alexander, an experienced artillery officer on his staff who was familiar with the Aleutian logistic requirements, and Lieutenant Colonel Carl Jones, his engineer, to San Diego in late January to lend Alaskan expertise for planning the Kiska invasion. They now turned their attention to Attu. With the invasion date set for May 7, they and their fellow planners had little time to plan the operation and collect the forces.

In addition to the limited time, lack of intelligence, inadequate forces, separation of commands (the joint staff at San Diego had to coordinate their plans with the staffs of Admiral Kinkaid and General Buckner on Adak), the planning process was hampered by a general lack of understanding of conditions in the Aleutians by those who did not have first hand experience there.[350] Eareckson noted at the time that the Alaska contingent's reception to the planning staff was similar to that of a "bastard at a family reunion."[351]

Castner, Eareckson and the others from Alaska tried to convince the rest of the need to properly equip and train the forces who were to be committed to battle. One of the colonels later remembered "that tears ran down my face" when he heard that the troops were to be equipped with leather boots and clothing more suited to a temperate climate.[352] Their efforts proved fruitless and the planning continued at a relentless pace in order meet the deadline established for the invasion.

Admiral Kinkaid ordered more photo reconnaissance missions flown over Attu. Based on the information obtained from them and other intelligence sources, the estimated Japanese strength on the island was upped to eighteen hundred. The intelligence analyst also noted that the Japanese had established fortified positions in the Holtz Bay and Chichagof areas and defensive positions in Massacre Valley. It would require more than an infantry regiment to overcome them. General DeWitt agreed to provide the 7th Infantry Division as the ground assault force.

"The Hourglass Division," garrisoned at Fort Ord on the Monterey Coast of California, had been equipped and trained for desert warfare in North Africa as a mechanized force. Most of its personnel were from the southwestern United States. However, it was the only division in the Western Defense Command that had reached a state of readiness where it could be committed to combat. The possibility of using the 35th Infantry Division was considered but rejected even though it was commanded by Major General Charles H. Corlett who had been the commander of the Army garrison on Kodiak Island. It was still in the process of being trained and equipped and would not be ready in time for the invasion.

The units in Alaskan were too small and committed to providing defense for various garrisons scattered throughout the territory. Therefore, even though experienced with Alaskan conditions, they were unsuited for offensive operations. A price had been paid for the decision to parcel out the forces in the defense of the many garrisons rather than maintaining a large force at a central location that could be rapidly committed to battle when needed.

The only sizable Alaskan unit, the 4th Infantry Regiment, was assigned the mission occupying Shemya Island along with the 18th Engineer Regiment. The force was commanded by Brigadier General John E. Copeland.[353]

Task Force 16 was formed and Admiral Kinkaid assumed overall command. Admiral Rockwell was designated the commander of the assault force and the World War I vintage battleships *Pennsylvania* and *Nevada*, veterans of Pearl Harbor, and the *Idaho* were placed at his disposal for naval gunfire support. This was the first commitment to battle for the three elderly warships following Pearl Harbor. They had become such a fixture at San Francisco that their crews were jokingly referred to as the "Market Street Commandos."[354]

The escort carrier *Nassau* (CVE-16), commanded by Captain Austin K. Doyle, was also assigned to Admiral Rockwell. The Bogue class carrier, built on a transport hull and commissioned August 20, 1942, had a flight deck that was four hundred and thirty eight feet eight inches long by eighty feet wide. Its air complement consisted of thirty pilots, an intelligence officer, twenty-eight enlisted men and twenty-six F4F-4 Wildcat fighters assigned to VF-21, commanded by Lieutenant Commander L.V.K. Greenamyer. The *Nassau* also carried three F4F-3Ps, a photo-reconnaissance version of the Wildcat, from Marine squadron VMO-155 and a SOC-3A Seagull nicknamed "Jeepers Creepers."[355]

In addition to the old battleships and the small carrier, three heavy and three light cruisers, nineteen destroyers, four attack transports and a variety of tenders, oilers, minesweepers, submarines, transports and smaller ves-

The escort carrier Nassau.
USN photo

sels were made available to Admiral Kinkaid. The force by now had grown to a considerably larger size than what had originally been intended when he first proposed the Attu operation.[356]

Admiral Fletcher, whose area of responsibility encompassed Alaska and who was providing the bulk of the naval forces for the planned operation, offered to give up his third star so that he could participate in the planned operations. As a vice admiral, he outranked Kinkaid, whose promotion had not yet come through. Admiral King refused to go along with the idea, and Fletcher graciously withdrew from direct involvement in the North Pacific and let Kinkaid have a free hand in running the operations.[357]

Major General Albert Brown, Commander, 7th Infantry Division began conducting amphibious training exercises off the sunny coast of California to prepare his division for the assault on the fog shrouded, cold and bleak Attu Island while General Butler and Commodore Gehres stepped up their air operations.

Following the frustrations of January, the aircrews of the Eleventh Air Force experienced better luck during February. The first successful mission was flown the 4th. The day got off to a good start when the gunners aboard the weather ship shot down one of the three Rufes that rose to challenge them. Other bombers arrived throughout the day to pound main camp areas while the P-38 pilots, strafed the ground installations, including the airstrip that the Japanese had begun work on near Salmon Lagoon.[358]

The next mission was flown four days later when five B-24s and equal number of B-25s accompanied by four P-38s were committed against the main camp. It was followed by another attack on the 10th, this time by six heavy and eight medium bombers accompanied by eight P-38s.[359] Two of the heavies were B-17Es on their last Aleutian bombing mission. Billy Wheeler noted in his diary:

A B-17E, 36th Bombardment Squadron, on a weather reconnaissance flight. Col Fred Ramputi collection

On this sad day the 36th flew its B-17Es into combat for the last time. Tomorrow we are to become, by order of bomber command, a B-24D outfit. Many an eye was moist as the big Boeing settled in their revetments for a well deserved rest. Someone even proposed a mad dash to Paramushiro in our remaining seventeens-a heroic gesture in the manner of J.W. Holmes' "Old Ironsides."[360]

The B-26 had also flown its last mission on January 18. The 73rd and 77th Bombardment Squadrons completed the conversion to B-25s by early February and the 406th Bombardment Squadron received its first Mitchells on February 15. There had been a general agreement that the Marauder had not been a suitable aircraft for Aleutian operations. Its replacement, the slab sided, twin engine North American B-25C and D model Mitchell proved to be a better bomber. It was an easier plane to fly and had a greater range, two very important factors in the Aleutians.[361]

On February 13, the crews of five heavy and six medium bombers pounded the main camp area and the landing strip that the Japanese were frantically trying to build while the pilots of ten P-38s from the 54th Fighter Squadron provided air cover and strafed the ground positions. The Japanese sent their float planes aloft. Captain Laven and Lieutenant Francis A. Evans received joint credit for shooting down a Rufe. The B-25D flown by

The North American B-25C and D model Mitchells that replaced the Martin B-26A Marauders were better suited to Aleutian conditions. They had a slight advantage in range, 1,500 versus 1,150, and were a more forgiving plane to fly. They stood up well under the primitive conditions of the Aleutians. Both bomber types could carry a maximum bomb load of three thousand pounds. The B-25C and D models were powered by two 1450 horsepower Wright R-2600-13 engines. The Mitchells were employed on medium and low level missions and against shipping. Charles Pinney collection

Several B-25Gs were sent to the Aleutians for test and evaluation. A conversion of the C model, the medium bomber featured a 75mm cannon and two 50 caliber machine guns in the nose. The concept for mounting an M-4 Army 75mm cannon in the B-25 had originated with the Fifth Air Force. The pilot used the 50 caliber machine guns to suppress flack and assist in aiming the cannon. The cannon proved an effective weapon against shipping. Its major drawback was its slow rate of fire. Each round had to be hand loaded by the navigator, and seldom could more than four rounds be fired during an attack. The B-25Gs reached the Aleutians too late to be used against shipping. AAF photo

This photograph, taken sometime during the early summer of 1943, shows the new recognition insignia being applied to one of the Eleventh Air Force B-25Ds. Because of the confusion experienced in telling the difference between the American star and the German cross at a distance, the national insignia on all American aircraft were ordered changed. Two bars were added to the white circle that surrounded the blue star and the insignia was outlined in red. The new insignia was adopted June 28, but because of complaints from the Pacific Theater that the red outline could be confused for the Japanese red ball insignia, the red portion of the American insignia was deleted in September 1943. Charles Pinney collection

Lieutenant Kendall W. Shepard Jr. from the 77th Bombardment Squadron was struck by anti-aircraft fire. Lieutenant Shepard managed to fly the medium bomber back to Davis Field on one engine and crash land it on Hill 302. Private Steve Rouchak, who was manning a nearby coastal artillery position, was killed.[362]

Another weather front moved in, and no more missions against Kiska could be flown until the 20th, when the crews of five B-24s and seven B-25s blasted the main camp area, North Head and the landing strip construction site. Eight P-38s were committed in support. Another mission was flown three days later when six B-24s, six B-25s and four P-38s were sent against the main camp and North

Head areas. Additionally, for the first time, the photo-reconnaissance version of the Lightning, the F-5, was sent to take photographs of the damage results.[363]

The Japanese gunners drew blood on the next mission, flown February 25. Six B-24s and six B-25s were sent out on an afternoon raid against Kiska. Lieutenant Jackson W. Lewis' B-24 was hit and his bombardier, Lieutenant Socrates S. Pappas, fatally wounded. In the terse words of the mission report, the crew of the 36th Bombardment Squadron Liberator:

> Approached Kiska from North in #3 position at 8000' over overcast. Turned 180 degrees and came through at 2500' approaching target (North Head) between Little Kiska and South Head at 2200'. Dropped 26 mixed demolition and phosphorous 100 lb bombs over South head, 4 hung up, bomb bay doors could not be closed. #4 engine shot out and on fire just after leaving harbor, a moment later nose shot out and bombardier hit in abdomen, several other hits; radio and intercom out but could receive; #3 engine began to lose manifold pressure, decided to try Amchitka. Reported AA heaviest seen, though new guns on South Head near turn of harbor. Landed with 4 100 lb demolition bombs.[364]

Lieutenant Lewis and his copilot, Lieutenant Douglas W. Hamilton, had managed to get their bomber as far as Amchitka, where they earned the dubious honor of making the first bomber landing on the island. The brakes locked and the bomber slid down the slippery rain soaked steel surface of the fighter strip and then off its end onto the soft ground.

The photograph was taken on February 27. Jackson Lewis' B-24 can be seen in the upper center.
USN photo via Lowell W. Bradford

Lieutenant Pappas died of his wounds while en route to Amchitka. Six other crew members including Lewis and Hamilton suffered an assortment of cuts and bruises from the crash landing. The others including a U.S. Naval Academy midshipman aboard as an observer escaped unharmed.[365]

Two more missions were flown against Kiska during February, bringing the total to nine. Altogether, thirty-two missions had been dispatched during the month of which twenty were weather and photo-reconnaissance that were flown as far as Attu. Four missions were aborted. Two hundred and fifty tons of bombs, mostly 100 pounders, were dropped, up from the less than fifty tons the previous month. The anti-aircraft fire was medium to light. Thirty Japanese airplanes were observed during the month, of which four were shot down by fighters. A fifth was credited to Lieutenant Shepard's crew. Only six Japanese pilots attempted to attack the bombers.[366]

With the mounting offensive against them, the Japanese were faced with the decision of withdrawing from the Aleutians or bringing in more reinforcements. Lieutenant General Hideichiro Higuchi, Admiral Hosogaya's army opposite in the North Pacific, wanted to abandon the effort. The Imperial Headquarters felt otherwise. A retreat would leave the Kurile Islands exposed to an invasion. On February 5, it issued orders that Kiska and Attu would be held "at all cost." Admiral Hosogaya realized that he had little more than a month's grace period before the Americans completed their base on Amchitka and began conducting air strikes against Kiska and Attu in earnest.

The Japanese struggled with the almost impossible task of carving out airfields on Kiska and Attu so that land based planes could be brought in to provide better protection against the steadily increasing bomber and fighter attacks and to provide air cover for the ships they were trying to sneak through the ever increasing blockade. However,

their efforts were hampered by the lack of heavy earth-moving equipment and the incessant air attacks. The strip on the ridge overlooking Salmon Lagoon was only half completed when the Eleventh Air Force offensive was stepped up during March and April.[367]

The twenty-eight hundred foot strip was not finished until June, but by then it was too late. The labor intensive project involved moving dirt and fill from the center of the ridge to build up the ends. The work had to done largely by hand, using picks, shovels and handcarts to move the dirt and fill over narrow gauge steel tracks. Most of the construction equipment had gone down with the *Montreal Maru* and the rest had never reached the island because of the blockade. The Japanese engineers were left with two small bulldozers, six rollers and five air compressors to work the airfield project. The Japanese were faced with an even more difficult task at Attu and were never able the complete the thirty-five hundred foot long strip they had planned to build in the Holtz Bay area.[368]

By the end of February, the 18th Fighter Squadron had settled into a routine. One flight maintained a two plane patrol over Amchitka from dawn to dusk. A second flight was dedicated to flying strike missions against Kiska. The third flight stood down to give the pilots and the maintenance crew a rest. The 18th Fighter Squadron flew a mission against Kiska on March 1. It was the first since the previous October when single engine fighter missions against Kiska from Adak had been called off as being too hazardous. Now that Kiska was 90 miles away from the fighter strip on the eastern tip of Amchitka, the flights could be made with some assurance that the pilots of the short range fighters would not be caught in the air by a sudden change in the weather and no place to land.

The four pilots assigned the mission arrived over Kiska to find the island obscured by clouds. They jettisoned their bombs and returned to Amchitka to find the landing strip

Bombs fall towards the runway overlooking Salmon Lagoon. AAF photo

The oblique photograph taken on a clear day shows the layout of Japanese facilities. The uncompleted runway is above Salmon Lagoon. To the left of the runway is the North Head area. The main camp area is located above the runway. The Nozima Maru *can clearly be seen beached off Trout Lagoon. The* Urajio Maru *is also visible immediately to the left where a bomb has exploded in the water. The submarine base and South Head areas can be seen in the upper center of the photograph.* AAF photo

The Japanese used narrow gauge rail tracks to move fill in push carts. *Frank Rosse collection*

One of the rollers the Japanese used in constructing the runway. Frank Rosse collection

One of the more graphic pictures of the attacks against the runway was taken during a low-level mission. A bomb burst can be seen in the lower center near one of the several anti-aircraft positions located near the end of the runway and puffs from exploding flack are visible. The efforts made by the Japanese to build up the ends of the runway with fill is evident. AAf photo

The Americans, using heavy earth moving equipment, were able to complete the runway within two weeks. The photograph of the east end was taken September 23, 1943. AAF photo

The photograph was taken on a foggy September 1989 morning at the east end of the runway. author photo

"socked in." After efforts to talk the pilots down by radio, Lieutenant Donald J. Crisp volunteered to take off and lead them down through a hole in the cloud cover. All five landed safely.[369]

After a further weather delay, Major James Dowling, Captain Joseph S. Littlepage, Lieuts Sidney M. Richman and George P. Tetrault took off from Amchitka at 2:15 PM in their P-40s. After dropping fragmentation bombs on the main camp, they landed at Amchitka at 3:20 PM.[370] The fighter sweep over Kiska signaled the beginning of a stepped up air offensive against Kiska and Attu. During March and April an average of forty-six sorties a day would be flown against Kiska.[371]

Following a pause due to weather, the offensive against Kiska was resumed on March 9. Six B-24s, six B-25s and four P-40s were committed against Kiska while a B-24

and four P-38s were sent against Attu. On completion of the mission, the six medium bomber crews from the 77th Bombardment Squadron landed at Amchitka where they joined the 18th Fighter Squadron. Other crews from the 77th arrived and the squadron began operating their heavily loaded bombers from the short fighter strip as the engineers rushed to complete a nearby bomber strip.[372]

Fighter and bomber missions were flown against Kiska on March 9 and 10. Fourteen float planes were observed at the seaplane ramp area and continued progress on the airfield at Salmon Lagoon noted. A fighter mission against the float planes was flown on the afternoon 13th by twelve P-40s and followed by another that day, flown by eight P-38s and eight P-40s. Hits were observed against the parked planes.[373]

General Butler, not waiting for the bomber field to be completed, began building up the air units on Amchitka, straining the small fighter strip to its very limits. In addition to sending in the aircrews of the 77th Bombardment, he moved the 54th Fighter Squadron forward. Four C-47s brought in the ground crew on March 12 and ten P-38 pilots arrived the same day in their fighters. The squadron historian commented: "The many months of aimless wandering along the chain had now finally made sense. Amchitka, to geographers, was only an insignificant spot of sand and tundra, but to us, it was the promised land; the land that promised real hell for the Japs."[374]

The first B-25 mission from Amchitka was flown on March 15 when six of the medium bombers with a maximum load of thirty-six 100-pound general purpose bombs and two hundred and six 20-pound fragmentation bombs were sent against installations on North Head. They were part of an effort that involved strikes by B-24s and the

Amchitka's nearness to Kiska resulted in a greatly increased number of air strikes frown against Kiska and Attu. The P-38s and P-40s were deployed to Amchitka shortly after the fighter strip was completed. The fighters were joined by B-25s and PBYs and the area took on a crowded look. The dock and Constantine Harbor are visible in the upper portion of the photograph. USN photo via AAHM

fighters that continued throughout the day.

Lieutenant Lyle Bean looked up after completing a strafing attack of North Head to see that the right engine of his friend's P-38 had been hit by anti-aircraft fire. Lieutenant John W. Livesay feathered the prop, and with smoke trailing from the badly damaged engine, headed for Rat Island, half way between Kiska and Amchitka. He managed to ditch his Lightning in the water three hundred feet from the shoreline and inflate his life raft.

Lieutenant John Geddes, who had accompanied Livesay, observed him clinging to the side of the life raft in the rough seas. Shortly afterwards, an OA-10 arrived. When its crew reached Livesay, he was face down in the water, dead. They took him ashore and buried him in a grave marked by a stone cairn and his identification tags.[375]

Lyle Bean and the other original members of the 54th Fighter Squadron were living on borrowed time. The squadron had suffered a fifty percent casualty rate in its pilots within less than a year. Lieutenant Livesay was the fifteenth to die. The survivors began to depart in March. Lieutenants Hasenfus and Long were the first to go. The squadron historian noted: "For men who were reluctant to leave; one had to admire the superb bursts of speed they showed in getting aboard transport planes."[376]

Another maximum effort against Kiska was flown on March 16 involving thirteen B-24s, sixteen B-25s, thirty-two P-38s and eight P-40 sorties that pounded the Japanese installations throughout the day. Bomb loads ranging from 20-pound fragmentation bombs up to 2000-pound general purpose bombs were dropped. The Japanese anti-aircraft gunners fought back, filling the sky with fire. Lieutenant Bertheau McCurdy and his four man crew from the 77th Bombardment Squadron disappeared. They were last seen in a diving turn after dropping their bombs.

The pilots of the remaining Japanese float planes took off and went into a defensive Lufberry circle to avoid being strafed on the water. A claim was submitted for one Rufe shot down. It was not substantiated.[377]

The number of float planes on Kiska continued to decline despite efforts by the Japanese to send in reinforcements. The *Kimikawa Maru* brought in ten Rufes and

General Butler and Colonel DeFord and the men celebrate the first anniversary of the Eleventh Air Force. AAF photo

General Butler reviewing the troops at Adak on the first anniversary of the Eleventh Air Force. AAF photo

Unlike Colonel Eareckson, Colonel DeFord was promoted. When this photograph of the XI Bombardment Command was taken in December 1943, he was a brigadier general. From left to right, front row: Col Robert H. Herman, Chief of Staff; Lieut Col Bearly, A-1; General DeFord; Lieut Col John W. Massion, Commander, 28th Bombardment Group; Maj Herold, A-2; and Capt Shedd, A-4. Second row, left to right: Lieut Wineman, A-2; Lieut Modermott, Weather Officer; Capt Byrnes, Flight Surgeon; Maj Millerry, Ordnance Officer; Lieut Craig, Assistant Adjutant; and Lieut Johnson, A-2. Third row, left to right: Lieut Maulick, Armament Officer; Capt Treaster, Chaplain; Lieut Blucher, Statistician Officer; Lieut Hoak, A-2; Lieut Howell, A-2; Lieut Teague, Public Information; Capt Renstrom, Engineer Officer; and Lieut Sheeshey, A-2. Fourth row, left to right: Capt Hamilton, A-2; Capt Wood, Commander, 404th Bombardment Squadron; Lieut Doell, Public Information; Lieut Doell, Public Information; Capt Schwin, Dentist; and Lieut Mecall, Asst A-4.

Bertrand Hoak collection

a Jake via Attu in February and six more Rufes during March before the American blockade put an end to the surface resupply operations. Eight Rufes were destroyed and seven others damaged in encounters with the Americans during the same period. Four Jakes were also badly damaged. By the middle of March, the Japanese float planes had ceased to be a threat to the Eleventh Air Force aircrews.[378]

On March 18, the first P-38 mission against Kiska from Amchitka was launched. More successful missions were flown on March 21, 22, 24, 25 and 29 without any serious incidents; and then on March 30 the luck ran out for Captain Fred Smith and his nine man crew from the 21st Bombardment Squadron. Six missions were dispatched against Kiska and Attu that day. The first consisting of six B-24s and six B-25s accompanied by four P-38s arrived over Kiska to find the island obscured by clouds. In the interim, four B-24s and four P-38s made it through to Attu where they bombed the airfield at Holtz Bay. They were accompanied by two F-5s which were used to take aerial photographs.

The third mission of the day, five B-24s and four P-38s, was flown against Kiska. Major Speer led the B-24s drawn from the three heavy bombardment squadrons on a course that took them to Kiska Volcano and then south across North Head at thirty-three thousand feet for a strike on the main camp. An anti-aircraft round exploded against Captain Smith's B-24 as he approached North Head. The bomber burst into flames and crashed into the waters one-half mile east of North Head. There were no survivors.

The next two missions were flown by P-38s followed by the sixth and final mission of the day. It was flown by medium bomber crews from the 73rd Bombardment Squadron who went after the main camp, submarine base, radar site and the landing strip. The Japanese anti-aircraft gunners blasted away as the six Mitchells swept in from the west at low level in three flights of two aircraft.

Four bombers were hit by cannon and machine gun fire. The B-25 flown by Lieutenant Everett Henricksen was hit by the blast from a bomb dropped by the bomber in front of it. The explosion blew the wing out of line, jammed the bombbay door in the open position, and left one of the 500-pound bombs armed and dangling in the slip stream. Lieutenant Arthur Horn, the bombardier, climbed into the bomb bay, and after a fifteen minute struggle, managed to free the bomb.

Lieutenant Henricksen and his crew made it safely back to Davis Field as did Lieutenant William E. Geyser's crew. A burst of machine gun fire had damaged their B-25's throttle, propeller pitch and mixture controls, forcing the engines into a fast cruising speed. On arriving at Davis Field, they discovered that the landing gear would not go down. Geyser and his copilot managed to make a safe wheels up landing. Other than the damages sustained by five of the bombers and two crew members who had been slightly wounded, the mission was a success.[379]

Altogether, the men of the Eleventh Air Force had flown twenty-five bomber, twenty-nine fighter and eight reconnaissance missions and dropped 550 tons of bombs during March, more than double any of the previous months since the beginning of the air offensive.[380]

With improvement in weather and the pending invasion of Attu, the air war took on a new intensity. The XI Bomber Command had dropped the provisional before its name on March 19. Its commander, Colonel Earl H. DeFord, who had replaced Colonel Donohew, the acting commander on January 23, implemented a more formal approach to the air offensive against the Japanese on Kiska and Attu that proved to be more effective. Many of the older members of the bomber command who had served under Colonel Eareckson resented DeFord. Larry Reineke, an enterprising intelligence officer with the 21st Bombardment Squadron, aptly described the situation when he noted that "Colonel DeFord ate steak while we ate Spam."

DeFord, the opposite of Eareckson, took a more traditional approach to his duties. He believed it was the responsibility of the commander to develop missions, oversee the production of plans, ensure that administrative and logistic requirements were taken care of and make certain his men had the resources they needed to perform their duties. Occasionally, he flew as an observer on the missions to get a feel for how they were carried out.

The fifty-three-year-old DeFord brought with him an impeccable career as a commander and staff officer with extensive pilot experience. Unlike Eareckson, who shared the dangers and discomforts of his men and led by example, DeFord held himself more aloof, insisting on the prerogatives of his rank and responsibility. He took some getting used to by the men who had grown accustomed to Eareckson's free wheeling style of leadership. In the end he proved more effective.[381]

General Butler continued to push forces forward to Adak and Amchitka. Aircrews and ground crews from rear echelon units were sent forward to take some of the pressure off the units on the two islands and gain combat experience, and the Canadians rejoined the air war.

Air Vice-Marshall Stevenson had discussed the possibility with General DeWitt during February of having his P-40 squadrons participate with the Americans in the planned fighter offensive against the Japanese from Amchitka. Wing Commander R.E. Morrow, who replaced Wing Commander McGregor as Commander, X Wing on March 1, also discussed the possibility with General Butler. The small fighter strip at Amchitka was already jammed with aircraft, but Butler agreed to accept Cana-

Curtis Kittyhawks, Number 14 Fighter Squadron, Cape Field, Umnak, April 1943.
Canadian Forces photo

A closer view of one of Number 14 Fighter Squadron's P-40s. While the squadron was forward deployed to Amchitka they flew American aircraft. Canadian Forces photo

dian fighter pilots who could alternate with the Americans in flying their fighters.

Number 14 Fighter Squadron was selected as the first squadron to send its pilots forward. The P-40 squadron, commanded by Squadron Leader Bradley R. Walker, had moved from Sea Island, British Columbia to Cape Field in early March to replace the 11th Fighter Squadron, which had been deployed to Davis Field. Number 111 Fighter Squadron remained at Kodiak.

On March 31, Squadron Leader Walker and eleven other pilots arrived at Davis Field where they began training in American P-40s in preparation for their deployment to Amchitka. The weather turned sour on April 3, preventing further training flights for the next ten days. The storm reached its peak on April 7, when winds gusting up to one hundred and six miles per hour blew the cups off the airfield's anemometer. Finally, on April 13, the Canadians made it back into the air, and on the 17th they departed for Amchitka.

The Canadians pilots were used to form a fourth flight of the 18th Fighter Squadron. Ten pilots who had arrived from the 11th Fighter Squadron on March 17 formed the third flight. The four flights soon settled into alternating routine of flying missions on one day against Kiska, followed by a day of standing alert and another day of flying defensive patrols around Amchitka. The fourth day was used as a down day for the pilots to allow them to rest.[382]

Fourteen Missions A Day

For Howard Nelson and Wilton Sass and the other mechanics, there was no rest as they worked the long hours necessary to keep their aircraft operational in the face of the heavy demands that were being placed on them. Staff Sergeant Jack Boyd, a medium bomber crew member who had arrived with the 73rd Bombardment Squadron in March 1941, recalled years later that April was an intense period for the ground and aircrews alike. Everyone was constantly busy loading bombs and servicing aircraft under the primitive conditions at Amchitka.[383]

New records were established for the number of missions flown and tons of bombs dropped that would not be broken for the remainder of the war in the North Pacific. General Butler ordered a max effort in preparation for the planned amphibious assault on Attu, and the men of the Eleventh Air Force began flying as many as fourteen missions a day.

Lieutenants John M. Duffy and Lawrence A. Duffy, brothers and pilots with the 54th Fighter Squadron, receive the Air Medal for missions flown over Kiska. AAF photo

The bomb and fuel dumps near Constantine Harbor, Amchitka. The Aleutians required an immense logistical system. AAF photo

A fused bomb being loaded aboard a B-25. AAF photo

Adjusting a 500-pound bomb hung from the wing of a P-38. The P-38s and P-40s were employed as fighter bombers during the Spring offensive against Kiska and Attu. AAF photo

The intent of the air offensive had a threefold purpose: to deceive the Japanese into thinking that the Americans were planning to land on Kiska, to prevent the garrison there from interfering with the planned assault on Attu, and finally, to neutralize Kiska as a threat. The majority of the missions were flown against Kiska during April and most of those planned for Attu had to be diverted to the island because of weather.

By now the air offensive against Kiska had turned into a shuttle bombing operation. The nearness of Amchitka allowed the Eleventh Air Force to take advantage of clearings in the weather to launch repeated fighter medium bomber strikes throughout the day. In addition to using bombers on the daily weather flight, fighters were now sent out at dawn to check the weather over Kiska. If it was clear, the missions were launched.

The P-40s were employed from Amchitka and the

P-38s from the island's fighter strip and from Davis Field on Adak. The Warhawks normally carried one 500-pound bomb while the Lightnings carried two 500-pound and occasionally two 1000-pound bombs. Depending on the mission, both fighters also hauled a load of 20-pound anti-personnel fragmentation bombs. The bombs were dropped during diving attacks at anywhere from five thousand to fifteen hundred feet. The longer range P-38s were also committed against Attu. The principal fighter targets were the airstrips on Kiska and Attu and the anti-aircraft gun positions.

The B-25s from the 73rd Bombardment Squadron were flown out of Davis Field while the medium bombers from the 77th Bombardment Squadron operated from the Amchitka fighter strip. The B-24s were operated from Davis Field. The bomb loads varied with the 500-pound general purpose bomb being the one most widely used. The

Nose art in the Aleutians ranged from the sublime to the profane, with most of it being in the latter category. One B-24, named "The Old Bitch," drew the anger of General Buckner who ordered the art work taken off. It was renamed "Viking Maiden." "Target for Tonight" was applied to a B 26 flown by the 15th Tow Target Squadron. John Litzenberger photo

The nose of the B-26 shows not only the art work, but also the general wear and tear of Aleutian conditions.
John Litzenberger photo

An example of less objectional art work on the nose of a B-25D. AAF photo

One of the more colorful pieces of work was "Myasis Dragon," a B-24L, 404th Bomber Squadron, flown later in the war. The photograph was taken at Elmendorf Field in 1946.
George A. Powell collection

Another example, this time Japanese characters.
Charles Pinney photo

bombs were dropped from the medium bombers between five and seven thousand feet and from the heavy bombers between thirteen and eighteen thousand feet on area targets.[384]

On April 1, the air offensive got underway when two bomber missions involving sixteen B-24s and five B-25s were flown against Kiska. Two P-38 missions, each consisting of twelve fighters, were also committed.

Two B-24 missions of eighteen bombers were flown against Kiska the next day and another mission of four B-24s was sent against Attu. A mission of six B-25s was also flown against Kiska. One of the medium bomber pilots barely missed a cable that had been strung across the pass behind the main camp by flying under it. The pilot of another B-25 collided with Lieutenant Everett W. Henriksen's medium bomber, shearing off its top turret and the roof of the pilots compartment. Henriksen and his copilot managed to fly their damaged bomber back to a safe landing on Amchitka. Five fighter missions were flown involving sixteen P-38 and twenty-four P-40 sorties.

After a break due to weather, another all day series of bomber and fighter strikes were flown against Kiska and Attu on the 5th. Another storm moved in which raged until the 10th, when five missions were launched from Amchitka against Kiska totalling three B-25 and six P-38 and seventeen P-40 sorties. Elsewhere, the crew of a PBY from VP-43 spotted two Japanese destroyers east of Attu and launched an attack. Four 500-pound bombs were dropped from five thousand feet in a glide bombing attack. The bombs failed to explode.

Four missions were flown the next day. A fifth was cancelled due to weather. Seven missions were flown on the 12th involving three bomber and thirty-seven fighter sorties. The anti-aircraft fire was heavy and four fighters were hit, three of which made it back to Amchitka. The fourth, a P-40 flown by Captain William F. Grund, 18th Fighter Squadron, made it as far as the west end of Amchitka, where Captain Grund ditched it in the ocean near Bird Cape. A crash boat, which had been dispatched to the scene, picked him up while a PBY orbited overhead.

Thirty bomber and forty-eight fighter sorties were flown in eleven missions throughout the 13th, dropping forty-three tons of bombs. The day proved unlucky for Lieutenant Edward A. Kercher who had joined the 54th Fighter Squadron as a replacement pilot in February. He was returning from a mission involving eight P-38s when Captain Harley S. Tawks and Lieutenant Royal E. McCarthy saw his Lightning slip to the right, slow up and then crash into the waters off Gareloi Island west of Tanaga Island. They and two other Lightning pilots circled. All that remained of Lieutenant Kercher and his fighter was an oil slick and some debris.

Ten missions against Kiska were flown on the 14th. All the records were broken the next day. The day began when Captain John Andrews from the 404th Bombardment Squadron and his copilot taxied their B-24 onto the runway at Davis Field, pushed the throttles forward. Their bomber began its takeoff roll at 8:00 AM. Another weather mission had been launched down the Aleutian Chain.

Captain Andrews and his crew proceeded to Kiska, arriving there at 9:55 AM. The anti-aircraft gunners on North Head slammed rounds into their cannons and Andrews counted twenty-seven flack bursts as they flew over the island at two thousand feet. The gunners on Little Kiska sent up another eight to ten rounds. After reporting that the weather was broken with fifteen hundred foot ceilings, Andrews and his crew departed the Kiska area at 10:27 and headed for Attu, which they reached at 11:32 AM. After flying a reconnaissance at one thousand feet three miles off Chichagof Harbor and Holtz Bay, the B-24 crew returned to Davis Field by way of Kiska and Amchitka.

The first bomber mission of the day, six B-24s from the 77th Bombardment Squadron arrived at 11:10 AM. Forty-eight 300-pound bombs were dropped on positions on South Head. Six bombers from the 21st Bombardment Squadron arrived next at 11:15 AM. Two hundred and ten 100-pound bombs were rained down on North Head and the main camp area from an altitude of seven thousand feet. The final mission of the morning, by three B-24s from the 36th Bombardment Squadron, arrived over Kiska at 11:17 AM. Thirty-six 500-pound bombs were dropped through holes in the clouds from an altitude of eight thousand feet. Hits were observed on targets on Little Kiska.

That afternoon, the first mission of nine B-24s from the 36th Bombardment Squadron, arrived over their targets at 5:20 PM at altitudes ranging from ninety-five hundred to fifteen thousand feet. Ninety-six 500-pound bombs were dropped on the submarine base, the radar sites and two of the stranded cargo ships in the harbor. The Japanese gunners below threw up a barrage of fire. The Liberator flown by Lieutenant Donald J. Gilliand was hit and burst into flames after its bombs had been dropped on the radar station. The bomber spun in from ten thousand feet and crashed into the waters three hundred yards east of North Head. Lieutenant Gilliand and the ten man crew, including a squadron cook who came along for the ride, perished.

Crews from the 21st Bombardment Squadron and 73rd Bombardment Squadron flew the last mission of the day. The five B-24s and six B-25s arrived on the heels of the first mission. The crews of the heavy bombers dropped one hundred and forty 100-pound bombs on North Head and the target, the landing strip, from an altitudes ranging between 10,500 and 11,500 feet. Twenty-four 500-pound bombs were dropped from the medium bombers on the anti-aircraft positions of North Head from an altitude of 8,600 feet.

The P-38 and P-40 pilots flew nine missions for a total of sixty-nine sorties. All the fighter pilots participated in at least two missions. A total of ninety-two tons of bombs ranging from 20-pound fragmentation to 500-pound general purpose bombs were dropped by the bomber crews and fighter pilots. Many hits were claimed, and when Captain Donald G. Kauffman arrived over Kiska in his F-5 to photograph the results of the raids he observed smoke pouring out of positions on Little Kiska and North Head.

For the next five days, the weather remained clear, enabling the bomber crews to fly seven missions over Kiska and two over Attu. The fighters accounted for forty-two missions, all against Kiska. Number 14 Fighter Squadron flew its first mission against Kiska on the 18th when Squadron Leader Walker led a mixed group of eight American and Canadian P-40 pilots on a bombing attack against installations on Kiska.

The weather turned sour following the raid on the 20th, and the next mission was not flown until the 24th when two P-38 pilots made it through to strafe Japanese positions in the Mutton Cove area of Kiska. The other missions planned for the day were cancelled. The attacks resumed with intensity the next day when two bomber missions were flown against Kiska and another against Attu. The fighter pilots pounded the Japanese on Kiska in eight missions.

Three more bomber and ten fighter missions were flown against Kiska on the 26th. Squadron Leader Walker led an all Canadian flight of eight P-40s on a bombing attack against positions on North Head. Each fighter carried a 300-pound demolition bomb and six 20-pound fragmentation bombs. The weather was overcast and the bombs were dropped though holes in the clouds. Three were observed exploding near the landing strip. The final two missions of the month, by the fighters, were flown on the 30th. The planned bomber missions were cancelled due to weather.

The Eleventh Air Force, during April, had flown one hundred and forty-four missions against Kiska and another five against Attu. Five thousand, seven hundred and forty bombs for a total of six hundred and thirty-eight tons had been dropped on all the installations of Kiska. Another one thousand, three hundred and forty-one bombs totaling one hundred and fifty-four tons had been dumped on the Japanese on Attu.

No Japanese air opposition was noted for the first time since the beginning of the air offensive the previous June. Additionally, other than a few barges, no shipping was observed in the harbors and bays of the two islands.

In exchange for the pounding given the Japanese on the two islands, the Eleventh Air Force lost one B-24 and its crew. Two fighters were destroyed and one pilot killed. Many aircraft returned from Kiska with battle damage, some with wounded aboard. The anti-aircraft fire over Kiska was especially heavy. One B-25 pilot, Charles Pinney remembered years later seeing the sky filled with flack bursts and looking down to see the ground below lit up with gun flashes.

No aircraft were lost over Attu where the Japanese had fewer anti-aircraft guns. Unlike Kiska, the air defenses there were less formidable. The Japanese managed to site fourteen 75mm dual purpose guns on Attu. Six were located on the West Arm area of Holtz Bay, five the East Arm area. The remainder were sited at Chichagof Harbor. Additionally, the Japanese had a plentiful supply of 20mm cannons which were effective against low flying aircraft.

Again weather had played a dominant role. Of the days available in April, only seventeen were suitable for bomber operations; and on many of the days when the crews got through, they found the conditions marginal. The weather at Attu was especially bad, and most of the missions planned for that island were diverted to Kiska.

Faulty bomb racks also plagued operations. Many of the bombers returned home with stuck bombs.[385] It was an altogether frustrating experience for the crews who had risked their lives, only to see a partial load, or worse, no bombs at all fall from their bombers over the target. Billy Wheeler, in the April 20 entry in his diary, noted: "Bad day, bombardiers practically in tears when they crawled into bed. Kiska was socked in and all three aircraft had rack problems."[386]

For the Japanese, the bombing offensive had become a nightmare. Documents captured later on Attu described the violence of the April offensive and the effect it had on morale. One noted that:

> Due to frequent enemy attacks we dream of enemy planes in our sleep and during our meals. The only really peaceful time that we can enjoy our meals and baths on Kiska Island is when the weather is stormy and then all the soldiers have pleasant expressions on their faces and they sing their military songs loudly.[387]

Another described the effects of the bombing, stating:

> Bombing is getting more violent month after month. The bombing technique used is not so superior, but if you drop enough of them there is bound to be some damage. Loss of personnel, installations, air defense arms, fuel and fire-arms influence us considerably, and it is deplorable that even the AA guns gradually lose their hitting efficiency.[388]

I Am To Die Here

While the Japanese suffered under the incessant bombing attacks, the Attu invasion force departed their West Coast ports on April 23 and 24. Envelopes were ripped open and their classified contents divulged to the men who were to assault the lonely island at the end of the Aleutian Chain. It ended the speculation on where they were going.

The Attu assault force (Task Force 51) dropped anchor in Cold Bay on May 1. The place lived up to its name. The men standing on deck were treated to a view of bleak snow-covered mountains and the sight of a huddled group of buildings on the shore line. Marine Captain John Elliott noted in his diary: "The ships look out of place in a world that belongs so little to man." While Admirals Kinkaid and Rockwell and their staffs made the final arrangements, the men conducted disembarkation drills and prepared themselves for the ordeal.

Admiral Rockwell ordered "up anchors," and his task force of 29 ships steamed out into the storm-lashed North Pacific. The force proceeded to Amukta Pass and entered the Bering Sea, sailing well north to avoid being detected by the Japanese on Kiska. The battleships and the other warships sped ahead to sweep the waters around Attu of any Japanese ships in the area. Finding none, they rejoined the rest of Task Force 51 on the evening of May 10 for the final run to the waters off the invasion beaches.[389]

Admiral Kinkaid, in preparation for the invasion, had placed all Alaskan based air units under the control of General Butler and Task Force 16.1 was formed April 21. The task force was further broken down into two entities. Task Force 16.1.1 was made up of the Army units and was responsible for neutralizing Japanese positions on Attu and Kiska, taking aerial photographs for intelligence use, serving as a reserve striking force and providing a combat air patrol during the battle to retake the island.

Task Force 16.1.2, composed of Fleet Air Wing Four, was responsible for flying patrols and providing antisubmarine coverage for the amphibious assault force. The *Nassau*, operating independently of General Butler, was responsible for close air support. Finally, the float aircraft from the cruisers and battleships were to be used to direct naval gunfire. The plan called for Admiral Rockwell to retain control of air operations until General Brown's forces were established on the island. At that point, the control would pass to General Brown.

Colonel Eareckson, back from the joint planning sessions at San Diego, was given the responsibility for coordinating the air activities over the island. A B-24 was placed at his disposal to serve as an airborne command and communications center during the battle. Liaison officers were exchanged and six forward air control parties

were assigned to the 7th Infantry Division.[390]

Colonel DeFord moved an advance post of the XI Bombardment Command to Amchitka on May 1. By now the engineers had completed constructing a five thousand foot long bomber strip. The 36th Bombardment Squadron was the first heavy bomber unit to be moved forward. The ground echelon arrived in late April to prepare for the arrival of the B-24s. They came thundering in on May 4, the same day General Buckner's third star was pinned on. Lieutenant Billy Wheeler recalled:

The first heavy bomber formation to land topside on the new strip at Amchitka departed from Adak at 0700 (7:00 AM) under a low overcast. Speer, Wernick, Brown, Katz, Davis, Francine and Sweet flew low over the 36th's new, tent studded area and buzzed it in the best p-shooter fashion as wondering dogfaces gaped wide-eyed and slack-jawed below. These same Air Corps glamour boys cursed and fumed shortly after landing as they struggled through mud and water to reach the tent area. No roads to this area existed: the most direct route to the tents led through numerous small lakes, and so did most of the indirect routes. We packed our barracks bags, B-4 bags, and foot lockers on our back, and settled down to life in tents again.[391]

Five of the original nurses who participated in the evacuation of the wounded from Attu were awarded the Air Medal a year later by Maj Gen Davenport Johnson, who succeeded General Butler as Commander, Eleventh Air Force. From left to right they are: Lieut Anna R. Hoover, Lieut Betsy Bradford, Lieut Helen F. Lyon, Lieut Alta M. Thompson and Lieut Winifred R. Zirkle. Lieutenant Ruth M. Gardiner was killed on July 26, 1943 when the transport she was flying in crashed near Naknek while en route to pick up patients. Gardiner General Hospital in Chicago was named in her honor.
AAF photo

Liberators from the 21st Bombardment Squadron were also dispatched to Amchitka as reinforcements. The 404th Bombardment Squadron remained at Davis Field, its crews given a reprieve from combat for the moment.

Navy nurses visiting with pilots of the 54th Fighter Squadron at Attu, Christmas 1944. From left to right, they are: Ensigns Elizabeth Morgan, Elaine E. Gallagher and Annabel McConnel. AAF photo

By early May there were 10,260 Army and 903 Navy personnel on Amchitka. Another 19,067 Army and 7,811 Navy personnel were on Adak. On the eve of the invasion General Butler's forces were concentrated on the two islands with twelve B-24s at Adak and sixteen at Amchitka. Twenty of the thirty B-25s were at Amchitka and the remainder at Adak. The entire 54th Fighter Squadron and all but two of its twenty-six P-38s and all three F-5s occupied the fighter strip area. Of the eighty P-40s, twenty-three were at Amchitka, twenty-two at Davis Field and the remainder operated out of Cape Field. The rest of the two hundred and twenty-nine aircraft assigned to the Eleventh Air Force were scattered throughout Alaska.[392]

On April 30, in anticipation of casualties at Attu, Flight A, 805th Medical Air Evacuation Squadron arrived at Elmendorf Field. Commanded by Captain George E. Johnson, it consisted of six flight nurses and eight enlisted men. The two troop carrier squadrons were assigned the mission of air evacuating the wounded from Attu. Flight A made its first trip to the Aleutians on May 18 to recover wounded. The event marked the first presence of women nurses in the Aleutians.[393]

The air offensive for May got off to a good start, when sixteen bomber and fighter missions were flown against all the Japanese installations on Kiska. More missions were flown against the island during the next two days. On the 4th, the 36th Bombardment Squadron, in its first mission from Amchitka, launched five B-24s against Attu. The crews bombed targets in the Chichagof Harbor area where the Japanese had established their headquarters. More bombs were dropped on the anti-aircraft positions at Holtz Bay.

A mission of eight P-38s and two F-5s was also flown. One flight strafed positions at Chichagof Harbor while the other conducted dive bombing attacks against the gun positions at Holtz Bay while the two F-5 pilots took aerial photographs. Elsewhere, a mission of six B-25s was turned back by the weather at Kiska.

With the invasion of Attu scheduled to occur within a week, priority was assigned to the island. Four missions were flown against the Japanese on the 5th which involved forty-nine sorties by fourteen B-24s, seventeen B-25s, sixteen P-38s and two F-5s. It was the heaviest going over that the Japanese on Attu received since their occupation of the island. While the strikes were being carried out against Attu, four P-40 missions involving thirty-two sorties including eight by Number 14 Fighter Squadron were flown against all the installations on Kiska. All the missions of the day were flown from Amchitka. For the first time, no missions were flown from Davis Field.

The next day, beginning at 9:55 AM and lasting throughout the day, all the targets on Attu were hit by two B-24 missions flown by twelve B-24s and two missions of an equal number of B-25s. The P-38s were also committed. A total of fifty-two bombs were dropped in what was the last air attack before the 7th Infantry Division landed on the 11th. Five P-40 missions involving thirty-two sorties were flown against Kiska.[394]

Number 14 Fighter Squadron flew its last mission for the month on the 6th. Pilots from Number 111 arrived at Adak on the 4th bringing with them their eight P-40Ks. The next day, the four section leaders flew on to Amchitka where they were briefed for a mission planned for the 7th. Number 14 Fighter Squadron was deployed to Cape Field, Umnak on May 15 after participating in fourteen missions against Kiska.[395]

The storm that halted the missions planned for the 7th also ended all missions against Kiska and Attu until the 11th. In preparation for the invasion, the men of the Eleventh Air Force had flown thirty-nine missions against Kiska and another twenty-three against Attu. Some 154.5 tons of bombs had been dropped on Kiska and another 95 tons on Attu.

Aleutian weather had played havoc with plans to soften up Attu. Between April 1, when the offensive was begun, until the landing on May 11, there were only eight suitable days in which missions could be flown against the island. Compared to the 792.3 tons dropped on Kiska during the period, the 155 tons dropped on Attu appeared insignificant.[396]

Colonel Eareckson arrived at Amchitka on May 7 to brief the bomber crews on what was expected of them on the forthcoming missions against Attu. The men of the Eleventh Air Force waited. Billy Wheeler's one diary entry for May 7 through 10 was: "grounded, weather."[397]

While General Butler's bombers and fighters pounded Kiska and Attu, Commodore Gehres' PBY crews had continued to fly their monotonous, but dangerous patrols over

A Lockheed PV-1 Ventura,
Fleet Air Wing Four. USN photo

Lockheed C-56 Loadstar,
Aleutians. AAF photo

the icy waters of the North Pacific and Bering Sea. In preparation for the pending invasion of Attu, Gehres moved his headquarters to Adak from Kodiak in late March. His patrol squadrons had already begun to shift forward. VP-43 moved to Adak on February 7 to join VP-62; and on February 23, the first PBY-5A landing on the fighter strip at Amchitka was recorded. It prophesied a change to land base operations.

The two original Alaskan squadrons, VP-41 and VP-42, had turned their PBYs over to the other squadrons in late January and departed for Whidbey Naval Air Station, Washington where they were decommissioned. Their pilots and crew members provided the experienced cadre for two new squadrons, VB-135 and VB-136, which were formed at Whidbey. Both were equipped with the Lockheed PV-1 Ventura bomber-reconnaissance aircraft.

The Ventura was a derivative of the Lockheed Electra commercial passenger plane from which the Hudson bomber reconnaissance and C-56 Loadstar passenger planes were also developed. The Ventura was powered by two 2000 horsepower Pratt and Whitney R-2800-31 Double Wasp engines which gave it a top speed of 312 miles per hour. It was equipped with two 50 caliber machine guns mounted in a Martin turret, another two 50 caliber

machine guns in the nose and two 30 caliber machine guns mounted in its underside, near the tail. The Ventura could carry three thousand pounds of bombs and had a range of 1,660 miles.

To achieve the extended range, the Lockheed engineers had crammed fuel tanks in every empty place they could find. Counting bomb bay tanks, the crew had to contend with eleven different tanks and associated pumps and plumbing. Although a patched up affair, the Ventura was a highly effective plane with many of the characteristics of a fighter. The Navy ordered sixteen hundred of them.

VB-135 and VB-136 arrived at Kodiak on April 3 and 25 respectively with a total of thirty PV-1s. The two squadrons were joined on April 27 by an advance detachment of five PBY-5s from VP-45. By early May, Commodore Gehres had completed deploying his squadrons forward where they could best support the Attu operations. VP-43, VP-45, VP-62 and VB-136 were at Adak while VP-61 and VB-135 were at Amchitka.[398]

By the early morning hours of May 11, all the forces were poised for America's third amphibious operation of the war. For the Army and for the men of the 7th Infantry Division, it was to be their first experience at assaulting an island from the sea.

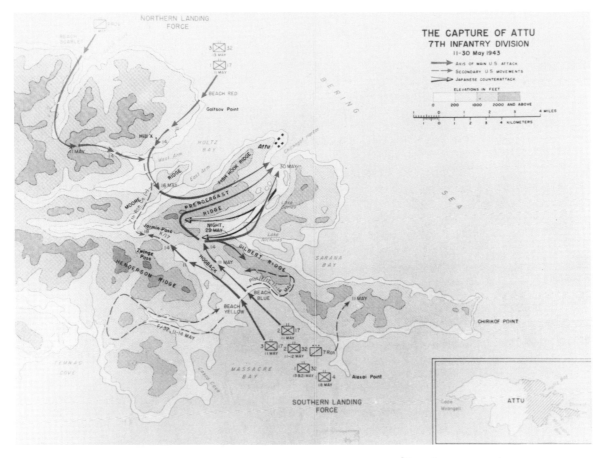

Map of movements, Attu

The Americans had developed five invasion plans. The one that was picked, drawn up by Colonel Alexander of General Buckner's staff and favored by General Brown, called for the landings at three separate locations.

The southern force under the command of Colonel Edward D. Earl and consisting of the 2nd and 3rd Infantry Battalions of the 17th Infantry Regiment and the 2nd Battalion of the 32nd Infantry Regiment reinforced by three 105mm artillery batteries was to be landed on the beaches at Massacre Bay. From there, it was to advance up the valley and seize the passes leading into Holtz Bay and Chichagof Harbor and link up with the northern force in Jarmin Pass separating Massacre Bay from Holtz Bay.

The northern force commanded by Colonel Frank L. Culin, consisting of the 1st Battalion, 17th Infantry Regiment under the command of Lieutenant Colonel Albert V Hartl, and a 105mm artillery battery was to go ashore at the West Arm of Holtz Bay, three miles north of the Japanese main camp. From there it would move overland to seize the high ground on Moore Ridge behind the Japanese camp before continuing its advance towards Jarmin Pass.

A third smaller force of five hundred men, commanded by Captain William Willoughby, composed of the division scout and reconnaissance companies, was to be landed by submarines *Narwhal* and *Nautilus* and destroyer *Kane* at Austin Cove on northeast side of the island. It was to ad-

vance across the mountains and attack the Japanese artillery positions at the head of the West Arm from the rear and then link up with Culin's force.

Once the link-ups were completed, the combined forces were to wheel east and push the Japanese off the high ground towards the Chichagof Harbor area where they would be destroyed by naval bombardment and aerial attacks. It was a classic maneuver of double envelopment. General DeWitt estimated the operation would take three days to complete. He and General Buckner, although not directly involved in the assault on Attu, had come along as observers since it was their forces that were being committed.[399]

On Attu, the Japanese waited. By now they had learned though a slip in the American security system that Attu would be invaded in early May. Vice Admiral Shiro Kawase, who had replaced Admiral Hosogaya, decided to defer sending reinforcements to Attu until the end of the month when fog conditions would be better and the project to equip his ships with radar completed. In the interim, he ordered Colonel Yamasaki, who had arrived by submarine in April, to hold out at all cost.

The stoic colonel ordered his troops to speed up preparing their defenses in the Holtz Bay and Chichagof Harbor areas and sent Lieutenants Hitoshi Honna and Yutake Goto, commanders of 2nd and 4th Companies, 303rd In-

The aerial photograph taken from a B-24 indicates the difficulty experienced by Captain Willoughby and his men. Holtz Bay divided by Moore Ridge can be seen in the distance. AAF photo

The photograph of the Chichagof Harbor, far left, and Holtz Bay center, was taken from Colonel Eareckson's B-24 on May 12.
Larry Reineke collection

Troops leave the attack transport Heywood (APA-6) the afternoon of May 11 for the beaches of Attu. USA photo

The seas off Attu were rough and the carrier was small, but there were brave men with a sense of duty who overcame the difficulties. In order to take advantage of infrequent clearings in the weather, Captain Doyle operated the Nassau within forty miles of the battle areas while on station off Attu. USN photo

A Wildcat flies past the Nassau. The photograph was taken from a B-24.
Larry Reineke collection

Pilots of VF-21 on return from Attu. Ted Condo collection

dependent Infantry Battalion to the head of Massacre Valley where they prepared defensive positions blocking access to Clevesy Pass. The two officers and their men dug in along Gilbert Ridge high above the valley floor and waited. From their vantage points above the fog line they controlled the routs into Chichagof Harbor and Jarmin Pass.[400]

The fog had rolled in, obscuring Attu from view of the assault forces that stood off the landing beaches of Holtz and Massacre Bays. The men waited in their landing barges until late afternoon when the order came through to head for the beaches. The fog still hung heavy in the air, hiding the landing beaches ahead as the coxswains aboard the landing craft slowly groped their way towards the undefended beaches.[401]

The fog also hampered air support operations on which part of the strategy for retaking the island hinged. A B-24 mission of nine bombers and two B-25 missions, each with six bombers, had been planned.

The B-24s under the command of Captain Speer from the 36th Bombardment Squadron arrived over Holtz Bay to find it covered by fog. Except for the crews of two B-24s who did not receive word that the mission was cancelled, the rest turned and headed for Kiska where they dropped their bombs before proceeding back to Amchitka. The two B-24 crews at Attu unloaded their bombs on Chichagof Harbor area and headed home. The crews of the B-25s never made it to Attu. Instead, Eareckson ordered them to bomb Kiska.

A final mission, flown by a lone B-24 on a resupply mission, arrived over Captain Willoughby's forces. Lieutenant Anthony N. Brannan's crew from the 21st Bombardment Squadron threw out the supplies. The wind caught the parachutes and the suspended bundles drifted out of reach of the men below, who by now had taken a wrong turn and were lost among the tangle of ridges and ravines behind Holtz Bay.[402]

The trip out to Attu from Cold Bay had been rough on the *Nassau*. Huge waves swept over her deck and the tiny escort carrier bobbed like a cork in the rough Aleutian waters. Captain Doyle's ships crew, many of whom were veterans of the *Lexington* who had been transferred to the *Nassau* after the sinking of their carrier at Coral Sea, managed the voyage without undue problems. By the morning of May 11, the *Nassau* was in position off Holtz Bay where she would operate anywhere from ten to forty miles off the coast during the next two weeks.

Captain Doyle began launching the first of three missions planned for the day at 6:23 AM in support of the Holtz Bay landing. Two of the missions consisted of eight and seven F4F-4 Wildcats respectively from VF-21. The third mission was composed of a mixed quartet of F4F-3P photo planes from VMO-155 and F4F-4 escorts. They were the first close air support missions flown from an aircraft carrier during the war.

Lieutenant Commander Greenamyer's VC-21 fighter pilots were relatively inexperienced at the business of close air support. The had received less than a week of training. Frustrated at not being able to see any ground targets because of the fog, several pilots spotted the rubber boats used by Captain Willoughby's party to land at Austin Cove and strafed them. Two others, unable to get back to the carrier, ditched their fighters near the destroyers *Aylwin* and *Monaghan*. Both pilots were quickly picked up. Several more Wildcats were damaged during the landings on the carrier and one, an F4F-3P, had to be pushed over the side.[403]

Air operations during the first day had been poor, primarily due to weather. They did not improve much during the succeeding weeks as the men of the 7th Infantry Division, poorly trained and equipped and new to the terrible ordeal of ground combat, battered themselves against well prepared positions manned by an enemy willing to fight to the death.

By the end of the second day of battle, the American admirals and generals sadly realized that the recapture of Attu would take far longer than the three days that General DeWitt had predicted.

Colonel Earl's force had advanced twenty-five hundred yards up Massacre Valley only to run into the determined opposition of the men led by Lieutenants Honna and Goto. The Japanese with two infantry companies of less than a hundred men each and a smaller number of supporting combat forces had stopped a task force of three thousand men consisting of three infantry battalions and three artillery batteries supported by the fire power of the *Nevada* and a host of lesser warships dead in its tracks.

Colonel Culin's northern force had managed to advance as far as Hill X overlooking the west arm where it also, despite the fire support of two battleships and a destroyer, became bogged down in the face of determined Japanese opposition. Captain Willoughby's force, lost and out of the action, continued to grope its way towards the Japanese rear positions at Holtz Bay.[404]

General Buckner had predicted that the battle to retake Attu would be tough, and "the soldiers, the infantry, will have to go in there with corkscrews to dig out the Japs."[405]

The weather cleared enough on the 12th for a mission of six B-24s and two missions consisting of six B-25s to get through. Colonel Eareckson, orbiting overhead in a B-24, directed the crews to drop their bombs on the landing strip and 75mm dual purpose gun positions in the Holtz Bay area. Three P-38 combat air patrol missions, each consisting of six aircraft escorted by a B-24, were flown over Attu to guard the forces below from an air attack by the Japanese. The 54th Fighter Squadron continued to maintain its fighters over the island, weather permitting, throughout the battle. The Lightnings were also flown in support of the ground forces.

Colonel Eareckson committed one the P-38 flights against Japanese positions in the Chichagof Harbor area. The Lightning pilots zoomed in at low level, dropping their 500-pound bombs and 20-pound fragmentation bombs on the Japanese positions. The P-38 flown by Lieutenant Robert A. Baker was hit by anti-aircraft fire. With the right engine on fire, Baker headed out into Holtz Bay where he ditched his fighter. The nearby destroyer *Phelps* sped to his, rescue. Within twenty-five minutes he was safely aboard, well along on recovering from the icy dunking.[406]

Lieutenant Brannan went looking for Captain Willoughby's force and found it. One of the crew members threw out a map providing Willoughby with directions to the Holtz Bay area along with the supplies. The map was found caught in the tail section when Brannan landed at Amchitka. Billy Wheeler noted in his diary: "The lost map had cost the Willoughby party unnecessary casualties and a crew of a B-24."[407]

Two days later, the 14th, Brannan headed in for another supply drop to Willoughby's forces. His bomber slammed into a mountain side behind Holtz Bay. All eleven men aboard died. They were later found by a party of infantrymen who buried their bodies near the bomber wreck.[408]

Two missions were launched from the *Nassau* on the 12th. The first was flown in support of the northern force, struggling to gain the heights of Hill X. The Wildcat pilots strafed the Japanese positions and dropped 100-pound "daisy cutter" bombs which had been designed to explode above the ground by adding a twenty inch extension to the bombs' nose fuses. The next mission consisted of nine Wildcats, which were launched in the late afternoon. The pilots went after several Japanese barges in Holtz Bay

A B-25D and a destroyer off the coast of Attu.
Larry Reineke collection

PBY-5s, VP-45, Casco Cove, Attu, May 1943. The air field was later built at the base of the mountain. USN photo via AAHM

One of the battle damaged OS2U Kingfishers. USN photo

from which the Japanese had been reported firing at the Americans ashore.[409]

Fleet Air Wing Four continued to fly long-range patrols and provide anti-submarine patrols over the waters near Attu. The *Casco* was moved into a cove in Massacre Bay that would later bear its name. The tender supported six PBYs from VP-45, another four from VP-61, and four OS2U Kingfishers from the battleships. The Kingfishers were used to spot naval gunfire, fly anti-submarine patrols, and on occasion, to provide close air support for the ground forces. For the latter, they were equipped with depth charges to which instantaneous fuses had been affixed.

On the late afternoon of the 12th, Lieutenant Rex Jolly's crew from VP-61 spotted the I-31 launching a torpedo at the *Pennsylvania*. They alerted the battleship crew in time for them to take evasive action. Jolly then went after the Japanese submarine by following the torpedo wake. After dropping depth charges and smoke lights, Jolly teamed up with the destroyers *Edwards* and *Farragut* to hunt for and destroy the I-31. The trio found the submarine around midnight. Depth charges brought the I-31 to the surface and the gunners aboard the destroyers began firing at her. However, the captain of the submarine was able to slip away in the darkness.[410]

The next day, the 13th, Colonel Eareckson arrived over

the battlefield to find it obscured by fog and turned back for Davis Field. Six B-24s were diverted and sent to Kiska. The crews of two bombers failed to hear the orders and continued on, blindly dropping their bombs on the Chichagof Harbor Holtz Bay areas. Elsewhere, two P-40 missions were flown against Little Kiska.[411]

On the ground, the men of the 7th Infantry Division continued to batter themselves against the Japanese defenses. The fourteen inch guns of the battleships thundered, hurling their shells into the ridge-lines and hill sides above the Americans, gouging out great chunks of earth, and occasionally sending pieces of bodies and equipment tumbling down the slopes. The Japanese hung on. Colonel Yamasaki reinforced his positions overlooking Massacre Valley. The Japanese, dug into positions above the fog line, poured down a withering fire. Within a two-day period, the Americans had suffered forty-four killed including Colonel Earl. It was only the beginning.[412]

The 14th was a clear day, and it turned out to be a bad one for the Wildcat pilots. Four were airborne at mid-day when a call came through that there was an unknown flight of planes heading for Attu. Eight more Wildcats were launched, one of which crashed into the sea. The destroyer *Aylwin* rushed over to pickup the wet and shivering pilot.

The alarm proved false. The planes were American. The Wildcat pilots were directed to attack positions on Attu. Four headed up Massacre Valley to drop their bombs ahead of the advancing American troops. As they streaked over the valley floor, a vicious williwaw swept down from the passes, hurling the two lead planes thousands of feet into the air and slamming the two trailing fighters flown by Douglas Henderson and Ernest D. Jackson into the ground. Both died. Lieutenant Commander Greenamyer,

An alert cameraman caught one of the Wildcats moments before it slammed into the ground. Colonel Talley, who was nearby, remembered a loud sound of an engine at full power. He looked up to see the fighter, out of control, coming out of the mist. USN photo

leading another attack against Japanese positions in the Sarana Bay area, disappeared, the apparent victim of anti-aircraft fire.[413]

Elsewhere, a mission of six B-24s and a mission of five B-25s succeeded in getting through from Amchitka. The crews dropped their bombs on the East Arm areas of Holtz Bay. No P-38 missions were flown over Attu because of the weather. A nuisance mission of two P-40s was flown against Kiska.[414]

By the 15th, the situation on the ground had reached an apparent stalemate. The Japanese were not budging despite repeated attacks and the bombardment by the battleships, two of which had run out of 14-inch-high explosive shells. Admirals Kinkaid and Rockwell were fearful for the safety of their ships. In addition to the attack on the *Pennsylvania*, another torpedo attack was made on the transport *J. Franklin Bell* from the two to three Japanese submarines lurking in the area. Fortunately, the four torpedoes missed their target.

Admiral Kawase also fretted. Colonel Yamasaki's notification that the Americans had landed set him in motion. He ordered the 24th Air Flotilla at Paramushiro to launch an attack with their Betty bombers and the captain of the *Kimikawa Maru* to dispatch his planes on a similar mission.

Elsewhere, the Japanese began forming a large armada that included the giant battleship *Musashi* and the carriers *Zuikaku* and *Shokaku* with the intention in engaging the Americans in a climactic naval battle in the north. The force, drawn from various locations in the Pacific, was being assembled in Tokyo Bay when Attu fell. All of this activity was not lost on Admirals Kinkaid and Rockwell, whose intelligence officers fed them a steady stream of intercepted and decoded Japanese naval messages.[415]

General Brown asked for more troops and road building equipment so that he could expedite the resupply of his beleaguered forces at the head of Massacre Valley. The request coming on the heels of the latest Japanese intelligence worried Admiral Kinkaid. Instead of the quick three day battle, the efforts to retake Attu were apparently turning into a protracted siege requiring the construction of roads and the other elaborate infrastructures of war. With the battle now into its fourth day, he decided to relieve General Brown in hopes a more aggressive and Alaska experienced general would break the deadlock.

His decision was based on incomplete information and the general frustration that the Japanese opposition was not at all like that briefed to him by his intelligence staff. Major General Eugene Landrum, who had commanded the occupation of Adak, arrived at Attu on the late afternoon of May 16 to assumed command. General Brown departed for Adak and a meeting with Admiral Kinkaid whom he had never met. To add more Aleutian expertise to his staff, Landrum brought with him Colonel Castner as his chief of staff. Colonel Wayne C. Zimmermann, the former division chief of staff, had been sent forward to replace the slain Colonel Earl.[416]

General Landrum's arrival coincided with the turning point in the battle. Colonel Yamasaki had decided on May 15 to evacuate the Holtz Bay area and transfer the forces to Chichagof Harbor. The dogged determination of Colonel Culin's men, the intense naval gunfire and the air strikes had made Japanese defense of the area untenable. At the same time, Captain Willoughby's force had fought its way out of the mountains to link up with the Culin's force.[417]

The weather cleared enough on the 15th for air strikes to be flown against the Holtz Bay and Chichagof areas. Six B-24s arrived from Amchitka. Bombs were dropped on the two areas. Strafing missions were carried out against the anti-aircraft positions at Holtz Bay by P-38s. No missions were flown from the *Nassau* because of the weather.[418]

Moore Ridge, separating the West and East Arm of Holtz Bay, held the key to the defense of the area. Stanley Titus photo

On the 16th, Colonel Culin, taking advantage of the fact that the Japanese had abandoned their West Arm camp, launched an assault to take Moore Ridge. The weather had cleared sufficiently so that the Wildcats from the *Nassau* could be flown in support of his attack. Fifteen were launched in two missions. Two did not return. Francis R. Register crashed into Holtz Bay after making a strafing run, and Marine Lieutenant Waldo P. Breeden from VMO-155 spun into the sea just after taking off from the carrier.

In addition to striking Japanese positions, several of the Wildcat pilots mistook a number of Culin's men moving across the rocky terrain in advance of the others to be Japanese and strafed and bombed them, causing a considerable number of casualties before attacks could be stopped.[419]

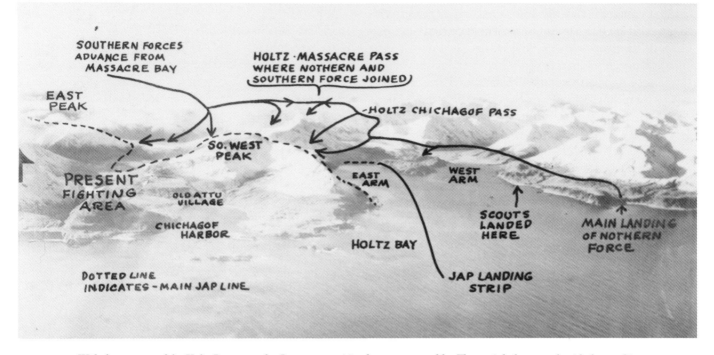

With the capture of the Holtz Bay area, the Japanese position became untenable. The aerial photograph with the markings graphically illustrates the progress of the battle. AAF photo

The Eleventh Air Force bombers were also committed on the 16th. However, of the one B-24, two B-25 and three P-38 missions that were planned, only the Lightnings, which were sent on combat air patrols, succeeded in completing their assignments. The bombers were diverted to Kiska and the P-38 pilots, once their patrol duties were over, strafed the Japanese positions and the Japanese who were making their way over the ridges to the east of Holtz Bay into Chichagof Harbor.[420]

By the end of the day, Moore Ridge was in American hands. From its summit, Culin's men dominated the rest of the Holtz Bay area. By the 17th, the Japanese had evacuated the rest of the Holtz Bay area, and on the 18th patrols from the northern and southern forces met in Jarmin Pass. The turning point of the battle to retake Attu had been reached. The next stage of the battle involved a series of hard fought battles to take one by one the series of ridges separating Massacre Valley from the last Japanese stronghold in Chichagof Harbor.[421]

Two air support missions were attempted on the 16th, but recalled due to weather. The next day another attempt was made to strike Attu, this time by six B-24s. Again, the mission was turned back and sent to bomb Gertrude Cove on Kiska. Four P-40s from the 11th Fighter Squadron in their last combat mission of the war were committed against Kiska.[422]

The venerable *Saint Mihiel* arrived and the 4th Infantry Regiment was landed on the 17th to join in the battle and take some of the pressure off the 7th Infantry Division.

Two days later, Admiral Kinkaid informed Admiral Rockwell that the amphibious phase of the battle was over. With it, the control of air operations was passed to General Landrum. All the ships, except three destroyers and the gunboat *Charleston*, which were needed for gun support, were withdrawn. General Landrum launched an assault against Clevesy Pass.

By the 20th, Colonel Zimmermann's forces had broken through. The next day, Point Able on Gilbert Ridge overlooking Massacre Valley was taken, clearing the area of

The Japanese can be seen as small dots as they make their way up a snow field towards Chichagof Harbor following the order to evacuate the Holtz Bay area. Bertrand Hoak collection

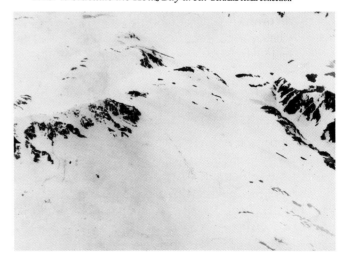

the last vestiges of the Japanese. Lieutenant Honna, who along with Goto and their men had held up the American advance for six days, was killed. He had served with great honor.[423]

With the *Nassau* gone, the Eleventh Air Force assumed the entire responsibility for supporting the ground forces on Attu. After a two day absence because of the weather, the attacks were resumed on the 19th, when six B-24s and eleven B-25s were committed in three missions against Japanese positions in the Sarana Valley area in preparations for the assaults against Clevesy Pass and Point Able. Colonel Eareckson had by now switched to a Kingfisher as a more suitable aircraft for controlling air strikes.

No missions were flown on the 20th due to weather, and of the ten B-24s, twelve B-25s and twenty-four P-38s dispatched to Attu the next day, only one B-24 and the six P-38s succeeded in attacking their targets. The weather was equally bad the next day, and no missions were flown as the ground forces advanced across Sarana Valley in a three pronged attack to seize the high ground behind Chichagof Harbor.[424]

There were thirty-six fighters and a equal number of Mitsubishi G4M1 Betty twin engine bombers assigned to the 24th Air Flotilla commanded by Rear Admiral Yamada. On the afternoon of the 22nd, twelve of the medium bombers came barreling out of the mist at low level, headed for the destroyer *Phelps* and the *Charleston* stationed outside of Chichagof Harbor. After launching their torpedoes, which missed the targets, the Japanese bombers headed for Chichagof Harbor where bundles were seen being dropped.[425]

The next day, Admiral Yamada sent sixteen of his bombers to Attu. They were spotted by a PBY crew on patrol west of the island, who passed their location to Lieutenant Colonel James R. Watt. The Commander, 343rd Fighter Group had taken off from Amchitka at 1:35 PM at the head of a flight of P-38s flown by Lieutenants Warren B. Banks, John K. Geddes, Harry C. Higgins, Marshall E. Hyde and Frederick Moore Jr. for a combat air patrol over Attu. It was the third and final patrol mission of the day.

Colonel Watt and his men were over Sarana Bay when they received word of the approaching Japanese bombers.

The Lightning pilots sighted the Japanese at 3:40 PM over the middle of the island at fourteen thousand feet. They were spotted by the bomber crews at the same time, who dropped their bombs and turned for Paramushiro. In the ensuing running air battle that lasted for approximately twenty-five minutes, five of the Betty medium bombers were shot down and seven were seen trailing smoke as they headed for their base at Paramushiro.

Colonel Watt, who was given credit for one bomber, radioed that his fighter's controls were vibrating badly and

Lieut Frederick Moore Jr. was credited with shooting down three Mitsubishi G4M1 Betty medium bombers west of Attu. It was the highest score achieved by a fighter pilot during the Aleutian Campaign. AAF photo

his right engine was losing its coolant. He disappeared on the way back to Amchitka. As Lieutenant Geddes pressed his attack, the entire right side of his canopy blew up, apparently struck by a 20mm shell. Geddes prayed and nursed his barely controllable fighter back to Attu, where he ditched off the coast. Navy Lieutenant Ferguson landed his Kingfisher and pulled the grateful fighter pilot from the water.

Lieutenant Higgins, after several passes at the retreating bombers, observed one go out of control and plunge to the sea below. He was given credit for one. Lieutenant Moore, who had decided against a stern attack to avoid the lethal 20mm cannon in the bomber's tail, climbed above the bombers, did a half roll and then dove at them at high speed. The tactic worked, and Moore succeeded in shooting down three bombers, the highest score for any Aleutian fighter pilot in a single day. Lieutenant Hyde experienced engine problems and was unable to keep up with the retreating bombers.[426]

The aerial victories over Attu were the last of the Aleutian Campaign. The fighter pilots accounted for thirty-four Japanese aircraft shot down during the Aleutian Campaign. The Eleventh Air Force claimed the destruction of approximately fifty-seven enemy aircraft, including those destroyed on the surface and by bomber gunners.

Of the thirty-four aerial victories that were validated, the 54th Fighter Squadron received credit for fourteen;

the 11th Fighter Squadron for seven; the 42nd Fighter Squadron, six; the 57th Fighter Squadron, three; the 18th Fighter Squadron, two; the 56th Fighter Squadron, one; and headquarters (Colonel Watt), 343rd Fighter Group, one. More Rufes, fifteen, were shot down than any other type. The other Japanese aircraft downed in aerial victories included six Jakes, five Bettys, four Vals, two Mavises, one Dave and one Zero.

The victories were concentrated in periods of intense air activity. Five Japanese aircraft were shot down during the Dutch Harbor attacks and sixteen during the September and October 1942 air offensive against Kiska. Six were destroyed in aerial conflict during the futile attempts by the Japanese to bomb Amchitka. Five occurred during the battle to retake Attu.

Claims for the shooting down of two Kawanishi H6K4 Mavis flying boats during the Japanese attempt to interfere with a planned naval bombardment of Kiska in early August 1942 were validated. However, Capt. Sukemitsu Ito, Imperial Japanese Navy, and Commander of the Toko Seaplane Squadron claimed during his post war interrogation by Capt. James S. Russell that none of his aircraft were lost to aerial combat.

The Aleutian Campaign produced no aces. Only two pilots, Captains Laven and Rice, achieved two aerial victories and Lieutenant Moore was the only one to shoot down three Japanese planes. The remainder were credited with one and in some cases shared in a victory. Of the fighters employed, the P-38s accounted for fifteen Japanese aircraft, the P-39s for ten and the P-40s for nine.[427]

Five Eleventh Air Force aircraft, a P-39, two P-40, a B-17 and a B-24 were shot down by Japanese fighters, and two P-38s and an OA-10 probably fell victims to enemy air attacks. Fleet Air Wing Four lost four PBYs to Japanese air attacks and another to a strafing attack during the Dutch Harbor raids.[428]

The Japanese in turn claimed their fighters shot down one B-17, four B-24s, nine P-38s, six P-39s, two PBYs and six other aircraft during the Aleutian Campaign. The figures do not include those aircraft downed during the Dutch Harbor attacks.[429]

The weather lifted at Attu on the 24th, allowing air strikes to be flown against Fish Hook Ridge in support of an infantry assault on the high ground overlooking Chichagof Harbor. Strikes were also flown against nearby Buffalo Ridge to the east. The first mission of six B-24s arrived shortly after noon, followed by another mission of five B-25s. Fourteen P-38s were committed to three combat air patrol missions, following the completion of which their pilots strafed Japanese positions on the ridges.

The planes crisscrossed the area all afternoon, the infantrymen, supported by artillery and naval bombardment hurled themselves against the Japanese dug into the side of the ridge line. Anti-aircraft fire was light and the bombers struck at low level, their gunners raking the Japanese positions with machine gun fire. Howard Handleman, a news reporter and author who observed the attacks, later reported that it was "the best air show of the war for Attu." Billy Wheeler noted in his diary that the bomber crews "had a field day."[430]

The attacks were marred by the accidental bombing of American positions by one of the B-24s. The troops below on the floor of Sarana Valley looked up in time to see the bombs falling out of the open bomb bay. Other than one shaken machine gunner, who had to be dug out of a collapsed trench, no damage was done. That and the Wildcat attack on the 16th were the only incidents where friendly troops on Attu were attacked by their own aircraft. It was remarkable that no other such incidents occurred, considering the problems posed by the weather and terrain. It was also a tribute to the air-ground procedures that had been worked out prior to the battle and the presence of Colonel Eareckson over the battle fields.

For the aircrews, the day was a success. Over fifteen tons of bombs had been dropped and not an aircraft lost. From their vantage point over the islands, they could see the first sights of Spring appearing as large patches of green grass against the snowy background.[431]

For the men down in the mud and cold of their own private hell, it was a different story. The attack to gain the heights of Fish Hook Ridge faltered and then failed in the face of the determined Japanese opposition. With the Japanese now bottled up in the Chichagof Harbor area and only the two ridge-lines separating them from the Americans, General Landrum regrouped his forces and ordered an anti-aircraft battery to move its 37mm guns from Moore Ridge to Prendergast Ridge where it could provide direct fire support for a renewed offensive.[432]

Fortunately the weather remained clear for the next three days so that air strike missions could be flown in support of the men battling their way up the ridge-lines overlooking Chichagof Harbor. On the 25th, fifteen B-24s and twelve B-25s were committed against the Japanese while thirty P-38 combat air patrol sorties were flown over the island in anticipation of another Japanese air attack. Eighteen tons of bombs were dropped on the Japanese positions.[433]

From his vantage point in the copilots' seat of a 36th Bombardment Squadron B-24, Lieutenant Billy Wheeler could see the infantry assaulting Fish Hook Ridge. Recalling later, Billy Wheeler noted: "To us the ridge, 2000 feet high, looked terrifically steep, like a wall in fact, to which the receding snow still clung."[434]

For the Japanese, the bombing and the assault on the ridge was the forewarning of pending doom. Paul Nobuo

Tatsoguchi, a Seventh Day Adventist medical missionary and a 1932 graduate of Pacific Union College at Angwin, California had kept a poignant day-by-day diary in which he described worsening conditions he and his fellow soldiers faced. In his May 25 entry, Tatsoguchi wrote:

> By naval gun firing it felt like Misaumi barracks blew up and things lit up tremendously. Consciousness becomes vague. Strafing planes hit the next room, two hits from a 50 calibre shell, one stopped in the ceiling and the other penetrated. My room is an awful mess from sand and pebbles that have come from the roof. First Lt. from medical corps is wounded. There was a ceremony to grant the Imperial Edict. The last line of Umanose (approach to Fish Hook Ridge) was broken through. We hope for reinforcements. Will die for the cause of Imperial Edict.[435]

No reinforcements were coming. Colonel Yamasaki and his men had been written off. They were to die on the lonely, weather tortured island at the end of the Aleutian Chain. Eight B-24s and eleven B-25s roared over the next day. The crews unloaded twenty-nine tons of bombs within the steadily shrinking Japanese perimeter. Twelve P-38 pilots tormented the Japanese with strafing attacks.[436]

The men of the 7th Infantry Division and 4th Infantry Regiment resumed their assault on Fish Hook Ridge. Men in small groups and occasionally individuals clawed their way upwards over the open, snow streaked slopes of the ridge. One man, frustrated with the slow progress and summoning up great courage from deep within himself, stood up and moved forward against the withering Japanese fire.

Twenty-three year old Private Joe P. Martinez from Taos, New Mexico, an automatic rifleman with Company K, 3rd Battalion, 32nd Infantry Regiment, with the rest of his company pinned down by machine gun fire, con-

Shortly after he assumed command from General Brown, General Landrum had stated that he would send his infantrymen up into the mountains. "I know this country and my heart bled for the boys I had to send up there. I knew how cold and bitter it was on the mountains. But I knew death was more bitter. I gave them a terrible task. I believed it kind to send them into the mountains to whip the Japs than to hold them in the valley where Jap snipers could cut them down." AAF photo

Attu was an infantryman's war that tested the spirit and soul of all those engaged in the battle. USA photo

Bringing down the wounded. USA photo

Replacements move up from the beach into battle. USA photo

General Buckner, fourth from right, looks up at the American flag over a former Japanese headquarters bunker in the Chichagof area. Colonel Culin, commander of the southern force is to his right. He is wearing a pair of Blucher boots that were issued the troops and which caused so much grief in the cold, damp climate of Attu. USA photo

tinued to climb alone up the steep slope. On reaching the first Japanese location where the ground began leveling out, he moved from position to position, firing a burst from his Browning Automatic Rife into each until he was finally cut down.

The single-handed assault by the lone, brave man stunned the Japanese defenders, and the rest of the 3rd Battalion, inspired by his deed, moved forward. By the early evening of the 26th, Fish Hook Ridge, except for isolated pockets of resistance, had been secured. General Landrum studied his map in preparation for the assault against Buffalo Ridge, directly behind Chichagof Harbor. For Private Martinez, the war was over. He died the next day from his wounds. He was the only man to be awarded the Medal of Honor during the Aleutian Campaign.[437]

Only a limited air attack was carried out on the 27th due to weather. A single B-25 arrived overhead. The crew dropped a bundle of aerial photographs taken the day before to the ground troops below. After unloading their bombs, the Mitchell crew headed back to Amchitka. Six P-38 pilots flew a combat air patrol over the island. No missions were flown on the 28th. By then the Japanese had been pushed back into an area four thousand yards wide and seven hundred yards deep along the shore of Chichagof Harbor. Their situation was hopeless.[438]

Lieutenant Oliver Glenn made a low, fast pass over Chichagof Harbor on the evening of the 28th in his PBY. Before the Japanese had time to react, a bundle of surrender leaflets were thrown out, and Glenn and his crew headed back to Casco Cove. The leaflets, addressed to Colonel Yamasaki from General Landrum, informed the commander and the approximately thousand men remaining in his command that their situation was hopeless and

asked for their unconditional surrender. Landrum also noted their "soldierly conduct" had "been worthy of the highest military tradition."[439]

Commander Yamasaki had three choices: surrender, evacuate or attack. The first was completely against the Bushido Code by which the Japanese military fought and died. To them surrender was a dishonorable act. Any hope of evacuation by now had long since passed. The third option was the only recourse. The plan that Colonel Yamasaki and his staff developed was a desperate one. Rather than wait for the final assault on their beach position, they decided to attack.

Colonel Yamasaki planned to assemble his remaining forces in the Chichagof Harbor area during the early morning hours of the 29th and launch an attack across Sarana Valley to seize the American artillery positions in the Clevesy Pass area. From there, his plans called for his force to continue down Massacre Valley, causing the maximum amount of damage before it was in turn destroyed.[440] Paul Nobuo Tatsoguchi made the final entry in his diary:

Today at 2000 o'clock (8:00 PM) we assembled in front of Hg. The last assault is to be carried out. All the patients in the hospital were made to commit suicide. Only 33 years of living and I am to die here. I have no regrets. Banzai to the Emperor. I am grateful that I could have kept peace of my soul which Enkist bestowed upon me. Goodby, Taeko, my beloved wife, Misaka who just became four years old will grow up unhindered. I feel sorry for you Mutsuko, born February of this year and never will see your father. Well, be good Matsue (brother), goodbye.[441]

At about 3:30 AM on May 29, approximately one thousand Japanese tore through the American front lines at the

Jim Fish Valley over which the Japanese launched their last desperate attack. Lake Cories can be seen in the distance. The sign, one of many, was erected shortly after the battle. It and others have long since been destroyed. Stanley Titus photo

The slopes of Engineer Hill where the final Japanese resistance was destroyed. Stanley Titus photo

The American cemetery at Little Falls. Individual identification tags can be seen nailed to the crosses and Stars of David. USA photo

A smaller burial site was established at Holtz Bay.
Stanley Titus photo

head of Lake Cories and continued across Sarana Valley, overrunning two command posts and a medical installation before smashing into a hastily organized defense of combat engineers, artillerymen and rear area troops under the command of Brigadier General Archibald V. Arnold dug into the crest of Engineer Hill. The Japanese repeatedly attacked the position only to be mowed down by the determined defense.

By the evening of the 29th, all effective Japanese operation had ceased. The Japanese who had charged up the slopes of Engineer Hill lay dead in grotesque heaps of bodies over a two mile stretch of bloody ground, many horribly disfigured by grenade blasts caused by those who chose to take their own lives rather than face the dishonor of capture. Colonel Yamasaki, sword in hand, died a warrior's death at the base of Clevesy Pass.

For the next two days, patrols hunted down and killed the few remaining Japanese on the island. After days filled

The Japanese were buried in communal graves. USA photo

Later, proper markings were erected over the burial sites. After the war, eighteen known and one hundred and seventeen unknown Japanese were reburied in the Fort Richardson National Cemetery.
Stanley Titus photos

with the thunder of artillery and bombs and crack of rifle and machine gun fire, the island suddenly fell silent. The wind could be heard again and the first signs of Spring began appearing on a land that had been the site of one of the hardest fought battles of the Pacific war.[442]

The sad business of cleaning up the battlefield of its melancholy debris of discarded equipment and supplies, expended ammunition, half eaten rations, and the terrible wastage of what had been young men, began.

The American dead, some 549 of them, were collected off the slopes and valley floors where they had fallen. Their bodies were stripped and personal effects collected, tagged and sent to a Quarter-Master depot in Kansas City for temporary storage until the next of kin could be notified. Their naked bodies were wrapped in blankets; and identified only by a single dog tag, they were laid to rest, eight at a time, side by side, in long graves hollowed out by bulldozers in a peaceful spot at the head of Massacre Valley, near a small waterfall in the shadow of Gilbert Ridge where so many had died. Another, smaller burial site was set aside at Holtz Bay for those who had died there.

Crosses and an occasional Star of David were erected over the site of each body and the mate to each dog tag nailed to them so that when the appropriate time came, their remains could be identified and taken home for reburial.

The bodies of approximately 2,350 Japanese that were found, many torn unrecognizable by the manner of their dying, were dumped into convenient holes near the place of their death and covered over; or unceremoniously, like so much rotting garbage, thrown into large communal graves scooped out of the earth. Crude and later more suitable markers were erected over their burial sites.

Only 29 Japanese, some deeply ashamed to be among the living, survived as prisoners of war. Attu provided the first indication of Japan's willingness to sacrifice its very existence for a belief. Attu was its Masada.[443]

In addition to the 549 killed in battle, 1,148 Americans were wounded and another approximately 2,100 were taken out of action, the victims of accidents, disease, exhaustion and the effects of not being adequately prepared for the weather, terrain and the terrible ordeal of ground combat. The largest number of non-battle fatalities resulted from trench foot, caused by the inadequate foot wear issued to the men. As noted in the official Army history:

> The price of victory was high. In terms of numbers engaged, Attu ranks as one of the most costly assaults in the Pacific. In terms of Japanese destroyed, the cost of taking Attu was second only to Iwo Jima: for every one hundred of the enemy on the island, about seventy-one Americans were killed or wounded.[444]

Colonel James Bush, who as a young major had commanded the engineer troops on Engineer Hill against the Japanese charge, remembered forty years later, "My God Almighty, to bring these people all the way from California in a desert climate . . . up here to bitter cold, freezing weather. . . ."[445]

The men had suffered needlessly from faulty intelligence and inadequate maps. They had been poorly trained, equipped and clothed; and had further compounded the problem by not taking proper care of themselves and their clothing and equipment. Loading and unloading of transports had been badly handled. Naval bombardment had been delivered from too long a range.[446]

Air support was to have played an important part in the battle. However, General Butler, because of the weather, could only commit his planes eleven out of the nineteen days the battle raged. A total of 132.36 tons of bombs were dropped and an untold amount of machine gun and cannon rounds expended. A B-24 and its entire crew of eleven perished. Two P-38s were lost and one pilot killed.[447]

The *Nassau* lost seven fighters and five pilots in carrying out nine missions under extremely hazardous conditions. The carrier, which was operated in close proximity to Attu, was able to launch attacks during breaks in the weather. Their attacks, particularly against Moore Ridge, proved effective in assisting the infantrymen in achieving their objectives.[448]

Catalina crews from Fleet Air Wing Four, flying out of Amchitka and Casco Cove kept an almost constant patrol over the waters near Attu, but not without a high cost. On May 10, on the eve of the landing, one PV-1 assigned to VB-136 crashed into Kuluk Bay and another squadron Ventura flown by Lieutenant Permeter disappeared with five aboard. On May 18, a PBY from VP-62 flown by Lieutenant William C. Leedy failed to return from a patrol. There were seven aboard the Catalina. Five days later, a PV-1 from VB-135 crashed on takeoff from Amchitka, killing Ensign P.P. Patterson and Aviation Machinist Mate 3rd Class A.D. Shaver. The next day another PBY from VP-62, piloted by Lieutenant Paul C. Spencer crashed into Kuluk Bay on return from a search mission. The plane and crew were lost.[449]

In the final analysis, Attu had been an infantryman's war in its truest form. It was a learning experience. The 7th Infantry Division had shown "little dash or initiative." The division was untested in battle, the junior officers and their NCOs had not been aggressive in closing with the enemy. However, in the end the men of the 7th Infantry Division had learned, become hardened and battle-wise and had prevailed. They would do better in the battles that followed in the Pacific.[450]

Into the Abyss

The Japanese tried to turn the loss of Attu into a propaganda advantage. Colonel Yamasaki's hopeless defense and "suicide charge . . . represented a tremendous stimulant to the fighting spirit of our nation." Axis military attaches and puppet governments expressed their admirations for the noble sacrifices that had been made. The Japanese ambassador reported that Stalin was so impressed that he ordered the story of Attu inserted into the text of primary school books.[451]

The Imperial General Headquarters met while the battle raged to decide the fate of Kiska. A directive was issued on May 21, stating in part: "The Kiska Garrison Force will be evacuated in successive stages, chiefly by submarine, as expeditiously as possible." After less than a year, the Japanese, with their supply line to their North Pacific bastion severed, had decided to abandon their lodgment in North America and use these forces to reinforce the northern Kurile Islands.[452]

By now, the Japanese were slowly sinking into the abyss of defeat; and the Americans and their allies, steadily building up a preponderance of power, were launching one crushing offensive after another. In March, following the fall of Guadalcanal, Admiral Halsey's forces occupied the islands to the northwest as a preliminary for the advance up the Solomon Islands.

While Halsey was carrying out his operations, American and Australian troops were clearing the Japanese from the Buna-Gona area of northeastern New Guinea. A Japanese force had landed there two months after the Battle of the Coral Sea with the intention of advancing against Port Moresby to the south over the forbidding Owen Stanley Mountains. The Australians stopped them thirty-two miles short of their objective.

The Australians then pushed after the retreating Japanese, while General MacArthur air landed troops south of Buna. When his first commander proved unequal to the task of taking Buna, MacArthur sent in Lieutenant General Robert L. Eichlberger with instructions "take Buna or die." The place was secured by January. From there, the Americans and Australians began a series of leap-frog attacks along the northern coast of New Guinea to clear the Japanese from the island.

To counter MacArthur's advance, the Japanese sent in a high speed convoy in early January with reinforcements to Lae on the northeast coast. Another convoy of eight transports crammed with five thousand troops of the 51st Infantry Division was dispatched from Rabaul in late February. The convoy was spotted by the crew of a patrolling B-24 on March 1 as it headed southwest across the Bismarck Sea. The air attacks began on March 2 and lasted until the 4th. When the American and Australian air crews finished their work, thirteen ships, including all the transports, had been sunk. Some twenty-nine hundred Japanese had been killed. Japan's control over the Southwest Pacific had been broken.[453]

Following the disasters of Guadalcanal and the Bismarck Sea, Admiral Yamamoto, to boost morale, decided to visit his bases at Buin on the southern coast of Bougainville Island and Ballale on Shortland Island to the south. His staff prepared an itinerary, which was encoded and transmitted to the places where he was to visit. American listening posts at Wahiawa on Hawaii and at Dutch Harbor intercepted the message. The code breakers at Pearl Harbor worked throughout the night, and early the next morning, April 14, Commander Edwin T. Layton, Admiral Nimitz's intelligence officer, entered the office of the Commander in Chief, Pacific Command, carrying in a worn manila folder what amounted to a death warrant for the Commander, Combined Fleet.

Admiral Yamamoto was unique. Next to the emperor, he was the most revered man in Japan. His loss would be a severe blow to the embattled nation. Admirals Nimitz and King and Secretary of Navy Frank Knox recommended he be killed. The Joint Chiefs of Staff concurred and President Roosevelt gave his approval.

The stillness of Fighter Strip Number Two on Guadalcanal erupted into a roar during the early morning hours of April 18 as sixteen P-38s under the command of Major John W. Mitchell lifted into the air and headed for the intercept point thirty-five miles northwest of Kahili on the southern coast of Bougainville Island. It was Palm Sunday and the anniversary of the Doolittle Raid.

The Lightning pilots arrived at the intercept point at 9:35 AM in time to spot the two Betty medium bombers carrying Admiral Yamamoto's party. The four fighter pilots assigned the mission of shooting down the two bombers streaked in.

Admiral Kakuta had just arrived at Truk from Rabaul to rejoin his fleet when a communications officer handed him a message as he stepped aboard the carrier Hiyo. Commander Okumiya, sensing disaster, later noted:

> Kakuta was a veteran combat naval air officer, known for his iron self-discipline under any circumstances. I was astonished to see the admiral's face grow pale . . . He uttered something unintelligible, and for some time could not or would not speak to anyone. Admiral Isoroku Yamamoto was dead.[454]

In the few dark moments over Bougainville, any chances the Japanese had of achieving an honorable end to the war had slipped forever from their grasp. For a time, they despaired and grieved for their lost warrior. It took the American invasion of Attu to end their lethargy and commit themselves to a strategic defensive war of exacting a terrible price against their tormentors.

Some of the principals involved in the retaking of Kiska. From left to right: Admiral Kinkaid, General DeWitt, Assistant Secretary of War John McCoy, General Buckner, General Landrum and Brig Gen Frank I. Whittiker, Deputy Commander, Alaska Defense Command. Secretary McCoy arrived in Alaska four days before the invasion force went ashore to witness the action. USA photo

Admiral Kinkaid, center, confers with other senior commanders during one of the planning sessions for retaking Kiska. To his immediate left are Generals Corlett, Buckner, Butler and G. R. Pearkes (Canada). To his right are Admiral Rockwell (head bowed and General DeWitt). USA photo

Admiral Kinkaid, near relief map of Kiska, and the other commanders involved in the planning for the Kiska invasion. To his right: Admiral Rockwell, General Corlett, General Buckner and General DeWitt. Note that the censors have scratched out DeWitt's shoulder patch. USA photo

Plans for the invasion of Kiska continued after the Joint Chiefs of Staff had issued their March 22 decision to retake Attu first. One month later, the Joint Chiefs gave General DeWitt the go ahead to organize and train an invasion force. Major General Charles H. Corlett, who had commanded the Kodiak army garrison, was selected as its commander. General Corlett, mindful of the problems encountered in planning for Attu, selected his staff from veterans of the Western Defense and Alaska Defense Commands based on their proven abilities and their knowledge of Alaska and the Aleutians.

On May 20, at the urging of Admiral Kinkaid and while the battle of Attu was reaching a decisive conclusion, Admiral Nimitz recommended to the Joint Chiefs of Staff that Kiska be retaken. His target date for the landing was set for the first week in September. Admiral Nimitz noted that he had the necessary shipping to support the invasion and that General DeWitt had already begun the planning. Admiral King supported him and four days later he informed Admiral Nimitz that he could proceed with the planning and begin organizing and training the invasion force. Admiral Nimitz and General DeWitt issued the joint directive for the retaking of Kiska on May 31. The Joint Chiefs of Staff approved it on June 22, and the invasion date was set for August 15.

With the bitter lessons of Attu fresh in everyone's memory, plans were made to gather a large force and train them under Aleutian conditions. The intelligence staffs estimated that there were nine to ten thousand Japanese on the island, who were well dug in and prepared to sacrifice their lives for the last vestige of Japan's North American holdings.

The forces to make the landing were identified. They included the veteran 17th Infantry Regiment from the 7th

The invasion fleet assembled in Kuluk Bay. Unlike the troops that landed on Attu, the ones that were to assault Kiska were put through a rigorous training program in the Aleutians to prepare them for the conditions they were expected to fight under. Craig D. Sorensen collection

Infantry Division, the 87th Mountain Infantry Regiment, the 53rd Infantry Regiment, the 159th Infantry Regiment, the 184th Infantry Regiment, the Canadian 13rd Infantry Brigade and the First Special Service Force.[455]

The latter organization was unique. Composed of Canadian and U.S. troops, it had been activated at Fort William Henry Harrison, Montana. Initially, it was intended as a special operations force with the mission of conducting raids to destroy hydroelectric plants in Norway and oil fields in Romania. The personnel were given parachute, amphibious, mountain and desert warfare training. The Norwegian and Romanian missions never materialized, so the First Special Service Force was committed to Kiska, as a reconnaissance force, in its first operational employment.[456]

Altogether, almost thirty-five thousand ground troops were assigned to retaking of Kiska. To support the force, Admiral Nimitz allocated two battleships, four cruisers, nineteen destroyers and host of transports and lesser vessels totalling over one hundred warships.[457]

The Eleventh Air Force was beefed up. At the conclusion of the battle of Attu, General Butler had at his disposal twenty-four B-24s, forty-four B-25s, twenty P-38s, sixty-three P-40s and three F-5s. The two Canadian fighter squadrons that were committed to the Aleutians contributed additional P-40s and the 407th Bombardment Group (Dive) was scheduled to arrive from Drew Field, Florida with twenty-four A-24s, the Army version of the Douglas Dauntless dive bomber.[458]

General Butler moved his full headquarters to Davis Field on Adak Island. The average number of Eleventh Air Force aircraft rose from 292 in June to 352 in July, peaking at 359 in August. The numbers included more transports for the 42nd and 54th Troop Carrier Squadrons. By now the two squadrons were airlifting a monthly average of 7,500 tons of cargo and 15,000 passengers.[459]

By the end of June, there were two more airfields, this time to the west of Kiska at Alexai Point on Attu and on Shemya. A third was being constructed by Navy SeaBees at Casco Cove. The fields provided the additional advantage of serving as places from which weather conditions could be reported.

On May 28, Colonel Talley, who had already selected the location of an Army airfield on Alexai Point as the battle for Attu raged, led a party of eighteen on a reconnaissance of Shemya.

After disembarking from the destroyer Kane, the party, whipped by a lashing wind, moved across the island in search of a runway site. Other than a dilapidated fox trap-

General Buckner pins the Distinguished Service Medal on Colonel Talley during an early February 1943 ceremony. The medal, the highest military award for meritorious service and achievement, was presented to Talley for his work on the construction of the air field at Otter Point. It resulted from a recommendation made by General Marshall. Colonel Eddie Post, Chief of Staff, Alaska Defense Command looks on. Colonel Talley, who went on to earn the Distinguished Service Cross for valor on Omaha Beach, retired in 1956 as a brigadier general after thirty years of distinguished service.

General Talley collection

per's cabin and a small grave site marked with Russian Orthodox crosses, Talley and his men found the island devoid of any human habitation. After selecting the site for a three thousand foot fighter strip which would be later expanded into a ten thousand foot bomber runway, Talley and his party waited for the arrival of the 807th Engineer Aviation Battalion, who came ashore on the 30th.[460]

His work in Alaska completed, Colonel Talley departed for England in June to assist in the planning for the Normandy invasion. Within little over three years he had completely transformed the infrastructure of Alaska. There were those, Governor Gruening among them, who complained that the military development had been poorly conceived, planned and wasteful, a condition not at all unusual in time of war.[461] However, in the final analysis, what Colonel Talley left behind provided the foundation of the postwar military in Alaska and contributed to the economic development of the territory.

In the last entry of the daily diary that he kept, Colonel Talley noted that in the course of his duties, he had flown over nine hundred hours, or approximately one hundred and thirty-five thousand miles, and had gotten to know many of the aircrews of the Eleventh Air Force and Fleet Air Wing Four well. To a man, he acknowledged them as being the "finest" in what for most was a temporary and very dangerous profession.[462]

The three thousand foot long fighter strip at Alexai Point was ready for use by June 7, seven days after the engineers had arrived to begin construction. The first landing was made by a C-47, which arrived on the 8th to evacuate

wounded. Four days later six P-40s from C Flight, 344th Fighter Squadron under to command of the squadron commander, Capt Robert L. Brocklehurst, arrived to provide air defense for Attu. The other two flights and the ground personnel were sent to Shemya.

The ground personnel from the squadron, twelve officers and one hundred and seventy-two enlisted men, had departed Cape Field in late May on a round-about journey aboard the former Alaska Steamship Line pleasure craft, the *Yukon*. The little ship arrived at Dutch Harbor on May 25 and the men were allowed to go ashore. Two days later, the *Yukon* departed for Adak. On arrival there, it was turned around and sent back to Dutch Harbor to pick up a battalion of SeaBees who had been accidentally left behind.

The *Yukon* then headed back to Adak, where on June 1, the men of 344th Fighter Squadron were put ashore. They remained there for two weeks until June 13 when the *Yukon* arrived back to pick them up. Four days later, they were in the middle of Massacre Bay wondering what their next destination was going to be. After another nine days, an LST arrived alongside, and the men were ordered to transfer themselves and their equipment and supplies to it. Finally, on June 25, the squadron's ground personnel arrived at their final destination on Shemya where they were to remain until the squadron was inactivated August 15, 1946.[463]

The fighter strip at Shemya was operational by June 21. The first landing, by a C-53, was made two days later. Two flights of P-40s from the 344th Fighter Squadron arrived on July 24 from Adak and Amchitka. The pilots had augmented the 18th Fighter Squadron in flying fighter-bomber missions over Kiska.[464]

On July 17, Major Ramputi arrived with a contingent of four officers and thirty-eight enlisted men as the advance party for the 21st Bombardment Squadron. The squadron's bombers began arriving on August 13, when the crews of six B-24s landed on Shemya's new runway. The squadron joined the 344th Fighter Squadron and the 54th Fighter Squadron, which began arriving on August 10, in the buildup of forces on the tiny, flat island near the end of the Aleutian Chain.[465]

With the construction of the airfields in the western Aleutians, Fleet Air Wing Four began converting from sea to land based operations in earnest. Two PBY squadrons returned to Seattle. VP-43 departed on June 1 and VP-62 on July 11, leaving VP-45 with fourteen PBY-5s at Attu and VP-61 with fifteen PBY-5As at Amchitka as the only Catalina squadrons in the Aleutians.

By August 10, Casco Field was ready and VB-135 moved in from Amchitka with eight PV-1 Venturas. VB-136 was split between Amchitka and Davis Field with five Venturas at the first location and eight at the second.

Also joining Fleet Air Wing Four at Adak was VS-56 with six Kingfishers, which were used for inshore patrolling.[466]

Never Miss A Break

With Attu secured, Admiral Kinkaid unleashed his full force on Kiska. The destroyers *Aylwin* and *Monaghan* were dispatched to blockade the entrance into Kiska Harbor and conduct periodic night bombardments of the positions ashore. Rear Admiral Robert C. "Ike" Giffin took up station to the west of Attu with a cruiser task force to repel any attempt by Admiral Kawase to reinforce or relieve the Kiska garrison. Commodore Gehres extended his PBY patrols further to the west to cover the waters near the Kurile Islands.

Unlike Attu, Admiral Kinkaid intended to subject Kiska to an prolonged and intense pre-invasion bombardment by air and sea. He urged General Butler to hit Kiska daily; to disregard the old Aleutian weather rule, "never take a chance," and adopt a new approach, "never miss a break." Unfortunately, the breaks were few and far between. The Aleutian weather, as usual, interfered.[467]

On May 30, the missions against Kiska resumed with intensity. Four P-40 reconnaissance and three B-24 and B-25 missions were flown. The pressure against the island was increased during the next two days as the P-38 and P-40 pilots flew eighty-five sorties against all the facilities on Kiska. The crews of six B-24s and ten B-25s unloaded their bombs on the Japanese on the 31st.

The next day eight Mitchells were committed; and for the first time, they were accompanied by five ASD-1 airborne radar equipped PV-2s from VB-135. The airborne radar added a new dimension to the attacks against the Japanese positions on Kiska. Unlike the older SCR-521 ASV, which gave only distance and bearing, the ASD-1 also provided a view, albeit distorted, of the topography on its round screen. By comparing the image on the scope with a map of Kiska, the radar operator could, with some accuracy, drop the bombs through the overcast on the target.

The crews of the five Venturas in addition to dropping their bombs on Little Kiska also guided the Army bombers to their targets in what would become a standard procedure during the weeks ahead. The PBY crews were also committed to flying bombing missions against Kiska, although most were flown at night to harass the Japanese and prevent them from getting any sleep.

In spite of the short distances between Amchitka and Kiska, the weather plane was still used because of the fickle nature of the weather. This fact plus the limited targets on Kiska led to the use of "canned missions" where charts and operations were drawn up and code words were established for specific targets. Medium and low-altitude attacks were the methods of choice because of the cloud cover at higher altitudes.[468]

After a break for weather, a mission of six B-24s guided by a Ventura was launched from Amchitka against Kiska on the 4th. Fourteen P-38 and P-40 sorties were also flown.[469] A small caliber anti-aircraft round slammed into the mid-wing section of the bomber flown by Major Speer, Commander of the 36th Bombardment Squadron. It failed to explode. With twenty-four months in theater and over one thousand hours of combat time, Speer was one of the senior veterans of the Aleutian air war. Billy Wheeler noted: "He has a charmed life, but this is too long a time for anyone to be in this theater."[470]

While the missions were being flown, the bombers of the 404th Bombardment Squadron arrived at Amchitka to replace the 36th Bombardment Squadron. Shortly afterwards, the aircrews of the 36th departed for Davis Field for a well-deserved rest. The ground personnel of the squadron remained behind to service the 404th Bombardment's Squadron's aircraft. The ground personnel of the 404th at Davis Field provided similar services for the 36th Bombardment Squadron's bombers. The 21st Bombardment Squadron remained on Amchitka in preparation for their movement to Shemya. By now, according to the historian of the "Pink Elephants," the crews and ground personnel "were becoming inextricably mixed."[471]

After being at Amchitka, the men of the 36th Bombardment Squadron were tired. On arrival at Adak they held a party which was "great for morale." The air crews were relieved from flying missions against Kiska, but not for long. They would be called back to duty as the air offensive was stepped up.

Duty during the battle of Attu, Wheeler recalled, had been "interesting and not too hazardous, but Kiska and its often terrible anti-aircraft fire was a complete mental hazard to flying officers and men."[472]

Adak by now had become a well appointed rear base that boasted a radio station, movie theaters, bathhouses with showers, comfortable quarters and a large Navy officers club with a twenty-six piece band. The place became a regular stopover for USO tours, which for the first time included women entertainers.[473]

In comparison, life at Amchitka remained primitive, a condition all too familiar in the newly established forward bases in the Aleutians. Ultimately they would improve, as army engineers and navy SeaBees first completed the mission essential airfield and other infrastructure construction projects before turning their attention to the creature comforts of the men who had to, in the interim, live in tents and slog to and from their destinations in a sea of mud and wet muskeg grass.

The navy did take more pains to provide its men with better facilities at the expense of completing other projects. While the army engineers were able to build an operational airstrip at Alexai Point with ten days, it took the SeaBees three months to complete one at Casco Cove. However, their quarters were comfortable and many for the senior officers featured fireplaces and the other amenities of civilization that made life more bearable in an otherwise bleak environment.

While the forward bases had plenty of bombs and gas, they lacked such essentials as fresh food and warm, dry quarters so necessary for a comfortable human existence. Billy Wheeler wrote during his stay at Amchitka:

> . . . our area lies in a swamp dotted with about twenty ponds. Between them lies mud, lightly coated with tundra. Tents are the only shelter from the foul weather and we wallow in mud inside them as well as out.
>
> . . . .
>
> The electric light generator goes off every few hours and those who have candles are lucky indeed. The S-2 (intelligence) double-tent does service for briefing, interrogation and pilots' alert tent, as well as the routine work of the S-2 section. A few benches for the flying officer personnel are ranged against the soggy walls; the floor is soft mud and the approaches to the tent are churned by countless boots.
>
> . . . .
>
> The mess tent stands on a dreary hillock vainly trying to repel the incessant rain, flapping and groaning in the Aleutian gales. The failure of the cursed generator was the last straw, and a few flickering candles dimly light the faces of the boys who from these quarters are daily attacking the stubborn enemy.[474]

The 404th Bomber Squadron flew its first mission from Amchitka on June 5 when it joined with the 21st Bombardment Squadron in a bomber mission over Kiska. Six B-25s were also committed and six P-40 sorties were flown. VB-135 provided one of its radar equipped Venturas to lead the bombers to their targets.[475]

The weather turned bad and no more missions were flown until the 10th. Major Richard Lavin, the operations officer for the 404th Bombardment Squadron had by now developed a system for alerting the others when a mission was on. The XI Bomber Command operations center at Davis Field usually called at around 4:00 AM to provide a weather report. If the report was bad, the planned missions were cancelled. If the weather was good, Lavin upended his cot in front of his quarters, which signaled the others to get out of theirs. The chief problem, one of the squadron members later remembered, was that "sometimes the fog was so thick one had to get within a few feet of the cot to see what position it was in."[476]

The skies over Kiska were clear on the 10th. One weather and two bomber missions were flown. VB-136

also committed six of its Venturas. The next day dawned beautiful and every available plane was launched from Davis Field and Amchitka. The missions continued throughout the morning and early afternoon as bombers and fighters shuttled back and forth between their bases and the targets on Kiska. Then the weather closed in during the late morning. A flight of P-40s managed to land at Amchitka before the fog rolled in. However, a flight of B-24s and another of P-38s were unable to get in and were advised to head for Davis and Cape Fields. Two fighter pilots did not make it.[477]

Five Lightening pilots, Captain Frank W. Friedman, Lieutenants John M. Duffy, John T. Larson, Glen B. Martin and Oscar Treland (in an F-5) headed for Davis Field. Friedman elected to make a forced landing on Tanaga Island, which he walked away from. Duffy, Larson and Treland landed safely at Davis shortly after noon. Lieutenant Martin, one of the 54th Fighter Squadron's oldest and most experienced pilots, was not so fortunate. At 12:15 he reported to the controllers at Davis that he was over the east end of the east-west runway and was planning to land. At 12:31, Martin reported "motor conked, landing in water three quarter miles north of runway." Martin's body washed ashore and was found June 17. He was the 54th Fighter Squadron's seventeenth fatality in less than a year.[478]

The summer Aleutian fog settled in and the weather remained bad. No missions were flown by the Eleventh Air Force until the 24th. VB-135, however, continued to keep up the pressure. Six Venturas were committed to day light attacks on the 15th and 20th. The bombs were dropped by radar through the overcast.[479]

On June 18, Lieutenant James H. Jones, 404th Bombardment Squadron, who had been forced to divert to Cape Field, was escorting a P-38 back to Davis Field only to discover the field obscured by fog on arrival. The P-38 pilot managed to make it through a hole in the overcast to a safe landing on Davis Field. Lieutenant Jones headed back to Cape Field low on fuel and with darkness approaching. He made it as far as Herbert Island in the Islands of the Four Mountains where he ditched his bomber in the sea off the shore line.

Jones suffered a fractured skull from the impact of the landing. Another man, Staff Sergeant Willard F. Crippen, disappeared in the confusion of evacuating the sinking bomber. The rest of the crew made it to shore. Lieutenant Jones died shortly afterwards despite efforts by the others to keep him alive under the bleak circumstances in which they found themselves. Two days later, the crew of a search plane spotted the forlorn little party. Supplies were dropped and shortly afterwards a rescue boat arrived to pickup the eleven survivors and the body of Lieutenant Jones.[480]

Flight of B-25Cs from the third B-25, 406th Bombardment Squadron led by Capt Vernan L Bonn, returning from mission against Kiska in late July. The photograph was taken from the third B-25. Part of the Kiska invasion force can be seen below.

406th Bombardment Squadron collection

Crew of one of the 406th Bombardment Squadron B-25Cs; from left to right: SSgt John Karlheim, flight engineer; MSgt Ralph Davis, radio operator; SSgt Louie Tyrone, armorer-gunner; Maj Russell L. Redman, pilot; Lieut Jack Roberts, bombardier; Capt John Mullican, navigator and Lieut Resnor, copilot.

406th Bombardment Squadron collection

The missions against Kiska were resumed on June 24 when sixteen bombers guided by three flights of Venturas from VB-135 dropped their bombs on the main camp and North Head areas. During the remaining days of June, the bombers and fighters of the Eleventh Air Force and Venturas and Catalinas from Fleet Air Wing Four pounded the Japanese installations on Kiska.[481]

The summer fog had plagued operations during June. The targets were only visible during eight days. Despite this, the Eleventh Air Force and Fleet Air Wing Four had dropped over 387 tons of bombs on the Japanese. No aircraft had been lost to combat. Six B-25s, five P-38s and two P-40s had sustained battle damage and one man was wounded. The anti-aircraft fire, while vigorous, was inaccurate. Most of the rounds had burst behind the bombers, an indication that the Japanese central fire direction center was unable to cope with the bomber and fighter attacks.[482]

The buildup of forces in the Aleutians continued. The 406th Bombardment Squadron was relieved of its anti-submarine patrols and convoy escort duties in mid-July, and the aircrews moved to Davis Field and Amchitka where they performed anti-shipping alert and participated in air strikes against Kiska with the other B-25 squadrons. The squadron flew its first combat mission on July 18 from Adak. Up until that time, individual crews had participated with the other squadrons in missions against the Japanese on the island and six crews had been at Davis Field since early June on shipping alert.

Colonel DeFord had promised Major Courtney, that his squadron would be sent to Amchitka to take part in the air offensive against Kiska. Courtney and several other of his officers had visited the island in early June to complete preliminary arrangements for moving the squadron there. However, the plans were delayed and the squadron remained split between the two islands and Elmendorf Field with a number of its aircrews on temporary duty with the other two medium squadrons.

During a staff meeting on July 19 and later during informal discussions with Colonel DeFord over a poker game, Major Courtney raised the issue of consolidating the squadron at Amchitka. By the end of the month the entire squadron, less three crews which remained with the 73rd Bombardment Squadron, was located on Amchitka and were flying missions against Kiska as a unit, weather permitting.[483]

The missions against Kiska in the interim had continued. After another break for the weather, five B-24 and B-25 and one P-38 missions assisted by Venturas from VB-135 were flown against Kiska on July 2 in one of the more intense efforts of the Aleutian Campaign. Over 56 tons of bombs were dropped on all the installations on Kiska. No aircraft were lost. One man, Lieutenant Paul A. Fine from the 404th Bombardment Squadron was killed.

A mission of six B-24s were sent against the main camp the following day. Fifteen tons of bombs were dropped. No missions were flown for the next two days due to weather.[484]

On July 6, Admiral Giffin's force of three heavy and one light cruisers and four destroyers steamed into position off the south shore of South Head; and in a repeat of Admiral Smith's bombardment of the Kiska Harbor area the previous year, lobbed 312 rounds of 8-inch, 250 rounds of 6-inch and 1,250 rounds of 5-inch high explosive shells at the well fortified Japanese. Particular attention was paid during the twenty-two minute bombardment to the coastal defense guns on North Head and Little Kiska.

Again, the fire was indirect and controlled by spotter aircraft from the cruisers. This time there were no Japanese float fighters to interfere with the operations, and the anti-aircraft gunners were only able to respond with sporadic fire. Other than to shake up the Japanese, the bombardment achieved little. Following the inconclusive bombardment, Admiral Giffin's force retired to their patrol station south of Kiska.[485]

The results turned in by the Eleventh Air Force were equally lackluster. The crews of six B-24s managed to drop their bombs through the overcast on targets on North Head, while those of eight B-25s, unable to make contact with their pathfinder Ventura, aborted the mission and returned to Amchitka.[486]

Another weather front moved in preventing any missions from being flown against Kiska until the 11th. However, by now the Eleventh Air Force and Fleet Air Wing Four had found a new target.

Mission to the Kuriles

The capture of Attu placed the two organizations within flying distance of the northern Kurile Islands and the Kamchatka Peninsula. The fact was not lost on the members of VP-45 and VP-62 who were operating out of Casco Cove, flying monotonous patrols over the North Pacific; or to Generals DeWitt and Buckner, who saw the capture of Attu as a means of carrying the war to the Japanese home islands.

In early June, Lieutenant Oliver Glenn from VP-61 decided to fly all the way to Petropavlovsk on the southern end of the Kamchatka Peninsula. He informed his squadron commander, who, although refusing to officially sanction the flight, did give tacit approval by suggesting that a photographer be sent along.

Oliver Glenn and his crew made it to the Russian port city as planned, where for the first time in months they saw trees, houses and streets. Two obsolete IL-16 Mosca fighters rose to intercept them. Seeing that the Americans meant no harm, the Russian pilots flew off the wing tips of the PBY as Glenn and his crew proceeded along the coast line, before turning and heading back to Attu.

The Russians apparently never complained of the violation of their airspace, and nothing official was said about the unauthorized flight.[487]

Lieutenant Commander Carl Amme, by now an old Aleutian hand who had moved up to become the commander of VP-45, also decided to try his luck with the Russians. On one flight out of Casco Cove, he flew past the north side of the Komandorski Islands where he observed construction going on. The next day he dispatched Lieutenant Stitzel, one of his patrol plane commanders to make an aerial reconnaissance of the construction site. Stitzel dutifully returned with a number of excellent oblique and vertical photographs. When Commodore Gehres saw them, he blew his top and directed that Amme discipline Stitzel for violating Russian neutrality.

Amme did not take any further action, but the episode did alert him to Gehres' feelings about unauthorized flights; so several weeks later when one of his pilots was forced to make an emergency landing on a lake on Bering Island, the largest of the Komandorskies, he was reluctant to seek official approval for a rescue effort. Instead, he ordered Roy Evans, another of his pilots to fly to the lake, rescue the stranded crew, recover the classified documents and sink the disabled PBY. He further cautioned Evans not to use his radio during the rescue operation.

To further make sure that higher headquarters did not find out what was going on, Amme directed his communications officer to fake a communications outage. The

THE KURILES

whole operations went as planned. Evans arrived at the lake just ahead of a Russian patrol. The Catalina was sunk and the crew and classified documents recovered. Gehres' headquarters on Adak remained ignorant.

Shortly afterwards, Commodore Gehres arrived at Casco Cove on a visit. Commander Amme gave him the royal treatment. Arrangements were made to put him up in style in VIP accommodations set aside in a recently erected Quonset hut. A salmon barbecue was held in his honor and several drinks of bourbon were consumed to mark the occasion. The subject of the communications failure was never brought up, and the Commander, Fleet Air Wing Four left Attu a happy if not wiser man.[488]

In the interim, General Butler's staff had pored over what information there was available on the northern Kuriles with the intention of launching an air strike against the Japanese installations there. The distance between the new field on Alexai Point and the nearest installation in the Kuriles was 750 miles.

The Japanese had built up a sizable defense complex on the northern islands. Most were located on Paramushiro, the largest of the Kurile islands. They included three air-fields and the Kashiwabara Army Staging Area. The Kotaoka Naval Base, headquarters for the Fifth Fleet, was located on Shimushu Island immediately to the north of Paramushiro.

Generals DeWitt and Buckner succeeded in obtaining the Joint Chiefs of Staff concurrence to conduct a raid against the Japanese facilities. Admiral Kinkaid liked the idea and General Butler's staff began planning the mission.

The orders were issued in early July. They called for eight B-24s from the 21st and 36th Bombardment Squadrons at Davis Field and ten B-25s from the 77th Bombardment Squadron at Amchitka to stage through Alexai Point where their gas tanks would be topped off before proceeding to their targets. Major Speer, the Commander, 36th Bombardment Squadron was assigned the mission of leading the heavy bombers and Capt James L. Hudelson, the B-25s.[489]

Other than a number of intelligence studies, translated documents captured at Attu and information gained from communications intercepts, the intelligence officers responsible for briefing the crews did not have a great deal of information to aid the bomber crews in finding their targets and avoiding the Japanese defenses.

One, a reserve officer who had temporarily left his insurance business in Middletown, New York, to do his part for the war effort, found himself on Adak as the assistant intelligence officer for the 21st Bombardment Squadron. Since the intelligence possibilities of Kiska had been virtually exhausted, there was not much else for Lieutenant Larry Reineke to do.

Larry Reineke, Eleventh Air Force reunion, August 1980 in Anchorage, Alaska. USAF photo

Tired of briefing essentially the same intelligence to the same bored bomber crews, Reineke looked for a diversion. He found it in the form of several Navy intelligence friends. They were able to provide him with additional information on the Kuriles. Using their information, translations of captured documents and diaries and prisoner interrogation reports from Attu and what little information that was available in the Eleventh Air Force intelligence files, Reineke pieced together a comprehensive assessment of the Japanese dispositions and capabilities in the northern Kuriles. Unfortunately, he failed to inform his superiors.

The intelligence officer from the 404th Bombardment Squadron who was supposed to brief the B-24 crews found out about Larry Reineke's project and asked him to assist in the briefing. Lieutenant Reineke offered to give him all the information. However, the major after a few introductory remarks, turned to the surprised junior intelligence officer and asked him to finish the briefing. Lieutenant Reineke proceeded to go into great detail on the target locations, geographical peculiarities, defense installations and other facts the bomber crews needed for planning their missions.

The bomber crews liked the information and asked Larry Reineke to provide the same information to the crews of the 73rd and 77th Bombardment Squadrons. The junior intelligence officer was happy. He felt he was at long last doing something for the war effort. About two days after briefing the bomber crews, Reineke recalled he was called into his boss's office and:

> . . . advised I had overstepped my authority and had broken channels of command and had no business to do that. I had embarrassed a lot of people. Maybe I did. I didn't know. I only did it because I came into the service after being in business for myself. I was used to being busy all the time and when I got to Adak and had all this time on my hands, I just had to do something. About three days after this episode I was put aboard an LST and was sent to Shemya to pull muskeg.[490]

Reineke, by his initiative, had embarrassed the intelligence staff of the XI Bombardment Command. Essentially, they had informed everyone that there was not very much information available. Larry Reineke was rewarded for his efforts by being sent to Shemya with the advance party of the 21st Bombardment Squadron to help set up camp area for the rest of the squadron.[491]

The day of the attack, July 10, arrived. The weather personnel predicted that conditions would be clear over the Kuriles. The B-24s were about to be launched from Davis Field, when suddenly, at the last moment, their mission was changed. A PBY crew had sighted two Japanese transports southwest of Attu, just across the International Date Line. From their location well south of the Koman-

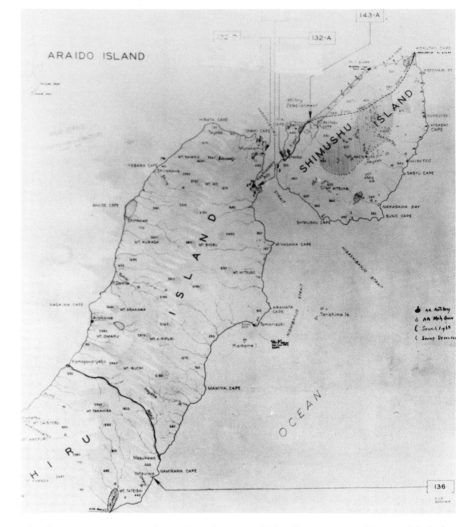

The map showing Japanese facilities on Paramushiro and Shimushu Islands was prepared by Larry Reineke for the target folders issued to the aircrews. Larry Reineke collection

dorski Islands, they were apparently part of a force sent to rescue the Kiska garrison.

While the PBY crew maintained visual contact, General Butler ordered the 73rd Bombardment Squadron to launch the five B-25s it maintained on shipping alert at Amchitka. Since the B-24s were already loaded with bombs and the convoy was a higher priority than the Kuriles, they were also dispatched. Captain Hudelson, whose bombers were loaded with general purpose bombs, was instructed to continue with his original mission.

The crews of the five alert B-25s were the first to arrive. By now, another PBY had relieved the first, whose crew had sighted two other, smaller transports. Deck level attacks were made in which one of the ships was sunk and another set on fire and was last seen in a sinking condition. One of the B-25s was hit by anti-aircraft fire, but its crew reached Amchitka safely.

Major Speer's force arrived over target shortly after the B-25s. The crews of two of the Liberators were unable to locate the cargo ships because of the extensive cloud cover in the area and returned to Davis Field. The others went in at deck-level under the clouds. However, the large four engine bombers were not as maneuverable as the smaller

medium bombers and the Japanese easily avoided the bombs that were dropped on them.

Lieutenant Lucian Wernick's B-24 was struck by a burst of anti-aircraft fire that severed hydraulics lines and punctured the nose wheel. Wernick and his copilot managed to manhandle the big bomber back to Davis Field. With no brakes and a flat nose wheel, Wernick decided to make a low approach over the water and touch down in a nose-high attitude. He ordered his men to begin slowly walking to the rear of the bomber as he and his copilot nursed the B-24 onto the runway.

With the men continuing to move to the rear to add weight to hold the tail down, Wernick and his copilot held the control wheel in their lap. The big bomber careened down the runway, its tail just off the surface. Gradually it slowed down. The nose dropped and the B-24 came to a stop near the end of runway.

While the attacks against the Japanese transports were being made, Captain Hudelson and his men had continued on the original mission. Taking off from Alexai Field at 5:44 AM, they arrived over Kuriles at 1045 AM to find their primary target, the Kotaoka Naval Base on Shimushu Island, and secondary targets on Paramushiro obscured

-304-

by clouds. Only the tops of the Kapochetka Mountains showed. The B-25 crews flew a time-distance approach from the mountain tops and dropped their thirty-two 500-pound bombs from nine thousand feet where they thought the targets were.

No opposition was encountered and the only sign of the enemy were six fishing boats seen through breaks in the clouds in the Paramushiro Strait area. Hudelson and his men headed back to Attu where they landed safely after a nine and one-half hour, 1,600-mile round trip flight. After refueling, they departed for Davis Field for a debriefing. The last bomber touched down there at 7:20 PM. The mission was billed at the time as longest B-25 one of the war, and according to the Eleventh Air Force Historian, the first land based air attack against the Japanese home islands.[492]

Fleet Air Wing Four also launched its own attack against the Kuriles the same day. Two Catalinas from Adak rendezvoused with two Catalinas from Attu at 10:15 the evening of June 10. Together, under the leadership of Commander Amme, they headed out on a night bombing mission. The crews of the two PBYs from Adak made it to within 70 miles of the Kuriles where they ran into a weather front and became separated from the rest. After jettisoning their bombs, they turned and headed back to Adak. The last crew landed there at 8:55 AM, July 11. They had been in the air for sixteen hours.

Amme and the crew of the other Attu based PBY continued on. They arrived over Paramushiro Island in the darkness to find it obscured by clouds. Using their radars, the crews dropped their bombs on what they estimated was the harbor area in Kashiwabara Bay before heading back to Casco Cove where they landed safely.[493]

As the PBY crews were returning from their nocturnal flight, Major Speer was leading another mission of five B-24s through the drizzling rain towards the northern Kuriles. They had taken off from Alexai Point a 6:27 AM. On arrival off the Kamchatka coast, Speer and the others turned south for a short distance before running into a heavy weather front.

The planes became separated and Major Speer decided to call off the mission. Major Edward Lass and his crew from the 21st Bombardment Squadron briefly caught sight of the green and sparsely timbered Kamchatka coast line through the swirling mist and continued on. Four bomber crews landed at Alexai Point between 1:55 and 2:45 PM. Major Lass landed at 4:20 PM after having proceeding within a few miles of Shimushu Island before being forced back by the weather.[494]

On July 18, Major Speer tried again in what was publicized at the time as the first bomber mission against the Kuriles. Six B-24s, three from the 36th (Majors Speer and Lass, and Captain Jacques Francine), two from the 21st

Major Robert Speer, leader of the July 18 raid against Japanese installations on Paramushiro and Shimushu Islands. Larry Reineke collection

(Majors Ramputi and Lucian Wernick) and one from the 404th (Major Lavin) Bombardment Squadrons, were staged out of Alexai Field under the leadership of Major Speer. All the bomber crews were volunteers and most were old hands at Aleutian operations. All had been on the first two aborted B-24 missions.

Each bomber carried a load of six 500-pound general purpose bombs with nose fuses in addition to tail fuses in case the bomber crews encountered shipping. Departing Attu at 6:32 AM, the bombers proceeded in two flights on a course of 236 degrees at an altitude of three thousand feet above the North Pacific. Landfall was made off the Kamchatka Peninsula. Billy Wheeler recalled, "We rubbed our eyes at seeing trees, some of us for the first time in a year." The bombers turned south, paralleled the coast and began climbing to twelve thousand feet.

Cape Kokutan on the north of Shimushu Island was sighted at 11:15 AM. Major Speer led Flight A over Shimushu Island. The bombs were dropped on the runway and adjacent buildings located near the Kotaoka Naval Base.

Major Ramputi led Flight B southwest over the Kataoka Naval Base on the southwest coast of the island before turning south and then east over Paramushiro Strait. After observing the shipping in the strait, Major Ramputi then turned his flight north over Shimushu, circled around to the east and made a bombing run on the shipping in Paramushiro Strait. No hits were observed and the bombs

Pilots of the first successful mission against the northern Kurile Islands pose before takeoff. Front row, left to right: Lieut Cox, copilot; Lieut Bollo, copilot; Capt Jacques Francine, pilot, 36th Bombardment Squadron; Maj Richard Lavin, pilot, 404th Bombardment Squadron; and Maj Frederick Ramputi, pilot, 21st Bombardment Squadron. Back row, left to right: Maj Lucian Wernick, pilot, 21st Bombardment Squadron; Maj Robert Speer, pilot, 36th Bombardment Squadron and mission leader; Capt Louis Blau, copilot, 404th Bombardment Squadron. Major Edward Lass was not present when the photograph was taken at Davis Field.
AAF photo

Major Wernick's B-24 turning away from the target over Shimushu Island during the July 18 raid. Larry Reineke collection

Crews being briefed for one of the missions against the northern Kurile Islands. Larry Reineke collection

The coast line of Shimushu Island. The photograph was taken later during the war from a low flying B-24.
Berthrand H. Hoak collection

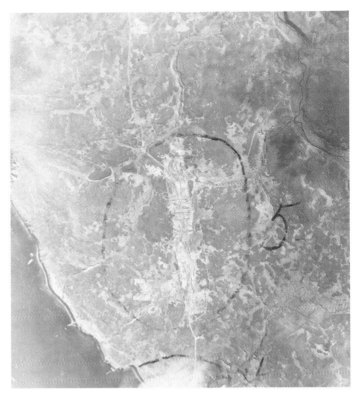

Runway under construction on Shimushu Island. The aerial photograph was taken during the July 18 raid.

Larry Reineke collection

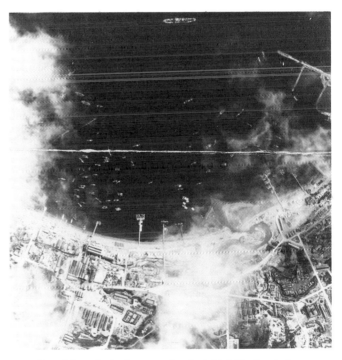

One of the principal reasons for the initial Kurile missions was to obtain aerial photographs. The Americans had been able to acquire information on the Japanese installation through documents captured on Attu, interrogation of prisoners and signals intelligence. However, they still lacked visual confirmation. The early raids provided the missing piece of intelligence. The July 18 aerial photograph is of the Kashiwabara Army staging area on Paramushiro Island. It shows docks, warehouses, shipping and a large number of small fishing boats. Larry Reineke collection

aboard Maj Lavin's B-24 refused to drop and had to be carried back to Alexai Point.

Five of the bombers arrived back at Davis Field between 5:28 and 7:28 PM. Two had stopped at Alexai Field to refuel. The sixth bomber, after landing at Alexai Field, had proceeded to Amchitka. Enemy opposition was light. Several Japanese planes were observed making feeble attempts to take off and intercept the American bombers. The attack in clear daylight had apparently caught the enemy by surprise despite the earlier raids. None of the bombers were hit by enemy fire.

The bombs that were dropped caused little damage. However, the intelligence that was gained from visual sightings and aerial photographs proved an intelligence bonanza. Practically the entire shoreline of Shimushu and the northeastern shoreline of Paramushiro were covered. Two airfields on Shimushu were observed being constructed and one on Paramushiro was in the final stages of completion. A great deal of activity was noted on the Kataoka Naval Base and the Kashiwabara Army Staging Area. A large number of ships were observed anchored in Paramushiro Strait below Kashiwabara Bay. The aerial photographs confirmed that the Japanese were in the process of a major military buildup in the northern Kuriles.[495]

A third raid was launched on August 11. Nine B-24s, six from the 404th Bombardment Squadron and the remainder from the 21st Bombardment Squadron were dispatched from Adak. Pausing briefly at Alexai Field to refuel and load bombs, the nine Liberator crews under the leadership of Louis Blau, now promoted to major, departed the forward field at 6:45 AM and headed out over the North Pacific on a compass course of 260 degrees.

Major Blau, a California attorney who had started out his Army Air Forces reserve officer career as a legal officer and then switched to flying, had assumed command of the 404th the previous day. He was one of the squadron's original members with over a year's Aleutian flying experience behind him.

The new commander had flown as a copilot on the July 18 mission, and was one the few officers present from that mission that had featured mostly majors as pilots who had pulled rank to be on the first successful land based air attack against the Japanese home islands. Other than Major Frank T. Gash, also from the 404th, and Captains Irvin Wadlington and Harrell Hoffman, all the other pilots were lieutenants. Although they were not to share in the glory of making the first successful bomber attack against the northern Kuriles they were to feel the sting of the now thoroughly aroused Japanese.

The weather on the way to the targets was clear with unlimited visibility. As the bombers approached the Kamchatka coast before turning south for the northern Kuriles,

the clear skies gave way to broken clouds with ceilings of two thousand to twenty-five hundred feet. The bombers arrived over their targets shortly after noon.

Major Gash led Flight A (Lieutenants Jerome J. Jones and James R. Pottenger) against the Kataoka Naval Base. Twenty-six 500-pound general purpose and fifteen incendiary cluster bombs were dropped from 11,500 feet. The two other flights, Flight B (Major Blau, Lieutenants Kemmerer and Robert Lockwood) and Flight C (Captains Wadlington and Hoffman and Lieutenant Leon A. Smith), were committed against the Kashiwabara Army Staging Area. Flight C, under the leadership of Captain Wadlington, was from the 21st Bombardment Squadron. The two flights flying at altitudes raging from 10,000 to 12,000 feet unloaded forty-five 500-pound general purpose and fifteen incendiary cluster bombs on the target.

Aerial photograph taken during the August 11 raid of the runway on the Kashiwabara Army staging area on Paramushiro Island. Larry Reineke collection

KISKA HARBOR   ← NORTH HEAD   ← SOUTH HEAD

LITTLE KISKA ISLAND

The panorama photograph was taken July 22 during the combined air-naval bombardment of Kiska. The five ships cruising about four thousand yards off the south shore of the island consist of from left to right: a Sims class destroyer and the cruisers Santa Fe, Louisville, San Francisco *and* Witchita. *The smoke from the funnels was caused by a sudden reduction in speed as the speed of the warships was reduced while they were maneuvered into firing positions. Flack bursts can be seen over Little Kiska in response to a B-24 attack proceeding the naval bombardment. In preparation for the naval bombardment, Admiral Kinkaid had divided his force into two groups. The two battleships,* Mississippi *and* New Mexico, *along with the cruiser* Portland *and an accompaniment of destroyers were responsible for bombarding the Japanese installations at the main camp, the submarine base and North Head. The second group consisting of the remaining five cruisers committed to the bombardment and their destroyer escorts were assigned targets on Little Kiska, South Head and in the Gertrude Cove area. Despite the intense bombardment by sea and air, the net result was one barracks destroyed and another damaged. None of the Japanese were killed. One Japanese diarist did admit that "Today's battle was the most furious since landing on Kiska."* AAF photo

Bomb hits were observed on a large group of buildings near the Kataoka Naval Base and several fires were noted in the base area itself. Bombs were seen to explode in the Kashiwabara Area and the adjacent airfield. Fires in the target area were seen. The anti-aircraft fire ranged from moderate and inaccurate over Kataoka to heavy but inaccurate over the Kashiwabara area. However, fighter opposition was intense and could have been much more lethal if the Japanese pilots had been more experienced and aggressive.

Flight A reported seeing twenty planes, Flight B, fourteen planes and Flight C, twelve to fifteen. Most were Zeros with a scattering of other types. Two fighters headed for Major Gash's bomber shortly after his flight had completed its bomb run. Gash turned towards his attackers and lowered the bomber's nose so that his top turret gunner could get a clear shot. The Japanese pilots broke contact.

Three other Zero pilots singled out Lieutenant Pottenger's B-24. With one of his bomber engines out and another running rough, Pottenger steadily dropped behind the other two bombers. Gash radioed him to head for an alternate field, which Pottenger correctly believed to be Petropavlovsk. Finally shaking his tormentors after his waist gunner Technical Sergeant Thomas E. Ring had shot one down, Pottenger headed up the east coast of the Kamchatka Peninsula for the Russian town and military base 150 miles away.

Major Blau saw his first Japanese fighters five minutes after completing his bomb run. One Zero pilot came barrelling at him from his front right, streaked passed and disappeared under the bomber. Three others attacked from the rear, two of which broke away before coming in range of the B-24s gunners. The third continued on and flew into a burst from the tail gunner's 50 caliber machine gun. Afire, it nosed down into the clouds, trailing smoke. Blau's tail gunner with the assistance from the waist gunner claimed a second fighter which pulled up into a stall, and then fell off and disappeared smoking into a cloud.

Elsewhere in Flight B, Lieutenant Kemmerer's B-24 was jumped by three Japanese fighters. One, the victim of the tail gunner, was seen going into a cloud trailing smoke. The waist gunner drove another off. Lieutenant Lockwood came out of the bomb run and was promptly pounced on by the fighters. His gunners fought back, shooting down two of the attackers. With one engine out and the rest of his bomber riddled, Lockwood headed back to Attu. He barely made it. As his bomber lost altitude, his crew threw out everything that could lighten the load of the struggling bomber; then the three remaining engines quit. In desperation Lockwood and his copilot managed to get them started moments before the bomber would have slammed into the cold North Pacific.

Captain Hoffman never made it over the target. The other two crews in Flight C saw him turning away as the rest of the flight commenced their bomb run. The tail gunner in Captain Wadlington's bomber later reported seeing Hoffman's B-24 being attacked by two Zeros as it headed north. The captain and his nine man crew disappeared without a trace.

As Captain Wadlington was leading the rest of Flight C across the target, he saw several fighters taking off from the runway and taxiway of the airbase at Kashiwabara. Both bombers soon became heavily engaged in a running battle with land based fighters and Rufe float fighters. Wadlington managed to break free, after his gunners drove away the attackers, claiming one shot down. Lieutenant Smith tailing behind was not so fortunate. A swarm of fighters continued to follow him for the next forty-five minutes before finally breaking off contact 100 miles east of Shimushu. Smith's gunners claimed two confirmed, one probable and two possible fighters shot down.

The seven surviving bomber crews made it back to Alexai Field by 4:30 PM after being in the air for almost ten hours. Lieutenant Pottenger was within 25 miles of Petropavlovsk before he had to crash-land his damaged bomber in a swamp. Two men were injured. One, Sergeant Ring, later died. The Russians rescued the men shortly afterwards. Pottenger's crew of ten became the first of two hundred and one men from twenty-five Eleventh Air Force and Fleet Air Wing Four crews to be interned in Russia during the air offensive against the northern Kurile Islands.

While the bombing results were not impressive, action against the fighters had been somewhat better. Four planes were confirmed shot down, one other was classed as a probable and two as possible. Again the aerial photographs indicated the Japanese were continuing to strengthen their defenses.[496]

The fact that they had accounted for two American bombers and inflicted damage on several others indicated the Japanese were now fully alerted to the new air threat. However, before any more missions could be flown, the final matter of retaking Kiska had to be settled.

Deliverance

The missions against Kiska were resumed on July 11 with the commitment of six B-24 and six B-25 sorties in three missions against the main camp and North Head areas. Four P-40 sorties were flown over Kiska and three Ventura sorties were flown in support of the army aircraft. No further missions were flown until the 15th when a mission of eight B-25s from the 77th Bombardment Squadron were sent against the main camp facilities. A mission of three B-24s bombed the Gertrude Cove area. One B-24 flown by Lieutenant Sheroen E. Van Blaricon from the 404th Bombardment Squadron crashed at Cape Adagdak on Adak. Lieutenant Van Blaricon and five others were killed.

The weather turned sour again and it was not until the 18th that two B-24s and six B-25s were sent against targets at Gertrude Cove. One Ventura sortie was flown against a tent area on North Head. Following another break for the weather, a mission consisting of nine B-24s pounded North Head on July 21. Other planned missions for the day were cancelled because of poor weather.[497]

On July 22, Admiral Kinkaid sent in the largest bombardment force ever committed against Kiska. Two prewar battleships, the *Mississippi* and the *New Mexico* along with five cruisers and nine destroyers were committed to the effort. The battleships and the cruiser *Portland* were placed under Rear Admiral Robert M. Griffin and the remainder under charge of Admiral Giffin. Together the team of Giffin and Griffin steamed into position just outside Kiska Harbor while General Butler prepared to launch one of the heaviest air attacks of the Aleutian Campaign.

The skies were clear as the bombardment force moved into position to subject the Japanese to a twenty minute bombardment. Some 212 tons of high explosives ranging from 14-inch to 5-inch shells rained down on the Japanese positions around Kiska Harbor, on Little Kiska and at Gertrude Cove.[498]

Bombers and fighters from the Eleventh Air Force also hit the Japanese hard before and after the naval bombardment. Three missions involving eighteen B-24 and sixteen B-25 sorties were flown out of Adak, and four missions consisting of eight B-24s, nine B-25s, twenty P-38 and thirteen P-40 sorties were launched from Amchitka.

One B-25 from the 73rd Bombardment Squadron was hit by anti-aircraft fire. Lieutenant Everett N. Hendrickson and his crew managed to ditch the bomber off Kiska where they were rescued by a nearby PBY.

In addition to the blasting by Admiral Giffin's fleet, the airmen of the Eleventh Air Force dropped over 63 tons of bombs on the Japanese positions.[499]

However, despite all the sound and fury, other than to jar the nerves of the Japanese burrowed deep in their dugouts, very little damage was done. One Japanese diarist who had previously derided the inabilities of the Americans to hit their targets as "sad case" did note that the naval and air attacks were "the most furious since landing on Kiska." The Japanese rightly regarded the July 22 bombardment as a prelude to an invasion.[500]

After a day's break for the weather, the runway overlooking Salmon Lagoon was singled out for special attention for the next two days as P-40s from the 18th Fighter Squadron and the Canadian Number 14 Fighter Squadron shuttled back and forth from early morning to late afternoon.

On the first of eight missions of forty sorties that were flown on July 24, Flight Officer Joseph Levy from the 18th Fighter Squadron was shot down. The Japanese buried his body near the airstrip. In a merciless world war fueled by racial hatred and acts of incredible, mindless violence, the Japanese on Kiska paused for a moment to honor a fallen foe. In one of their last acts before leaving the island, they erected a cross and a sign over Levy's grave on which was written: "Sleeping here a brave air-hero who lost youth and happiness for his mother land."[501]

The fighter-bomber assault resumed the afternoon of the 25th. Relays of P-40s carrying 500-pound bombs were sent against the Japanese runway. By the end of the day, a total of forty sorties had been flown. However, for all

The grave site of Pilot Officer Joe Levi, 18th Fighter Squadron, left behind by the Japanese. USA photo

A seemingly direct hit on the seaplane area, main camp, Kiska. Despite the intensity of the bombardment effort, very little damage was done to the Japanese who expended a considerable effort to protect their installations from aerial and sea bombardments. General Butler admitted that despite ten months of bombing, the Japanese were stronger at the end because of their fortifications. AAF photo

the effort, the runway had only been cratered in seven places.[502]

The largest and most intensive bombing and strafing effort to date was mounted the next day as General Butler committed every operational combat aircraft in the Eleventh Air Force including the few B-17Es that had been retained by the 36th Bombardment Squadron for reconnaissance duties. The weather over Kiska was clear for a change. Two missions, one of eight and the other of ten B-24s, were launched from Adak followed by two B-17 and one B-24 reconnaissance missions. One hundred and forty-five 500-pound bombs were dropped from altitudes of eighteen to twenty thousand feet.

The major effort was from Amchitka where the bomber crews waited their turn on the bomber strip to take off while the fighter pilots flew in relays from the fighter strip. The day was filled with the thunder and roar of engines as ground crews assisted by the aircrews worked frantically to service and rearm the aircraft. Eleven missions were flown that day involving fourteen B-24, twenty-four P-38 and thirty-nine P-40 sorties. A total of 104 tons of bombs ranging from 20-pound fragmentation to 1,100-pound general purpose bombs were dropped on all the Japanese installations by American and Canadian airmen from both bases.[503]

Anti-aircraft fire was weak. However, Flying Officer John R. Bradley's P-40 was hit in the cooling system as he flew over Little Kiska. Reporting his position and problem to Captain George Ruddell, leader of the 18th Fighter Squadron flight, Bradley headed for nearby Rat Island. His fighter continued to lose altitude as the engine lost power. Finally, the engine, out of coolant, froze.

While Ruddell and the others of his flight orbited overhead, Bradley, following prescribed ditching procedures, slid the canopy back, tightened his seat belt and shoulder harness, lowered his flaps and made a stall landing on the water near Rat Islands. The fighter hit the water in a great plume of spray, stopped abruptly, nose deep in the water, bobbed back to the surface, and then immediately sank nose first for the last time. As it went under, Bradley was still trying to free himself from the shoulder harness and seat belt. With the water turning to a dark green, Bradley finally broke loose from the confines of the cockpit. On reaching the surface, he looked up to see a PBY circling overhead.[504]

Oliver Glenn had been orbiting in his PBY off the coast of Kiska when he heard Bradley's call for assistance. Glenn landed beside the downed pilot. One of the crew members pulled him aboard and the pharmacy mate stripped off Bradley's heavy leather flying suit, wrapped him in an electric blanket and gave him a two ounce bottle of brandy. Captain Ruddell and the other P-40 pilots, seeing that Bradley was safe aboard the Catalina, departed, leaving Lieutenant Glenn to begin the most hazardous part of the rescue, the open water takeoff in ten to twelve foot swells.

After slamming into two swells with a bone jarring wrench, Glenn's PBY lifted off just as it was about to hit the third swell. The rest of the flight back to Amchitka was uneventful, and Bradley had recovered enough so that he could walk unaided off the amphibian.[505]

On the 27th, six B-24s and five B-25s were sent against Kiska from Davis Field while two missions of eight P-38s and eight P-40s were committed from Amchitka. Ninety 500-pound bombs were dropped.[506]

Admiral Akiyama's forces on Kiska, huddled in their dugouts, waited for their deliverance. Initially Admiral Kawase planned to evacuate the garrison by submarine. His staff figured it would take forty to fifty round trips to bring home the approximately six thousand men on Kiska. Thirteen I Class submarines from 1st, 7th, 12th and 19th Submarine Division were committed to the effort. The evacuation got underway when the I-7 arrived the night of May 26 with a cargo of weapons, ammunition and food. After unloading the cargo and taking aboard sixty passengers, the submarine slid out of Kiska Harbor and headed for Paramushiro.

Despite the initial success, the evacuation by submarine proved to be a time consuming and dangerous undertaking in the face of the incessant patrolling by Fleet Air Wing Four and the vigilance of Admiral Kinkaid's warships.

On June 10, the crew of the sub chaser PC-487 picked up the I-24 on sonar forty miles northeast of Shemya. Depth charges were dropped and the submarine was forced to the surface. Lieutenant Wallace G. Cornell, despite the fact that his 170-foot long vessel was one eighth the tonnage of the submarine, elected to ram the I-24. The bow of his vessel rode up over the hull of the submarine with a loud scraping noise. Lieutenant Cornell backed off, and after raking the I-24 with his deck guns, rammed her again in the conning tower. This time, the large submarine

Evacuees crowd aboard one of the submarines sent to their rescue. Japanese photo via Larry Golden

rolled over and sank with all hands.

The I-9, which had served as the flagship of Admiral Yamasaki during the Dutch Harbor attack, was sunk by the destroyer *Frazier* off the coast of Kiska on June 13. The destroyer *Monaghan*, on patrol with *Aylwin* off Kiska Harbor, caught the I-7 while on her third trip to Kiska and drove her ashore near Little Kiska with long range gunfire. The captain was trying to put back to sea with his damaged submarine when three patrol boats arrived and finished the job. The I-7 sank near Twin Rocks south of Kiska Harbor. Only a handful of the crew made it ashore.

One other submarine disappeared without a trace and three others were damaged. On June 21, Admiral Kawase decided to halt the operations after evacuating 820 Army and Navy construction workers.[507] The Commander, Fifth Fleet next decided to commit virtually all of his warships in a maximum effort to save the isolated garrison on Kiska.

It was a desperate gamble fraught with risk in the face of Admiral Kinkaid's seemingly impenetrable air and sea blockade which extended from the very entrance of Kiska Harbor, where the two destroyers lurked, to the waters west of the Aleutian Islands towards the Asian mainland over which Fleet Air Wing Four kept a constant vigil. However, Admiral Kawase had three important factors in his favor: the summer fog of the North Pacific; American military bungling; and plain, old fashioned luck.

The mission of saving the Kiska garrison was entrusted to Rear Admiral Masatomi Kimura, at the time Commander, 1st Destroyer Squadron. Of great patience and determination, and with a cool head, Kimura possessed a knowledge of the North Pacific waters gained during the

Japanese prewar probing of the Aleutian Islands. The light cruisers *Abukuma* and *Kiso* and ten destroyers along with an oiler and escort vessel were placed at his disposal.

On July 2, Admiral Kimura's force headed out from its anchorage at Paramushiro, turned due south and then east again along the 45th parallel to avoid the patrolling PBYs, before turning northeast for the final high speed run to Kiska. After two days they had reached a point 500 nautical miles southwest of Kiska. The fog was too thin, and Admiral Kimura ordered his force to return to Paramushiro. He sortied out again on July 12 with the same dismal results.

While their rescue force steamed back and forth across the North Pacific, Admiral Akiyama's men continued to practice their evacuation drill. Akiyama had sent one of his staff officers to Paramushiro aboard a submarine to work out the details. The officer returned in late June. The garrison at Gertrude Cove was withdrawn to Kiska Harbor; and beginning five days after the first departure date of the rescue force, the Kiska garrison began assembling on the beaches between the hours of 9:00 PM and midnight. Some of the personnel were required to come as far as five miles away from positions on North Head and in the hills behind the main camp and the submarine base.

On July 21, Admiral Kimura's force headed out again. By now his force was running low on fuel. This was the last effort he could make. Fortunately, weather conditions were right. A thick fog hung over the North Pacific. Fortune also smiled on his endeavor, for during the early morning darkness of June 26, the Battle of the Pips was fought.

It began on the 23rd when a PBY crew reported a radar

contact with seven vessels 200 nautical miles southwest of Attu. Admiral Kinkaid and his staff reasoned that the Japanese were trying to reinforce Kiska and ordered Admirals Giffen and Griffin to intercept the Japanese. At the same time the *Aylwin* and *Monaghan* were pulled from their stations off Kiska Harbor and sent to participate in the anticipated battle. Unfortunately, the PBY sighting proved to be a bogus one, but the damage had been done. The team of Giffen and Griffin had been distracted and the entrance into Kiska Harbor left wide open despite belated attempts to plug it with patrol boats.

Shortly after midnight on June 26, as Admiral Giffen's force was steaming towards the bogus Japanese fleet, the radar operator aboard the *Mississippi* spotted what he thought were the Japanese on his scope heading on a course due east. Radar operators aboard several other ships confirmed the sighting. Giffen's force had by now reached a point 80 nautical miles southwest of Kiska. Battle stations were sounded and Admiral Giffen's ships crews, using their radars, began firing at the sightings. When it was over, the battleships had pumped 518 14-inch and the cruisers 487 8-inch shells into the empty expanse of the North Pacific.

When dawn broke, the Americans were greeted with the sight of the cold, grey heaving seas of the North Pacific. There was no debris, not even a dead whale. Admiral Giffen's force had slugged it out with a phantom fleet. The radar operators through some quirk in the atmosphere or equipment, or both, had picked up false returns on their radar scopes.

Admiral Kinkaid then compounded the problem by ordering the ships to refuel from the oiler *Pecos* at a point

105 nautical miles south east of Kiska. While the Americans were engaged in this operation, Admiral Kimura's force steamed through the scene of the Battle of the Pips and into Kiska Harbor.

Admiral Kimura had broken radio silence briefly to inform Admiral Akiyama that he was inbound and ask for a weather report. By the time his ships emerged like grey ghosts into view, the garrison was waiting on the beach, their hearts filled with joy in the knowledge that they had been delivered from certain death. The anchors were lowered at 1:40 PM. The men quickly clambered into the barges with only their personal possessions and weapons and headed out for the waiting ships. The empty barges were sunk and ships got underway at 2:35 PM.

Kiska receded into the mist and memory, as the Japanese warships sped towards the Kurile Islands. The stillness ashore was broken by the sound of explosions as timed explosive charges went off, blowing up the facilities that had been hastily abandoned. After over a year of sound and fury, the guns stood silent and useless, their vital parts removed and thrown away. A few dogs, Explosion among them, abandoned by their owners, wandered through the empty camps in search of food.

For Commander Nifumi Mukai, who was among the last to leave, the world had changed greatly since his invasion force had first come ashore the evening of June 6 the previous year. Japan's brief occupation of North America had ended. She was now faced with the terrible, well organized, led, trained and equipped American juggernaut that was advancing with relentless, merciless fury across the vast expanse of the Pacific.[508]

Admiral Kimura's force arrived back at its anchorage in

The Japanese wait on the beach near their main camp for their deliverance.
Japanese photo via Larry Golden

Paramushiro Straits on August 1. The Navy personnel from Kiska were set to work building an airstrip and gun emplacements at Kataoka Naval Base while the Army personnel moved into the Kashiwabara Army Staging Area.[509]

The Fury

Admiral Kinkaid's forces continued to pound Kiska despite nagging indications that the Japanese were no longer there. The weather cleared sufficiently on August 1 for missions to be resumed, and Lieutenant Bernard J. O'Donnell from the 21st Bombardment Squadron flew a reconnaissance mission over Kiska during the morning. He reported "no anti-aircraft, no enemy aircraft or shipping observed." A seven B-24 mission was flown later that day and eighty-three 500-pound bombs were dropped through the overcast on the main camp area.[510]

The next day, Kiska was subjected to another naval bombardment. The *Mississippi* and *New Mexico* along with five cruisers and nine destroyers pumped 2,315 rounds totaling 200 tons into the deserted facilities ashore. The Eleventh Air Force added its weight to the softening up of Kiska prior to the invasion planned for the 15th. Two bomber missions, one of eight B-24s and the other of nine B-25s were flown from Amchitka while a Ventura from Davis Field was committed to a weather reconnaissance mission. Eight P-38 sorties were also flown. A total of 268 bombs ranging from 20-pound fragmentation to 600-pound general purpose bombs were dropped on all the facilities.

In addition to the daily bombardments by the Eleventh Air Force, the destroyers *Farragut* and *Hull* which had taken up station off Kiska Harbor shortly after the Battle of the Pips, subjected the facilities ashore to nightly bombardments. Fleet Air Wing Four also continued to fly nocturnal "Black Cat" missions over Kiska with its PBYs.[511]

Six attack missions were planned for August 4, two of which were aborted. The two B-24 missions from Davis Field were turned back by weather. A mission of five B-25s from Amchitka made it through as did the twelve P-38, seven P-40s and a PV-1.[512] The next day the weather improved and Kiska was subjected to the most intensive aerial bombardment of the Aleutian Campaign.

Between 8:55 AM and 6:46 PM, the valleys and hillsides on Kiska rumbled with the sound of explosions as 153 tons of bombs were rained down on the silent Japanese gun positions and abandoned facilities. Six missions were flown from Davis Field involving twenty-three B-24 and sixteen B-25 sorties.

The fury of Amchitka was turned loose. Twelve missions were launched from the island consisting of five B-24, twenty-seven B-24, forty P-38 and eight P-40 sorties. And for the first time, Lieutenant Colonel Mark E. Hubbard's 407th Bombardment (Dive) Group was committed to battle. Carrying a maximum bomb load, the Douglas A-24 Dauntless dive bomber pilots flew sixteen sorties from Amchitka and dropped forty-six 500-pound bombs on two anti-aircraft batteries in the main camp area. Altogether, the bombers and fighters from Amchitka unloaded one thousand five hundred and fifty seven bombs. Only the wildlife and the abandoned dogs cowered in fear below.[513]

Following the maximum effort of the 4th, the weather closed in and no more missions were flown until the 10th. On 6 August, Colonel Tom Hutton, General Butler's intelligence officer released a bomb damage report based on aerial photographs taken between July 27 and August 4. According to it, twenty-three buildings at the main camp and nine at the submarine base had been destroyed. The two radio stations had apparently been moved and the radar station had been damaged or dismantled. An examination of the photographs also showed the Japanese had made no attempt to fill approximately thirty bomb

Douglas A-24 Dauntless dive bombers, 407th Bombardment (Dive) Group.
Frank Harvey collection

craters in the runway on North Head.

The aerial photograph interpreters who poured over the photographs were disturbed by what they found. "It is significant," they noted, "that most of the buildings affected show no evidence of having been bombed and shelled . . . It is also significant that the photographs of 2 August and 4 August show all the trucks in identical positions and show ten to twelve less barges than usual in the Kiska Harbor area."[514]

There were other indications. The Japanese had ceased radio communications on the date they left the island. However, pilots returning from missions immediately after the Japanese evacuation had reported light anti-aircraft fire. One claimed that he had been hit by ground fire. Another stated he had strafed a Japanese soldier and seen him fall. Still another reported seeing the Japanese digging defensive positions at the base of Kiska Volcano. Admiral Kinkaid ordered the attacks continued despite comments by his staff that the reports had been rendered by green pilots.[515]

The missions against Kiska resumed on August 10th when Major Blau's nine B-24 crews en route to Attu for the mission against the northern Kuriles the next day dropped 12 tons of bombs on all the installations on Kiska. A further nineteen missions involving five B-24, fourteen B-25, seventeen A-24 and eighteen P-40 sorties were flown from Amchitka. Sixty-three tons of bombs were dropped. Twenty P-40 and three F-5 strafing and reconnaissance sorties were also flown.

The next day, two missions were flown by six B-24s and twenty-two B-25s from Davis Field and eleven missions consisting of eleven B-24s, twenty-seven B-25s, fourteen P-38s and twenty-six P-40s from Amchitka. Four F-5 and one Ventura mission were flown to document the 104 tons of bombs dropped on Kiska.[516]

On the 12th, Admiral Kinkaid sent five cruisers and five destroyers into the waters off Kiska. When they had finished, the crews of the warships had lobbed 60 tons of high explosive shells at the deserted positions ashore.[517]

General Butler's bombers and fighters added another 87 tons of ordnance. Four B-25 missions were flown from Davis Field, and the 75mm cannon equipped B-25Gs were employed for the first time. Twenty-two shells were fired at targets on Kiska. Another fifteen missions originated from Amchitka involving eighteen B-25, eighteen P-38, sixteen P-40 and fourteen A-24 sorties. Four reconnaissance and photographic missions were flown by the crews of two B-24s and the pilots of two P-40s and two F-5s. Finally, the crews of six Liberators returning from Attu to Adak dropped one hundred and five 100-pound bombs on Kiska.[518]

The effort marked the last commitment of Canadian fighter pilots to the attacks on Kiska. Ten pilots and an intelligence officer from Number 14 Fighter Squadron had replaced a similar number of personnel from Number 111 Fighter Squadron at Amchitka on July 9.

Number 14 Fighter Squadron flew thirty missions and one hundred and ninety sorties during its two Aleutian deployments. Number 111 Fighter Squadron flew a similar number of missions during its two deployments. The squadron was also the first to be committed to combat in the Aleutians when four P-40 pilots flew an escort mission on September 25, 1942 against Kiska. The Americans awarded one Distinguished Flying Cross and fifteen Air Medals to individuals of both squadrons. Most qualified for the Worn Out Aleutian Pilot diploma.

Seventeen Canadian airmen gave their lives for the allied cause. Seven are buried in the Fort Richardson National Cemetery.

The Aleutian Campaign was the first time the two nations had conducted joint air operations during wartime. In the course of the campaign, the Canadians learned something of the American desires to provide an air defense of North America and the Americans in turn were made aware of Canada's strong desire to maintain its national sovereignty. The campaign also proved that Canadian squadrons could operate within the American command system, yet maintain their identity. The lessons learned helped provide a framework for the later establishment of the North American Air Defense Command.[519]

Amid the sound and fury of the August attacks, the airmen of the Eleventh Air Force and Fleet Air Wing Four began realizing for certain that there were no Japanese on the island. One P-40 pilot returning to his alert shack on Amchitka exclaimed in disgust: "If there are any Japs on that #@ island, I'll eat em all." Billy Wheeler noted in his diary: "The whole thing looks suspicious and baffling."[520]

By now the fighter pilots were making low-level passes across the empty positions and reporting no anti-aircraft fire. One, Capt George Ruddell, decided to make a first hand investigation. He and three other P-40 pilots of a flight from the 18th Fighter Squadron that he was leading made several low and slow passes over the main camp area, the numerous gun positions there and on North Head and the Salmon Lagoon runway. After studying the bomb cratered runway in some detail, they decided they could thread their way around the holes and debris for a safe landing.

Recalling the experience during an August 1990 reunion of the Eleventh Air Force in Anchorage, Ruddell, a retired Air Force colonel, stated: "All four of us got down OK, although we almost lost No 4. He almost went off the end of the runway and down a 100-foot drop. We knew there were no Japanese there, and we wanted to prove it and get

The photograph of the Kiska runway was taken in 1946. The effects of the bombing attacks can be clearly seen around it. Despite the efforts expended to make it unusable, Capt George Ruddell and three other P-40 pilots from the 18th Fighter Squadron were able to land on it shortly after the Japanese evacuated the island and before the Americans and Canadian invasion force landed. The runway was repaired after the reoccupation. Even after years of abandonment and the ravages of Aleutian weather, the runway is still in a good state of repair.

FAA collection, Anchorage Museum of History and Art

The remains of the control tower built by the Americans near the approach end of the runway. The photograph was taken on a foggy September morning in 1989. photo by author

back and say so."[521]

Captain Ruddell and the other pilots got out of their fighters and walked around the areas near the runway. They found Joe Levi's grave. Satisfied that there were no Japanese on the island, Ruddell and the others safely negotiated a takeoff from the bomb pitted runway. On return to Amchitka, he informed his superiors of his discovery. Ruddell recalled:

> I got called to the head man's office and got a real good chewing out, because we weren't authorized to land there. Apparently nothing else came of our information, because the invasion, which I thought was a terrible waste, went as planned."[522]

General Butler, who had flown over the island, was also convinced that the Japanese were not on the island as was Major General Holland M. Smith, who suggested that a scouting party be sent ashore to have a first hand look. Admiral Kinkaid, however, felt that the Japanese had retreated into the hills to prepare defensive positions similar to those encountered on Attu. He did not want to take a chance on exposing the scouting party on the open terrain of Kiska where it might be spotted and wiped out. In any case, even if the Japanese were not on the island, the invasion, Admiral Kinkaid believed, would be a "super dress rehearsal, good for training purposes." With the invasion date only days away and the troops trained and

The Japanese left behind the remnants of
aircraft and discarded fuel barrels.
Souvenir hunters, salvage and technical
teams removed virtually all the aircraft.
Very little remains today to indicate that
the Japanese once had an air base in the
Aleutians. The photograph was taken
August 19, 1943. USA photo

American and Canadian troops prepare to disembark as
others make their way up the fog shrouded slopes off the
landing beach. USA photo

One of the badly damaged submarines left on the beach. USA photo

The Japanese left behind three of the original six midget submarines they shipped to the island. The three were badly damaged by explosive charges set by the Japanese and by the air and naval attacks. The remnants of one of the submarines can be still found on the beach and another rests in what used to be the repair and service area. Part of the marine railway also remains. The photograph, looking towards North Head shows the expanse of Kiska Harbor and the shipping in it. The float planes are Kingfishers. USA photo

The remains of Type O Aichi El3Al Jake three-seat, twin float reconnaissance monoplane found on Kiska. The Jake and the Rufe were the most common aircraft the Japanese employed on Kiska. USA photo

Panoramic view of Kiska Harbor taken from the high ground behind the submarine base. North Head can be seen in the distance. Alaska Historical Library

ready for action, Kinkaid gave the go-ahead.[523]

The Eleventh Air Force flew eleven more missions during August 13 and 14, bringing the total flown by it and Fleet Air Wing Four between June 1 and August 15 to two hundred and ninety-one missions against Kiska. One thousand, two hundred and fifty-five tons of bombs were dropped, slightly over a third of the total tonnage dropped on Kiska since the start of the Aleutian Campaign. The air assault reached its highest peak during the four days preceding the landing when 400 tons of ordnance ranging from 20-pound fragmentation to 2000-pound demolition bombs were unloaded on the empty positions below.[524]

General Corlett's forces, after making a feint towards the south shore near Kiska Harbor, landed on the north and west sides of the islands and began moving into the mist-shrouded interior. For the next several days, American and Canadian patrols probed deeper into the island. Occasional shots were heard as friendly forces unexpectedly came upon each other in the mist.

The accidental encounters resulted in some of seventeen American and four Canadian soldiers who died during the invasion. Booby traps left behind by the Japanese also contributed to the lives lost. Another one hundred and twenty-one men suffered from sickness and wounds. The largest number of casualties occurred when the *Abner Read* struck a floating Japanese mine during the early morning hours of August 18 off the northwestern landing beach. The explosion crumpled the destroyer's stern, which broke off and carried seventy-one men to their death. Forty-seven others were wounded.[525]

As the American and Canadian soldiers moved across the island, they came upon the melancholy remnants left from over a year of violence and human perseverance. A climbing team from the 87th Mountain Infantry Regiment found what was left of Lieutenant Vasataka's OA-10 on the slopes of Kiska Volcano. The bodies were still in the rescue aircraft. Another patrol found Flying Officer Levi's grave. A photographer took several pictures, one of which later appeared in *Newsweek* magazine.

In their haste to abandoned the island, the Japanese left behind all their supplies and equipment. Piles of wrecked aircraft and abandoned vehicles lay about. Uneaten meals and discarded games of chance were found in hastily vacated quarters lending mute testimony to the hurried departure of the Japanese. A copy of Margaret Mitchell's *Gone With the Wind* was found in a deserted gun position.

The Japanese also took time to scribble crude caricatures of American leaders on the wall with misspelled statements such as "We shall come again and kill out separately Yanki-jocker," and "You are dancing by foolish order of Rouserbelt." Someone had left a message

on one of the ships in the harbor, "You gave us this ship, now take the damned thing back."

Deserted gun positions stood intact, a mocking example of the ineffectiveness of the aerial and ship bombardment that the Japanese had been subjected to. Not one of the coastal defense gun positions had been put out of action. Most of the 75mm dual purpose gun positions remained unharmed. The 120mm dual purpose guns, although their splinter shields were riddled, were still standing despite their exposed positions near the tip of North Head. Many of the smaller anti-aircraft positions were unharmed. The barrels of all the guns were badly worn.

Most of the buildings, some badly damaged, still stood. Underground facilities remained relatively intact. The runway that the Japanese so laboriously built on North Head, although pitted with craters, was easily repaired.[527]

To achieve this destruction, the Eleventh Air Force alone had dropped 26,910 bombs ranging in size from

Japanese messages scribbled on the walls of one of their underground bunkers. Frank Rosse Collection

Canadian soldiers hold a captured Japanese flag in front of one of the former occupant's quarters. USA photo

20-pound fragmentation to 2,000-pound demolition bombs. In total weight, the figure came to 3,024.76 out of the 3,662.00 tons dropped on both islands. Fleet Air Wing Four and sea bombardments had upped the tonnage considerably.[527]

The aerial and sea bombardment of Kiska had failed in destroying the Japanese and their installations. Although the Japanese complained of the bombardment in their diaries, they had in the end endured. Robert Sherrod noted in an August 30, 1943 Time magazine article: "The sooner we acknowledge the relative ineffectiveness of precision bombing on small, well dug-in, expertly camouflaged positions, the better we will be."[528]

As the Americans and Canadians searched the island, they came across three dogs, including Explosion. One of the Eleventh Air Force flyers, when he heard about them, quipped: "We dropped one hundred thousand propaganda leaflets, but those dogs couldn't read." The dogs also gave rise to a sarcastic ballad, "Tales of Kiska," with the refrain:

> O here's to mighty ComNorPac
> Whose kingdom lay at cold Adak
> Whose reign was known in fame for fog
> And capture of two couple dogs.[529]

Admiral Kinkaid, ComNorPac, tried to put an optimistic face on the situation, stating: "We got what we set out to do. The lives saved by the withdrawal of the enemy made it even more successful. It was a darned good dress rehearsal under combat conditions."[530] Robert Sherrod coined a new word, Janfu: joint army-navy foul-up.[531]

On August 17, Major Gash and his crew took off from Shemya at 7:45 and headed for Kiska. After three days of fog and clouds the skies over Kiska were clear. As Gash and his crew looked down from their B-24, they could see

One of the dual purpose 120mm gun positions on North Head which experienced a near miss by a 500-pound bomb.
USN photo

The Americans also found a cemetery on Kiska marked with Russian Orthodox Crosses. USA photo

men moving about the positions formerly occupied by the Japanese. The Eleventh Air Force had flown its last mission over Kiska.[532]

Shortly afterwards, President Roosevelt met with Prime Minister Churchill in Quebec, Canada to affirm the decision to invade France and discuss future strategy. While there, he and Canada's Prime Minister Mackenzie King issued a joint statement announcing the successful conclusion of the Aleutian Campaign. On August 21, Robert Atwood's *Anchorage Daily Times* informed Alaskans that the "last vestige of North American territory" had been freed from Japanese forces.[533]

The Price of Pride

For little over a year, a force of approximately 8,500 Japanese at its peak strength had tied down a considerably larger American and Canadian force which had grown to 144,000 in the Alaska-Aleutian area on the eve of the Kiska invasion. The strength of the Eleventh Air Force had climbed from 4,489, the first day the Japanese bombed Dutch Harbor, to 16,526, the day the troops were landed on Kiska.[524]

Approximately one thousand men died in battle or were counted missing in action during the course of the Aleutian Campaign, which lasted from June 10, 1942 to August 15, 1943. The bulk of the casualties, 549, were born by the ground forces in the retaking of Attu. The Navy, excluding Fleet Air Wing Four, lost around 200 personnel. The Eleventh Air Force in the course of the campaign sustained 114 killed in action and 42 missing in action. Fleet Air Wing Four lost 10 killed in action and another 16 missing in action. Accidents claimed the lives of approximately 46 Eleventh Air Force, 34 Fleet Air Wing Four and 17 Royal Canadian Air Force airmen. The 406th Bombardment Squadron was the only Eleventh Air Force combat flying unit that did not experience any fatalities.

The fighter pilots suffered an accident rate far out of proportion to their combat losses. Twenty died in accidents while nine were killed in action and another three were reported missing in action; and of the fighter squadrons, the 54th sustained the highest loss. Eight pilots lost their lives in accidents, seven died in battle and two disappeared while engaged in combat with the enemy.

The names of all those who died, to include the deaths sustained during the bombing of Dutch Harbor, can be found either in the text of this book or in the end notes that cite each occurrence. The known non-battle deaths are included in this endnote.[535]

In terms of equipment lost, the Aleutian Campaign cost the Eleventh Air Force, Fleet Air Wing Four, the RCAF and the other air units in the Aleutians 225 aircraft of which 41 were destroyed during combat. The others were classified as operational losses, most of which were due to accidents. Weather was the prime culprit. The table below shows the loss by type of aircraft.

Aircraft	Cbt Losses	Ops Losses	Total
Fighters	18	108	126
Light Bombers	0	2	2
Medium Bombers	7	18	25
Heavy Bombers	10	22	32
Patrol Planes	5	34	39
Float Planes	1	0	1
Totals	**41**	**184**	**225**

The fighter losses included the eight F4F-4 Wildcats lost during the battle of Attu and those P-40s lost by the Canadians. The two light bombers were A-24s from the 407th Bombardment Group deployed to Alaska for the Kiska invasion. The medium bombers included B-18s, B-25s and B-26s. The heavy bombers were the B-17Es and the B-24Ds flown by the three heavy bombardment squadrons. The patrol planes included the Catalinas and Venturas of Fleet Air Wing Four and the A-29 Hudsons of the 406th Bombardment Squadron. All the combat losses were sustained by Fleet Air Wing Four during the Kiska Blitz and the course of their patrol activities over the North Pacific and Bering Sea. The 406th Bombardment lost three of its A-29s to accidents elsewhere. The float plane loss occurred when the SOC-1 Seagull from the cruiser *Indianapolis* was shot down during the August 7, 1942 naval bombardment of Japanese installations in Kiska Harbor.

In compensation for the loss of life and aircraft, the Eleventh Air Force, in addition to the pounding of Japanese facilities on Kiska and Attu, was credited with the destruction of the *Borneo Maru, Nissan Maru, Nozima Maru* and *Urajio Maru* at Kiska; the *Cherryboune Maru* at Attu; and the *Kotohira Maru, Montreal Maru* and another unknown transport on the open sea. Bomber crews also sank the destroyer *Oboro* and damaged the RO-65. The Vickers class submarine later sank in Kiska Harbor. The Eleventh Air Force was also credited with damaging the destroyer *Hatsuharu* and a transport.

Fleet Air Wing Four received credit for the sinking of

The flags of Canada and the United States fly over Kiska.
USA photo

-322-

the RO-61, finishing off the *Kano Maru* and damaging the destroyer *Hibiki*.

In addition to the losses from air attacks, the Japanese lost the destroyers *Arare* and *Nehohi* to submarine attacks. The destroyers *Kasumi* and *Shiranuhi* and the transport Kano Maru were also damaged during submarine attacks. Two Japanese I class submarines, I-7 and I-24, and the transport *Akagane Maru* were sunk by surface gunfire. The I-9 was sunk by ramming.

The Japanese, besides losing their entire garrison on Attu and approximately 500 men on Kiska, also admitted to the loss of about 1,000 men at sea as well as the loss of 150 of its Navy airmen.[536]

The Japanese committed a folly in trying to secure a lodgment in the Aleutians which they had little hope of sustaining; and which gave them little advantage other than the false hope that it was blocking a military invasion route and the knowledge that their presence was an embarrassment to their foe. The retaking of the two strategically worthless islands represented not a military victory, but the erasure of a psychological blot.

The command arrangements, already badly flawed, were made even more difficult by the egos of the senior commanders and their unwillingness to work in joint har-mony. Despite the urging by General Marshall and the suggestions by General Buckner, General DeWitt had refused to agree to the creation of a separate theater of operations in Alaska. General Buckner, shunted aside in a supporting role at the outset of the Aleutian Campaign, failed to fully cooperate with the overly cautious Admiral Theobald and then compounded the problem by his un-professional slurs on the admiral's courage and abilities.

Admiral Kinkaid, aggressive, battle experienced and more diplomatic, proved more able in securing General Buckner's cooperation. However, in his drive to destroy the Japanese lodgments, he optimistically underestimated the Japanese strength and will on Attu and then refused to heed overwhelming evidence that they had evacuated Kiska.

In the final analysis, the Aleutians should have been left to the Aleuts. The troops employed there could have been put to better use elsewhere and the billions of dollars hastily spend on building and sustaining a military infrastructure on the islands used more wisely in other theaters.

In the end, the price of pride was paid for by the young men, American, Canadian and Japanese who fought with great bravery and then were forgotten by history.

A few of the Aleutian Warriors gather at Elmendorf AFB on August 9, 1990, to commemorate the rebirth of the Eleventh Air Force. USFA photo

NOTES
. . . .

Chapter 1: Old Alaska New Alaska

1. George W. Rogers, *The Future of Alaska: Economic Consequences of Statehood*, (Baltimore, MD, 1959), p. 63.

2. Lieut Jerry N. Ransohoff, Hist, Eleventh Air Force, 15 Jan 42-Sep 45, pp. 4-5.

3. Intvw., John H. Cloe with Brig Gen Benjamin B. Talley, USA (Ret), 14 Sep 1979.

4. Lieut Arthur B. Ferguson, *Alaskan Air Defense and the Japanese Invasion*, Army Air Forces Historical Study No 4, p. 4.

5. Stetson Conn, Byron Fairchild and Rose C. Engelman, *The Western Hemisphere, Guarding the United States and Its Outpost*, (Washington DC, 1964), pp. 228-229.

6. Hist, Vol. I, Alaska Div, Air Transport Command, 1939-41, pp. 36-38.

7. Conn, Fairchild and Engelman, *Guarding the United States and Its Outpost*, p. 225.

8. "Hepburn Report," submitted by Sec of Navy to 76th Congress, 27 Dec 1938.

9. Conn, Fairchild and Engelman, Guarding the United States and Its Outposts, p. 227.

10. Testimony, Gen George C. Marshall, Chf of Stf, USA, before House of Representatives Subcommittee on Military Appropriations, 76th Congress, Feb 23, 1940.

11. Intvw, Cloe with Robert Atwood, June 1980. Robert Atwood came to Alaska in 1935 with his bride Evangeline Rasmuson; and with a loan from his father-in-law's National Bank of Alaska, he bought *The Anchorage Daily Times*. In the years ahead he would turn the small paper with a staff of five and a circulation of around 700 into the most influential publication in Alaska. Atwood, a pro developer, first championed the military buildup and later oil development, statehood and the unsuccessful attempt to move the state capital from Juneau to a more accessible location. On November 20, 1989, Robert Atwood announced that he was selling his paper, now known as *The Anchorage Time,* to Veco International, an oil field services company. The sales came on the heels of declining circulation and the intense competition of the Pulitzer Prize winning and well financed morning newspaper, *Anchorage Daily News*.

12. *The Anchorage Daily Times, Apr 5, 1940.*

13. *Philip Paneth, Alaska, Back Door to Japan*, (London, England, 1943), p. 41.

14. Frank Wesley Craven and James Lee Cate, editors, *The Army Air Forces in World War II*, Vol I, *Plans and Early Operations, January 1939 to August 1942*, (Chicago, IL, 1948), p. 40.

15. Dr Terrence Cole, draft manuscript, *A Regional History of South Central Alaska,* prepared for the Alaska Historical Commission history textbook program, p. 182.

16. *Ibid.*, p. 184.

17. *The Anchorage Daily Times*, May 21, 1940.

18. William Gilman, *Our Hidden Front*, (New York, 1944), p. 250.

19. Cole, draft manuscript, p. 191.

20. Jean Potter, *Alaska Under Arms*, (New York, 1942), pp. 95-96.

21. *Ibid.*, *pp. 148-150.*

22. *Ibid.*, *p. 24.*

23. *Stanton Patty, "Alaska Sprouts Wings," Aerospace Historian, Spring, 1969, pp. 15-16.*

24. *William L. Mitchell, The Opening of Alaska,* edited by Lyman Woodman, (Anchorage, 1982), p. viii.

25. Archie Satterfield, *Alaska Bush Pilots in Float Country*, (New York, 1969), pp. 12-15.

26. Patty, "Alaska Sprouts Wings," pp. 15-21.

27. Capt Arthur H. Rosein, Hist, Alaska Department, Jun 40-Jun 44, pp. 283-284.

28. Ransohoff, Hist, Eleventh Air Force, pp. 4-5.

29. Conn, Fairchild and Engelman, *Guarding the United States and Its Outpost*, pp. 224-228.

30. Lieut Richard W. Fagen, Hist, Fort Richardson, 1944, pp. 10-11.

31. Lieut Henry E. Fleischer, Hist, Elmendorf Field, 1940-44, pp. 16-17.

32. Fagen, Hist, Fort Richardson, pp. 18-19.

33. Fleischer, Hist, Elmendorf Field, pp. 16-17.

34. Pat Lawler, "Taking The Territory By Storm," *The Alaska Journal, 1981 Collection,* p. 85.

35. "Buck's Battle," *Time,* April 16, 1945.

36. Ltr, Buckner to DeWitt, Feb 4, 1942. General DeWitt politely ignored the slanderous comment and Buckner's wishes.

37. Lawler, "Taking Alaska by Storm," p. 95.

38. *Ibid.*, p. 95. Among the cadets at West Point during Buckner's tenure as Commandant of Cadets were: General Raymond J. Reeves, later Commander-in-Chief, Alaskan Command, and Major General C. F. "Nick" Necrason, who served as Commander, Alaskan Air Command from August 1959 to July 1961. Both became Alaskans.

39. *Ibid.*, p. 91.

40. Conn, Fairchild and Engelman, *Guarding the United States and Its Outpost,* p. 231.

41. *The Anchorage Daily Times*, Jul 14, 1940. Those accompanying General Arnold were: Lt Col Arthur McDaniel, Lt Col Ira Eaker, Maj Harold L. Clark, Capt Eugene H. Beebe, TSgt H. B. Puzenski and Sgt Robert Meade.

42. Gen Henry Arnold, "Our Air Frontier in Alaska," *National Geographic*, Oct 1940, pp. 487-501.

43. Gilman, *Our Hidden Front,* p. 34.

44. *The Anchorage Daily Times*, Jul 22, 1940.

45. *Ibid.*, Aug 31, 1940.

46. Lawler, *Taking Alaska by Storm,* p. 91. The tradition of a close friendship between Anchorage and its military neighbors, although strained by the events of World War II, has continued throughout the years.

47. Conn, Fairchild and Engelman, *Guarding the United States and Its Outposts*, p. 231. The chain of command that was established required General Buckner to answer to General DeWitt. It did not prove to be a satisfactory arrangement. The problem was solved with the creation of the Alaska Department on November 1, 1943. It gave Alaska the same independent status enjoyed by Hawaii and the Panama Canal. However, by then the Aleutian Campaign was over and the benefits that would have been derived from a separate command had been squandered.

48. Fleischer, Hist, Elmendorf Field, pp. 19-22.

49. Ransohoff, Hist, Eleventh Air Force, p. 19.

50. Fleischer, Hist, Elmendorf Field, p. 22.

51. Ltr, Davis to Maj Oliver S. Ferson, Off, Ch of Army Air Corps, Sep 11, 1940.

52. Fleischer, Hist, Elmendorf Field, pp. 22-23.

53. Ak Def Comd Gen Order 9, Dec 2, 1940.

54. Fleischer, Hist, Elmendorf Field, p. 15.

55. *The Anchorage Daily Times*, Dec 14, 1940.

56. *Ibid.*, Aug 2, 1940.

57. Ransohoff, Hist, Eleventh Air Force, pp. 20-21.

58. Conn, Fairchild and Engelman, *Guarding the United States and Its Outposts*, pp. 240-241.

59. Ltr, Buckner to DeWitt, Jul 16, 1941.

60. *The Anchorage Daily Times, Nov 8, 1940.*

61. Ransohoff, Hist, Eleventh Air Force, pp. 17-18.

62. *The Anchorage Daily Times*, Nov 26, 1940.

63. Fleischer, Hist, Elmendorf Field, pp. 22-23.

64. *The Anchorage Daily Times*, Sep 23.1940.

65. *Ibid.*, Oct 3, 1940.

66. *Ibid.*, Oct 4, 1940.

67. *Ibid.*, Oct 29, 1940.

68. Intvw, Cloe with Frank O'Brien, Aug 8, 1980.

69. Intvw, Cloe with Maj Gen Norman Sillin, USAF Ret, Aug 8, 1980.

70. Capt Alvin R. Winzeler, Hist, 18th Fighter Squadron, Feb 1940-Jan 1944, pp. 1-8.

71. Charles R. Hyer, "The Curtiss P-36 In Squadron Service," *American Aviation Historical Society Journal*, Winter 1988, pp. 248-249.

72. Fleischer, Hist, Elmendorf Field, pp. 24-26.

73. *Ibid.*, p. 24.

74. Hist, 28th Bomber Group, Feb 1940-Mar 1943, p. 19.

75. O'Brien Intvw.

76. Written Notes, Col Fred Ramputi, USAF Ret, undated.

77. Conn, Fairchild and Engelman, *Guarding the United States and Its Outposts*, pp. 247-248.

78. West Point Vital Statistic Questionnaire, William Olmstead Eareckson, Apr 2, 1930; Info extracted by Larry Reineke from cadet file, West Point Library; "William Olmstead Eareckson," *West Point Assembly*, Spring 1968.

79. *Ibid.*

80. Ransohoff, Hist, Eleventh Air Force, pp. 252-253.

81. Ramputi Notes.

82. Ransohoff, Hist, Eleventh Air Force, p. 35.

83. *The Anchorage Daily Times*, Jan 8, 1941.

84. Fagen, Hist, Ft Richardson, p. 29.

85. Biography, Brig Gen Benjamin B. Talley, 1980.

86. Speech Transcript, Brig Gen B. B. Talley, "Building Alaska's Defense of World War II," given before Cook Inlet Historical Society Meeting, June 26, 1969.

87. *The Anchorage Daily Times*, Jan 16, 1941.

88. Conn, Fairchild and Engelman, *Guarding the United States and Its Outposts*, pp. 246-248.

89. Ltr, Buckner to Marshall, Nov 24, 1941.

90. Conn, Fairchild and Engelman, *Guarding the United States and Its Outposts*, pp. 246-247.

91. *Ibid.*, p. 245.

92. Ltr, Buckner to DeWitt, Now 25, 1941.

93. Ransohoff, Hist, Eleventh Air Force, pp. 41-42.

94. *Ibid.*, p. 56.

95. Ltr, Buckner to Marshall, Jul 24, 1941.

96. Ltr, Marshall to Buckner, Sep 23, 1941.

97. Vincent J. Esposito, editor, *The West Point Atlas of American Wars*, Vol II, (New York, 1960), pp. 112-113.

98. Samuel Eliot Morison, *History of United States Naval Operations in World War II*, Vol III, *The Rising Sun in the Pacific*, (Boston, 1982), pp. 42-47.

99. Edwin P. Hoyt, *Japan's War*, (New York, 1986), p. 207

100. John Toland, *The Rising Sun*, (New York, 1970), p. 119.

101. Robert Goralski and Russell W. Freeburg, *Oil and War*, (New York, 1987), p. 93.

102. *Ibid.*, pp. 336-337.

103. *Ibid.*, p. 102.

104. John Toland, *The Rising Sun*, pp. 24-25.

105. Hiroyuki Agawa, *The Reluctant Admiral, Yamamoto and the Imperial Navy*, (New York, 1979) p. 173.

106. Ltr, Arnold to Buckner, Nov 15, 1941.

107. Conn, Fairchild and Engelman, *Guarding the United States and Its Outposts*, pp. 249-250.

108. *Ibid.*, p. 236.

109. *Ibid.*, pp. 236-237.

110. Ferguson, AAF Study No. 4, p. 4.

111. Memo, Col Frank M. Kennedy and Lt Col Harold L. Clark to Maj Gen Henry H. Arnold, Ch of Stf, AAF, "Report on Alaska," Sep 3, 1941.

112. Ferguson, AAF Study No 4, pp. 43-43.

113. Ransohoff, Hist, Eleventh Air Force, p. 80.

114. Ltr, Lt Col Everett Davis to Lt Col Emil Kiel, Off of Ch of Stf, AAF, 5 Dec 1941.

115. Conn, Fairchild and Engelman, *Guarding the United States and Its Outposts*, p. 242.

116. Rosein, Hist, Alaskan Department, 1940-45, p. 316.

117. Terrett Dulany, *Signal Corps, the Emergency*, (Washington, 1956), pp. 276-277.

118. Hist, North Pacific Forces, U.S. Navy, Aug 14, 1945, pp. 54-56.

119. Conn, Fairchild and Engelman, *Guarding the United States and Its Outposts*, pp. 245-246.

120. Col James D. Bush, *Narrative Report of Alaska Construction, 1941-1942*, Const Div, Engrs, Alaskan Department, 1944.

121. Craven and Cate, *Plans and Early Operations*, pp. 307-308. The SCR stood for Signal Corps radio. Both the mobile 270 and fixed 271 required an unobstructed 360 degree sweep, which necessitated they be located on a high promontory or mountain top. It created considerable construction difficulties since access roads or tramways had to be build along steep slopes to the sites. Additionally, the sites were located in remote, difficult to reach places. Other types of radars included the SCR-268 antiaircraft searchlight radar, the SCR-296 surface vessel detection radar, the SCR-521 air to surface vessel or ASW radar and the SCR-588, an improved long range aircraft warning radar. This radar with 180 degree sweep greatly eased the construction problems, since it could be sited at lower elevations. SCR-171s were in the process of being installed on Unalaska Island when the Japanese bombed Dutch Harbor.

122. Hist, North Pacific Forces, p. 10.

123. Conn, Fairchild and Engelman, *Guarding the United States and Its Outposts*, pp. 241-242.

124. Chronology, Fleet Air Wing Four, Aug 11, 1940-31 Aug 1945. The chronology, contained in the history of Fleet Air Wing Four, provides a detailed day-to-day account of the wing's operations.

125. Biography, Admiral James Russell, USN Ret.

126. James Russell, "Foatplanes and Flying Boats," *Naval Aviation Museum Foundation*, Fall 1984.

127. *Ibid.*

128. Conn, Fairchild and Engelman, *Guarding the United States and Its Outposts*, pp. 243-244.

Chapter 2: A Primeval Battleground

1. Lael Morgan, editor., The *Aleutians, Alaska Geographic*, (Anchorage, 1980), pp. 206-21.

2. Joan M. Antonson and William S. Hanable, *Alaska's Heritage*, (Anchorage, 1984), pp. 85-91.

3. *Ibid.*, pp. 113-19.

4. Intelligence Center Pacific Ocean Areas Bulletin 5-42, "Information of Enemy Positions North Pacific," Dec 20, 1942, p. 6.

5. Vincent Ponko, Jr., "The Navy and the Aleutians Before World War II," *The Alaska Journal*, Spring 1983.

6. Ernest H. Gruening, *The State of Alaska*, (New York, 1954), pp. 307-309.

7. Presidential Executive Order 1733, Mar 3, 1913.

8. Samuel Flagg Bemis, *A Short History of American Foreign Policy and Diplomacy*, (New York, 1959), p. 458. Thanks to an erratic genius, Herbert O. Yardley, who had broken the Japanese diplomatic code in 1920, the Americans were aware of the terms the Japanese were willing to accept. In 1926, an unsung cryptanalyst known only as "Miss Aggie" cracked the Japanese Admiral's code. These two achievements allowed the United States to monitor Japanese diplomatic and military communications during the years leading up to World War II.

9. Joint Army-Navy War Plan Orange, Jun 27, 1928, revised 1938, cancelled 1942. The Japanese counter plan was to draw the U.S. Navy westward into waters near their islands and annihilate it in one climatic battle.

10. Ponko, "The Navy and the Aleutians Before World War II."

11. *Ibid.*

12. D. F. Griffin, *First Steps to Tokyo*, (Toronto, 1944), p. 18.

13. *The Campaigns of the Pacific War, United States Strategic Bombing Survey (Pacific)*, (Washington, 1946), p. 85.

14. Encyclopedia Americana, Vol I, (New York, 1963), p. 360.

15. Draft Environmental Impact Statement for World War II Debris Removal and Cleanup, Aleutian Islands and Lower Alaskan Peninsula, prepared by the Alaska District Corps of Engineers with assistance of Tetra Tech, Inc., 1980, pp. 30-44.

16. Morgan, *The Aleutians*, p. 6.

17. A. R. Cahn, *War Diary, Naval Operating Base, Dutch Harbor,* 10 Sep 41-31 Dec 45, p. 12; Cuttlefish Five, *The Aleutian Invasion, World War II in the Aleutians,* (Unalaska, 1981), pp. 1-5.

18. Conn, Fairchild and Engelman, *Guarding The United States and Its Outpost*, p. 242.

19. Ransohoff, Hist, Eleventh Air Force, p. 37.

20. O'Brien Intvw.

21. Conn, Fairchild and Engelman, *Guarding the United States and Its Outposts*, p. 242.

22. *Ibid.*, pp. 36-37.

23. Ltr, General DeWitt to General Marshall, Jul 24, 1941.

24. Talley Intvw.

25. *Ibid.*

26. *Ibid.*

27. Ferguson, AAF Study No 4, pp. 15-16.

28. Ransohoff, Hist, Eleventh Air Force, p. 66.

29. Lieut Hyman Diwinsky, Hist, Fort Randall Army Air Base, (also referred to as Thornborough AAB), May 15, 1941-May 31, 1944, pp. 1-2.

30. Ransohoff, Hist, Eleventh Air Force, p. 55.

31. *Ibid.*, p. 91; Capt Joseph L. Cutler, Hist, Fort Glenn Army Air Base, (also referred to as Cape AAB), Aug 26, 1941-Jul 1944, pp. 1-8.

32. Richard K. Smith, "Marston Mat," *Air Force Magazine*, Apr 1989.

33. Cutler, Hist, Fort Glenn, pp. 1-4.

34. Talley Intvw.

35. Simon B. Buckner, "The Cannery That Wasn't There," *Scholastic,* Apr 12, 1943. Another popular but inaccurate account given for disguising the construction of the bases was the need to keep it a secret from the Navy. Even if Buckner wanted to do so, it would have been very difficult since the movement of transports between the western United States ports and Alaska were managed by the Navy. Additionally, the Navy was already aware of the two airfields since they had given their approval for construction.

36. Hoyt, *Japan's War*, p. 206.

37. Michael Carver, editor, *The War Lords,* (Boston, 1976), p. 397.

38. Hoyt, *Japan's War*, p. 115.

39. Agawa, *The Reluctant Admiral*, p. 232. Other sources have quoted the admiral as saying that Japan would be able to wage offensive war for only six months. In reality, this became the case.

40. Hoyt, *Japan's War*, pp. 216-217.

41. *Ibid.*, 93.

42. *Campaigns of the Pacific War*, p. 3.

43. Karl C. Dod, *The Corps of Engineers: the War Against Japan*, (Washington, 1966), p. 50.

44. Conn, Fairchild and Engelman, *Guarding the United States and Its Outposts*, pp. 250-51.

45. Ransohoff, Hist, Eleventh Air Force, pp. 84-85.

46. Esposito, *The West Point Atlas of American Wars*, p. 115.

47. Ronald H. Bailey, *The Home Front: U.S.A.,* (Alexander, VA, 1982) p. 8.

48. Potter, *Alaska Under Arms*, pp. 112-13.

49. *Ibid.*, pp. 9-11.

50. *The Anchorage Daily Times*, Dec 7, 1941.

51. *Ibid.*, Dec 10, 1941.

52. Potter, *Alaska Under Arms*, pp. 9-11.

53. Gilman, *Our Hidden Front*, pp. 55-56.

54. Forrest C. Pogue, *Organizer of Victory, 1943-1945, George C. Marshall,* (New York, 1973), p. 140.

55. Hist, *Aleutian Campaign, Northern Pacific Intel Center,* Dec 15, 1944, pp. 13-14.

56. *Life's Picture History of World War II*, (New York, 1950), p. 27.

57. Ltr, DeWitt to Gruening, Aug 6, 1941.

58. Otis E. Hays, Jr. "The Silent Years in Alaska," *The Alaska Journal, A 1986 Collection*, pp. 140-47.

59. Ltr, Gruening to Secretary of Interior Harold Iches, Nov 10, 1942.

60. *Ibid.*

61. Entry, personal diary, Ernest Gruening, Jan 27, 1947.

62. Potter, *Alaska Under Arms*, pp. 87-79.

63. *Ibid.*, p. 145.

64. James Richardson, *Alaska Guard,* an unpublished and undated manuscript, p. III-7.

65. Gilman, *Our Hidden Front*, (New York, 1944), pp. 126-27.

66. Ransohoff, Hist, Eleventh Air Force, p. 86.

67. *Ibid.*

68. Hist, Fleet Air Wing Four, Aug 11, 1941-Dec 14, 1944, pp. 5-6.

69. Ransohoff, Hist, Eleventh Air Force, pp. 86-87.

70. Craven and Cate, *Plans and Early Operations*, p. 303.

71. Hoyt, *Japan's War*, p. 264.

72. *The Anchorage Daily Times*, May 6, 1942.

73. Craven and Cate, *Plans and Early Operations*, p. 294.

74. Ltr, Gen DeWitt to Gen Buckner, Jan 3, 1942.

75. Conn, Fairchild and Engelman, *Guarding the United States and Its Outpost*, p. 255.

76. Ransohoff, Hist, Eleventh Air Force, pp. 88-89.

77. *Ibid.*, p. 89.

78. Ltr, General DeWitt to General Buckner, Jan 9, 1942.

79. Ltr, War Dept to Western Def Comd, "Allotment of Aircraft for Alaska," Jan 26, 1942.

80. Lieut William S. M. Johnson, Hist 11th Ftr Sq, Jan 15, 1940-Dec 31, 1945, pp. 13-15.

81. *Ibid.*

82. *Ibid.*, pp. 19-21.

83. *Ibid.*, p. 19.

84. *Ibid.*, p. 20.

85. Intvw, Cloe with Lt Col Albert Aiken, USAF Ret, Oct 20, 1986.

86. Ltr, General Buckner to General DeWitt, Feb 4, 1942.

87. Lieut Bailey K. Howard, Hist, 77th Bomb Sq, Jan 15, 1941-Dec 31, 1943, pp. 1-4.

88. Lloyd S. Jones, *US Bombers*, (Fallbrook, Cal, 1974), pp. 88-90.

89. Paper, "Suitability of Aircraft in the Aleutian," Col Richard D. Salter, USAF Ret, 1982.

90. Howard, Hist, 77th Bomb Sq, p. 5; Chronology, 77th Bomb Sq, undated; Hist, Fourth Air Force, *The First Phase of the Battle for the Aleutians,* Oct 31, 1943, pp. 1-2.

91. Ltr, Brig Gen John B. Brooks, Comdr, 2nd Air Depot Comd to Col Lawrence H. Douthid, Eleventh Air Force, Oct 31, 1942; Aiken Intvw. An account of the later recovery of the B-26s for shipment to a collector by Robert Shepherd, a member of the salvage party, appeared in the Spring 1976 edition of "Air Classics Quarterly Review."

92. Hist, Fourth Air Force, pp. 1-2.

93. Ltr, General Buckner to General DeWitt, Feb 4, 1942.

94. *Ibid.*

95. Aiken Intvw.

96. Intvw, Cloe with Col Joe Schneider, USAF Ret, Aug 17, 1980.

97. Memo, HQ AAF, Investigation-Movement of Air Corps Units to Alaska, Jul 11, 1942.

98. Memo, Col William O. Butler, Ch of Stf, Fourth Air Force to Maj Gen Millard F. Harmon, Ch of Stf, Office of the Ch of AAF, "Ferrying of P-40s and B-26s to Alaska," Feb 16, 1942.

99. Aiken Intvw.

100. Ransohoff, Hist, Eleventh Air Force, p. 137.

101. *Ibid.*, p. 105.

102. Hist, *Aleutian Campaign*, p. 56.

103. Fleischer, Hist, Elmendorf Field, p. 41.

104. Pitt, *Wide Open On Top*, pp. 312-313.

105. Dod, *The Corps of Engineers: The War Against Japan*, pp.

299-300.

106. *Ibid.*, pp. 314-315.

107. M. Vincent Brezeau, *RCAF Alaskan Commitment, 1942-1943*, draft manuscript, National Defense HQ, Canada, Directorate of Hist, 1980, pp. 1-13.

108. Pitt, *Wide Open On Top*, pp. 73-74.

Chapter 3: The Side Show

1. Ferguson, AAF Study No. 4, pp. 44-45.

2. General Order No 3, HQ, ADC, Jan 9, 1942; General Order No 4, HQ, ADC, Jan 10, 1942; Charles Ravenstein, *Organization and Lineage and Lineage of the United States Air Force*, (Washington DC, 1986), p. 16.

3. Ransohoff, Hist, Eleventh Air Force, p. 120.

4. *Ibid.*, p. 111.

5. *Ibid.*, p. 113.

6. *Ibid.*, p. 105.

7. Talley Intvw., p. 29.

8. O'Brien Intvw.

9. Biography, Maj Gen William O. Butler, Fourth Air Force, undated.

10. Ltr, Buckner to DeWitt, Apr 22, 1942.

11. Ransohoff, Hist, Eleventh Air Force, pp 121-22.

12. *Ibid.*, pp. 122-23.

13. Ferguson, AAF Study No 4, pp. 42-43.

14. Conn, Fairchild and Engelman, *Guarding The United States, and Its Outposts*, pp. 253-54.

15. Ransohoff, Hist, Eleventh Air Force, pp. 110-1.

16. Lieut Billy Wheeler, "Diary, Bombardment, Two Years in Alaska," p. 2, found in Hist, 36th Bomb Sq, Feb 40-Jun 43.

17. Maurer, *Combat Squadrons of World War II*, pp. 223-24, 226-27.

18. Esposito, *West Point Atlas*, pp. 114-30.

19. Donald MacIntyre, *Aircraft Carriers*, Ballantine Books, 1968, p. 79.

20. Hoyt, *Japan's War*, pp. 271-73.

21. Potter, *Alaska Under Arms*, p. 142.

22. Hoyt, *Japan's War*, p. 278.

23. Thomas E. Griess, editor, *The West Point Military History Series, The Second World War, Asia and The Pacific*, (Wayne NJ, 1984), pp. 7-11.

24. *Ibid.*, pp. 12-16.

25. *The Campaigns of the Pacific War*, p. 32.

26. Japanese Monograph No 88, *Aleutian Naval Operations, March 1942-February 1943*, HQ Army Forces Far East, Mil Hist Sec, Japanese Research Div, not dated, pp. 1-2.

27. Carver, *The War Lords*, pp. 390-403.

28. Richard Humble, *Japanese High Seas Fleet*, (New York, 1973), p. 23.

29. Japanese Monograph No 88, p. 6; *Campaigns of the Pacific*, p. 3.

30. *Campaigns of the Pacific War*, pp. 31, 52-53.

31. *Ibid.*, p. 4.

32. A. J. Barker, *Midway the Turning Point*, (New York, 1971), pp. 42-45.

33. Japanese Monograph No 88. p. 9.

34. *Ibid.*, p. 7; *Campaigns of the Pacific War*, pp. 78-79; Conn, Fairchild and Engelman, *Guarding the United States and Its Outposts*, p. 259. Although the Japanese showed great skill in planning and executing complicated operations, they were weak when it came to logistics. Their intelligence staff, which consisted of plodders, were good at collecting information, but demonstrated little flair for analysis and the proper use of intelligence.

35. Japanese Monograph No 88, pp. 13-14; *Campaigns of the Pacific War*, pp. 99-101.

36. *Ibid.*, p. 24; Samuel Eliot Morison, *History of United States Naval Operations in World War II*, Vol IV, *Coral Sea, Midway and Submarine Actions, May 1942-August 1942*, map, p. 94.

37. Walter Lord, *Incredible Victory*, (New York, 1967), pp. 25-27; E. B. Potter, *Nimitz*, (Norwalk, Conn, 1976), pp. 81-82.

38. Msg. Chf of Naval Ops to CINCPAC. 21 May 1942.

39. Potter, *Nimitz*, pp. 80-81.

40. Morison, *Coral Sea, Midway and Submarine Actions*, p. 166.

41. Intvw, Cloe with Admiral James S. Russell, USN Ret and Lt Gen Masatake Okumiya, JSDF Ret, Jan 18, 1980.

42. Morison, *Coral Sea, Midway and Submarine Actions*, p. 166.

43. Memo, Capt James S. Russell, USN to Lieut Jerry N. Ransohoff, Historian, Eleventh Air Force, not dated; Intvw, Cloe with Russell, Jan 18, 1980.

44. Ltr, Parker to Buckner, Feb 20, 1942.

45. Memo, Russell; Russell Intvw.

46. Ferguson, AAF Study 4, pp. 47-48.

47. Wheeler Diary.

48. Chronology, Fleet Air Wing Four, 1941-1945.

49. Russell, "Floatplanes and Flying Boats," p. 27.

50. Paul Carrigan, "Weathermen at Dutch Harbor," *Aleutian Airdales*, published by the Pat Wing Four Reunion Committee, 1987, p. 24.

51. *Ibid.*

52. *Ibid.*, pp. 27-28.

53. Capt Leo J. Nocenti, Hist, 54th Ftr Sq, 15 Jan-31 Dec 43, pp. 7-9.

54. *Ibid.*, pp. 10-11.

55. *Ibid.*, pp. 11-15.

56. Hist, 406th Bomb Sq, Jun 42-Oct 43, prepared by former members of the squadron under the direction of Col Courtney, 1987.

57. Extract, draft autobiography, Ward T. (Tommy) Olsson, *A Career in the United States Air Force*, Feb 7, 1987.

58. Hist, 406th Bomb Sq.

59. Bezeau, *The RCAF Alaskan Commitment*, pp. 24-43.

60. Talley Intvw.

61. *Ibid.*

62. Morison, *Coral Sea, Midway and Submarine Actions*, p. 166.

63. Hist, North Pacific Forces, pp. 17-18.

64. Edwin Layton with Roger Pineau and John Costello, *And I Was There: Pearl Harbor and Midway-Breaking the Secrets*, (New York, 1985), p. 434.

65. Hist, North Pacific Forces, pp. 166-167.

66. Morison, *Coral Sea, Midway and Submarine Actions*, pp. 170-71.

67. *Ibid.*, p. 171.

68. *Ibid.*, p. 165.

69. Johnson, Hist, 11th Ftr Sq, pp. 29-31.

70. Intvw, Cloe with Capt John R. Melter, USAF Ret, Aug 5, 1983.

71. Ferguson, AAF Study No 4, p. 4. The problem was corrected in July 1942, when the cable ship, *Restorer*, laid the communications cable between Dutch Harbor and Otter Point.

72. *Ibid.*, p. 50.

73. *Ibid.*, p. 171.

74. Ransohoff, Hist, Eleventh Air Force, pp. 149-150.

75. Wheeler Diary.

76. Morison, *Coral Sea, Midway and Submarine Actions*, p. 167. Life aboard a S class submarine in the northern waters was miserable. There was insufficient heat and condensation kept everything, including bedding, wet.

77. Potter, *Nimitz*, p. 88

78. Johnson, Hist 11th Ftr Sq, p. 34.

79. *Ibid.*, pp. 33-34.

80. "The First Phase of the Battle for the Aleutians," Produced by Historical Section, Fourth Air Force, Oct 30, 1943.

81. Johnson, Hist, 11th Ftr Sq, p. 43.

82. Cahn, War Diary, pp. 1-5.

83. *Ibid.*, p. 65.

84. Commander Paul F. Foster, USNR, "Report of Inspection of U.S. Naval Air Station, Dutch Harbor, Alaska, Made in May 1942," contained in "War Diary, Naval Operating Base, Dutch Harbor."

85. Hist, *Aleutian Campaign*, p. 5.

86. Walter Lord, *Incredible Victory*, (New York, 1967), pp. 87-88.

87. Japanese Monograph No 88, pp. 18-19; U.S. Strategic Bombing Survey Interrogation 97 (of Okumiya), "Aleutian Campaign, Carrier Aircraft Attack on Dutch Harbor," Oct 10, 1945.

88. Carrigan, "Prelude to Attack on Dutch Harbor," *Aleutian Air-*

dales, pp. 40-42.

89. Japanese Monograph 88, pp. 18-19; Interrogation Report 97.

90. Ransohoff, Hist, Eleventh Air Force, pp. 144-145.

Chapter 4: Many Foolish Things

1. Intvw, Cloe with Adml James Russell and Lieut Gen Masatake Okumiya, Jan 18, 1980; Mitsuo Fuchida and Masatake Okumiya, *Midway, The Battle That Doomed Japan,* (Annapolis, Md, 1955), pp. 137-39.

2. U.S. Strategic Bombing Survey (Pacific) Interrogation No 97, "Aleutian Campaign, Carrier Aircraft Attack on Dutch Harbor," Capt James S. Russell, USN with Comdr Masatake Okumiya, IJN, Tokyo, Oct 10, 1945; Ltr, VAdml Hiroichi Samejima to Adml James S. Russell, Mar 5, 1969, with account of Dutch Harbor raid, compiled from records in War History Section, Japan Defense Agency.

3. Transcript, sound tape eight, Intvw of Col Zenji Abe, JSDF (Ret), used in the making of the 1986 film, *Alaska at War.* On file in Univ of Ak-Anchorage archives.

4. USSBS No 97; Ltr, Samejima to Russell; Intvw, Cloe with Adml Hiroichi Samejima, Jun 7, 1982. Unlike many of his contemporaries, Admiral Samejima survived the war, possibly because he was engaged as a test pilot during the latter part of the war.

5. Intvw, Cloe with Lieut Col Otis Boise, USA Ret, Aug 1983.

6. *Ibid.*, Hist, Fleet Air Wing Four, pp. 33-34.

7. Report, Commander, Dutch Harbor to Commander, Alaska Sector, "Bombing of Dutch Harbor-Report On," Jul 6, 1942, contained in War Diary, Naval Operating Base, Dutch Harbor.

8. Personal account, Chief Photographer Mate Dean Freiday, contained on pages 64-69, War Diary.

9. Carrigan, "The Japanese Attacks on Dutch Harbor," p. 45.

10. "Bombing of Dutch Harbor-Report On."

11. Thomas P. O'Neal, "Bombing of Dutch Harbor, Eyewitness Account," contained in pages 32-37, *The Aleutian Invasion.*

12. Hist, Fleet Air Wing Four, pp. 33-34; Carrigan, "The Japanese Attack on Dutch Harbor," *Aleutian Airdales,* pp. 45-46.

13. USSBS No 97; Ltr, Samejima to Russell.

14. Samejima Intvw.

15. U.S. Strategic Bombing Survey (Pacific) Interrogation No 606, "Information on Japanese Second Mobile Force and the Kiska Garrison from U.S. Prisoners of War," Capt James S. Russell, USN with Lieut Wylie M. Hunt, USNR and Aerographers Mate First Class William C. House, Tokyo, Dec 20, 1945. Hunt, Brown and Creamer survived the war as prisoners of war. Killed as a result of the attack were: Lieut Jean C. Cusick, RM3c John F. Collins, AMM2c Alton J. Davis, AMM2c Burdette B. Siler, ARM2c Louis E. Yurec, and AP1c Clark W. Morrison.

16. Walter Karig and Eric Purdon, *Battle Report,* (New York, 1947), pp. 269-70.

17. Chronology, Fleet Air Wing Four, pp. 8-9.

18. "The First Phase of the Battle for the Aleutians," prepared by the Historical Section, A-2, Fourth Air Force, 30 Oct 43. Contains an interview of Captain Meals.

19. O'Neal, "Bombing of Dutch Harbor, Eyewitness Account."

20. Ltr, Samejima to Russell, Mar 5, 1969.

21. Johnson, Hist, 11th Fighter Squadron, pp. 37-38.

22. Japanese Monograph No 88, p. 29; USSBS No 97.

23. Ltr. Samejima to Russell, Mar 5, 1969.

24. Hist, Fleet Air Wing Four, p. 35; "Bombing of Dutch Harbor, Report On." Those killed in the Zero attack were: Ensigns Albert E. Mitchell and Joseph M. Tuttle, AMM1c Wheeler H. Rawls, AMM1c Frank G. Schadl, ARM3c Burton J. Strom, ARM3c Neal R. Sparks and S1c James D. Pollit.

25. "Bombing of Dutch Harbor, Report On."

26. *Ibid.*, Transcript Intvw, Abe, *Alaska at War.*

27. "Bombing of Dutch Harbor, Report On."

28. D. Colt Denfeld, Ak Dist, U.A. Army Corps of Engrs, "The Defense of Dutch Harbor, Alaska from Military Construction to Base Cleanup," Dec 87, p. 173. The National Park account of Dutch Harbor prepared by the Alaska Region's History Office claims that the *Northwestern* was towed to Seattle as planned. However, long time residents at Dutch Harbor have maintained otherwise. The presence of the ship was confirmed on August 13, 1986 by an on-site survey which noted the presence of its name on the port bow and the fact that the bomb damaged matched that of wartime photographs.

29. "Bombing of Dutch Harbor, Report On."

30. Intvw, Cloe with Col Zenji Abe, JSDF (Ret), Jun 7, 1982. Abe was captured by the Americans during the Battle of the Philippine Sea, June 1944.

31. Johnson, Hist, 11th Ftr Sq, pp. 39-40. Although, Lieutenant Cape was officially credited with shooting the Zero down, Japanese records after the war indicated that only one Zero had been lost in the attack on Dutch Harbor, that of Tadayoshi Koga.

32. Intvw, Cloe with Capt John R. Melter, USAF (Ret) and former enlisted member of the 11th Fighter Squadron, Aug 5, 1983. Melter also witnessed the Japanese attacking Captain Marks' B-17B, which according to him was still had its Cold Weather Test Detachment aluminum finish with the wing tips and tail painted day glow orange. However, a U.S. Army Corps of Engineers film taken of the construction of Cape Field shows a brief glimpse of the bomber in wartime olive drab paint.

33. Johnson, Hist, 11th Ftr Sq, pp. 39-40.

34. Melter Intvw.

35. Abe Intvw. Forty years later the gentle Abe still remembered the names of the crews and the tail numbers of the four Vals he lost that day.

36. Craven and Cate, *Plans and Early Operations,* p. 467.

37. USSBS No 97.

38. Carrigan, "The Japanese Attack on Dutch Harbor," pp. 52-53.

39. Chronology, Fleet Air Wing Four, 11 Aug 41-31 Aug 45, pp. 8-9. Killed were Lieut Eugene W. Stockstill, AP1c Henry M. Mitchell, AM1c Cyril A. Day, ARM3c Glen E. Ray, ARM3c Oscar J. Alford, S1c David D. Secord, S1c Frank E. Birks and AP1c Merlyn B. Dawson. Commander Okumiya told Captain Russell, who was collecting information for the Strategic Bombing Survey, that he had a photograph of Stockstill's burning PBY, but unfortunately had destroyed it.

40. Hist, Fleet Air Wing Four, pp. 34-35; Chronology, Fleet Air Wing Four, p. 10. Those who disappeared without trace were: Ensign James T. Hildebrant, Jr., Ensign Leonard J. Hurley, AP1c William B. Laing, ARM2c William J. Glover, ARM1c Lester W. Dietrich, AMM3c Anthony H. Duessing, AP1c Frank D. Geiger, S2c Willis H. Sweeny and RM3c Thomas W. Lowery.

41. Ferguson, AAF Study No 4, pp. 56-57.

42. RAdml Leslie E. Gehres, USN (Ret), "When Alaska was Attacked-Footnote to World War II," *U.S. News & World Report,* Nov 30, 1962.

43. Karig and Purdon, *Battle Report,* p. 274.

44. Memo, Capt James S. Russell to Lieut Jerry Ransohoff, Historian, Eleventh Air Force, subj: History of Eleventh Air Force, undated.

45. Ransohoff, Hist, Eleventh Air Force, p. 151. Those killed with Capt Thornborough were: Lieut Norman A. Nysteen, Lieut James L. Smart, Lieut James F. Lee, SSgt Joseph. L. Wiseman, Sgt Roy E. Jordan and Sgt Howard K. Jaycox. They were from the 73rd Bombardment Squadron. The Carlson and Brodsky account in *No Mean Victory* also list Lieutenant John J. Jarvis as killed in action on the same day. He could have been one of Taylor's crew.

46. Russell Memo.

47. Ferguson, AAF Study No. 4, p. 58. Craven and Cate, *Plans and Early Operations,* p. 468. Missing were: Capt Thomas F. Mansfield, Lieut Irvin Berman, Lieut Francis C. Cornwell, Lieut Lyle A. Slocum, Sgt Orval V. Paul, Cpl Edgar L. Rogers, Pvt Edwin T. Bottelson, Pvt John W. Labar Jr., PFC Don B. Harris and Pvt Wilfred W. Hellenbrand. Except for PFC Harris, all were from the 36th Bombardment Squadron. Harris might have been sent along as the photographer. Both Craven and Cate and Masatake Okumiya claim that one of Mansfield's crew was rescued from the sea. Unfortunately there is no other record

of the incident and the name and what became of the prisoner remains a mystery.

48. "The First Phase of the Battle for the Aleutians."

49. *Ibid.*

50. "Report on the Aleutians," *The Readers Digest*, May 1943.

51. Morison, *Coral Sea, Midway and Submarine Actions*, p. 180.

52. Ransohoff, Hist, Eleventh Air Force, pp. 159-60.

53. Ferguson, AAF Study No 4, p. 109; Morison, *Coral Sea, Midway and Submarine Actions*, pp. 180-81.

54. *Ibid.*, pp. 110-1.

55. Chronology, Fleet Air Wing Four.

56. Hist, *Aleutian Campaign*, p. 9.

57. Ltr, Butler to Arnold, Jun 6, 1942.

58. 1980 Notes, Col Owen "Jack" Meals on a copy the first edition of *The Deck Leveler,* a paper published by the 77th Bombardment Squadron during World War II.

59. Army Signal Corps film, *Report from the Aleutians*, produced by Darryl Zanuck and narrated by John Huston. The filming was done on Adak during the Fall of 1942, and included a sequence shot during a bombing mission over Kiska. It was intended for popular consumption and to boost morale. Another similar film on the Aleutians was produced by the Japanese.

60. USSBS No 97.

61. Brian Garfield, *The Thousand Mile War,* (New York, 1983), pp. 48-49.

62. Ltr, Minoru Kawamato, Tokyo to Jim Rearden, Homer, Ak, with atch translation of Yanagida's account of the Akutan Zero.

63. Report, Comdr, VP-41, "Salvage of Japanese Nagoya Type Zero Discovered on Akutan Island, 10 Jul 42," 22 Jul 42.

64. Ltr, Kawamato to Rearden.

65. "Defiance Rewarded," *Military History*, Jun 1989. The article is an oral history interview of Thies by Joseph S. Rychetnik and covers Thies' experiences in the Aleutians.

66. *Ibid.*, Salvage Report.

67. Technical Aviation Intelligence Brief No 3, Aviation Intelligence Branch, Navy Department, "Performance and Characteristics Trials, Japanese Fighter," Nov 4, 1942.

68. David A. Anderson, *Hellcat*, (New York, 1981) p. 17.

69. Intelligence Brief No 3; Report, Intelligence Services, U.S. Army Air Forces, "Information Intelligence Summary No. 5," Dec 1942.

70. Jim Rearden, "The Akutan Zero, Part 11," *Alaska Magazine*, Oct 1987. Jim Rearden who is an authority on the Akutan Zero is also the author of the book *Cracking the Zero Mystery*, published by Stackpole in 1990.

71. USSBS No. 606.

72. *Ibid.*

73. Gordon W. Prange, *Miracle at Midway*, (New York, 1982), pp. 253-54.

74. Morison, *Coral Sea, Midway and Submarine Actions*, p. 117.

75. *Ibid.*, pp. 102-159.

76. The information was extracted from the table on pages 176-177, *Zero*, by Masatake Okumiya and Jiro Horikoshi, published in 1956; and pages 29-33, *Supplement and General Index, History of United States Naval Operations in World War II* by Samuel Eliot Morison.

77. Morison, *Coral Sea, Midway and Submarine Actions*, p. 144.

78. U. S. Strategic Bombing Survey (Pacific) Interrogation No 101, "Aleutian Campaign, Planning and Operations Through November 1942," Capt James S. Russell, USN with Capt Taisuke Ito, IJN, Tokyo, Oct 11, 1945. Captain Ito served as the air officer on Admiral Hosogaya's staff.

79. Walter Lord, *Incredible Victory*, (New York, 1967), pp. 285-86.

80. Morison, *Coral Sea, Midway and Submarine Actions*, p. 161.

Chapter 5: A Time For Courage

1. Prange, *Miracle at Midway*, pp. 335-36; USSBS No 101.

2. U.S. Strategic Bombing Survey (Pacific) Interrogation Report No 99, "Japanese Occupation of Kiska, the Kiska Garrison and Operations in the Kuriles," Capt James S. Russell, USN with Comdr Nifumi Mukai, IJN, Tokyo, Oct 22, 1945.

3. USSBS No 606. William House survived the war and retired from the Navy as a commander in 1959. He (1990) lives in Valley Center, California, where he owns a vineyard. His other companions also survived their imprisonment. The Japanese film that was taken on their capture was later incorporated into a documentary on the capture of the Aleutian Islands that was shown to the Japanese public. After the war, the same scenes were in "The Magnetic North," part of the epic "Victory at Sea" series first televised in 1953 by NBC.

4. USSBS No 99.

5. Morison, *Coral Sea, Midway and Submarine Actions*, p. 181.

6. Howard Jones, "Etta Jones . . . P.O.W.," *Alaska Life*, Dec 1945. From San Francisco, Etta Jones went to Seattle to attend to personal business. She planned to visit a brother, Russell T. Sherman, in Atlantic City, New Jersey. Nothing was heard from her again.

7. Record of Research Form, Office of History, Alaska Air Command, Mar 30, 1979. Sergeant Lucas, Mortuary Officer at Fort Richardson called on March 27 to ascertain the cause of death of Charles Foster Jones. A check was made of office and other records at the Air Force Historical Research Center. The Center suggested that Sergeant Lucas contact the American Graves Registration Service. He did so, and they informed him that Charles Foster Jones remains had been examined after they were disinterred from their burial place on Attu. The report stated that there was a hole, probably caused by a bullet, in his skull. Professor Henry Stewart, in his December 1978 report to the law firm representing the Aleutian/Pribilof Islands Association, states that the Joneses attempted to commit suicide by slashing their wrist. The information was based on an account provided him by the Japanese present on the island. Dr Gary Stein, a historian at the time with the Alaska State Department of Natural Resources, in January 1979 interviews with two of the surviving Attuans, ascertained from them that the Jones had in fact slit their wrist. A personal account by Alex Prossoff in Ethel Ross Oliver's *Journal of an Aleutian Year* also states that when the Aleuts buried Charles Foster, they noted that his wrist had been cut.

8. Report submitted by Professor Henry Steward to the law firm of Cook and Henderson, Washington DC, Dec 1978, on the evacuation and internment of Attuans in Japan. In his account, House notes that it was the *Nagata Maru* that took him and the Aleuts to Japan. There is also a number of discrepancies in the times of various Japanese activities. Since Professor Steward's information was based on the research of Japanese documents, much of the information used is this section is derived from his report.

9. Ethel Ross Oliver, *Journal of an Aleutian Year*, (Seattle, 1988), Appendix 3.

10. Ltr, Butler to Arnold, Jun 16, 1942.

11. Paper, presented by Col Stan Long, USAF (Ret) at "Wings Over Alaska" conference in Anchorage Feb 1980.

12. *Ibid.*

13. Nocenti, Hist, 54th Ftr Sq, p. 18.

14. Wheeler Diary.

15. *Ibid.*

16. Ransohoff, Hist, Eleventh Air Force, pp. 154-55.

17. Wheeler Diary.

18. Chronology, Fleet Air Wing Four.

19. Carl Amme, "VP-43 Joins the Airdales," *Aleutian Airdales*, p. 88.

20. Chronology, Fleet Air Wing Four.

21. *Campaigns of the Pacific War*, p. 94; Discussions, author, with Admiral Russell.

22. Ransohoff, Hist, Eleventh Air Force, p. 157.

23. *The Anchorage Daily Times*, Aug 8, 1944.

24. Report, Col Eareckson to Comdr, Eleventh Air Force, dated "Sunday, I think." The report also describes the disposition and condition of aircraft, gives a short account of Thornborough's attack against the *Ryujo* in which Eareckson expresses his displeasure at the captain ignoring his orders to proceed to Otter Point. Someone, to his credit, did submit Thornborough for the award of a posthumous Distinguished Service Cross. The rest of the report was taken up with mundane but

vital things such a request for additional mess personnel.

25. *Campaigns of the Pacific War*, p. 80.

26. Morison, *Coral Sea, Midway and Submarine Actions*, p. 182.

27. Ransohoff, Hist, Eleventh Air Force, pp. 156-57.

28. Pitt, *Wide Open on Top*, p. 130.

29. Gilman, *Our Hidden Front*, pp. 118-19.

30. *Ibid*.

31. Navy Department News Release, "Small Scale Jap Landing on Tip of Aleutians," Jun 12, 1942.

32. "Alaska War Continues," *The Anchorage Daily Times*, Jun 13, 1942.

33. Pogue, *Organizer of Victory*, p. 150.

34. Morison, *Coral Sea, Midway and Submarine Actions*, p. 183.

35. JCS Memo 61, "Estimate of Situation in the North Pacific Area," Jun 13, 1942.

36. Notes on JCS 20th Meeting, Jun 15, 1942; Extract from Minutes, JCS Meeting, Jun 15, 1942. The United States was fortunate in having three exceptional military leaders who composed the Joint Chiefs of Staff. General George C. Marshall, honest, patient and modest commanded the greatest army ever fielded in American history. His genius was that he could pick, with a few exceptions, the right field commanders. Many, such as Bradly, Eiesenhower and Patton, were to achieve greater public fame; but it was the quite, unassuming Marshall who forged the force they used in battle. Admiral King, stern and gaunt, fought for his beloved navy and the war it waged across the vast expanse of the Pacific. Difficult at times and unbending, he was the architect of victory in the Pacific. The genial "Hap" Arnold believed air power was the key to victory. Although subordinated to Marshall as Commander, Army Air Forces, Arnold was given an equal voice because of the mighty power his force wielded. His most cherished dream was realized when the United States Air Force was created in 1947. The Joint Chiefs met under the leadership of Admiral William Leahy, the president's personal military representative, to decide the major issues of the war. Their decisions had to be unanimous, otherwise the issue was referred to the president who exercised the ultimate authority. Although an informal organization, the Joint Chiefs of Staff proved to be a winning combination.

37. Chronology, 21st Bomb Sq, May 18, 1943.

38. Ransohoff, Hist, Eleventh Air Force, pp. 161.

39. USSBS No 99.

40. Ransohoff, Hist, Eleventh Air Force, pp. 162-63. In addition to Capt Todd and Lieut Hood, others killed were: Capt Virgil C. Alleman, Lieut Henry F. Hubbard, Lieut Robert R. Rieman, SSgt Roy Ellis, SSgt John S. Ferguson, Cpl Charles Jimick, Cpl Harold Denson and Pvt Stanley A. Douglas Jr.

41. Wheeler Diary.

42 Kit C. Carter and Robert Mueller, compilers, *The Army Air Forces in World War II, Combat Chronology 1941-1945*, (Washington, 1973), p. 20; Wheeler Diary.

43. Wheeler Diary.

44. Ltr, Butler to Arnold, Jun 16, 1942.

45. *Campaigns of the Pacific War*, p. 92.

46. Amme, *VP-43 Joins the Airdales*, pp. 90-92.

47. Leonard Engel, "PBY Saga," *Air Trails Pictorial*, Feb 1944.

48. Hist, Fleet Air Wing Four, pp. 39-40. The history provides only a brief account of the "Kiska Blitz." Its chronology does contain a casualty list. Inflated claims are not uncommon during the heat of battle. It is easy to understand in the confused conditions that existed over Kiska Harbor how the participants, who trying to stay alive while performing their missions to the best of their abilities, believed their bombs had hit home.

49. *Campaigns of the Pacific War*, p. 92.

50. Chronology, Fleet Air Wing Four. Those killed in addition to Davis were: Ensign Robert F. Keller, AP3c Albert L. Gyorfi, ARM3c Robert A. Smith, ARM3c Elwin Alford and AMM2c John H. Hathaway. Japanese still and motion picture cameramen documented the attacks. The photographs show aircraft being shot down and near misses of dropped bombs.

51. USSBS No 99.

52. Hist, Fleet Air Wing Four, p. 41.

53. U.S. Strategic Bombing Survey (Pacific) Interrogation No 100, "Japanese Flying Boat Operations in the Aleutians," Capt James S. Russell, USN with Comdr Sukemitsu Ito, IJN, Tokyo, Oct 9, 1945.

54. Hist, Fleet Air Wing Four, pp. 40-41.

55. USSBS No 100.

56. Hist, Fleet Air Wing Four, p. 42.

57. RAdml Paul Foley, Jr. USN (Ret), "VP Squadron Forty-One in the Aleutians (1941-1942)," *Aleutian Airdales*, p. 79.

58. Craven and Cate, *Plans and Early Operations*, pp. 358-59.

59. Rosein, Hist, Alaskan Department, p. 43.

60. Pogue, *Organizer of Victory*, p. 150.

61. Pitt, *Wide Open On Top*, p. 145.

62. Wheeler Diary.

63. Aiken Intvw.

64. Carter and Mueller, *Combat Chronology*, p. 20; Wheeler Diary. During September 1989, the National Park Service's Submerged Cultural Resources Unit from Santa Fe, New Mexico and the Navy's Global Diving and Salvage Unit One from Pearl Harbor conducted a series of dives on the *Nissan Maru* to document her conditions. The U.S. Third Fleet provided the salvage and towing vessel USS *Safeguard* (ARS-50) to support the effort.

65. USSBS No 99.

66. USSBS No 606.

67. Wheeler Diary; Ltr, Adjutant, 21st Bomb Sq to Historical Officer, XI Bomber Command, Feb 22, 1943.

68. Wheeler Diary.

69. Craven, Wesley Frank and Cate, James Lea Jr (editors), *The Army Air Force in World War II*, Vol IV, *The Pacific, Guadalcanal to Saipan*, (Chicago, 1955), p. 365.

70. *Ibid., p. 363*.

71. *Wheeler Diary.*

72. *Carter and Mueller, Combat Chronology*, p. 24; U.S. Strategic Bombing Survey (Pacific) Interrogation No 98, "Aleutian Campaign, Seaplane Operations, the Naval Battle of the Komandorski Islands, and the Defense of the Kuriles," Capt James S. Russell, USN with Comdr Kintaro Miura, IJN, Tokyo, Oct 20 and 23, 1945.

73. Craven and Cate, *The Pacific, Guadalcanal to Saipan*, pp. 367-68.

74. Ransohoff, Hist, Eleventh Air Force, p. 164.

75. Lieut H.D. Beland, Hist, 404th Bomb Sq, Jan 14, 1941-Jan 1, 1944, pp. 7-11.

76. Maurer, *Air Force Combat Units of World War II*, pp. 101-2.

77. Beland, Hist, 404th Bomb Sq, pp. 9-10.

78. Maj Thomas P. Wright, Hist, 54th Ftr Gp, Jan 15, 1941-Dec 31, 1943, pp. 1-2.

79. Intvw, Cloe with Lieut Col Leslie Spoonts, USAF Ret, Jul 9, 1982.

80. *Ibid.*, Wright, Hist, 54th Ftr Gp, pp. 1-3; Special Order #3, HQ 54th Ftr Gp, Jun 12, 1942.

81. *Ibid*.

82. Wright, Hist, 54th Ftr Gp, Section 3.

83. Carter and Mueller, *Combat Chronology*, pp. 23-30.

84. Martin Caidin, *Zero Fighter*, (New York, 1970), p. 68.

85. Chronology, Fleet Air Wing Four, p. 12.

86. Wheeler Diary; Hist, 36th Bomb Sq, p. 12. Those lost were: Maj Jack L. Marks, Lieut Harold E. Mitts, Lieut John R. Giddens, SSgt John E. Cane, Cpl Edward P Dwelis, Sgt Bill Von Diehl, Cpl Hubert D. Smith, Pvt Theodore A. Alleckson, Pvt Robert G. Brown and Pvt Consetto J. Castagna. Wheeler does not list Diehl as a crew member; however, in the Carlson and Brodsky account, Diehl was listed among those killed. He was probably a photographer.

87. Wheeler Diary. Those lost in the crash were: Maj Marvin E. Walseth, Lieut James A. Daughtry, Lieut William R. Ware, SSgt Norman Holm, Sgt Leland E. Taylor and Cpl Kenneth E. Nelson. The Carlson and Brodsky account does not list the crew members of Walseth's crew. However, they list Lieutenant W. H. Berntson as missing in action on the 18th. He could have been aboard Walseth's aircraft

(B-17B, 38-215).

88. Japanese Monograph No 88, p. 33.

89. *Ibid.*, USSBS No 99.

90. Report, G-2 (intelligence), Ak Def Comd, *The Enemy on Kiska,* Sept 1943, p. 13.

91. *Ibid.*

92. *The Enemy on Kiska,* pp. 97-98.

93. USSBS 98.

94. USSBS 98. Commander Miura was the senior air officer aboard the *Kamikawa Maru. The Enemy on Kiska,* pp 7, 33.

95. *Ibid., The Enemy on Kiska,* p. 3.

96. USSBS No 100.

97. *Ibid.*, pp 17-19, 31. Because of the British markings on the 4.7 and 6 inch guns, it was rumored that the Japanese had used guns captured at Singapore to defend Kiska. Like so many other aspects of the Aleutian Campaign, the rumors were converted into facts by authors seeking to embellish the story. In fact, all but three of the coastal defense guns at Singapore were destroyed in battle. The Japanese did not remove the surviving guns.

98. *Ibid.*, p. 34.

99. James Gleason and Tom Waldron, *Midget Submarines,* (New York, 1975), p. 156-57.

100. *The Enemy on Kiska,* pp. 27, 47 and 49.

101. *The Enemy on Kiska,* p. 49.

102. *Ibid.*

103. Radio Transcript, Point Grey Monitoring Center, "News Broadcasts from Radio Tokyo for Today," 31 Jul 1942.

104. *Ibid.*

105. Dr Gary C. Stein, "A Transportation Dilemma: Evacuation of the Aleuts in World War II," *Transportation in Alaska's Past,* Alaska Historical Society, 1982. Dr Stein presented the account of the forcible removal of the Aleuts from their homes at the annual meeting of the Alaska Historical Society in Fairbanks in 1982. It was published along with the other papers by the Office of History and Archaeology, Alaska Department of Natural Resources, State Division of Parks. To date, it remains one of the few definitive accounts of the evacuation of the Aleuts and their relocation to southeastern Alaska.

106. *Ibid.*

107. *Ibid.*

108. "Aleuts Seek Damages for World War II Treatment," *Anchorage Daily News,* May 12, 1980.

109. "Commission Recounts Trauma of Aleut Relocation," *The Anchorage Times,* Mar 6, 1983.

110. Eric Scigliano, "The Other Internees, The Untold Story of the Aleuts' WW II Exile," *We Alaskans, The Anchorage Daily News Magazine,* Mar 6, 1983.

111. Intelligence Center Pacific Ocean Areas Bulletin 5-42, p. 6.

112. Scigliano, "The Other Internees."

113. "Panel Exhumes Ills of Aleut Relocation," *The Anchorage Times,* Sep 6, 1983.

114. Gen Lawrence S. Kuter, USAF Ret, "How Hap Arnold Built the AAF," *Air Force Magazine,* Sep 1973.

115. Ltr, Buckner to DeWitt, Jun 23, 1942.

116. Craven and Cate, *The Pacific: Guadalcanal to Saipan,* p. 368. Alaska was one of the few places that General Arnold did not visit during the war.

117. Radiogram, DeWitt to Marshall (personal), Jun 23, 1942.

118. Radiogram, Marshall to DeWitt, Jun 23, 1942.

119. Conn, Fairchild and Engelman, *Guarding the United States and Its Outposts,* pp. 265-66.

120. Kuter, "How Hap Arnold Built the AAF."

121. Statistical Summary, Eleventh Air Force, prepared by the 27th Statistical Control Sq, Eleventh Air Force, Aug 1945.

122. Intvw, Cloe with Lieut Col Charles Pinney, USAF Ret, Jan 17, 1980.

123. Tom Love, "Carrier Squadron 42," *Alaska Life,* Jul 1944.

124. Russell Intvw.

125. "Senator Chandler Announces Alaska Trip," *The Anchorage Daily Times,* Aug 7, 1942.

126. Preliminary Report, "Subcommittee to Investigate Military Establishments," Sep 1, 1942.

127. Pitt, *Wide Open On Top,* p. 134.

128. *The Anchorage Daily Times,* Sep 5, 1942.

129. Preliminary Report.

130. Ltr, President Roosevelt to Senator Chandler, Oct 13, 1942.

131. Report, Col H.W. Shelmire to Gen Arnold on Alaska trip.

132. Hist, North Pacific Forces, p. 30.

133. Spector, *Eagle Against the Sun,* (New York, 1985), p. 179.

134. Pogue, *Organizer of Victory,* pp. 151-52.

135. Spector, *Eagle Against the Sun,* p. 179.

136. Ltr, Theobald to Adml Ernest King, Comdr-in-Ch, U.S. Fleet, Aug 19, 1942 with attached poem.

137. *Ibid.*

138. *Ibid.*

139. Ltr, Theobald to Buckner, Aug 20, 1942.

140. Ltr, Buckner to Theobald, Aug 26, 1942.

141. Pogue, *Organizer of Victory,* p. 152.

142. Ltr, Marshall to DeWitt, Sep 3, 1942.

143. *Ibid.*

144. Memo, General Marshall to Admiral King, Sep 3, 1942.

145. Pogue, *Organizer of Victory,* p. 140.

146. Ltr, DeWitt to Marshall, Sep 3, 1942.

147. *Ibid.* Generals Marshall and DeWitt used the terms Dear DeWitt and Dear George in their correspondence, as was common for general officers of their generation who often expressed their innermost thoughts and feelings in their correspondence to each other. The correspondence of Marshall, DeWitt and Buckner show an amazing amount of candor that would never have been found in the carefully crafted letters prepared by staff officers.

148. Potter, *Nimitz,* p. 186.

149. Ltr, DeWitt to Marshall, Sep 8, 1942.

150. Ltr, DeWitt to Marshall, Sep 23, 1942. Admiral Theobald, at the September 19 meeting, asked General Buckner to destroy his letter to him complaining of the poem incident. However, a copy of the letter, the poem and the high level correspondence the episode generated survived and can be found in the Marshall papers at the George C. Marshall Research Library in Lexington, Virginia.

151. Memo, General Marshall to Admiral King with King's hand written comments, Sep 28, 1942.

152. Ltr, Marshall to DeWitt, Oct 2, 1942.

153. Morison, *Aleutians, Gilberts and Marshalls,* pp. 6-9.

154. Hist, Fleet Air Wing Four, pp. 46-47.

155. Morison, *Aleutian, Gilberts and Marshalls,* pp. 9-10.

156. Carter and Mueller, *Combat Chronology,* pp. 30-31; Wheeler Diary; Chronology, 21st Bomber Sq. Those lost in Lieutenant Heald's crew were: Lieut Scott H. Neal, Lieut William R. Maloney, Lieut John P. Wright, SSgt Jack R. Conklin, SSgt John M. Norquist, Sgt Toxie B. Blackwell, Sgt Edward Evans and Sgt Hoyt A. Pollard. They were from the 30th Bombardment Group.

157. Chronology, Fleet Air Wing Four.

158. Morison, *Aleutians, Gilberts and Marshalls,* p. 10.

159. Chronology, Fleet Air Wing Four.

160. Morison, *Aleutian, Gilberts and Marshalls,* p. 12; Karig and Purdon, *Battle Report,* pp. 287-93. Both accounts claim that the Japanese returned fire with a coastal defense battery on South Head. Commander Nifumi Mukai recalled during his interrogation by Captain Russell that the Japanese did not return fire because they lacked a radar fire control system and the fog was too thick for visual sighting. In any case the heaviest guns they had on South Head were the 75mm dual purpose guns and they would not have been very effective at the extended ranges the Americans were operating from.

161. USSBS Nos 100 and 101.

162. Karig and Purdon, *Battle Report,* p. 293.

163. Carter and Mueller, *Combat Chronology,* p. 31.

164. Hist, Fleet Air Wing Four, p. 48.

165. Chronology Fleet Air Wing Four, p. 16. Missing, VP-41, were: Lieut Julius A. Raven, Ensign Thomas D. Moore, Ensign Reuben M. Smith, AMM2c John L. Riley Jr., AMM2c Steve Cuvar, ARM1c Delburt F. Cox, ARM2c Erven F. Falquist and AMM3c David C. Wren. Killed, VP-62, were: Ensign Fergus F. Kelly, Ensign Leroy H. Dougherty, Ensign Julius O. Hodges, ACMM Harold A. Spencer, AP1c Paul H. Witham, ARM3c Nathan Silvers and Comdr Malcolm P. Hanson.

166. Atchm 4, Chandler Report.

167. Bezeau, *The RCAF Alaskan Commitment,* pp. 42-49. In addition to Sq Leader John William Kerwin, those killed were: Pilot Officer Dean Edward Whiteside, Flight Sgt Frank Robert Lennon, Flight Sgt Stanley Ray Maxwell and Flight Sgt G. D. Baird. Their bodies were found at the crash site on Unalaska Island. They are now buried in the Allied Plot, Fort Richardson National Cemetery. The crash site of the fifth pilot, Sergeant Baird, was never found.

168. Ransohoff, Hist, Eleventh Air Force, pp. 169-70.

169. Intel Summary, XI Ftr Comd, Aug 4, 1942.

170. Long paper, "Wings Over Alaska."

171. Carter and Mueller, *Combat Chronology,* 31. Commander Ito in response to his interrogation by Captain Russell after the war, claimed that his operational losses occurred during the navy bombardment of Kiska. He did not acknowledge loosing any of his Kawanishi flying boats to an aerial engagement. However, the claims by Lieutenants Ambrose and Long were validated and they were given official credit for destroying two Mavises.

172. Nocenti, Hist, 54th Ftr Sq, p. 27.

173. Ransohoff, Hist, Eleventh Air Force, p. 169; USSBS No 100.

174. Carter and Mueller, *Combat Chronology,* p. 31.

175. Chronology, Fleet Air Wing Four, p. 17.

176. Chronology, 21st Bomb Sq, May 18, 1942.

177. Beland, Hist, 404th Bomb Sq, p. 12.

178. Carlson and Brodsky, *No Mean Victory,* p. 229.

179. Pitt, *Wide Open on Top,* p. 163.

180. Carter and Mueller, *Combat Chronology,* p. 35.

181. *Ibid.,* Wheeler Diary: In addition to Wilsey, those lost were: Lieut Raymond L. Adair, Lieut Charles H. Cooper, Lieut John W. Sheppard, Cpl Paul W. Lyden, Pvt Charles W. Fantner, Pvt Rudoph S. Olensevich, Pvt Harold N. Knutson and Pvt Donald W. Brown.

182. Report, Lieut C. D. Y. Ostrum to Comdr, Western Def Comd, "Landing Operations and Initial Unloading Operations at Longview," Oct 4, 1942.

183. Chronology, Fleet Air Wing Four, p. 17.

184. Carter and Mueller, *Combat Chronology,* p. 36.

185. Ostrum Report.

186. *Ibid.,* pp. 116-117.

187. Samuel Eliot Morison, *The Struggle for Guadalcanal, August 1942-February 1943,* (Boston, 1984), pp. 79-107. 188. Potter, *Nimitz,* pp. 185 and 200.

189. Morison, *The Struggle for Guadalcanal,* pp. 130-138.

190. *Ibid.,* pp. 182-83.

191. *Ibid.,* pp. 200-224.

192. *Ibid.,* pp. 225-87.

193. Craven and Cate, *The Pacific, Guadalcanal to Saipan,* pp. 369-70.

194. Bush, *Narrative Report of Alaska Construction,* p. 180.

195. Ransohoff, Hist, Eleventh Air Force, p. 173; Maurer, *Combat Squadrons of the Air Force, World War II; Wheeler Diary.*

196. Bush, *Narrative Report of Alaska Construction,* pp. 178-80.

197. Ransohoff, Hist, Eleventh Air Force, pp. 171-72. Tests had been conducted on July 21, 1942 to determine how long the P-38E could remain airborne. The 54th Fighter Squadron pilots determined that by using a power setting of 1600 revolutions per minute and 24 inches of manifold pressure, and carrying two 150-gallon drop tanks, they could keep their fighter aloft up to eleven hours.

198. Wheeler Diary.

199. Ransohoff, Hist, Eleventh Air Force, pp. 173.

200. William S. Carlson and George D. Brodsky, editors, *No Mean Victory,* a draft history of Army Air Forces' activities, dated June 15, 1945, p. 252. The scene from *Report From the Aleutians,* which shows a P-38 skidding along on its belly is probably that of Lieutenant Hasenfus making his wheels up landing.

201. Pitt, *Wide Open on Top,* p. 174; Nocenti, Hist, 54th Ftr Sq, pp. 32-33.

202. Nocenti, Hist, 11th Ftr Sq, p. 21.

203. *Ibid.,* Killed in the July 5 crash were: Lieuts Robert W. Foss, Robert W. Neal, Harlin E. Helgeson, William D. Thompson, TSgt Edward J. Weidenbenner, TSgt Mark E. Greer, Sgt Mathis F. Unger, Sgt Woodrow W. Cole, Sgt Samuel E. Thomas and Cpl Donald F. Mahoney.

204. Hist, Fleet Air Wing Four, p. 51.

205. Hist, *Aleutian Campaign,* p. 132.

206. Talley Intvw.

207. Hist, *Aleutian Campaign,* p. 13; Chronology, Fleet Air Wing Four, p. 18. Killed were: Slc John H. Brumfield and S2c Lawrence L. Davis. Missing were: CMM Cornelius N. Cremer, Flc Wilson Manar, EM2c Dail I. Richard. Wounded were: SC2c John W. Jacobs, RM3c William W. Portor and SK2c Elmer H. Kracke.

208. Carl Amme, "Casco Torpedoed by Jap Sub RO-61 and Avenged by Three PBYs," *Aleutian Airdales,* pp. 96-99.

209. Hist, *Aleutian Campaign,* p. 13.

210. Ransohoff, Hist, Eleventh Air Force, p. 175; Pitt, *Wide Open on Top,* p. 176.

211. Ransohoff, Hist, Eleventh Air Force, pp. 175-79. Lieutenant Dewey Crowe had been with Major Jackson they day they narrowly missed crashing into the mountain. The other survivor from that day, Lieutenant Ambrose, was fated to die November 28, 1942, while ferrying a P-38 to the states. Although the claims for the shooting down of the three Japanese aircraft were included in the history of the Eleventh Air Force, they were not recognized in *Air Force Aerial Victory Credits, World War I, World War II, Korea and Vietnam,* USAF Historical Research Center, 1988.

212. Ransohoff, Hist, Eleventh Air Force, pp. 179-82. Carter and Mueller, *Combat Chronology,* p. 41. Conflicting claims were submitted after the attack, which make it difficult to determine what the actual damages were. Accounts providing in the unit histories add to the confusion. According to the manuscript *Wide Open On Top,* none of the ships were damaged since the bomb fuzes had been set for a too long delay, resulting in the bombs passing through the vessels without exploding. The account provided here is from *Combat Chronology* and from the intelligence summaries prepared on the mission.

213. Carlson and Brodsky, *No Mean Victory,* p. 263.

214. USSBS No 99.

215. Pitt, *Wide Open On Top,* p. 184.

216. Samuel Kostenuk and John Griffin, *RCAF Squadron Histories and Aircraft, 1924-1968,* (Toronto, 1977), pp. 29-67.

217. Hist, 406th Bomb Sq.

218. Ransohoff, Hist, Eleventh Air Force, p. 372.

219. Howard, Hist, 77th Bomber Sq, p. 9.

220. Howard, Hist, 343rd Ftr Gp, pp. 7-8.

221. Lieut Clair E. Ewing, Hist, 344th Ftr Sq, Oct 10, 1942-Jan 1, 1944, pp. 1-2.

222. Hist, 54th Troop Carrier Sq, pp. 1-2.

223. Hist, *Aleutian Campaign,* pp. 52-53.

224. Beth Day, *Glacier Pilot,* (New York, 1957), pp. 238-83.

225. Ransohoff, Hist, Eleventh Air Force, pp. 189-91.

226. *Ibid.,* pp. 217-18.

227. Wheeler Diary.

228. Intel Summary No 1, HQ Prov XI Bomb Comd, Sep 21, 1942; Intel Summary No 3, HQ Prov XI Bomb Comd, Sep 23, 1942; Intel Summary No 7, HQ Prov XI Bomb Comd, Sep 27, 1942.

229. Summary of Intel Rpt, Longview (Adak), Ops Sep 23, Sep 25, 1942.

230. Intel Summary No 9, HQ Prov XI Bomb Comd, Sep 29, 1942.

231. Wheeler Diary.

232. Summary of Intel Rpt, Longview (Adak), Ops for Sep 22, Sep 25, 1942.

233. Aiken Intvw.

234. Intel Summary No 4, HQ Prov XI Bomb Comd, Sep 24, 1942.

235. Ransohoff, Hist, Eleventh Air Force, pp. 195-97; Johnson, Hist, 11th Ftr Sq, p. 48; Hist, Prov XI Bomber Comd, p. 3.

236. Intel Summary No 7.

237. Intel Summary No 8, HQ Prov XI Bomber Comd, Sep 28, 1942.

238. *Campaigns of the Pacific War,* p. 93.

239. Nocenti, Hist, 54th Ftr Sq, p. 33.

240. Johnson, Hist, 11th Ftr Sq, p. 95.

241. Wright, Hist, 54th Ftr Gp, p. 7.

242. Aiken Intvw.

243. *Ibid.*

244. Pitt, *Wide Open On Top,* pp. 179-82.

245. Intel Summary No 9.

246. Wheeler Diary.

247. Ransohoff, Hist, Eleventh Air Force, pp. 211-12.

248. Craven and Catc, *The Pacific, Guadalcanal to Saipan,* p. 372.

249. Ltr, Arnold to Butler, Oct 30, 1942.

250. First Partial Report of Alaskan Inspection—Organization and Morale Problems of the Provisional Bomber Command, HQ AAF, Nov 12, 1942.

251. *Ibid.*

252. Ransohoff, Hist, Eleventh Air Force, pp. 214-15.

253. Nocenti, Hist, 11th Ftr Sq, p. 54.

254. Intel Summary 12, Prov IX Bomber Comd, Oct 2, 1942. 255. Intel Summary 13, Prov XI Bomber Comd, Oct 3, 1942

256. Ransohoff, Hist, Eleventh Air Force, p. 218.

257. Carter and Mueller, *Combat Chronology,* pp. 46-48; Intel Summaries for Oct 2-11, 1942, HQ Prov IX Bomber Comd. The Japanese anti-aircraft gunners on the island usually cut the fuzes of their rounds so that they would explode at predetermined altitudes. Because of this, it was difficult for them to make last minute changes when to Americans arrived overhead. The Japanese also sent their aircraft aloft during the attacks to provide information on the altitudes of the bombers. The introduction of American fighters discouraged this practice. As a result, the effectiveness of the large caliber guns was reduce. The smaller caliber guns, because of the greater flexibility and rapidly of fire, proved to be the most effective defense the Japanese had against the American attacks. Most of the damage inflicted against the bombers and fighters came from small rounds.

258. Howard, Hist, 77th Bomb Sq, pp. 9-10.

259. Ransohoff, Hist, Eleventh Air Force, p. 230.

260. Wheeler Diary.

261. Ransohoff, Hist, Eleventh Air Force, pp. 231-32.

262. Hist, 10th Emergency Rescue Boat Squadron, prepared by Ralph Bartholomew based on the war time official history compiled by First Sergeant Wilson G. Crompton.

263. *Ibid.*

264. "WW II Crash Boat Vets to Reunite on Alaska Day," *Ketchikan Daily News,* Oct 4-5, 1986.

265. Bartholomew, Hist, 10th Emergency Rescue Boat Sq.

266. Intel Summary No 24, HQ Prov XI Bomber Comd, Oct 15, 1942.

267. *Campaigns of the Pacific War,* p. 93.

268. Chronology, Fleet Air Wing Four, p. 20.

269. Carlson and Brodsky, *No Mean Victory,* p. 283.

270. Intel Summary No 25, Prov XI Bomber Comd, Nov 16, 1942.

271. *Campaigns of the Pacific War,* p. 93.

272. Hist, 73rd Bomber Sq, Oct 26, 1927-Jul 1, 1943, p. 18; Howard, Hist, 77th Bomber Sq, p. 18.

273. Intel Summary 25.

274. Carter and Mueller, *Combat Chronology,* pp. 49-54.

275. Wheeler Diary.

276. *Campaigns of the Pacific War,* p. 80; *The Capture of Attu: As Told by the Men Who Fought There,* (Wash D.C., 1944), p. 3.

277. Morison, *Aleutians, Gilberts and Marshalls,* p. 15.

278. *Ibid.* The language was cleaned up in Morison's version. In other accounts it is more graphic.

279. Jim Rearden, *Cracking the Zero Mystery,* (Harrisburg, Pa, 1990), p. 66.

280. Russell Intvw.

281. Morison, *Aleutians, Gilberts and Marshalls,* p. 16.

282. Ltr, Lieut Comdr Oliver Glenn, USNR Ret to author, Nov 8, 1978.

283. Ltr, Lieut Comdr Oliver Glenn, USNR Ret to author, Dec 26, 1979.

284. Wheeler Diary.

285. Carter and Mueller, *Combat Chronology,* p. 56.

286. Wheeler Diary.

287. Nocenti, Hist, 54th Ftr Sq, p. 37.

288. Intel Summary No 38, XI Ftr Comd, Nov 9, 1942.

289. Carter and Mueller, *Combat Chronology,* pp. 57-63.

290. Ransohoff, Hist, Eleventh Air Force, p. 239.

291. Intel Summary, Prov IX Bomber Comd, Nov 26, 1942.

292. Carter and Mueller, *Combat Chronology,* pp. 62-64.

293. Ransohoff, Hist, Eleventh Air Force, p. 239.

294. Nocenti, Hist, 11th Ftr Sq, p. 37.

295. Carter and Mueller, *Combat Chronology,* pp. 46, 77 and 92.

296. Hist, 54th Ftr Gp, p. 6. Three pilots who served with the group in the Aleutians, Thomas B. McGuire, Gerald R. Johnson and Samuel J. Brown went on to become leading aces in other theaters.

297. Maurer, *Air Force Combat Units of World War II,* p. 116.

298. *Ibid., p. 221.*

299. *Carter and Mueller, Combat Chronology,* p. 65.

300. Wheeler Diary.

301. Ransohoff, Hist, Eleventh Air Force, p. 241.

302. Intvw, Cloe with John Andrews, Oct 13, 1982.

303. *Ibid.*

304. *Ibid.*

305. Carter and Mueller, *Combat Chronology,* p. 68.

306. Howard, Hist, 77th Bomber Sq, p. 11; Intel Summary, Prov XI Bomber Comd, Dec 20, 1942.

307. Intel Summary No 96, Prov XI Bomber Comd, Dec 26, 1942; Intel Summary 84, XI Ftr Comd, Dec 26, 1942.

308. Intel Summary, Field HQs, 11AF, Dec 30, 1942; Ransohoff, Hist, Eleventh Air Force, pp. 244-45. Those killed in Lieut Constantin's crew were: Lieut Sam R. Couris, Lieut Thomas Pfeiler, Lieut Edward A. Supinski, SSgt Henry S. Jones Jr, and SSgt Andrew A. Maichau. In addition to Lieutenants Vasataka and Thorton, SSgt Harold A. Forbes, SSgt Howard D. Friestead, SSgt Albert Katz and Sgt Lew Goldstein were killed. Lieutenant Knute Flint, General Buckner's aid, was supposed to have been on the OA-10. However, he stayed behind to write an account of a rescue for Corey Ford, who was doing research for his book, *Short Cut to Tokyo.*

309. Pitt, *Wide Open on Top,* pp. 185-86.

310. *The Enemy on Kiska,* pp. 6, 45-46; *Schedule for Transportation to West Aleutian Islands (1 Nov 42 to 11 Feb 42),* a translation of a captured Japanese document.

311. Carter and Mueller, *Combat Chronology,* p. 75.

312. Pitt, *Wide Open on Top,* pp. 184-85.

313. Potter, *Nimitz,* p. 211.

314. Conn, Fairchild and Engelman, *Guarding the United States and Its Outposts,* pp. 273-75; Talley Intvw.

315. Hist, *Aleutian Campaign,* pp. 67-68. Questions have been raised on why the 7th Infantry Division was selected for the Aleutian operations and much has been made of the fact that it had been trained for desert operations in North Africa. At the time the 7th was selected, General DeWitt also had the choice of the 35th Infantry Division. However, the 7th Infantry Division was in a better state of training and its location at Fort Ord, California facilitated amphibious training on the nearby beaches.

316. *Illustrated World War Encyclopedia,* Vol 8, (Monaco, 1966), pp. 1115-25.

317. Craven and Cate, *The Pacific, Guadalcanal to Saipan,* pp. 377-78.

318. Biography, Admiral Theobald.

319. Ltr, Buckner to DeWitt, Jan 5, 1943.

320. Biography, Admiral Thomas Cassin Kinkaid. The admiral was the recipient of two Distinguished Service Medals and a Presidential Unit Citation for his participation in the Guadalcanal Campaign. He would earn a third Distinguished Service Medal for his work in the North Pacific.

321. Carter and Mueller, *Combat Chronology,* p. 78; Hist, 73rd Bomber Sq, p. 8; Chronology, 21st Bomber Sq; Schedule for Transportation.

322. Carlson and Brodsky, *No Mean Victory,* p. 300.

323. *The Japanese Navy in World War II,* (Annapolis, 1969), pp. 88-9.

324. Carter and Mueller, *Combat Chronology,* pp. 78-9.

325. Morison, *Aleutians, Gilberts and Marshalls,* p. 18.

326. Ransohoff, Hist, Eleventh Air Force, p. 247.

327. Bush, *Narrative Report of Alaska Construction,* pp.193-97.

328. Carter and Mueller, *Combat Chronology,* pp. 80-90.

329. Ransohoff, Hist, Eleventh Air Force, p. 248.

330. Arthur Unknown, Chronology, 21st Bomber Sq.

331. *Ibid.* Missing in Lieutenant Bloomfield's crew were: Lieut Marvin H. Bryant Jr., Lieut Charles R. Davis, Lieut Nunnery Wilson, TSgt Curtis G. Burgdorf, TSgt John H. Crowder, SSgt Jessie Ç. Easterling, SSgt Eric E. Rundle and SSgt Ralph W. Thomas. Missing in Lieut Hamilton's crew were: Lieut Bill W. Carpenter, Lieut Judson K. Shirer, TSgt John B. Byars, SSgt Edward L. Beavers, SSgt Ranford R. Patterson, SSgt Carl B. Reigh, SSgt Roger P. Vance and Sgt Milton Kalter.

332. Wheeler Diary.

333. Craven and Cate, *The Pacific: Guadalcanal to Saipan,* p. 375.

334. Ransohoff, Hist, Eleventh Air Force, p. 249; Craven and Cate, *The Pacific, Guadalcanal to Saipan,* p. 376; Handleman, *Bridge to Victory,* pp. 23-25. Lieutenant Saxhaug was killed March 2, 1943, when he tried to do a slow over the fighter strip on Amchitka, lost speed and crashed into a nearby ravine.

335. Wilton Sass, editor, *The Heart of the 18th Pursuit and Fighter Squadron, 1940-45,* draft manuscript, p. 12.

336. Ransohoff, Hist, Eleventh Air Force, p. 251.

337. Japanese Monograph 88, p. 47.

338. *Ibid.,* pp. 48-50.

339. Morison, *Aleutians, Gilberts and Marshalls,* pp. 19-20.

340. *Ibid.,* 24; USSBS No 102.

341. Morison, *Aleutian, Gilberts and Marshalls,* pp. 23-36.

342. Ransohoff, Hist, Eleventh Air Force, pp. 262-63.

343. Morison, *Aleutians, Gilberts and Marshalls,* pp. 23-36; *The Japanese Navy in World War II,* p. 89.

344. Conn, Fairchild and Engelman, *Guarding the United States and Its Outposts,* pp. 280-81.

345. Hist, *Aleutian Campaign,* pp. 58-60.

346. Potter, *Nimitz,* p. 238.

347. Craven and Cate, *The Pacific, Guadalcanal to Saipan,* pp. 378-79.

348. Wheeler Diary.

349. Craven and Cate, *The Pacific, Guadalcanal to Saipan,* pp. 378-79.

350. Hist, *Aleutian Campaign,* pp. 66-69.

351. Ransohoff, Hist, Eleventh Air Force, p. 253.

352. Talley Intvw.

353. Conn, Fairchild and Engelman, *Guarding the United States and Its Outposts,* p. 282.

354. Morison, *Aleutians, Gilberts and Marshalls,* pp. 38-9.

355. William T. Y'Blood, *The Little Giants* (Annapolis, 1987), p. 30.

356. Morison, *Aleutians, Gilberts and Marshalls,* pp. 38-9.

357. Potter, *Nimitz,* p. 241.

358. Intel Summary, Field HQ 11AF, Feb 4, 1943.

359. Intel Summaries, Field HQ 11AF, Feb 5&10, 1943. 360. Wheeler Diary.

361. Salter paper.

362. Intel Summary, Field HQ 11AF, Feb 13, 1943.

363. Intel Summaries, Field HQ 11AF, Feb 20&23, 1943.

364. Intel Summary No 7, HQ XI Bomber Comd, Feb 25, 1943.

365. *Ibid.*

366. Intel Summary, Feb 1943, HQ XI Bomber Comd.

367. Hist, *Aleutian Campaign,* pp. 18-9.

368. *The Enemy on Kiska,* pp. 32-3.

369. Winzeler, Hist, 18th Ftr Sq, Sec II.

370. Intel Summary No 11, XI Ftr Comd, Mar 3, 1943.

371. Hist Data, 11AF.

372. Howard, Hist, 77th Bomber Sq, p. 18.

373. Carter and Mueller, *Combat Chronology,* pp. 102-6.

374. Nocenti, Hist, 54th Ftr Sq, p. 43.

375. Intel Summary, Field HQ 11AF, Mar 15, 1943.

376. Nocenti, Hist 54th Ftr Sq, p. 42.

377. Intel Summary, Field HQ 11AF, Mar 16, 1943. Missing in Lieutenant McCurdy's crew were: Lieut William F. Paulett, SSgt Lloyd L. Accord, SSgt William A. Holbrook and PFC Harry J. Danaiker. Killed during the mission were Lieut John A. Rozboril, 404th Bombardment Squadron and Lieut Robert T. Kissinger, squadron unknown.

378. Paper, Masatake Okumiya, "Air Operations of the Imperial Japanese Navy-Aleutian Operations," undated.

379. Intel Summary, HQ 11AF, Mar 30, 1943. Those killed in Captain Smith crew were: Lieut James J. Dresher, Lieut Lawrence L. Laberge, TSgt Victor V. Probst, SSgt Gerald I. Grubb, SSgt James F. O'Brien, SSgt Roy L. Price, Sgt Floyd H. Gwin, Cpl Clifford C. Foster and Cpl Herbert L. Paillette. Dresher, Gwin and Paillette were from the 404th Bombardment Squadron.

380. Statistical Summary, Eleventh Air Force.

381. Intvw, Cloe with Larry Reineke, Aug 7, 1980.

382. Brezeau, *RCAF Alaskan Commitment,* pp. 83-5.

383. Taped experiences of SSgt Jack C. Boyd on his experiences in Alaska, 1941-43, Mar 3, 1987.

384. Hist, *Aleutian Campaign,* pp. 70-73.

385. The information was extracted from the mission reports for the period, which were very comprehensive in their coverage. Those killed in Gilliland's crew, all from the 36th Bombardment Squadron, were: Lieut Donald G. Walker, Lieut Travis V. Hodges, TSgt John D. Helm, Sgt Jess S. McArthur, Sgt Lonnie I. Sewell, Sgt Harold A. Swetland, Cpl John V. Beulick and Cpl Stanley G. Harmon, Jr.

386. Wheeler Diary.

387. Document, "What the Japs Think of Us," extracted from Japanese diaries and documents captured on Attu. Larry Reineke collection. Reineke, an intelligence officer with the 21st Bombardment Squadron, had the foresight to collect and retain many important documents and photographs that otherwise might have been lost. They are deposited in the University of Oregon Library.

388. *Ibid.*

389. Morison, *Aleutians, Gilberts and Marshalls,* pp. 38-41.

390. Hist, *Aleutian Campaign,* p. 70.

391. Carter and Mueller, *Combat Chronology,* p. 130; Wheeler Diary.

392. Craven and Cate, *The Pacific, Guadalcanal to Saipan,* p. 381.

393. Fleischer, Hist of Elmendorf Field, p. 61.

394. Mission reports for period.

395. Bezeau, *The RCAF Commitment,* pp. 86-7.

396. Hist, *Aleutian Campaign,* p. 27; Ransohoff, Hist, Eleventh Air Force, p. 270.

397. Wheeler Diary.

398. Hist, Fleet Air Wing Four, p. 59.

399. *The Capture of Attu: As Told by the Men Who Fought There,* (Washington, DC, 1944), pp. 6-7.

400. Morison, *Aleutians, Gilberts and Marshalls,* p. 39-40; Final Report, Asst Ch of Stf, G-2, Western Def Comd, "Reduction and Occupation of Attu from the Combat Intelligence Point of View," Aug 9, 1942.

401. *The Capture of Attu*, p. 5-6.

402. Intel Summary, XI Bomber Comd, May 11, 1942.

403. Y'Blood, *The Little Giants*, p. 30.

404. Conn, Stetson and Engelman, *Guarding the United States and Its Outposts*, pp. 291-2.

405. Handleman, *Bridge to Victory*, p. 78.

406. Ransohoff, Hist, Eleventh Air Force, pp. 274-5.

407. Wheeler Diary.

408. Wheeler Diary. Those killed were: Capt Miles A. Warner, Lieut Brannan, Lieut Albert F. Danek, Lieut Edwin C. Hill, Lieut George W. Moyen, Lieut Francis R. Siebenaler, SSgt Cleo A. Ronning, SSgt Albert D. Crandall, SSgt Francis A. Cole, TSgt George R. Shaffer and Cpl Jack J. Watson.

409. Y'Blood, *The Little Giants*, p. 31.

410. Hist, Fleet Air Wing Four, p. 60; Morison, *Aleutians, Gilberts and Marshalls*, p. 44.

411. Carter and Mueller, *Combat Chronology*, p. 134.

412. Morison, *Aleutians, Gilberts and Marshalls*, p. 45.

413. Y'Blood, *The Little Giants*, p. 31.

414. Carter and Mueller, *Combat Chronology*, p. 135.

415. Morison, *Aleutians, Gilberts and Marshalls*, pp. 43-4.

416. Edmund C. Love, *The Hourglass*, (Washington DC, 1950), p. 35.

417. *Ibid.*, p. 42.

418. Carter and Mueller, *Combat Chronology*, p. 136.

419. Y'Blood, *The Little Giants*, p. 33; Love, *The Hourglass*, p. 42.

420. Carter and Mueller, *Combat Chronology*, p. 136.

421. Conn, Stetson and Engelman, *Guarding the United States and Its Outposts*, pp. 293-95.

422. Carter and Mueller, *Combat Chronology*, pp. 136-7; Johnson, Hist, 11th Ftr Sq, p. 82.

423. Hist, *Aleutian Campaign*, pp. 85-6. Except for a brief appearance in support of operations in the Gilberts and Marshalls, the battle of Attu was the last time the *Nassau* saw combat. As scheduled, she was assigned the task of transporting aircraft to forward areas. She was decommissioned October 28, 1946.

424. Carter and Mueller, *Combat Chronology*, pp. 137-8.

425. Hist, *Aleutian Campaign*, p. 91.

426. Nocenti, Hist, 54th Ftr Sq, pp. 50-51.

427. USAF Historical Study No 85, "USAF Credits for the Destruction of Enemy Aircraft During World War II," 1978.

428. Carter and Mueller, *Combat Chronology; Chronology, Fleet Air Wing Four.*

429. Okumiya, Chronology, "Air Operations of the Imperial Japanese Navy (Aleutian Operations)," undated.

430. Carter and Mueller, *Combat Chronology*, p. 139; Handleman, *Bridge to Victory*, p. 188; Wheeler Diary.

431. Ransohoff, Hist, Eleventh Air Force, p. 282.

432. Hist, "Battle of Attu," prepared by Intel Sec, 208th Inf Bn (Sep), Jan 1945.

433. Carter and Mueller, *Combat Chronology*, p. 139; Ransohoff, Hist, Eleventh Air Force, p. 282.

434. Wheeler Diary.

435. Diary, Paul Nobuo Tatsoguchi, captured on Attu; translated and distributed August 1943. Notations at the end of the diary, apparently taken from documents found on Tatsoguchi's body, state that he attended the Pacific Union College from September 1929 to May 1932, and received his California medical license September 8, 1938. His diary has been the subject of a number of articles and a novel, *Allegiance*, by Paul Green, publish in 1983 by Crown Publishers, New York.

436. Carter and Mueller, *Combat Chronology*, p. 139.

437. Love, *The Hourglass*, pp. 78-80.

438. Ransohoff, Hist, Eleventh Air Force, pp. 282-83.

439. Ltr, Oliver Glenn to Cloe, Jan 14, 1979; Surrender Note, Comdr, Army Forces, Attu to Comdr, Japanese garrison, Attu, undated.

440. Short Hist, Battle of Attu.

441. Diary, Paul Nobuo Tatsoguchi. Paul met his wife Taeko Miyake, while he was in California. Her parents were Hawaiian missionaries. They married before returning to Japan. After the war, Taeko and her children Joy Misaka and Lori Mutsuko returned to the U.S. and became naturalized citizens. Both daughters attended Pacific Union College.

442. Short Hist, Battle of Attu, pp. 10-11.

443. Robert Sherrod, "Burial In the Aleutians," *Time*, Jun 28, 1943; Conn, Fairchild and Engelman, *Guarding the United States, and Its Outposts*, p. 295.

444. Conn, Fairchild and Engelman, *Guarding the United States and Its Outposts*, p. 295.

445. Intw, Cloe with James D. Bush, USAR Ret, May 24, 1982.

446. Morison, *Aleutians, Gilberts and Marshalls*, p. 50; Rosein, Hist, Alaskan Department, p. 44. According to the Rosein account, much of the blame for the high number of non-battle casualties were caused by the failure of the individual soldier to properly take care of himself and his clothing and equipment. He compared the experiences of the Alaskan Scouts with the 7th Infantry Division's provisional scout battalion. The thirty Alaskan Scouts who fought throughout the battle lost two killed in action, two wounded and one slight case of trench foot. The provisional scout battalion was rendered ineffective by the elements and enemy action after five days, and could only muster forty men who were able to walk.

447. Craven and Cate, *The Pacific, Guadalcanal to Saipan*, p. 386.

448. "Battle Experience: Assault and Occupation of Attu, May 1943," republished in *U.S. Naval Experience in the North Pacific During World War II*, Naval Historical Center, Wash DC, 1989, p. 25.

449. Chronology, Fleet Air Wing Four. Those lost in Lieutenant Permenter's crew were: Ensign Elton W. Cooke, AMM3c Robert S. Matthews, AMM3c Frank S. Tall and AMM3c John R. McClennan. Crew members missing from Lieut Leedy's PBY were: Ensign Earl C. Alter, AP1c Preston Bright, AMM1c Walter B. Kerr, AMM2c Edwin H. House, ARM2c Allen F. Walker and ARM3c Roland L. Hughes.

450. Morison, *Aleutians, Gilberts and Marshalls*, p. 50.

451. *Ibid.*, 51.

452. *Campaigns of the Pacific War*, p. 82.

453. *Ibid.*, pp. 174-5.

454. Burk Davis, *Get Yamamoto*, (New York, 1969), p. 198.

455. Rosein, Hist, Alaska Department, pp. 119-20.

456. Standly Dziuban, *Military Relations Between the United States and Canada, 1939-45*, (Washington DC, 1959).

457. Hist, *Aleutian Campaign*, p. 100.

458. Ransohoff, Hist, Eleventh Air Force, p. 290.

459. Craven and Cate, *The Pacific, Guadalcanal to Saipan*, p. 387.

460. Hist, Shemya Army Air Field, May 28, 1943-Apr 30, 1944, pp. 405.

461. Claus M. Naske, "The Battle of Alaska Has Ended and the Japanese Have Won It," *Military Affairs*, 1985. 462. Talley, Daily Diary. General Talley is an unofficial member of the Eleventh Air Force.

463. Ewing, Hist, 344th Ftr Sq, pp. 24-28.

464. *Ibid.*; Hist, Shemya, p. 11.

465. Hist, Shemya, pp. 20-1.

466. Hist, Fleet Air Wing Four, p. 60.

467. Morison, *Aleutians, Gilberts and Marshalls*, p. 54.

468. Hist, XI Bomber Comd, Mar 18, 1943-Mar 31, 1944, pp. 16-17.

469. Carter and Mueller, *Combat Chronology*, pp. 140-41; Hist, Fleet Air Wing Four, pp. 62-63.

470. Wheeler Diary.

471. Beland, Hist, 404th Bomb Sq, p. 25.

472. Wheeler Diary.

473. Handleman, *Bridge to Victory*, pp. 234-5.

474. Wheeler Diary.

475. Carter and Mueller, *Combat Chronology*, p. 143.

476. Beland, Hist, 404th Bomber Sq, 27.

477. Nocenti, Hist, 54th Ftr Sq, p. 53.

478. Intel Summary (Supplementary) Field HQ, 11AF, June 18, 1943.

479. Chronology, Fleet Air Wing Four.

480. *Ibid.*, pp. 28-9.

481. Carter and Mueller, *Combat Chronology*, pp. 149-51; Chronology, Fleet Air Wing Four.

482. Ransohoff, Hist, Eleventh Air Force, p. 291.

483. Supplement Hist, 406th Bomber Sq, pp. 13-20.

484. Carter and Mueller, *Combat Chronology*, pp. 152-3.

485. Morison, *Aleutians, Gilberts and Marshalls*, p. 55.

486. Carter and Mueller, *Combat Chronology*, p. 154.

487. Ltr, Oliver Glenn to author, Nov 8, 1978.

488. Carl Amme, "VP-45: First Squadron Based at Attu," *Aleutian Airdales.*

489. Ransohoff, Hist, Eleventh Air Force, p. 293.

490. Intvw, Cloe with Reineke, Aug 7, 1980.

491. *Ibid.*

492. Ransohoff, Hist, Eleventh Air Force, pp. 293-5.

493. Mission Report, Fleet Air Wing Four, July 11, 1943; Amme, "VP-45: The First Squadron Based at Attu."

494. Intel Summary, 36th Bomber Sq, Jul 11, 1943.

495. Intel Summary, Field HQ, 11AF, Jul 18, 1943; Wheeler Diary.

496. Intel Summary, Field HQ, 11AF, Aug 15, 1943; Ransohoff, Hist, Eleventh Air Force, pp. 296-98; Carlson, *No Mean Victory,* pp. 393-97; Otis Hays, Jr., *Home From Siberia,* (College Station, Tex, 1990), pp. 57-9. Killed were: Capt Harrell R. Hoffman, Lieut Robert J. Riddle, Lieut Carroll W. Cramer, Lieut Edward R. Bacon III, TSgt Myron M. Brown, TSgt John J. Antonions, SSgt Sammie C. Benton, SSgt Raymond G. Brown, SSgt Richard H. Quakenbush and Sgt John N. Mesa. Interned were: Lieut James Pottenger, Flying Officer Richard Filler, Lieut Charles K. Hanner, Jr., Lieut Robert R. Wiles, TSgt Anthony Homitz, TSgt James Dixon, TSgt Thomas Ring, TSgt Peter Bernatovich, SSgt Donald Dimel, SSgt Charles Day and Cpl Richard T. Varney.

497. Carter and Mueller, *Combat Chirology*, pp. 157-61. Killed in the crash were: Lieutenant Van Blaricon, Lieut Edward P. Poyner, Lieut Owen L. Day, Lieut Norman Lyle Jr., TSgt Robert M. White and TSgt Donald G. Gerstenberger.

498. Morison, *Aleutians, Gilberts and Marshalls*, p. 56.

499. Intel Summary, Field HQ 11AF, Jul 22, 1943.

500. Morison, *Aleutians, Gilberts and Marshalls,* p. 56.

501. Intel Summary, Field HQ 11AF, July 23, 1943; Winzeler, Hist 18th Ftr Sq, p. 19. Commander Mukai after the war stated to Captain Russell that the body of a man who fell to his death from a bomber during the winter was also buried on North Head.

502. Intel Summary, Field HQ, 11AF, July 25, 1942.

503. Intel Summary, Field HQ, 11AF, Jul 26, 1943.

504. Supplementary Rpt to Intel Summary No 158, HQ 18th Ftr Sq, Jul 26, 1943.

505. Ltr, Oliver Glenn to arthur, Nov 8, 1978.

506. Intel Summary, Field HQ, 11AF, Jul 27, 1942.

507. Japanese Monograph 88, pp. 52-3; Morison, *Aleutians, Gilberts and Marshalls*, pp. 56-7.

508. The Japanese Navy In World War II, pp. 91-96; Morison, *Aleutians, Gilberts and Marshalls*, pp. 56-61.

509. USSBS No 99.

510. Intel Summary, Field HQ, 11AF, Aug 1, 1943.

511. Morison, *Aleutians, Gilberts and Marshalls,* p. 61, Intel Summary, Field HQ, 11AF, Aug 2, 1943.

512. Intel Summary, Field HQ 11AF, Aug 3, 1943.

513. Intel Summary, Field HQ, 11AF, Aug 4, 1943.

514. Craven and Cate, *The Pacific: Guadalcanal to Saipan*, p. 390.

515. *Ibid.*

516. Intel Summaries, Field HQ, 11AF, Aug 10, 11, 1943.

517. Morison, *Aleutians, Gilberts and Marshalls,* p. 61.

518. Intel Summary, Field HQ, 11AF, Aug 12, 1943.

519. Dziuban, *Military Relations Between the United States and Canada,* pp. 258-9; Hatch, "Allies in the Aleutians." In addition to the pilots listed buried in the Fort Richardson Cemetery in endnote 167, the following are also interred there: Sgt Pilot Harold Grandville Anderson, Apr 1, 1943; Pilot Officer Rodney Shavalier, Sep 6, 1943; and Pilot Officer John Whiteford, Mar 28, 1943.

520. Ransohoff, Hist, Eleventh Air Force, p. 1; Wheeler Diary.

521. Nancy Price, "11th Air Force Vets to Begin Reunion Today," *The Anchorage Times,* Aug 9, 1990.

522. *Ibid.*; Phone call, arthur to Col George Ruddell, USAF Ret, Aug 25, 1990. Colonel Ruddell is seeking the names of the other pilots to verify his account. The account he kept in his personal diary was latter lost when the plane, a war-weary PBY in which he was a passenger returning home to the states, crash landed and sank just off Amelia Island in the Aleutians. Also, he was unable, after 57 years, to recall the name of the Amchitka colonel who chewed him out for landing at Kiska. Colonel Ruddell did recall that the craters were positioned in such a manner on the runway that he and the others were able to avoid them. Colonel Ruddell retired after a career in the Air Force in which he saw service in the European Theater during World War II and during the Korean and Vietnam War Conflicts.

523. Conn, Engelman and Fairchild, *Guarding the United States and Its Outposts*, p. 297.

524. Hist, *Aleutian Campaign*, p. 98.

525. Conn, Engelman and Fairchild, *Guarding the United States and Its Outposts*, pp. 297-98. Samuel Eliot Morison's account puts the casualties ashore at twenty-five men dead and thirty-five wounded. The two Canadian soldiers are buried in the Fort Richardson National Cemetery.

526. Pitt, *Wide Open on Top,* p. 242; *Hidden Front*, pp. 222-26; "The Miracle of Kiska," *Alaska Sportsman,* Jun 1946.

527. *The Enemy on Kiska,* Table I.

528. Robert Sherrod, "Janfu," *Time,* Aug 30, 1943.

529. Morison, *Aleutian, Gilberts and Marshalls,* p. 64.

530. Battle Report, p. 343.

531. Sherrod, "Janfu."

532. Intel Summary, HQ 11AF, Aug 17, 1943.

533. *Anchorage Daily Times*, Aug 21, 1943.

534. Conn, Engelman and Fairchild, *Guarding the United States and Its Outposts*, p. 299; Statistical Summary, Eleventh Air Force.

535. Carlson and Brodsky, *No Mean Victory,* sect II, atchms 2 & 3; Chronology, Fleet Air Wing Four. Also consulted were unit histories and mission reports. While the Carlson and Brodsky provided the most comprehensive list of KIAs and MIAs, there were a number of discrepancies with the spelling of names and the categories under which the names were listed when compared with the histories and mission reports. In one instant they list the names of five crew members (Lieut William R. Ware, Lieut James A. Daugherty, SSgt Norman Holm, Sgt Leland E. Taylor, Cpl Kenneth E. Nelson and Seaman 1C1 W. F. Boyce) as missing in action July 18, 1942. However, there is no mention of it in the histories. Every effort was made to correct the discrepancies. The Fleet Air Wing chronology provided concise and with a few exceptions, complete information. The exceptions were the failure to list the names, in a several incidents, where lives were lost due to accidents. The Carlson and Brodsky account did not list the names of individuals who lost their lives to accidents; however, most of the unit histories did. The fighter squadrons histories provided a complete account. The bomber squadron histories were more sketchy. The following is a list by squadron and names of those who died in aircraft accidents during the Aleutian Campaign: 11th Fighter Squadron: Lieut Mike J. Buku (Sep 10, 42), Lieut Edward G. Butler (Dec 22, 42), Lieut Carl Bigger (Mar 20, 43) and Lieut Robert H. Combs (Aug 10, 43); 18th Fighter Squadron: Lieut Roger P. Stein (Oct 29, 42), Lieut Robert L. Mrag (Jan 21, 43), Lieut Kenneth Saxhaug (Mar 2, 43) and Lieut John C. Gorman (Apr 24, 43); 54th Fighter Squadron: Lieut Carl Middleton (Jun 27, 42), Lieut Robert W. Foss (Jul 5, 42), Lieut Robert E. Helgerson (Jul 5, 42), Lieut Robert W. Neal (Jul 5, 42), Lieut William D. Thompson (Jul 5, 42), TSgt Edward J. Weidenbenner (Jul 5, 42), TSgt Mark E. Greer (Jul 5, 42), Sgt Mathis F. Unger (Jul 5, 42), Sgt Woodrow W. Cole (Jul 5, 42), Sgt Samuel E. Thomas (Jul 5, 42), Cpl Donald F. Mahoney (Jul 5, 42), Lieut Kenneth W. Ambrose (Nov 26, 42), Lieut Thomas Archer (Nov 26, 42) and Lieut Glen B. Martin (Jul

11, 43); 54th Fighter Group: Lieut Robert J. Neal (need info); 344th Fighter Squadron: Lieut Melvin Thomas (Aug 4, 43); ; 21st Bombardment Squadron: No Record; 36th Bombardment Squadron: Pvt Nuel S. Curtis (Sep 30, 42), Capt Robert H. Bennington, Lieut Major H. McWilliams, Lieut Bernard M. Dowd, Lieut Richard M. Johnson, Lieut William B. Osburn, MSgt Henry Fretwell, SSgt Samuel L. Herron, Cpl Clinton J. Chaosey, Cpl Stanley Earls, Cpl Harold Homcombe, Cpl Royal C. Kinsman, Cpl Louis T. Madore, Pvt Julian W. Meeks and Pvt Wright (Jan 21, 43); 73rd Bombardment Squadron: SSgt

William W. Chapman (Aug 16, 42), 77th Bombardment Squadron: Lieut Lee W. Wright, SSgt Peter P. Verbich, Sgt Paul G. Yahoney, Sgt Rolan C. Moehpic, Sgt Fred J. Robinies and PFC Robert A. Norby (Sep 2, 42); 404th Bombardment Squadron: Lieut James H. Jones and SSgt Williard F. Crippen (Jun 19, 43); 42nd and 54th Troop Carrier Squadron: No Record. SSgt James S. Vickers is listed in the Carlson and Brodsky as KIA on January 23, 1943. However, no missions were flown that day.

536. *Campaigns of the Pacific War*, p. 90.

INDEX

• • • • • • • • • • • •